ALSO BY MEL GUSSOW

Theater on the Edge: New Visions, New Voices
Conversations with and about Beckett
Conversations with Stoppard
Conversations with Pinter
Don't Say Yes Until I Finish Talking: A Biography of Darryl F. Zanuck

Edward Albee:

A Singular Journey

A Biography

Mel Gussow

Simon & Schuster

SIMON & SCHUSTER
Rockefeller Center
1230 Avenue of the Americas
New York, NY 10020

Manufactured in the United States of America

10 9 8 7 6 5 4 3 2 1

Library of Congress Cataloging-in-Publication Data
Gussow, Mel.
Edward Albee : a singular journey : a biography / Mel Gussow.
p.   cm.
Includes bibliographical references (p.   ) and index.
1. Albee, Edward, 1928–   . 2. Dramatists, American—20th century—Biography. I. Title.
PS3551.L25Z684 1999
812'.54—dc21
[B]   99-26558
CIP
ISBN 0-684-80278-3

Photo credits:
Philippe Halsman © Halsman Estate: 1; Edward Albee collection: 2, 3, 4, 6, 11, 30, 32, 36;
New York Times Pictures: 5; Jack Manning/*New York Times* Pictures: 24;
Fred Conrad/*New York Times* Pictures: 35;
William H. Wharfe Collection: 8; Bettmann Archive: 9;
Alix Jeffry, Harvard Theater Collection: 10, 14, 15, 16, 19, 20, 25, 26, 29, 31;
Howard Atlee Collection: 13; *Newsweek* cover photo by Burt Glinn-Magnum: 17;
Newsweek, Tony Rollo: 18; Elaine Steinbeck Collection: 21;
Photofest: 22, 27, 28, 38, 39; Carol Rosegg: 33, 41;
Alastair Muir: 34, 40; Carol Marcus: 37

For Ann

I shall walk the earth and search
For something that I shall not find.

EDWARD ALBEE, 1945

Contents

Prologue

JAMES AGEE'S autobiographical novel, *A Death in the Family*, opens with a preface, "Knoxville: Summer 1915," the author's brief, eloquent elegy of his childhood. Agee begins, "We are talking now of summer evenings in Knoxville, Tennessee, in the time that I lived there so successfully disguised to myself as a child," and he goes on to speak about his plangent memories of spreading quilts on the grass and lying under the stars, alongside members of his family. Agee writes, "All my people are larger bodies than mine, quiet, with voices gentle and meaningless like the voices of sleeping birds . . . One is my mother who is good to me. One is my father who is good to me. By some chance, here they are, all on this earth; and who shall ever tell the sorrow of being on this earth, lying, on quilts, on the grass, in a summer evening, among the sounds of the night." With a prayer, he blesses his family and then concludes:

"After a little I am taken in and put to bed. Sleep, soft smiling, draws me unto her: and those receive me, who quietly treat me, as one familiar and well-beloved in that home: but will not, oh, will not, not now, not ever; but will not ever tell me who I am."

London, November 10, 1994. Edward Albee is on top of the world. We are having lunch at the restaurant at St. George's Hotel and are seated at a window overlooking the city. Albee's new play *Three Tall Women*, starring Maggie Smith, is opening next week at Wyndham's Theater. The previous season, the play, in a production starring Myra Carter, was a great dramatic success in New York, all at once reviving Albee's reputation, reaffirming his position as a major American playwright, and winning his third Pulitzer Prize for Drama and the New York Drama Critics Circle award for best new play. Suddenly, people who had disparaged him in the last decade or more, who thought he was bankrupt as a playwright, were surrounding him with adulation.

I had known Albee for more than thirty years, from the time of the opening of *Who's Afraid of Virginia Woolf?* on Broadway in October of 1962, when he was proclaimed as the playwright of his generation. I reviewed the play for *Newsweek* magazine and early the following year wrote a cover story about him for that magazine, a profile entitled "Odd Man In." At the time, Albee lived across the street from me in Greenwich Village. During the intervening years, we had met often and I had written a number of pieces about him and his work. Recently we had begun the conversations that were to lead to this biography. At lunch in London, with a newly revitalized creative life before him, we talked about the roots of *Three Tall Women*, about his adoptive parents, and his childhood. For the first of many times, I suggested that he try to track down his natural parents. As always, he was ambivalent about the subject: He was reluctant to exhume old facts about his birth, but he retained a curiosity about his genetic origins (and about his medical history). This was, he agreed, an essential part of his story, part of the search for "who I am."

Then he said, with seeming casualness, "Here's something that may be of interest to you. Do you know Samuel Barber's piece for voice and orchestra called 'Knoxville: Summer 1915?' " He explained that it was based on the James Agee text of that title. "Listen to it. Read it. It is a piece of music that I cannot listen to or even think about without crying. If you look at the text of that you will understand a good deal about me. I'm getting teary now thinking about it. It's so odd, you see, that's a very important text to me." That passage was, he said, "one of the most moving things I have ever experienced in my life." More than anything he was touched by Agee's last line, which he now quoted: "They 'will not now . . . not ever tell me who I am.' "

From then on, any time that he or I mentioned the Agee passage, he was overcome with emotion. Where did this powerful feeling come from? How different could two artists be—Agee, a poet and novelist of America's heartland (and a film critic), looking back to 1915 and writing about his presumably idyllic childhood; Albee, a playwright with bitter memories of his marred childhood, growing up at midcentury as the adopted son of parents so distant from him as to make it seem as if he had come from another planet. A contemporary theatrical experimentalist, he was known as the cool, cynical surveyor of marital angst and the damage provoked by parents. What could the two disparate writers possibly have in common? Perhaps it was that disparity that drew them together: What Agee had, Albee longed for.

As with many things, Albee hesitates to offer self-analysis. As psychologically probing as he can be in his work, he is not eager to apply such questions to his own life. But clearly, when he thinks about "Knoxville," he is contemplating his own identity. Here is Agee, in the bosom of a loving family, but still not knowing who he is, and there is Albee, accidentally placed within an unloving family, an outsider from the earliest age, not knowing who he is— and with an urgency trying to find himself within his work, and with lovers and friends trying to find a family. If even Agee wondered about his identity, what does that leave for Albee? Through the prism of "Knoxville," he can look back to a dream of childhood he never experienced.

The passage, he said, "is less about home than about a sure sense of belonging and being comforted and protected." And about his own life: "I never felt protected in my environment. Being adopted, I always felt like an interloper. I never felt that I belonged and therefore I didn't feel that this was home to me. I felt like a transient, as if I were a visitor in a strange land." His parents' world, the world of Agnes and Tobias in A Delicate Balance, was WASP, upper class, and impersonal, very distant from Agee's world. "Maybe I loved the simplicity and the purity of that environment," Albee said, referring to Agee. "Maybe I would have loved to have been able to grow up in a place like that. Maybe I thought this is the kind of family that I would have had if I hadn't been adopted. I guess it would have been nice to have grown up with people that I could love. This was clearly a place where everybody was loved, and was welcome to come, all the time." He remembered a line from his play Box, "The memory of what we have not known." "Maybe I missed what I had never known. Yes." He qualified the statement, "Never having had it, I couldn't have literally missed it. Missed out on it."

There are three other moments in literature, all of them in plays, that move him almost to that degree. Two are in plays by Thornton Wilder: In The Skin of Our Teeth, during the Great Storm when Mrs. Antrobus cannot find her son and, for the first time, calls out his real name, "Cain! Cain!"; and in Our Town when Emily Webb returns from the grave to relive one day of her life, and her father comes bounding down the stairs saying, "Where's my girl? Where's my birthday girl?" The other is in Krapp's Last Tape, the most poignant passage in all of Beckett, when Krapp recalls a time of deep love in his youth. Drifting in a boat through the reeds, he looks down at the woman he loves. As she opens her eyes, he says, "Let me in." In all three instances, there is a moment of intense connection, a bonding—between mother and son, between father and daughter, between lovers. Each is a moment wished for, but seldom achieved.

In Albee's own life, these moments represent a longing for the unattain-

able. Paradoxically, such moments rarely exist in Albee's plays. His work pro-
vokes laughter, anger, and rage, offering insights into human nature as well as
linguistic delight, but with certain exceptions they stop short of catharsis and
the kind of emotional release that he finds in the passages just mentioned.
The exceptions include two plays that are closest to his own biography, *The
Sandbox*, a cameo tribute to his maternal grandmother, the relative who was
closest to him, and *Three Tall Women*, an act of peacemaking with his formidable mother. The scene in *Three Tall Women* that always moves him is in
the second act when the son, Albee's surrogate, comes onstage and sits by the
bedside of his mother.

More than many artists, Albee is his own invention: He is a self-made
writer who has created an environment in which he can exist and can find
some kind of contentment, and he has molded his character out of his life.
He has discovered a life of his own. "By nature, I was a solitary creature," he
says, explaining that very early he realized that life was "a solo journey," that
"one is making that journey through wonderful consciousness toward the end
of consciousness. I've always had a sense of it, and it doesn't make me feel
lonely. I am aware that it is I who am living this life, I who have to make some
kind of sense of it for myself," and "the older you get, the more solo you become."

Martha Coigney, head of the International Theater Institute (ITI), says,
"He's a lone traveler," and she means that in a metaphorical sense. Irene
Worth, who is a friend of his as well as an actress in his plays, says, insightfully,
"I think he suffered from every possible kind of neglect, except physical, but
he received reassurance through his friends—and also by fighting for his own
balance, his own ego, his own dynamic center. I think that makes an artist
very strong. Isolation can be a great booster."

What he had lost (or never had) in his childhood, he has been seeking as
an adult, and as an artist. His identity is in his art, more than anyone might realize. Writing his plays he has intuitively explored and plundered his past. All
his work has deep autobiographical roots, although in many cases characters
and events have been so transformed as to be virtually unrecognizable, even
to those who are the models. The plays are filled with cross references from
his life. "I'm there in all of the plays," he says, unequivocally, "in all of the
characters." In common with other artists, Albee is exceedingly skeptical
about linking the art with the life, about the idea of biography, but the art can
shed light on the life, and vice versa. Repeatedly he would warn me about trying to find themes and motifs in his life. "Oh God," he would say, with mock
exasperation, "you're trying to do connective tissue. Everything is going to re-

late to his life." But things do relate to the life; attitudes and opinions can be traced back to childhood. Through Albee's plays, one can see the shaping of his character and the reasons why he is who he is and how he became Albee the playwright.

With the aid of Elia Kazan as their mutual director, Tennessee Williams and Arthur Miller dominated Broadway during the 1940s and the early 1950s. After them, there were followers and imitators, some with talent but none with a definable and durable vision. Then in the 1960s there was Albee as innovator, the American agent of the absurd, our homegrown equivalent of Beckett. He is, said José Quintero, "the last great playwright that we have." By that he means that Albee is the fourth, after O'Neill, Williams, and Miller.

Because of *Who's Afraid of Virginia Woolf?*, and the explosive love-hate relationship between its principal characters, Albee's writing is often linked with that of Strindberg. But the three playwrights he most admires and who have been most influential on his work are Chekhov, Pirandello, and Beckett—Chekhov for his plays of character and apparent inaction, Pirandello for his treatment of reality and illusion, Beckett for both those reasons plus his language and his humor. Albee's signature is his use of language, playfully, as a weapon and as a revelation of character through storytelling. In addition to the trio of influential playwrights, one must add as influences the names of two expatriate American writers, Henry James and T. S. Eliot, for their intellectualism and the atmospheric resonance behind the words (especially in a play like *A Delicate Balance*). With Albee, intuition is married to intellect, in plays that boldly challenge expectation and convention.

With *The Zoo Story*, he opened up Off-Broadway, and with *Who's Afraid of Virginia Woolf?* he threatened to transform Broadway, which was badly in need of transformation. For a variety of reasons, many of them economic, Broadway did not substantially change, except to make room, for a time, for Albee. His influence on other playwrights, however, was to be extraordinary. After Albee came Sam Shepard, Lanford Wilson, John Guare, David Mamet, and others, all of them deeply affected by his work. As for Albee, he has written at least four major plays (*The Zoo Story*, *Who's Afraid of Virginia Woolf?*, *A Delicate Balance*, and *Three Tall Women*), others (*Tiny Alice*, *Box* and *Quotations from Chairman Mao Tse-Tung*, *All Over*, *Seascape*, and *The Lady from Dubuque*) that demand a second look, and one-acts that remain models of their kind. This is a substantial body of work, one with constantly renewable vigor from a playwright who always experiments, who never allows himself to be locked into predictable positions.

In 1983, after *The Man Who Had Three Arms* had opened on Broadway and Albee was being viciously and personally attacked by critics, his oldest friend, Noel Farrand, wrote to him, saying, "Nothing can alter your impregnable position as the outstanding imaginative dramatist of your generation." It was a claim with which Farrand would allow no contradiction, and it remains an accurate assessment of Albee's position in the American theater. His art is continually surprising, and nothing was more surprising than *Three Tall Women*, which began the second act—or was it the third act?—in his life (and was followed by the mordant, mysterious *The Play about the Baby*). *Three Tall Women* represented the kind of later-in-life success that Tennessee Williams so craved and was unable to accomplish. Albee achieved that success after enduring a long period of critical neglect and abuse and after winning a battle with alcoholism.

One difficulty for a biographer is that Albee has never kept a journal or a diary; he has not notated his own life. Intentionally, he and his closest friends sometimes exchanged what they called "posterity letters"; but the correspondence was sporadic, and some of the letters have been lost. Not all letters can be trusted, nor can all memories. Legends have sprung up about Albee, causing him to suggest as a title for this book, "Apocrypha." Perhaps a greater truth about Albee's life, at least his interior life, can be found in his writing, and he has been writing from a very early age. At the root of the myth of Albee, as perpetuated by the playwright himself, is that he was born at the age of thirty, when, just before his birthday, he sat down at his kitchen table in his apartment in Greenwich Village and wrote his first play, *The Zoo Story*, as a present to himself. According to this story, his only previous plays were *Aliqueen*, a three-act sex farce written when he was twelve ("which my mother threw away, and therefore does not exist") and *Schism*, a long one-act play written when he was a student at Choate preparatory school and published in the Choate literary magazine.

The truth is, of course, far more complicated. Before *The Zoo Story*, there was a long apprenticeship, including hundreds of poems, two novels, and nine plays, two of them full length. None of the plays was, of course, *The Zoo Story*, which was an astonishing leap of his imagination, but there are several plays that reveal his dramatic promise and one that was an early version of *The American Dream*. His plays, from *The Zoo Story* onward, are his journal— transformed, transmogrified, but true to the events and the people and to his understanding of them.

His mother, the tall, imperious, and striking Frances Albee, is the model for so many of his characters. She acted as a kind of anti-muse. From *The American Dream* to *A Delicate Balance* to *Three Tall Women*, she appears in various incarnations: a demanding, domineering figure who, from her son's perspective, never knew him, understood him, or recognized him for what he was or wanted to be. In *Three Tall Women*, he recreates her with honesty and compassion. After her death, he could come to terms with her life and with the effect—the damaging effect—that she had on his life. One amazement of that play is that after all the conflicts between them—the grave unhappiness of his childhood, his rude departure from his home at the age of twenty, the years in which they did not speak, the years in which they spoke but did not really communicate, his lingering feelings of resentment and what he considers to be his disinheritance—he can look back more with rue than with anger while still maintaining his ironic perspective. In *Three Tall Women*, he is able to tell the family's story from his mother's point of view, empathetically as well as sardonically. This is all part of Albee's unique talent. In his plays, he can turn himself into so many different people. And which one is the closest to the real Edward Albee?

Like many artists, he is a figure of contradictions. A critic in life, he can be witheringly cynical and abusive (especially about pomposity, pretension, and venality in all its guises), and he is unforgiving about those people (especially critics) who have wounded him. His mother is an exception, and in *Three Tall Women* he offers her a kind of absolution. Sometimes he will make cutting remarks about his peers, and even some who might be considered his friends, though these remarks are more often private. In public, he can be exceedingly discreet. To some, he exhibits a prickly personality, marked by malice. That malice is generally—though not always—an act of reciprocity: Hurt him and he hits back. On the other hand, he has demonstrated a great fidelity and loyalty to those whose friendship he values, and they reciprocate in kind. He is generous with his time and interest, making himself readily available to teach and to encourage new playwrights and artists. Through his work with ITI and PEN, he has been a constant battler for human rights and other social causes.

Asked to draw a self-portrait, he underscores the paradoxes of his character: "Certain words come to mind: cool but passionate at the same time. Standing off observing, but not disengaged. I get as enraged and angry about things as anybody does. I am involved in political and social matters, but I also think of myself as a bit of an observer, not a removed observer, a clinical observer so that one can make valid and objective decisions about things. It ties in with the ability to participate in something and at the same time observe oneself participating. It's a sort of schizophrenic thing that a lot of writers have. I can be involved in an intensely personal moment of my life, and I can also observe myself participating in it." That artistic "schizophrenia" is at the core of his work. "And that ties in with the impression I give to other people of distancing myself. Some people say it is hard to get to know Edward." Some of the people closest to him say it is hard to know Edward. Each has his own story to tell, and often those stories diverge as people remember what they want to remember. In other words, they subjectify. His response: " 'I tell what ought to be true,' as Blanche DuBois said." He adds, "All my friends are like Blanche DuBois. They tell what ought to be true."

"I've always felt this vague, unreasonable kinship," says Mike Nichols. "I feel connected with him in some way. All artists are susceptible in the dark part in the middle that Dante told us about. I think he's lived an exemplary life for an artist and I'm glad he got through the tough part. I really salute him." Stephen Sondheim, who knows him at more of a distance, says, "He has a kind of dark, strong personality. That's a combination I don't know if I ever met before. Edward is a recessive fellow. He's like a litmus test: he reflects the viewer rather than himself."

The composer William Flanagan, Albee's mentor, partner, and confidant for many years, was, along with Albee's mother, one of the most important and catalytic people in his life, the one person who did the most to shape Albee as an artist. In 1962, he told me that he thought Albee was "a mysterious number." If Flanagan, the man who knew him best at the most crucial time of his life, felt that way, that leaves little room for outsiders to understand him. He *is* a mysterious number, keeping close watch over his cards of identity, revealing only so much of himself, disguising himself in his art and playfully watching—and gauging—himself as he moves through and overcomes crises. While all this is true, there are clues to his life and art, beginning with "Knoxville: Summer 1915."

1
Eddie

*It's lucky that he was adopted. He would not get much
talent from those two.*

Larchmont: Summer 1928

*E*DWARD ALBEE prides himself on his visual memory. Although he
can forget names and dates of events, he remembers with precision where he
was at certain times and what the environment looked like. It is a talent that
aids him in his creativity. When it came time to write an introduction to
Three Tall Women, he asked himself how long it took him to write a play. His
answer was "all of my life." As proof, he projected himself back to his very first
visual memory, and the spark of an idea that eventually led to *Three Tall
Women*. In this childhood reflection, he was one of four people on a knoll: his
adoptive father and mother, Reed and Frances Albee; his nanny, Anita
Church; and himself at three months (though later in conversation he suggested that he may have been six months, still very young to have such a vivid
memory). The family house at 5 Bay Avenue (the number was later changed
to 7) in Larchmont, New York, was "being built or renovated and I remembered seeing the scaffolding all over the house." He was in Nanny Church's
arms, and his parents were looking down at the house. It was "my first awareness of being aware, and so I suppose I treasure it." In its own way, this is a
peaceful, idyllic moment, one that proved to be rare, if not unique, in his
childhood. Did he really experience it or was it a memory stirred by a photo-

graph or a family recollection? Truth or illusion? We will never know, but the fact is that from an early age he was watching everything around him. He was always, in Saul Bellow's phrase, "a first-class noticer."

On March 12, 1928, a woman named Louise Harvey gave birth to a son in Washington, D.C. All that is known about her and the father of the baby is that, according to adoption papers filed in Washington, the father "deserted and abandoned both the mother and child and had in no way contributed to the support and maintenance of said child." The baby was "surrendered" for adoption. On March 26, "Said minor was delivered into the care and custody of the Alice Chapin Adoption Nursery" at 444 West 22nd Street in Manhattan. On March 30, when the baby was eighteen days old, he was placed by the adoption agency with Reed A. Albee and Frances C. Albee, a childless couple living in Larchmont, New York. They brought him back to their home in Westchester, and on February 1, 1929, after ten months of living with the Albees, the child was formally adopted. The papers were processed, and he was named Edward Franklin Albee III, after Mr. Albee's father, who was the head of the Keith-Albee chain of vaudeville theaters. Albee later referred to himself as "tiny me, a little twig of a thing." "They bought me," he said. "They paid $133.30," explaining that was the cost for "professional services."

He says that he is unsure of the date but thinks that, from the age of six, he knew that he was adopted, and that both his paternal cousins, Barbara and Nancy, the daughters of his aunt Ethel, were also adopted. As he said, "The whole family was barren: the end of the line. Skidding to an awful halt. The whole bunch of them." The reason for his adoption, he said, was because his grandfather wanted a grandson, a male heir. When he was told that he was adopted, he pretended that he already knew. After his mother died in 1989, he found his adoption papers buried in a trunk with old photographs and other mementos. It was then that he learned that his birth name was Edward Harvey. His name was always Edward, the one continuing link to his otherwise unknown past.

His feeling about his adoption was to become one of the most important factors in his life. Repeatedly he would ask himself questions: Where did he come from, where did his talent come from, who were his natural parents, what effect did they have on his character, and did it really matter who they were? What does it mean to be a parent and what are the responsibilities of parents to children, children to parents, siblings to siblings? Did he have a brother or sister, perhaps even an identical twin, who, as was the case with

Thornton Wilder, was stillborn? These and related questions were to be posed again and again in his life and in his work. At the same time, he had no sense of history about the family into which he entered.

Edward F. Albee III became a member—certainly the most famous member—of an old American family. The Albees can trace their New England lineage back to the late seventeenth century in Machias, Maine, where they were sea captains. There are Albees buried in the hilltop graveyard on Monhegan Island, Maine, where Edward Albee's oldest childhood friend, Noel Farrand, summered. William Albee, Edward Albee's great-great-great-grandfather, was one of the original Minute Men in 1776, but in the late nineteenth and early twentieth centuries the family was most closely allied with the world of show business. Albee's grandfather Edward Franklin Albee was born in Machias in 1857, and at nineteen ran away to join the circus, which is where he met Benjamin Franklin Keith.

In 1883, B. F. Keith opened a museum-cum-freak show in Boston, exhibiting a chicken with a human face, a pig that was billed as the biggest hog in America, and other strange creatures. Keith also presented variety acts (including the comedians Weber and Fields). He soon brought in E. F. Albee, his old friend from circus days, as his partner. It was Albee's idea to expand performances. Together they offered a pirated version of *The Mikado*, along with vaudeville. Then they jettisoned any pretense of presenting art and limited themselves to vaudeville. With success, their business expanded. Adding theaters in Providence, Philadelphia, and New York, they became real estate tycoons. Eventually they owned some four hundred theaters across the country, featuring popular entertainment. E. F. Albee, who was referred to as Keith's "lord high executioner," was known as a tough negotiator and a firm opponent of labor unions. He broke the White Rats of America ("rats" is "star" spelled backward), the union of vaudeville performers, and then bought their midtown Manhattan clubhouse and turned it over to the Vaudeville Managers' Association, a rival organization run by the Keith-Albee circuit. E. F. Albee had lunch in the clubhouse "in imperious splendor—and loneliness—almost daily." When Keith died in 1914, Albee took over the Keith-Albee circuit.

Groucho Marx, who knew Albee well from his days in vaudeville, referred to him as "the Ol' Massa" who regarded the performers as his slaves. Despite—or because of—the bawdiness of vaudeville, he was known as a rigid enforcer of censorship on the Keith-Albee stages. In 1927, Keith-Albee merged with the Orpheum circuit. Through the purchase of stock, Joseph P.

Kennedy took over the company. He is supposed to have told Albee that he was "washed up" and then edged him out of the business. None of this interests E. F. Albee's grandson and namesake in the slightest. He thinks of the Albee family and the family history as something completely separate from himself.

In 1910, E. F. Albee moved to Larchmont, where he owned two houses, one on Bay Avenue, the other on Hommocks Road. Occasionally he would sponsor visits to Larchmont by famous entertainers like Lillie Langtry. As a wealthy local patron, E. F. Albee often played Santa Claus at Christmas and gave presents to all the children of the village. According to a local history, he was toasted at a testimonial dinner as "Larchmont's first citizen" and "Santa Claus to young and old." He died in 1930, at seventy-two, two years after his only grandson was born, and the $15 million he left was the root of his wife's estate and of their son's fortune. Reed Adelbert Albee inherited the Bay Avenue house, and E. F. Albee's widow, Laura Smith Albee, kept the Hommocks residence and their home in Palm Beach, Florida. With private railroad cars to take her and her relatives from one place to the other, she became the dowager empress of the family. To her grandson, she looked like the Queen Mother of England, a regal woman who wore her hair in a large bun and often had a lace collar around her neck. E. F. and Laura Albee's son, Reed (who was born in Boston, September 8, 1885), was for a time the assistant general manager of the family theater chain, and a far more popular figure among vaudevillians than his despotic father. He retired in 1928; his adopted son, who was born that year, has, of course, no memory of him ever working. It was said that Reed Albee devoted the rest of his life to "owning and showing three- and five-gaited saddle horses." More accurately, it could be said that his wife, Frances Albee, devoted her life to that pursuit.

In 1914, after an earlier unhappy marriage, Reed Albee married Louise Williams, an actress and a widow, then divorced her ten years later. In the divorce papers, his wife mentioned several corespondents, including one "well-known actress," whose name was not disclosed. It was a friendly parting, with Mrs. Albee giving her husband a farewell party. Several months later, on March 12, 1925, Reed married Frances Loring Cotter. It was her first marriage. One newspaper headline read: ALBEE, SON OF MILLIONAIRE, MARRIED TO SALESGIRL IN JERSEY CITY. Throughout her life, especially in articles about her son, she was identified as a former mannequin (or model) in Bergdorf's department store on Fifth Avenue. When she was married, however, a newspaper article said she had been "in charge of the wholesale millinery department" of J. Thorpe and Company on Fifth Avenue, and that she met her husband the previous year at a party he gave in his apartment. Why she was invited to that party remains a mystery. The portrait of A and her unnamed husband in *Three Tall Women* is an almost exact replica of the Albees. As in *Three Tall Women*, Reed was very short and Frances, who was known as Frankie, was very tall; he liked tall women. Before he married Frankie, he had been involved romantically with many women, including the actress and comedienne Charlotte Greenwood (presumably the unnamed corespondent in the divorce papers). Greenwood was tall and gangling and specialized in doing handstands and backflips on stage. As the character of A, the old woman in *Three Tall Women*, says about her husband, "He was going with that comedienne did the splits, the eight-foot one." Later, Edward Albee was to consider the possibility that Charlotte Greenwood could have become his adoptive mother. He said, "He got my mother instead," and added that he might have preferred Greenwood. Then, he said, "There would have been some laughs."

Reed had a glass eye (as a young man, he had been hit in the eye by a golf ball), wore pince-nez, was reserved but liked to dance. He was, said his son, "a funny-looking little man with one eye." Frankie loved clothes and horses and was considered to be glamorous. She made a reputation for herself as a Westchester horsewoman, winning ribbons in shows. As one of her acts of vanity, she, in common with A, lied about her age, but took off only one year. When she died, she was ninety-two, not ninety-one as she had said.

Claire, the witty, astringent sister played by Elaine Stritch in the Broadway revival of *A Delicate Balance* and by Maggie Smith in the subsequent London revival, is based on Frankie's younger sister Jane, who was an alcoholic. Jane did not live with the Albees, but she was often at their house, and when she was there she would generally be drinking. As in the play, she had an apartment by the Larchmont railroad station. As Claire says in *A Delicate Balance*, "Do you remember the spring I moved out, the time I was *really* sick with the stuff: was drinking like the famous fish? Was a source of great embarrassment? So that you and Agnes set me up in an apartment near the station, and Agnes was so good about coming to see me?" Paralleling the characters, Frankie would say to her sister, "Why don't you go away for a vacation, go to Kentucky or Tennessee and visit the distilleries?" or "Why don't you find a bar with an apartment in the back and move in there?" As should be clear in *A Delicate Balance*, Edward was fond of his aunt, with an affection that he did not feel for his mother.

Soon after *A Delicate Balance* opened on Broadway in 1966 (starring Hume Cronyn, Jessica Tandy, and Rosemary Murphy as Claire, the role based on Aunt Jane), Jane had lunch with Edward and his mother and then went to see the play. She sent him a note saying how much she was impressed: "It is superbly written with just the right balance of wit, humor and near tragedy. The cast could not be 'more right'—especially Rosemary Murphy." Then she added, with discretion, "There is so much 'food for thought' after you leave the theater." She did not explain what she was thinking.

When Edward was in his early twenties, he wrote a play called *The Merry Month of May*, about the tortured relationship between a son and his parents. In his stage directions, he describes the father: "Neal, 65, short, a paunch, grey-haired, is dozing in a chair, an evening paper across his lap. He is blind in his right eye; he has a deep voice which can, and does frequently, rise to a whine. His clothes (suit and tie) expensive but dull, tiny feet encased in highly polished custom-made shoes; on each little finger he wears a ring; on his right hand an emerald set in gold, on his left hand a massive gold signet ring. His nails are polished and his jowled face is tanned." The mother is described: "Agnes, six feet in her heels, and her fine figure is just slightly overblown. She is 53, colors her hair an expert dull blond, wears a summer dress that is youthful but which does not make her look foolish; she is a big woman and, on her, the heavy jewelry she wears does not look out of place, but on a smaller woman the huge diamond she wears on her marriage finger would be absurd; four strands of real pearls she wears wound into a rope; she walks erect, proud of her height; her voice has great range." These are, Albee acknowledges, portraits of his parents.

From their son's point of view, the Albees were the oddest and most removed of couples. Frankie was imperious, demanding, and unloving, though she was an active, if often an offstage, presence in her son's life. In contrast, Reed was uncommunicative and disengaged. At least, as their son remembers, they hardly ever spoke. Others in their circle had different feelings about them. Depending on the point of view, Frankie could be seen as a charming, gregarious woman, someone with an easy way at least in her local society. Reed, however, seemed to be one-dimensional, but there were two areas of his life that always remained something of a mystery to his son: his friendship with theater people and his supposed sense of humor, which never was in evidence to his son.

Harry and Edna Winston (of the Fifth Avenue jewelry firm) were good friends of the Albees. Frankie bought jewelry—her signature pearls—from Harry Winston, and the two couples saw each other socially. The Winstons' son, Ronald, said that, within his family, Frankie was always "billed as my favorite woman." In many ways he was closer to her than her son was. "I found her very amusing because she was full of spunk. I think that feeling was generated more by my father than by me, but I was very fond of her. She was an extremely vivacious woman and had a rather powerful, sonorous voice. She was a big-boned woman, six feet tall. I remember that she'd wear off-the-shoulder evening dresses and had blond bouffant hair and very white skin." Others outside her family, considered her to be a stylish, elegant figure.

People have far fewer memories of Reed. "He was a kind of dapper chap, a mousy guy," says Ronald Winston. "Reed didn't have a lot to say. My impression of him was, in an expression of the thirties, that he was 'a rich man's son.' He didn't seem to have a lot of interests. I don't think he ever worked. He obviously liked the camaraderie with my father, but I don't think they were soulmates. My father was a very driven, dynamic guy. He was a great raconteur and highly motivated in his thinking. Reed didn't seem terribly motivated. I remember my father wanted to talk to him about business, but said that Reed was hopeless. He wasn't interested and didn't understand business affairs. He would just sit there with his glass of scotch. It was definitely Frankie who held forth." And about the relationship between the Albees: "He used to call her Mommy" as the character of Daddy does in *The American Dream.*

Why did Frankie marry Reed? As the character says in *Three Tall Women*, "Because he makes me laugh. Because he's little and he's funny looking—and a little like a penguin" and "he's rich—or his father is." Reed Albee was also famously unfaithful, with a penchant for showgirls. Many years later, long after his parents had died, Edward received a letter from his mother's personal maid, who said that Reed Albee had tried to rape her in the root cellar. She said that she had reported the incident to Mrs. Albee, who paid her never to mention it again. Edward's comment: "I don't think he was the 'maid kind.' " However, in *Three Tall Women*, the character of B, the middle-aged version of A, says sarcastically that her husband has the "morals of a sewer rat." She continues: "Chasing the chambermaid into closets, the kitchen maid into the root cellar, and God knows what goes on at the stag at the club! They probably nail the whores to the billiard tables for easy access." In a conversation in 1995, Albee paraphrased that last sentence in direct reference to his father: "I don't think my mother had much of a sex life with my father. He was often nailing the whores to the billiard table at the Lotos Club in New York."

There is still a question about Frankie's personal life before she met her husband. In *The American Dream*, Grandma says to Daddy, "It's Mommy over there makes all the trouble. If you'd listened to me, you wouldn't have married her in the first place. She was a tramp and a trollop and a trull to boot, and she's no better now." Asked directly if his mother was "a tramp and a trollop and a trull to boot," her son says, "I certainly thought she was," but admits that he had no proof. "I can't say that I knew she was a tramp or that she married him for money. But I suspect so. It certainly must have crossed her mind." Then he remembers another quotation from *The American Dream*, where Grandma says that her daughter at the age of eight had vowed that she was going to marry a rich man. In baby talk, she says, "I'm going to set my wittle were end right down in a tub o' butter." Albee says that line is "a paraphrase of something that my mother is supposed to have said. It means 'I've really got it good.' "

In *Three Tall Women*, in a long, passionate monologue, the character known as B talks about a sudden fling she had with the groom in a stall in the stable, an encounter that her son discovered. The woman later fires the groom, "because it's dangerous not to, because it's a good deal I've got with the penguin, a long-term deal in spite of the crap he pulls." Albee says the scene was an invention and also a kind of wish fulfillment: He liked to think his mother had had an affair with the groom. But no, he did not catch her in the act, as the character does in the play. Then he adds quickly, "I was in love with the groom's son"—one of his early stirrings of homosexuality—and the groom's son did not know of his feeling. In a playful mode, Albee later wrote about the groom's son's hairy wrists in *Tiny Alice*. Julian (the character originally played by John Gielgud) conjures a childhood memory of a groom, "a young fellow who always scowled and had . . . the hairiest hands I have ever seen." Albee recalls that at least at one point in his childhood there was talk of divorce because of his father's infidelity. "My mother and her mother had caught him with some floozy. They heard about it or found out about it somehow, and they were in alliance against this man. There was a period when nobody was talking to anybody." But the couple decided to remain together. "I don't think they were enormously happy together, but they stayed together. I think she sort of liked him. It's fairly accurate in the play [*Three Tall Women*]. Unless one heard the vile remarks about niggers and kikes, they would pass as a perfectly normal middle-class WASP family."

How close was Reed to Tobias, the patient paterfamilias in A *Delicate Balance?* Says Albee, "My first instinct is to say, not terribly, but there are certain similarities. He didn't want the boat rocked, he wanted everything kept quite quiet, and he let everybody run things for him." In Albee's original notes for that play, he wrote, "Tobias retired from the usual battles of life, maybe through not having to face them, the insulation of position, money, a wife who runs things as he wants them run, it's a life for him that's least discomforting." While agreeing on the parallels, Albee said, "I don't know whether he could have risen to the occasion as Tobias does in the third act of the play."

In the third act, Tobias invites his frightened friends to move into his home, to accept his offer of sanctuary.

The Albee house was one of the largest and grandest manor houses in an exclusive section of Larchmont, at that time a small village of 5,284 people. As Edward remembers, "It had lots of lovely lawns and big trees, all on the coast, on the water," the water being Long Island Sound. Putting his visual memory to the test, he describes the house. As if walking through it, he says: "A big mock Tudor house. A three-car garage over on the left. Circular driveway. Go in the front door, little vestibule, then a large paneled entrance hall. Straight ahead is the solarium, the sun room. To the right, down three stairs, the big formal living room, piano on the left, fireplace on the far wall, arches on either side going to another sun room at the end of it. On your immediate left are stairways going up to the second floor, a little further on, the formal dining room paneled in pine, leading to the pantry, which led to the second pantry, which led to the kitchen. Upstairs, go down to the hall to the left: my room, a long narrow room. My grandmother's room off to the left, or maybe no; that was a guest room. Go along the long narrow corridor, another room. I forget who lived in it. Another room upstairs and then way off on the right my parents' room. And then my mother's room with two beds and huge dressing areas and closets. Then a stairway, going up to the third floor, where seven or eight servants' rooms were, and a big attic."

And his room? "A bed with a sort of wicker background. I actually clawed through it, until it broke. The croup tent. I had croup a lot. Nobody has croup anymore, do they? Influenza, terrible fluid in the lungs. And the croup tent. There was my little desk where I did all my drawings [as a child, he had a penchant for art as well as for music]. All those windows, even though I was on the second floor. Nine windows in this room. No air conditioning. I remember the screens were attached with those little hooks to eyes in the wood, making sure they were locked every night so that I would not be kidnapped. And the bow and arrow under the bed. That's all in a play somewhere."

In the third act of *Who's Afraid of Virginia Woolf?* Martha remembers the childhood of their imaginary son: ". . . with teddy bears and transparent floating goldfish, and a pale blue bed with cane at the headboard when he was older, cane which he wore through . . . finally . . . with his little hands . . . in his . . . sleep . . . and a croup tent . . . a pale green croup tent, and the shining kettle hissing in the one light of the room that time he was sick . . . those four days . . . and animal crackers, and the bow and arrow he kept under his bed." Why, asks George. "For fear," says Martha, "for fear of . . ." and does not finish her sentence.

Larchmont, especially in the 1930s and early 1940s when Edward was growing up, was an exclusive suburban community, primarily Protestant, but with a sprinkling of Roman Catholics. No outsiders need apply. The neighborhood around Bay Avenue was its own enclave, decidedly upper class and snobbish. To a great extent, the people who lived there were untouched by World War II, just as they had been untouched by the depression. Nearby was the Larchmont Yacht Club, which the Albees occasionally visited (more often they went to the Westchester Country Club in Rye, the model for the country club referred to in *A Delicate Balance*). The Farrands—Mr. and Mrs. Clair L. Farrand and their children—lived next door to the Albees in a smaller house, and next door to them in a large house was Frank Campbell, who owned the Campbell funeral homes. Down the street was R. J. Schaeffer of the Schaeffer brewing company. Of all the neighbors, the Farrands were by far the closest to Edward. The father, Clair L. Farrand, was an electronic engineer and inventor. He invented the cone loudspeaker in 1921 and later worked for Warner Bros. in Hollywood during the time that sound replaced silent movies. Noel Farrand, the youngest of Clair Farrand's four sons, was a year and a half younger than Albee; he became Albee's best friend and remained one of his closest friends for his entire life.

Noel Farrand knew Albee "almost from the cradle" and always spoke about him with the fondness of family. He was the nearest to a brother of all the people that passed through Edward's life. Projecting himself back to his first memory, Farrand said: "I can remember being in the front yard in a playpen and being conscious of Edward upstairs in his bedroom." The play *Tiny Alice* is dedicated to Farrand, and he thought of the Albee house as the model for that mysterious mansion that dominates the play and the stage. "Our house had three stories," said Farrand, "but it didn't have the distance and darkness of the Albee house. The Albee house seemed uninhabitable." As children, the two boys used to wander freely through the house and gardens and the neighboring woods. It became their world for exploration. Putting the lie—or at least a question—to the tales of Edward's unhappy childhood, Noel could find a salutary side: "For a kid, it was a wonderful life we led in Larchmont: the water and the wild birds, the herons. Larchmont was such a little place then, and you could play almost any game. There were enough kids to do that with." On the other hand, as Edward said, "Noel didn't fit very well into his family. We were both outsiders"—in every sense of the word.

From the earliest of ages, Noel and Edward sparked each other's creative imagination. Both were great readers and were interested in music. Both thought about becoming composers. Noel eventually did become a composer and was Albee's entrée into the world of music and musicians; many years later he introduced Albee to William Flanagan. Noel's own career never reached the heights of others in his life (beginning with Albee), but he was a highly articulate and intelligent man, a colorful and likeable character. He also had deep psychological problems and periods of manic depression, some of which could be traced back to his rigid Roman Catholic upbringing and the lack of encouragement he received for his creativity in his own home. It was said that his father treated his sons as if they were in boot camp. He wanted them to follow him into the family business and, disappointed with Noel, would refer to him as "the piano player." When Noel did not do well in school, his father would lock the piano (Noel, with Edward's help, learned to unlock it). About the Farrands, Albee summarizes tersely: "Redneck Irish family with a lunatic mother."

Through many ordeals, physical as well as emotional, Noel always received support from Albee, who remained loyal to him even when others jettisoned him from their lives because of his bizarre behavior. At his most manic, he decided to have a music festival on Monhegan Island, ordered a piano to be shipped over from the mainland, and invited Robert F. Kennedy and Leonard Bernstein, among others. Until his death in 1996, through all his difficulties, Noel retained the clearest of memories: He could remember dates and details that would escape others. He also had a lifelong devotion to Albee, whom he trusted implicitly and greatly admired as an artist.

Once, while pondering Albee's ancestry, Noel decided that his friend was the illegitimate son of Eugene O'Neill and "proved" it through various dates, declaring that chronologically O'Neill could have been Albee's father, adding that there was a physical resemblance between the playwrights. When told of Noel's figment, Albee said, quite coolly, "On the whole, I would have preferred that William Faulkner were my father." He then offered as possible "proof" that both he and Faulkner wrote long sentences. In photographs of them at a mature age, there is a passing resemblance among all three writers, O'Neill, Faulkner, and Albee: a distant look of sadness in their eyes, as if each had firmly resolved not to smile. In common, all three had serious drinking problems.

Farrand said that as playmates he and Edward (who was called Eddie and Ed at the time) suffered a great deal of interference from Mrs. Albee: "Sometimes she didn't think Edward should play with me or my brothers. We played games that had to do with robbery and jewel thefts. There was a time when I enjoyed great favor with Mrs. Albee and used to have breakfast with her in her bedroom. I realized when I was sitting with her that she was a very bigoted woman. She had this anti-Semitic thing about 'the Jews in Washington.' She had all the nouveau riche prejudices. I first encountered prejudice in her sa-lon. I wasn't very sophisticated at that age, but I definitely had the impression that she was intolerant and that she was ruling Edward in a far from benevo-lent way." To Noel she seemed "tall, regal, and rather forbidding."

To Peter Alexander, another of Edward's childhood friends, she was a Valkyrie, Brunhilde towering over Edward and his playmates. "When she came in the room, there was tremendous presence and power." She kept watchful guard over her son, who "was kept in a glass cage." As a child, Ed-ward was short and a bit overweight. Looking back, Alexander thought of Mrs. Albee's prejudices as being typical of the community: "It was probably a bee-hive of anti-Semites. Nobody would cross the line. Nobody even had black help; it was all Irish and Scottish." That area of Larchmont was "a tight little island" in several senses: It was filled with secret and not so secret drinkers, though as Edward remembers, drinking was not a problem with his parents.

As a pampered child, he had every wish indulged. He had an enormous, expensive collection of Grenadier Guard toy soldiers, thousands of them, enough to fill three rooms when they were on maneuvers. (Interestingly, when Hume Cronyn first met Frankie Albee, he thought that she seemed like a Grenadier Guard.) Because Edward had so many toy soldiers it was natural that the boys would come to his house to play. Edward, Noel, Noel's brother Robert, and Peter Alexander, who also lived in the neighborhood, had mock battles with the soldiers. Edward, dressed in a smoking jacket (which he owned and wore from the age of seven), would act as the emperor. "I thought he was autocratic," says Alexander. "He always wanted to be the boss." Robert Farrand recalled that Edward wore his hair slicked back and sometimes would have a cigarette holder in his mouth (but not a cigarette). Robert said he seemed like Genghis Khan, though in retrospect the image seems far more like Noël Coward. Edward had "the whole FAO Schwarz catalog" of toys, including a gilded chariot and a beautiful four foot long model sailboat, which, because of his age, he was not allowed to sail. Robert Farrand, being older, sailed the boat for him and Edward watched from his backyard. The boys also invented games about Sherlock Holmes, Nero Wolfe, Robin Hood, and other favorite fictional heroes. In addition, Edward would invent games for himself, war games and baseball games, and sit for hours and play them by himself. "My memory tells me I was always a bit of a loner," he says, "and that I didn't mind being a loner."

Both Edward and Noel had the most active fantasy lives. As a child, Noel imagined that he was a bird. He drew pictures of birds, constructed models of them, and decorated them with his mother's rhinestone jewelry. Sometimes he would add pieces borrowed from Mrs. Albee's collection (probably one reason Mrs. Albee later turned against him). He would place the fake birds in trees, which might be considered a Farrand attempt to confuse nature. Once the two boys were on a nearby dock, tossing stones and other objects into the water, and Noel threw a brick, which struck Edward's hand. As a result, Albee lost mobility of one of the joints in a finger. Before or after, Edward made mischief of his own: He had a guinea pig pen on his property and when Noel was four he locked him inside, which frightened Noel and apparently delighted Edward. Years later when told that Noel felt that was a traumatic experience, Albee dismissed it by saying, "I thought he liked it." Edward's friends would often tease him and take advantage of him, at least partly because they considered him the richest kid in the neighborhood. "We didn't treat him very well," said Noel. Despite their own friendship, "We would take possession of his toys and break his soldiers." They built a toy guillotine and would chop the heads off the expensive soldiers. Of course, Edward always had replacement armies at the ready: "He was a little rich boy treated cruelly by his peers." Noel remembers several times, including one at Edward's own birthday party, that his friend broke down in tears. Birthday parties were lavish, impersonal affairs for the children; Mrs. Albee was not there.

Inside the Albee house was another world, populated by his parents and their circle. Edward's life was with Noel and his other friends; with Nanny Church and the servants; and with his favorite relative, his maternal grandmother, Grandma Cotter (the model for Grandma in *The Sandbox* and *The American Dream*). He grew up with surrogates, several of whom acted as substitute parents, and the idea of surrogate parents was to become an important theme in his plays. In the family, Grandma Cotter was by far the closest to him. She was, he said, "an outlaw like me." For much of Edward's childhood, she was upstairs in her room with her asthmatic Pekingese dogs. She and her grandson formed an alliance against the world, or, rather, against his father and mother. It was, he said, "two ends against the middle." His mother, once her own mother's friend, eventually turned against her. As A says in *Three Tall Women*, "She becomes an enemy. She dies when she's eighty-four—seventeen years of it, of staying up in her room in the big house with us. The colitis, the cigarettes, the six or seven Pekingese she goes through. I stopped liking her." Edward never stopped liking her. But it was his other, paternal grandmother whose largesse was to enable him to live on his own at a crucial time of his life.

Lenore (later Lin) Emery, a childhood playmate of his, his first female friend and later in life a successful sculptor and very good friend, knew him both in Larchmont and Palm Beach. Their families lived near each other in both places. "Our governesses were friends, but our mothers were not," she said, explaining that her mother had married for money and was envious of Edward's mother for marrying more money. "My mother was very much like his mother. My mother was a very beautiful, ambitious woman, from no money, no family background whatsoever. Her only interest was jewels and furs; she was very antagonistic to me. She was very anti-intellectual." In contrast to Mrs. Albee, she was Jewish, a fact that she tried to keep secret but, when it was discovered, eventually led to problems in Palm Beach. Because of the anti-Semitism in that community, there was an attempt to have Lin excluded from the Palm Beach school. Her mother, who had severe psychological problems, had episodes of violence. Ironically, Mrs. Emery and Mrs. Albee, who were often not on speaking terms, ended up in the same place many years later, as residents in retirement at the Westchester Country Club, a scene that sounds like something out of *The Gin Game*.

Lin Emery said of her childhood friendship with Edward, "My memories are of myself with Edward, a shadowy playmate in our playrooms, with my Mrs. Oliver and his Mrs. Church standing guard." Anita Church was a large woman; Bertha Oliver was small. Both governesses were strong intellectual forces in the children's lives. Mrs. Oliver had been part of the Fabian group in England and knew Bertrand Russell and George Bernard Shaw. She had also corresponded with Einstein. Nanny Church nurtured Edward's interest in the arts from an early age.

Lin Emery participated in what must have been Edward's first brush with theater: "I know we made up plays because I remember being severely punished for tying him up with imaginary ropes in one of our plays. It was in the center of the room and he was sitting on the chair. I was acting as an angel or some sort of spirit dancing around him. He started screaming, and both the governesses rushed in. I got scolded for whatever I was doing to Edward that would make him so terrified."

Albee recalls it as a time of great inquisitiveness: "We used to get under the dressing table and poke around." That, he said, was in one of his plays. Lin adds a curious note to her recounting of their relationship, "I envied Edward (and his cousins Barbara and Nancy) for being adopted and longed to have been adopted also." Lin disliked her mother even more than Edward disliked his. She ran away from home at fifteen during one of her mother's violent fits of temper and found shelter with the family doctor. Then her nanny took her to Manhattan, and Lin moved in with a grandmother. She had an even worse childhood than Albee did.

One of Albee's recurrent fantasies, developed when he was quite young, was that, in the tradition of Victorian novels, Nanny Church was his real mother and had been hired secretly to take care of him (this was years before Olivia de Havilland played a related role in the movie *To Each His Own*). Similarly, Lin dreamed of belonging to her governess. In any case, Edward felt closer to his nanny than to his mother and father. For one thing, he does not remember having meals with his parents. One family friend offers a snapshot image of Edward having his supper in his bed: "a grave, handsome child with beautiful eyes." Periodically he would be brought down, as if for inspection, and, always, he was kept at a cool distance.

When Edward was almost four, Nanny Church was called out of town and Mrs. Albee asked Ida Hughes, whose husband ran a local drugstore, if she had any suggestion as to who could fill in for the governess for that weekend. Mrs. Hughes's younger sister, Ethel Hofer, then seventeen, was visiting her relatives from her home in Minnesota and was drafted as babysitter. Many years later, after Edward had become a celebrated Broadway playwright, Ms. Hofer, as Ethel Erickson, a practicing pathologist, married with two children, sent him a letter recalling what was for her a euphoric weekend: "The first night we stayed up as late as we could and ate too many gum drops. The next day we went to the stables and I watched you ride a silver horse. That afternoon we went to 'boxing lessons.' . . . That evening there was a big dinner so we stayed upstairs and whooped it up, as three-year-olds and teenagers can." In her recollection, the guests at the Albee dinner included Jimmy Walker, the mayor of New York City, and Mr. and Mrs. William Todd, wealthy shipowners and friends of the family. "On Sunday it was a ride to the stables and meeting the whole family, and finally that afternoon you and I walked miles and played in a half dozen backyards with other kids, arriving home completely disheveled, dirty and happy. But unfortunately for me, Mrs. Church was back." For Ethel, it was a memorable and momentous time. For Edward, hearing a voice from the past was like hearing about someone else's childhood. Answering her letter, he wrote, "You remind me of things that I do recall, and you also bring up things that I only might have recalled — things that are so misty and dreamlike that they may never have happened at all, though I'm sure they did."

Around the age of four, during a visit to church with his nanny, he had what he regards as a religious experience. It was Easter, and for the first time he heard the story of The Crucifixion: "I was deeply upset by it. I think I somehow related to the fact that the Episcopal Church was responsible for The Crucifixion." He started weeping and cried so much Nanny Church had to take him out of the church. That, he said, wryly, "leads to a plethora of Christ symbolism in my plays." Going one step further, he suggests—with a smile—that that moment began his loss of faith. The fact is from that time onward he has had an obsession about Christ, as man and martyr.

The private life of his parents often revolved around entertaining. Because of his vaudeville connections, Reed Albee would invite actors and clowns to their house: Walter Pidgeon, Ed Wynn (who would come with his son Keenan), Victor Moore, and William Gaxton—by then all of them were major stars. Some of them would sail up from New York on their private yachts, docking them at Larchmont harbor and then taking a tender to the Albee house. When the neighborhood children heard that Shirley Temple, at that time the most popular star in America, was going to visit the Albees, they were excited at the prospect. They were greatly disappointed when it turned out that it was merely a rumor.

From their perspective, his parents' friends thought Edward was well cared for. "There was never a kid more indulged in," said Ed Wynn in 1962. "When he was five or six, his father bought him the biggest St. Bernard he could find. The kid looked like he was leading an elephant." What Edward remembers most about that St. Bernard, Laddie, was that one snowy winter day, the dog was tied to his sled and, dog and boy, they rode around the family grounds. Laddie apparently saw a rabbit, swerved, and ran the sled directly into a large tree. Edward fell forward and struck his head on a nail in the tree. As always, Nanny Church was quick on the scene. She picked him up and carried him to the house. Edward was in tears and he remembers Nanny Church saying again and again, "For crying out loud," which "had nothing to do with the fact that I was crying." Luckily a doctor was at that moment visiting the Albees. He cleaned the wound but he did not take stitches, leaving Edward with a scar that is still visible on his forehead. Later Albee wrote about Laddie that he was "an unhappy St. Bernard who became fat and lazy, for he didn't get to run much or sink deep in snow, or rescue anybody, or anything." Then and later, dogs and cats were to play an important part in his life. One of his most vivid childhood memories is of crying at The Biscuit Eater, a movie about a dog that is punished for stealing eggs.

Looking back on his childhood, he says, "I was given all the things that money can buy: electric trains, private schools, a nanny" and a man named Al Zerega who acted as an athletic trainer and a kind of paid companion. In the absence of Edward's father, who always seemed otherwise engaged, Zerega was the closest to a strong male presence in the household. One of Zerega's roles was to teach Edward the art of self-defense. Lin Emery remembers boxing with Edward and has a photograph to back up the memory. There was a stable with saddle horses (and Dalmatians) on the property. Because Frankie was a horsewoman, she encouraged her son to ride, which he did from an early age. Later, Don Budge taught him how to play tennis at the Westchester Country Club, where Budge, a former tennis champion, was the professional in residence. Every day, the family chauffeur drove him to and from Rye Country Day School. Albee's memories of the Rye school are mostly of athletics; he played both soccer and baseball.

In the family collection there is a photograph of Edward next to his mother and his cousins Barbara and Nancy, each on a horse, "tiny little me on top of a huge gray gelding." Neatly groomed, wearing a checked jacket, he looks princely, a perfect picture of Larchmont royalty. In an earlier photograph, he is sitting in his mother's lap next to one of the many Albee pet dogs, a terrier. Frankie's hair is marcelled in the current fashion. Edward has a chubby face, long ringlets, and a cheerful smile. In this and other pictures, he looks happy and content: a pose, of course, for the camera. About those photographs, he said, "All unhappy families are alike," meaning, in part, that despite everything people look happy in the family album.

Often the chauffeur drove Edward and his nanny into New York in one of the family's two Rolls-Royces to see a matinee of a Broadway show. Edward habitually sat in the front seat next to the driver. He and Nanny Church always saw musicals, beginning with Billy Rose's *Jumbo* starring Jimmy Durante (which opened in November 1935, when Edward was seven). Many years later, Rose was to become an important figure in Edward's professional life, but that was the boy's first brush with theater. His two most indelible memories of the show are seeing a live elephant on stage and the Krazy Kat wooden toy that he took home as a souvenir, a toy that could be manipulated like a puppet. He vividly remembers Durante leading the elephant by its trunk. Every time anyone would ask Durante about the elephant, he would say, "What elephant?" The following year, he saw Rodgers and Hart's *On Your Toes*, which featured George Balanchine's *Slaughter on Tenth Avenue*. In 1937, the show was *Hooray for What!*, a Harold Arlen–E. Y. Harburg musical that made room for Ed Wynn to insert his vaudeville routines. One was a telephone sketch in which Wynn said hello to a long list of people. When Wynn learned that young Albee was in the house, he ad-libbed his name on that list. Another of Edward's favorites was Bobby Clark, who "played a Mexican tortilla maker: He came out with a cart and a lot of dough, which he lassoed into great long strings." He also enjoyed the outrageous nonsense of Olsen and Johnson in *Hellzapoppin'*. Ushers would intentionally put theatergoers in the wrong seats and then make them crawl over the heads of others to get to their right places. A small plant was carried through the audience, "and every time it went through, it grew larger and larger." This was, as Albee later realized, his first experience with the Theater of the Absurd.

At the same time, Nanny Church encouraged his interest in classical music. On Saturday afternoons, if they were at home, they would listen to the broadcast of the Metropolitan Opera: They would lie down on a bed together and lift off into a world of music.

Hovering over the house was a fear of kidnapping, as there was for many other wealthy families at the time, because of the kidnapping of the Lindbergh baby. "I remember my family talking a lot about kidnapping, and maybe they even put a guard on the property for a while. [One friend said that there were guards.] They were afraid that there might be a spate of kidnapping, and that their son might be a prime target." It was in response to these precautions that Edward grew so fearful that he started sleeping with the bow and arrow under his bed and began to check that all the screens on the windows in his room were locked before he went to bed. When his nanny came into his room to say goodnight, he would say, for luck, "See you in the morning," and persist until she said, "Yes, I'll see you in the morning." Only then, with that promise, would he go to sleep. He asks himself, "Was I afraid of dying or of being removed? I don't know which." In later years, he made a few futile attempts to run away, to remove himself: a kind of self-kidnapping.

If there was little communication with his mother, there was none with his father, who sat silently in his favorite chair or walked around the room jingling the coins in the pocket of his trousers or dressing gown (an image repeated by Tobias in *A Delicate Balance*). Noel Farrand recalled, "The sound of his jingling coins usually heralded his entry into the room, and often you heard it while he was there. He rarely spoke. He would say hello to me and then listen to his wife talk." Albee says simply, "He was such a negative, quiet person that I never even got to know the man." He adds, "I have the memory that I once did try to have a conversation with him about how I felt, that I did try that, and it didn't work. We were both terribly embarrassed by it. I wanted it to be over as soon as possible, and I think he did too." Once, Edward and his father and Noel played poker together. "He beat us, and he giggled about that. He had that laugh: ha-*ha*. That's the way he laughed. I'm told that he was a very funny man, a raconteur. I have no memory of any of this." Almost everyone who visited the Albee house has a clear recollection of Mrs. Albee, but few have anything to say about her husband. He seemed to be invisible.

With bitterness, Edward says that whenever his mother became angry with him, she reminded him that he was adopted. The inference was in the air that, if he did not behave, if he did not measure up, he could be returned to the orphanage, like an unwanted possession. As he said, "I will never forgive her for that. . . . She kept saying things like, 'Just wait until you're eighteen and I'll have you out of the house so fast it will make your head spin.' The only thing I could possibly say for her is that she had a lot of pressures on her. But I don't think that excuses any of that kind of behavior."

He felt a curious kind of ambivalence about his relationship with his mother. In an early Albee play called *End of Summer*, a young man speaks about a memory of his mother crawling into bed with him, an image that appears several times in Albee's apprentice work. When that image was mentioned to him, he said, "in life, too," and added, "I don't remember how old I was," but he has a clear picture of times when his mother got into bed with him. It was not at all like those times when he and his nanny would lie on a bed and listen to the opera. His mother's action made him feel "sexually uncomfortable. I haven't the faintest idea what was going on in her mind, and whatever it was, I'm sure she wouldn't have admitted it to herself."

Pressed about his childhood, he says, "When I was a kid, I can't remember being unhappy or happy. I don't remember much of my emotional state between the age of four and eleven." When did he first realize he was unhappy? "Obviously not when I was going through it." But looking back, the perspective changes: "I was not happy being away at school. I was not happy being at home. Obviously I wasn't happy anywhere." About one thing he is adamant: He suffered no physical abuse in his family, no corporal punishment. On the other hand, neither did he feel love or affection, and has no memory of his parents embracing him, or, as he says, "no touchies, no feelies." Even as he began to express himself artistically, drawing as well as writing poems (from the age of six) and at least thinking about becoming a composer, there was not the slightest interest from his parents. Very early, their son responded by maintaining his distance from them.

There is, as always, another side to the story. Even at a young age, he was clever and had a certain amount of guile. Muir Weissinger Jr., one of his closest childhood friends, said, "He was consciously contrary at home. He enjoyed pushing the button to see what would happen. He would say, 'Let's press the button.' He would treat his parents like puppets. Reed Albee would make different grunting sounds. He hardly ever said complete sentences. If

Ed pressed the right button, his father would tell his story about meeting the Pope. His mother would say things to Ed like, 'Why don't you go out into the world and make a man of yourself?' He would always have a great comeback. There was lots of arguing in that house." Recalling the disparity between parents and child, Weissinger concluded, "It's lucky he was adopted. He would not get much talent from those two."

Reflecting on Edward's childhood, his friend Joanna Steichen, who is a psychologist, says, "He was particularly sensitive and observant and intuitive about what was going on. He was in this environment in which his mother wanted to be a perfect Republican aristocrat. She was so anxious, engaged in having to survive in that family, and terrified that her son might ruin her chances of survival: If he was bad enough, they might all get thrown out. His father wanted to be a playboy and have a good time. The in-laws were there demanding certain standards, and there was the drunken aunt, and Grandma in her room. I try to make sense of his life."

The Albees did not socialize with their neighbors, as did the Farrands, who frequented the Yacht Club. Often they visited the Winstons, going to dinner parties at their home in Scarsdale, but rarely did they return the invitation. Ronald Winston, who continues to run the family jewelry business, barely knew Edward (Edward was several years older), but has always been fascinated by the fact that Harry and Edna are the names of the characters who suddenly move in with Agnes and Tobias in A Delicate Balance. Edward says that the reason he borrowed the Winstons' names for the characters is that they would have been the last people that his parents would have taken in. For all of Edward's memories of his mother's casual prejudices, in particular her anti-Semitism, their friends the Winstons were Jewish. This, Edward suggests, is one reason that in real life his parents would not have given them shelter.

Every winter, the Albees all went to Palm Beach to Edward's paternal grandmother's house. Even more than Larchmont, this was a very conservative community where people were equally devoted to golf, bridge, and cocktails at the club. It was a place that he would remember with regret: "a highly prejudiced community with exclusionary clubs, a fortress against reality and the world." The journey south was a major expedition, like a scene out of a novel by Henry James or Edith Wharton. Gathering up possessions, they traveled from Pennsylvania Station in Grandmother Albee's two private railroad cars, linked to the end of a regular passenger train. The entourage included Reed and Frankie, Grandma Cotter, aunts, uncles, cousins, and servants. These were grand festive events, greatly anticipated within the family. Reed's sister Ethel would bring down her husband of the moment. Her first was a dentist, Ted Lauder; her second, George E. Vigouroux Jr., had been a dance instructor at an Arthur Murray dance studio and then opened an art gallery in Palm Beach. According to Albee, Vigouroux was homosexual and, both in Palm Beach and at his wife's house in Nantucket, indulged in activities that scandalized the family: he would "pick up and be beaten by tough black guys" and he would bring male lovers back home. Eventually he was ostracized from both resorts. Edward's Aunt Jane would also visit Palm Beach with her husband Hamilton Bendilare. As with her sister Frankie, she had been a department store model; then she became a buyer of women's clothes and moved to Washington where she worked for Garfinkel's department store. Edward liked her but not her husband. He recalls one episode: "I was ten or eleven. A swimming pool in Washington, probably in the apartment where they lived. I remember swimming, playing around, and throwing myself in the water at Bendilare, no sexual intent on my part that I can recall. But I remember him complaining that I was all over him. Interesting."

Edward loved to swim. He learned early and seemed to regard swimming, or life under water, as a kind of escape, a sea escape. In *Seascape*, Charlie, the middle-aged character played on Broadway by Barry Nelson, speaks for the author in his reverie about his childhood: "When I was tiny, I would go in the swimming pool, at the shallow end, let out my breath and sit on the bottom; when you let out your breath—all of it—you sink, gently, and you can sit on the bottom until your lungs need air. I would do that—I was so young—sit there, gaze about. Great trouble for my parents. 'Good God, go get Charlie; he's gone and sunk again.' "

During the three or four months he was in Florida, Edward would be taken out of Rye Country Day School and transferred to the Palm Beach Private School. "Then around Easter I'd be shipped back north again and put back in the Rye Country Day School, where they were teaching nothing I had been paying attention to down at the Palm Beach Private School." Among the children in Palm Beach were Lin Emery, Edward's cousins Barbara and Nancy Lauder, and as Lin Emery recalls, Fred Gwynne (later, the actor), and an exceedingly disruptive little boy named James Merrill. She remembers a Merrill birthday party: "All the governesses were on one side of a long table and all the children on the other side, and Jimmy got up on the table and ran up and down on it knocking over all the sugar pots. Then everybody started throwing creamed chicken at each other." Merrill was to cross paths with Edward at Lawrenceville Academy; much later he would become celebrated as a poet.

The annual journey to Florida left Edward with one especially bad memory. Once in class at the Rye Country Day School, the teacher was talking about the first American colonies, and in particular about Jamestown in Virginia. Edward piped up that he passed through Jamestown on the way to his grandmother's house in Florida. He recalls: "I said, 'Every winter we go down by train to Palm Beach, in my grandmother's private car. We go by Jamestown and I see all the lights in the windows.' I was just making this up because I wanted to participate. And he humiliated me by saying, 'There are no lights in the windows of Jamestown.' I shut up for three years after that. I never said another word to anybody about anything. I was enormously tongue-tied, pathologically shy." He adds, "Maybe part of that shyness was a form of loneliness."

Nanny Church was part of the Albee entourage to Palm Beach and, as usual, spent more time with Edward than his parents did. In one photograph, Edward, at a very young age, is seen with Nanny Church and his mother, in one of the rickshawlike bicycle coaches popular in that resort. To the rear is a black man, riding the bicycle that drives the wicker chair on the boardwalk. At Edward's feet is a spotted dog that looks like the one in the old RCA Victor phonograph ads. Looking at the photograph, Albee says, "I don't remember that dog at all. It must have been somebody else's. God, I am a fat little thing." When that photograph first turned up, he wrote to the family friend who had sent it to him: "Thank you for the photograph. You have sent me so far into the past that I don't know if I shall ever recover. I don't remember the specific incident of the photograph, but I imagine the cameraman was Mr. Brady, on his way south for a rest after covering the Civil War."

During the summer Albee was usually at the Adirondack Camp in upstate New York and later at Lake Sunapee Summer School in New Hampshire. One summer, when Edward was ten, his father called Harold Hughes at the Larchmont drugstore and said he would pay him to give his son a job. Taking an ethical stand, Hughes said that would violate state labor laws, but offered to hire the young boy and give him a salary. Naturally, Edward was driven to work by the family chauffeur, which, said Hughes, gave his modest store added dignity. Beginning as a delivery boy, he was soon promoted to mixing sodas at the fountain. When he was paid at the end of the week, he would ride the bus into New Rochelle and buy classical records. Sometime earlier, he decided he would take piano lessons and signed on with a local teacher. Without telling his parents, he visited her in her home and took private lessons. He did not pay her and finally she told his parents. As he tells the story, that was the end of his piano study.

In 1940, his paternal grandmother died. At the funeral, the casket was open and, one by one, each of the relatives had to view the body. "I remember exactly what my father, this reticent man, said. He stood at the coffin and said in a very loud voice, 'Good-bye, Mom.' And I think he cried. Was he talking to the dead, or was he talking to be heard? It always has to be a little bit of both." That death considerably altered the lives of the rest of the family. Reed Albee was wealthy enough to be unaffected by the depression, but the death of his mother increased his fortune. His sister inherited the house in Palm Beach and he inherited his mother's house in Larchmont, "the Hommocks" on Hommocks Road, at the very end of the street. It was grander and more beautiful than the Albee home on Bay Avenue, which they then sold. A handsome shingled house across the harbor from Bay Avenue, the Hommocks resembled grand estates in Newport, Rhode Island. It had nine acres, six or seven gardeners, and five or six servants indoors (the number varied according to the Albee's needs).

This was Edward Albee's favorite childhood home. As he described it: "All around three sides were great porches, open porches with white Doric pillars. It was a three-story house. Entering through the solarium—everybody had a solarium—it was an informal sitting room. Enter: a huge living room with sezesson walnut paneling, very much like the one in the play [A *Delicate Balance*]. Everywhere there were sixteen foot ceilings. Off to the right, a large formal dining room, off white, as I recall. At the end of it was a less formal breakfast room, but still very formal. Looking straight from the solarium into the living room, straight ahead of you is the staircase. Fireplace off to the left, bookshelves going into a paneled library, where I used to make old-fashioneds for my grandmother at cocktail time." At twelve, he was already the family bartender. "Upstairs there were five bedrooms. Mine was way off on the right, a guest room, another upstairs solarium, my grandmother's room, then my mother's room and my father's room. They didn't sleep in the same room. I think there was another upstairs sitting room where we had one of the early early television sets: a huge box with a tiny screen."

Edward loved the library, with its wall of leatherbound books. It was "a wonderful, wonderful room," and filled with an air of mystery. The library was for show, not for use, but he was overcome by his curiosity. One day, browsing the shelves, he came across the collected works of Ivan Turgenev. The books were unread; the pages had not been cut, and that fascinated him. "I took one out and cut the pages, and took it upstairs and started reading." He was thrilled by the stories of Russian country life, at least partly because they were so distant from his own world. After reading a book, he would put it back and take another one up to his room. "One day I guess I had fallen asleep with a book. When I came down to breakfast, my mother and my father were there, and Grandma Cotter and Aunt Jane. The whole scene in the dining room was emotionally chilly. I found out why. My mother announced, 'Suzie,' or whatever the maid's name was, 'Suzie tells us that there is a book that has been taken out of the bookcase. There is a hole where the book belonged.' " Edward explained that he had been reading the book and mentioned the author, an announcement that was met with stony silence. No one else at the table had read Turgenev or cared about him.

Years later, Aunt Jane asked Frankie if she remembered scolding her son for taking the books off the shelves. She replied, "Oh no, dear. I didn't scold him for taking them down. I scolded him for not putting them back." The important fact, as Albee recalled, was "the gap tooth in the bookshelves." In other words, the books were decoration and not to be disturbed. "Turgenev? Balzac? Zola? Madame de Sévigné? Who's going to read that stuff? I was in my early teens. It was a nice introduction to serious literature."

As a young teenager, Edward's other closest friend (besides Farrand) was Muir Weissinger Jr., who was born in England and emigrated to the United States in the late 1930s. Muir carried with him a sense of good breeding, combined with a devil-may-care, hedonistic attitude toward life. After meeting Muir at the Larchmont Yacht Club, Noel introduced him to Edward. The three formed a triumvirate, and Edward spent a great deal of time at the Weissingers' house. He called Muir's mother, Florence, "Mummy," as did other unrelated children, and to a certain extent the Weissingers became a kind of substitute family for him. Florence was English, while her husband was "a white-haired Southern gentleman with a cane: Judge Weissinger." Edward and Muir both went to Rye Country Day School and, later, Choate, and still later, Trinity College. They would hang up loudspeakers in the Weissinger garden and present recorded concerts. Edward, Noel, and Muir would go sailing in Muir's boat. None of them knew anything about boats and on at least one occasion, all three fell overboard. Later, Edward dated Muir's sister Delphine; he was her escort at her coming-out party. Before they ended their long and intense relationship, they were, he said, "unofficially engaged." In contrast to his own family, he thought the Weissingers were "a perfectly nice family," and, he adds, "I don't think my mother liked them." She thought he was spending too much time at their house. Long after he left home, he remained in contact with the Weissingers, at least with Mrs. Weissinger and Muir.

During World War II, the Albees split their time between the Hommocks and their apartment on Park Avenue in Manhattan. By then, Edward was away most of the time, at school (a succession of schools) or summer camp. But he wrote poetry and fiction at the Hommocks and he lived there until he left home. His childhood may not have been as unhappy as it seemed to him in retrospect, but it is clear that he always felt at a remove from his parents. It was not the first time that he thought of himself as an intruder.

Many years later, Albee and Noel Farrand were having lunch in Taos, New Mexico, where Farrand was in residence as a composer. They were both in their fifties, and well into their careers, although as always with Farrand his career was a struggle. Farrand recalled: "Edward said, do you feel that you have grown up or matured? I said no, I feel I'm very much the same as I was when I was a child and lost in that big house of yours, just like in *Tiny Alice*. He nodded and said with some bitterness, 'They didn't tell us this.' They didn't tell us that we wouldn't mature. He asked, 'Are we going to be the same way when we're seventy?' I repeated, 'They didn't tell us this,' and he laughed."

2
Santayanian Finesse

An ultra-poetical, super-aesthetical out-of-the-way
young man.

W H E N Albee gives a speech, he often begins with a cautionary tale about his education, or, rather, his noneducation. It goes like this: "I'm not sure I am representative of the average creative artist in the United States today—by either background or career. I was adopted into a wealthy family. I received a private school education—a private schools education. No sooner would my well-intentioned family get me into one—Lawrenceville, for example, in Princeton, New Jersey—when I would get myself thrown out. I think it was nothing more complex than my desire to be at home and my family's desire to have me away. Well, they knew me better than I knew myself in those distant days, and I suspect they were right. I went to many, many schools. There was a law on the books, I think, in those days that said, in effect: No matter how despairing your well-intentioned family may be at your refusal to be educated, they may not have you put into a reform school. There was no law on the books, however, that said they could not do the next worst thing and put you in a military academy. And so, at the age of fourteen, for my sins—and it is amazing the number of sins I must have committed by the age of fourteen—I found myself at the Valley Forge Military Academy, wittily located in Valley Forge, Pennsylvania."

Then after a discussion of the two courses taught at Valley Forge, "sadism and masochism," he talks about the Choate School in Wallingford, Connecticut, "the only place in my life from which I have ever graduated," and

Trinity College in Hartford, which he left after a year and a half. He was to become one of many contemporary playwrights (others are Harold Pinter, Tom Stoppard, and Alan Ayckbourn) who did not have a college or university education, yet became known for the brilliance of their dialogue. Like everything else in Albee's life, Lawrenceville, Valley Forge, Choate, and Trinity were all consequential parts of his self-education, and the truth about each is more or less than he imagined. Each was a way station on an interior journey.

In 1940, when Edward was twelve, he and his mother were driven to Lawrenceville to meet the headmaster, Alan Heely. As Albee later described it, his first encounter with Lawrenceville began with a moment of acute embarrassment. He sets the scene: "Albee and Ma driving to Lawrenceville to get me into the joint. She must have loosened the side of her dress to be comfortable in the car driving down. We were sitting in the outer room of the headmaster's office. I was hunched on a sofa while she was sitting properly alert at a round table. I noticed that she had not zipped up the side of her dress, and one could see her corset. To show you how shy and tongue-tied I was, I could not bring myself even to say, 'It's unzipped.' Now, I know I wasn't doing it to humiliate her. The idea of saying something so embarrassing"—to him and to her—"I couldn't bring myself to do it. I was paralyzed."

On June 24 of that year, Reed Albee formally submitted an application for his son's admission to Lawrenceville. At the time, Edward was just finishing the seventh grade at Rye Country Day School. Although the application was signed with his father's name, it was Frances Albee who filled it out and signed it. Asked for the reason for the applicant's leaving his last school, she wrote, tersely, "Want boy in boarding school." To the question, "Has applicant ever failed to be promoted in his school career?" she wrote, "This year." The applicant's reading preference? "Edward is very fond of reading worthwhile material," she stated, without naming his favorite authors. But with maternal pride, she listed his sporting interests (boxing, riding, rifle marksmanship, tennis, swimming) and his hobbies (making airplane and ship models). Then in a moment of candidness, in a rare comment on what she thought were her son's deficiencies, she said that Edward has to learn "to give and take—as an only child, everything around belongs to him—he must learn to share."

Albee was admitted to the prep school on July 9, and returned in September. Away from home for the first time, he remained shy and remembers having no close friends. James Merrill and Frederick Buechner (later famous, respectively, as a poet and as a novelist) were also in the lower school, but they were two classes ahead of him. Charles Chaplin's sons, Sydney and Charles Jr., were among the other students there at the time. Merrill and Buechner were best friends at Lawrenceville. As Merrill said in his memoir *A Different Person:* "I began writing poetry in my second year at Lawrenceville, soon after meeting Freddy. He had shown the way by publishing in the school literary magazine eighteen lines (they gave it a whole page) in a delectable pre-WWI mode." Merrill set about modeling his writing on that of his friend. At the same time, his teachers "were busily exposing us to the whole of English poetry from Wyatt to Browning." While Merrill and Buechner were immersing themselves in an intellectual and aesthetic atmosphere, Albee, the new boy, remained apart. He remembers: "I tried to pal around with Jimmy and Freddy. Obviously I gravitated to them, something about their personality and creativity. But I was sort of the puppy tagging along occasionally." They were "very sophisticated," and he was "a tot."

The disparity in their Lawrenceville experience, Buechner said, was that he and Merrill stayed on and went from the lower school to the upper school, where they found "tremendous encouragement" from the teachers, especially those on the English faculty. Buechner remembers Albee as "small for his age, a lonely little boy." He continues: "I can see him sitting there in study hall, a little sad boy with a tiny scar over one eyebrow, looking like a mark of anxiety. I liked him as much as I was aware of him." He allows himself one conjecture: If Albee had continued at Lawrenceville and made friends, "it might have made all the difference in the world."

Academically, Lawrenceville draws a blank from Albee: "I didn't really care much about classes." Setting what was to become a pattern, he only went to the classes that interested him. He did poorly in all his subjects. The first year his housemaster reported, "Stubbornness and a kind of selfishness are the chief stumbling blocks he has to overcome before he can really begin to realize his abilities more fully." As usual, Edward is unsure about exact dates, but along about the time of his first year at Lawrenceville, he decided to leave home and go abroad. He went so far as to make a reservation on an ocean liner to go to France, thinking that he would pay for the ticket with money that he had saved (his grandmother habitually gave him $100 at Christmas and on his birthday). Typically, when Edward thought about running away from home, he was not about to hitchhike west, but to escape to Paris at least in semi-grand style. Imagine young Albee arriving in Paris in the late 1930s, and meeting Ernest Hemingway or, more important, James Joyce and Samuel Beckett. Naturally, the voyage was abandoned.

Before returning to Lawrenceville for his second year, he wrote a letter to the headmaster announcing his plans to settle down and take advantage of the educational opportunities. The threat of military school was already hanging over his head like a Damoclean sword. In his letter, he said, "Truthfully, I like Lawrenceville very much. Mother and Dad doubt that and they have a perfect right to. But I think that I should know better than anyone else if I like it. In connection with my getting down to work my mother does not consider that possible . . . In short, I plan to. That is the main gist of it. If you are willing to have me return and give it a try I will be eager to do so. If not just say so."

"Maybe I thought I was punishing them by not doing well," he said later. "It's like suicides: I'll kill myself and then they'll be sorry. My discontent with the environment I lived in was so profound, or maybe my discontent with everything was so profound. I would not participate. I was a non-participator." He did, however, participate in extracurricular activities, including the theater. Appearing in a Noël Coward one-act, he played "a middle-aged British dowager trying to get a meal at a Cockney restaurant, and being spritzed with water." He decorated his room with reproductions of Van Gogh, Cézanne, and Picasso, rented from the school library, expressing an interest in art at the same time the other boys had pictures of "naked babes and sports figures" on their walls. He traces his earliest sexual adventures to Lawrenceville. Just before he reached puberty, he began to realize that he was attracted to other boys. He has memories of sexual experimentation among the students. The students slept in a dormitory rather than in individual rooms: "I remember everybody going from one bed to another all night, the patter of little feet." It was at Lawrenceville, he said, that he had his first sexual experience, "probably with an older boy," unnamed. "The day of puberty," he said, "and bang— and I took to it, as they say, as a duck to water."

Despite all promises, the second year was not an improvement. As his housemaster wrote:

Ed's four failures in five subjects were entirely unnecessary. He simply has not interested himself in the work, and instead of doing even a minimum job he has deliberately wasted his time. In other respects his record is no better. He has made few friends because of an unfounded attitude of superiority. As manager of the house football team he was largely a failure. I have made no real progress in numerous talks with him because he prefers glib conversation to honest discussion and because he politely resents every offer of advice and help.

The housemaster's irritation was clearly showing. One phrase is curious: "unfounded attitude of superiority." As was also the case with Samuel Beckett during his school days in Ireland, Albee projected an air of being smarter than his classmates and his teachers. In both cases, the attitude was not unfounded. But how were Edward's teachers to know about his intelligence? He was often absent, and when he was in class he refused to do assignments.

In the eighth grade he failed both math and science and got a bare 60 in English. He finished the year with a weighted average of 55. Occasionally there was a glimmer of hope. In his second year of English, he scored an 85 on his final. His teacher said that "climaxed a drive that began after the April Quarterly Report" and suggested that "there is nothing he can't do in English if he will work." In the fall of 1942 he failed English, history, French, and science and was put on probation. Oddly, he passed math. At mid-year when his probation was terminated he was still failing everything but math, with a weighted average of 49. Before the end of his second year, he was dismissed from Lawrenceville for not attending classes.

For Albee, reading Merrill's memoir evoked thoughts about Lawrenceville: "He seems to have much more of a handle on how he felt at the time than I did, than I do. Or maybe if he was going to write the book he had to develop more of a handle on it." Quietly and privately, Albee wrote poetry at Lawrenceville, and at twelve he wrote his first play, a three-act sex farce called *Aliqueen*, which his mother supposedly threw away. John Joseph, who later was one of Edward's favorite teachers at Choate, said that he understood why someone like him would dislike Lawrenceville. That school, he said, promoted "a Lawrenceville norm, the apotheosis of the successful American, the rugged athlete and he-man, the no-culture, no-sensitivity-permitted type of boy." In other words, Merrill and Buechner were exceptions.

As might be expected, Frances Albee was very upset at her son's failure and wrote to the Lawrenceville headmaster saying that he must know "what a large size lump I have in my throat." If Edward thought that Lawrenceville was restrictive, his next stop, Valley Forge Military Academy in Pennsylvania, was ice water, a shock to his system. J. D. Salinger had preceded him at Valley Forge by seven years. With his creation of Holden Caulfield in *Catcher in the Rye*, he unwittingly wrote about a rebel like Albee. Think of Holden Caulfield at Pencey Prep (in Agerstown, Pennsylvania) or of Ben Gazzara in the stage adaptation of Calder Willingham's *End as a Man*, and you have a picture of Albee at the time. As Albee said, "I did not write *Catcher in the Rye* or *End as a Man*, I lived them." Salinger graduated from Valley Forge, and Albee did not.

In a school photograph in uniform at Valley Forge, Albee looks starched and steely-eyed. Albee regarded the militarism of the environment as perverse and the school as a kind of prison. "It was an awful place. Reform school, basically." At other times, he would refer to it as the Valley Forge Concentration Camp. Despite, or because of, the authoritarian air, he wrote poetry, some of which was published in the school newspaper. In one bizarre series of incidents, he would be called upon to read poems to one master "who would beat students in front of me because he thought I would like it." Paradoxically, this was the one teacher who expressed interest in his writing. Albee himself was never beaten by his masters. But he was surrounded by the latent brutality of the students. Though always dismissive of his juvenalia, Albee remembers the first stanza of one of his Valley Forge poems and recites it on request. It sounds like a drumbeating lyric by Vachel Lindsay or Rudyard Kipling:

> Darkness stole the scene's full power
> Darkness hit the watcher's plight
> Darkness hit the very hour
> Darkness, watchword of the night.

"Pretty good for fourteen," he says.

At Valley Forge, he became nostalgic and wistful about Lawrenceville. He sent a letter to Dr. Heely, the headmaster, offering to stop by and see him that Christmas, either in New York or at Lawrenceville. Looking back on his time there, he wrote:

> I suppose the customary thing to say is that I don't really miss Lawrenceville and am quite content where I am.
>
> I guess I don't dislike it here at Valley Forge, but it is so different from Lawrenceville. I will admit that I was sent to Valley Forge for discipline, and, discipline I got. I also admit that it was entirely my own fault that I was forced to leave Lawrenceville. I just didn't study. Yes, I made up excuses that sound perfect, and which I believed, after a time. You might say that I just didn't care.
>
> Now I understand what I left. The whole atmosphere at Lawrenceville was so friendly, while here it is all "military." But what do you expect at a military school?
>
> I hope that you won't consider this just a lot of "talk," because I really mean it . . .

While Edward was at Valley Forge in the early 1940s, presumably training to be a cadet, America was at war. The Albees, with their wealth, were scarcely affected by the war until it proved difficult to obtain fuel for the furnace of their large house in Larchmont. Eventually, they closed the house and moved to their apartment at 299 Park Avenue, which was then called the Park Lane Hotel. So much for their participation in anything that might be regarded as the war effort. When their son was home from boarding school, he stayed with his parents on Park Avenue. A curious memory of embarrassment: On one vacation, he was out walking his mother's two French poodles and happened to be outside of the Liberty music store on Madison Avenue when Frank Sinatra, then at the very height of his fame, came out the door. "He saw me standing there in my military school outfit with those poodles. I've never seen a stranger expression on anyone's face."

After a trying year and a half, Albee was out of Valley Forge, for medical as well as academic reasons. He suffered an assortment of illnesses, including measles and chicken pox, and spent much of his time in the school infirmary. Somehow, despite his disastrous academic record at his first two prep schools, he managed to transfer to Choate, a highly regarded prep school in Wallingford, Connecticut, later to be known for such famous political alumni as Adlai E. Stevenson and John F. Kennedy, and much later, as the school that educated Edward Albee. Why was Albee admitted? The reason for his acceptance was hidden for many years in his student file at Lawrenceville.

On June 6, 1944, C. Wardell St. John, the assistant headmaster of Choate (and the son of the headmaster George C. St. John), wrote Dr. Heely, the Lawrenceville headmaster, who was an old friend of his. He said that Mrs. Reed Albee had applied for admission for her son, Edward (then sixteen), and he asked if Heely could send him a description of the boy's record at Lawrenceville.

How was Heely to respond? It was a straightforward request, and normally it would have been followed by an equally straightforward response. The average headmaster would have simply looked up the boy's academic record and told Choate about his failure, or at best, he would have been noncommittal in his reply, wanting to free himself of all responsibility. However, this was not the case. In response to the request from Choate came a life-changing—and a life-saving—letter, probably the most crucial letter in Albee's life. It is the kind of letter that some people might think about writing but would never write because they were bound by expectation and tradition, or they were simply afraid of taking a chance. Throwing caution away, and disregarding Edward's disastrous record at Lawrenceville, Heely focused on the young man, his character, and what he regarded as his great potential. In a letter to St. John, dated June 7, 1944, he wrote:

Young Edward Albee is a very bright boy indeed. He was with us from September, 1940, to February, 1942. He scored an I.Q. of 125 on the Otis Form A in May, 1941, and an 83rd Independent School percentile on the American Council Psychological test a little later. He was an omniverous [sic] reader of very good taste, with a keen, interesting mind. In short, he is an exceedingly promising young man.

He had, however, an uncontrollable inertia toward his academic duties. [Then he described Albee's scholastic failure and explained] So we had to let him go. [Carefully, but with full knowledge of the chance he was taking, he continued:] His academic deficiencies are not to be credited to a conscious and deliberate neglect. Ed is an adopted child and, very confidentially, he dislikes his mother with a cordial and eloquent dislike which I consider entirely justified. She and we used to see each other socially when Ed was here and she has always been very nice to us. She is, however, in my opinion a selfish, dominating person, whereas Ed is a sensitive, perceptive and intelligent boy. He feels he is not really loved and the psychological hurdle which had been built up in front of him was simply insurmountable. I can think of no other boy who, I believe, has been so fully the victim of an unsympathetic home background or who has exhibited so fully the psychological effect of feeling that he is not wanted. The parents are constantly attentive and solicitous about him but I believe Eddie is right when he says his mother really doesn't like him and is disturbed by his failure simply because she thinks it reflects upon her.

The boy and I have written to each other and seen each other once or twice since he left here and a very friendly feeling exists between us. He realizes that he let himself go to pieces here and that he got what was coming to him when he was dismissed. As far as I am concerned, however, I should be very glad indeed to have him come back here, and I don't think I can say handsomer than that. If you can take him into Choate, with the knowledge of his background I have given you, I think you might find he is ready now to do you great credit and himself too.

At the time, Edward did not know about the letter. Reading it many years later, he expressed his gratitude and said, "Obviously he was aware that I was waving flags, that I was drowning. Either that or he just hated her so much." He paused. "He had her pegged and saw the situation." And seeing it, Dr. Heely did his best to rectify it.

In retrospect, one has to wonder what would have happened if Heely had given the usual formula response: Edward had failed academically, had promised to rectify his mistakes but had not, and was dismissed from the school for all appropriate reasons. It is always possible that Edward's parents would have found some way to exercise their influence and he would have been accepted at Choate or at some similar institution. It is equally possible that he would have been shipped off in disgrace to some lesser school, or as a final act of youthful rebellion, he might have given up entirely on the idea of education, run away from home, or fallen into a depression. His conclusion: "I think I probably would have gone on being very unhappy at whatever school I was." In any case, none of these last resorts was necessary. He was accepted at Choate. Disregarding Edward's past, and perhaps emboldened by Heely's response, Frank C. Wheeler, the director of admissions at Choate, wrote with rare prescience, "I have a feeling he will distinguish himself in literature."

It was at Choate, Albee said, that he learned how to educate himself, something that had eluded him in his previous schools. Moving from Valley Forge to Choate was "like moving from Purgatory to heaven." To catch up to his classmates, he went to the 1944 summer session at Choate, and in typical fashion almost got thrown out of school for misbehavior. One night with four or five other students, he sneaked out of the Hillhouse dormitory. The group drove to nearby Meriden, where they went to a bar and got drunk on beer and boilermakers. Two teachers found them there, brought them back to the school, and the incident was overlooked. In the fall, Albee began his first year at Choate.

George St. John, the longtime headmaster, was considered to be something of a benevolent despot. In 1946, Albee's graduating year and the fiftieth anniversary of the founding of the school, the *Brief*, the Choate yearbook, was dedicated to Dr. St. John for erecting "in Choate a noble and aspiring monument to scholarly and human ideals." The solemnity of such a sentiment was also reflected in the Choate Hymn: "In life's gladsome morn, thy spirit compelling / Thy sons, ever faithful, respond to thy call," and by the fact that students had to attend chapel every day.

Entering Choate, Albee could not have been optimistic, and neither could Choate, despite the comment from the director of admissions. His previous academic record was abysmal, and, physically, he was out of shape. He had gained considerable weight, at one point ballooning to 207 pounds. Looking back, he blames the weight on puberty and depression, "and a growing sense of disenchantment." It was at Valley Forge that he was at his lowest.

At his new school, he could have continued to go his own way, to do the absolute minimum of work while finding time for what he considered to be more important pursuits: reading, writing, and listening to music. Instead, he put himself on a strict diet and lost weight. With a determination that had not been previously apparent at his other schools, he fit himself into the Choate routine—in direct contrast to his approach at his previous schools. He scored "superior" in IQ tests, with a high aptitude in math and science, but only average verbal aptitudes. This was soon reversed. His report cards showed a satisfactory record in English and history, a very poor one in physics and French. In one of his periodic reports, Albee's housemaster, Edwin Proctor, said that he was performing poorly in physics and "worst of all is that Ed treats the matter so lightly."

Up at 6:45 every morning, twenty minutes to get down to breakfast, compulsory chapel every day. To his surprise—and pleasure—he found at Choate the kind of stimulation that Merrill and Buechner had discovered at Lawrenceville. For the first time in his life, he applied himself to his schoolwork and began achieving. Teachers encouraged his academic pursuits and also his acts of the imagination. In contrast to the disregard that surrounded him at home, there was genuine appreciation from an array of teachers: Charles Rice, John Joseph, Edwin Proctor, Porter Dean Caesar, Alexander (Sandy) Lehmann, and others. "They all were supportive," he said. "They were sympathetic, I suppose, to somebody who had delusions of grandeur." Some of them were to remain his friends long after he had left the school.

Choate became his first intellectual home. Rice, an English teacher, was astonished at the prolific nature of his poetry: "I remember sitting hour after hour in my study with him reading his many, big, hand-filled pages. One night I was faced with fifty of them." In 1962, a *Newsweek* stringer tracked down Rice at Athens College in Greece to ask him about his former pupil. At the time, Rice wrote to Albee about this journalistic inquisitiveness:

> The press is obviously trying to nose out the cliches that bursting genius presumes. They wanted "anecdotes." Having been "dumped out of many schools," you're supposed to be a psychotic Tom Rover, caught in nightly escapades involving billy goats in teachers' closets. Alas, I could think of no anecdotes at all. I could only tell about the talent that persisted in raising its head every once in a while through the dozens of pages of dialogue you used to let me read. I happened to have a Choate *Brief*, for the year of '45, and was faced with a far more somber Albee than exists in my memory. After all, what about that laughter that rang through the Homestead when you arrived for what I think of as almost daily visits?

In his report for the first term, 1944–45, Porter Caesar, who taught English, wrote, "Ed has done a splendid job this Term in his English, learning memory passages accurately, submitting articles to the literary magazine, writing profusely, and showing a mature understanding of Macbeth and Richard II." But years later, when he was interviewed by Newsweek, Caesar expressed his ambivalence about his pupil. "He was moody, eccentric and self-absorbed. He was smug and proud and had feelings of persecution following Lawrenceville and Valley Forge. On the surface he was a poser, a posturer, underneath he was passionately honest, mature and perhaps even wise, with boundless energy for poetry, plays and literature and a bald unwillingness to be forced to do what he had no interest in doing."

John Joseph said that Albee was brighter than many of the masters, but in contrast to other boys, "he never curled his lip or arched a brow when one of the masters was showing how dull he was." He added, "His great conversational interest was music." He felt that Albee thrived in the Choate atmosphere of emphasizing "individual development" and wrote "one sweet hell of a lot" while he was there. The wife of one housemaster evidently agreed with Joseph's assessment: "He was very mature, witty, entertaining, bright, precocious, creative, deeply interested in music, and his conversation was far more interesting to adults than to the other boys. He was the kind of young man who sought adult company, and whom adults could enjoy."

Home on vacation, he and friends from Choate would occasionally meet in New York for an evening of underage drinking at a receptive bar. One excursion left a particularly deep impression on Albee. When he was sixteen, they went to Nick's, a popular jazz club on Seventh Avenue at Tenth Street, featuring such jazz stars as Muggsy Spanier and Pee Wee Russell. One of the teenagers in the Choate group had apparently accidentally killed both his mother and father. When the boys ordered drinks, the young man fumblingly asked for "bergin" instead of "bourbon." "I'll have a bergin," he said, "Give me some bergin please . . . bergin and water." Albee and his friends laughed at the mistake, and the laughter soon spread. Almost everyone in Nick's started to laugh. The laughter would die down, then someone would say "bergin," and it would begin again. With its shared camaraderie and euphoria, Albee said he remembered that incident "as the grandest day of my youth."

Eighteen years later in his first Broadway play, Who's Afraid of Virginia Woolf?, Albee replayed that scene, transposing it to the 1930s during Prohibition and making it a childhood memory of George, the history professor who is married to the daughter of the president of his college.

GEORGE

When I was sixteen and going to prep school, during the Punic Wars, a bunch of us used to go into New York on the first day of vacations, before we fanned out to our homes, and in the evening this bunch of us used to go to this gin mill owned by the gangster-father of one of us . . . and we would drink with the grown-ups and listen to the jazz. And one time, in the bunch of us, there was this boy who was fifteen, and he had killed his mother with a shotgun some years before—accidentally, completely accidentally, without even an unconscious motivation, I have no doubt, no doubt at all—and this one evening this boy went with us, and we ordered our drinks, and when it came his turn he said, I'll have bergin . . . give me some bergin, please . . . bergin and water. Well, we all laughed . . . he was blond and he had the face of a cherub, and we all laughed, and his cheeks went red and the color rose in his neck, and the assistant crook who had taken our order told people at the next table what the boy had said, and then they laughed . . . and no one was laughing more than us, and none of us more than the boy who had shot his mother. And soon, everyone in the gin mill knew what the laughter was about, and everyone started ordering bergin, and laughing when they ordered it . . . We drank free that night, and we were bought champagne by the management, by the gangster-father of one of us. And, of course, we suffered the next day, each of us, alone, on his train, away from New York, each of us with a grown-up's hangover . . . but it was the grandest day of my . . . youth.

Although St. John stressed the family aspect of his school and encouraged parents to visit their sons, the Albees never came to Choate. Except for Frances Albee's first visit to Lawrenceville with Edward, there is no indication that they ever visited him at any of his schools. However, the masters at Choate conducted a prolific correspondence with Mrs. Albee, one letter telling her that "his danger lies in spreading himself too thin over his range of interests." Those interests focused on the Choate literary magazine and the *Choate News*, the weekly newspaper, but he also acted (in *Androcles and the Lion*) and was active on the debating team and at the school's radio station. Sports took sixth place, though he played fullback in intramural soccer. Although Porter Caesar respected Albee, he also noted what he saw as his problems: "He was lazy, conceited, undisciplined and never worked up to his ability except in creative writing."

With a demonic intensity, Albee wrote poems in his copy books: sonnets, narrative poems. In retrospect, he considered most of them to be "terribly self-pitying" and derivative. In common with the young Eugene O'Neill, he was influenced by the English poets Swinburne and Ernest Dowson, and also by Rupert Brooke, Eliot, and Yeats. Almost immediately he began publishing verse in the Choate literary magazine.

One poem, "To whom it may concern," which appeared in the February 1945 edition, sounds a bit like Dorothy Parker, with a line suggesting, "That we don't know / What side our gin / Is bittered on." A poem called "Eighteen" was accepted by a Texas monthly, *Kaleidograph*, and printed in its September 1945 edition. Albee was seventeen and it was his first professional publication. The poem soared with the passionate intensity of a young man desirous of a creative future.

> You must let me live!
> I have not as yet begun . . .
> The world has need of life, not death.
> And I have not as yet begun.

Albee's roommate at Choate was David Aldeborgh, a young man from Pough-keepsie, New York. It was chance that brought them together. Under ordinary circumstances, they would not even have been acquaintances. They seemed to have nothing in common, although Aldeborgh gives Albee credit for awak-ening his interest in classical music. Many years later, Aldeborgh said proudly that he was "a nineteenth-century, white male chauvinist pig," someone who politically was "to the right of Patrick Buchanan." In almost all respects, Alde-borgh was Albee's opposite.

Aldeborgh said that at Choate Albee "liked to dominate people. I think he had a penchant for psychological domination of somebody else. His name for me was Caliban," as if Albee were Prospero and Aldeborgh were his slave. In actuality, that was far from the truth. Each followed an individual path. They were never close friends, but Aldeborgh was able to have a close view. He re-members that Albee was always writing, and despite their distance, it was clear to him that he had a talent. As he said, "There was never any doubt in my mind that he would be a success. There was never any doubt in his mind that he was going to be a writer. He would sit on his bunk and he would write sonnets with a pen. He might cross out a word, or a line, but aside from that, there were no cross-outs, no erasures, nothing. And he would toss these things off, sitting on his bunk." Scholastics took second place. "He didn't have to study. He would do what was necessary to get through the exam, in as short a time as possible, and he would devote the rest of the time to doing things he was interested in. I think our mentalities went in two very divergent direc-tions. But I enjoyed him as a person. Ed was definitely a charismatic person-ality—and authoritative. He was articulate and authoritative. He was not reticent about his opinions, and he was given to a little pontification. I think Ed was always on a pedestal of sorts, of his own design, and people came to him for his pontifications. He did not go to his superiors except at least as an equal. I always liked him. But I'm not about to be the moth flying around a lamp, if you know what I mean."

At night Albee sat on his bed and wrote his first novel, *The Flesh of Unbelievers*, longhand in a copy book, taking the title from an opera by Howard Hanson. He dedicated the novel to Muir Weissinger ("the reasons being too numerous to mention") and drew on himself, Muir, and his other friends. In 537 pages (some of them typed), he tells the story of an insanely romantic young man named Michael Crawford, who comes out on top of every situation and can silence anyone with a glance or a quip. Michael dislikes his father for "his gruff remarks . . . his air of omnipotence, his blind spots, his intolerance, his unawareness of what was fine and beautiful and meant so much to Michael, and, above all, his impatience and discrediting of Michael's every trivial accomplishment." As for his mother, she "assumed an air of scornful martyrdom which disgusted Michael." There were three siblings, a baby sister who died and two brothers. Michael is pictured as a "shy, frail, and intelligent youth," who spent his earliest years "in happy oblivion." Moving through a series of parties in Manhattan, lunching at "21" Club with his friends, he is like a character in a novel by Dawn Powell. At one point, he is picked up by a male prostitute who says, "You're either a virgin or a fairy," and sends him back to the party where he found him. Occasionally there are poetic moments: "Occasionally on a wonderful night he would lie on his back and look as far as he could into the sky and wonder what lay beyond."

At seventeen, Albee also wrote his first play (other than the elusive *Aliqueen*). It was called *Schism* and it was written at the suggestion of Noel Farrand. While Albee was at Choate, Farrand was at Iona Prep in New Rochelle. Farrand was unhappy about the restrictive Roman Catholic attitudes he found at school, as in his home. "I was about to graduate," said Farrand, "and I asked Edward if he could write me a play that would satirize some of these Catholic attitudes. He set to work and produced a play in Irish brogue." Dismayed by the brogue, Farrand edited it out of his copy, "and that made it much more viable as far as the language was concerned." Simultaneously, Albee submitted the play (with the brogue intact) to Choate for a literary contest and Farrand submitted it, under his own name, for an Iona literary contest. *Schism* won prizes in both schools. "They were always in cahoots," says Noel's brother Jack (later a Jesuit priest). "They wanted to see if they could get away with it."

"This particular fraud never turned up," said Noel. "Nobody ever found out about it." Both he and Albee enjoyed the deception. Farrand further complicated the schoolboy hoax by directing a performance of the play at Iona (*Schism*, written and directed by Noel Farrand). William Ball, a fellow student at Iona and later a highly regarded though eccentric theater director, played the role of Mrs. Monohan, a dying eighty-three-year-old grandmother confined to a wheelchair, thereby unwittingly acting in the first produced play by Albee.

In keeping with Farrand's suggestions, *Schism* was a long one-act play about the rebellion of a young Irish couple against Roman Catholicism and Irish customs. The hero Michael Joyce was as heartless as the play was humorless. Despite the Irish background, the play seemed more shadowed by Clifford Odets than by Sean O'Casey. "You've been brought up by a misguided bunch of people under a rotten philosophy," says Michael to his girlfriend Alice Monohan. In the play's most melodramatic scene, he has a battle with Alice's grandmother who accuses him of being "a stupid, blaspheming, radical atheist." Finally, Mrs. Monohan has a stroke and asks Michael to get her a doctor and a priest. Instead, he wheels her into her bedroom and closes the door. Within minutes, Alice appears and the two leave, with Michael saying, "There is no past for you, anymore, darling, only a golden future." With that statement, Albee could have been speaking to himself.

The May 1946 commencement issue of the Choate literary magazine, with Albee now the managing editor, published three pieces by him, a sonnet entitled "Nihilist," a short story, and *Schism*. The poem began:

> Upon his pedestal of self he strikes
> The pose of studied carelessness, or plays
> The role, with Judas-like humility,
> Of priest confessor to his following.
> With Santayanian finesse he spikes
> Existing principles, old, trusted ways,
> And offers in their place sterility
> Of soul and thought; these are his plundering.
>
> What causes him to mouth the purple grape
> Of life experience, then spit the seeds
> Back at the world? . . .

In the *Choate News*, the school's weekly newspaper, various faculty members reviewed the work of the students, as was the school's custom. Sandy

Lehmann, one of Albee's mentors, reviewed the issue of the "Lit," focusing on Albee as "a campus force to be reckoned with." Then he proceeded to give him his first play review, "my first bad review," said Albee. About *Schism*, he wrote, "There is a really clever plot, full of suspense, and the right number of characters to carry it. There doesn't seem to be too much of anything unless it be the necessary mumbojumbo pseudo religious talk which gives them stagey force. It's Albee's first play, yet I think it will act well, in spite of its heavy theme." Lehmann felt less kindly toward the story, "Lady with an Umbrella," saying "It's so unmotivated, so unworthy of Albee's capabilities, which I hasten to restress, are enviable," adding, "Maybe I'm just jealous."

Then he took a swipe at "Nihilist," saying that the invented adjective "Santayanian" "lends his poem all the grace of a walking crow." That was a phrase that Albee (and Farrand) never forgot. It became a kind of running joke between them. Nineteen years later, the line reappeared on Broadway. In the third act of *Tiny Alice*, the character identified as Lawyer, played by William Hutt, reminisces to Miss Alice (Irene Worth) about a troublesome schoolboy experience in his past. An English teacher reviewed one of his poems in his school's literary magazine, saying that the words "Santayanian finesse" had "all the grace of a walking crow." The poet demanded an explanation and the teacher said, "Crows don't walk much . . . if they can help it . . . if they can fly." After Lawyer repeats the criticism, the character of Butler (John Heffernan) says about the critic, "Bright man."

Charles Rice, at least in retrospect, was much more indulgent of Albee's early work. After the success of *The Zoo Story*, he offered his congratulations: "It's wonderful that the talent that showed as unmistakably as a light deep in the water—murky water, sometimes—in these dramas you produced for the Lit, should have made its way to the surface and put you on the road to becoming a household word."

At school, David Aldeborgh dabbled in art, and in that same issue of the *Choate News*, the ubiquitous Lehmann reviewed an art exhibition that included work by Aldeborgh, which he somehow compared to Van Gogh and Picasso. Aldeborgh had also painted his roommate. Lehmann said, "His portrait of Ed Albee, though it may seem to you to be a most original kind of vengeance to wreak on one's roommate, strikes me nevertheless as Dave's most original, least derivative job. It bespeaks Ed's love of words and music."

Schism was not the only play Albee wrote at Choate. *Each in His Own Way* (written in 1945) was an eleven-page one-act play about music and morality in Nazi-occupied Poland. In it, a piano teacher tries to keep the spirit of

Frédéric Chopin alive even as Germany destroys his country. His prize pupil is a thirteen-year-old boy named Josef. In the melodramatic denouement, as Nazis arrest Josef's parents, the teacher makes plans to flee with the child to England. "The heart of Poland beats in England," he says. "We'll leave tonight." The play ends with a revolutionary anthem by Chopin. Sentimental and polemic, the play has no currency, except as an early demonstration of Albee's political conviction, his interest in and knowledge of music, and his ability to move characters around a stage. The play was rediscovered in 1996 by a Choate classmate going through old scrapbooks in preparation for their fiftieth reunion. When the play surfaced, Albee said he had no recollection of writing it. He read it, laughed at its naivete, and said that he felt "somebody was out to destroy my reputation."

At Choate, Albee was friendlier with his teachers than he was with his fellow students. "I figured I might learn a little bit more from them than from other people," he said. Those students who were his friends were often outsiders like Augustus "Gus" Eddy, who was overweight and effeminate. He also liked Covington "Covey" Allen, who was "a great scarecrow of a boy. Covey was quite mad," he said. "He got into the same sort of trouble that Joe Orton did, going to the school library and cutting things out of bound volumes of magazines." Albee said that both Eddy and Allen were gay. Both have since died.

In addition to all his other activities at Choate, Albee had a record program on the school radio station, was the music editor and reviewer on the newspaper, and also wrote a column for the paper called "Off the Record." In that year-end issue of the *Choate News*, he played the game of desert island discs and named his favorite composers, Rachmaninoff, Mozart, Brahms, Bach, and Tchaikovsky, and his favorite symphonies. Rachmaninoff would remain at the top of the list. With Albee's help, Noel Farrand later formed an American Rachmaninoff society.

During the summer of 1945, Albee worked without pay at WNYC, the New York City municipally owned radio station, writing continuity for music programs. It was there that he met Celeste Seymour, a lovely blonde Finch student who also had a summer job at the station. They were both seventeen. At the time she was thinking about becoming an actress. Her father, Luther Reed, was a movie director. Her parents were divorced and she and her younger brother Dana lived with their mother in Manhattan. The Seymours, as it turned out, knew the Albees. To both families, she and Edward seemed like an ideal match. "My mother was crazy about him," said Celeste. "He really was a wonderful, wonderful young man." For the two teenagers, what was perhaps most encouraging to their relationship was that they had met at work and not at a country club or at one of their parents' parties.

Drawn together by a natural affinity and common interests, beginning with music, they began dating. They went to the theater and to night clubs, the Blue Angel, the Monkey Bar, and especially Larue, a supper club (on 58th Street between Madison and Park) that seemed welcoming to prep school teenagers. The war had just ended and, in common with other young couples, they had a grand and glorious time, drinking underage, dancing, and talking incessantly. At that stage, Edward was, in Ronald Winston's phrase, "Holden Caulfield manqué." At Larue, they would often find friends from Choate. It was, said Celeste, "a fun period of our lives, an exhilarating period," with the entire future before them.

On a personal level, she was very impressed by him, by his knowledge of music, by his interest in the arts, and by his own creative instincts: "You knew that he was special." Because of his manners and his sensitivity, she thought that he could be "of another era," perhaps the eighteenth century. Some of her fondest memories are of the two of them having dinner at the Blue Angel and other places. "We didn't really need or want other people," she said. "We'd enjoy whatever we were going to do." In 1945, they were at the Blue Angel on the day that Harry Truman became president.

In a rare familial event, one evening Edward and Celeste had dinner at the "21" Club with Reed and Frances Albee. It was Celeste's first visit to that restaurant, then at the height of its popularity, and she remembers it as a glamorous and elegant time. Her memory of the Albees is in stark contrast to that of their son. Reed was quiet, but friendly, Frances was domineering, but not in any malicious way: "She did take over, but I didn't find that an objectionable kind of manner." In that respect, she was in fact somewhat like Celeste's mother. She was also a gracious hostess, and Celeste remembers being invited to dinner at the Albee house. "She was tall, blond, handsome, a strong personality. She liked me, and it was fun being with them. I did not feel a tension in that house. I did not see it as a dysfunctional family." When she was there, the atmosphere was civilized.

Seeing *Three Tall Women* many years later was a revelation for her. She was aware of all the autobiographical connections. "There were so many insights about Frances that I never knew, and the whole thing about Reed being a chaser—that was just amazing to me. I would have thought that he adored his wife and would never look at anyone else. She certainly did have strength. Boy, she was a survivor." She continued, "I couldn't stand what she did to Ed.

I just hated it: the pushing him out of the house and the coldness later. It just wasn't her way to be a loving, warm kind of person, at least not to Ed. But that doesn't mean she was a bad person, at least not to me when I was young."

From a very early age, Edward was a faithful reader of *The New Yorker*. He read every issue and, along with Noel, had a particular fondness for the work of James Thurber. He saved his copies (years later, one of his producers gave him a complete collection of the magazine). In emulation of Thurber, Dorothy Parker, and others, he wrote many *New Yorker*–style short stories. One of them, "Sort of a Test," was published in the Choate literary magazine and concerns in part a young woman named Celeste. The plot was far removed from events in his life. It is about a man who apparently has killed his wife by pushing her off the terrace of their apartment and then becomes involved with another woman, named Celeste. But there are certain personal aspects. At one point, he wrote that the husband "wanted very much to marry her, to settle down to certainty, to have a home and children and all the conventionalities that were becoming more important to him every day, every moment." Later "they laughed and danced the evening away at Twenty-One and then the Stork," before returning home for a cliffhanging conclusion in which he leads the new woman . . . out to his terrace.

In the summer, Edward and the real Celeste went to Playland in Rye and rode the rollercoaster. They also visited the Westchester Country Club, sometimes along with Celeste's brother Dana. Reaching back to the past, Celeste has one sad memory: "Ed had given me a ring that his grandmother had given to him, a wonderful signet ring. I knew it meant something to him," and by his giving it to her that "I meant something to him." She wore it all the time. "For some inexplicable reason, I wore it to the beach one time, and I lost it in the surf. I just felt so awful about it. It's one of the great guilt things I have. I think he was very sad about it. It was a loss to him, and I've never forgotten it." Curiously, he says he does not remember the ring or the incident. But of course he does remember Celeste. "She was nice," he said. "She was approved of. I thought she was older than I was. Certainly she was a lot more mature."

The relationship between Edward and Celeste continued when both returned to school. In February 1946, she joined him at Choate for the annual "midwinter festivities," a weekend of dancing, dining, and a glee club concert. In the school paper, the lead story announced that "180 beautiful girls," a record number, had arrived on the Choate campus, and in "tonight's starting lineup," Celeste Seymour was paired with "Ed Albee."

Gradually they drifted apart, or in Celeste's recollection, he "disappeared" from her life. But she kept up with his career and occasionally they would run into each other, in the early 1960s at one of his plays (she thinks it was *The American Dream*), and years later at the ballet. Soon after the opening of *Who's Afraid of Virginia Woolf?* in 1962, she went to see it and found it "devastating; it left me speechless. I was proud for him." But she did not contact him, feeling it would be a personal intrusion. She did not see him again until the early 1990s, by which time she was married to her second husband, had two children, and a career as an art dealer. She was living for most of the time in New Orleans and Albee had come to that city for a revival of *The Death of Bessie Smith*. After the performance, people were standing in line to meet him. Celeste waited and then when it was her turn gave him her card. He looked up and said, "Celeste? You haven't changed." It was a brief meeting; he was leaving the next day, but she remembers that he was in a "jubilant and joyous" mood.

Asked if marriage to Albee had ever crossed her mind, she said, "Well, only when we were seventeen, eighteen years old. I'm sure our mothers were saying, 'That would be very nice.' But we were just good friends. It was not a romantic sensual thing. We were close, but there wasn't that for me at that point, which didn't take away a thing from my caring for him and being a friend." Albee's response: "I suppose she was one of the ones I might have married." And if they had? "Think about it," he said. "What an unhappy time for the two of us, and the kids, if there had been kids, which I doubt. It would have been an unhappy time."

For inexplicable reasons, Albee's picture appears in both the 1945 and 1946 editions of the Choate yearbook. In the 1945 edition under his photograph were the words: "An ultra-poetical, super-aesthetical out-of-the-way young man," and an emblematic line drawing of a figure wearing clown shoes, with his back turned. In the 1946 *Brief*, there were no mottoes, but the line drawing for Albee was now of a man writing and tossing sheets of paper into a wastebasket. While his classmates were voted Most Likely to Succeed, Most To Be Admired, and Wittiest, Albee, along with two others, was named Class Diversion. Asked what that meant, he said, "I suppose people used to think I was amusing. 'Let's laugh at Albee, let's look at Albee and see what he's doing now.' " Evidently there was still some lingering academic question. On June 18, 1946, Dr. St. John wrote to Reed Albee: "I am thankful Ed won his diploma—he had frightened me!"

In 1972, twenty-six years after he graduated, Albee returned to Choate to receive the school's Alumni Seal Prize. Accepting Choate's accolades, he gave a speech entitled "Building Responsibility," in which he spoke about "the state of art in the United States." The speech was reprinted in the *Choate Alumni Bulletin*, alongside a photograph of Albee: In double-breasted blazer, with long hair and a handlebar moustache and a fixed look of dour concern, he looked nothing like the preppy of a quarter of a century ago. By that time, he was of course a famous, prize-winning playwright, and people listened to what he had to say.

While criticizing the commercialism of Broadway, he praised the proliferation of Off-Broadway in the 1960s. Then he spoke about the turn on college campuses toward the theatrical avant-garde. In the mid-1960s, he had been startled to read the names of the four most frequently performed playwrights in schools and universities. Shakespeare was first, followed by Albee, Ionesco, and Beckett. There had been 292 productions of 29 plays by Shakespeare and 137 productions of five plays by Albee. The three most produced plays were *The Sandbox*, *The Zoo Story*, and *The American Dream*, followed by *Twelfth Night*. The fact of his position filled Albee with "wonder and pleasure," but it was also unnerving as he wondered what happened to that theatrical interest after students graduated. In an aside, he looked back on his days at school: "I didn't come to Choate to study. I hadn't gone to any other school to study. I came to Choate to learn how to educate myself: that, I consider, to be the function of an educational institution . . . For better or worse, Choate was the only educational institution I ever went to where I began to get a glimmering of how I could educate myself."

After Choate, he had hoped to go to Kenyon College. Perhaps his father still thought he might make Princeton. Instead he ended up at Trinity College in Hartford, and it was not a happy experience. It was, he said, "a less controlled, less contained society," and once again he neglected his studies, failing math and science while focusing his attention on extracurricular and nonacademic activities. Disregarding his required freshman courses, he audited senior subjects like nineteenth-century literature. He joined the college theater group, the Jesters, and played a small role in *Golden Boy* ("an old Jewish handler with a cigar") and was the emperor Franz Joseph in Maxwell Anderson's *Masque of Kings*. The reviewer for the *Trinity Tripod*, the school newspaper, said "Ed Albee's presentation of Franz Joseph was superb. His stage presence and understanding of character set the tone for [the play about the] twilight of the Hapsburg dynasty." His performance was "cynical, wise, restrained."

Following tradition, he pledged to a fraternity, Sigma Nu, but resigned before his pledge period was completed, because of the house's exclusionary practices. Coincidentally, David Aldeborgh was also a student at Trinity, but they rarely saw each other. With the exception of his boyhood friend Muir Weissinger, who was also enrolled, he spent more time with the older students, the veterans who had entered the college under the GI Bill. Among his friends was Michael R. Campo, who later taught at Trinity. Campo had joined Sigma Nu and acted with Albee in the Jesters. Looking back on their schooldays, Campo said about his friend: "He played the role of the inscrutable person, with a few wisps of a moustache, hissing, clucking Mephistophelian gestures, refusing to answer you sometimes, histrionic. He was so advanced culturally compared to me that I didn't know how to interpret his befriending me." There were moments when Campo wondered if he were "being used as a study, as a 'type,' " but he said, "I liked him very much. He was exciting and amusing company."

Campo was invited to visit the Albees in Larchmont at Christmas. He remembers having cocktails in the afternoon with the family, something he never would have done at home. "When I saw him in the context of that Larchmont mansion and his family, he seemed to me mature beyond his years. His attitude was one of forbearance, of endurance. His mother was unquestionably a tyrant, his father a short, weak man, and his grandmother— who I recognize in *The Sandbox*—was trying desperately to be two generations younger than she was. He introduced me to the New York theater on that vacation, much the way he had chosen to expose me to certain poets and writers I had never known. Albee is at the origin of my intellectual life."

During his brief time at Trinity, Albee published a poem in the college literary magazine *The Trinity Review*. Called "Cocktail Party—The Women," it was clearly influenced by T. S. Eliot. The poem begins:

> They scream each other's names across the room
> Already numb with voice, and call dead words
> To faces fixed in smile.

He spent a great deal of his time in Hartford drinking and "experimenting with how to get drunk." It was also a time of sexual experimentation. He said that he slept with three different women. Noel Farrand remembered meeting one of them, "an attractive dark-haired girl," whom he thought might have been the inspiration for an Albee poem called "Spring Song," written to a woman "darkly beautiful and sad." Exploring a double life, Albee visited gay bars in Hartford, recalling with a laugh that one was located on Asylum Street.

One Trinity teacher, Kenneth Cameron, made a particularly deep impression on him. A leading scholar in the works of Emerson and Thoreau, Cameron was, said David Aldeborgh, "a quiet, dedicated presence—constructive and positive." For Albee, he represented urbanity, and something else. He became the model for the character of George Cameron in a three-act play that he wrote in 1949, called *The City of People*, one of the most interesting of his apprentice works. In it, a professor acts as mentor, ruling his menage with an iron hand. Arrogant and controlling, he plays at being Plato in his home, saying, "Here we may sit for two hours at dinner if we like, drink wine and talk of Aristotle." He subjects everyone to his will—his son, Alan; his assistant, who writes essays on French poets; and a series of attractive young women acolytes. The son is described as "Byronesque blond, perfect but lame." His father tells him, "Your foot doesn't matter. It's only when you're alone in the world, walking before a city of people, that you're not perfect." For the first time in Albee's work, the words "delicate balance" appear, referring to that "shading between love and hate that exists between anybody who cares for one another." The professor dismisses one acolyte after many years because she has become too close to Alan and brings in a new young woman to take her place. Eventually, the two young people fall in love and run away together. "I'll regret going," Alan says, "but I'd rather have freedom instead of security."

Although Albee is generally dismissive of all his writing before *The Zoo Story*, calling the poems and plays "jejune" ("They don't exist. They're written by somebody I don't know"), he seems to have a particular tolerance, if not affection, for *The City of People*. As he says, "I know I wrote it with some enthusiasm. I can't remember if I realized how foolish the play ultimately was." During his short time at Trinity, Albee was evidently gathering material. But he certainly was not paying attention to his studies. In February 1947 he received a telegram from his old Choate headmaster, George St. John, who through some private network always seemed alert to Albee's scholastic deficiencies:

> Your irresponsible record of cutting at Trinity disgraces you and your school. You have fine ability and yet you are on the edge of being dropped. Right about face. Make the distinguished record of which you are capable. Don't be a fool.

After three semesters of skipping classes and refusing to go to compulsory chapel, he was dismissed from Trinity. His formal education had ended. His long apprenticeship was about to begin.

At first, he moved back into the family house and commuted to New York, where he worked at Warwick and Legler advertising agency, a job that had been arranged for him by his parents. He was an office boy with aspirations of writing advertising copy. On his own, he came up with a campaign for Seagram's whiskey: a large photograph of thousands of people milling around in a square, with a caption that would read, "There's somebody here in this crowd who doesn't know about Seagram's V.O. Find him and tell him." Albee thought it was brilliant; the account executive did not. His career as a copywriter ended before it began. He took several courses at Columbia University, including a short story class. About the same time, he and Muir Weissinger joined the Army reserves in order to avoid being drafted; they were to be attached to an intelligence unit. Eventually he was called before the draft board. When he was asked if he was homosexual, he said yes, "and that was the end of that. I never heard from them again. It was 1946 or 1947 and I wasn't trying to get out of serving in the war zone." Serving in the military was simply not "part of my plan." Albee, Weissinger, and Farrand continued their interest in music. Led by Farrand, they focused their attention on Rachmaninoff, going to concerts featuring his work. As recounted in Farrand's unpublished musical memoir, they visited Rachmaninoff's widow in Manhattan, and she invited the three young men to come to her home, Villa Senar, on Lake Lucerne in Switzerland. Albee and Weissinger accepted "with the blithe assurance of the rich and mobile." Farrand did not see how he could accept, "but the remote possibility begins to fester in my jealous heart." Eventually, he was the only one to take Mrs. Rachmaninoff up on her invitation.

During this period, Albee dated Muir's sister Delphine. In common with Celeste Seymour, she was lively and pretty. In 1949, he was her escort at her coming-out party. They talked about marriage and were informally engaged. In 1962 *Newsweek* contacted Delphine, who had married a Royal Marine and was living in England. After the *Newsweek* cover story was published, she wrote an affectionate letter to Albee, reawakening old memories. She said that on the day she and her husband and their daughters moved to Plymouth, in the midst of chaos, the phone rang. It was a reporter from *Newsweek*, asking, "Is it true that you were escorted to your Debutante Dance by Edward Albee?" "That brightened moving day for us all. I can see that I shall have to prepare clever statements, i.e., 'I always knew he had it in him,' etc." She said she couldn't be more delighted with his success. "The only thing that disturbs me is that in the various articles . . . your seriousness is stressed and *Newsweek* says you hardly laugh. This isn't in keeping with my memories—or maybe it was me who was laughing at what you had said."

Clearly they had a good time together, but gradually he came to the realization that their relationship was deceitful, and he ended their unofficial engagement. "I don't know what I thought I was doing with her. She was nice. I liked her. I really can't believe that I came close to making that terrible mistake. That went out the window with the whole family and everything else. That was another part of life: living at home, being the dutiful son, engagement, and the rest of it. I knew that I was supposed to become the kind of person they wanted me to be, which meant business or something, turning into a commuter, marriage, two and a half kids. For God's sake, what did I think I was doing? I was going to bed with boys from age thirteen on and enjoyed it greatly. If I went to bed with girls, I never felt the same pleasure from it." He added that he did not sleep with Delphine.

He and his mother often had arguments. One of the worst was over the question of mail. She began opening his letters. He was furious. They fought and she picked up a crystal ashtray and threw it at him. The next turning point came after a late night of partying and drinking in Manhattan. He came home at five o'clock in the morning, and somebody (other than himself, he said) had thrown up in the car. He hurriedly parked the car, left the lights on in the driveway, and went up to his bedroom. At 8:30 in the morning he was awakened by his mother, who demanded that he come downstairs. With a terrible hangover, he made his way to the dining room for a confrontation with his parents. "There were a lot of ultimatums flying around the dining room. How dare you come home at five in the morning. How dare you leave vomit in the car for the chauffeur to clean up." Years later, with the age altered, the scene was attributed to the character of Tobias in A Delicate Balance. His wife, Agnes, remembers "when you were very young and lived at home, and the servants were awake when you were; six A.M. for your breakfast when you wanted it, or five in the morning when you came drunk and seventeen, washing the vomit from the car, and you, telling no one." With Albee's parents, the accusations moved on to, "How dare you get thrown out of college. How dare you not like our friends. How dare you not do this. How dare you not do that." Absurdly, the angriest charge was: "How dare you leave the lights on in the driveway." Quietly seething, Edward found himself pushed over the edge.

"At that moment, it became, do it our way or get out. I didn't want to have anything to do with those people. I'd learned to hate their politics, their morality, their bigotry. I was really very very unhappy in that whole environment. And when my father said, either you straighten up or get out, I knew this was it. I remember going upstairs and packing one suitcase and leaving the same day." He said good-bye to his grandmother and to her Pekingese. In typical Albee fashion, he telephoned for a taxicab, which took him to the train station. He never looked back, although several months later, when the family was away, he did return briefly to pick up more of his clothes. "Was I thrown out or did I leave?" he asks. "I didn't feel I was left any alternative. And it had nothing to do with homosexuality. That's another fiction. That was never discussed between us. She could never bring herself to discuss the subject, and my father didn't talk about anything. I was aware of my own sexual nature and that I would never be able to function according to their standards. I'm sure that in the background that helped motivate me in my decision to take off. It was clear to me: I was not what they bargained for, what they thought they had bought."

Later, in a play called *The Dispossessed*, an early version of *The American Dream*, a young man comes home after a long night of drinking and leaves the driveway lights on. The lights shine into his father's room, keeping him awake. After their altercation the next morning, the son says, "Why didn't you go out and turn the lights off?" That was, of course, a scene from life. What if his father had turned the lights off? "My life would have been different." More likely, his departure would simply have been postponed. It was impossible for him to stay, and it was time to break away.

Up to then, friends called him "Eddie" or "Ed." When things were going well, his mother had called him "Ed," but whenever she was angry she called him "Edward." Leaving home, he decided that " 'Edward' was my proper name." This was not, of course, as consequential a change as Tom Williams renaming himself Tennessee Williams, or William Falkner distinguishing himself from his family by turning into William Faulkner, but it was a significant act of self-definition. "Edward" had the ring of maturity, or at least formality, and from then on, he was "Edward Albee"; and he was not to see his mother again for seventeen years. Looking back on his departure, he summarized it by saying, "Left school; left home; left everything." When he left, he had no plans ever to see his parents again. He did not leave home thinking, "This will show them. They'll love me after this." Instead, "I walked out because I was fed up with it. It's hard for anybody to understand completely the pressure I was feeling at home, the pressure and the unhappiness—and the enormous release that I had when I left. I was not anxious to be taken back, to be reaccepted. That part of my life had absolutely ended."

3
Albee's Village Decade

I've been to the zoo.

W ILLIAM FLANAGAN was a talented young composer with a commanding presence and a strong self-destructive streak. Noel Farrand, who
studied composition with Flanagan, described him to Albee as "the most brilliant person" he had ever met, an estimation that would have been echoed by
any number of Flanagan's friends. He was born August 14, 1923, in "lower
middle-class depression-ridden Detroit," where his father worked for the telephone company. Coming from an Irish-American, Roman Catholic background, he had thought about becoming a priest until, as his friend Francis
James ("Jim") Brown said, "he became totally disillusioned with the church."
He soon switched his attention to music. "When I told my family I wanted to
study music," Flanagan said, "they thought of either putting me away or sending me away. Then they thought they might just as well let me be, since I was
being so pigheaded around the house anyway." When Flanagan studied at the
University of Rochester's Eastman School of Music, his classmates included
Jim Brown, Charles Strouse, and Laurence Rosenthal. "We were," said
Brown, "the four shining lights of the composition class." In 1946, the composer Howard Hanson, as a member of the Eastman faculty, led a purge that
was both sexual and political. Flanagan was dismissed from the school because he was homosexual. As Brown explains, "They threw out all the people
they thought were gay, and all the people they thought were Left. They threw
out all the best people."

Strouse, later a popular Broadway composer (*Bye Bye Birdie, Annie,* and other shows), regarded Flanagan as his best friend. Only fifteen when he entered Eastman, Strouse was younger than his classmates. "I was very young, so Bill was not only my friend, but he was a mentor in many ways. He was the first person who ever had anything to say about my being talented. I looked up to him tremendously. He shaped my attitude toward literature, poetry, the awareness of certain kinds of music"—and in that regard he was soon to play a somewhat similar role with Albee. When Flanagan was forced to leave school after three years, Strouse said, "He had a very hurtful time about it, and this was in the days, needless to say, when nobody was going around flaunting his gayness." Strouse, who is heterosexual, stayed on at Eastman and graduated while Flanagan moved to New York. They remained close friends and in 1949 went to Europe together to study composition with Nadia Boulanger.

Flanagan also studied with Aaron Copland and David Diamond, and Leonard Bernstein gave him early encouragement. With his charismatic personality, Flanagan quickly became the center of a circle of younger composers. The Carnegie Tavern behind Carnegie Hall was a regular meeting place for a group that eventually included Strouse, Brown and Rosenthal, Farrand, Ned Rorem, Edward Lewis, Russell Smith, and Israel Citkowitz—and Edward Albee, the one noncomposer in the group. In this circle, there were rivalries as well as friendships. Flanagan was, said Strouse, "the leader of the pack. He was the one that all of us looked up to."

While writing his art songs, Flanagan also worked as a music critic for the *New York Herald Tribune* and the *Stereo Review*. He was one of a number of composers brought to the *Tribune* as critics by Virgil Thomson, who seemed to favor those like himself who were also composers. John Gruen, one of Flanagan's fellow reviewers on the *Tribune*, wrote, "One of the most intellectually stimulating people I have ever known, Bill could analyze a piece of music with the deftness and precision of a surgeon, and he could talk about friends and acquaintances and stars with a kind of bitchy insight that nevertheless took people's vulnerabilities and weaknesses into account. I suppose the major event of his personal life was his long and turbulent friendship with Edward Albee." In 1959, writing about a concert of songs by Rorem and Flanagan, Marc Blitzstein said about Flanagan: "His melodic curve is sensitive, personal, and remarkably sure." The artist Roger Baker, who was a friend of both Flanagan and Albee, said, "If there was a contemporary Voltaire, Flanagan was it. He was so sharp and perceptive and skillful in his writing. He saw around corners. He had savage humor. En point!"

At the time, Flanagan was living with Brown at the Garden Hotel across from Madison Square Garden, "a wretched and, as it turned out, mildly notorious hotel on the periphery of Manhattan's theatrical district." Many years later Brown was married and living in London. Remembering Flanagan, he said, "Every homosexual in New York wanted to go to bed with him. He could have whoever he wanted, and he had most of them one way or another." He added, "Bill loved to have sycophants. He couldn't live without people admiring him."

In 1948 on a visit to Manhattan from Larchmont, Farrand introduced Albee to Flanagan. When they met, it turned out to be a historic encounter, something like the meeting of Rimbaud and Verlaine: Flanagan, the sharp-witted, acidulous older man; Albee, the younger, impressionable and hopeful artist, but with his own strong though momentarily submerged individual personality. Actually at twenty-five, Flanagan was only five and a half years older than Albee (and he had a habit of shaving off three of those years to make himself seem younger). He exuded a greater maturity and worldliness. In contrast, Albee seemed subdued. Flanagan's first impression of him: "He was kind of on the plump side, very very quiet, very prep school." Years later, Flanagan wrote about their first meeting: "I can't recall a word Edward said that evening. He was dressed in a somber, voluminous and quite obviously expensive double-breasted suit. Its style might have been considered unnecessarily old for a man of sixty. And his hair was slicked back flat. He was engaged at the time to an extremely pretty English girl [Delphine, who was not with him at the time]. And it must have seemed reasonable to him that *he* should speak with a British accent too."

Coincidentally, when Albee left home in 1949, so did Noel Farrand. He had quit the Eastman school after two years and, accepting Mrs. Rachmaninoff's invitation, had gone to Europe on a pilgrimage to learn more about Rachmaninoff. When Farrand ran out of money in Switzerland, he wired home, referring formally to the "necessity for the allocation of many monies," borrowing the expression "monies" from Albee. Noel's father responded with irritation: "Sending money. Pretty well disgusted. Dad." Returning to America, Farrand decided it was time to be entirely on his own. "Edward and I both left home at the same time for something like the same reason. I quarreled with my father and he quarreled with his mother." Continuing their friendship, they shared an apartment at 60 West 10th Street. As Flanagan said, "The next I heard of Edward, he had effected his now-celebrated break with family and environment and had fled—rather too dramatically, I thought—to Greenwich Village. For his double-breasted suit he substituted more casual attire. He unslicked his hair into a crew cut he retains to this day. And he dropped his accent."

It was not until 1952 that Flanagan and Brown separated, and Flanagan and Albee moved in together and began their close, often tempestuous relationship. "There was a tremendous physical attraction between them," said Brown. "Edward and I were at opposite ends of the turnstile: one going in, one going out." About Albee, he said: "He had a very open face, very clean shaven, sort of cherubic. It was a very beautiful face at that age—and so was mine, and I hated it. Like him, I looked very very young." About Brown, Albee said: "He was a good-looking kid, and he fancied himself as a great homme fatale." At one point, Albee and Brown wrote a blues song together. It was called "River Blues," and Brown took it to Billie Holiday, who was not interested in singing it. Albee recalls it as a song about a woman who was going to kill herself. He quotes a lyric: "The river blues have got me. The deep and dreary river blues have got me." It was, one might say, an example of Albee's gift of mimicry: It sounds like a blues song.

With a greater frequency, Albee and Farrand were also collaborators. Together they wrote what was to be Albee's first published work in New York. Farrand asked Albee to write prose versions of Rachmaninoff song texts for the Rachmaninoff Society. In July of 1950, the society published fourteen songs with "prose realizations by Edward Albee," and the following year, they were released on a record. It was at Farrand's suggestion that Albee met W. H. Auden. Farrand did not know Auden, but he looked up his number in the telephone book and insisted that Edward call him, telling his friend that it would be "a wonderful chance to show him some of your poetry." Following Noel's advice, Albee telephoned Auden, who invited him to visit. "I rang his doorbell on Cornelia Street, shoved a bunch of poetry in his face and said, 'Read it.' He did." Asked to return, Albee took along a jug of red wine as well as more poems. At that second meeting, Auden asked him if he were queer and Albee said that he was not. Auden responded, "Somehow I have the feeling it would be much better if you were," without explaining whether that was a reference to his poetry or the possibility of the two of them having a relationship. Said Farrand, "I've always assumed there was a buttoned-up quality to Edward's poetry that Auden was trying to correct." Auden suggested that Albee write pornographic verse.

On March 12, 1949, his twenty-first birthday, Albee came into a small inheritance from his paternal grandmother, $25 a week from a $100,000 trust fund, with the principal coming to him when he turned thirty. Every week, he dutifully collected a small check at his father's New York office. He received his dole from his uncle, Ted Lauder, the dentist, Ethel's first husband, who had been named the family's financial adviser. (His uncle is mentioned in *Three Tall Women:* "The dumpy little . . . dentist was he? What did *he* know about running an office. What did *he* know about handling money? Enough to steal! Enough to line his *own* pockets.") Once, by accident, Edward arrived early and ran into his father. It was "a brief, cold exchange." They had little to say to one another, and the meeting was not repeated. The weekly stipend helped to pay the rent. At the time, Noel was not working and briefly Edward supported him. By the summer, Noel had moved out, and each was on his own.

During the next few years, as Albee moved from apartment to apartment, from Greenwich Village to Chelsea, to a $16-a-month cold-water flat on Henry Street, he had a series of brief, stopgap jobs. "He was unable to make a commitment to a decent job," said Flanagan. "He was willing to go to any end to avoid it. Anything that ever involved getting up at eight in the morning lasted only a few weeks, anything that tended to limit his nocturnal freedom." When he worked, he did so with a certain wiliness. As a clerk at Schirmer's record store on 47th Street, he kept his silence as music students stole musical scores and slipped them into their briefcases. Occasionally, Albee himself would steal books. His explanation was that he—and the music students— needed the books and the scores more than the store did. He appropriated only what he thought he needed, and he was never caught for his thievery. Adjusting the cash register, he would also pay himself an extra five or six dollars every day. At other times, he worked in the record department at Bloomingdale's and the book department at Gimbel's and for less than a day he was a desk clerk at the Warwick Hotel on West 54th Street. His longest, steadiest employment was as a messenger for Western Union. But these were all interim jobs, to give him time (and money) to write and to enjoy himself.

With Farrand, Flanagan, and others, he was caught up in a swirl of social and cultural activity. Across the arts, it was a heady period in New York. Wherever one turned, especially in Greenwich Village, there were artists on the move, and many on the rise. To a great extent, New York in the late 1940s and early fifties was the equivalent of Paris in the twenties. While Flanagan and his friends in the music world met at the Carnegie Tavern, painters and sculptors (Willem de Kooning, Jackson Pollock, and Franz Kline, among others) frequented the Cedar Tavern on University Place, and writers (James Agee, Delmore Schwartz, Allen Ginsberg, William Styron) went to the San Remo, an Italian restaurant on MacDougal Street—and Dylan Thomas was drinking himself to death at the White Horse. Many of the composers were homosexual and many of the artists were womanizers. In common, they were drinkers and carousers and also experimentalists in their art form. Abstract Expressionism overlapped with absurdism in theater, which itself was influenced by Surrealism. Sometimes artists crossed the line and visited one another's hangouts. The San Remo, in particular, drew a mixed crowd. Painters knew composers and they all knew writers, who for the most part led more solitary lives.

Attached to the world of composers, Albee, still "pathologically shy," remained quietly in the background. "I was glum, taciturn, closemouthed, nonparticipatory," he said. He listened as they talked—incessantly. "We talked all the time," said Farrand, "and we were always acting out something," spontaneous plays in life, in which they would often dress up as characters. Farrand, impetuously, would arrive at the Carnegie Tavern with fake moustache and cigar, in the guise of Groucho Marx. Flanagan and the others were also friendly with Aaron Copland, Virgil Thomson, and Leonard Bernstein. "They were a generation older and were always treated that way," said Farrand. Copland, for one, would have gatherings at his house in the Village. "Everyone treated Copland with kid gloves," said Brown, indicating that he was instrumental in the careers of younger composers: "He could make you or break you."

When Ned Rorem first met Albee, he thought of him simply as Flanagan's latest boyfriend: "Bill always had a boyfriend of one sort or another, and I never paid much attention to them because they were accoutrements of him. When Edward appeared on the scene, all I knew was that he was a nice, affable, slightly overweight kid with some money, and whenever I needed to cash a check, he would cash it. But I never paid any attention to him." And apparently neither did anyone else, except to think, as Rorem did, that he was the wealthiest person in the crowd. In that sense, it was a repeat of the atmosphere that surrounded him as a child when he was the richest kid in the neighborhood. In New York, he did not have immediate access to money, but he retained an air of well-being. The truth is that Albee himself was often in need of money and at one point borrowed from Richard Howard (later a prize-winning poet and translator) and was very slow to repay his debt, an act that left him with considerable remorse.

In a letter to Howard, Albee spoke of his misgivings as a borrower:

> Of the many distresses my life is subject to high on the list is the anxiety I
> suffer by having to, from time to time, assume that the give and take of friend-

ship includes within it the give and take of aid and succor. And one step closer to the things that eventually rot the soul is the anxiety suffered by these friends of mine who experience the perhaps extraordinary calls I put upon an essentially social relationship. In this regard I suffer most with you because, among all my friends, you suffer most from me.

Money, dear Dick, I have sadly learned to be not a system of exchange and barter but, rather, a tangible extension of the psyche. How much better one could deal in pots of pate de foi [sic] or bottles of wine!

Vowing to pay back the debt, he signed the letter "Yr (humble) creditoree." Soon he paid back a quarter of "the money you were kind enough to let me have during a season of high water and expenses. It is, in truth, all I can manage at this exact moment without hocking my jewelry (and I never know when Mother will want at least the tiara back)."

In Rorem's view, Albee generally kept to himself: "He would sit quietly in a corner. He loved music and he admired musicians. Friends of Bill's who were bigshots like Aaron Copland—Edward was in awe of them. I never even knew he was a playwright, or that he was interested in anything." Although Rorem had reservations about Flanagan's musical talent, he admired his intelligence and his insightfulness: "Bill never talked about what he didn't think was important." Howard agreed with Rorem and Farrand about Flanagan's brilliance, saying that he had "this wonderful Jesuit-trained mind, and he was very quick and sharp and funny." He had a somewhat different attitude toward Albee at this time, whom he thought had a streak of meanness. About every third night Flanagan, Albee, and Howard would see each other, and Albee would make harsh comments about both private and public matters.

Drinking heavily, often going on binges, Flanagan and Albee frequented a round of gay bars in Greenwich Village, including Goody's, Mary's (on Eighth Street); the Old Colony; and Lenny's Hideaway, a basement bar on 10th Street between Seventh and Eighth Avenues. Robert Heide, a hopeful playwright recently arrived in New York, remembers Lenny's as a seedy place with a tacky Bohemian feeling. A typical evening for Flanagan, Albee, and others would begin at 11 P.M. and go on until 4 A.M. Then they would often sleep until four in the afternoon. Albee drank for pleasure, then from habit, eventually from a kind of inner necessity. Frequently he drank excessively.

During this time, he had his first overt immersion in a gay world. As Heide recalled, "It was a tribal gay scene—you have to remember that gay life at that time was very oppressed in certain ways. It was clandestine. These were Mafia bars and the guy who ran Lenny's was kind of a goon. It tended to attract creative-type gay people as well as neatniks in little sweaters with gold chains, looking like they were from the land of Peter Pan—waiting around the bar for the knight in white armor to arrive and meanwhile being very rejective of everybody else in the place." A popular song on the jukebox at Lenny's was Chris Connor singing Billy Strayhorn's "Lush Life," with a double meaning seemingly directed at the clientele ("I used to visit all the very gay places / Those come what may places / Where one relaxes on the axis of the wheel of life / to get the feel of life / from jazz and cocktails"). One of the regulars at Lenny's was Ian Orlando Macbeth, an eccentric Village character who had pink hair and dressed in flamboyant Renaissance clothes. Albee found him fascinating and watched as he ordered a drink called a clinker (a combination of brandy and vodka) and then threw it in the bartender's face. Rarely would women visit Lenny's. More likely they would be at Page Three, a lesbian and gay bar around the corner. To a great extent, the bars remained underground and were unknown to a more general public, although occasionally there would be police raids on these establishments.

Rorem recalls, "In those days, friends meant getting terribly drunk with an awful lot of sex." Within the group, there was a certain fidelity. "There wasn't sex in the family. People slept out of the family, but when I think back on it, the amount of promiscuity and the amount of drinking that went on in this milieu was astonishing." It was long before the Stonewall rebellion and, for the most part, homosexuals kept their sexual proclivities within the group. In private, and in gay bathhouses, in a time before AIDS, promiscuity was rampant. With a wildness that seemed second nature to his character, Flanagan was given to acts of indiscretion. Once he told Strouse about an incident that happened at the bar at the Astor Hotel. A man made a pass at him, they went outside, and then the man flashed a badge revealing himself as a detective. Flanagan was arrested and taken to the Tombs, the detention center, from which he called Strouse. "Flanagan was into more of a furtive kind of thing," said Heide, "whereas I think Edward was more direct about his physical need." Heide said that a gay relationship was expected to be an open relationship: "There was no sense of monogamy."

One of the most popular gathering spots was the San Remo, which drew a very heterogeneous crowd, including college students visiting New York. Heide remembers Flanagan and Albee standing at the bar, "Edward usually in a black leather jacket, Bill in a brown leather jacket. Beer in hand." The two of them affected a somber, moody look. In photographs, they often looked like twins, though in actuality they were a contrast. Albee still seemed preppy while Flanagan was more casual and often haggard looking. Flanagan looked like a poet. At Lenny's Hideaway, said Heide, "They used to call them the two owls, because they stared straight out." He adds, "When I think of Flanagan and Edward, I think of all that anger and rage. There was something in their presence that was fearful. You felt, where is this going?"

Rorem agrees with the picture: "Before Bill and Edward were famous, they would go to the Eighth Street bars, the Old Colony, the Eighth Street, or Mary's, and they would go to opposite ends of the bar. They were known as the Sisters Grimm because they wouldn't smile. They would sulk and they would swill down straight shots of whiskey with beer." At the time, he felt there was an element of anger and rage in the relationship between Albee and Flanagan, and also something "fearful, a feeling of danger."

"We called them clones," said Strouse. As Flanagan and Albee grew closer and closer, Strouse, for one, felt excluded and was somewhat jealous of the tightness of the Albee-Flanagan relationship. Eventually Strouse and Albee also became friends.

If he hadn't met Flanagan, what would Albee's life have been like? "I have no idea," he said. After praising Flanagan as a teacher, he added quickly, "I know he started me on the road to alcoholism. He turned out to be an alcoholic, and I think he encouraged me in that direction, not that I needed much encouragement." He remembered, in particular, one long night of drinking, in which the two of them worked their way up Sixth Avenue going from bar to bar, drinking martinis. By the time they had finished their expedition, each had had twenty-one martinis, or so Albee remembers, as if anyone could keep count after having so many cocktails.

It was after one such night that Albee wrote a cautionary poem about drinking. One verse reads:

Avoid martinis after dinner
Drink the sluggish beer instead
The gin and wine may keep us thinner
The malt and hops more sure of bed
Though either way you have a winner
More apt to rise—or quicker dead.

For Albee, it was a time of education and experimentation. "I was soaking a lot up, but obviously I was involved," he said. "I was writing, not very well, the entire time, but I did a lot of absorbing. I was always around people who were somewhat older than me, somewhat more sophisticated, informed, people who could teach me something."

In 1952, Flanagan and Albee went off to Europe for six months, the first time that Albee had been abroad. They traveled through France and Italy, and it was in Italy, said Albee, that he and Flanagan became lovers. They spent much of their time in Florence, where they immersed themselves in art. David Diamond was living there and they looked him up—despite a previous conflict he had had with Albee. When they first met in New York, they had taken an almost immediate dislike to one another. Later in a letter to Diamond, Albee tried to explain their differences and the distortions that had been made by mutual friends:

> Whatever remarks I have made about your music in the past have been objective judgments, and I believe myself entitled to them under our form of government. But I can promise you that I will never again so much as open my mouth about your stuff again. It's bound to be twisted somewhere and come out as slander.

In Florence, Albee wrote love poems as well as 150 pages of his second novel, a mysterious story about a lawyer and "twins, a brother and a sister, who carry chaos around with them." About his trip and about Flanagan, Albee said, "It was part of the learning experience. Looking, learning, seeing, hearing. Being hectored and lectured at by Flanagan all the time. Every sentence beginning with 'You see,' or 'Do you understand?' He was terribly bright and a great teacher. He molded and shaped my aesthetic. He was much more knowledgeable in the ways of the world and in the ways of the arts. It was a lover relationship, but also a teacher-student relationship. He pointed out to me very, very clearly that this is the way one should be exploring one's life with the arts." As a pupil, Albee was a quick study and began investigating areas of culture on his own.

When they came back to New York, they took an apartment together and, said Flanagan, "He went distinctly Bohemian, but not in a self-conscious way. He kept uncanny hours and did anything he pleased." Even as Flanagan came to know him better than anyone else during this period of his life, he felt there was always something removed about Albee. As he said, "He's a chronically ambivalent man—in his human relationships and with his family." For one example, he pointed to Albee's attitude toward his parents. "There's a certain calculation when he talks about his home life. It disturbed him less than he makes it. He hated his mother—and he adulated her. I'm not opposed to ambivalence as an aesthetic, but it has to be a willful aesthetic, couched in a structure. With Edward, there tends to be an emotional involvement in human terms, but specific emotional reactions lack urgency." He added, "Edward is widely reputed to be a mysterious number." His conclusion: "He's been exorcising ghosts all his life."

In 1953, Flanagan was awarded a fellowship to the MacDowell Colony in Peterborough, New Hampshire, and Albee, still writing poetry and working at odd jobs, visited him there for a week. He carried a valise filled with his poems, having decided he would show his work to Thornton Wilder, who was also in residence at MacDowell at the time. Wilder drove Albee and Flanagan to the nearby Dublin Pond, where, said Albee, "We sat by the edge drinking bourbon and lake water" out of paper cups. Having read some twenty of Albee's poems over several days, Wilder commented on them, one by one. As the years passed, Albee elaborated on the story, so that it became a comic yarn. In Albee's favorite retelling, Wilder would criticize a poem and gently set it on the surface of the lake until it floated away. Then he would repeat the process, launching poems like ships until the lake was filled with a flotilla of verse. The story was, of course, an exaggeration. Returning to the truth, Albee said, "Because Wilder was a little drunk, by some mistake he put one of the pages in the water rather than on the shore." The important point of the story, in all its variations, was that, having read the poems, Wilder subjected each to serious criticism. Then, suddenly, he asked Albee, "Have you ever thought about writing plays?"

"When I tell the story," said Albee, "I usually conclude by saying I am not trying to suggest that Wilder saw in the poetry the incipient playwright. I think he was trying to do a very, very good deed, to save poetry from me. And that becomes a good story." Whatever Wilder's motive, the effect was inspirational. Albee had, of course, written plays, along with short stories and poetry, but at that point had not thought seriously about being a playwright. Theater was simply one of several possible outlets for his creativity. As he liked to say, having failed as a poet, novelist, and essayist, it seemed like the next natural step.

In 1962, Wilder recalled the encounter in a letter to Garson Kanin and Ruth Gordon:

> When I was at the MacDowell Colony, two young men came to see me, one
> of them with some poetry for me to read. I've never seen them since and

wouldn't recognize them in the street. Last week *Newsweek* wrote me they were doing a cover story on Edward Albee. He had told them that after reading his poems I had urged him to be a dramatist. That I was responsible, etc. Had I any comment? Well, that I was very proud. The satisfaction that this little story gives me is that it lets me believe that it is a swell way I can pass the torch. The torch that Gertrude Stein gave to dozens and me. Nice, eh?

Wilder commented to *Newsweek*, "A reading of his poems had prompted me to urge him to write plays. His poems were good; but the specific imagery gave the impression that he would be fine in drama—and he is." Wilder sent Albee a note acknowledging the magazine's query: "I told them that I was very proud."

In a letter to Wilder, Albee recounted the episode:

Well, maybe memory plays funny tricks, and mine is notoriously witty, but I seem to recall that during that evening that Flanagan, you and I sat there and drank whiskey and lake water—and during which you commented on all those poems I gave you to read—I seem to recall that you dropped a couple of hints suggesting that I might find the theatre a more comfortable medium than the poem.

Although it is questionable how much the meeting meant to Wilder, it was extremely important to Albee. For the first time, a serious professional in his field (whatever that field was) treated him as an artist and made what seemed to be a valid suggestion. Trying to cross the bridge from poetry to playwriting, Albee began writing a play, a masque in rhymed couplets. He sent Wilder a letter telling him about the work in progress and asking him whether it was necessary to have published anything in order to apply to the MacDowell Colony. Wilder neatly avoided any encouragement about MacDowell except to say that if Albee applied he would write in support of his application but would have to see a considerable amount of the applicant's work, ignoring the fact that he had already read many of his poems. He asked to see the play when it was finished and said that the Poet's Theater in Cambridge accepted dramas in verse.

Albee's verse play, *The Making of a Saint*, seventy-six pages long, takes place in a way station between heaven and hell. A wise old man says (a line Albee can still quote), "People live in a world of ruses / Platitudes, and poor excuses."

One verse read:

The speculation of why we're on earth
Should be a continual subject for mirth;
There is no purpose; there is no equation.
It's a lot of rot; it's just evasion.

Albee dedicated the play to Wilder and sent him a letter telling him he had completed it. In his letter, Wilder offered the following advice:

> You say that the answer to your finding acceptance by editors is: "Time and work."
>
> Yes, but . . .
>
> That's not enough.
>
> Cultivate also a deeper concentration of all yourself on the poetic act. One preparation for it is this: let me beg you not to read too much contemporary prose and poetry. Expand your imagination's picture of what poetry does by withdrawing into yourself for a short time daily to read some of the great writing of the past. It's often valuable to do this in some foreign language. It wouldn't hurt if you made a sort of ceremony of it: quietly shut the door, sit down, relax, open the book, make your mind a serene blank cup for a minute—then slowly read Baudelaire or Mallarmé or Rimbaud—for instance.
>
> Something like that.
>
> And remember: don't only *write* poetry; *be* a poet.
>
> I like the poem you have sent me. The mood is admirably conveyed. But wasn't the poem on its way to a greater intensity? Before you used the title: *Letter from Florence*. This too has something of the "letter" quality—that is, talking. The talking cries out to pass to the next stage of singing, of praying, of bursting . . .
>
> Something like that.

While one can give Wilder credit for offering the suggestion that art needed tranquillity, there is something of Polonius in his comments, especially in the advice, "Cultivate a deeper concentration . . ." This above all, Albee, to Wilder be true. The play was sent to him, but if Wilder ever commented on it, those comments have been lost. Albee also sent the play to Virgil Thomson, suggesting that he might make an opera out of it. Thomson declined, saying that he had already done a "saint" opera, meaning *Four Saints in Three Acts*. Albee went back to his desk and continued writing.

To their friends, he was still Flanagan's shadow, at best his protégé, although some knew of his writing aspirations. But he never stopped writing, somehow fitting it in amid all the late night drinking and carousing, and day-long sleeping. "He was vitiating his emotional resources," Flanagan said. "He knew if he didn't find something soon, he wouldn't find anything at all." Although Flanagan was correct in his emotional estimation, it turned out to be a long, intense apprenticeship. Over a period of ten years, Albee wrote nine plays, dozens of stories, and more than one hundred poems, and in each form there is some value.

In all this work, there are recurrent themes (and even character names, like Agnes, Amy, Ann, Toby, Fred): twins (male and female), sometimes separated at birth; children who died or were lost; strong mothers and weak fathers; dreamers and questers who are misunderstood and confused about their identity, sexual and otherwise. The range of Albee's apprentice plays was wide, including *The Recruit*, a short play about soldiers in battle, five of them talking about one who is dead; one act of a play called *In a Quiet Room*, about two school friends meeting after a twenty-year absence. One of the men has had a broken marriage and has lost his baby daughter. *Ye Watchers and Ye Lonely Ones*, a short play in three scenes, parallels the lives of two boys (one a homosexual indoctrinating the other) with two older men, who have been together for seven years. One man asks, "Why do homosexuals always write rotten love poetry to each other?" and the other answers, "Because homosexual love is rotten, too."

There were four different versions of a one-act play called *The Invalid*, about an artist who, like Oblomov, "refuses to participate" and is overcome by "an extraordinary lethargy." In it, one character says, "It is one thing to see a man struggle against public indifference, or some psychological stumbling block or even against a lack of talent . . . and it is another thing to see a person realize that he is unable to be what he wants, and then try to make the adjustment toward something commonplace." A young man replies, "We are concerned with something a great deal more painful—the determination to fail without trying." He adds, "I fear for that terrible day maybe when you're thirty, maybe later, when you find yourself skidding toward middle-age with nothing to show for your youth, all of it a blank, a waste." Along the way there is the line, "The balance has been delicate now for some time."

End to Summer concerns the relationship between a fifty-year-old widow and two young men and poses the question: If a father and child are drowning, which one should you save first? The widow thinks, the father, because one can always have more children, as if to say that children are dispensable and interchangeable. There are four versions of *The Merry Month of May*, also called *Black Is the Color of Mourning*, the play whose leading characters,

Neal and Agnes, are stand-ins for Reed and Frances Albee. The most fully formed of the early plays is *The Dispossessed*, written in 1958. The four characters are a brother and sister (Toby and Ann), a nurse (Mrs. Meadows), and a grandmother. Toby, a version of Albee, was thrown out of five schools, left home four years ago, and lives in Greenwich Village. When he refers to his parents as "the one who was supposed to be my mother, the one who was supposed to be my father," his sister says, "If that's the way you feel about it, you should have arranged to get adopted by some other family." There is a spark of wit in the character of the grandmother, a precursor of Grandma in *The American Dream* and *The Sandbox*. She weighs eighty-seven pounds and explains, "It's mostly water, too; every fourth day I get drained . . . like a swimming pool." One thing that is missing in the other plays is Albee's humor. In his own life, he always retained a comic perspective, but he was as yet unable—or unwilling—to transmit that into his work. A feeling of seriousness, of portentousness, shadowed much of his apprentice writing.

Occasionally, though, a story had a certain lyricism and even a theatricality. One of the most intriguing is "Excelsior," an overheard conversation in the Excelsior Hotel in Rome, a story that clearly derived from his trip to Italy with Flanagan. At the center is a boorish American woman. Albee says he was influenced by Tennessee Williams's novel *The Roman Spring of Mrs. Stone*. He sent his poems to various poetry and literary magazines and to *The New Yorker*, and they all were rejected, some of them by Howard Moss, who was the poetry editor of *The New Yorker* (and, later, a very good friend of Albee). For years, as a writer, Albee was the equivalent of a painter in a garret, producing work in private, work that no one saw.

Flanagan later wrote that a great deal of nonsense had been printed about "Albee's Village Decade":

> Curiously enough, its most characteristic segment was passed in an airy, comfortable and altogether proper floor-through in Chelsea. And I consistently find it all but impossible to determine from the accumulated probings of the press whether Edward, soggy with privilege and inherited wealth, was a slippery Bohemian *poseur* or merely an obscure, insecure, poverty-ridden poet reduced by circumstance, inertia and material want to delivering death notifications for Western Union.

As his closest friend and his most demanding critic, Flanagan believed that "The truth lay at neither extreme. He was, to be sure, adrift and, like most of the rest of us, he had arrived in town with an unsown wild oat or two. But from the beginning he was, in his outwardly impassive way, determined to write—even as he realized that his facile, morose and sharply talented poetry was something less than distinguished in itself."

To a great extent, Flanagan considered Albee's poetry to be uninspired: "He was dabbling around in poetry, taken by the neoclassic religious rhythms of Eliot and Auden. His poetry had lots of facility—some of it staggers the imagination—but it couldn't be taken seriously. There was no intellectual commitment. I don't remember any sustained, systematic approach to his work. He'd go on a writing binge. In three months he would produce a lot, but he wouldn't go back and revise." Albee's life up to then, he said, "was largely a matter of stopped writing altogether," a statement that proved to be prescient in regard to Flanagan's own life.

Flanagan and Albee were "not pleasant together when they were drunk," said Howard, "and there was a lot of drinking and a lot of jockeying for power in the relationship." Beneath it all, Howard felt a great sympathy for Albee. "He was very much an orphan of the storm at that point. There was no family. There was only Bill and the home they made together against the world."

One of their favorite hangouts was Julius's on West 10th Street, and down the street was a restaurant and bar called the College of Complexes (later the Ninth Circle), between Greenwich Avenue and Waverly Place. Behind the bar at the College of Complexes, there was a large mirror, on which patrons would write slogans and messages with soap, "what they pleased," said Albee, "short of obscenity." On an evening in 1954, he noticed a graffito, "Who's Afraid of Virginia Woolf?" Placed there by an unknown hand, the line made Albee laugh. He said he "dropped it from mind." Actually he lodged it deep within his mind.

Often Albee would go to concerts of friends. He also went to concerts given by Billie Holiday and Judy Garland, among others, and continued to read widely, but theater remained a sidelong interest. Flanagan said that Albee "could all but hoot himself out of the balcony at the zanier moments of Leonard Sillman's *New Faces of 1952*," and that he was moved by "the elegantly sustained combination of rueful mockery and wintry sadness of Jean Anouilh's *The Waltz of the Toreadors*." Several plays made an even stronger impact, beginning with the Broadway premiere of Eugene O'Neill's *The Iceman Cometh* in 1946. Albee was struck by the play and by its treatment of the theme of truth and illusion. Through the character of Hickey, it was O'Neill's conclusion that man needed to keep his pipe dreams in order to survive. Albee was fascinated by O'Neill's drama, and for him it became a kind of time bomb, ticking away until he was able to come to grips with its message.

The Iceman Cometh failed on Broadway. It was not until the Circle in the Square revived the play in 1956 in a production starring Jason Robards that it took its rightful position in O'Neill's body of work and in the American theater. Another, earlier production at Circle in the Square, a revival of Tennessee Williams's *Summer and Smoke* (starring Geraldine Page), performed a similar service for Williams and also represented the beginning of what was to become the modern Off-Broadway movement. Although Williams, Arthur Miller, and William Inge continued to open plays on Broadway through the 1950s, and O'Neill's posthumous *Long Day's Journey into Night* was a success there (in 1956), there were already rumblings of dissatisfaction with the main marketplace of the theater. There seemed to be little room for real experimentation, and the failure of *Waiting for Godot* in 1956 made it clear that Broadway, confronted by competition from television, was becoming increasingly timid and insular.

Although Off-Broadway can be traced back to the early part of the twentieth century when O'Neill began at the Provincetown Playhouse, there was a resurgence in the early 1950s. Led by Circle in the Square, Joseph Papp's New York Shakespeare Festival, and the Phoenix Theater, among other companies, Off-Broadway provided other options for actors and directors as well as playwrights. In smaller theaters, with lower production costs and lower ticket prices, companies could produce Chekhov and Ibsen as well as contemporary writers. The Living Theater, which Judith Malina and Julian Beck began in 1948, opened the door to plays by Paul Goodman, Gertrude Stein, and Jean Cocteau. Along with Ellen Stewart at La Mama and Joe Cino at Caffe Cino, the Living Theater had a renegade quality that helped to make it one of the guiding forces behind Off-Off-Broadway. The late 1950s turned out to be a particularly exciting time in the New York theater, with initial productions of works by Eugène Ionesco and Jean Genet, among others, all of which were shattering theatrical expectations.

When Albee went to the theater, generally it was Off-Broadway. He saw Picasso's *Desire Trapped the Tail*, E. E. Cummings's *Him*, and the Auden-Isherwood *The Dog Beneath the Skin*. Albee and Flanagan, Richard Howard, and Sanford Friedman became a foursome, on their limited budgets doing and seeing as much as they could. When Albee saw T. S. Eliot's *The Cocktail Party* in 1950, he said about Irene Worth: "If I ever write a play I would like her to be in it." On the other hand, in 1955, when the four friends saw Ugo Betti's *Island of Goats*, Albee was dismayed by Uta Hagen's performance. In addition to *The Iceman Cometh*, two productions proved to be catalytic:

Genet's *Deathwatch* in 1957 and Williams's *Suddenly Last Summer* the following year. Albee was gripped by Genet's prison drama and was also drawn to George Maharis, who played one of the three convicts in it. Maharis was later to create the role of Jerry in the New York premiere of *The Zoo Story*. Albee and Flanagan saw *Suddenly Last Summer* together, and, said Flanagan, "It had a profound hypnotic effect on both of us." Albee was particularly taken not just by the grotesque story of cannibalism but also by Williams's use of the monologue, the long reminiscence delivered by Anne Meacham about the horrors that happened, suddenly last summer. Robert Heide said that, for Albee, seeing the Genet and the Williams "was like a light bulb going off, or as if they were a release for his own pain."

Of all the jobs that Albee had, his favorite was as a messenger for Western Union. He explained, "Outdoors. Exercise. Interesting people. Typewriters to be borrowed or stolen." His coworkers included "heroin addicts and old people who had missed their way somewhere along the line." For three years, beginning in 1955, he worked at several Western Union offices but principally at a branch at 74th Street and Broadway. "I liked three things about the job. You came in when you wanted to and left when you wanted to. You didn't have to work every day if you didn't want to. You met a lot of interesting people. And it was a good job because I love walking. I was out in the air a lot. I didn't mind climbing stairs, and I didn't have to wear a uniform." He liked the salary, $1.10 an hour, about $44 a week, and he was good at getting tips, usually a quarter or thirty-five cents, three or four dollars a day. His shift ran from 3:30 P.M. to midnight. During his dinner break, he would often go to the cafeteria in the Manhattan Towers Hotel on 74th and Broadway. "You could get a huge, huge bowl of borscht, and all the black bread you could eat for thirty-five cents. If I had fifty cents, I would get kasha varnishkes. And there were bookstores close by to steal from."

Following Albee's lead, Flanagan also got a job delivering telegrams. Wearing sweaters and sneakers, the two of them would often sit together at the end of a long bench, clones waiting to receive an assignment. Toward the end of *Who's Afraid of Virginia Woolf?*, George tells Martha that a telegram has been delivered, one, as it turns out, announcing the death of their imaginary child. "It was good old Western Union," says George, "some little boy about seventy." "Crazy Billy?" asks Martha. "Yes, Martha, that's right . . . crazy Billy." That was a joking reference to Flanagan. As Albee explained in a *Paris Review* interview with Flanagan: "I did that because as *you* might recall, Mr. Flanagan, you used to deliver telegrams for Western Union, and you are very old and your name is Billy." The inference was that if Flanagan stayed on the job he would become the oldest living Western Union delivery boy, which, of course, could also have been said about Albee.

In the course of his work, Albee covered an area from 66th to 86th Street, from Central Park West to the Hudson River. He met a cross-section of New Yorkers covering a wide economic range, from the very rich to the very poor. He became friendly with the actor Laurence Tierney (who had played John Dillinger in the movies). Tierney was living in a seedy rooming house and was receiving money orders from his brother, the actor Scott Brady. One of Albee's routine extra assignments was to pick up Leonard Lyons's nightclub column on Sunday evening and deliver it to the *New York Post*. Many of the telegrams that he was called upon to deliver were notices of death, and they were sent collect. "I always knew when there was a death message because I learned the symbol, something subtle like a *D* in the upper part of the telegram, visible through the cellophane. I had to get a signature for any death telegram: 'Aunt Sarah died yesterday at 3 P.M., pick her up by 4 this afternoon, or we'll charge you.'" Sympathetic to the recipients, he would suggest that they read the telegram before they paid for it, and then he would return the message unpaid to the central office. This was an act of mercy but also one of pragmatism: "Not long after I started doing this I noticed that I was getting fifty cent tips. That taught me a very interesting lesson; you are not always punished for good deeds." The result was that he saw many people whom he would have never met, and he saw them up close and confronting sudden tragedy. Whatever he witnessed, he tucked away in his mental filing cabinet: characters, incidents, and images.

In retrospect, he would attack the "fiction of the waste land years," the years of anonymity and struggle. "I was living in Greenwich Village at a high point of Greenwich Village's existence. I was surrounded by creative people: painters, writers, composers. I was sitting around listening and learning. I was at just about every avant-garde event: theater, poetry reading, art show, concert. It was an exciting time. I don't remember being unhappy. I may have felt somewhat unfulfilled." This is partly hindsight. As was clear to Flanagan and others, his frustration was self-evident. At the beginning of 1958, as his thirtieth birthday approached, Albee felt a sense of dissatisfaction bordering on desperation. Despite his incipient talent and his ambition, he had written nothing of consequence. Was he a writer or simply an observer, destined to play a secondary role in other people's lives? Increasingly there was a feeling of emptiness and, perhaps, the idea that he would become another Flanagan, whose creativity never measured up to his potential. As he said several years later, he was "fed up with everything, including myself." He was also drinking far too much.

In February, one month before his birthday, he sat down in a folding chair at a rickety table in his kitchen in his apartment at 238 West 4th Street. Using a standard typewriter he had stolen (or "liberated") from Western Union and yellow copy paper from the same source, he began to write a play, single space, filling the margins. Everything had led him to this moment. For the first time in his life, the writing seemed to flow from some inner need and conviction. He was to remember it as "sort of an explosion." The first lines came swiftly:

I've been to the zoo. I said I've been to the zoo. MISTER, I'VE BEEN TO THE ZOO!

And the words never stopped.

The title of the play was *The Zoo Story*, and the character speaking was named Jerry, "a man in his late thirties, not poorly dressed, but carelessly. What was once a trim and lightly muscled body has begun to go to fat; and while he is no longer handsome, it is evident that he once was. His fall from physical grace should not suggest debauchery; he has, to come closest to it, a great weariness." The scene was Central Park on a Sunday afternoon in summer, and seated on a park bench is a man named Peter: "A man in his early forties, neither fat nor gaunt, neither handsome nor homely. He wears tweeds, smokes a pipe, carries horn-rimmed glasses. Although he is moving into middle age, his dress and his manner would suggest a man younger." (Albee borrowed the names from two friends of his, Peter Dellheim and Jerry Farmer.)

As the play begins, Peter is reading a book. At first, when Jerry speaks, Peter does not notice him. Finally Jerry gets his attention. He teases, taunts, and threatens him. Peter gradually rises in self-defense. What follows is a blistering confrontation between opposites. In turn, each gains a certain dominance, as the action rises and falls. Jerry works his way to "the story of Jerry and the dog," describing how he tried to communicate with his landlady's dog, "a black monster of a beast," which growls at him the first time he sees him and soon becomes his nemesis. Jerry decides, "First, I'll kill the dog with kindness, and if that doesn't work . . . I'll just kill him." He feeds the dog poisoned hamburger. The dog becomes deathly ill but survives. From then on, says Jerry, he and the dog "regard each other with a mixture of sadness and suspicion, and then we feign indifference." It is the beginning of an understanding. From the experience he learned that "neither kindness nor cruelty by themselves . . . creates any effect beyond themselves; and I have learned that the two combined, together, at the same time, are the teaching emotion." For Jerry, life is a zoo, and people are at war, and finally he challenges Peter to fight him for possession of the bench. Jerry gives Peter a knife, prods him into anger, and rushes toward him, impaling himself. In the shocking ending, Jerry dies. Only through his self-sacrifice is Jerry able to pass on the suffering of his experience.

It took Albee two and a half weeks to write *The Zoo Story*. He made pencil revisions on the manuscript, then retyped it. The play was finished on March 10, two days before his birthday. Narrowly, he had beaten the self-imposed deadline. There were stops and starts, occasional second thoughts, but for the most part, the play was a clear outpouring. From first line to last, it flowed. As he said, "There was a click."

The play was written with a pitch-black humor and an odd air of abandon. Despite the undertones of symbolism, it seems like the most direct of confessionals, a report from the front line of urban life and death. For the first time, as he wrote a play, he could see three-dimensional people and he could visualize the play onstage. He could see Jerry enter; he could imagine what his moves would be. Previous plays had been limited by a kind of artificiality. Frequently he had written about the meeting of two men, one young, one old, one aggressive, one passive, but never with the impact of *The Zoo Story*. Albee said, "All these other plays are filled with sturm und drang and self-pity" and have a character who is "the Author Slightly Disguised." Those plays were juvenalia, and the person who wrote them "disappeared completely from the earth because I am no longer that person." Years later, Albee went back and looked at *The Dispossessed* again. "I read it objectively," he said, "and it doesn't sound like me. It sounds like it was influenced by a great number of people, Salinger and others. It doesn't have my voice. The thing that happened with *The Zoo Story* was that I suddenly discovered myself writing in my own voice. It was that simple. Between those two plays, that occurred."

One definite change was that he discovered his sense of humor, or rather found a way to use it onstage. "I wrote somewhere once that I've never been surprised by anything that happened to me, that everything seemed to make a certain amount of logical sense. My memory tells me that when I wrote *The Zoo Story*, I was suddenly aware that I had written something worthwhile." In effect, he had written his first play. It was, he said, "my thirtieth birthday present to myself." With that, his life had changed. Edward Albee had become a playwright.

4

Die Zoo-Geschichte

I am dislocated, quite alone, homesick, and, I assume,
very happy.

IN subsequent years, critics and academics would overanalyze *The Zoo Story*, looking for hidden meaning and comparing Jerry to Jesus Christ. If such thoughts passed through Albee's mind at the time, he kept them to himself, although later he was to suggest such parallels. Drawing on his life in New York and the people he met while delivering telegrams, he made an imaginative leap. Some people naturally came to the conclusion that Jerry was based on Albee, or to those who knew them both, on Flanagan. Physically, the character, as a once handsome man going to seed, seemed closer to Flanagan. From Albee's point of view, both characters were based on himself. They were, he said, "the two Edwards, the one who lived back in Larchmont, and the one who lives in New York City," and by indirection the play was an attack on the life he led, and could have continued to lead, at home. Then and later he insisted that everything he wrote was an amalgamation of what he observed and experienced and what he invented.

The first person to read the play was Flanagan. He was astonished. "There was no preparation for that sudden emergence of a full-blown talent. He arrived with nothing coming before. I was overpowered by it. It's as if he didn't exist creatively before he was thirty." Asked what triggered the creativity, Flanagan said, "A sense of his own mindlessness, having reached a crisis in his sense of disinvolvement. He was vitiating his emotional resources. His lack of a sense of order; he knew he had to order his life. If he didn't find something soon, it wouldn't happen at all. As he approached thirty, for a number of reasons related to his family, a life so harmlessly and abstractly wasted, he was running into an area of personal turmoil."

Part of that turmoil was with Flanagan himself. Their relationship, always a rocky one, was on the verge of terminating (although after they broke up they renewed their friendship). On a more positive side, Albee's approaching birthday represented a certain financial freedom. He would receive the principal, $100,000, from his grandmother's trust. He would no longer have to go to his father's office for his weekly check, his stipend, but would finally be independent of family. That would be, he said, "a freeing of the bonds from the adoption. Thirty years with these people. No longer beholden, no longer obligated. They can't control me, they can't do anything to me anymore. Obviously there was a profound relationship between my being able to cut my last links with that family and the freedom to write." All these factors came together on that crucial day that he began to write *The Zoo Story*, a play that surprised even him. The hesitancy and the artificiality of his earlier work had disappeared. In its place was an assurance, a self-assurance. For the first time, Albee wrote about what he knew and experienced and not about what he thought. *The Zoo Story* was ripped from his life in New York and, in particular, from his life at Western Union, where he acted as a kind of angel of death.

Laurence Tierney's rooming house was itself a rich repository of West Side characters. Jerry was describing that building when he said,

I live in a four-story brownstone rooming-house on the upper West Side between Columbus Avenue and Central Park West. I live on the top floor; rear; west. It's a laughably small room, and one of my walls is made of beaverboard; this beaverboard separates my room from another laughably small room, so I assume that the two rooms were once one room, a small room, but not necessarily laughable. The room beyond my beaverboard wall is occupied by a colored queen who always keeps his door open; well, not always but *always* when he's plucking his eyebrows, which he does with Buddhist concentration. This colored queen has rotten teeth, which is rare, and he has a Japanese kimono, which is also pretty rare; and he wears this kimono to and from the john in the hall, which is pretty frequent. I mean, he goes to the john a lot.

At the end of this passage, Jerry says, "And in the other front room, there's somebody living there, but I don't know who it is. I've never seen who it is. Never. Never ever."

As Albee was aware, "There was such a tremendous shift of the author's point of view with *The Zoo Story*. I suddenly was able to breathe. I guess I must have felt some kind of suffocation before. I knew the freedom to breathe and to be an individual was tied in with being able to write, to write something I realized was good and was a kind of objectifying of my writing ability. I knew when I wrote *The Zoo Story* that this was invention, this was creativity. This wasn't a 'what if,' taking ideas from other people." It was an authentically personal response. Playwriting was no longer a private preoccupation. He wanted people to read his play and he wanted to see it produced, but as a novice he had no idea how to go about it.

With Flanagan's help, Albee began sending the play around. In retrospect, it is astonishing how shortsighted the initial criticism was. Charles Strouse, who by this time had a friendly, bantering relationship with Albee, read *The Zoo Story* and thought it was "fantastic." He volunteered to show it to a friend at the William Morris Agency. The agent read it and liked it but said it was too short to be produced. Remembering Thornton Wilder's encouragement, and his suggestion that he move from poetry to playwriting, Albee sent him a copy of the play.

On August 17, Wilder responded. He began by saying that he was "much impressed" by the play, that it had "many far-plunging insights." He offered his congratulations, and then he began to tear the play apart.

> I don't think it would play half as well as it reads—the men—the concrete men there—would get in the way. Not a matter of acting. Talent: a matter of *how*.
>
> The trouble is that your *content* is real, inner, and your own, and your form is tired old grandpa's . . .
>
> The number of plays I've had to read (obliging Wilder, judging contests) about chance encounters—Central Park benches. Whimsy, or stark or dear Romance. 'Do you mind if I talk to you?'
>
> It may well be that someday a Kafka or a Beckett will come along and show that it can be done, but oh! what difficulties you made for yourself before you'd really started.
>
> Why does your sense of form, your vision of the *how* lag so far behind your vision of the *what*: It's as tho you were frozen very young into the American 'little theatre' movement. Because this gulf between the stage-mode and the inner gift means that finally you have no style. You don't even have a slightly ironic play on the kind of theatre you are employing—as I think I remember you having had before. [Just as Kafka's style is a constant play on very matter of fact bureaucratic documents.]

Anyway, I wish you well. I think you have much to say. And I have the recommendation which I urgently bring before you: write much, write many
things. Only that way will your imagine [sic] teach you to make your mode as
original as expressive as your thought.

Give my regard to Mr. Flanagan and he can illustrate my point, I'm sure, for
the principles of musical composition.

Coming after Wilder's initial interest in Albee's work during their meeting
at MacDowell, his comments seem exceedingly grudging. "Much impressed," "far-plunging insight," and then a boredom with both the style and
the content. How many plays had he actually read or seen about a chance encounter in Central Park? Many such plays came after *The Zoo Story*. Then he
had the effrontery to suggest that Albee's earlier play in rhymed couplets bordering on doggerel was better. The most wounding references in Wilder's letter were probably those to the "little theatre" movement and the fact that he
thought *The Zoo Story* had "no style" and no irony. He offered no suggestion
of what Albee might do with the play, except perhaps to rewrite it according to
Wilder's instruction. Wilder apparently could not cope with the play's directness, or with the visceral quality of the language. At the time his reaction must
have hurt. Albee certainly hoped he might have greeted the play with enthusiasm. But despite Wilder's dismissal, Albee continued to admire the older
playwright's work.

Balance was supplied by Aaron Copland, a totally objective voice and
someone, at least in Albee's case, with no ax to grind. After reading *The Zoo
Story*, Copland wrote to Albee:

> I was very impressed with your play. It seemed to be written with real exper-
> tise—carefully planned and beautifully carried out, like a musical piece. At the
> same time, it's a little frightening—as you well know (I guess I identify with 'Pe-
> ter'!). So it doesn't make for pleasant reading; in a way, seeing it on a stage
> would make it easier to take, I think. I'm not sure I understand all the subtle un-
> derpinnings, but that doesn't matter, since the wallop is there. What seems
> most familiar is the over-all mal-de-siecle theme, the atmosphere of controlled
> hysteria. But it's powerful stuff as you treat it, nonetheless.

Albee had hoped that if Copland liked the play, he might pass it along to
his friend (and distant relative) Harold Clurman, but Copland reported that
Clurman was busy casting two plays and said that he turned over all new
scripts to Robert Whitehead's play reader. The composer thought *The Zoo*

Story might be Off-Broadway material and suggested that Albee find a good agent. He concluded, "Anyhow, I was impressed. Knowing you only as Bill's alter ego, a dark young man who doesn't say much, I was unprepared for so articulate and literate a piece! Whatever happens, I think you ought to go on. And maybe I ought to know you better!"

As a composer, Copland was less able than Wilder to help set a production in motion. But he did send the play to William Inge, who was then at the peak of his celebrity, with three Broadway hits in a row, *Picnic, Bus Stop,* and, in 1957, *The Dark at the Top of the Stairs.* Along with Tennessee Williams and Arthur Miller, Inge was one of the top Broadway playwrights of the moment. A word from him to a producer, director, or agent would have made a great difference.

On August 13, 1958, Inge returned the script to Albee with the following comment:

> *The Zoo Story,* I think, is a very good play. I read it with a lot of interest and was quite moved by the ending. I wish I could give you some suggestion of what to do with it (commercially), but that's hard, things in the theatre being as they are. However, you might try writing a few more and then show them to an off-Broadway producer (you can't get anyone on Broadway interested in one-acts); or you might try a full-length. Anyway, I'm glad to have read it.

That letter sounds like a thank-you note for an unwanted gift. Perhaps Inge did not understand the play; perhaps he was envious of it. It is possible that he really did not like it. In any case, *The Zoo Story* simply did not matter to him. August was not a good month for Albee.

Despite Inge's tepid response, Albee went to see him in his apartment on Sutton Place. Having liked *Come Back, Little Sheba* and, to a lesser extent, *The Dark at the Top of the Stairs,* Albee was at his most respectful. Inge was polite, but he had nothing more to say about *The Zoo Story.* Albee said, "I remember very little about him except that he seemed soft, quiet-spoken and reserved. We were both fairly shy people. I don't think it was a very interesting or important meeting"—except of course in one crucial aspect. Always the acute observer, Albee took in the entire elegant apartment and the ambiance of a playwright at the height of his success. The younger playwright had the last word. Very soon after his visit, he wrote *Fam and Yam,* a brief dialogue with a very Beckettian title. It was a malicious spoof of a meeting between a famous American playwright (like Inge) and a young American playwright (like Albee).

Fam is described as "a no-longer thin gentleman, a year or so either side of 50," who looks like "a slightly rumpled account executive" or "a faintly foppish Professor of History." Yam is "an intense, bony young man, whose crew cut is in need of a trim." The setting is a duplicate of Inge's apartment, with "a view of the bridge, white walls; a plum-colored sofa, two Modiglianis, one Braque, a Motherwell and a Kline." Yam has come to interview Fam, who tipples sherry, laughs nervously, and comes across as an insecure intellectual lightweight. In a self-parodying portrait, Yam, who is interviewing him for an article he is writing about the theater, has a *Zoo Story*–like play Off-Broadway called "Dilemma, Dereliction and Death." To Fam's amusement, Yam lists the villains of theater, who include "ignorant, greedy, hit-happy" theater owners, critics who set themselves up as social arbiters and "the pin-heads" on theater parties. The word "pin-heads" makes Fam giggle. "Let 'em all have it," he says. "Mow 'em down!" By the end of the sketch, the paintings on Fam's wall are reacting against him. A Modigliani frowns and the Motherwell crashes to the floor.

In September, out of pride and as an act of amelioration after an argument, Albee sent a copy of *The Zoo Story* to Richard Howard, together with a letter: "The bulky object attached is a play you have heard the piano noises about; I hope you will read it and I hope that Sandy will read it, and I hope that you will, the two of you, let me have your candy opinions of it—between the eyes even." Then came an apology for his misconduct:

> My shoddy behavior in the face of your many kindnesses and your generosity horrifies me still; I wish I could excuse it by saying I was possessed by demons, but I can't. I was thoughtless, selfish and rude. Nor can I help but shudder remembering how I used to expose you, poor Dick, who wanted nothing more than a good friendship with the two of us, to sordid displays of malice and aggression. You were right to withdraw, but now, while it is still the same country and the wench is not dead, she is older, a good deal wiser, wears a sunflower hat of regrets, and wonders if we might not be able to. . . . what?. . . . to begin by touching fingertips, perhaps.

Howard, who had read Albee's poetry and dismissed it for its derivativeness, was amazed at the play's language and power of evocation. He and Sandy Friedman had but one suggestion. They did not like the title and suggested that he change it to "The Black Dog." Friedman gave the play to José Quintero, who with his productions of *The Iceman Cometh* and *Long Day's Journey into Night* was the most acclaimed director in New York. He recognized Albee's talent and wanted to do *The Zoo Story* on a double bill with O'Neill's long one-act *Hughie;* but the project was not approved by Carlotta Monterey O'Neill, O'Neill's widow and executor, and the production did not happen.

One other theater person who was interested in *The Zoo Story* was Herbert Machiz, who had directed *Garden District*, the two-part Tennessee Williams production that included *Suddenly Last Summer*. Ned Rorem, who had written the music for *Suddenly Last Summer*, interceded for Albee and gave Machiz a copy of *The Zoo Story*. Machiz liked it, but in emulation of his successful Williams evening, thought that it needed a one-act to go with it. Albee had already started writing another short play *The Death of Bessie Smith* and hoped that might be acceptable as a companion piece.

The Death of Bessie Smith began with the cover of a record album, although Albee can trace his interest in Bessie Smith and jazz back many years before. "I had loved gospel music and early jazz for a long time. I used to hear those gospel shows Off-Broadway and Off-Off-Broadway in the fifties, Clara Ward and all those wonderful people. And of course I liked Billie Holiday a lot. I followed her career and saw her the last time she appeared at Loew's Sheridan. She wasn't allowed to be in night clubs anymore because she was a convicted drug addict. Her voice was shattered, but she was so very moving and touching. I'd also been listening to Bessie Smith's records. An LP had come out and I happened to read on the album cover the story of how she died, the automobile accident outside of Memphis, her arm outside the window of the car, her arm almost cut off, how she was taken to a white hospital and was refused admission and died on the way to a second hospital. That generated the play. How long after I became aware of that information did I write it? It can't have been very long. I made the necessary additional step, the gift of the dead Bessie Smith to the second hospital. That was totally my invention. But those facts prompted the play."

The Zoo Story remained the playwright's first priority. Flanagan thereupon wrote to David Diamond in Florence. Diamond was a close personal friend of Flanagan's as well as one of his teachers. In the letter, Flanagan said:

Edward, who one day about six months ago just upped and decided that he would stop drinking, and *has*, has written a beautiful one-act play which looks set for an off-Broadway production soon. Everyone who has read it—from Aaron, to William Inge, to Thornton Wilder—has been anywhere from mildly enthusiastic to wildly impressed by it. It has been a big boost for him and has finally set him to working with a fury. I've taken the liberty of having him send you a copy of it, for one, because I'm proud of him, and for another, because I think he'd like to read your comments about it.

It was with trepidation that Albee sent a copy of the play to Diamond. This was not likely to be a warm response. At least Wilder seemed to like him and to be interested in his work, whereas Albee was aware that he and Diamond had had the testiest of relationships. Nevertheless, he took the chance. In a letter sent October 2, 1958, Albee said, "Attached is my play, *The Zoo Story*. When Bill asked me if I'd like you to read it, I was surprised that I hadn't thought of it myself. Your temperament and imagination make you the sort of man whose opinions I'd like, and whose criticism I'd value." With abashment, he added, "The play is the first half-way satisfying thing I've done (late enough!) and the first I've wanted lots of people to see. So, if you have the time, I'd appreciate your comments."

Diamond's answer came three weeks later. To Albee's astonishment, the composer was unhesitating in his enthusiasm. In common with that headmaster way back at Lawrenceville, Diamond jettisoned all doubts and restraints—and ignored the past. For Albee, it was the equivalent of Ralph Waldo Emerson's letter to Walt Whitman, greeting him at the start of a brilliant career, and it came from a most unlikely and unexpected source. Diamond embraced the play and offered some extraordinarily astute comments about it:

I have finally come to a point when I can write to you about your play, *THE ZOO STORY* (I don't think that should be the definitive title). First let me tell you that I read it through at one reading. I was impressed just as an experience of interpersonal relationship. The same day, I read it through before going to bed, analyzing it some—as a director would do. And I was even more impressed. Then yesterday I performed it with a friend (I played Jerry) before two other friends who understand English very well and are admirers of Inge and Williams. I am certain you have a very playable and valuable creative contribution. I want to congratulate you fully and respectfully for having written a very moving, disturbing and thoroughly ruthless expose of human conflicts and the pathetic inability of interpersonal communication. What Carson McCullers did in her way, Ten in his and Bill Inge in his you do in your way: in a more forthright way. The long soliloquies are gems for young actors to play. And this is what I want to ask you: have you plans for it? Has anyone valuable in the theater world (among directors) seen it? I for one think Lee Strasberg or Kazan would be pleased to see it and might even use it with their actors in lab sessions. I think Stella Adler and Harold Clurman should see it. Therefore, let me know whether you care to have me intervene and write Lee, Harold and Stella. If you do, I will do so and tell you when to send the scripts to them. I would also like you to send it to a Swiss actor named Pinkas Braun who would be interested in it for television in Germany.

I await further word from you and again congratulate you on a stunning (and I mean it in the sense of the verb) accomplishment.

PS/ May I keep the copy you sent me?

Even more than admiring the play, Diamond was prepared to do something about getting it on, setting off a chain reaction that was to start Albee's career. Albee answered, thanking him for the letter and for his comments on the play. He began with an apology:

I don't mean thanks specifically for the good things you had to say about the play, although I appreciated hearing them, because I don't think you thank a man for his honest opinions; but thanks for taking the trouble to read the work of a guy who has made trouble for you and been unpleasant during an earlier and badly screwed-up part of his life. That was really good of you, David.

You ask what plans I have for the play. Well, here is how things are now: Herbert Machiz, who directed *Garden District* in New York, London and L.A. is taken with my piece and wants to do it—if he likes the second play I've just finished to go along with it. He promises an off-Broadway production if nothing else, but has his sights on doing it as part of the series of plays at the Bijou Theatre this season. Naturally, I'm hopeful about this but, at the same time, I'm wary (should I be?) of these loud-fast-talking, extroverted types who can let you down as quick as they set you soaring. Also, New World Writing had asked for the play to see if they want to publish it. Inge and Wilder are among the people who have read it and reacted favorably [a clear misrepresentation of their reactions], and Machiz tells me that Williams likes it, too. So, that's how things are now: A lot and at the same time, nothing.

Aaron introduced me to Clurman at Tanglewood this summer . . . but it was a fleet meeting, and I doubt I made any impression. All considered, then, I'd appreciate it more than you can know if you would, as you have suggested you might, let a few people know about me, that I might send them some of my work. I'm a serious boy now, wet behind the ears yet, but determined to do the most I can with whatever ability I have. And this is funny: The people who have helped me most so far have been composers! If they *all* helped each *other* as much. . . . !

And certainly I want you to keep your copy of *The Zoo Story*. What should I do about Pinkas Braun? Send you a copy to send him?

At this point, Pinkas Braun seemed like an afterthought.

When Albee gave Machiz *The Death of Bessie Smith*, his surprising reaction was, "Who wants to see a play about a dead nigger?" Albee's answer: "That was the end of my association with Herbert Machiz."

In December, Diamond replied to Albee's last letter, with apologies for the delay. First, in response to the comments about composers, he said, "Well, I must be an exception for I have found that while there is a snake always around in the grass, most composers have been extraordinarily good to me, in my beginnings and now in the middle; and I have been likewise to them." He was irritated only at the fact that some of the people he helped did not come to performances of his pieces. "I prefer to not interpret it as anything else but a terrible weakness known as *Envy*. The mystery is how you can be envious of someone who helped you." Then he gave him Braun's address and suggested he send the play after January 10. "As for Lee S and someone else I have in mind, let me hear from Lee first. Better this way."

Albee sent the play to Braun in Hemishofen, Switzerland. While waiting to hear from Braun, he wrote to Diamond saying that he was reworking *The Death of Bessie Smith*, which deals "with the people and the circumstances surrounding her death. You know the story, don't you? I'll send you a copy of the play, if you'd like to have it." Diamond answered, "You ask me whether I know 'the story' about her. Mon cher. I *knew* B.S., when I was quite young in Cleveland."

Braun responded quickly with an endorsement of *The Zoo Story* that equaled that of Diamond. "I was convinced," Braun said, "that—by David Diamond's kind offices—I had come across a theatrical masterpiece." He wrote to Albee, saying that he did not think it was appropriate for television but thought he could find a German theater to produce it. He suggested that, because of its brevity, it should be done together with another short play, not necessarily by Albee. Braun, who was a translator and director as well as an actor, immediately translated *The Zoo Story* into German and, playing both roles, made a tape recording of it. Fearful that the play might languish on someone's desk, he telephoned Stefani Hunzinger, head of the drama department at S. Fischer Verlag in Frankfurt, the company that published O'Neill, Williams, and Wilder, as well as Thomas Mann. Braun at the time was married to Gisela Fischer, one of the daughters of the owner. Braun persuaded Mrs. Hunzinger to listen to the recording and, said Braun, "She was gripped by Albee's enunciative power, by his work's magnetism, and after having heard it she wanted to have the rights on the spot." Mrs. Hunzinger was so fascinated by the play that she blocked all her telephone calls at her office for ninety minutes while she listened to Braun's enactment of *The Zoo Story.*

Braun wrote to the author about the play:

> I have read it several times with increasing interest and I think it is a fine piece of craftsmanship. I have been deeply touched by the two characters' human qualities. The solitude of men in over-populated cities, the forlorn hope of lives, the incapability of finding contact—apart from the purely local New Yorkese references in your play—is a subject which concerns audiences all over the world.

Mrs. Hunzinger took the next step, calling Boleslaw Barlog, the director of the Schiller Theater in Berlin. He asked to see a script and, upon reading it, agreed to present its world premiere. Because of the brevity of *The Zoo Story,* he agreed that it should be presented on a double bill with another play. Mrs. Hunzinger suggested that it be paired with Samuel Beckett's *Krapp's Last Tape* (which had its world premiere in London in 1958). This was to be the first linking of Albee to Beckett, who had already created an international reputation with *Waiting for Godot* (in Paris in 1953 and on Broadway in 1956) and *Endgame* Off-Broadway in 1958. Although the two playwrights were born twenty-two years apart and came from very different backgrounds, they shared an ironic attitude to life and a stylistic approach to theater that would later be described as absurdist. Both *The Zoo Story* and *Krapp's Last Tape* would be performed in German by German actors during the 1959 Berlin Festival.

There was also a chance that Gian Carlo Menotti would do *The Zoo Story* at the Spoleto Festival in Italy. Albee had an audience with the maestro:

> Gian Carlo Menotti received me last week in bed—his bed, he in bed me not—to say that he likes the play, and might do it, or my new play—if he likes it when he sees it—at Spoleto this summer. But I am wary of this; I have heard too much about the Barber-Menotti axis, know what they do to fairly young people, pretending to be interested in their work—they gobble them up and then spit them out—that's what they do. Nasty people. But he *has* asked me to compose a short (7 minutes at most) play for a project . . . for Spoleto.

If accepted, Albee's play would join works by Ionesco, Cocteau, and others. Then, after commenting that there had been a mention of him in *Variety,* he said, "But swamped as I am by all this nonsense, I try to keep my head down and my eyes on the sparrow, remembering that I am the rankest of be-

ginners, the most undisciplined of men-types." Albee's new play was to become *The American Dream*, and to fulfill the seven-minute slot at Spoleto, he
took several characters from that work and wrote *The Sandbox*. Menotti did
not do any Albee plays, not *The Zoo Story*, *The American Dream*, or even *The
Sandbox*.

While waiting for the major event, Albee had a minor debut. A song, "The
Lady of Tearful Regret," with text by Albee and music by Flanagan, was presented as part of an evening of songs by Flanagan and Rorem on February 24,
1959, at Carnegie Recital Hall. This was the first time a piece by Albee was
performed on a professional stage. In a letter to Diamond, Flanagan said that
the poem "is a mess, both in itself and for musical purposes, but I thought I
saw possibilities for it with regard to doing the coloratura study that has been
on my mind for years . . . But it was begun before there were any 'Zoo Stories'
around and I was terrified of offending and discouraging Edward when I realized that it wouldn't work; by the time I had finished scoring it he decided he
didn't like it either, and I was stuck with it." Then he added, "Edward—and I,
for that matter—couldn't be more grateful for the marvelous things you did
about his play. It's been a big boost for a boy who has had a hell of a time
pulling himself into some sort of shape for living a useful, directed life."

While the Berlin production was taking shape, the script was still making
the rounds in New York. In March, Albee sent a copy to his friend Howard
Moss, the poet and poetry editor of *The New Yorker*, with a note saying it was
"dog-eared, high-middle Polish translation of my zoo play, which you must already regret having asked to see." From his home in Florence, the ever helpful Diamond sent *The Zoo Story* and *The Death of Bessie Smith* to Priscilla
Morgan at the William Morris Agency, and she gave them to a new young
man in the office, Edward Parone. She asked him if he would handle the
contract for Fischer Verlag's publication of the plays. Neither Morgan nor
Parone had ever heard of the playwright. Parone, who had served his apprenticeship with the Phoenix Theater and with the theatrical agent Audrey Wood
(as a play reader), had been engaged to look after foreign rights and to perform other lesser tasks at William Morris. On his own, he had taken as his
mandate a search for new American plays. He read *Bessie Smith* at lunch that
day and felt "the characters seemed emblematic, not quite alive. It wasn't bad
work but it seemed more a *foray* into writing a play, an exercise, a test run."
Then he read *The Zoo Story*, and it "leaped off the page into unmistakable
life. The sparseness of the stage directions sent the first message: everything
you need to know is in the text that follows. A confident first chord of music
had been struck. There was interesting listening ahead. It read, and subse-

quently played, like a piece of music, although it was language, words, that drove it . . . It played out its scary, funny story with an assurance and a voice all its own. The real thing, it seemed to me, had arrived." Parone became a crucial factor in the history of the play and the playwright.

He telephoned Albee and they met the next day. Parone recalled, "He had the good manners of Auden, a sly we'll-see-won't-we smile and a catlike way of observing." It turned out they both had been at Trinity College at the same time (in contrast to Albee, Parone graduated, in 1950; while he was at Trinity, he had seen Albee act in Maxwell Anderson's *Masque of Kings*). Albee signed on as a client with the William Morris Agency (where he has remained ever since, though he has gone through a series of individual agents). It was clear to Parone that Albee "already knew what he was doing and had more than an idea or two about his future . . . He seemed more than able to row his way among the sharks who would no doubt come to patrol his boat. The life of a successful playwright would suit him well." The playwright would soon leave for Berlin, and, said Parone, "I set about finding a New York producer for his work."

Before leaving for Germany, Albee had some pressing personal matters to sort out. Sandy Friedman had broken the trust of the four-way friendship he and Howard had with Albee and Flanagan. Later Albee recounted the episode in a letter to Howard in which he said that their friendship, their "quadruple communion" had been shattered and he was "hurt, bewildered, deeply angry and sad."

> The facts are simple. Sandy decided to have an affair with Bill. Now, I need not point out that this decision was foolish—doomed to frustration from the start. But what gets me is that Sandy could have been so blind, willfully or no, to the effect that this ill-chosen infatuation would have on the four of us. It embarrassed Bill; it must have put some strain on you; it hurt me that he could treat his friendship with me in so cavalier a fashion; and his own reaction to rejection would seem to be that we are all to be punished for his indiscretion . . . This is absurd, petty, childish!

In one of his poems, Howard wrote with self-mockery about Albee, Flanagan, and himself. The poem "Duet for Three Voices" was published in 1962 in *Quantities*, Howard's first collection of verse. In it, he wrote of a conversation among three symbolic characters: Failure (Flanagan), Phony (Howard), and Feral (Albee), with Feral clearly a reference to an artist in a natural state. The poem ends:

> The night that is falling
> > Confirms our disguises
> Determines our calling
> > And darkens our grief.
>
> For Failure what future
> > For Phony what prizes
> For Feral what creature
> > Can sanction our life?

"Phony" was eventually to win a Pulitzer Prize and a MacArthur "genius" prize for his work as a poet and translator of French literature, and "Feral" was to win three Pulitzer Prizes for his plays. Flanagan would continue to play the role of "Failure."

On July 15, 1959, a controversial new play opened Off-Broadway. It was emblematic of a turbulence that was to help change the face—if not the heart—of the American theater. The play was Jack Gelber's *The Connection*, a graphic, seamy slice of life about drug addicts waiting for a fix. *The Connection*, which opened at the Living Theater in its loft on 14th Street, was to polarize critics as well as theatergoers. A *New York Times* reviewer dismissed it as "nothing more than a farrago of dirt, small-time philosophy, empty talk and extended runs of 'cool' music." This was about as wrongheaded an assessment as one could imagine. Fortunately, other critics weighed in with more serious and perceptive comments. Harold Clurman (in *The Nation*) thought that the play was arresting in its authenticity. "The play reeks of human beings," he wrote, and warned, "if we turn completely away from people of any kind we can know little of anything worth knowing." Within six months, he would be able to say something similar about *The Zoo Story*.

Before Albee sailed for Germany and the opening of his play, he and Flanagan separated after seven years together. The breakup had a classic symmetry. As the student's fortunes rose, the mentor's confidence waned. Looking back, Albee said, "The relationship collapsed when I started having a career. He just sort of deflated, as I started going up. He became a dependent. It wasn't that I needed to break away. It was that he ceased being what he had been. Or maybe the relationship had just come to an end of its usefulness." In a sense, it was a safer role for Flanagan as mentor, and perhaps Albee simply had a deeper commitment to his own creativity: "I remember he told me quite near toward the end of our knowing each other well that he couldn't conceive of writing a piece of music unless he wrote it for somebody, unless there was an emotional need to write that piece for somebody. And I said, 'That is an immense sign of weakness.' I write because I have to—for me."

One other reason that the relationship collapsed was the fact that Albee met Terrence McNally. That meeting took place in February 1959 at a party given by the actor Michael Wager. Wager and McNally were both great opera fans. Many years later, the character of Mendy (Wager's nickname) in Mc-Nally's play *The Lisbon Traviata* was inspired by Wager, though, to the actor's irritation, he never was asked to play the role. Wager and McNally had quarreled and Wager had disinvited him from his party. McNally came anyway, and, said Wager, "thereby hangs a tale." Albee was one of the guests. He had written *The Zoo Story* but it had not yet been produced. Albee remembers: "I noticed this nineteen-year-old, a ravishing-looking blond kid lurking around the place. I found out he was a college student named Terrence McNally who wanted to be a playwright. Well, Terrence and I started talking and the next thing I knew, so to speak, we were living together." Fresh in from his home in Corpus Christi, Texas, McNally was at the beginning of his career. He may have been as much in awe of Albee's talent as Albee was of McNally's looks. Much later, it would be said that when Martha in *Who's Afraid of Virginia Woolf?* described her imaginary son she was really describing McNally ("... and he loved the sun! ... He was tan before and after everyone ... and in the sun his hair ... became ... fleece ... beautiful, beautiful boy"). At the time, Albee was living at 31 Eighth Avenue, just south of 14th Street. Then he moved with McNally to 345 West 12th Street. When Flanagan needed a place to live, Albee let him stay in the basement while he and McNally were living upstairs. It was something Albee later regretted. It put Flanagan in a lesser, demeaning position. Robert Heide remembers visiting Albee in that apartment. While they were having coffee in the living room, Flanagan came up the stairway from the cellar: "He popped his head up and saw me sitting in the living room, and Edward said, 'You get back down there,' and the head went back down like a turtle returning to its shell."

Flanagan knew that this living arrangement was impossible and finally decided to move out. In a letter to Albee, he wrote:

> I'm sorry—sorrier than you will ever know—for the trouble I caused you last winter ... I'm likewise sorry that our experiment in living together was so dreadful a fiasco. I believe—inevitably—that it would have ended badly no

matter my behavior. If you love Terrence—and you seem to have decided quite positively that you do—it can't have been brought about by anything I did . . . I will always, I guess, love you, Edward. Or, if not that, I will never love any one as I have you . . . I'm nostalgic about the past, rueful about the image of us in the future that I've clung to so stubbornly; but the grief, the mourning—thank God for both of us—is over . . .

From somewhere in last winter's fog I remember your saying to me that you thought I was making your career a vicarious substitute for the inhibited rewards of my own. I want you to know now that, to the best of my knowledge, this is not and never was true. But if what *is* true is to be known, then know this: I'm proud of you, proud to have been at one time so intimately connected with you, one of your number-one-on-line fans. You see, Edward, I *couldn't* feel anything like envy, resentment, or vicarious substitution; I couldn't feel anything unsavory about it . . .

Gathering his books, records, and his piano, Flanagan left. He and Albee continued to meet and to correspond, and at least in his letters Flanagan retained a distant cordiality about McNally, asking about him and his plays. About his involvement with McNally, Albee said, "I think it was a doomed relationship to begin with. I'm sure Terrence thinks it was." The relationship lasted a little more than five years. Whenever they were apart, McNally flooded Albee with passionate love letters, a hothouse of flowering verbiage dense with sexual imagery. In one letter he compared himself to a giant firecracker; in another, he wrote about love being an uncontainable demon. These extravagantly romantic, almost operatic confessions are in lush contrast to Flanagan's letters, with their unflagging wit and cynicism even as he was enduring his own heartache and professional defeat.

Occasionally McNally speaks in his letters about his work and Albee's, and there are insights into Albee and into their relationship. In one, he wrote:

If one's life is the source of his art, then I'm happy to be taking inventory. As I write to you now, I remember you telling me that I would never be as important to you as your career. Those words hurt me then but for some reason I hear them without wincing today. And I cannot tell you why unless it is because I am thinking that what is true for me is also true for you: there is no separation between an artist's career and his life.

Then he added, "If I truly believed that I was always to be second place to a progression of a talented writer's theatrical triumphs I would know a despair besides which the feelings caused by our separation this summer would seem imperceptible by comparison." Eventually McNally left Albee and moved in with the actor Robert Drivas. Somehow through all the changing partners, Albee and Flanagan remained friends. For years after Albee and McNally broke up, they did not speak. Eventually they, too, became friends.

At the time of his split with Albee, Flanagan was distraught. "It has been a difficult, terrible, nerve-wrecking struggle," he wrote to Diamond after Albee had left for Germany. "It's curious . . . that our trouble started with the 'beginning' of his 'career'; and, just as it was I who wrote you about his play—a gesture that resulted in his REASON for being in Europe now—it was I who put at his disposal contacts that had taken me 13!! painful [years] to build for myself. And I'm glad that I did. Still, I wonder if we would have hit the trouble that we did if I *hadn't*." But Flanagan and Albee were still speaking—and writing. After the opening in Berlin, Flanagan sent a congratulatory cable to which Albee responded with a long, journal-like letter in September.

Albee had been sick before he left New York, and he began by describing the voyage to Bremerhaven in detail, and his feeling of alienation from his fellow passengers:

> The last few days on the boat were better than the first five. I got my health back, came to terms with the ocean, and fell in with a bunch of kids, more or less out of desperation: A medical student from Afghanistan on his way to study in Germany after two years in the U.S., a cartographer from Scotland (he makes maps, or, parts of maps), an Irish medical student who got on at Cobh, Ireland, for a breath of fresh air, took the rest of the trip, to Bremerhaven, was going to stay on the boat and go right back to Cobh, which strikes me as a pretty funny thing to do; a French boy who kept asking me how about the Beatniks, thinking that there is in N.Y. a tidy little group of student-intellectuals (called Beatniks which corresponds to his set in Paris; There isn't, is there). I'm afraid I gave him the impression that we don't sit around and think much in N.Y. (We don't, do we? At least, my dealings with people eight to twenty in my fair city the last year or so doesn't give me the impression that we do), and . . . a boy from Berlin, who is very strange, and about whom I shall write, down a bit. Aside from these people, who were all really very nice, friendly . . . interesting in themselves, but all, I'm afraid, quite a good deal too young (which made me kind of sad. Am I sort of out of place everywhere?) there were girls, girls, girls. Hundreds of them, Delphine-types, but American, going in awful groups to live a year and study in Paris and/or London. Since I was the only guess-what on the whole boat (you don't believe this?) these girls were all around me and the kids mentioned

above with the result that I was thrown in to a post-adolescent heterosexual society, which is a funny business, especially on an international level. I mean,
they didn't drink much, just sort of sat around, talked and played cards, walked
the decks, formed tiny little romances, none of which got beyond the hand-
holding stage, and, when the hour got late, grouped, and sang songs. It was this,
or the sixty-year-olds. Nothing in between.

In a letter to Richard Howard, he viewed the passengers from a somewhat
different perspective: "The ship is full of priests, for God's sake! (Naturally)
They walk the decks, muttering to themselves, whilst I bumbled into a chair,
peek out my blanket, avoiding the rapacious eyes of a platoon of unattached
Amurican girlies. What is a good, healthy, Villagey, N.Y. homosexualist to do?
Even if you have the answer for me, it will arrive too late."

The boat arrived in Bremerhaven at midnight on Saturday. Since he had
been scheduled to be in Berlin by 6 A.M. on Sunday, he decided to go immediately by train. He was accompanied by the young man from Berlin, acting as his
interpreter. They arrived by taxi in Bremen at 2 A.M. and found they had three
hours to kill before the train left. So they went sightseeing. "It was lovely. Most
of the city was bombed out in the war, all except for the old city, which, especially at two A.M. in Germany for the first time in my life, was one of the most
stunning things I have ever seen. The moon was up, the street lights were on."

After changing trains in Hamburg, they rode through East Germany.

The East German authorities checked my passport at the border, and were
polite. Naturally I didn't sleep a bit this whole trip, but who would? At noon the
train stopped for half an hour, just outside the outskirts of Berlin. I decided to
doze, got half asleep when Berndt, this Berliner boy, shook me and pointed out
the train window. I opened my sleepy eyes, looked out, and do you know what I
saw, looking in the window at me? Can't you guess, buddy-boy? Right: Two
Russian soldiers. These Russian soldiers, hung with enormous sub-machine
guns, got up in green uniforms, were small, burly, handsome and young. They
looked at me; I looked at them. What to do. So, I smiled and nodded my spinning head. They smiled, nodded back, and walked on. Strange and jarring bit.

He got out of the train, stood on East German ground, then got back on
and rode into Berlin. He arrived early in the morning of September 27.

There, goodbye for the day to the Berliner boy, and hello to Stefani Hunzinger (the lady who bought the play), and Pinkas Braun, David's friend, who

translated it . . . Pinkas is a wonderful man, about forty, I guess, apparently one of the best actors, and, the press says, a magnificent translator. We all ate, then went to theatre, not mine, thank God, considering how tired I was, but to an English play by a guy named Willis Hall, whom I got to know, and who promises to help me in all ways if and when I get to London this trip. His play was, of course, in German, and I sat there, all bleary-eyed, trying to make some sense out of what was going on. It being a real conventional-type play, I followed it pretty good. I confess, though, it was funny to see a bunch of German actors pretending to be British soldiers in Malaya, in W.W.2. After that, still no bed, but on, on, on.

As arranged by his hosts, he stayed in Pension Sheira, which catered to theater people, including a scenic designer and a young man he characterized as "the German Elvis Presley." "Marlene doesn't stay here, or anything, but the lady who runs the place tells me (in her Berliner-French, which is even funnier than my Roumanian-French) that I should be impressed." His room was actually a suite: a bedroom with a twenty foot high ceiling and a sitting room that looked out on the Kurfurstendamm, all for two dollars a night. He ("I and a wasp") had breakfast on his balcony. After visiting East Berlin, he described it as "the most depressing sight I have ever seen." In contrast, in West Berlin, "The sidewalk cafes are packed, the streets full of shiny new cars, the people clean and well-dressed." The rubble was well covered as the Berliners "integrated the old and the new." They are "all cheerful, working like crazy and, unless you try hard and remember that these folk were the ones who did all that ghastly business, just like people. Anyway, West Berlin is alive, noisy, exciting, handsome," while East Berlin is "rubble, ruins, smashed palaces, houses, railroad terminals, cathedrals, Nazi edifices (boy), embassy row, with the gutted remains of the mansions, shattered museums, theatres, on and on and on . . . In the middle of all this horror there stands, in the center of a beautiful park, the enormous Russian Memorial for the 20,000 dead Russian soldiers lost in taking the city."

On Monday, September 28, 1959, *Die Zoo-Geschichte* opened at the Werkstatt, the studio theater of the Schiller Theater, on a double bill with Samuel Beckett's *Das letzte Band* (*Krapp's Last Tape*). Both plays were directed by Walter Henn, and Albee's play starred Thomas Holtzmann as Jerry and Kurt Buecheler as Peter. Pinkas Braun had translated the play into German, a language that was completely foreign to the author. Albee sat in a box, stage left, at the front of the theater. He had seen the play at a dress rehearsal, but this was the first time he was seeing it with an audience; he spent most of the time looking at the audience rather than at the stage. As he said, "I was very interested in what effect my play, through the actors, was having on the audience. They were rapt, laughing when they were supposed to. The most amazing thing was that at the end of the play, when Jerry ran on the knife and Peter ran off and Jerry was left there dying, there was absolute silence for what struck me as being a minute or so, though it could not have been more than a few seconds before thunderous applause started . . . During that absolute silence before they started applauding, I remember thinking, oh-oh."

After the actors had taken their first curtain calls, there was a call for the author, and in the European tradition he allowed himself to be brought out onstage. "I don't remember any cheers when I climbed up on stage, but there may have been. There *was* a lot of applause, and I took several bows, alone & with the actors and the director."

He later wrote that he wouldn't have missed that opening for the world,

despite the fact—as I have learned since—that, for this author, at least, opening nights do not really exist. They happen, but they take place as if in a dream: One concentrates, but one cannot see the stage action clearly; one can hear but barely; one tries to follow the play, but one can make no sense of it. And, if one is called to the stage afterwards to take a bow, one wonders why, for one can make no connection between the work just presented and one's self. Naturally, this feeling was complicated in the case of *The Zoo Story*, as the play was being presented in German, a language of which I knew not a word, and in Berlin too, an awesome city. But, it has held true since. The high points of a person's life can be appreciated so often only in retrospect.

Following what was to become a lifelong pattern, Beckett was not in attendance at opening night. Albee appeared alone at a press conference, where he was asked only one question: Who do you write like, Tennessee Williams or Samuel Beckett? Albee answered, "Neither; both; I write like me."

About the opening night performance, Albee wrote to Flanagan:

The two actors are wonderful, the guy who plays Jerry, Thomas Holtzmann, is one of the best up-and-coming actors here, and he does a thrilling job. Alas, a few things distress me. For example: it is terribly important that Jerry not touch Peter until the first of the three specific physical actions leading up to the knife bit. This first action is the tickling. But, the way they do it, Jerry has his hands all over Peter, all the time. After the opening, someone asked me if Jerry was homosexual, then went off and argued among themselves as to which one was. Nobody asked me if I was. And, the big speech at the end of the play, after the knifing, in which Jerry explains to Peter what happened at the Zoo, is cut. Almost completely. I miss it. After all, it does help explain what the title means. But, all in all, I can't complain.

The Death of Bessie Smith was scheduled to open in the same theater at the next festival, next year. He wrote Flanagan, "They want a long play as soon as I get one. Know where I can get any?" He had been given 500 marks, around $125, for spending money, which he didn't seem to be able to spend. For the first time in his life, he was recognized. "Lots of people here seem to know who I am, which is a damn funny experience, and the kids, student types, who come to talk to me are all intelligent and well informed."

After the opening night party, carried on a wave of euphoria, he went out to dinner with Stefani Hunzinger, Pinkas Braun, and his wife, Gisela, now all good friends. They drank champagne and ate oysters, followed by stewed pears covered with whipped cream, vanilla ice cream, and crystalized violets (Albee never forgot those crystalized violets, and neither did Flanagan once he heard about them). It was a heady time. Then he went back to his pension, where, by himself, he could contemplate the evening and try to put it in perspective. Later he wrote: "I am on my balcony; there is a moon. From where I sit, I can see the shattered hulk of the Kaiser Wilhelm Cathedral—left standing, in ruins, in the center of the almost rebuilt city as a testimony to war. I am dizzily tired; I am dislocated, quite alone, homesick, and, I assume, very happy."

The next day, a brief paragraph appeared in *The New York Times*, stating that a first-night audience at the Berlin Art Festival "warmly applauded Edward Albee's one-act play, 'Zoo Stories,' " doubling the "story" and then leaping to the conclusion that the play would be produced on Broadway later that year. For the first time, a description of the play appeared in a New York newspaper, indicating that the play was a forty-minute dialogue "between a lonely, despairing young man and a prosperous businessman," and adding that "the young man finally commits suicide."

The Berlin reviews, which appeared on September 30, were quickly and awkwardly translated for Albee. It was the first time he had heard any professional critical comments about his work, and he quoted from them in his letter home.

Friedrich Luft in *Die Welt:* "E. Albee has mixed out of his knowledge of

Beckett, Poe, Kafka, Freud and the thrilling low-hit technic of Hollywood . . . a thrilling drama of the very clever kind; desire of death in blue jeans; twilight of the Gods in the gutter. Very talented, and the dialectics of the absolute evil often has a chilly gleam."

Walter Karsch in *Tagesspiegel*: "There was much applause for the extraordinary proof of talent of Mr. Albee."

Dora Fehling in *Telegraf*: " 'The Zoo Story' was a touching experience of the Berlin festival . . . Albee . . . is a geologist of our souls."

An unsigned critic in *Berliner Morgenpost*: " 'The Zoo Story' is unusual but very talented."

Florian Kienzl in *Der Tag*: "What an inexorable play full of despair. Incredible that this comes from the new world, the bright continent of the unlimited possibilities."

Albee wrote, "Well, that's all I have in English (or something like English) for the present. Four O.K. And one not so hot. Anyway, all the reviews are much longer, and we shall see them soon. The play is selling out at the box office, anywho, and plans for new productions are popping up all over the place. Vienna, Frankfurt, Mannheim, Baden-Baden, and God knows where else here in funny Germany. People in the theatre here tell me that it is a hit."

That night he was off for another visit "to the flesh pots . . . a number of bars, and they all seem to cater to something different." It was more than twenty years since Christopher Isherwood had gone to Berlin and discovered the original of Sally Bowles, as well as rising Nazism. But despite World War II and its aftermath, the spirit of Berlin night life remained. In many of the bars, Albee said, were boys from East Berlin, who earned money that they brought home to their mothers. "Most of the boys seem pretty gay for me; they all dance at these saloons, with each other. Other places do this: One bar caters to middle-aged and old men, who go there, dance with each other etc. One bar is for drags, one bar is for drags over fifty and on, and on. One bar which, damn it, doesn't reopen until after I leave, has boxing and wrestling matches, with the winner going to the highest bidder. And then, there are some plain bars too. Just bars, with just people." He added a note about the Berliner boy he had met on the boat coming over. His story "has to do with America, the land of dreams as opposed to this trapped island. The boy was so taken with the U.S. while he was over that he has taken on everything American: Clothes, speech (he won't talk German), attitudes, with the result that he is . . . a parody of the Amurican in Yerp."

The letter closed: "I have been so busy, running around from one thing to another, all my time occupied, that I just haven't had time to be depressed,

really gone depressed. At the party opening night I was struck by the fact that
I was alone so far from home with no one I loved nearby. But the important
thing, I guess, is that I haven't fallen apart, cracked up. The controls are pretty
good, but not too good in that I think I'm feeling things. I feel greatly the
need to get back to work." He said he planned to stop in Paris to talk to the
man who was directing *The Zoo Story* there and in London to see a few plays,
"and then home, to my ivory plants, my sissy cat, the booby-hatch over on
Grove Street, all the problems which will afflict me, and the sight of you,
which is worth the going away for, after so long a removal."

During his last few days in Berlin, he went to the Berliner Ensemble and
saw Brecht's *Galileo*, "which is exactly the stunning experience that Tynan
and everybody else yaps about. It made 'Sussen Vogel der Jugend' (one guess
what *that* is) the following evening one of the most dismayingly funny
evenings I've ever had. Chance Wayne turned into a more than slightly
swishy gigolo, Miss de Lago sort of a steely Nazi hausfrau; the other people all
got up in boots and wide metal-studded belts. You would not believe it. It was
an embarrassing flop, even though they *did* add, illegally, and to all sorts of
law suits, the scenes from the Esquire version." There was a production of
Two Gentlemen of Verona, "done by an East German director, in the Brecht
manner; I guess only Brecht could do Brecht-manner." He also saw a Chinese
opera-drama troupe in East Berlin, with an audience

full of Russians, Red Chinese in their frightening blue smock regulation civil-
ian dress. East Berlin is full of these types; is also full of huge red banners, loudspeakers blaring marching music down on the poor people who pick their way
through the ruins. It's chilling, and every day that I read Alsop in the Paris Trib
I shudder. I shall never forget this particular part of my trip. East German flags
sprouted all over West Berlin the day before I left, put up at night by the Reds in
celebration of the 10th anniversary of the 'People's Democratic Republic.' The
next day, the West Berlin police started to tear them down; riots ensued and 17
people were killed in gun fights.

Before Flanagan received Albee's long letter, he anxiously telephoned him
in Berlin and ended by "having asked none of the questions that I had been
popping with curiosity about. Like how were the reviews, like what's the future of the play, like are you being carried, nude and penis-erect, through the
Brandenburg Gates by those people who always make such scenes in European cities and are usually called 'students'; are you, in other words, the darling of Berlin, the toast of Central Europe. Has that guy who lurks around in

'The Third Sex' spotted you yet and taken you to one of those crazy orgies accompanied by 'Musique Concrete?' Have you seen dirty Lola? Have you been to a beer garden? Have you been getting any? Or does the overlay of Nazi fascism haunt every nook and cranny of the town?"

In characteristic Flanagan fashion, he continued:

> I dropped off at your apartment yesterday and threw away one loaf of bread that had turned to penicillin, some milk that had turned to black yougurt, and a lot of polywags and frogs and sea horses. The latter congregation of lower animal life has forever changed my opinion of growing things like pretty flowers; you'd left some old gladiolas around and in emptying the vase in which they were encased I came upon this strange swamp; the smell was unthinkable and strange bats and winged creatures emerged. It's a good thing you didn't leave the care of the apartment to Norman; it would have set him back several years in his analysis. As it was, I had just a few days before taken a Roar Shock (I spell euphonically, as you see) test and was to a certain extent immune.
>
> Things go on here as usual except that the rush is on so far as work and things go. Virgil [Thomson] threw a cocktail party at several people whose innocence was variable; to the shock and horror of one and all Elsa Maxwell hobbled in, availed herself of the red-velvet love seat; in an antic mood, I took the other part of it and engaged her in stylish conversation about Aristotle Onassis and Maria Callas. She says Callas is 40 NOT 35 and that she is a monster til she comes onstage. Then, she becomes a VIBRANT monster who is irresistible [sic]. She said she was enchanted by me and told Virgil that she would tell all her readers about that CHARMING young man. Since she did nothing but lie all the time I spoke with her, I won't lose any sleep, hold my breath or count anybody's chickens (even yours) until she does.

To Flanagan's relief, he received Albee's letter and he rushed to reply:

> I don't know if distance makes *this* easier to accept or no, but believe it you had better!!! I couldn't be happier about your success with 'The Zoo Story' if it had been my own. It's all yours, though, and savor every bit of it. Once you get the taste of it—of status as a creative person—it won't be easy for you to settle back to or for anything less—here, where it will be more difficult, or within thee, where it will be *impossible* to . . . I can see you through the last year or so as someone to be thoroughly admired. It isn't easy to have decided to *want* to say YES to life instead of NO; it isn't easy to have gone so far in so short a time (quite—and I mean this honestly—apart from the things that may have made it

easier for you); it isn't easy to *want* a good life, a healthy one, and a useful one to one's self.

Then he spoke about their breakup, in what sounded like an analyst-couch confession: "I can't feel anything but shame for most of my behaviour . . . Raging, self-pitying, self-righteous; obsessive, self-indulgent, pseudo-martyred where a show of charm, where a sense of proportion, where a little 'class' might have helped . . . I sense that my lost relationship with E. is more to be put at my feet than I have ever admitted . . ."

From there, he moved to events in his own life, which seemed to verge on the delusionary: "THEY'RE AFTER ME. And, Buster, I mean it. The phone is a janglin', the appointment calendar is a maze of inescapable late-comings; people want articles, books, rehearsal time, pieces on commission, me for DINNER, me for COCKTAILS, an obsession with me now . . . I won't say I haven't missed you, because I have; but I won't say that I *have* missed the torment of the last year—when the 'needing' stopped—because I haven't . . . You must be practically in Paris by now. Hurry home and we will see what is going to be."

Within several years, Albee was to look back at his relationship with Flanagan and say to him, "You were the teacher then," meaning, "I am the teacher now."

Leaving Berlin, Albee went to the Frankfurt Book Fair, at the suggestion of the people from S. Fischer Verlag. "I don't know how I got roped into going to Frankfurt," he wrote, "but I did (get roped) and am fleeing the dismal city with all haste. The hqtrs of S. Fischer . . . is here, and I have for too many days now, been lying round in Dr. Fischer's falcon lair, way outside the awful town, strolling the halls, peering with greedy emotions at the Picassos, the Roualts, the Miros, and quietly going batty." After four days of wandering, of going to parties and looking at books, he felt restless and longed to be out of the country. David Diamond had not attended the opening in Berlin, but sent a letter to Braun "sighing heavily that of course he could be no part of the Albee triumph he had so much to do with, but wasn't that the way the world turned." So Albee decided to take "a lunatic side-trip to Florence" to see David Diamond, the "other" (Michelangelo's) David, and "the city I loved so many dim-distant years ago; but I fear it will be glum-making, this time without Bill."

Later, on the train from Florence to Paris, alone and filled with youthful enthusiasm—and expectancy—he took out his portable typewriter and typed a letter to Pinkas and Gisela Braun:

It is nine-thirty at night, and it has begun to rain. I have spent four full and happy days in Florence—in glorious weather—discovering that in seven years I had lost none of the sense of that city . . . Naturally I still haven't even begun to sort out my impressions of this crazy trip I've been on for exactly one month now—is it possible to digest Berlin in Florence? I don't think so. But some things are already clear to me, and high among them is the deep pleasure and satisfaction I have received from knowing the two of you. You are exceptional people, and exceptional people are pretty rare these days.

In Paris, he went to a dress rehearsal of Genet's *The Blacks* ("a stunning work and, from what I could tell through my bad French, an important one") and saw two plays on the same bill at the Comédie-Française ("a most lamentable rendering of Sophocles' *Antigone* and a thoroughly delightful staging of the short de Musset piece, *Un Caprice*"). As arranged by Richard Howard (who had already left Paris), Albee met with Genevieve Serreau about a French production of *The Zoo Story*. Most significantly, he met Samuel Beckett. Beckett "asked after the fortunes of our two plays in Berlin, and was nice enough to ask me to send him a script of *The Zoo Story*, in English." As soon as he returned to New York, Albee complied. Beckett responded, "Many thanks for the play. I like it very much. I want to read it again a couple of times. Then I'll write you again." Two months later, he repeated his praise in a letter, adding "it is good news that our show is still doing well and that you have a new play coming on."

The final stop on Albee's journey was London, where, still unknown, he checked into a bed and breakfast near the British Museum and spent most of his time in the theater. He had mixed feelings about most of the plays that he saw, except for *The Hostage*. The Brendan Behan play, as staged by Joan Littlewood, was, he said, "one of the most exciting new theatrical concepts I have encountered in a long time." And then it was back to New York, for what he hoped would be another triumph.

Looking back at the Berlin experience, he said, "A month before I was delivering telegrams for Western Union, and there I was in Berlin with a very successful play in a language I didn't understand. I was no longer a Western Union messenger. I was a playwright. It was unnerving and bewildering." And there was a feeling of elation about what he referred to as "my own faintly idiotic but damn gratifying happy-making play-success."

5
YAM

That's the best fucking one-act play I've ever seen.

THROUGH all the Berlin preparations, Ed Parone, acting as Albee's agent, kept showing *The Zoo Story* and *Bessie Smith* to various people in New York. Parone's confidence in Albee's talent was not shared by the first producers who read the plays. One of the first was Clinton Wilder (who was not related to Thornton Wilder); he turned them down. (Later, after he joined Richard Barr in partnership, Wilder would have a change of mind; together he and Barr became Albee's producers.) Next, Parone went to David Merrick, who had created a nonprofit foundation to do new plays. He rejected the plays with a tone that Parone remembers as "how dare you." Trying to get them published, Parone submitted them to Barney Rosset at Grove Press (which published Beckett) and to *Esquire.* Both filed rejections, although Grove later printed *The Zoo Story* in its *Evergreen Review.*

The Actors Studio was starting the Playwrights Unit and was looking for new work. Parone called Molly Kazan, who was in charge of the unit and then sent over a copy of *The Zoo Story.* Both she and Michael Wager, who was her associate in the Playwrights Unit, read it and were enthusiastic. They issued an invitation for Albee to join the group when he returned from Berlin and agreed to give *The Zoo Story* a reading, and a hearing at the Studio. Then Wager looked for a director to stage it. He was turned down by Arthur Penn and Arthur Storch, among others. Storch, an actor as well as a director, also rejected the suggestion that he might play Peter. Finally Wager gave the play to John Stix, who greeted it warmly.

"It was different from anything I had read," said Stix. "It seemed to have its own form. It was at times poetic, at times shocking, but it had such a 'liveness.' " He agreed to direct it. Then he met Albee and thought he was the opposite of his writing: "very subdued, withdrawn, detached, cold—and that fascinated me all the more. He was mysterious." Stix enlisted Sheppard Strudwick to play Peter and Lou Antonio for Jerry. There were five days of rehearsal, sometimes with Albee watching. He was, said Antonio, "this very quiet buttoned-up young man, with short hair, and he spoke hardly at all, more an observer than a participant." The play was presented in the fall of 1959 for one performance at the Actors Studio.

Lee Strasberg and Elia Kazan, the two most important members of the Studio, were not at the reading, but the theater was filled with about ninety people, including Molly Kazan, Arthur Penn, and Norman Mailer (and other members of the Playwrights Unit), as well as Studio actors. Outsiders like Parone were not invited. Some may have wondered at the identity of the young man in a corduroy sports jacket lurking in the background: He was, of course, the playwright. This was the first time *The Zoo Story* had been performed in America before an audience. With scripts in hand and with a bench as scenery, the two actors acted out the play. As was customary, Studio members joined in a colloquy after the performance. Traditionally these sessions were harshly critical, often leaving a wounded playwright. When *The Zoo Story* was over, there was a brief silence. Then people started to hedge and even to quarrel with the play, saying things like "Well, you should do this" and "It doesn't go anywhere."

Suddenly Mailer jumped up. Without a moment's hesitation, he cleared the air of criticism by saying, "I'm surprised no one has said what a marvelous play this is. That's the best fucking one-act play I've ever seen."

Mailer's pronouncement did not stop others from continuing their dissent. He remembers that in the discussion the verdict was about twelve to four or five—against the play. "During the Strasberg era," he said, "everyone was savage in their criticism." Stix, who was not entirely happy with his own work on the production but had great admiration for the play, said, "What has struck me with such irony through the years is that only one or two recognized the merit in the writing, and one of them was Mailer. He recognized its greatness." Explaining the adverse reaction of others at the reading, Antonio said, "They just weren't used to a play like that. The theatrically stodgy just couldn't get it." For that moment, Mailer was Albee's champion, and his praise had a dramatic effect: This was a play and a new playwright to be reckoned with.

Also in the audience was Romulus Linney, then an aspiring young actor trying to learn how to write novels, not yet a playwright, and that day beginning a job as stage manager at the Actors Studio. "Sheppard Strudwick was not the most charismatic actor," he said, "but Lou was wonderful, and the play worked like a pistol." He found the reaction bewildering. Except for Mailer, "people talked in generalities." Everyone was wondering what to say in what Linney came to know as "the Strasbergian manner. Strasberg had a pedagogical side. He would begin slowly, then give an oration."

As a nonmember and a hired hand, Linney was not allowed to contribute to the discussion and remained on the sidelines, but looking back at the event, he said, "The first reading of *The Zoo Story* showed me how the theatrical cobwebs that eternally hang over stages—then and now—can be swept away by a bench, two characters, and the plain truth. All the splendors of seemingly profound films, beautiful musicals, dazzling performances, electrifying directorial concepts, and all that, were suddenly childish compared with the bone simple shattering truth that play dramatically expresses, which a whole country faced thereafter."

In May of the following year, Stix directed a reading of *The Death of Bessie Smith* at the Studio, but the group did not pursue the idea of producing either one-act (and later there was to be a contretemps over a possible production of *Who's Afraid of Virginia Woolf?*). Still searching for a producer, Parone spoke to Richard Barr, whom he had met through Virgil Thomson. Barr had begun his career in the late 1930s as an actor and stage manager with Orson Welles and the Mercury Theater and had also worked with Welles on *Citizen Kane*. He spoke the first line of the movie (after "The March of Time" theme has played). "Stand by," he says. "I'll tell you if we want to run it again." Later he became a Broadway producer, for many years in partnership with Charles Bowden. In a sudden change of direction, he was now turning his sights Off-Broadway. He wanted to start his own theater, with a playwright, a new playwright, at the center of it. Eventually Barr was to become Albee's devoted producer—presenting most of his plays on Broadway—and a major force in producing new and adventurous work on and Off-Broadway, from Samuel Beckett to Stephen Sondheim's *Sweeney Todd*. For now, more than other producers, he was looking for challenging material. One day, Barr told Parone that he was considering producing two one-act plays, both of which Parone, as an agent, had read. They were, Parone told him candidly, "workmanlike, produceable, forgettable." Wouldn't Barr prefer to produce the real thing? He offered him *The Zoo Story*.

Barr recalled in his unpublished memoirs, "I distinctly remember my first reading the play. Sitting alone in the attic, I began with my usual cynicism accorded to a new script by a new writer. By the third page, I guessed I was on to something. By the tenth page, I hoped I was on to something. By the last page, I knew I was on to something. Here in my lap was one of the best one-act plays ever written. Certainly, it was the best written by an American writer." He called Parone, who told him that *The Zoo Story* had been done in Berlin on a double bill with Beckett's *Krapp's Last Tape*.

Krapp's Last Tape had already been optioned by another New York producer, with the added stipulation that it be directed in New York by Alan Schneider, who had staged *Endgame* Off-Broadway at the Cherry Lane Theater and was Beckett's chosen American director. Barr said, "Having no money to produce the play, no companion piece, no theater, and an author in Europe, I could only sit by and wait." However, for $250 (he told Parone that it was his last $250), he took an option on *The Zoo Story*. It was, of course, a wise investment.

Albee went to see Barr in his attic apartment on West 11th Street. Barr wrote, "Up the stairs came a remarkably shy young man with extraordinarily expressive eyes. The conversation was somewhat formal, but from time to time, I caught a glimpse of humor in the eyes and felt more comfortable." Barr told him about his interest in encouraging playwrights Off-Broadway, and his plan to present *The Zoo Story*. Sanford Friedman had shown the play to Milton Katselas, a hopeful young New York director whom he knew from Carnegie Tech. Katselas read the play and contacted Albee. They met and, later, Albee suggested to Barr that Katselas should be the director. He also said that he hoped that, as in Berlin, Barr would produce the play together with *Krapp's Last Tape*. That meeting between Albee and Barr was the beginning of one of the most mutually rewarding producer-playwright relationships in the American theater. As for Parone, it was his last deal as an agent. He had quit William Morris to run the New York office of a film production company set up by Arthur Miller and Marilyn Monroe. In 1963, Parone returned to the theater as the managing director of the new Albee-Barr-Wilder Playwrights Unit.

All Barr needed to produce *The Zoo Story* and *Krapp's Last Tape* was $9,000. He first sent a letter to David Merrick, asking him to join in this plan to produce plays Off-Broadway. Merrick, who had already turned down Parone, never answered. Barr's "second long shot" was Evie and H. B. (Whitey) Lutz. Evie Lutz was an heiress to the Lilly pharmaceutical fortune and her husband was a writer with an interest in the theater. Barr wrote Lutz, "There is a whole crop of American writers waiting to be heard, and I feel it's time to do something about it. I am bored with Broadway, and no longer wish to cater to its system with my blood and guts. Those I intend to save for things I really want to do . . . I consider it disgraceful that a new American playwright, Edward Albee, had to get a hearing in Berlin first. He has written a play, *The Zoo Story*, which is walking off with raves in several spots in Europe. The play is superb, and I have it." Lutz had taken out an ad in the *Village Voice*, supporting the Living Theater, and Barr thought perhaps he could influence that newspaper to write about the new play project, though privately he may have been hoping that Lutz would invest. To Barr's surprise, when Lutz came to see him, Lutz asked Barr how much money he needed. On the spot, Lutz decided that he and his wife would be Barr's sole backers. Later, when it turned out that Harry Joe Brown Jr. had bought the option on the Beckett play, half the investment was returned to Lutz. Eventually the production became a three-way partnership: Lutz, Brown, and Barr. It was still 1959 but, looking ahead, Barr decided to name his company Theater 1960 (and then to update it, year by year).

He began gathering a team: William Ritman as scenic designer, Mark Wright and Michael Kasdan as stage managers, a group that was to work together with him for many years. Alan Schneider was named to direct *Krapp's Last Tape*, with Donald Davis, a Canadian actor, and Katselas was signed to direct *The Zoo Story*. Davis met Albee for the first time, in Barr's office: "I remember him sitting on the floor practically with his head between his knees, absolutely silent. He never said anything. Perhaps the word morose is a little strong, but he was sort of everybody's outsider in those days. And Richard was anything but quiet and morose. He tended to be on all the time."

William Daniels came in to read. To lure him into playing the role of Peter, Katselas said that he could read for Jerry. "I was very torn about it," Daniels recalled. "It seemed to me that one guy [Jerry] had all the words and the other guy [Peter] just sat there. All I could see were the problems. It was a rather static situation. It has to be filled in with an emotional life, a reactive reality between the two men." Gradually overcoming the actor's hesitations, Daniels's wife and Gerald Freedman (a director and later associate producer of the New York Shakespeare Festival) talked him into accepting the part. Barr proposed Peter Falk for the role of Jerry, but Albee wanted a younger actor (later when they were seeking a replacement for the role, he turned down Peter Fonda because he was too young). Albee's choice for Jerry was George Maharis, whom he remembered from *Deathwatch*. Maharis had just made a television pilot for a show called *Route 66* (later the source of his fame, and the reason he left *The Zoo Story* very early in the run). Each actor was to make $50 a week, the Off-Broadway scale.

As preparation for the play, Katselas decided to imitate Jerry in life in order to see what reaction Jerry's manner might bring. Riding the subway one day, he said to an elderly woman sitting next to him, "I've been to the zoo." She looked at him as if he were crazy. Ten seconds, he edged closer to her and said in a louder voice, "I've been to the zoo!" He repeated the line: "I said I've been to the zoo." Finally she responded, "So, *nu?*"

By the third week of rehearsal, there was trouble on *The Zoo Story*. Mark Wright, the stage manager, told Barr that there was a conflict between Katselas and Maharis. From here on, the story of the production of *The Zoo Story* becomes one of Rashomonic complexity. According to Barr, he sat in on a rehearsal and was upset with Katselas's direction, which, in Barr's words, "loosened the tension" and pushed the play toward the maudlin. From Daniels's point of view, the problem was much simpler. "Barr got very nervous that we were sitting around a table for so long, just reading the play. The meat of the play had to be worked out, sitting around a table, reading it, absorbing it, creating the background of the people. It had nothing to do with getting us on our feet." Barr disagreed and said that he gave Katselas an ultimatum: "He could resign, he could be fired, or he could sit and watch me direct the play. Milton chose the last of the options, and rehearsals continued"—under Barr's direction. In his memoirs, Barr claims that he staged the play. Daniels says that Barr directed it for only about three days. Then Maharis became upset with Barr's instructive approach: "On that line you go over there and on that line you go over here."

"Maharis hadn't had that much experience on the stage," said Daniels. "He started to flip out. I went to the management and said, 'you better bring Milton back or you're going to lose this kid, and if he goes, I go.' They brought Milton back. Milton being a hothead, said, 'if anybody comes near me again, I'll punch him in the nose.' That was that, and he finished directing the play." Katselas confirms Daniels's story, Barr in his memoirs insists that he directed the play, and Mark Wright says that to his knowledge Katselas did not come back. Albee prefers not to make a judgment. A directorial switch, or a double-switch, could have happened without his knowledge.

At the first preview, the actors were startled by the audience reaction. Daniels recalls: "I'm sitting on the bench reading a book and George walks up to the bench and says, 'I've been to the zoo.' All I did was look up, and there was a huge laugh. So I looked in the opposite direction, thinking maybe he was talking to somebody else. Another huge laugh." After the performance, Barr and Albee rushed backstage and said, "You're getting laughs. Don't do that." Daniels said, "I'm not doing anything. I'm not playing for laughs." He explained that none of them, including Daniels himself, knew in advance that the play would get such a response. "But these were not joke laughs. They were recognition laughs: People were thinking, haven't I been in this position before," or they were afraid that something like that might happen to them. As he realized, "These laughs are absolutely essential to the play." The audience must feel Peter's discomfort: "If you're not made uneasy by this man, I'm not doing the job right." During a preview, three people walked out when Maharis, telling the dog story, delivered the line, "Malevolence with an erection." Katselas was standing in the back of the theater: "Bang! They got up like a jack-in-a-box and just walked by me. That's when I knew it was a hit."

On January 14, 1960, the double bill of *The Zoo Story* and *Krapp's Last Tape* opened at the Provincetown Playhouse, many years earlier the scene of Eugene O'Neill's first triumphs. After the performance, Barr, his partners, Albee, and a few others went back to Barr's apartment to wait for the reviews. At 1 A.M., Howard Atlee, Barr's press agent, called in with the reviews of Brooks Atkinson in the *Times* and Walter Kerr in the *Herald Tribune*. Although both critics had favorable things to say about the actors, and for once Kerr seemed to be admiring of Beckett, both had serious reservations about *The Zoo Story*. Four years earlier, Atkinson had been confused by *Waiting for Godot*, saying that it was "a mystery wrapped in an enigma." Now he wrote glumly about the Beckett and Albee one-acts, "Both plays are interesting, and both of them are well acted by intelligent professionals. Nothing of enduring value is said in either play. But each of them captures some part of the dismal mood that infects many writers today." In his first encounter with Albee, Kerr said that he wrote "with a certain wit and a promising degree of theatrical intensity," but that the play "sags in the center because it is a soliloquy rather than a play." Giving an inch, he concluded, "And while en garde remains the proper spirit in which to approach the avant garde, I think you will find that each of these curios creates a genuine, and a tantalizing mood."

Hearing those reviews, Barr "immediately went into a deep slump and threatened again to quit the theater." The next morning he was at the Blaine-Thompson advertising agency to talk about a possible advertising campaign to rescue his plays. He was greeted at the door by one of the agency's executives, who said, "Boy, have you got a hit!" Then Barr looked at the afternoon newspapers, and lost his despondency. In the *New York Post*, Richard Watts Jr., who was to become one of Albee's most articulate critical supporters—during the reign of Atkinson and Kerr, he was the one daily New York newspaper critic who consistently embraced innovative new theater—praised

Krapp as "the most human" of Beckett's plays. Then he said, "It is actually the unknown Mr. Albee who provides the interesting bill with the major event of the evening. 'The Zoo Story' demonstrates that the hitherto unproduced American is a dramatist who writes with power, skill and freshness, and he is clearly a man with a claim to attention." Critics in the *Journal-American* and the *New York Daily News* were also enthusiastic. Despite Albee's opening night feeling of the "deepest gloom," the "next morning dawned (as they all will) and I found that the plays were a big fat hit."

By the time that Atkinson did his Sunday follow-up piece, he seemed to have changed his mind, deciding that "the two short plays at the Provincetown provide one of the few stimulating theater evenings of the season." Although Harold Clurman, writing in *The Nation*, had certain qualifications, he was unequivocal in welcoming Albee. He said that *The Zoo Story* "interested me more than any other new American play thus far this season." On the other hand, Robert Brustein in *The New Republic* made his debut as a critic of Albee with a sour review dismissing *The Zoo Story* as Beat Generation "claptrap." Albee immediately shot off a letter to Brustein, suggesting that he read the play. In his response to the playwright, Brustein remounted his critical high horse and proclaimed:

> To judge from 'The Zoo Story,' you have a tendency to disguise unconventional ideas as religious affirmations, and it is my duty to try to pierce this disguise. If you are going to be the American Jean Genet (I assume you know who *he* is), then you will have to call a pickup a pickup, and not a direct telephone connection to the navel of God. My own prejudice is that I cannot equate alienation and sainthood; I can accept anything on stage but religious revivals.

Reading that letter in 1998, Brustein expressed his remorse about writing it: "I must confess I am not happy with the insufferable tone of the young man who wrote the 1960 letter." Over the years, it was assumed that certain Albee plays received favorable reviews *(The Zoo Story, Who's Afraid of Virginia Woolf?)* while others received negative ones. As Albee has asserted, with justification, all his plays have had mixed reviews. *The Zoo Story*, his first play and his first success, was no exception.

Culling the reviews, Barr and his associates put together a quote ad that naturally emphasized the positive side of the critical reception. The producer made one other wise decision. He decided that the playwright was the star. He put Albee's name over the title and had Atlee send his photograph to newspapers and magazines. This meant that Albee's brooding, boyish face, with his brush cut and what he calls "the surly, angry young man look," establishing him as an American equivalent of John Osborne, stared out at readers and became an immediate point of identity. Beginning with Albee's next play, that photograph appeared in the advertisements. Why was this man not smiling? There was a simple, reasonable answer. He had uneven teeth and, protectively, kept his mouth shut, especially when facing a camera. In time, his teeth were fixed. Soon his face, in a variation of the same photograph, was appearing in news and feature articles and on television. Albee's first formal interview was with Frances Herridge in the *Post*, following up Watts's review. Herridge said that the success of the play in New York was "a vindication, here where it meant most, of the choice he had made 10 years before at great emotional cost." She quoted him as saying his mother, "a strong-minded woman," had insisted that he give up writing and "amount to something." They had fought until he left home. In this interview, he mentioned for the first time that he was working on a full-length drama "about two faculty members and their wives." The play was tentatively called *Exorcism*.

After *The Zoo Story* opened, Barr sent Katselas a formal letter:

> As you know, I have never been satisfied with your interpretation of "The Zoo Story," feeling that it lacked tension, and that you permitted the actors to go too far in the direction of comedy—thus killing the essential struggle which occurs on stage. Following the opening, Edward, Harry Joe [Brown] and I had a long discussion and have decided to relieve you of further responsibility in the production. We will continue to pay your royalties and give you credit. However, for further casting, replacements, and the road company, including the redirection of the present material, we will not require you to be present.

Albee objected to that letter, saying that "no such summary dismissal of Milton was agreed to." Barr admitted only that he was undiplomatic. Daniels is unwavering: "They were so vindictive about Milton. He directed this play!" "I was there to the end," says Katselas.

With *The Zoo Story*, as Flanagan quickly realized, "It looks as if he is the hottest young playwright since Tennessee Williams." Whenever Albee went to Julius's or another favorite bar, he was instantly recognized. One night, soon after the play opened, the San Remo was packed with famous people. In the room were Tennessee Williams, Simone Signoret, Bill Flanagan, and Ned Rorem. Leonard Bernstein was at a table with Judith Malina and Julian Beck. Then Albee walked in, wearing a white Irish knit sweater. He stood at the bar and, in Robert Heide's memory, he looked like Eugene O'Neill in the photograph on the book jacket of Long Day's Journey into Night, standing moodily on the porch of his house in Connecticut. And, said Heide, "All eyes turned toward Edward."

Within several weeks after the opening, Albee privately expressed his criticism of the production, saying it was "something less than Elysian-like ideal (and so is the play, for that matter, I suspect)." Two months later, he wrote Barr: "I begin to wonder if there may not be, built-in to the play, by yours truly's own hand, some sort of disaster device which sabotages the best efforts of directors and actors . . . Keeping the play at a correct level of intensity would seem to be just as difficult a task as sculpting in mercury." Then he criticized Katselas and both Maharis and Mark Richman, who had replaced Maharis in the role of Jerry:

> Milton's direction and George's acting tended to slop the piece over in the direction of sentimentality, introspection and whining togetherness. This flaw, to be fair to George (and, despite his dereliction to the money madness bit, we must try to be fair to such a yum-yum), showed up most when young Michael went into the part . . . Now, with Mark at it . . . The play has slowed down, slopped over into being a silence-ridden drudge. The wings of danger no longer flutter in the background; the claw of the seapuss ain't going to get no one! . . . The whole play has, curiously, become nothing more intense than a polemic.

One month after The Zoo Story opened, another new playwright, Jack Richardson, was introduced Off-Broadway with The Prodigal, an antiheroic reinvention of the Orestes story. Clurman paired it with The Connection as "the two most striking 'social' plays of the past year." As dissimilar as their first plays were, Albee, Richardson, and Gelber were linked as a trinity of discoveries, outsiders who were shaking up the old order and redefining the boundaries of what was desirable or even permissible in the theater. At the end of the 1959–1960 theater season, the Vernon Rice Award, which previously had gone to actors, was given to four Off-Broadway playwrights: Albee, Richardson, Gelber, and Rick Besoyan, author of the nostalgic musical Little Mary Sunshine. Richardson (and Besoyan) proved to have no staying power as playwrights. Although Gelber was never able to equal his early success, he continued to be quietly productive as a director and teacher. Only Albee became a durable and dominant voice in the theater.

His influence on younger playwrights like Sam Shepard and Lanford Wilson was of inestimable value. One could trace a direct path from The Zoo

Story to David Mamet, to the harsh, street realities of *American Buffalo* and *Edmond*. As John Guare wrote, "You can't imagine the debt that every American playwright writing after 1960 owes to Edward Albee." When the double bill of Beckett and Albee opened at the Provincetown Playhouse, it was on the crest of the Off-Broadway movement. Guare came up from Washington to see it. He becomes rapturous as he tries to describe the effect of the experience: "The production ended. I was in a daze. I was lost but I was home. I was at sea but not drowning. The future had finally shown up. Whatever theatrical revolution had started in England and France had finally hit America. I walked around the Village for hours in a fever afraid to let go of the spell. Holy Christ, maybe I could be a playwright." He went home and with great enthusiasm told the story of the play to his parents, who wondered if this was something that had happened to their son.

Guare said that after Albee, "We all wrote our own version of *Zoo Story*. Albee spawned an entire generation of park bench plays. Theater for years became littered with park benches. To show you were avant-garde, you needed no more than a dark room and a park bench" (as in Mamet's *Duck Variations*). Guare's admiration for Albee was unbounded. "A generation had a figurehead," he said, remembering "a great bohemian time in New York when everyone was young and how Edward Albee created the very heart of it."

Just as John Osborne's *Look Back in Anger* had awakened a legion of new working-class playwrights in England, sweeping out the gentility of a theater bred by the tradition of Noël Coward and Terence Rattigan, Albee's *The Zoo Story* aerated the American theatrical environment with an earthiness and an immediacy. Certainly, Arthur Miller and Tennessee Williams had provoked their own theatrical revolution on Broadway, but with *The Zoo Story* Albee opened the doors even wider, making a direct connection with the disaffected and disenfranchised. Albee's impact was also felt in Osborne's country. For Tom Stoppard, it was *The Zoo Story* even more than *Look Back in Anger* that encouraged him to be a playwright. The theater of *The Zoo Story*, he said, was where things were happening and "where one wanted to be."

Together with Gelber and Richardson, Albee represented a seismic shift in the theater. Suddenly Off-Broadway was alive with new plays. In the 1950s, the modern Off-Broadway began with Circle in the Square and its revivals of Tennessee Williams's *Summer and Smoke* and Eugene O'Neill's *The Iceman Cometh*, and with Joseph Papp's founding of the New York Shakespeare Festival. At the same time, David Ross was reinvestigating plays by Chekhov. At the end of the 1950s and at the beginning of the 1960s, there was a turn toward adventurous new plays. Jean Genet, the ultimate outsider, was represented by *The Balcony* at Circle in the Square, and a year later by *The Blacks*, the play that Albee had admired so much in Paris. *The Blacks* became one of the most successful Off-Broadway plays, arresting audiences with its exploration of the nature of blackness, at the same time it uncovered the richness of actors from the black community. The success of Off-Broadway at least momentarily encouraged Broadway to be more daring. Eugène Ionesco was on Broadway with *Rhinoceros*, in which Zero Mostel offered a virtuosic display of acting anthropomorphism in this black comedy about the wages of conformity. Broadway also proved hospitable to Brendan Behan, Harold Pinter, and Arthur Kopit, whose *Oh Dad, Poor Dad, Mamma's Hung You in the Closet and I'm Feelin' So Sad* moved there from Off-Broadway (very early Albee spotted that play as "ODPD," or short for Oedipus). Kopit joined Albee, Richardson, and Gelber as the radical leaders of the new American theater. In one of the most ridiculous examples of the playwrights' sudden celebrity, *Mademoiselle* magazine featured a photograph of the four of them (plus Arnold Weinstein, author of *The Red Eye of Love*) crowded into a wooden packing crate labeled with the names of their fellow absurdists Ionesco and Arrabal. It was, Albee said, "rather as if we were about to be shipped somewhere."

As *The Zoo Story* moved from theater to theater, it became a long-running Off-Broadway success, establishing the author's reputation and also that of Barr's company. Among other things, it proved to be the springboard for William Daniels's subsequent career. He continued in his role, with a series of actors as Jerry, playing it at various Off-Broadway houses and during its South American tour. Looking back at the play and the author, he says that he never got to know Albee, but remembers one special gracious act. When the actor and his wife adopted a baby, Albee sent them a letter of congratulations: "These little bumbles can, I'm told, and do believe, with proper love and care, turn out to be very nice people." With proper love and care. Moved by that letter, they framed it and hung it on the wall: an Albee sampler.

A national touring company of *The Zoo Story* was launched, with Albee directing, for the first time and with great trepidation. "Picture me," he said, "never having directed a play, let alone a playlet, in my whole hundred years or so, working eight hours a day . . . with two frightening professional actors . . . trying to make contact with *them* in order to make contact with the play. Naivete, or megalomania: one or t'other; that's all it could be . . . Any rate, I am doing this—and while it is fascinating—I am horrified at what I have wrought."

In August, *The Zoo Story* opened in London on a double bill with Tennessee Williams's *This Property Is Condemned*. Kenneth Haigh played Jerry, Peter Sallis, Peter. In their mixed reviews, the London critics often compared Albee to Pinter, with Milton Shulman in the *Evening Standard* grumbling, "No doubt Mr. Albee will have his frenetic disciples just as has Mr. Pinter." Fifteen years later, the play was revived as a classic with Robert Stephens playing Jerry to Michael Gambon's Peter. That time it was performed outdoors at the Open Air Theater in Regents Park, "very near the zoo," said Stephens, "as a lunchtime diversion," the closest it would come to a simulation of the actual location. For Stephens, the play was "a torrential suicide note about the ugliness of existence, the squalor and misery of the downtown apartment block where the character lived, and a general outpouring of unassuaged anguish."

Other productions were done throughout America and Europe. Frequently, directors called upon Albee for help in understanding how best to present *The Zoo Story*. In one typical letter, he said that Peter was the key to the audience's response: "I find as a general rule, the audience identifies completely with Peter and is taught as he is and is attacked as he is. I won't give you any absolute indications beyond saying that you must make Peter the sort of person who cannot leave the bench, and by this I don't mean that he must be a cypher. His humanity and withdrawal must always be in conflict, and absurdity must always be just under the surface." He warned against making Jerry seem neurotic or insane. "This approach completely disturbs the balance of the play as well as my intention."

Years later, when Albee would do public readings from his work, he would often begin with *The Zoo Story*, and he would read the story of Jerry and the dog. He would introduce the passage by saying:

All you need to know about *The Zoo Story* is the fact that it concerns a meeting in New York's Central Park, deep in New York's Central Park, back in the days when a meeting deep in New York's Central Park was not a suicidal act, between a man named Peter, a nicely settled, young middle-aged middle-class rather bright man, who, I think, has probably accommodated to his life too much, a meeting with a man named Jerry, who is an outsider, who some people feel has not accommodated enough, a man who in various critical and scholarly journals has been referred to a., as a psychopath, and b., as Jesus Christ . . . Certainly Jerry is a man who has not closed down, who is a man who is trying during the course of this play to persuade Peter that closing down is dangerous and that life for all of its problems, all of its miseries, is worth participating in, absolutely fully. Jerry tries to persuade Peter of this, cannot because Peter refuses to understand and Jerry by the end of the play must therefore sacrifice himself to make the point. But during the course of the play he tells Peter a number of stories about his past, about his life, some of which are true, some of which are not. It's always fun for the actors who are doing the play to figure out which ones are true and which are not . . ."

On the basis of a single short play, running less than one hour, Albee was heralded as a savior of the American theater. Seemingly overnight, a star playwright had been born. Typical of the overstatement was an article that appeared in *Horizon* magazine in 1961, opposite a full-page photograph of Albee (very serious, very brooding) with a white cat: "As a playwright, Albee sprang almost full-grown from Zeus's forehead. There were no abortive scripts, no produced failures, no old dresser drawers stuffed with rejected manuscripts, and (discounting a sex farce written at the age of twelve) no amateur efforts." The author of that article had not checked the dresser drawers.

By the time that *The Zoo Story* opened in New York, Albee had already written two new short plays, *The Death of Bessie Smith* and *The Sandbox*, and the sketch *Fam and Yam*. As already stated, *Bessie Smith* was inspired by the cover of a record album. Among his plays it is an anomaly. In contrast to all his subsequent plays (except, much later, for *The Lorca Play*), it was based on a real event. It is the most overtly political of all his works, and it is the one nonadaptation that has nothing to do with his life.

Looking back on *Bessie Smith*, he said:

> Stylistically, it's enormously different from both *The Zoo Story* and *The American Dream*, but that was the manner in which that play had to be written. Take those three plays: *Zoo Story*, totally naturalistic, aside from some elevated prose; *Bessie Smith*, a kind of Brechtian structure; and *American Dream*, French, Ionesco, avant-garde, absurdist. So who is the author of those three and why are they so different? Simply, that is the way each of those plays had to be written. Whenever I start thinking about a play, I start getting ideas about its style. Form and content co-determine each other. I have a sense of how naturalistic or stylized a play is going to be probably even before I've written a word of it.

He had started writing *Bessie Smith* right after he finished *The Zoo Story*. The play began "as a statement of (somewhat tardy) outrage over the racial prejudice in the South in the '30s which resulted in the singer's death, and emerged on the page as that, but became, as well, a socio-economic examination of a time and place." As early as January 1959, before *The Zoo Story* was set for Berlin, Albee had written to Pinkas Braun about the new play, which, he said, he was "rewriting" and thought might work as a companion piece for *The Zoo Story*. In the letter, he explained that Bessie Smith was "probably our greatest blues singer. In 1937 she was in an automobile crash in the South . . . She was taken to a hospital near the Tennessee border and there refused admission because of her color. She died, from loss of blood, on the way to a second hospital. My play deals with several people in the second hospital, their lives and attitudes, and the effect the arrival of the dead Bessie Smith has on them." As he once said, the play is about "people trapped in the skin of their environment and people trapped in the environment of their skin."

When Mrs. Hunzinger visited him in New York, Albee gave her a copy of *The Death of Bessie Smith*, and she passed it on to Braun. In April, Braun sent a candid letter to Albee expressing his doubts about the play. Apologizing for his bluntness, he said that he thought that the effect of the play on an audience might be the opposite of what was intended by the author:

> If the characters whom you described so well are such big exceptions to the rule, so near the edge of being abnormal, that the average citizen in the audience would never agree to identify himself with them; it makes it so easy for everybody in the audience to say: "These awful people. How could they ever allow themselves to let such a terrible thing happen? If Bessie would have come to us, we would have saved her; she might still be living." And this cannot be what you wanted. In my opinion you wanted to brand the phantom prejudice which haunts our society and with which almost everybody is at least a little bit "sicklied o'er". . . . You should not take for granted that people know her and know her destiny . . . You should try to make the audience understand the tragic measures of this human failure.

Braun's letter confirmed Albee's own doubts. As he wrote back:

> Your comments on my Bessie Smith play, and the questions you raise, are ones which occupy me—plague me is closer to it—many hours of each day. When I began work on the play I thought it would be a fairly simple matter to do what I wanted to do. And what I still want to do . . . To take a point in time and three people; expose the areas of their relationships, their environment, their attitudes in relation to their environment, build conflict, and then expose these three people, and the effect this would have on them considering the co-incidental crisis in their own lives . . . and the extra consideration, and, I had hoped, thunderbolt effect of this arrival being of a dead Negro . . . *beyond* help,

yet brought both as a symbol of the basic unreality of their preoccupations, and as a gesture of hope beyond hope.

Obviously, I have been successful in none of this. But I am going to work on this play until I have done what I want to do. I would not have written the play in the first place if I were only interested in the rejection of a dying Negro at a white hospital. But the significance of the arrival of a *dead* Negro, brought there knowingly, brought as an unconscious symbol of the responsibility man is tragically unable to assume for his fellow man even under *ideal* circumstances, but in these twisted circumstances . . . THIS is the thing that fired my imagination, that made me *have* to write this play.

So, you can see that I am concerned with something more than sociological values with this play. And I have used Bessie Smith, rather than just *any* Negro, because I feel the special identification with this specific woman helps to emphasize my point.

But let me tell you that your objections to the play as it stands are valid; in fact, considering my failure in dealing with a matter so cryingly in need of lucid and affecting treatment, your comments are far softer than they should be.

In his revised, improved version, he added two new scenes, beginning the play with a brief meeting between two black men in a bar. One of them, we learn later, is traveling with Bessie Smith. This was followed by a long scene at home between the nurse and her bigoted father, casting some sympathy on the overworked nurse. Albee said about the second new scene, "I think it helps to clarify one or two possibly unclear motivations for the Nurse's later actions." In its final form, the play moves inexorably to the moment that a nurse in another hospital refuses admission to a dying Bessie, shouting at Bessie's companion, "I don't care who you got out there, Nigger. You cool your heels!" As always, there was the final irony, the attempt to deliver a dead black woman to a white hospital in the South. Albee decided to dedicate *Bessie Smith* to Ned Rorem and sent him a copy of the revised script. Rorem responded, "As a play now it dazzles with terror: we know where *we* are and who *they* are, and the theatrical 'trouvailles' seem original and should work."

The new scenes were written too late for insertion into the Berlin premiere. *Der Tod von Bessie Smith* opened on April 21, 1960, at the Schlosspark Theater, on a double bill with Arthur Miller's *Zweimal Montag (A Memory of Two Mondays)*. Albee was not there for the opening, but Braun, who translated the play into German, reported back to him that the director Walter Henn did a very good job and the evening was a success despite the fact that the cast "was not as good as it should have been." *The Death of Bessie Smith* was not presented in New York until January 24, 1961, when it joined *The American Dream* on a double bill at the York Playhouse, replacing *Bartleby*, a one-act opera by Flanagan and Albee.

Momentarily stumped for an idea for another play, Albee went back and looked at *The Dispossessed*, the last play he had written before *The Zoo Story*. From his new perspective, and very much with Ionesco in mind, he began reconceiving *The Dispossessed* as *The American Dream*. When Gian Carlo Menotti asked him to write a short piece for the Festival of Two Worlds at Spoleto, Italy, he took the characters of Mommy, Daddy, and Grandma from *The American Dream*, turned the Young Man into a kind of Angel of Death, put them on a beach, and presto, *The Sandbox*. *The Sandbox* was never done at Spoleto, but was given its first performance April 15, 1960, at the Jazz Gallery in Manhattan, with a score by Flanagan. It was one of a quartet of plays (two by Fernando Arrabal, one by H. B. Lutz, who paid for the cost of the production). The next year, *The Sandbox* was presented on the *Omnibus* television show, together with excerpts from *Krapp's Last Tape*, Ionesco's *The Killer*, and William Saroyan's *The Time of Your Life*. Albee was unhappy with the program. Everything was handled badly, he said, "the camera work, the direction, the acting (except for *The Sandbox*, where everyone was O.K." except for "the aging, muscle-brained" actor who played the Young Man). Only fourteen minutes long, *The Sandbox* moved Albee the most of his four short plays. It has remained one of his favorites, "an absolutely beautiful, lovely, perfect play."

The Sandbox was written for (and about) his grandmother, Grandma Cotter, his closest relative, the one member of the family with whom he had formed a lasting attachment. A crotchety and very amusing woman, she considerably brightened Albee's childhood and was a natural ally against his mother (her daughter)—and everyone else. When he left home, his one regret was having to leave Grandma Cotter behind. She died in 1959 at the age of eighty-three before her grandson's first play was produced in New York. Still estranged from him, his parents did not tell him of his grandmother's death, and he missed her funeral. He found out later, from "spies in the house of love, so to speak," that is, from a secretary in his father's office. *The Sandbox* is dedicated to his grandmother.

Grandma in *The Sandbox* and *The American Dream* was also inspired by the puppet Beulah Witch on Burr Tillstrom's *Kukla, Fran and Ollie* television puppet show. When Albee became successful, he was immediately asked to name his primary influences. He answered that he had been influenced by everyone from Sophocles to Noël Coward. Pressed for more names, he would

put Beckett, Genet, and Ionesco on the short list along with Chekhov, Pirandello, and Williams. Unmentioned but of equal importance to him were
James Thurber and Burr Tillstrom. This was no joke. In the case of both the
humorist and the puppeteer, Albee was a great admirer, not just of their sense
of comic absurdity in everyday life, but of the spontaneity of their dialogue
and their theatricality. In particular, Tillstrom was to be a major influence on
the writing of *The American Dream.*

As for Thurber, he had been a favorite since Albee's childhood. Albee read
every story he wrote and savored all his cartoons. He also savored *Winnie the
Pooh,* not, he makes it clear, Christopher Robin, but Pooh, Eeyore, Tigger,
and their animal friends, in his eyes a warming family, a group, one might
suggest, like *Kukla, Fran and Ollie.*

Albee said, "I do think the style of *The American Dream* has far less to do
with the influence of Ionesco, as some of our brighter pedants have said, than
with the influence of Burr Tillstrom." On his popular television show, Tillstrom created an amazingly lifelike contemporary version of Punch and Judy.
His characters slapped each other with wit. Though ostensibly a children's
show, it also became a favorite with adults. With Tillstrom, Albee went from
fan to friend, and one of his dream projects (unfulfilled) was to have the puppeteer stage a Kuklapolitan Player version of *The American Dream.* In his
mind, Albee had cast all the characters: Kukla as Daddy, Madame Oglepuss
as Mommy, Fran Allison as Mrs. Barker, and Oliver J. Dragon as the American Dream. Beulah was his particular favorite, and a natural to play
Grandma: To him, she *was* Grandma.

One time when Albee was in Chicago, he visited Tillstrom at his home.
"We were sitting in the living room having an after dinner drink, and Burr
said, 'Excuse me,' and went into another room. I wandered around, looking at
posters and photographs. I heard some rummaging back there and all of a
sudden, I heard a voice coming from the other room, 'Edward! It's Beulah.
Come in here.'" He went to the other room and there was the Kuklapolitan
stage all set up, with Tillstrom hidden behind it. "There was Beulah right on
stage, saying, 'Edward, I missed you. Come talk.' I pulled up a chair and we
sat and we talked for twenty or thirty minutes. It was wonderful. I remember it
being very, very exciting to be talking to Beulah. I liked her a lot. I had become a Kuklapolitan!"

Once, Tillstrom was driving Albee to his house in Montauk for the weekend, and there was a sudden proliferation of voices in the car. Tillstrom remembered, "The Kuklapolitans held forth in the driver's seat, with Beulah
calling out directions and Madame Oglepuss cautioning Ollie to slow down

for the next curve, etc., etc. I thought Edward was asleep during all this but when we finally stopped for breakfast, he opened one eye and very wryly said, 'If you think you can win me over with cheap imitations of your friends, you're mistaken.' I loved it! It's one of the best backhanded compliments I've ever heard—and I might add that I shut up for the rest of the trip."

In *The Sandbox*, Mommy and Daddy put Grandma out to pasture, or rather, they leave her at the beach (the sandbox) in the hands of a Young Man who is the Angel of Death (later he will be the title character in *The American Dream*). Grandma, "a tiny, wizened woman with bright eyes," is carried on-stage like a piece of sculpture and dumped in the sand. Her first intelligible words, spoken directly to the audience, are, "Honestly! What a way to treat an old woman! Drag her out of the house . . . stick her in a car . . . bring her out here from the city . . . dump her in a pile of sand . . . and leave her here to set. I'm eighty-six years old!" A musician is playing and she cuts him off. "I'm a feeble old woman . . . how do you expect anybody to hear me over that peep! peep! peep! There's no respect around here!" Then she reminisces about her life with her daughter and her husband, "They moved me into the big town house with *them* . . . fixed a nice place for me under the stove . . . gave me an army blanket . . . and my own dish . . . my very own dish! So, what have I got to complain about? Nothing, of course. I'm not complaining." For all practical purposes, Grandma is a housecat, though a family pet probably would be treated better.

Onstage, Grandma was personified by Sudie Bond, who was then in her early thirties, but was somehow able to transmogrify herself into an octogenarian. She had played Agnes Gooch in Barr's production of *Auntie Mame* on Broadway. Barr took Albee to see her as the Queen of Norway in *Bertha*, a comedy sketch by Kenneth Koch at the Living Theater. Albee fell in love with her. His favorite moment was when the Queen of Norway was so bored with everything she was doing that, in desperation, she turned to her generals and said, "Invade Norway!" Later he wrote about the actress, "She is young, she is tiny and I suspect she is crazy. Rather, she is either crazy or she is a genius—because, if she is not one of the two, one cannot explain the wild, antic humor she brings on the stage with her, the wild antic humor in tandem with a depth and poignancy of characterization that is absolutely staggering." All those qualities Bond brought to Grandma in the two Albee plays, in which she acted "with the wit and wisdom of the aged and the bouyancy and objectivity of the intelligent young. She is—well, perfect. She is my favorite grandmother." Beginning with *The Sandbox*, she made a career out of playing Albee's grandmother.

Fam and Yam was printed in the September 1960 issue of *Harper's Bazaar* (published in August just before the sketch was staged at the White Barn theater in Westport, Connecticut). Inge was horrified at what he considered to be an intrusion. In a letter to Ned Rorem, he said, "Don't become famous all of a sudden and turn around and write nasty pieces about me like your dirty little friend Edward Albee, in Harper's Bazaar. It's a piece that should bring him a great deal of embarrassment in time to come. God, what a smug little creature he must be, to write as though perfectly assured about his own future prestige." Apparently forgetting, or choosing to forget, their one meeting, he said, "And *where* did he find out all about *my* apartment?" Inge's astonishing Broadway success was soon followed by a series of disappointments. His plays closed quickly and critics and theatergoers deserted him. It was a sudden turnabout and the playwright soon found himself with no outlet for his work. In 1973, overcome by depression and acute alcoholism, he killed himself. He was an artist with a meteoric early career who was unable to survive failure.

6

Mommy and Daddy

Is the play offensive? I certainly hope so.

READING *The Dispossessed* and *The American Dream* side by side, it is difficult to see how one gave birth to the other. *The Dispossessed* is straightforward and naturalistic. *The American Dream* is an outlandish cartoon. The two plays have only one character in common, Grandma, and even she is different in each play. The grandmother in *The Dispossessed* is a bit of a nuisance. In *The American Dream* (and, of course, *The Sandbox*), she is devilish, daft, and a constant source of amusement. Where the two plays converge (and also differ in their attitude) is in their consideration of the American family. Long before the word dysfunctional was popularized, Albee stepped in with his scalpel and, without anesthesia, performed an exploratory operation on Mommy, Daddy, and their traditional values of marriage and parenting. Trying to trace the transition from *The Dispossessed* to *The American Dream*, I once said to Albee that *The Dispossessed* was *The American Dream* without a sense of humor. He laughed at the idea and then accepted it.

Even at his most depressed, Albee has never lost his humor, finding relief in bantering with his friends, reading Thurber or watching *Kukla, Fran and Ollie*. However, his writing before *The Zoo Story*—his plays as well as his poems—had a certain sobriety and self-consciousness. It was Writing, and, except for an occasional amusing line or phrase, it was not fun. *The Zoo Story*, for all its mordancy, opened the floodgates of his comic sensibility. One can ridicule Albee's announcement that he was born at the age of thirty, but it has a kind of ironic truth. The author of *Ye Watchers and Ye Lonely Ones* and *The*

Making of a Saint was not the author of *The Zoo Story* and *The American Dream*, and there is a good reason why he has rejected all his juvenalia. For one thing, the titles are steeped in pretension. From *The Zoo Story* on, the titles are exactly what the plays are about: Read a title, see a play.

As a child of luxury (and lovelessness), Albee was indoctrinated in the American dream. Work hard, study hard, apply oneself, take advantage of opportunity, and become a success. Get to know the right people, make a good impression, belong to the correct clubs. Marry well, generate a family, and live happily in consanguinity. Just like his parents? Who were his parents? As he realized, his adoptive parents were indolent, unproductive, uncommunicative, and prejudiced. As Noel Farrand said, he learned bigotry from Frankie Albee, and it was not just her casual racism, her cracks about ethnic minorities, but her dismissiveness about homosexuals, about any behavior she considered aberrant. Then there was Daddy, Reed Albee, whom his son could not touch emotionally or physically. Only with Grandma Cotter and with his growing family of friends could he find sanctuary and share a laugh. But the Albees at home were amusing, if unintentionally so. Edward (and Noel) could laugh at them. Edward could spoof them, privately; why not as a playwright onstage? And we would laugh (and possibly, secretly, if she were watching, Frankie Albee would be amused).

Albee is frank about his theatrical inspiration: "*The American Dream*, at least in its beginning, is a homage to Ionesco. I couldn't have written it in the manner I wrote it without him. It's also very clear that in *The American Dream* I go to a dehumanizing degree beyond Ionesco, certainly beyond *The Bald Soprano*, or any other of his short plays." With Ionesco—and Tillstrom—looking over his shoulder, he wrote *The American Dream*. After he wrote it, he freely admitted that the opening few minutes "had been intentionally stolen from *The Bald Soprano*." In common with *The Bald Soprano*, it begins with a middle-class married couple chattering about the inconsequentialities of their everyday life, or rather the wife is chattering while the husband pretends to listen. In the Ionesco, the husband "continues to read, clicks his tongue." Ionesco's Mr. and Mrs. Smith are definably English; everything about them is English, from his English pipe to the English clock that "strikes 17 English clock strokes." In *The American Dream*, everything about the unnamed couple is American, and in the American tradition, they call each other Mommy and Daddy, though in fact there are no offspring in this American household. The parents have already mutilated and dismembered their own child. The sterility of the characters is mirrored in the fact that there are no pictures in the frames on the wall.

Line after line rings with the sound of the Albees at home. "We were very poor!" says Mommy. "But then I married you, Daddy, and now we're very rich." Then Grandma intrudes with a rude remark about her own daughter: "If you'd listened to me, you wouldn't have married her in the first place. She was a tramp and a trollop and a trull to boot." In common with her real-life prototype, Grandma has a blind Pekingese dog. Soon the "van people" will come, to tote the old woman off to the nursing home. But first, here is Mrs. Barker, the paradigmatic clublady who makes herself at home. "Are you sure you're comfortable?" asks Mommy, adding with politesse, "Won't you take off your dress?" And so she does, in a single moment tilting the comedy into cuckooland.

When the play was first performed, the dress removal was a moment of shock, followed by a gasp of laughter. "The play was also about the break-down of language," the author explains. "That's why that scene was in there, not to shock, not to titillate. 'Take off your dress.' 'Don't mind if I do.'" One of his early attempts at a play, two untitled pages of dialogue, is entirely about the breakdown of language. A husband and wife cannot communicate. She speaks in gibberish because she has a hairpin in her mouth. "Bobble," she says over and over again.

Even as the comedy in *The American Dream* flirts with nonsense, it stays on the path of sequitur and it is filled with references to scenes from Albee's life. Grandma remembers a lady very much like Mrs. Barker who came from the Bye-Bye Adoption Service twenty years before and left off "a bumble of joy" that turned out to be the opposite: a troublemaker. Without a warranty, Mommy and Daddy wanted their money back. With that, in comes a new young man, handsome, happy, a real "bumble of joy," the American Dream incarnate, an identical twin to the late lost youth, another version of the "By-ronesque, blond perfect" male in *The City of People*. Later, in a different form, he will reappear as the imaginary child in *Who's Afraid of Virginia Woolf?* He is, the young man announces narcissistically, "almost insultingly good-looking in a typical American way." Momentarily, the play becomes serious as the title character confesses his inability to "touch another person and feel love" (that is his tragic flaw, like the lameness of the youth in the early play, *The City of People*). As orchestrated by Grandma, *The American Dream* quickly returns to comedy and ends in irony as everyone seems to get what he or she deserves. For Albee, *The American Dream* was a definite contrast to *The Zoo Story*, adding satire to his comic arsenal. The play was to qualify him as a charter member of the Theater of the Absurd, the phrase that the critic Martin Esslin coined to link the diverse experimentalists of the time. In his groundbreaking

1961 book *The Theatre of the Absurd,* Esslin traced influences back to James Joyce, the Surrealists, and Franz Kafka, but made a persuasive case for its newness in theater. For him, the "sense of metaphysical anguish at the absurdity of the human condition is, broadly speaking, the theme of the plays of Beckett, Adamov, Ionesco, Genet" and other writers discussed in his book, including Albee and Pinter. Esslin said that with *The American Dream,* Albee translated the Theater of the Absurd "into a genuine American idiom."

During the summer of 1960, with a production of *Bessie Smith* still not set in New York, Albee finished *The American Dream.* Adding to the work already done by James Hinton Jr. (who had withdrawn from the project), Albee had also completed the libretto for Flanagan's one-act opera *Bartleby,* a longtime project based on Herman Melville's story about a man completely divorced from reality. Whenever asked to do anything, Bartleby responds, "I would prefer not to." Barr decided to present *The American Dream* and *Bartleby* as a double bill, this time with Clinton Wilder as his coproducer. He gathered his production team, with Alan Schneider as the director. The cast included Gladys Hurlbut and John C. Becher as Mommy and Daddy, Jane Hoffman, Ben Piazza (as "the American Dream") and, of course, Sudie Bond as Grandma. Albee decided to dedicate *The American Dream* to Diamond and sent him a note telling him about the approaching opening. In passing, he talked about his success, "which has been gratifying, but certainly not sufficient to turn the head of anyone except the most gullible." It made him "only much busier with extraneous things than I would like, and has given me confidence in what I want to do."

Rehearsals began on January 3, 1961, while Schneider was still at the Actors Workshop in San Francisco. He sent a letter of advice to Albee, in effect telling him how to direct a play. First he should encourage the actors to familiarize themselves with the text. "Let them ask you any questions of specific nature . . . I would beware of philosophical or metaphysical speculation as much as possible. While this is going on I think it is valuable for you to tell them anything *you* want about the play's nature or meaning for you, give them every idea possible regarding the play's style, tone, texture. For example, what you said to me about the need for doing it 'loud and flat,' the question of Grandma's and the Young Man's being 'in and out' of the play, whatever else you feel important." Schneider suggested that he work on the scenery with William Ritman. "Middle-class bourgeoise inanity—whatever that is—is what we need . . . Then we need some way of having Daddy try to hang himself and then be able to get rid of the rope . . . What is critical is the right kind of unity, style, comment." If he were there, Schneider would tell the cast the play is "a

study of emptiness, of hollowness . . . a comedy of manners, a tragedy of feeling . . . a play about the corruption of values in the bourgeoise family . . . about
the substitution, without awareness, of the artificial for the real, of vacuity for
substance, of surface for essence." The style is "cartoon-like" but not stylized in
the sense of being distorted, the "logic is oblique but always present in character and situation," the characters "prototypes but also individuals."

Then he labeled each character: Mommy, a "tumescent monster"; Daddy,
an "acquiescent blob"; Mrs. Barker, a "professional woman . . . a cheerful
predatory robot"; Grandma, a "gentle shrewdie—knowing what's going on
and wanting to survive the emptiness and have the satisfaction of dying with
dignity"; and the Young Man, "like a 'homing pigeon' he heads for some kind
of personal completion somehow in spite of the emptiness. Does he get it?"
The last, he said, was the most difficult question for him. Although Schneider
seemed to understand the play instinctively, he did not understand his actors,
alienating many of them almost from the moment that he took over rehearsals several weeks later. As Hoffman remembers, he would often be overcome by a temper tantrum.

Two weeks before the play was scheduled to open, Hurlbut withdrew from
the cast because she was offended by some of her character's dialogue. Hoffman was moved up to the role of Mommy and Nancy Cushman took over the
role of Mrs. Barker. The double bill opened at the York Theater on January
24, 1961, with *Bartleby* as the curtain-raiser. Hoffman was appearing simultaneously in *Rhinoceros* on Broadway, fortunately only in the first act. Barr supplied a car for her and immediately after she left the stage, she was driven
across town to the York for *The American Dream*. One complication was the
fact that on Saturday, there were two evening performances of *The American
Dream*. For the actress, this meant a double trip across town. On the opening
night of *The American Dream*, there was a snowstorm, and Hoffman almost
missed the Off-Broadway curtain.

Howard Taubman, who had succeeded Atkinson as the *Times* drama critic,
praised the first scene of *The American Dream* and then proceeded to tear the
play apart. On the other hand, Walter Kerr was amused by an image "genus
Americanus 1961" that was "cruel and funny and hollow and eerily familiar,
and I'm pretty sure it serves us right." Neither liked *Bartleby*. Again, it was
Richard Watts who captured the spirit of an Albee play—and also noticed the
touch of Ionesco, saying it "is packed with untamed imagination, wild humor, gleefully sardonic satirical implications and overtones of strangely
touching sadness, and I thought it was entirely delightful."

Barr quickly axed *Bartleby* and substituted a dance piece by Valerie Bettis while waiting to bring together a production of *The Death of Bessie Smith*. Albee was angry at the treatment of *Bartleby*, more at the critics ("Damn those drama men for being dull-headed when they have to listen to anything more demanding than Richard Rodgers") than at his producer. He did, however, see the problems in an opera "that is concerned with the reverse of accepted action, with, in other words, regression, absence of the usual physicality; add to this the dilemma of the piece is moral and that the title figure is a pure non-hero, and the other major figure a contemplative man. Seems to me that valid theatricality can be made from these valid devices; but it makes it hard." In other words, how do you write an opera or even a play about a character who would prefer not to?

Albee was irritated, but Flanagan felt "damaged." In a letter to David Diamond, he said that the reaction to *Bartleby* "was the straw that broke not the camel's, but *my* back. But my general despondency—one that I can't seem to shake loose and one that has produced dismaying psychosomatic illnesses—is a two-year accumulation of many things." His woes included the breakup with Albee and the fact that he had been fired from his job as a music critic for the *Herald Tribune*. He grumbled about "the *Bartleby* fiasco" and "the shoddy way" Barr reacted. "Like replacing it hastily with Valerie Bettis, who got infinitely worse press than I did and did worse business." There had also been a problem with *Bessie Smith*. He had written a score for three instruments, but union rules would not allow him to use only one standby. In one day, he had to reduce the trio to one. Beneath it all was another heavier burden: He was also feeling the effects of Albee's sudden celebrity and his own eclipse.

As Diamond observed in a letter to Albee, "I wish it were *only* the *Bartleby* fiasco that is torturing Bill. I sensed something in Bill . . . I had not felt before: that he was agonizing for compensatory gain, if you get me: in other words, he liked stewing in his own juices if I may quote a great platitude . . . As the analyst would say: 'if you want to get well, it's all up to you; I can only help you get well.' " He added, "May I repeat again how happy I am about *The American Dream?* and bless you for cracking down on the USA imbeciles in the great tradition of an older friend of mine, Estlin Cummings!"

On March 1, *Bessie Smith* joined *The American Dream*, and critics returned, this time, it seemed, with an even greater respect for Albee's talent—except for Judith Crist, reviewing in the *Herald Tribune*. She called the play a "heavy-handed diatribe." On the other hand, Clurman said, "The writing of the play is biting, tensely risible, euphonious—making for heightened speech which approaches stylization. It marks Albee once again as a new American playwright from whom much is to be expected." As Clurman observed, the true tragedy of the play was not that of Bessie Smith but of the nurse, who was "caught in the same blind alley of a 'closed' society" as the ineffectual intern and the angry but passive black orderly. By the end of the play, the nurse flails out at "the disparity between things as they are, and as they should be." In this crucial speech, Albee evokes images that were to preoccupy him in all his subsequent work. Rae Allen as the embittered nurse was the center of a vibrant cast. As with *The Zoo Story* and *Krapp's Last Tape, The American Dream* and *The Death of Bessie Smith* settled in for a long run.

In May, Albee received an extraordinarily sympathetic letter from his uncle George Vigouroux, apologizing for not keeping in contact while Edward was estranged from his mother. He had seen *The American Dream* and had been very moved by the resonances it had of the Albees at home:

> A little I knew about your family life, and your growing up seemed you had hell on the ears and a boot in the ass. Whenever I wanted to communicate with you I was told no. You'll hurt Frances or Reed. There seemed no milk of human kindness, but I wanted you to have even a Christmas card or anything to know we were thinking about you and if you ever needed someone to lean on we'd be there.
>
> Since seeing your heart laid open on stage in *The American Dream*, the tender poignancy in your writing I realize more than ever your suffering. Your writing has the ring of truth and a positive force that your imagination might never bring to it. Strictly speaking my dear Edward you turned this emotional force into intellect, and rose above the situation, sadly no doubt, but for the world now to see, and be stirred, moved, and involved with. The casting superb, the direction excellent, and the guts on stage. Your guts. Solitary brooding can't help, but work can. This you have achieved. But love aches and the emptiness is always there.
>
> There never is anyone to confide in honestly and openly for fear, but your modesty impels me to give you a key to some of the double punches I've had also. It must depend on you whether I should open the door, many things you're involved in and very busy but if you have the time and my confidence will be kept secret I should like to.

And he closed, "So proud of you and my humble congratulations."

Albee responded with his own understanding of his uncle's double life as a gay man married to Aunt Ethel and besieged by other members of the family. In his response, Vigouroux unburdened himself of other resentments. After Ethel's first husband, Ted Lauder, died—the dentist who supervised the family's finances—Ethel was worried about who would take over that task. Then, said Vigouroux, Edward's mother, "Big Frances," as he called her, moved in. "Ted and Ethel's mother always said be careful of Frances—she's not to be trusted." He remembered that when Grandmother Albee died, Frances rushed over to the house and immediately walked away with the old woman's black bag containing jewelry and cash. According to Vigouroux, Frances had saved Edward's short stories, and one day in Reed Albee's office, she brought them out and said to her sister and brother-in-law that she was keeping them "in case I have to prove he wanted to kill me," that they would show that her son was insane. Vigouroux's comment: "What a strange horror she is and how lucky you are to be out of it. Edward you cannot be disinherited, you are entitled to one third of everything your father had and you must fight if necessary ... I hope I'm not sounding like a bastard but they have acted like ignorant, conniving children."

When *The Zoo Story* was performed with Strindberg's *Miss Julie* for a week in July at the Westport Country Playhouse in Connecticut, John M. Lupton, a state senator from Weston, compared the plays to "all the filth we export in our B movies and dirty plays." The plays, in repertory with John Van Druten's *I Am a Camera* and a shortened version of Tennessee Williams's *Sweet Bird of Youth*, were on their way to South America as part of a cultural exchange program. "There was a great to-do in Westport," Albee said. "Ladies formed committees, sent telegrams to the Secretary of State [Dean Rusk], protesting that the play was a disgrace, that it falsified the America we all know and love, that it was, in fact, thinly disguised communist propaganda." At Rusk's request, Adlai Stevenson went to Westport to check it out and "he said it was just swell." On the other hand, at Lupton's prodding, Prescott Bush (George Bush's father), a United States senator from Connecticut, got up on the floor of the U.S. Senate and denounced *The Zoo Story* as "filthy"—and demanded to know why it was going to represent America in Argentina. At the time, Albee was teaching a summer session at Wagner College on Staten Island. As he said, "That's where it all stands now. *The Zoo Story* is rotting inter-American relations in Buenos Aires, and I am furthering the Red cause on Staten Island."

Later that month, Albee traveled to Argentina with the acting company (drawn from the roster of the Actors Studio), and between making speeches and public appearances, he reported home on local conditions in Buenos Aires and on the state of his play. "Mr. Peron ruined this place when he ran it," he said. "Also, a kind of cultural isolation has produced ferocious intellectual activity in a vacuum, sort of unconsciously eclectic and very naive." *The Zoo Story*, with Ben Piazza and William Daniels, was presented in an eighteen-hundred-seat theater, "too big for the play, of course, but the great old Spanish renaissance theater—the Cervantes—we were supposed to go into burned down the day before the company arrived." His play "was received better than ever anywhere and plays to good houses." Piazza, Albee noted, "threatens to kill himself with homesickness," a feeling that, to a lesser degree, was shared by the playwright. The U.S. State Department, he said, "has ignored this tour like it was a turd . . . with the result that everyone else likes us very much." On July 31, Albee went to Rio de Janeiro for a rest. While he was there, on August 2, his father died; he did not return home for the funeral. "I never knew him at all," he said at the time. "That's the kind of sorrow I feel: for somebody I never knew."

Early in September, McNally went to Europe for ten months to travel with John and Elaine Steinbeck, as tutor to Steinbeck's two sons. His trip overlapped and occasionally intersected with a trip that Albee took to Germany and England. In October, in a reverse of the New York order, *The American Dream* joined *Bessie Smith* (and *The Zoo Story*) in the repertory at the Schiller Theater in Berlin, and later that month Tony Richardson directed a double bill of *The American Dream* and *Bessie Smith* at the Royal Court Theater in London. At the same time, *The Zoo Story* was a hit in Ankara, Turkey.

Albee decided to see the English and German productions. First he flew to London. He put up at the Park Lane Hotel, a far shot from his former bed and breakfast near the British Museum. He had dinner with McNally: "sat right on top of old Margaret Leighton and her faggy escort; he hissed; she chinkled her many, many rings—seven on three fingers—and looked around waiting to be recognized." Then he sat in on rehearsals of his play and reported: "The boy who plays the Dream has orange hair, scarlet gums, hips up around his armpits. But he acts so good. The director is pliant (to me) to the point where I lose respect for him daily; but I don't know what the English *want*! Maybe they'll love it all. More likely no. I don't know." From New York, Flanagan informed him, "Your fame continues to grow even in your brief absence, your name appearing in the public prints now rather than daily, hourly." Before he had left, Albee had seen Schneider's production of *Happy Days* and been disappointed in the play and in Ruth White's performance as Winnie. At the time, he hoped the show would run "if nothing less to spite that new idiot on *Time* who shuffles around like a drama critic." That unsigned critic had linked Beckett, Ionesco, and Albee as The New Exquisites. The Old Exquisites, Oscar Wilde "and the fin de siecle dandies," were "anti-bourgeois snobs." The new ones were "anti-life snobs." After Albee left New York, Flanagan went to see *Happy Days* and disagreed entirely with Albee's assessment; he was "terribly shaken" by the play. Later Albee agreed with Flanagan and decided it was probably the best performance of the play he had ever seen. In his next letter, Flanagan addressed Albee as "Dearest of the New Exquisites."

Before his plays opened in London, Albee went to Berlin for *The American Dream*. He stayed at the same pension, "the same dirt-cheap two room set-up, with the high ceilings, the enormous bed, the balcony, breakfast on it looking five flights down onto the main street, the same pumpernickle [sic] bread and jam, the same . . . most things. A lot different, though." One of the major changes was the erection of the Berlin Wall, separating the East and West sectors. "Last time, two years now, the city was booming, and while it's still pretty prosperous and content-looking on the surface, there are subtle differences: Fewer people out at night, fewer cars, fewer tickets sold to the Festival . . . all because the border is closed." After seeing the penultimate rehearsal of *The American Dream*, he said,

> *Der Americanische Traum* ist ein Deutsche traum if ever I saw one. Traum or night-traum I can't tell, yet. It's not really bad, except in this rehearsal they played it at just under one and three quarters hours, which is, nicht war?, a teensy bit slow. I told them to get it down to as close to an hour as they could manage, which will be an hour and a half. German speaks slower than U.S.—I mean it takes longer to say the same things—which accounts for part of it. The beast playing Mommy is the most incredible thing I've ever seen. She looks like a cross between Mae West and my mother, and is eight feet tall. Daddy is a wonderful lump, and Grandma is played by a spry 81 year old thing named something-Wagner, and she is quite wonderful. Mrs. Barker stinks, and the young man is not all what I hoped . . . you know: a magnificent young Nazi with blond hair, teeth and cheekbones; but he's not bad; dark, though, and a little too old.

He added, "I may go to the Kleist Kasino tonight or tomorrow night, to sit on the high bar stools, watch the German boys jitterbug, and make goo-goo eyes at the Kraut lovelies. Ach, such a feast to look at after the West End snits. Beautiful, beautiful boys. Shame they're all murderers at heart."

Flanagan's response was addressed to "Brunhilde, dear": "Your semi-literate pastiche arrived in yesterday's mail just as I had come to wonder if your continent-bound plane had fallen from the air and sagged into the waters of the English Channel." Recounting a story about a music critic being knocked down by a hit-and-run driver and left in the gutter on 12th Street as a drunk, almost dying, Flanagan expressed his "near-pleasure." He said he had never really hated anyone, but that critic had "caused me more grief and hurt than even I knew for me to react thus. Am I sick or just getting well-adjusted? Well adjusted *a la mode* Albee, I mean." Then he offered a cultural rundown from Manhattan: "Harold Pinter, you will be distressed to learn, is the *dernier cri* hereabouts: *The Caretaker* picked up a Krop of Klassy Klippings and even Walter Cur, who broached his customary reservations about non-sense-meaning avant-gardism, said he was a writer of quality. If reviews count, a hit it will be."

Albee returned to England for the out-of-town opening in Cambridge. He had doubts about both productions. *The American Dream* "will be lovely; there is no question about that. Whether it will be liked, or not, is another matter." He was still angry over the fact that British Equity would not allow black American actors to be in *Bessie Smith*. Richardson had cast Trinidadian actors "who talk in an English accent with a Calypso inflection" and "who can't act." Worst of all, the director "thinks the play is a piece of Chayevskian neo-television-realism. I scream as hard as I can, throw my hat down on the counter, and all the rest, insisting that the speeches must be arias, the gesture larger than life. They look at me like I'm an hysterical American queen (which, when you come right down to it, I suppose I am) and go right on. I go on television tonight, in part to pre-refute everything and everybody, which is probably a bad idea, but I will take it easy. People here have been generous and kind to me, which is nice, if foolish of them." McNally, who had been in Scotland, met Albee in Dublin for a few days, then Albee returned to London, "having decided to stay for the opening, come what may."

As he anticipated, the plays received mixed reviews. In the *Daily Mail*, Robert Muller praised *Bessie Smith* as "one of the most shattering exposures of Southern hysteria that I have seen on an English stage," but shrugged off *The American Dream* as "a sleeping pill." The reaction of Bernard Levin in the *Daily Express* was the opposite. He said *The American Dream* was a "sharp-eyed, funny, oblique look at the universal human passion for trivialities," while *Bessie Smith* "makes no memorable impact."

After Albee returned to America, McNally kept him posted on the English reception of *The American Dream* and *Bessie Smith*. McNally was furious at the Sunday reviews by Harold Hobson and Kenneth Tynan, especially the one from Tynan whom he accused of pontificating. "He writes about you as if you were dead, no longer in the process of developing your art, in a sense as if you were an Established Fact, like Shakespeare, and not as the still living, still maturing person that you are." Tynan, McNally said, "stubbed his toe mightily Sunday and I cannot help but be indignant that . . . the very best young playwright I know of, is the cause—and victim—of this fall from grace." With a certain snobbishness, Tynan said that Albee was "one of the few young American dramatists—Arthur Kopit and Jack Gelber are among the others—about whose future I feel more than a passing curiosity." Then he pigeon-holed *Bessie Smith* as a "safe protest" and *The American Dream* as a "safe chuckle." Trying to explain the hostility of the reviews to Albee, Tony Richardson said, "A lot of it is based on sheer prejudice against Americans generally" and was also part of a backlash against plays written in this style, "of the Pinter/Ionesco/Simpson school."

In response to his critics (and his censors), Albee later wrote about *The American Dream:*

> The play is an examination of the American Scene, an attack on the substitution of artificial for real values in our society, a condemnation of complacency, cruelty, emasculation and vacuity; it is a stand against the fiction that everything in this slipping land of ours is peachy-keen.
>
> Is the play offensive? I certainly hope so; it was my intention to offend—as well as to amuse and to entertain. Is it nihilist, immoral, defeatist? Well, to that let me answer that *The American Dream* is a picture of our time—as I see it, of course. Every honest work is a personal, private yowl, a statement of one individual's pleasure or pain; but I hope that *The American Dream* is something more than that. I hope that it transcends the personal and the private, and has something to do with the anguish of us all.

Albee now had four plays produced, but all were short and even as he was surrounded by crosscurrents of adulation and invective, people wondered what was going to be his next move. Could he, would he write a full-length play? And if so, what would it be like? Would the promise fade or would there be at least a kind of fulfillment? Back in 1960, after the opening of *The Zoo Story,* Albee had talked about writing a play about two faculty couples. The following year, after seeing *The American Dream* in Berlin, he drove with Stefani Hunzinger to Frankfurt. On the way, he told her that he was writing a new play and summarized the story. She recalled, "I know that he said, 'She has a son and she and her husband are talking about that son—and she hasn't a son.' I said, 'You mean she has a son and she hasn't a son?' He said, 'You'll see.'" Later, back in New York, thinking about the play in progress, he remembered a line from his past, a scrawl in soap on a barroom mirror, "Who's Afraid of Virginia Woolf?"

7

Blood under the Bridge

*Albee . . . is currently . . . writing a two-act play that
seems unlikely ever to appear on a midtown mar-
quee. Its title is* Who's Afraid of Virginia Woolf?

TIME MAGAZINE, FEBRUARY 2, 1961

A s Albee describes the genesis of *Who's Afraid of Virginia Woolf?* or any
of his plays, there is something almost mystical about the process. As he says,
"I will discover one day that I am thinking about a new play, which means
that it's been in my unconscious and I am informing my conscious mind that
I have been thinking about it. I'll put it back again. I'll forget about it. It will
pop up again a few weeks later and I will discover that I have thought more
about it." The characters appear: " 'Hello, here we are.' Pirandello time." In
effect, they say, *Write us.* "I make experiments with my characters before I
trust them in a play of mine. I will do a form of actor's improvisation. I'll take
a long walk on the beach with the characters, who I plan to have in the play
that I haven't written yet. I will put them in a situation that won't be in the
play, and I will improvise dialogue for them to see how well I know them."

Gradually the play takes shape—before a word is written down. In contrast
to those playwrights who are, as he says, "hopelessly didactic and plot everything out," Albee makes no notes and there is no outline. In his head, there is
"the playwright's file cabinet," in which he places things he has heard or seen.
"I make the assumption that the play knocks on the conscious part of my
brain, which is why it keeps coming into focus before I write it down." When
he senses that the work is ready, he begins to write in longhand (his handwrit-

ing is difficult to read—even for him). "When I start putting a play to paper, I have no idea what the first line is going to be. I have some idea of the destination, some flash of how it's going to end, but I have no idea how I'm going to get from the beginning to the end. But then the reality of the situations and the characters take over."

Sometimes this process is brief, other times it takes place over a period of years, in a few cases as long as ten years. This is, one might suggest, something like the birth of a baby, and as Beckett said, it can be "a difficult birth." The baby—the play—emerges intact. It would not be a reach of the metaphor to add that some "children" are healthier than others, but that Albee, as mother and father, loves them all.

From his point of view, the early plays were as long as they needed to be, but having experimented with style as well as thematic substance, he was now ready to try something larger and more deeply textured. The one-acts were written in a relatively short period of time. Naturally, the full-length play, almost four times longer than any of the short plays, took considerably longer to write. He says that he wrote most of *Virginia Woolf* within four to six months in 1961. But the earliest documentation of the play goes back as far as February of the previous year when he was working on a full-length play called *Exorcism*. Early in what he calls the "thinking-as-opposed-to-writing part of working on the play," he realized that the characters were going to use the quotation, "Who's afraid of Virginia Woolf?" Four or five months later, when he was well into the writing of the play, he decided to use the sentence as a subtitle. Then *The Exorcism* became the title of the third act and the play became *Who's Afraid of Virginia Woolf?* Despite the skepticism of that unsigned writer at *Time* magazine, *Who's Afraid of Virginia Woolf?* became one of the most memorable catchphrases in theatrical history.

It is relatively easy to trace the sources, both personal and theatrical, of the one-acts. *The Zoo Story* came out of Albee's experiences living in New York in the 1950s and working as a Western Union messenger, and the play was influenced by Jean Genet and Tennessee Williams. *The American Dream* and *The Sandbox* were inspired by his childhood experiences with his parents and his grandmother, and they were influenced by Ionesco and Burr Tillstrom. At first glance, *Who's Afraid of Virginia Woolf?* would seem to have no precedents in his own life. Albee lasted only a year and a half at Trinity College and he is homosexual; and yet the play deals with modern marriage in academia. He is, of course, an intuitive expert on both matters, as a survivor of his parents' marriage and a veteran of three exclusive prep schools, as well as Trinity.

As he readily admits, the play owes a thematic debt to *The Iceman Cometh*, taking a position the reverse of O'Neill's. In *The Iceman,* O'Neill had demonstrated the psychological ravaging that can occur when people are stripped of their pipe dreams. In his play, Albee demonstrates the need to free oneself of such fantasies. "O'Neill says you have to have false illusions. *Virginia Woolf* says get rid of them." He also said, "The play is about people of more than average intelligence getting to the point where they can't any longer exist with a whole series of games, tricks and false illusions, and then knocking down the entire untenable superstructure. The end result: something may or may not be built in its place. Everybody plays games. I think the games that my family played were far more traditionally structured," games about role-playing and keeping up appearances. "The play was built around the destructive forces of various falsities in relationships, the self-deceptions." Whenever he has been asked the meaning of his title, Albee has answered, with variations, that it "means who's afraid of the big, bad wolf, which means who's afraid of living life without delusions?" Although the academic environment is essential to the play, the foreground is the marriage itself; the battle (and the love) between George and Martha; the lies, deceits, and futile hopes that have held them together; and the contest of wills they play with their guests, Nick and Honey.

When he first revealed the title, Albee said, "But it's not a funny play. It deals with two couples in the course of a degrading, drunken two A.M. party. The older couple have created a fantasy child of nineteen, whom they drag out to advance their divergent viewpoints. The father eventually decides the child must be exorcised."

In November 1960 Albee said in a letter to David Diamond that he was halfway through the play. There were problems in the writing, and it was not until the summer of 1961 that he was able to resolve all the difficulties. For three months, he rented Morris Golde's house on Water Island, an outlying stretch of Fire Island. Golde was a good friend of Albee, Flanagan, and Rorem, among others, and was known as a great benefactor of contemporary American music. Whenever Golde himself was in residence on Water Island, his house was a gathering spot for celebrated composers and writers. Frank O'Hara had been on his way from Golde's house when he was fatally struck by a Fire Island beach taxi. For much of the time that Albee was there that summer, Terrence McNally was his housemate before McNally left to travel with the Steinbecks. Because McNally was at Golde's, Flanagan declined to visit. In any case, the focus for Albee was on his work in progress. He vowed to finish the play, then in two acts, by the end of the summer or "die trying." The house, which was not electrified, was isolated and Albee's workdays were long and uninterrupted.

He finished the first act in June, "right on schedule," he reported to Rorem. "The first of two acts, and the damned act is one hundred two pages long." In contrast, the whole of *The American Dream* was seventy pages. "I'm afraid I shall have an irritated and snappish audience (what's left of it), at intermission. Maybe the second act will be no more than twenty pages. But that would be lopsided, wouldn't it?"

Taking a break from writing, Albee left Water Island in July to be a writer in residence (along with Saul Bellow and Robert Lowell) at the Wagner College Writers Conference on Staten Island. Two of the hopeful playwrights at the conference were Paul Zindel and Loree Yerby. Together they interviewed Albee for a piece that appeared the following year in the Wagner literary magazine. Speaking to them in July 1961 about his work in progress, Albee said, "The play—I think—is going to be three acts, although I don't know at the moment, and I don't care . . . The only thing I can tell you about the action is that it concerns the exorcism of a nonexistent child, and that most of the last part of the play is going to be in Latin. I think it has something to do with what I thought *The American Dream* had to do with—the substitution of artificial for real values in this society of ours. It's sort of a grotesque comedy."

While Albee was at Wagner College, he and Rorem exchanged letters in which each spoke about the fact that Flanagan had spent a brief time at Bellevue Hospital for his acute alcoholism. Albee said about Flanagan: "He is chastened (horrified and remade) by his experience in Ward 07 at Belleview. I imagine he will not drink *at all* for a year or so (like the fifteen months I was off it), and if he ever goes back I also imagine it will be manageable."

When he returned to Water Island, he worked on *Virginia Woolf*, finishing the first two acts and twenty pages of the third act. Before McNally left to join the Steinbecks, Albee read part of the play aloud to him. At the end of the summer, he returned to New York. As Rorem remembers, one night the two of them were out drinking until 3 A.M., when Albee suggested that Rorem come back to his apartment and he would read the first two acts of his new play to him. "I'm bored when people read aloud to me," said Rorem, "but the minute he started, I was taken, grabbed by it. He read and read—and you know how long the play is—and one climax followed another, and another wave of theatricality would come over. Then he told me how the third act would end. To make me attentive—Ned, drunk, at three in the morning—that means a play has to have strength."

Throughout the fall, McNally wrote Albee from his various stops with the Steinbecks and invariably asked about the progress on *Virginia Woolf*. In De-

cember, McNally wrote from Venice, calling the play "Betty Wolfe," a reference to the fact that from the beginning, Bette Davis was Albee's choice to
play the leading role. In his letter, McNally said that the play should be on
Broadway, that to do it Off-Broadway would be a retreat. He had thought
about it a great deal since Water Island: "The dilemma of George/Martha will
not leave me. You have written brilliantly before, but not like this. There is a
quality of razor-blades here. Clean slices, one after the other. How does the
dissection come out? I think I know but send the final conclusions." In letter
after letter, McNally impatiently awaited the arrival of *Who's Afraid of Virginia Woolf?*, aka "Miss Wolfe," aka "Betty Wolfe."

By January 1962, Albee had finished the play. It was three acts and three
hours, and with revisions it was to get even longer. In a letter to David Diamond, he acknowledged completion of the play and spoke about Flanagan:
"Bill's collapse, as Bill will have it, came not so much from Terrence's presence in my life as from the loss of me in his. But, who knows? Bill is func-
tioning now, though without any great enthusiasm, for anything, and
whatever decisions he has made about cause and effect are the ones he can
live with."

As *Virginia Woolf* evolved, it dealt with the hellish marriage of a middle-
aged faculty couple: Martha, the termagent daughter of the president of New
Carthage College; George, her somewhat younger, acerbic husband, once a
faculty prize as history professor, now an academic failure. In Martha's word,
George is a "bog." Returning home from a late party at the president's house,
George and Martha continue their habit of mutual abuse, in which each
ridicules the other and purposely misunderstands the other. The difference
this evening is that Martha has asked a new young faculty couple, Nick and
Honey, back to their house for a nightcap. That nightcap turns into a long
night's journey into truth and illusion.

In the course of the play's three tumultuous acts, four games are played,
Get the Guests, Hump the Hostess, Humiliate the Host, and Bringing Up
Baby, and more are hinted at. The house is a field of games. The principal
contest is between George and Martha, who seem to live in a kind of marital
boxing ring: gloves off, no-holds-barred, no referee. The other couple are
pawns in their assault: Nick the opportunist, the personification of historical
inevitability, the man seemingly on the rise who will do anything to get there,
including bedding the college president's daughter; and Honey, his childlike,
childless bride, who drowns her unhappiness in alcohol. They are easy prey
for George, and a great deal of the play's humor comes from his attack on
them as he pounces on their words and on their vulnerabilities. Martha is his

primary target, as he is hers. In one of many moments of truth, Martha says George married her for her ability to fight with him. They are locked into their life together, and Nick and Honey are momentary witnesses to the self-destruction and the odd but lingering love that Martha and George share.

As Martha finally says to Nick, George is her one true love: "George who is good to me, and whom I revile; who understands me, and whom I push off; who can make me laugh, and I choke it back in my throat; who can hold me, at night, so that it's warm, and whom I will bite so there's blood; who keeps learning the games we play as quickly as I can change the rules; who can make me happy and I do not wish to be happy, and yes I do wish to be happy. George and Martha: sad, sad, sad."

"George who is good to me." Remember James Agee: "One is my mother who is good to me. One is my father who is good to me." The pivotal line in Martha's speech is "who keeps learning the games we play as quickly as I can change the rules." Each gauges the other for marksmanship: They are co-equals on the field of battle.

George is a storyteller, and as always, the truth is "for me to know and you to find out." Did he accidentally kill his mother with a shotgun, or is this a fanciful creation simply meant to jar his guests? It is, in any case, a wild, hilarious, and horrifying tale ("When I was sixteen and going to prep school, during the Punic Wars . . ."), an Albee set-piece that has come to be known as "the bergin" story. One night the boy who killed his mother orders drinks with friends and fumblingly asks for "bergin" instead of bourbon. As was noted earlier, the story came from an incident in Albee's life, when he was a student at Choate and drinking with his friends at Nick's in Greenwich Village. In George's telling of the story to Nick, the boy later is driving with his father on a country road and swerves to avoid hitting a porcupine and crashes into a tree. The father is killed and after the boy recovers from his injuries, he is placed in an asylum. George says that he is still in the asylum and has not "uttered one sound" for the past thirty years. Despite that ending, the inference in the air is that George was the young man who had killed his parents. Martha says that George wrote a novel about a boy who killed his mother and father. That, he said, is "blood under the bridge." A second inference could also be drawn: that for Albee the accidental deaths were also a kind of wish fulfillment for a boy who felt so removed from his adoptive parents.

The strangest section in *Virginia Woolf* deals with George and Martha's imaginary son, referred to as "sunny-Jim," whom they have made up and use as a kind of cement in their marriage. They have vowed never to talk about this secret in public. Tonight, Martha breaks that vow, which leads George to declare open season on Martha and their "child," finally "killing" him on the eve of his twenty-first birthday as the guests watch in horror and disbelief. The idea of an imaginary child probably has its origin deep in Albee's past. His parents, in common with George and Martha, were unable to have children of their own. They were, in his word, "barren," as was also true of his father's sister Ethel and her husband. The Albees of that generation were barren, and, again in Edward's phrase, they had come "to the end of their line." In that generation, it would probably not occur to couples to decide not to have children. The absence of children was generally seen as something biological, and in some cases, cause for embarrassment. Why could they not have children, and whose fault was it? Years later, of course, attitudes would change, and there would be methods to counteract a couple's infertility.

It could be suggested that Reed and Frances Albee "made up" Edward, although, of course, he was the equivalent of their real son. When he left home (just before his twenty-first birthday), he banished himself—and they banished him—from their lives. After Edward left, one wonders if they spoke about him, and if so how often they spoke about him and in what circumstances. Perhaps like George and Martha, they imposed a restriction against such conversation—or perhaps not. It is possible that some, or all, of these thoughts were going through Albee's mind, or his subconscious, as he invented the idea of an imaginary child.

Skeptics—and there were many—repeatedly held the play up to a mirror of expectation, not realizing that Albee had written a different kind of play, partly a reinvention of Strindberg, for a time when the world was spinning awry. The political commentary in *Virginia Woolf* is not only playful, it is also integral. George's commentary on chromosomes and genetic alteration leads him into a prophecy about the decline of history. Albee says that the reference to George and Martha Washington was supposed to be "a small irony, not a large truth." The problems of all the characters are endemic to their time, continuing through today, beginning with sexual and academic politics. As much as anything the play is about lost illusions (as in Balzac), the price of failure, and the methods that people use to survive and to postpone inevitability.

With *The Zoo Story* and *The American Dream*, Albee had mastered the short play form. People were anticipating a full-length play, but no one expected him to write such an ambitious one—a direct challenge to O'Neill and other daring playwrights: an all-through-the-night, deeply personalized duel that ended in a catharsis, as George poses the title question and Martha admits, "I . . . am . . . George . . . I . . . am." *Virginia Woolf* was to break dramatic ground, creating its own style of heightened naturalism. In a time when plays were shrinking to two acts, it was expansive, drawing its audience in for three and a half hours. In a time, when—with Walter Kerr's encouragement—domestic comedies like *Never Too Late* and *Any Wednesday* were turning Broadway into a desert (one that would later shift its light weight to television situation comedies), *Virginia Woolf* would force theatergoers to confront themselves. Cynics and self-appointed censors were lying in wait, determined to shoot down the author at all costs, but as it turned out, the play was to prove to be both innovative and remarkably resilient. The one-acts were a warm-up for the main attraction, a play that fully established Albee's reputation as a playwright. He was to write many more plays, but *Virginia Woolf* was to be the cornerstone of his career: One play feeds all. In it, we can see strands reaching back to *The Zoo Story* (the act of confession, death as the final relief) and *The American Dream* (the household as microcosm) and forward to *A Delicate Balance* (the meaning of friendship and loyalty) and *Three Tall Women* (the price of parenting, the tricks of memory).

Some friends of Albee have said that some of the linguistic sparring between George and Martha—the brilliant, snappish dialogue, the matching of insult and retort—sounds like Albee and Flanagan. In their circle, they were legendary for their wit and also their malice, and friends were quick to say that the general tenor and even specific lines came from life. Richard Howard believes that the foursome of himself, Flanagan, Albee, and Sanford Friedman, at least partly inspired the dialogue. Charles Strouse had a curious feeling of déjà vu when he saw the play. With its sharpness, it was "like hearing Bill talking," and there were also echoes of Farrand, Albee, and even of Strouse himself. He said to his wife at the time: "It's like all of us talking." A line like "hump the hostess," he said, was pure Flanagan.

Albee freely admits that Flanagan influenced the play. "Some of it obviously came from the arguments Bill and I used to have together," he says, "but the invention of the university setting, the invention of those other two characters—I have no idea where they came from. Obviously my mind was using things in my own experience, and translating them completely." His days at Choate and Trinity and his closeness to members of the faculty clearly filtered into the play, but as always, transformed into a fictional reality. The characters are also not strictly academic, though they are clearly academically inclined. "I knew a lot of people who were intelligent, stayed up late and drank a lot. I was not thinking at all that I was writing about Bill and me when I was writing about George and Martha. I knew that I was inventing characters."

Asked where Martha comes from, he says, "I don't remember," words often heard from him. From your mother? "Oh, no." More Flanagan than your mother? "Yes, certainly, but I don't think that's very important. I really don't know what the sources are." He has always been adamant about one subject. The play was written about two heterosexual couples and that is how it is meant to be performed. If he had wanted to write about two homosexual couples, he would have written the play that way, and to have men play the women's roles would subvert the essence of the work. As he says, "I know I did not write the play about two male couples." At the same time, it is also clear that a great deal of the dialogue could be said alternately by gay or straight people. "There's not that much difference between straight and gay couples in their fights," Albee says. He sees the universality in relationships and of language, as exemplified in his own personal life. He has had several sequential relationships, the equivalent of marriages. Elaine Stritch says, "It is mind-boggling what Edward Albee knows about the heterosexual relationship."

In April 1961, he told Diamond that "Mommy and Daddy, disguised, turn up again in *Who's Afraid of Virginia Woolf?*, the two act job I'm trying to make sense of now, and I suspect (as you suggest) that they will turn up again." By "Mommy and Daddy," he could have meant his adoptive parents or their stand-ins, Mommy and Daddy in *The American Dream*, or more likely, some combination of the two couples. As it grew, *Virginia Woolf* departed widely from what we know of the Albees, but in George and Martha's contest—his weakness, her strength—there is at least a semblance of his parents' real-life relationship, and metaphorically their talk about their imaginary child bears a connection to the Albees' attitude toward their adopted child. In terms of that child, George and Martha are akin to Mommy and Daddy in *The American Dream*. Those earlier characters have dismembered their own son. That theme itself, the theme of the lost or forgotten child, the imaginary child, of parents playing games with paternity, is one that is endemic to Albee's work, from his apprentice plays and stories all the way through to *The Play about the Baby*, which was written in 1997. So many of his plays, not the least *Who's Afraid of Virginia Woolf?*, center on the Baby. Who is the Baby? And did Edward Albee himself have a twin (in his mind if not in reality), a better behaved, more cherished twin, the apple of his parents' eye, the best behaved bumble on the block? Is there a doppelganger in the house?

Or did he simply make it all up: an imaginary imaginary child? Pressed to explain the relationship between the use of reality and the use of fiction, he said, "We're all scavengers. We scavenge anything. We use anybody who will be useful to us. We appropriate. And we even take our own past and translate it into another character, and it is no longer our past. It carries no emotional baggage—from its source to its new appropriation."

Albee denies that George and Martha have any relevance to his father and mother, saying, "I liked George and Martha. I did not like Mommy and Daddy very much. I think that may be a false lead." He adds that unlike George, his father was a passive character. But he does admit that the two characters evoke "the Mommy/Daddy syndrome," with reference to the "nonexistent child and the destroyed child in *The American Dream*—I mean obviously I was aware of some connective thematic tissue."

The concept of the imaginary child was to become a subject of great controversy, an obstacle to those who otherwise appreciated the play and evidence of Albee's failure as a dramatist to those who disparaged the play. Some were to wonder if the child were necessary. Later, when Ernest Lehman was writing the screenplay for the Mike Nichols movie version of the play, he was determined to make the child real, alive then dead, which would, of course, have been a corruption of Albee's basic premise. What was often overlooked is that the child is the fulcrum of George and Martha's fantasy. It is their major invention, and it holds them together in their own imaginary world. Could two otherwise intelligent, sophisticated people create such a fiction? Parents are always creating fictional images of their children, of what they want them to be, what they think they can be, and when expectations are unfulfilled, fantasies can continue. Albee simply took this to a symbolic level and dramatized it cleverly and craftily. Still it was a difficult theory for some theatergoers and critics to accept.

Asked if he always knew there was going to be an imaginary child, he said, "I must have. I like to keep these things secret from myself. If I begin to analyze the implications, the meanings, the metaphors of everything in the play before I write it down, I don't think I'd have as much enthusiasm for going on with it."

In contrast to Harold Pinter and others who can remember the exact image, visual or verbal, that sets off a play, Albee is usually unsure about such matters. However, he says he remembers the moment he began *Virginia Woolf*: "Bare stage, nobody there. A lot of laughter offstage. Door open. I remember seeing somebody very much like Martha come in, kick her shoes off and say, 'Jesus H. Christ.' I knew that she was going to say 'Jesus H. Christ,' but I didn't know that I knew it, because I hadn't done that transition yet from author to character into play. I don't know if I even knew 'What a dump' was happening. Not knowing what I was going to write after the first couple of lines." Those words sprang into his mind? No, "they sprang into Martha's mouth." And the play was off and running, as George and Martha invited us in to share their vituperation, and as Nick and Honey arrived, just in time for the first game of Get the Guests (another phrase that was to enter the American lexicon).

"What a dump," of course, derives from Bette Davis. It was a line that she spoke in the 1949 movie *Beyond the Forest* (in which she costarred with Joseph Cotten). Some of Bette Davis and the characters she played in that film and others rubbed off on Martha. Martha is partly Bette Davis, or at least she is playing at being Bette Davis, a doubly interesting fact when one considers that Davis was Albee's first choice for the film version of *Virginia Woolf*, and, at least covertly, for the stage version. For stage or film, she would have been ideal casting. The Davis persona, as we know it, was harsh, acerbic, diabolic, bitchy, sexy, a little vulgar, and when she wanted to be, hilarious. All these adjectives apply equally to Martha.

As always with Albee, the play is resonant with literary and theatrical imagery. The third act begins with Martha entering like the drunken porter in *Macbeth*. She is, in her words, "deserted" and "abandon-ed." In her monologue, she suddenly mentions "The Poker Night," which was the original title of *A Streetcar Named Desire*. Albee says he put that in the play "to amuse Tennessee." At one point, George and Martha have an insult contest ("Monstre!" "Cochon!" "Bete") that is a homage to Didi and Gogo's insult contest in *Waiting for Godot*.

In terms of influence, the obvious one—besides O'Neill—is Strindberg, especially *Dance of Death*, as a long-married couple play marital war games with one another. There is also, Albee admits, "a lot of Thurber in *Virginia Woolf*," especially in the beginning of the second act as George mimics Nick and intentionally misinterprets what he says, and as George and Martha move into their ritual ordeal of attack and counterattack. In common with Thurber, in Albee's work there is great disparity between what people say and what people think. Albee's Thurber is not the fantasist of *The Secret Life of Walter Mitty* (one of his least favorite Thurber stories) but the comic realist of *One Is a Wanderer* and *The Evening's at Seven*. *One Is a Wanderer* is about a man who has had "too many nights alone." A walker in New York City, he goes from his hotel to his office and back to his hotel, where he has several brandies in the lobby. "Out of remembrance comes everything," he thinks, and whistles to keep from remembering: "disturbing fragments of old sentences, old scenes and gestures, hours, and rooms, and tones of voice, and the sound of a voice crying." Similarly, in *The Evening's at Seven* a man finds his home alone in a hotel. Outside in the city, "a siren screamed its frenzied scream . . . a little like an anguish dying with the years."

Albee and Thurber share a comic sensibility and an understanding of the difficulty of trying to maintain an equilibrium on the marital tightrope, of the secrets that bind couples together and also tear them apart. In Thurber's story *The Breaking up of the Winships*, a married couple, Gordon and Marcia Winship, have a bruising argument after seeing Garbo in *Camille*. As they move on from Benedictine to Scotch and soda, "their words came out sharp and flat and stinging." In the beginning, the battle is about the movie, which Gordon had not liked very much and which Marcia had been crazy about. Thurber writes:

> Her sentences were becoming long and wavy, and her words formal. Gordon suddenly began to pooh-pooh her; he kept saying "Pooh!" (an annoying mannerism of his, I have always thought). He wouldn't answer her arguments or even listen to them. That, of course, infuriated her. "Oh, pooh to you, too!" she finally more or less shouted. He snapped at her, "Quiet, for God's sake! You're yelling like a prizefight manager!" Enraged at that, she had recourse to her eyes as weapons and looked steadily at him for a while with the expression of one who is viewing a small and horrible animal, such as a horned toad. They then sat in moody and brooding silence for a long time, without moving a muscle, at the end of which, getting a hold on herself, Marcia asked him, quietly enough, just exactly what actor on the screen or on the stage, living or dead, he considered greater than Garbo. Gordon thought a moment and then said, as quietly as she had put the question, "Donald Duck."

Substitute George and Martha for Gordon and Marcia and this passage could have been written by Albee, and the dialogue could have come from *Who's Afraid of Virginia Woolf?* It is even possible to imagine that Thurber, in common with Albee, had thought of his characters, Gordon and Marcia Winship, as stand-ins—at a considerable remove, of course—for George and Martha Washington.

Or one could regard Albee himself as a surrogate for Thurber's Bernard Hudley, who in *Afternoon of a Playwright*, says, "I'm trying to outline a drawing-room comedy of horror . . . but a note of hope, even of decency, keeps creeping into it." A drawing-room comedy of horror is actually a suitable description for *Who's Afraid of Virginia Woolf?* And haunting Albee was the image of Douglas Bryce in *The Waters of the Moon*, an author who "ran out of ideas and his command of sentence construction at the same time, on a

Wednesday. He died in 1932, on his chinchilla farm, and only the hat-check girl, Dolores, was at his bedside." Scribbled on the bathroom wall were the words, "The Shore; The Plain; The Mountain, a trilogy by Douglas Bryce," under which he had written "A monumental achievement," signed Van Wyck Brooks. Thurber wrote, "The reservoir of his natural talent had run dry and he had been reaching for the waters of the moon." Under everything, he wrote, "a trilogy wilogy by Brycey-Wycey."

For all Albee's appreciation of Thurber, Albee is himself the more probing artist. Thurber cartoons instill the dialogue of Albee's plays, but with Albee there are currents beneath the captions. His game is a blood sport, and the stories told by his characters—the story of Jerry and the dog, the bergin story, the cat story in *A Delicate Balance*—are not only hilarious, they are also horrific.

Long after Thurber died and long after some people dismissed him as a humorist, Albee's admiration continued unabated. For years, he and Noel Farrand would quote chapter and caption to one another, and Albee on his own still does. He is obsessive in his devotion to the writer (and is on the board of Thurber House, the museum that was the writer's boyhood home in Columbus, Ohio). "Thurber was a very serious social commentator and also sadly funny," he says, using words that also describe himself. These facts of Thurber have not been clear in the stage and film adaptations of his work. With a laugh, Albee becomes heretical: "To hell with Beckett, to hell with Ionesco. It's Burr Tillstrom and James Thurber. They're the real influences on me."

One might have thought that after *The Zoo Story* and *The American Dream*, *Who's Afraid of Virginia Woolf?* might have sailed into production, but the opposite was true; and one of the problems was the language. For some potential producers, it was too outspoken. Both Barr and Wilder had their doubts about it; Cheryl Crawford and others at the Actors Studio were afraid of it. But Billy Rose, an emblem of Broadway commercialism, loved it. On the other hand, many actors who were approached were hesitant about taking the risk.

Among the first to read the manuscript were Barr and Alan Schneider. Both had been waiting for the play, and Schneider was already somewhat familiar with it. He had read and worked on the first scene, eighteen minutes long, in 1961, using it as part of a program on WNET, Channel 13 in New York, called *Playwright at Work*. As it turned out, that program was delayed until after the play opened on Broadway in October 1962. In the television excerpt, Schneider had cast Sheppard Strudwick and Peggy Feury in the two principal roles. Recalling that scene, he said, "The dialogue crackled" in an encounter in the "battle game" of marriage. About a year later, in the spring of 1962, he and Barr read the completed version of the play. With the two sitting side by side, Barr passed him pages after he had read them. Schneider kept thinking of Strindberg and O'Neill—and Albee, who, he said, "was piercing the darkness with these unexpected, pulsating flashes of light." Martha and George "were like dinosaurs battling on the cliff of emotional survival." After that initial reading, Barr called the play "remarkable, maybe too remarkable for Broadway," and the director thought Barr might be correct in his assessment. Schneider telephoned Albee and told him he loved it. Although he obviously kept his feelings to himself, Barr already had second thoughts.

The artist Roger Baker, who was a friend of Albee's and Barr's, was an early reader of the play. Albee gave him a copy and Baker stayed up all night reading it. "I felt like I was riding some wave," he said. "It would lift me up and then come crashing down, then lift me up again. I was not prepared for this. Dawn came, and I went out and walked. I was so happy for him. I called Barr and said if you don't produce this play, don't ever call yourself a producer again." Barr told his press agent Howard Atlee that Albee had written a full-length play and he was planning to take it to Broadway. Clinton Wilder gave a script to Atlee and commented, "Here it is, if you can get through it." Atlee read it through at one sitting and immediately telephoned Barr and Wilder and told them they were going to win a Tony award for the play. "I was just so sure about it," said Atlee. "It was so dynamic on the page."

The first reading of the play took place on an evening in late winter of 1962 in the living room of Barr's apartment at 26 West 8th Street. Albee read the role of George and, in exceedingly odd casting, Barr read Martha and Clinton Wilder was Honey. Ben Piazza read Nick. At that point (and for some time) Nick had no name. He was simply identified as Dear, just as Honey was Honey (and stayed Honey), because nobody called her by her name; and the two referred to each other only with those terms of endearment. Present at the reading were Barr's stage managers Mark Wright and Michael Kasdan. Schneider was not there. Wright remembers the evening vividly: "By the time they got to the second act where George and Nick have that drunken conversation, I was in hysterics; rolling with laughter." To Wright, that scene between George and Nick evoked a memory of *The Male Animal*, the James Thurber–Elliott Nugent play about academic freedom. He had just reread that play and was reminded of a scene between the two leading male characters: He thought that Albee's scene was funnier and better. One of the odd parallels between the two plays is that in *The Male Animal*, the professor who is condemned as a Communist for wanting to read a letter from Bartolomeo Vanzetti to a class mocks his accusers by singing "Who's Afraid of the Big Bad Wolf?" Wright was overwhelmed by the reading of *Virginia Woolf*, but others apparently felt differently. "The reactions were not mixed," Barr wrote in his memoir, leaping to the false conclusion that "no one liked the play." No one, of course, except for Albee and Wright and perhaps several others. In Barr's memory, he was one of the few who wanted to go ahead, "with some reservations." But his partner, Wilder, "felt it needed about six months' more work; the others on the staff thought we should not do it at all."

From the first, the idea had been to do *Virginia Woolf* on Broadway, in spite of Albee's innate suspicion of it as a place for adventurous theater. In a February 1962 essay entitled "Which Theater Is the Absurd One?" in *The New York Times Magazine*, Albee praised the avant-garde theater as "free-swinging, bold, iconoclastic and often wildly, wildly funny." He said that when he was told he was a member in good standing of the Theater of the Absurd, he was "deeply offended because I had never heard the term before and I immediately assumed that it applied to the theater uptown—Broadway." Broadway, he said, was a theater, in which a "good" play was one that made money and a "bad" play was one that did not. The aim of Albee and his producers was to upset Broadway, to root it out of its complacency. But at least in the beginning, Barr seriously questioned the vulgarity of the language, especially the scattered use of the words "fuck" and "motherfucker." Such words had been heard Off-Broadway but not yet on Broadway. "I was nervous," said Barr, "because I felt the sensationalism of breaking the 'word-barrier' would prejudice" some people and "revolt" others. "It did not seem worth the risk. I told Edward: 'I'll take one fuck uptown!'" Albee decided, however, to take them all out. "Shit" became "hell" and "crap," "bullshit" became "nuts," and "fucked" became "screwed." When Albee directed the Broadway revival in 1976, he simply restored all the original words and "nobody knew the difference."

Barr sent the play to Billy Rose, who was both a producer and theater owner. He thought that the Billy Rose Theater on West 41st Street would be ideal for the play. Despite his highly commercial background, Rose completely committed himself to the play and said that if they produced it properly, it would be a certain hit. As Barr said, "Clinton and I were not so sure." In fact, Barr was so worried about the commercial success of the play that he came up with what he called "a daring plan." In retrospect, it seems a disastrous plan. Barr wanted to open the play at two different theaters on the same night, on Broadway and Off-Broadway, with two different casts, two different directors, and, presumably, two different sets of critics delivering two different sets of reviews. This, he thought, might "soften the blast." Of course, it could also mean a double disaster. Rose thought this was crazy and told Barr it would demean an important play. He refused to give him the Billy Rose Theater if he insisted on doing something so foolish.

Barr's next thought was to do it as a coproduction with the Actors Studio, which had just announced its plan to create a theater company on Broadway. In part, that theater was Lee Strasberg's envious response to the fact that his old friend and rival Elia Kazan had been named (together with Robert Whitehead) as the artistic director of the theater at the new Lincoln Center. Barr called Michael Wager, who was then executive administrator at the Actors Studio, sharing his title with Roger Stevens and Cheryl Crawford. With them and, of course, Strasberg (the ultimate arbiter), Wager was responsible for the Studio's choice of plays to produce. At the time, he was acting in *Brecht on Brecht* at the Theater de Lys. Wager began reading *Virginia Woolf* immediately, finishing it before that evening's performance. During the intermission, he telephoned Strasberg at home and said, "Lee, I have just read the best American play since *Long Day's Journey into Night*." Strasberg answered, "If you say that, we'll do it." Wager had already cast three of the roles in his mind, drawing from the Studio's roster of actors: Geraldine Page as Martha and Rip Torn and Sandy Dennis as Nick and Honey (Sandy Dennis was to play Honey in the movie). For the moment, he could not think of a George at the Studio. (Later, Schneider said the initial Studio casting was Page and Eli Wallach, with either Lou Antonio or Ben Piazza as Nick and Lane Bradbury as Honey.)

With Strasberg's assent, Wager sent the play to Page in California. She telephoned him, and as he recalled, she said, "I don't want to play a part like this. I want to play something where I can look beautiful." She had last done Tennessee Williams's *Sweet Bird of Youth* on Broadway (in 1959), in which she played the faded movie star Alexandra del Lago. Wager was dismayed at her response, but when Page returned to New York, she met with Wager and Strasberg. Strasberg insisted that she play the role "for the Studio." She reluctantly agreed. The idea was to begin the Actors Studio Theater on Broadway with *Virginia Woolf*.

Then the play was shown to Cheryl Crawford and Roger Stevens. Crawford remembered that neither Page nor Stevens liked the play and that Stevens questioned the language, "saying he would not help subsidize the speaking of dirty words on the stage." As for Crawford, "I was scared of its bitterness and brutality. So we passed it up. Of course we made a mistake." She said that Page later wrote her, "It would have put a stamp on us of bitterness, hostility and infantilism that would have taken us years to struggle out from under." "Perhaps," said Crawford, speaking from the vantage point of commercialism, "but we could have used a big hit." Instead the Studio opened with a revival of *Strange Interlude*, with an all-star cast headed by Page (who looked beautiful onstage). That dutiful but uneven production turned out to be the high point of two unfortunate seasons of the Actors Studio Theater. If the company had begun with *Virginia Woolf*, it might have made all the difference. As Wager said years later, "If we had opened with that play, the Studio would still have a theater today."

Stevens has his own version of the story. He said he opposed producing the play because of what he considered to be potential tax problems and the fact that the production had already been put together by a commercial management. Arthur Penn, for one, believes that Strasberg himself was at the heart of the Studio's decision not to do the play: "There was a real break in the ranks of the decision-making group about whether or not to do it." Penn and others were in favor of doing it, "but Lee didn't want to, and that swung it. I'm not sure I ever heard him enunciate his reasons. Very often with him, it was by fiat: 'I don't want to do it!' He was a volatile personality."

Albee remembers the story differently, saying that Page wanted to do the play, but when she told Strasberg, he insisted that he would have to be at all the rehearsals. Whoever was most negative about *Virginia Woolf*—Page, Strasberg, or Stevens and Crawford—the play was dropped and the Studio lost its second and last chance to originate a play by Albee.

As it turned out, there was no difficulty in raising the financing. Both Barr and Wilder had a list of backers from their previous shows, and when Milton Sperling, a Hollywood producer, offered $15,000, the production was on its way. As it turned out, Sperling was the largest single investor. With four actors and one set, *Virginia Woolf* was budgeted at $75,000, but came in at $47,000 (eventually, the twenty-eight backers made more than thirty times their investment). As a partner, Albee received 20 percent of the managerial share. One small way the thrifty producers kept down the cost was not to have the actors sing the title of the show to the tune of "Who's Afraid of the Big Bad Wolf?" For the rights to that song, they would have had to pay two hundred dollars a week. Wilder realized that the words could also be sung to the tune of the nursery rhyme, "Here We Go Round the Mulberry Bush," which was in the public domain.

With his own doubts about the play intact, but assuming that they would be overcome in rewriting and in the production, Barr forged ahead with casting. At the top of the list to play George and Martha were Henry Fonda and

Judith Anderson. Fonda, who had played the beleaguered professor in the film version of *The Male Animal*, seemed an obvious choice, but Anderson was known for *Medea*, and not for having anything approaching a comic touch. In each case, the actor's agent turned down the play without showing it to the client. In a conversation with me several years later, Fonda confirmed the fact that he had never seen the script. He said that if he had read it and been offered the role, he would have accepted it. In his autobiography, he said his agent John Foreman read the play and sent a memo to his colleagues at CMA: "This no-balls character is not for my Henry." According to Schneider, Richard Burton was also an early possibility for George, as was Katharine Hepburn for Martha. She turned it down, he said, because she felt she was not a good enough actress to play the role. Burton presumably was too busy; perhaps he hesitated about playing an American character.

Then Uta Hagen's name was mentioned. She had had a long distinguished career in the theater and her talent and her temperament made her seem to be a natural for Martha; but her recent appearances on stage had been sporadic. She had been devoting most of her artistic energies to teaching at HB, the acting studio she ran with her husband, Herbert Berghof. In July, Barr gave Hagen a copy of the play. She started reading it between her acting classes. By the end of the first act, she knew she had to do it. "There was no question about it," she said. "I thought it was a great part." By the time she finished the last act, she was "so gripped and moved by it" that it took her "quite a while to recover." She taught her second class "in a daze." Her only hesitation was that Alan Schneider had been named as director, and she did not want to work with him. Berghof had been hired to replace Schneider as director of *Waiting for Godot* before the play moved to Broadway and she had heard horror stories about Schneider from other actors. Through his work with Beckett and Albee, Schneider became known as a playwright's director, someone who respected the writer's intention. At the same time, he had a reputation for alienating actors. Habitually he would choose one of the actors in the cast, usually a woman, always the one he thought was the most vulnerable, and he would provoke that person with abuse during rehearsal. Mark Wright remembers, "Alan had a sadistic streak. He always had to have somebody to pick on. He would just not let them alone. It was almost as though they could do nothing right. That sort of constant pressure could drive an actor nuts." In *The American Dream*, his target was Sudie Bond. In *Virginia Woolf*, it was to be whatever actress played the role of Honey.

At 5:30 that day, Hagen met with Albee, Barr, and Wilder. In her diary, she wrote, "I was floored that Albee was so young (34—looks 24) and college-boyish. He was very quiet but I felt there was immediate rapport. We talked for an hour and I told them my hesitations about Schneider very openly." She also told Albee his play was "like a great modern Bosch canvas." The next day she was at her country home in Montauk and Barr telephoned her to discuss her contract, in "such high terms that I got dizzy." In his autobiography, Schneider said that he had to spend five hours convincing Uta to do the role, to which she responds, as she does to most of the comments about her in Schneider's book, "That's a total fiction! There was no persuading. Immediately, I just flipped." And later: "They kept saying this is an arts project and will have a short life. I said, wanna bet? This is going to be a smash hit. I said it from the time I read the script. I just knew it." In the beginning, however, she had questions about the last act. She said that days later Schneider called her and they had a long talk on the telephone. "He was wooing me, being overly pleasant. It embarrassed me and I was relieved when it was over." In her diary, she wrote, "It's decided I *will* do the play. Glory be I can't believe it. What will it be like! . . . I sure do think it's a great play though."

Still undecided about an actor to play George, the producers asked Uta for ideas. She suggested Fritz Weaver, but when she contacted him, Weaver told her not to push for him; he had had a bad acting experience with Schneider in *Miss Lonelyhearts* on Broadway and did not want to work with him again. There was a report that Uta had also suggested her husband. She denies that vehemently: "Herbert had an accent. I would no more suggest him for the part of George than the man in the moon. That's nonsense." At one point, she supplied a list of actors with asterisks next to the names of leading candidates. For George, she starred Weaver and then named a wide range of actors: Gig Young, Jason Robards, Richard Kiley, José Ferrer (her former husband, next to whose name she wrote "eeek"), and Art Carney. Her list of possible Nicks was headed by Paul Roebling and James Ray and also included George Peppard, James Lipton, George Segal, Ben Piazza, and Lee Richardson; and for Honey, Olga Bellin and Barbara Barrie were followed by Penelope Allen, Gaby Rodgers, and Monica Lovett.

By the end of July, only the role of Martha had been cast. Schneider wrote to Albee from California, approving the idea of the British actor Robert Flemyng as George and adding that another possibility, Arthur Kennedy, worried him and "already worries our leading lady. Uta, of course, I am tickled about." He said that Robert Lansing would be acceptable as Nick, "though I've heard he's difficult," and wished that Albee would reconsider Schneider's suggestion of George Grizzard. In his autobiography, Schneider said that, to find someone to play George, they "had gone through every actor in the United

States and England who was even remotely possible, starting with Richard Burton and ending up with Robert Flemyng." At one point Flemyng accepted the role and then changed his mind.

Grasping for an idea, Schneider remembered Arthur Hill, who starred on Broadway with Colleen Dewhurst in *All the Way Home,* Tad Mosel's adaptation of *A Death in the Family.* Although Barr was also familiar with Hill's work, for most of the others he was an unknown quantity, at best a Henry Fonda without Fonda's name recognition. In passing, Schneider contacted Arthur Penn, who had directed *All the Way Home,* and asked him how deep Hill was as an actor. Although Hill's role in *All the Way Home* was small—his character died in the first act—Penn assured Schneider that he had "a surprising range" and "could do anything." Penn had also directed Fonda in *Two for the Seesaw* and thought that Hill was a far better choice for George. The script was sent to Hill in London, where he was filming *In the Cool of the Day* with Jane Fonda.

Reading the play, Hill said, "I was just absolutely knocked out by it. It was staggering. I thought this is a play that has to be done. It'll never make a nickel, but it's got to be done." He cabled his acceptance. In London, he started learning his lines and thinking about his character. "Sometimes you have a part where you just say, 'Stand back everybody, I think I know what I'm doing here.' This was one of those cases. It doesn't happen very often. I was terribly confident. I knew the whole academic scene. I knew who this person was. I knew how I could fit myself into it." He was concerned about the length of the play and asked his agent to find out when they were going to cut it. She told him there were no plans to reduce the script. He then asked her where the company was going to try out the play, and she said they were opening cold in New York. Hill remembers, "I said, 'Whaaat! Get me out of this play.' Fortunately, she didn't."

The role of Nick had gone through many possibilities, including Lansing, Piazza (who had played Nick in the first reading at Barr's apartment and later was to take over the role), and George Segal (although at the time the producers felt that Segal was "too Jewish," he later played the role in the movie). From the first, Schneider favored George Grizzard, whom he knew well and had worked with many times before. Although Grizzard did not fit the physical type suggested by the script—Albee wanted someone rugged, like a halfback—Schneider insisted that he was strong and resilient enough for the role, that Nick could also be a quarterback. The director gave the play to the actor in California. Grizzard read it and decided it was "an absolutely brilliant script and a rotten part."

When Grizzard came east, he went out to Montauk for a reading of the play at Uta Hagen's house. She, of course, read Martha and Grizzard read Nick. Albee played both George and Honey. There was no audience: Hagen's husband Herbert Berghof left the group after dinner. Grizzard accepted the role because of Schneider and because he loved the play (he later invested $750 in it, a sum he was to make back many times over). But he continued to have grave reservations about his role. As he explained: "It was painful to get stabbed every night. It was like multiple stabbings. The more they stuck knives in me, the more the audience laughed. Edward wanted Nick destroyed, and he destroyed him." In order to do the play, Grizzard had to resolve a conflict in his schedule. He was going to play Hamlet at the opening of the Tyrone Guthrie Theater in Minneapolis the following spring and asked to be released from *Virginia Woolf* after three months. The producers agreed to the actor's terms.

Albee had seen Lane Bradbury in a play at the Actors Studio and liked her performance. She was going out with Lou Antonio (they would later marry and then divorce). Antonio remembers driving her to Albee's apartment to see about a role in his play. After the meeting, he said, she came out "with the thickest-looking play I'd ever seen." Antonio had played Jerry in the Actors Studio version of *The Zoo Story* and was later to have a leading role in *The Ballad of the Sad Cafe*. On Albee's recommendation, Bradbury was chosen to play Honey.

Harold Clurman was among the many early readers of the play. Possibly regretting not having read *The Zoo Story* when Aaron Copland offered it to him, he had been asking Albee for a copy of *Virginia Woolf* from the time he first heard about it. Finally in August 1962, Albee gave him the script. Clurman read it and rushed to comment, "The play is quite extraordinary." He added,

There is no play this season I look forward to seeing as much as I do to yours. (I shall know much more about our "uptown" audience when the play opens. The play in a sense will be an "experiment" on the audience!) . . .

I'd like to keep the script—to refer to when I review the play. I have made preliminary notes for myself. But my impressions may change after seeing the play on the stage and I'm curious to know how my first impressions—on two readings—vary from the later ones . . . What I know of the cast (three actors only) it seems to me just about perfect.

Long before rehearsals began, Uta Hagen was working on her role. As she says, "The first homework I did alone was on Martha's life, her relationship to her father and to faculty life, what it meant being nonfunctioning. She was not an academic. What it was like being raised by her father. All these things I would take from my personal experience and put them together to make somebody new." After a meeting with Albee and Barr, she wrote in her workbook: "Everything in my [Martha's] past—lawn mower, life with Daddy, boxing match, etc. is *true* (except for child). George's novel and Majorca—he doesn't know if it's true, but will tell me. Bases it being untrue on one line— 'Book-maker-child-maker.' In which case, what I [as Martha] expose or make naked is purely one of George's failures—a creative work." At another point, she wrote, "The party at Daddy's house tonight. A dozen new faculty members. Particularize them! Especially meeting with Nick and Honey . . . *How* did I show off?—how much to provoke George? Or to impress Daddy? I sang 'Who's Afraid of Virginia Woolf?' I'll bet I read *Orlando* last week!"

Finally, on September 7, she and Schneider met at Sardi's for their first extended discussion of the play. She brought along a notebook filled with questions. At the end of the meeting, she said to him, "We start rehearsing in a few days, and I'm afraid I know this play better than you do." As Hagen recalls, Schneider replied, "I'm afraid you do." Earlier, she asked him, "How are you going to deal with the imaginary son?" To her memory, he said, "I don't know. Ask Edward." "So I asked Edward," she said, "and he said, 'I don't know. Ask Alan.' And I ended up making up my own mind about that. After I had been playing it for about three weeks, the stage manager said that Alan wanted to tell me that now he knows what the child is. I said, 'What does he think it is?' 'It's Jesus Christ.' I said, 'In that case that makes me Holy Mary Mother and I don't know how to play Martha like that.' "

Rehearsals began without Hill because his movie had been delayed in London. Said Hagen, "I distinctly remember praying that he would show up." By September 12, Hill had still not arrived. Albee filled in for him as George, and by Hagen's estimation, he was reading "badly. I think Edward is a genius so *naturally* I have a crush on him but he can't act!" She was critical of Schneider: "Alan says things that are intelligent, but I know them already. He also says things that are not intelligent—because he doesn't know them yet, and he says *nothing* which is truly creative or anything which will set an actor into creative motion." The following day, in a note to herself about Martha, she wrote, "I wear the pants because somebody has to."

On September 14, Hill finally arrived. He was concerned because he had to catch up to the other actors and there were only two and a half weeks before the opening. This would have been difficult in any circumstance, especially so considering the length of his role and of the play. "I was so doggone busy I didn't have time to be frightened." As the four actors read *Virginia Woolf* aloud, Schneider said, "The play exploded like a sudden storm, one stroke of lightning, one thunder clap after another."

Whatever initial animosity there might have been between Hagen and Hill, including her resentment at his late arrival, dissolved as they began working together. Their approaches to acting were decidedly different. She worked from the inside and was filled with psychological questions about the roots of her character. She tried to imagine a biography of Martha before she played her.

On the other hand, Hill concentrated on the script itself, drawing his character only from the dialogue: "I listen to the author's words, to see what they're giving me." He felt that intuitively he had a connection with George. "I had a pretty good notion who this person was anyway. He's having difficulty in the college. The wife was riding him and the father-in-law was a pain in the neck to him. I think he felt his own qualities weren't being drawn upon. A certain amount of anger going on inside him, and the realization that Martha was looking elsewhere." To him, George was not a weak person. "There are different kinds of strength. He is not the kind to have his fists flying, but I think he has a stiff spine. There are certain principles that he would not back down on." He found that Hagen was open to ideas, and he also admired her daring: "She had no fear about swimming right out there and seeing what happens. 'If you don't find any land to get to, then you swim back. Don't worry about it.' And she encouraged that in the rest of us."

Five days into rehearsal, there was a problem that should have been foreseeable. Schneider had been hounding Lane Bradbury, easily zeroing in on her as the most vulnerable member of his cast and attacking her performance in front of the other actors. Finally he fired her, and she was replaced by Melinda Dillon, who also fell under Schneider's fire, but managed to survive. "He tortured Melinda Dillon," said Hagen. "I think he drove her nuts. He would say, 'You're no good. You're an amateur.' I was the only one he didn't torture. Maybe he was scared of me." That was an understatement. If he had tried to, said Albee, "Uta would have chewed off his head and spit it out."

Grizzard was furious that Bradbury had been replaced: "She was darling and tiny and Southern. I felt I had been betrayed. It was like I was given a divorce without being asked about it. And then this tall girl came in." The immediate difficulty for Grizzard was that of Dillon's height. In contrast to Bradbury, she was several inches taller than Grizzard. Suddenly, he felt out of place: He had become the shortest person in the cast, and he had to look up to his stage wife. Soon his grumbling stopped and he came to appreciate his new mate. "Of course Melinda was brilliant and she did everything a tall girl would do if she were married to me. She slumped and she wore flat shoes and if you'd say anything to her, she'd get three inches shorter."

Giving Schneider latitude, Albee would appear at rehearsals only about once a week. The communication was between Schneider and Albee and not between the author and the actors. Almost every day of rehearsal, Grizzard wondered why Nick and Honey stayed on at George and Martha's house after all the insults. Schneider responded, "Why doesn't Hamlet kill Claudius?" Grizzard said, "I can give you six reasons why he doesn't kill Claudius, but I can't find one reason why I stay in this house. Why don't I take my wife and leave? Their answer was tenure, which meant nothing to me. It was that she was the president's daughter and I was a guy on the make."

Along the way, there were changes from the original script, some of them slight, some consequential. In an early reference to Martha's father as "the white mouse," it was said that he "was wearing his pince-nez," an obvious reference to Reed Albee. That was cut, as was a passage about Martha's father getting "hootch" from "Mafia types." Instead, George was given an earlier speech in which he said that "the old man is not going to die," that he has "the staying power of one of those Micronesian tortoises." In such a fashion, many of the insertions added humor. In speaking about age in the earlier version, George told Nick that he was forty-six, not, as in the final script, "forty-something," and that Martha was fifty-two, not 108, and that "she weighs somewhat more than that."

In the first version of the play, the third act began with a nine-page scene between George and Honey. They are onstage alone. In a stage direction, the author says about Honey, "it is evident that she is very drunk but, at the same time, under a kind of possessed control." Honey tries to explain herself and says she does not remember anything that happened earlier in the evening. That scene was inessential and was cut, so that Act Three could begin more swiftly, with Martha barging onstage, talking to herself. At the end of that act, several pages were cut in which George reiterates things that are self-evident. In all substantial ways, the play remained the same—and it remained very long.

About ten days into rehearsal, Ritman's set was installed onstage and the cast moved into the Billy Rose Theater. Using the props and the scenery, the actors began inhabiting the environment and their roles. "There were so many cockeyed things in that production," said Hagen. "I hated that set. I thought it came right out of the Goodman Theater. And when I saw all those books, I thought, we've got to play in front of all those books: red and blue and green. At one point they were picking fabrics for the sofas, Richard Barr, Clinton, Edward, and Alan picking these fabrics. Then Alan said to me, 'Which do you like?' I said I'm not a designer. Where the fuck is the designer? I said you're playing games up there decorating living rooms without a designer. I thought the whole thing was put together like that. It's just a *miracle* to me that it worked so well."

Several days later, Schneider had the cast do a run-through of the play. Barr and Wilder were there, the first time that they had seen the entire play in its proper setting. Sitting in an empty theater, watching the actors bring the play to life, Barr was "astonished, excited and ineffably moved," words that had not come to his mind at the first informal reading. At the end of the performance, said Barr, he and Wilder "were so shaken, that outside of a few mumbled words of conventional necessity, we left the theater at once" and went to Wilder's house "where we finally exploded. We both knew that something very, very special was happening on the Billy Rose stage."

Billy Rose, ever the tinkerer, had a few final thoughts. In a long letter to the playwright, he said, "I think you're a nickel phone call away from a memorable and distinguished success." Then he went down the play, act by act. Act One: "It's superb. Almost every line and situation is dead on target. A few lines fizz, sputter and fall flat. To mix my similes, they're like fly specks on a Rembrandt." Act Two: "Better than Act One. One of the most powerful and penetrating pieces of writing in years." Then he criticized Schneider's direction and "the off-stage groans and grunts to telegraph the lovemaking in the kitchen," explaining "when a gentleman strikes out, the lady doesn't moan that loud—at least not the ladies I've been fortunate enough to know." Act Three. Twice in this act, he said, the play is in trouble, when George "informs the audience that we're going to play another game, the game without a name," and the long soliloquy about the child, which he "never understood a word of," and "was badly played and badly staged." Finally, the ending: He remembered in the script he read, "after the misery of the long night, the woman and the man she loved went up to bed." Last night, he said, George "sang the little jingle about Virginia Woolf and it left me cold." Despite all these quarrels, "I love the play," and felt "with a smidgen of work," it would "be around, in one form or another, for years to come." The "game without a name" was Bringing Up Baby. Rose's suggestions were disregarded; his prediction about the play's longevity came true. Having not yet performed before an audience, the actors remained doubtful about the play. Grizzard said that before the previews began, "We didn't know if we had the biggest bomb in the world, or a hit."

Since the decision had been made not to take the play out of town, there were ten preview performances, five unpaid and five paid. To boost sales, Rose took out an ad in the *Times* saying that he was selling preview tickets at a top price of three dollars including tax, less than half the usual price ($6.90 at the time). He explained, "Mr. Albee's first full-length play is for that segment of the population which reads good books, likes good music and occasionally visits an art gallery. Unfortunately, such people are seldom rich." In response, he was lowering prices "to where the Proust-reading stenographer can afford to blow herself to an intellectual binge." Then he issued a warning to that stenographer's boss "who used to smirk at the naked tootsies at my Diamond Horseshoe nightclub a few years back. Pass this one up, sire. Edward Albee and *Virginia Woolf* are not your cup of oolong."

Quietly expressing their confidence in the play, the producers encouraged theater people, in particular, to come to previews. At the first preview, there were no programs. Barr made a pre-curtain speech, listing the actors. Then the curtain went up for the first time. Word soon began to spread through the theater community. "Once we had an audience," said Hill, "we were running on all eight cylinders." The previews sold out.

On the Sunday before the play opened, Albee wrote a piece for *The New York Times*, deriding, as it said in the headline, "the excessive importance attached to Broadway." He joked about the fact that he and his fellow Off-Broadway playwrights, Jack Richardson and Rick Besoyan, had been photographed for the *Times* standing next to a Broadway billboard because all three were about to have plays on Broadway. He said that he knew *Virginia Woolf* was going to be a "big test" for him, but didn't know exactly why. He had been told that "if this play is a success it will be a more important success" than his other plays, "and that if it is a failure the failure will be more disastrous than it could be downtown."

As the play headed toward its opening, there was sobering political news. The Cuban missile crisis was a daily concern, and the confrontation seemed to be posing a threat of nuclear war. On October 13, a rainy Saturday night, *Who's Afraid of Virginia Woolf?* opened on Broadway. Years later, the single opening night would be eradicated and critics were invited to a selection of preview performances. That night, all the critics were there at the same time.

The scene is "the living-room of a house on the campus of a small New England college." Act One: the Fun and Games begin. "Set in darkness. Crash against front door. MARTHA's laughter heard. Front door opens, lights are switched on. MARTHA enters, followed by GEORGE." Martha is "a large, boisterous woman, 52, looking somewhat younger. Ample, but not fleshy." George, "her husband, 46. Thin; hair going gray.

Uta Hagen, as Martha, delivered the first words of the play, "Jesus H. Christ," followed by laughter from the audience. Later, the play was to become legendary, make several fortunes, and establish Edward Albee as the first playwright since Eugene O'Neill to break through from Off-Broadway to Broadway and continue his exhilarating ride into theatrical history. On opening night, Albee and Barr were in the back of the Billy Rose Theater, nervously pacing from one side to the other, as the actors took charge of the play.

8

FAM

FOR DIRTY-MINDED FEMALES ONLY.

•

A brilliantly original work of art—an excoriating theatrical experience, surging with shocks of recognition and dramatic fire.

T H E evening was astonishing: laughter followed by gasps, as the characters wounded one another with words, as the play moved inexorably to its final catharsis. When the play ended at 11:40, there was a moment of silence, then thunderous applause, followed by curtain call after curtain call for the actors, who were high on the adrenaline of the evening. Amid the bravos, a cry was heard for the author, but Albee did not go onstage. Tennessee Williams was at the opening and came back again and again the following week. I, too, was at the opening, as was Tom Wenning, the drama critic of *Newsweek*. Tom and I shared an office, and I wrote and reviewed for that magazine. For some time, I had been following Albee's career Off-Broadway and telling Tom about his talent, priming him for this Broadway debut. As we left the Billy Rose Theater, Tom gave me a thumbs up sign. "You've found one," he said, meaning Albee as playwright.

At that performance, Abe Burrows said to Albee, "Welcome to the theater, young man," disregarding the playwright's Off-Broadway success. It was as if Albee were now a member of the "real" theater. There was no formal opening-night party, although Uta Hagen remembers hosting a party upstairs at Sardi's, and Arthur Hill remembers going to Albee's apartment for a celebratory drink. Because the play opened on a Saturday, reviews were not printed until Monday, although some of them were available in advance on Sunday night. With no performance on Sunday, this meant that everyone would have a day off—to worry. Late Sunday afternoon, the principals (except for the actors) met at Wilder's apartment: Alan Schneider (and his wife), Barr, Albee, the stage manager Mark Wright, William Ritman, and the press agent Howard Atlee. "We sat around pretending to be relaxed, pretending not to be concerned," said Albee. "We sat around, actually, in quiet hysteria." Billy Rose called and asked if he could stop by.

Because Rose was a whiz at taking shorthand, he agreed to transcribe the reviews as they were received over the telephone. The first review to come in was from Robert Coleman in the *Daily Mirror.* He called it "a sick play for sick people." Next was John Chapman in the *New York Daily News.* He said that it was "three and a half hours long, four characters wide and a cesspool deep" and suggested that someone should have taken "young Albee out behind a metaphorical woodshed and spanked him with a sheaf of hickory switches." Chapman's follow-up Sunday piece was to be headlined, FOR DIRTY-MINDED FEMALES ONLY, words that summed up the reviewer's opinion. As Albee said, Chapman's remark "added six months to the run." There was, however, a fan in the Chapman family: After the opening, his wife booked a theater party for her garden club.

Although Coleman and Chapman were known as critical Neanderthals, the harshness of their reviews was unexpected. Those at Wilder's apartment began to sink into a state of depression, with the exception of Billy Rose, who continued his shorthand chores while announcing brightly, "I'm willing to buy you guys out as a favor." It was Albee's belief that Rose's offer was not altruistic but pragmatic: "Somehow he had access to information that the good reviews were coming."

Walter Kerr's review in the *Herald Tribune* was an improvement. There were positive comments and quotable adjectives, but in his first paragraph, he said that the play was "a brilliant piece of writing with a sizable hole in its head," a phrase for which Albee never forgave him. Interestingly, when Kerr published that review in a book of collected criticism the following year, he rewrote it, and in all respects, it was reductive of his original opinion. He took back the word "brilliant" and it dwindled to "admirable," "two stinging acts" became "two exacerbating acts," and no longer was the play a "work of energy and distinction." In his review in the *Times,* Howard Taubman concluded that Albee's "new work, flawed though it is, towers over the common run of contemporary plays." In anticipation of the opening, Paul Gardner had written a "Man in the News" column on Albee for the *Times,* and in an unusual move, it ran in the same issue as the review. The article announced that Albee was "the first new important playwright to shake Broadway from its lethargy." In the afternoon *Post,* Richard Watts led the critical bravos. With his customary enthusiasm for Albee, he said the play was "the most shattering drama I have seen since O'Neill's *Long Day's Journey into Night.*" For Albee and his colleagues, depression was soon replaced by euphoria.

On opening night, I had no idea that *Virginia Woolf* was going to represent my debut as a Broadway critic. I knew that Tom Wenning was ill, but I did not know he was suffering from terminal cancer. On Monday he quietly told me that he was unable to write his review of *Virginia Woolf.* He asked me if I could fill in for him, which I did, for that play and for the rest of the season. Having taken no notes on opening night, I reviewed the play with some trepidation. The review was printed the following week under the headline GAME OF TRUTH. (Since this was still a time when there were no bylines in newsmagazines, my name did not appear on the review.) In part, I wrote:

> Albee's new play . . . is not only shocking and amusing, but is also as emotionally shattering, in its own way, as Eugene O'Neill's *Long Day's Journey into Night . . . Virginia Woolf* is a splendidly acted, electrically staged (by Alan Schneider), brilliantly original work of art—an excoriating theatrical experience, surging with shocks of recognition and dramatic fire. It will be igniting Broadway for some time to come.

On Monday, there was a long line outside the theater. The box office sold $12,000 worth of tickets, more than the show's entire advance sale. The treasurer announced that he was "wrapping" one thousand dollars an hour. As the weekly reviews came in, it was evident that the critics continued to be divided. Harold Clurman, who was so enthusiastic about the play when he read it, began his review in *The Nation* by saying that *Virginia Woolf* was "not only the best play in town now; it may well prove the best of the season. Its significance extends beyond the moment. In its faults as well as in its merits it deserves our close attention." He had high praise for the dialogue, which he called "superbly virile and pliant." At the same time, he felt that the author's pessimism was unearned and immature. Robert Brustein praised Albee's wit and imagination, then took it back by saying, "Despite its surface brilliance, however, the play is hollow at the centre, and ultimately claustrophobic." Brustein's "hollow at the centre" echoed Kerr's remark that it was a play "with a sizable hole in its head." In the end, the passion of the response worked to the play's advantage. In a curious reversal, even the negative reviews seemed to sell tickets. Within the week, the show was building into the season's biggest dramatic hit.

Because the play was so long and so demanding on the actors, the initial idea was to limit performances to six a week, but when Rose said he was going to charge the producers rent for eight performances as in the contract, Barr came up with the idea of having a separate matinee company. Hagen insisted that she was ready and able to do all eight, or even "twelves times a week" if necessary, but Hill was not sure he would have the energy. A different company of four actors was brought in and agreed to serve as standbys for the evening company. Kate Reid, Sheppard Strudwick, Bill Berger, and Avra Petrides were hired, and the matinees sold out as well.

On Thursday after the play opened, I met Albee for the first time, for a feature story that would appear in *Newsweek*. Neatly dressed, with his hair cropped short, he looked younger than his thirty-four years. He seemed modest and reserved while still exuding an air of confidence, or rather, an air of someone who had received his just deserts. He seemed clearly capable of handling his sudden success. It was also obvious from that first encounter that he was a man who watched his words—and the words of others. He was always listening, observing, and analyzing. Over a Campari and soda, he said, "I don't feel any kind of elation, just relief. Maybe elation will come."

How did he feel about being compared with O'Neill? "If you mean that both *Long Day's Journey into Night* and *Who's Afraid of Virginia Woolf?* have four characters and they talk a great deal and nothing happens, if you mean that, that's pretty superficial. If it's a more serious comparison, then I think it's premature and I get embarrassed." About O'Neill, he said, "I was enormously involved in, enveloped by *The Iceman Cometh* and *Long Day's Journey*. I'm sure *Long Day's Journey* influenced *Who's Afraid of Virginia Woolf?*, just as *Suddenly Last Summer* influenced *The Zoo Story*"—especially in his use of the long monologue reflecting on the past.

He added, "I've been influenced by everybody, for God's sake. Everything I've seen, either accepting it or rejecting it. I'm aware when I write a line like Williams. I'm aware when I use silence like Beckett. I like silence in my own life, solitude and stuff like that. In a play it's like music—sound and silence." Looking ahead to the life of the play, he said, "There is no virtue in failure. There is no virtue in commercial failure. Nor should it be a god."

As it turned out, this was to be the first in a series of meetings between us over the next few months. Because of the success of *Virginia Woolf*, I suggested to the editors that *Newsweek* do a cover story on Albee. The idea was accepted, and I was assigned to write it. When Albee and I met for the second time, it was in his new apartment on West 10th Street, which happened to be directly across the street from mine. It was a large, high-ceiling duplex apartment, with cork-lined walls and a feeling of solitary splendor. Among many other things, we talked about the reviews—as he emphasized, the "mixed" reviews—and he singled out for praise the *Newsweek* review, assuming that it had been written by Tom Wenning, whose name was listed as drama critic on the masthead. When I told him I had written it, it caught him completely by surprise. For once, he was at a loss for words.

After only thirty-one performances, the play paid back its investors, who from then were able to reap profits. In retrospect, *The Zoo Story*—and the ensuing acclaim and celebrity—was like a pilot program for what happened to Albee with *Who's Afraid of Virginia Woolf?* Broadway did make a difference. He was put on a pedestal, occasionally knocked down from that pedestal; repeatedly interviewed, he was quoted, courted, and invited. On November 19, he went to the White House and as part of a delegation of tastemakers met President Kennedy.

In December, he flew to Italy to talk to Franco Zeffirelli about an Italian production of *Virginia Woolf*. He spent New Year's Eve in Rome, "as much as anything to witness the Roman custom of throwing bottles, furniture, and people out the windows into the streets at exactly midnight." With McNally, he visited Diamond in Florence and traveled to Venice and Milan, where they saw *Rigoletto* and also *The Zoo Story* in Italian.

Meanwhile, the *Newsweek* cover story moved ahead. Although reporters were unable to talk to Beckett, Genet, and Ionesco, one did speak to Tennessee Williams, and either misheard what Williams said or Williams himself misspoke and then had second thoughts. In the article, he was quoted as saying, "Edward Albee is the only great playwright we've ever had in America." Reading that in print in the February 4, 1963, issue, Williams immediately sent a telegram from Key West:

> I am sure that Edward Albee is even more embarrassed than I am by the misquotation attributed to me that he is the only great playwright that America has produced. Since I know that he must feel as I do that the mark of Eugene O'Neill is a great one yet to be reached by any of us late comers. After all true theatre is not an athletic competition and comparisons are better left to critics if they wish to make them sincerely.

For all the differences in their approach to theater, both Williams and Al-

bee had a marked respect for O'Neill. Parenthetically, Williams also said in
that *Newsweek* interview, "Albee is much handsomer than he appears in his
photographs. Most playwrights don't photograph very well anyway. In fact,
most of them look like a dog's last dinner." That quotation, of course, was not
used in the article. Nor was Harold Pinter's: "His work exhilarates me. He's a
cool, quiet, self-contained chap, a very amiable, charming host but not a gar-
rulous man. He's a shrewd observer with a gimlet eye on life around him."

Flanagan sent me a letter offering to check the article for facts, an offer
that I did not accept. Explaining his interest, he wrote:

> You see, from about 1952 through 1959, let's say, I guess I'm the only person
> Edward knows who had any kind of complete picture of his life. And I know, for
> example, that you've talked a good bit to Noel Farrand who, with the best in-
> tentions in the world, is quite capable of confusing opinion for fact—this out of
> a desire to warm The Past with a sort of Proustian glow . . . I realize that, so far
> as *you* are concerned, word from any *one* of Edward's friends is as good as an-
> other's. And it's quite possible that closeness to Edward, and my resultant ten-
> dency to want to protect him, makes me a fair share *more* suspect than anyone
> else.

The *Newsweek* cover photograph was of Albee, his brooding, somber face,
hand on chin, in front of the cast in performance. For a cover banner that
would appear under the words, PLAYWRIGHT EDWARD ALBEE, the editor, Os-
born Elliott, chose the sensationalism of SEX + SADISM = SUCCESS. After a
strong objection, my choice for a banner was used: ODD MAN IN. When the article was published, Albee sent a letter thanking me for writing "an honorable
piece." He added, "Of course, as I whined at you all the time, I would have
preferred that the piece consider mine instead of me, maybe only because a
man's work is the man, and a man is not his work—not completely . . . by the
way, where *did* you get the T. Williams quote from, the quote which he so
graciously qualified."

The offers began to flow in to Albee—for productions of *Virginia Woolf*
around the world and for him to write articles, stories, screenplays, and plays
on commission. To help clear the air of pretension, he wrote a self-interview
on the subject, "How *Who's Afraid of Virginia Woolf?* Has Changed My Life."
He approached this as a child's theme or schoolboy's essay. Naturally he began by avoiding the question. Then he said, "People should be more interested in a writer's work than in the person of a writer. Writers, in other words,
should be heard and not seen. It is very dangerous for a writer to become a

public personality; I can think of one American novelist [Ernest Heming-way], recently dead, who became so convinced that he was, in fact, the public image of himself that it did serious damage to his work. And the better the writer, of course, the more interesting his work in comparison to himself." Asking himself what he meant when he wrote his play, he said, "If I could tell you what I meant by the play in any fashion other than reading you the play from beginning to end then I should have written the play in a different fashion." He added that six months after completing a play, "I can no longer really recall either the experience of writing the play or the motivation for writing it." "An exorcism of devils?" asked his self-inquisitor. "You say it, I don't," he answered, in a variation of George's comment, "That's for me to know and for you to find out," which itself could serve as a motto for Albee's interviews at the time.

He admitted that some things had changed: "I'm busier, I have less privacy, I'm solvent, I travel a good deal more, I meet many more people," and he discovered, to his sadness, that people did not take Off-Broadway seriously. Despite his Off-Broadway success, it was not until he had a play on Broadway that he was admitted "into the fraternity." When people came up to him and said, "I saw your play, and I loved it (or, hated it)," they meant one play, *Virginia Woolf.* One reason why audiences were seeing it was its "reputation, unfounded . . . of being dirty and sick." Did he mind people going to his plays for what he considered to be the wrong reason? "Not so long as they don't come out of them with the same opinion. Besides, a playwright has two alternatives—either people go to his plays or they don't. And while there are only two bad things for a playwright—failure and success—the second, I think, nurtures him better."

With the waning of Inge, Albee joined Tennessee Williams and Arthur Miller in the reigning Broadway triumvirate of playwrights, though, of course, at that point he had but one Broadway play. But he was already working on his adaptation of Carson McCullers's *Ballad of the Sad Cafe,* and he had several projects lined up, including a play called *The Substitute Speaker,* which years later surfaced as *The Lady from Dubuque,* and a play about Attila the Hun, often announced and never written. There was also the opera *The Ice Age* that he was writing with Flanagan. It had been commissioned by Julius Rudel at the New York City Opera. Albee wrote one act of the libretto (dealing with Utopia in an insane asylum) and Flanagan wrote very little music. As the months passed, Flanagan was becoming increasingly frantic while lying to Rudel about progress being made. The opera was never finished.

After *Virginia Woolf* opened, countless people emerged from academia claiming to be the models for George and Martha. Often when Albee would speak on a college campus, which he now did frequently, he would be approached by someone saying, you must have been writing about so-and-so and his wife. How did you know them so well?

At Wagner College on Staten Island, there were many people who thought that Jack and Elaine Boies were the originals for George and Martha. Jack Boies taught English at Wagner and his wife occasionally acted. In July of 1962, months before *Virginia Woolf* opened, Wagner had held a writers' conference, the second one in which Albee participated at the college. That year he, Kenneth Koch, and Kay Boyle were the writers in residence. In the fall, the Boieses saw the play on Broadway. They began talking about it at a party at their house—*Virginia Woolf* was a favorite topic on campuses—and Boies said, "Who do you think it was about?" There were stares and doubletakes. The rumor started that evening and spread. A mutual friend, Dominic Lagotta, recalled, "From then on, they were under constant scrutiny. We would look for a glimmer of Martha in Elaine's eyes, a trace of Arthur Hill in Jack's voice." Elaine Boies always categorically denied the report and, of course, the chronology was wrong. In the summer of 1962 Albee had already finished writing the play. But the story continued to spread. Thirty-two years later, the long-running rumor appeared in an article in the *Staten Island Advance* suggesting that Albee was "inspired by the people he met on campus at Wagner College." Albee has always rejected such possibilities, except in one instance. If anybody inspired George and Martha, he said, it was Willard Maas, a teacher and poet, and his wife, Marie Menken, who was a documentary filmmaker. Maas had been the faculty liaison at the 1961 Wagner College Writers Conference and the director of that conference the following year.

Paul Zindel believes the suggestion that Maas and Menken, as a titanic couple, could have been the real models.

Here you're talking about two people who were intellects, who had a marvelous vocabulary, two people of extraordinary polarities—and they brought Edward to Staten Island. Willard was small and rotund of varied sexual appetites, very nice, sweet, provocative, knew everybody in show business. Anything bizarre, cutting edge, freakish—he knew them, and people sometimes spoke of him as a B poet. His wife was huge, six foot if she was an inch—she was built like a football player. She had a Great Dane or a German shepherd that most of us thought was her second husband. There was a definite liaison between the two of them. It was not a warring relationship in public, but you could see these were two great combatants, almost like Colleen Dewhurst meeting Michael Dunn [in *The Ballad of the Sad Cafe*]. They were larger than life. Willard Maas died two or three days after Marie Menken did. It sounded like a fiction that they had created, that Willard had committed suicide—which we assumed—in order to create another story about their lives.

Zindel is himself an intriguing peripheral figure in Albee's life. A Staten Island high school chemistry teacher who was thinking about becoming a playwright, he took a brief ten-day course in playwriting with Albee at Wagner College. Simultaneously, he and Loree Yerby did their 1961 interview with him. Zindel was an ardent fan, or as Albee says, a "neurotic fan." He followed Albee, hounding him with his presence. Zindel recalls, "I was the world's worst horror, stalking Edward Albee, and wanting his whole career and wanting everything about him, and not the least bit fitting in with any of his thoughts. I wanted all the fun and glamor that he had." At one point, he said, he also "stalked" Tennessee Williams: "Tennessee felt my sting, but Edward Albee was my supreme stalk." Zindel went to the opening of all Albee's early plays and was "blown away" by most of them. He flooded Albee with scores of letters, filled with wild fantasies and manic theories, and once sent him a present of a bronze crab because he thought he was being "crabby." Trying to explain his obsession, Zindel said, "I might have been in love with him. I think I was in love with a fantasy I was projecting. I was saying, hey, look at me, hey, notice me, let me into your life, let me be a playwright, let me have this exciting world."

He went to a preview of *Virginia Woolf* in early October and had the audacity to send the author a letter enclosing two reviews he had written, the first one unfavorable, the other favorable. In the first, he said it was "a sloppy half-formed play" written by "the Glimmering Hack of Coffee House Hetairae." In the second, he said that Albee "assured his place in history as one of the most powerful and important playwrights of the 20th century." With a kind of irresistible urge, he ended the second review by saying about the author, "This magnificent young man is vulgar only in that he doesn't pay enough attention to Paul Zindel." Albee generally did not respond to Zindel's letters, although he did read his plays. Occasionally he went to see them, always, said Zindel, "with a kindness, but hardly letting me into the privacy of his world."

Receiving this bizarre double review before his play had opened on Broadway, Albee felt obliged to comment: "I am in the middle of severe facial neuralgia, in great pain. If you didn't mean what you said about my play, please write me immediately and let me know. If you did mean what you said, go fuck yourself." Looking back on his correspondence and on his one-sided relationship, Zindel said, "I felt that was the first time I got through to him." He also believed that "the two reviews marked the end of Edward being nice to me." In fiction, such aberrant behavior might lead to an act of violence. In Zindel's case, it led him to become a playwright who would always be indebted to Albee as mentor. In 1971, he won the Pulitzer Prize for drama for *The Effect of Gamma Rays on Man-in-the-Moon Marigolds*, a play that owes a greater artistic debt to Williams than to Albee. Ironically, that was the year that Albee failed to win the Pulitzer for his play *All Over*.

Virginia Woolf was such an enormous hit that it freed the playwright and his coproducers from financial concern. One of the direct results of the success of *Virginia Woolf* was the formation of the Playwrights Unit, created by Albee, Barr, and Wilder, to encourage the work of new playwrights. The workshop was founded in 1963 with profits from *Virginia Woolf*, and later received additional financing from the Rockefeller Foundation. During the eight years the group was in existence, it became one of the primary training grounds for new writers, and along with La Mama and Caffe Cino made a major contribution to the theater. Some 100 plays were presented, including works by Lanford Wilson, Sam Shepard, Paul Foster, Jean-Claude Van Itallie, Israel Horovitz, Terrence McNally, Adrienne Kennedy, John Guare, Megan Terry, Paul Zindel, and A. R. Gurney Jr. Its two most notable successes were *Dutchman* (by Leroi Jones, later Amiri Baraka) and *The Boys in the Band* by Mart Crowley.

Most of the people connected with *Virginia Woolf*, from the stars to the stage manager to the press agent, had at least a small percentage of the profits, which continued to provide them with income for the next twenty-one years, until the rights to the play reverted to the playwright. With his profits, Albee was able to buy a house in Montauk. It cost him only sixty thousand dollars and proved to be a very shrewd investment. Eventually he began improving his property, adding another house and a tennis court.

As the author of a Broadway hit, he was flooded with fan mail. A woman from the midwest wrote him a letter saying that she and her husband had gone to the second night of *Who's Afraid of Virginia Woolf?* and greatly admired his work. As the mother of an adopted daughter, she wondered if his deep sensitivities were the result of his being adopted. He answered: "Adoptions are like all things, aren't they—marriages, friendships? Some are good, some are bad, even if they are entered into in good faith. The chemistry may not be 'just right.' And maybe the saddest of all things is an attempt at something in good faith where for some reason or another, that nobody can help, things don't work out."

The actress Peggy Wood, who was at the opening, wrote, "I must tell you how moved I was by the play and the performance. Moved to laughter, moved to pity and moved by the impact of greatness which is in that play." She added, "I will repeat to you now that I felt no one since O'Neill had brought such power to the theater, and I think you are better than O'Neill because O'Neill's dialogue was never brilliant." The scenic designer Boris Aronson wrote, "Seeing your play was a great experience. Never was terror more delightful—a complicated theme more simply handled—bravo!"

One of the more personal letters came from a woman who had taken care of children of neighbors in Larchmont at the same time that Nanny Church was looking after Edward. Seeing a photograph of Albee in a newspaper, she said, "Although you have gone a long way and so successful, yet there are still the same dreamy searching eyes of yours, and often a little sad—that is really the way I remember you most."

By the end of the season, *Virginia Woolf* deservedly collected the major awards. The New York Drama Critics Circle named it the best new play by the narrowest of margins. The vote was nine to eight, with three votes going to Brecht's *Mother Courage* (which had its New York premiere twenty-four years after it was written) and two votes to *The Hollow Crown*, the Royal Shakespeare Company's compilation of scenes from Shakespeare. Two of the dissenters, Robert Coleman and John Chapman, voted for Tennessee Williams's *The Milk Train Doesn't Stop Here Anymore* and Sidney Michaels's *Tchin-Tchin*, respectively, and there was one ballot for Peter Ustinov's *Photo Finish*. Despite the reservations expressed in his review, Walter Kerr agreed with the majority that *Virginia Woolf* was the best play of the season. It was nominated for six Tony awards and won five, for best play, best production, best director, best actress (Uta Hagen), and best actor (Arthur Hill). It missed only best supporting actress (Melinda Dillon), with that honor going to Sandy Dennis (for Herb Gardner's *A Thousand Clowns*), who would play the role of Honey in the movie of *Virginia Woolf*.

Albee's play was the obvious choice for the Pulitzer Prize for drama, which would have meant that it had won the triple crown for theater, a rare feat for any work. John Mason Brown and John Gassner, the critics who made up the Pulitzer jury that year in the area of drama, strongly recommended it. As was the custom in those years of the Pulitzer, it was the jury's only nomination. In his letter to the Pulitzer advisory board, Brown said, "Although I can't pretend that *Who's Afraid of Virginia Woolf?* makes for a pleasant evening in the theater, I do know it provides an unforgettable one." Gassner said that the play "towers over the other plays and makes it impossible to make a second nomination" and added that it was "a flashing and penetrating work by the most eminent of new American playwrights." The advisory board of journalists has the final say over the awards in the arts. Three years earlier the board had rejected the nomination by Brown and Gassner of Lillian Hellman's *Toys in the Attic* and had given the drama prize to the musical *Fiorello!* Again rejecting a Brown-Gassner nomination, the board of journalists decided to give no theater prize in 1963. There were fourteen members on that board, and the vote was split. Barry Bingham, publisher of the Louisville *Courier-Journal*, and Turner Catledge, managing editor of *The New York Times*, both voted for *Virginia Woolf*, Catledge saying that it was "the best play I knew of in New York." W. D. Maxwell, vice president and editor of the *Chicago Tribune* and a self-styled censor in his home city, voted against it because he thought it was "a filthy play," which, he said, was "purely my personal opinion and it's narrow-minded and bigoted and anything else you want to call it."

The advisory board's decision was a shocking disregard of the advice of its expert jury and also a radical attack on the theater. When their Hellman nomination had been rejected, Brown and Gassner said that "if the trustees overruled us on future occasions and gave the award to a play other than the one we selected, then the trustees would have to announce what our selection was." By not giving any prize, Gassner said, it seemed "to be an indirect way of getting around our vote." As a result, Brown and Gassner resigned in protest. "This is a case of advice without consent," said Brown, accusing the board of making "a farce out of the drama award." He added, "Whether you like it or not, Mr. Albee's play is the biggest and the strongest play written by an American this year."

Albee's public response was seemingly without rancor: "I'm glad my play was recommended by the jurors, but I really don't see what reaction one can have to an award that wasn't made . . . I wasn't counting on the award. If you start counting on winning prizes, you get disappointed. And if you don't count on them, it's a very nice surprise if you do win them." On the other hand, Barr rose in high dudgeon. He was "shocked and appalled," and because some board members had voted against the play without seeing it, he suggested that the awards be "reformed or discontinued."

The Pulitzer rejection turned out to be a foreshadowing of controversies to come. In common with poems and novels of the Beat Generation and with *Lolita*, *Virginia Woolf* was condemned by self-proclaimed moralists as a decadent work. In part that was a manifestation of the times, the early 1960s, be-

fore the assassinations of the Kennedys and Martin Luther King Jr. and long
before Watergate, when cynicism was not yet endemic. Albee's play was a
shocker, especially because it was on Broadway, an arena known more for its
timidity than its temerity.

While the play was still running on Broadway, other productions began
spreading out. Nancy Kelly and Sheppard Strudwick led the American touring company. The play was censored in Boston, where the head of city li-
censing said "it would be a mortal sin to sit back and do nothing while this
cesspool backs up." He sent a letter to the theater manager asking for alterations in nine "irreverent references to the Deity." The producers agreed.

After about a year on Broadway, the play was licensed for foreign production. The first, starring Jerome Kilty and his wife, Cavada Humphrey, toured
South Africa, where the actors had previously traveled with *Dear Liar*, Kilty's
dramatization of the letters of George Bernard Shaw and Mrs. Patrick Campbell. At Albee's insistence, *Virginia Woolf* was to be presented only before integrated audiences. The play opened in Port Elizabeth and then moved to
Durban, receiving strong reviews (favorable and unfavorable) in both cities,
with a more negative response in Durban, where one critic called it "dirt-
laden debris." In Johannesburg, the press was more positive. But people who
may or may not have seen the show expressed their outrage in letters to the
government. In response, Jan de Klerk, the South African minister of the interior, ordered that performances be suspended in Johannesburg while waiting
for a report from the official Board of Censors to insure that the play was "not
contrary to public interest or good morals." In effect, the play was banned.
Molly Reinhardt, writing in the *Sunday Times* of Johannesburg, was furious,
saying that the banning made South Africa "once again the laughing-stock of
the thinking world." In order to resume performances, the producer suggested possible alterations in the text, including the substitution of ridiculous
euphemisms like "jeepers" and "hell's bells." Imagine Martha bursting into
her home and saying "Jeepers H. Christ" or "Hell's bells, what a dump." In
spite of that attempted whitewash, the censors still continued the ban. In the
Cape Argus newspaper, Owen Williams objected—to no avail—calling the
play a masterpiece and "a very moral" work.

Looking ahead to the first anniversary of the New York production, Hagen
wrote to Albee with deep affection, as "Eduardo mio": "A year ago you didn't
have two homes and I didn't have this one which I can only *bear* to leave because I have to be *so* grateful to the play that I can't (shouldn't) let it down
now . . . Well neighbor mine. I can't wait to see you on any occasion. I keep
telling you I love you and I REALLY do."

Three foreign language productions of *Virginia Woolf* followed in quick succession in October 1963: in Venice, directed by Franco Zeffirelli; in Stockholm, directed by Ingmar Bergman; and in Berlin by Boleslaw Barlog (who had presented the original production of *The Zoo Story*). Barr and Mark Wright went to all three European openings. Albee was otherwise engaged with *The Ballad of the Sad Cafe* in New York.

The day before the critics came, Zeffirelli wrote Albee a long letter about the play and his production. He explained that his changes in the text were largely to clarify American expressions for Italian audiences. Then he confessed to a great loss in the production—Honey, a character that could not be translated. Melinda Dillon was in fact the most underappreciated member of the Broadway cast. Then Zeffirelli mentioned the fierce opposition to his production, the anti-Americanism in Italy, the bitterness of Italian authors, and the skepticism of authorities. As Mark Wright remembers, "Franco's production was full of vitality and Italian expression, the German one was what I would have imagined as German Expressionism. In my recollection, there was nothing on the stage except big gray furniture and people in gray costumes, and very dour lighting. Of the three, I remember the Swedish one the least, but with the exception of the woman in the Italian one, it was the best acted."

In the Ingmar Bergman production, Karin Kalvi and Bibi Andersson were Martha and Honey (with Thommy Berggren as Nick). Andersson had seen the play on Broadway and suggested that Bergman do it at the Royal Dramatic Theater. "I thought it was Bergman's universe," she said, "with the endless problems with relationships and also that it was very symbolic." The imaginary child was "a symbol of the destruction of love. I've experienced it myself: there can be one word, one line, and it's irreparable and you fall out of love." In the play, "it's a night where everything is becoming clarified. They're testing their love to such a degree that they're destroying themselves. They go down together. It's not one who wins. It's like being in hell." Bergman staged the play starkly, with four chairs and bookshelves, "a little bit abstract, Walpurgis nacht, all in grey and black," she said. It was a highly eroticized production, one of the few Bergman did of a contemporary play. The fight was about castration, said Andersson: "The fight between the sexes was very Strindberg. Although it was a small part, it was the most important role I've done because before that I was always cast as very healthy. Suddenly they realized I had some character. I said, if she's called a mouse, I want to play a small town Marilyn Monroe, very sexy. She wanted to be something she wasn't. After that, I did Maggie in *After the Fall*."

In December, the play was done in Prague, and in a case of local adaptation, the title was changed to *Who's Afraid of Franz Kafka?*, thereby losing something in the translation.

Virginia Woolf ran for two years on Broadway, giving 664 performances and earning a profit of $750,000. Hagen and Hill were in the show for the entire run, with Ben Piazza and Rochelle Oliver taking over the other roles. Another company continued to rotate at matinees, with Elaine Stritch and Haila Stoddard, among others, playing Martha. Then, led by Hagen and Hill, the play went to London for a limited engagement of three months early in 1964.

With the announcement that the play was going to be done in London, Albee immediately collided with the Lord Chamberlain, who at that time was still the official English censor. His role, said Albee, was "to make plays safe for the Royal Family, if they ever went to the theater." In May 1963, Clinton Wilder and Donald Albery, who was coproducing the play, went to the Lord Chamberlain's office to discuss the matter with two of the censor's colleagues. Albery had made that journey many times before, with *Waiting for Godot* and other plays. Before the visit, Wilder decided that if the Lord Chamberlain proved to be intractable, he and his partners were going to make it "a big scandal in the press." Wilder began in a lighthearted fashion, making it clear that they were not taking the possibility of a rejection seriously. The response was good-natured and friendly. As Wilder reported to Albee, "What followed was a hilarious hour of absolutely filthy conversation. Their primary worry is 'bugger.' I felt that we should fight for 'bugger' and then back down after we had won everything else since we don't need 'bugger.' This way we might get 'screw' when it means 'fuck' which is the secondary objection."

The play was approved for production but despite Wilder's optimism, the Lord Chamberlain took exception to much of the dialogue. There were pages and pages of requested changes. When Albee arrived for the opening, he posted the list backstage. "We laughed until we wept," said Hagen, "and we had long meetings about it. You couldn't say, 'screw, baby,' but you could say, 'hump the hostess,' because hump was in Shakespeare. We were allowed three Jesus Christs out of ten." The first line cut was the first line, "Jesus H. Christ." Going over changes in the Lord Chamberlain's office, Albee suggested sardonically that perhaps Martha could say Mary H. Magdalene. To the playwright's astonishment, the censor agreed. But Hagen was so accustomed to the original line that when she came onstage for opening night, she accidently said, "Jesus H. . . . Magdalene," which confused everyone. Hill was not allowed to say "scrotum" in "tiny little slicing operations on the underside of the scrotum." It was suggested that he use the English expression, "privacies." On opening night, he said, "tiny little slicing operations on the underside of the . . . privacies." Later Hill said, "I'm never going to say that again." Among the Lord Chamberlain's other requests: "cheese" for "Jesus," "bastard" for "bugger," "bowel" for "right ball," and "propaganda machine" for "screwing machine." Barr and Albee suggested that the actors simply forget the Lord Chamberlain's requests, and for the most part that is exactly what they did.

After writing the play, Albee had sent a letter to Leonard Woolf, telling him that he was planning to use his wife's name in the title. Woolf gave his approval. Soon after the play opened in London, Woolf and Peggy Ashcroft saw it together and Woolf wrote to Albee: "We both enjoyed it immensely. It is so amusing and at the same time moving and is really about the important things in life. Nothing is rarer, at any rate, on the English stage. I wonder if you have ever read a short story which my wife wrote and is printed in *A Haunted House?* It is called "Lappin and Lapinova." The details are quite different but the theme is the same as that of the imaginary child in your play."

In the strange and mysterious story, a married couple in England invent an alternative reality for themselves as an imaginary pair of rabbits named Lappin and Lapinova, and use it as a method of survival. In the end, the wife, suffering what seems to be a breakdown, announces that her character, Lapinova, has been "caught in a trap" and killed. And that, says Virginia Woolf, was "the end of that marriage." Albee says he never read the story. In his play, of course, he suggests the opposite: The loss of George and Martha's illusion will lead to the continuation of their marriage.

"Our" Ballad–and
Travels with Steinbeck

Who else is directing the play?

ALTHOUGH it might be said that adaptations have been Albee's undoing, each one he has chosen to do has been undertaken with high hopes and a promise of fidelity. Perhaps it is the fidelity that is the primary problem. From *The Ballad of the Sad Cafe* through *Malcolm* and on to *Lolita,* he has tried to mimic the original author, in effect, to be that author: Albee as substitute speaker. He hides or rather disguises his own voice. The most satisfying collaboration—although it was only partly successful—was with Carson Mc-Cullers in *The Ballad of the Sad Cafe,* and perhaps that was because it was with her that he had the closest emotional kinship.

Albee had read the McCullers novella in the early 1950s and was struck by its lyrical quality and its visual possibilities. In the summer of 1960, after writing his one-acts and while working on *Virginia Woolf,* he sent a letter to the author saying that he wanted to adapt the book to the stage and offered to write a sample scene. He also sent her a copy of *The Death of Bessie Smith.* McCullers read his play and said that she was "delighted with the brilliant dialogue," but thought that the premise "that bigotry and prejudice are evil" did not have the desired dramatic build-up. At the time she was "still having a tough time" writing her novel, *Clock Without Hands,* so that a staged *Ballad* would have to wait for her serious consideration. "Whenever the spirit moves

you," she said, "I would be most anxious to read that first scene" of his dramatization. She closed by saying, "I have a feeling we are going to be very good
friends." He wrote the scene, and she gave the go-ahead for the project.

Then Albee wrote to David Diamond about the prospective adaptation,
and Diamond responded by saying that it was a fine idea. Coming from a
man who had been the closest of friends with both Carson and her husband,
Reeve McCullers (who had committed suicide in 1953), this was a great encouragement—not that Albee really needed encouragement. Although Mc-
Cullers was fully cooperative on the venture, Albee was wary of becoming too
involved with her. In January, he wrote Diamond again, saying "I have stayed
out of contact with her once the *Ballad* deal was set . . . for the simple reason
that I cannot work when someone needs to look at every page, every day. It
was enough of a struggle to convince her that the piece should not be a musical. . . . with chorus line and all." Before Albee entered the scene, McCullers
had considered doing her own adaptation, turning the story into a musical
drama. She said that he convinced her "the words would be coarsened by the
music."

With her friend Dr. Mary E. Mercer, McCullers spent part of the summer
of 1962 with Albee and McNally at Water Island, several months before Albee's Broadway debut with *Who's Afraid of Virginia Woolf?* After writing for
about four hours every morning, he would take long walks on the beach. At
night, he would read aloud to his guests. One evening, he read Beckett's
Happy Days and another, after an early dinner, he read *Virginia Woolf.* He
also read aloud the first act of his adaptation of *The Ballad of the Sad Cafe.* After returning to her home in Nyack, New York, McCullers sent Albee a letter
thanking him for "the sun, the hay, the suntan, not to mention Virginnia
Woffe [sic] and all the fun, *Happy Days* and 'our' *Ballad.*" Dr. Mercer followed with a letter, saying she thought he was "accomplishing all you hope to
do with the *Ballad.*"

That fall, McCullers saw *Virginia Woolf,* and later she wrote in *Harper's
Bazaar,* "This play, as luminous as the stars, is about the destruction of a
dream. It has the passion of a Greek drama although the setting is in an Eastern college town. It shows malicious humiliation and love and tenderness and
bitterness. It has in it compassion, the wildest humor and the dark brilliance
that, to me, is peculiar to the genius of Edward Albee." In a parallel piece, Albee returned the praise, calling McCullers "a curious magician . . . both
Child and Sage; Pain and Joy. She has mastered the card tricks of both art and
life, and she has seen equally clearly the sleight of hand of reality and the
truth which resides in legerdemain." Away from public print, he offered his

personal feeling about her: "I wouldn't like to have had her as an enemy. She could be vicious and terribly selfish, but she was very bright and a good friend. I enjoyed her company." McCullers had suffered from a variety of debilitating illnesses including cancer and had had several operations on her paralyzed left arm. When she and Albee were working together, she had difficulty getting from place to place.

The immediate obstacle Albee faced was that the novella was almost entirely narrative, with very little dialogue. He had to discover a language for McCullers's characters, in particular for the three relatives who are locked in a grotesque triangle: the Amazonian Miss Amelia; her husband, Marvin Macy; and her cousin, Lymon, who is a dwarf. In conversation, he would ask McCullers for clarification: "What went on upstairs when Marvin Macy tried to get into bed with Miss Amelia? Was Miss Amelia a lesbian?" Intentionally, she left these questions ambiguous.

By February 1963, he was halfway through the adaptation, which he identified as "Carson's play." From the beginning he planned to incorporate some of the author's words through the use of the device of a narrator. The original plan was to have McCullers herself act as narrator. She would record her role and it would be replayed on tape at every performance. In May she sent him a letter, saying that when he typed "the McCullers part," could he type it in capital letters and triple space, "so that I will be able to read it easily and perhaps memorize it by the time we record it. I ask this because I have an obscure neurological defect that makes me skip two or three lines at a time (that is why I cannot read out loud)." Because of her disabilities, she was unable to do the narration herself. Maintaining her authorial interest in the adaptation, she said, "Do let me know when you think we should start to work on our ballad." By mid-July, he was "just about done" with it. McCullers and Mercer returned to Water Island for a week and he read the play aloud to them.

In August, he had a momentary diversion. Picking up the Sunday *Times*, he read a piece by Joseph Hayes, author of *The Desperate Hours*, attacking what he considered to be the negativism of writers of "so-called 'serious' plays," namely Williams and Albee. Hayes heatedly posed some questions: "Are all children the braying monsters of those in *Cat on a Hot Tin Roof?* Is marriage itself the stultifying trap, the wasteland of illusion and cruelty and betrayal described in this play and many others, notably *Who's Afraid of Virginia Woolf? ...* Does the waspish bitchiness of the dialogue in *Virginia Woolf,* for instance, correspond to a recognizable pattern of the speech in a marriage or to some other relationship out and beyond the experience of most of us?" If we responded positively to these visions, then "the forces of darkness and despair and destruction have moved that much closer."

Putting his work aside, Albee moved into polemical action. His reply to Hayes appeared the following Sunday in the *Times:* "Mr. Hayes *appears* to suggest that Mr. Tennessee Williams and I are bent on bringing about a thermonuclear war, thereby destroying the United States and Our Way of Life." Therefore, it seemed "sensible that either Mr. Williams or I should reply to Mr. Hayes's piece, and since Mr. Williams is, at the moment, meeting with Anastas Mikoyan in a Russian sub off Key West, the job has fallen to me." Swiftly he attacked Hayes's "untruths, half truths, intentional and/or unintentional distortions of purpose and fact . . . jingoism, sophistry, spuriousness and sophomorics—not to mention humorlessness." It is "men like Mr. Hayes who will, truly and finally, corrupt the taste of our theater audiences, destroy our theater, undermine the national morality and bring things to a point where it will not matter if the bombs fall." Then, after taking a jab at Hayes as a purveyor of "escapist commercialism for our stage," he plunged to the heart of the argument:

> If the theater must only, as Mr. Hayes puts it, "reflect or express the fundamental beliefs, feelings, convictions, aspirations" of our audiences, then, say I, down with all the debate; down with all playwrights who have questioned the underpinnings of all the fundamental beliefs, etc.; down with all the playwrights who have not been content merely to reassure their audiences that all their values were dandy; down, then, say I, with Moliere, Ibsen, Shaw, Aristophanes. Down with the theater as an educational as well as an entertainment medium. Down with the theater as a force for social and political advancement. Down with the theater! And up with the Fascism of a theater dedicated to satisfying only the whimperings of a most unworthy audience.

Albee's piece was printed under the headline WHO'S AFRAID OF THE TRUTH? Soon, readers were angrily attacking both Hayes and Albee, with the novelist Evan Hunter wading in with an assault on Albee's "strident hairpulling reply." Taubman, the *Times*' critic, followed with an act of attempted fence-straddling saying that Hayes was not the escapist that Albee made him out to be, nor was Albee the nihilist that Hayes described. In the tone of a sermonizer, Taubman confessed a preference for "the yea-saying writer who digs into the depths of his soul to emerge with hope and affirmation," while suggesting that one should not misunderstand "those who speak, whether hol-

lowly, agonizingly or even hysterically, from the deeps of personal abysses."
Moving to Beckett, he said that there was something alien in his "parched
landscape," but made a plea for theater as "an enormous mansion," with
room for "the Ibsens, Shaws, O'Neills, Hellmans and Millers on the one hand
and the Strindbergs, Becketts, Pinters and Albees on the other." One fallacy
of his argument was that arbitrary division, as if the first group were entirely
yea sayers, the second naysayers. And where did Williams fit? Somewhere in
the "deeps of personal abysses?"

Hayes had the next word. In a letter to the *Times*, he said: "I am ignoring
Edward Albee's personal, hysterical, finger-clawing attack on me: it reveals
the kind of human being he is." It was, of course, Hayes who seemed hysterical. It is impossible to read these charges and countercharges, particularly
Evan Hunter's description of Albee's remarks as "strident hair-pulling" and
Hayes's reference to "hysterical, finger-clawing," without wondering whether
the attack on Albee was aimed in some part at his homosexuality, which, in
that more restrictive time, had not yet been publicly acknowledged. Even
Taubman the peacemaker seemed to be dealing with such innuendo when
he spoke of Albee having "secrets about his people" and visions he was not yet
exposing to public view.

As a joke, Richard Barr sent a letter to Albee, signed with Hayes's name:

> Thank you so much for your kind words about me in last Sunday's *Times*. It
> is refreshing to know that one's colleagues are so perceptive — nay, flattering. I
> was a bit disappointed that you took such a whack at your producers (whom I
> understand are extremely nice fellows) in *Transatlantic Review*. [Albee had said
> in that journal that his producers "should be given medals hammered out of
> solid gold because they don't know what the term Broadway means".] One can
> feel from your two columns . . . that we see eye to eye, and share happily a truly
> objective evaluation of reality.

Returning to his writing, Albee revised his adaptation of *Ballad*, polishing
it for Broadway production in the fall. It was to be produced by Lewis Allan
and Ben Edwards (also the set designer), and not by Barr and Wilder. Albee
estimated that the actual writing took him about seven weeks, but it was extended over a year's time. Flanagan wrote the musical score.

Alan Schneider once again was Albee's director. From the beginning he
seemed to have doubts about the work. In his autobiography, Schneider
speaks about a visit that he and Albee made to McCullers's home:

Carson's relationship with Edward was always a mysterious one to me . . . I felt that she didn't really like Edward's script but that she respected his theater sense and craft. I respected that sense and craft also—how could I not?—but felt that *Ballad* had been constructed too rapidly, without carefully considering its structural and stylistic problems. Edward's adaptation contained some beautiful scenes and some exquisite speeches, but the whole piece didn't seem to connect.

Schneider had Geraldine Page's agreement to play Amelia, but Albee insisted on Colleen Dewhurst, an ideal choice for this commanding character. McCullers's own role was soon referred to as the Narrator, and it was decided to have an actor play the part. In one version of the script, that role was identified by the name of the actor who had been chosen, Roscoe Lee Browne. Lou Antonio played the husband, and William Prince and Enid Markey were cast in other roles. Searching for a dwarf to play Cousin Lymon, they discovered Michael Dunn, who was three feet ten, had a genius IQ, and seemed extraordinarily self-possessed. Accustomed to holding court by perching on bars in theatrical restaurants, Dunn said, "I don't have a midget mentality."

On the first day of rehearsal, September 2, Albee addressed the actors: "You're good actors. Alan's a good director. Ben's built a nice set. So if the play's lousy, it's my fault. And that's why the first day of rehearsal is depressing to me." In his log of the production, Lou Antonio said that when the cast sat down to read the play, Schneider said that it was a play about loneliness and love, but mostly loneliness. At that point, the play was a long three acts. The playwright promised that it would be cut, and within several weeks, it had been reduced to one long act.

As had been true of Uta Hagen in *Virginia Woolf*, Dewhurst was not eager to work with Schneider. In her posthumous autobiography, she is quite clear about her antipathy, which increased as the rehearsals continued. Approaching previews, she said, he "was beginning to show signs of cowardice. He was frightened by the material, and to relieve himself of his fright, he began to put Roscoe, Enid and especially Michael under his thumb." Browne, who could certainly take care of himself, denies there was any such attempt in his case, and he had previously worked effectively with Schneider in a production of *The Threepenny Opera* at the Arena Stage in Washington. "I didn't notice that he was picking on Enid, but I did see him confusing Michael to the point of harassment. Michael said to me, does he want me to dance?" Dunn could sing, play the piano, and fly a plane, but he could not dance. "I have a good sense of rhythm," he said, "but a lousy leg." Dunn proved to be surprisingly resilient, despite the fact that he was not healthy and was in physical pain for most of the production. "It was a virtue for him to have that confidence," said Browne. "To wear a cockiness even if he didn't have it. He would strive not to have you notice his infirmities. He even managed a kind of jauntiness in his walk."

In his notes to Antonio, Schneider told him to show "more restraint—like Edward, like lava: no eruptions. Better to be controlled. Edward's definition of a fable: where nobody shouts." Dewhurst felt that the director was not giving her the help she wanted: "With each succeeding day, the tension mounted. Worst of all, a feeling of fear began to invade the cast . . . a fear of being unexpectedly humiliated by some unprovoked or snide remark from Mr. Schneider." Among other things, the actress wanted a clarification of her character's sexuality. She was also worried about the brutal, climactic battle between her and Antonio. Would an audience believe a woman could be such a tough fighter? At one point, the director brought in a choreographer to do the fight scene, which disturbed the actors because they were playing mountain people: They felt that they needed movement rather than choreography. Next, Schneider hired a stunt man from *The Naked City* on television, and, said Antonio, the fight "looked fake."

Getting no support from Schneider, and with Albee attending few rehearsals, Dewhurst asked Antonio to her house in Riverdale, where they received an uncredited and unofficial assist from Dewhurst's husband, George C. Scott, a director as well as actor. At Dewhurst's request, Scott helped them restage the fight scene. "We wanted to take out all the fancy, all the cliches," said Antonio. They threw themselves into the fray. "I remember using my arm as a club and coming down on top of her shoulders." The next day at rehearsal, Dewhurst and Antonio did the scene not as they had before, by circling each other like wary animals, but directly engaged in combat. Schneider objected; Dewhurst protested. As the cast watched in awe, Dewhurst shouted at Schneider, accusing him of being a destructive human being and stormed off the stage. As she tells the story, she became a heroine to the other actors, but by walking out and refusing to take any further notes from the director, she was erecting an obstacle for herself as well as for the play. As an adversary, Schneider was simply not in Dewhurst's class. "Alan would not dare shout anything rude to Colleen," said Browne. "She couldn't stand him," Antonio said, "and he was afraid of her." As Ben Edwards said in understatement about *Ballad*, it was a "troubled production all around."

The Narrator continued to present a problem. He was there to set the scene and connect the narrative, but he was not supposed to be part of the action, or even to relate to any of the other actors onstage. Browne remembers: "Alan would say almost childish things: 'He's not there! You don't see him!' You can't say that to actors who hear you, who know that you're onstage and they hear you speak about their characters." Browne, for one, thought that the Narrator should somehow be integral to the action. There was a reference in the text to a chain gang. Perhaps he could be a former member of that chain gang designated to sweep the floor and do odd chores around the cafe. Perhaps he could be something of a balladeer (one name that was considered for his character).

Browne also thought that some of his lines more properly belonged to Marvin Macy's brother, Henry (William Prince). Schneider agreed, at least after the fact: "All through rehearsals, I kept thinking that the brother, Henry Macy, should be telling the story instead of an impersonal Narrator," but "Roscoe was too much of a delight to relinquish." For the most part, Schneider concentrated on the drama in the foreground and allowed Browne to follow his own lead. Browne remembers one moment of Schneider direction, when he said, "Roscoe, my love, do you think you should be on that side of the stage?" Browne answered, "Alan, my love, let me put it this way: nooo." Schneider laughed, took his baseball cap off (he always wore a baseball cap when he directed), tipped it, put it back on, and returned to the play.

As Albee rewrote scenes, the role of the Narrator kept getting larger. Browne said that every morning "I would have a new speech incorporating most of a scene they had just deleted. They didn't realize I was complaining when I said, 'Gentlemen, there's something wrong with this fellow who comes to tell you what you've just seen, what you're now looking at and what you're going to see." In reaching for greater fidelity to McCullers, the play was becoming less dramatic, and it was making Dewhurst's role more difficult. Constantly she was aware of the Narrator encroaching on her territory. One added problem was the fact that Browne, the Narrator, was one of her best friends. Browne recalls, "In her rage, she would say to Schneider, 'you have this wonderful actor [meaning Browne] stuck out there.' By the time we were in previews, Colleen was in deep trouble with the piece. She knew of course she needed another eye to see what she was doing. It couldn't be anybody onstage, and she would not allow the director to do it." And protocol would not have allowed Albee to take part in the direction.

Enter George C. Scott. Finally, at his wife's urging, he came to watch rehearsals. He sat unobtrusively in the back of the theater and returned again as an observer. Scott, Dewhurst, and Browne drove back to the house in

Riverdale, and over a long evening they went through the play line by line, with Scott acting as director, editor, and play doctor. All this was, of course, completely unofficial and not known to either Schneider or Albee. Browne remembers: "I had more than twenty entrances, which means as many speeches and as many exits." Scott would say, "You don't really need this speech," and Browne would agree, realizing that what he was saying should have been self-evident from the preceding scene. With Browne's assent, Scott slashed entire speeches as unnecessary, "whittling" Browne's role "down to about eight speeches."

Browne greatly admired Scott's effort. Then it became his job to present the suggested cuts to Schneider, without, of course, revealing who was responsible for them. The next day, with great tact, he told Schneider how his role should be reduced, an astonishing thing for an actor to tell a director. Schneider admitted that the cuts made sense, but said they would have to be approved by the playwright, and that he was in Montauk and unavailable. Then Browne went to Lewis Allan and asked him if he could contact Albee.

That evening, as the signal came for half hour before curtain, there was a knock on Browne's dressing room door. It was Albee, and Browne repeated to him what he had told Schneider. To the actor's relief, Albee responded, "You're still saying those dreadful words? Take them out!" Browne recalls, "He couldn't have been more charming and generous of spirit." They went straight through the script, as Browne pointed out the suggested cuts. "Only one he wanted to keep. That put me at such total ease that I could institute all those cuts that evening." Did he tell Albee that Scott was involved in the rewriting? "Never! Never, never, never. It would have been most indiscreet to mention it." And if Schneider found out, says Browne, he "would have wondered, who else was directing the play?"

Along the way, there were other small changes in the dialogue. At one point, the Narrator used the word Negro; at Browne's urging it was changed to "field hand." In at least one other way, Browne helped Dewhurst. She had to make her first entrance laughing. To induce that laughter, Browne whispered to her in the dark just before she went on stage: "Do you know who played Jane to Elmo Roper's Tarzan in the silent film." "Who?" she said. "Enid Markey," he said, and Dewhurst howled with laughter. Part of the humor, Browne explained, was because "you cannot imagine this sweet lady swinging on a tree." Every night from then on, the conversation was repeated, until all Browne had to say were those magic words, "Enid Markey," to trigger her laughter.

McCullers came to a preview in her wheelchair. By this time, she was not in good shape. She had great difficulty in speaking and after the performance she haltingly asked Browne what his character was called. He showed her the prompter's script, and her face lit up. The Narrator was still identified as "Mrs. McCullers." Browne said that the reason for the oversight in the script was that there was "enough turmoil not to pay attention to things like that." At one point, Albee took Noël Coward to see *Ballad*. It was, he said, "a great mistake." Coward kept sighing through the performance and finally said, "Dear boy, this is not my kind of play."

On October 30, the day of the opening, the cast had a double-quick run-through of the play, led by Schneider, who had a *New York Post* headline affixed to the back of his jacket, which read "Control your tension." McCullers was at the opening in her wheelchair, along with a contingent of her friends. Although the actors missed some of their lines, the play went as expected. The reviews were mixed. Chapman in the *New York Daily News* surprised himself—and Albee—by rolling out every favorable adjective in his glossary: "magnificent . . . beautiful, absorbing, exciting, touching and absolutely enthralling." It was up to Kerr to provide the negative. He said it was "silent at the core, an act of refusal, a warning tacked to the fence-post that says: 'move on.'" He also called it "the possible shell of a play." Brustein took the opportunity in panning *Ballad* to assail *Virginia Woolf*, which he now regarded as "an ersatz masterpiece." Criticizing both Albee and McCullers, he said that with *Ballad*, Albee was imitating "an inferior writer" and had written "a trivial and a tedious play." Albee's faithfulness to McCullers left the play curiously underdramatized.

The Ballad of the Sad Cafe did only moderate business. "It was a very delicate piece," said Browne. "It was illusory and strange. I had difficulty deciding if it worked. On different evenings I thought, we've just done a lovely poem. There were evenings when we knew the audience and we were wed, and that we loved doing it." Other nights it seemed less like a play and more like a staged reading. "I think the other actors all had a good feeling for me but if anybody was unhappy it was really because that fucking narrator was going on and on and on. No one ever said so, but I thought so."

While *Ballad* struggled, *Virginia Woolf* continued to thrive on Broadway, which apparently irritated McCullers. According to McCullers's biographer Virginia Spencer Carr, the author was not happy with the adaptation and resented the fact that Albee left New York immediately after the play opened and did not stay to help with any possible changes. As Flanagan suggested in a letter to Diamond, Albee's presence in New York might itself be enough to help the run of the show: "He could insult somebody publicly and get his name in the newspapers and *Time* the way he's wont to do when he's here—and thereby send the public flocking to the theater."

In the absence of Albee (and Schneider), the actors had continued to search for a way to make *The Ballad of the Sad Cafe* work. Finally in one performance, said Antonio, "it clicked," and everything fell in place. Through it all, he greatly enjoyed working with Dewhurst. She was, he said, "the easiest to break up onstage of anyone I've ever acted with—that big laugh of hers." In one scene, he had to come down to the apron of the stage and open a box with their engagement ring in it. One matinee, he opened the box and the ring fell to the floor and rolled off the stage. He could not continue the scene without it, so he went to the edge of the stage and looked at a man in the front row and said, "Gimme the ring." The man gave the actor the ring, and when Antonio turned around Dewhurst was lying flat on her back laughing. He went up to her, said his line—and then her line because she was still laughing. She left the stage to a burst of applause from the audience. At one point, Antonio and Dewhurst talked about doing a revival of *Virginia Woolf*, with Scott and Dewhurst as George and Martha and Antonio and Lane Bradbury as Nick and Honey. That never happened, but it would have been a powerhouse production.

Along with Dewhurst, Michael Dunn had gotten the best reviews in *Ballad*, and was soon appearing on the Johnny Carson show and being interviewed extensively (by me, among others). The sudden fame seemed to turn his head. "He started showing off onstage," said Antonio, "not doing the play so much, but trying to be cute." He and Dewhurst both noticed that and tried to keep Dunn in line. At one performance when Dunn started acting up, Antonio walked in front of him, swinging his arm and obliterating him from the view of the audience, upstaging the upstager. Two years later Dunn performed a nightclub show, but *Ballad* was to prove the single highlight of his brief career.

On Sunday, November 3, 1963, three days after the opening of *Ballad*, Albee left for Moscow to meet John Steinbeck. Their visit, part of President Kennedy's cultural exchange program, had been planned the previous spring. In October 1962, Steinbeck had been awarded the Nobel Prize for literature, and as a friend and admirer, Albee was one of many who immediately congratulated him. When Steinbeck saw *Virginia Woolf* at the opening night, he sent the playwright his congratulations, saying that "the flash of the moment of truth is blinding." Taking a cue from Ralph Waldo Emerson, he continued, "When Whitman sent his home-printed copies of *Leaves of Grass* to the so-called giants of his time, only Emerson deigned to reply. He said and I want to plagiarize — 'I salute you on the threshold of a great career.' Isn't it interesting that only the vulgar papers found your play vulgar? But that was inevitable, I guess." He added, "I want to see it again and again."

When President Kennedy invited Steinbeck to go to the Soviet Union, Steinbeck was hesitant. In a letter to Leslie Brady, the cultural attache to the American Embassy in Moscow, he said that he was concerned that he would be asked to comment on racism in America, that he would have to explain the Birmingham church bombing (in which four young black girls were killed) to people whose minds were closed. He also felt "a kind of grey weariness" creeping over him. In spite of that, he wanted to go, in his words, "to kick up some dust," and he asked if his wife Elaine could accompany him. He also thought it might be a good idea to include another artist. Elia Kazan, who had directed several Steinbeck films, was a possibility, but he was busy. Steinbeck then thought of Albee, "our newest and perhaps most promising young playwright," and a friend of the Steinbecks.

For Steinbeck, one of the advantages of having Albee along was the fact that they had different opinions about political issues and also about literature. In contrast to the playwright, the novelist supported the U.S. involvement in Vietnam. Because *The Ballad of the Sad Cafe* was due to open in the fall, Steinbeck suggested that the journey be postponed for Albee's convenience.

In September, Steinbeck sent letters to Mikhail Sholokhov, Ilya Ehrenburg, and other Soviet writers he had met on previous trips. The next month, he and his wife left for Moscow, where they were to meet Albee after his opening. The journey, beset with problems during the Cold War, was to cement the relationship of Albee and both Steinbecks. Years after John Steinbeck's death, Elaine Steinbeck would remain one of Albee's closest friends.

Albee spent a month in the Soviet Union and a week each in Poland, Hungary, and Czechoslovakia. He and Steinbeck met publicly with writers and sought out dissidents. Both writers gave talks, were interviewed, and, especially in Albee's case, went to the theater. Albee's guide for the journey was William Luers, then an officer in the administrative section of the American Embassy in Moscow, several years later the United States ambassador in Prague, and still later the president of the Metropolitan Museum of Art. At the time that Luers and Albee met in Moscow, Luers had not yet seen any of his plays, but had read several of them and had had copies sent over and circulated. Despite his growing international success Albee was largely unknown in the Soviet Union, in contrast to Steinbeck, who through his novels and his Nobel Prize was a great celebrity. Because of censorship questions about *Virginia Woolf*, Albee was also a controversial choice.

On arriving in Moscow, Albee was immediately taken to a U.S. Embassy reception. Rocky Staples, an embassy official, greeted him at the door by saying, "If I can call you Ed, you can call me Rocky." Albee replied coolly, "Nobody calls me Ed." That, said Luers, "sort of established their relationship" and showed him "a certain quality of Edward's that I came to have affection for and a certain fear of during that trip"—his candidness and directness. Albee was not afraid of confrontation. Luers continues, "That was a period when he was drinking a good deal. He and John both drank a lot on that trip. It was a pretty depressing trip for them, particularly for John, but I think Edward absorbed a lot of John's frustration. It was a tough period both internally in Russia and in our relations with the Russians even though we were beginning this cultural exchange."

The Soviets had decided that Steinbeck was "a closet Communist, who had been writing Communist tracts all his life." *The Grapes of Wrath* and some of his later novels were perceived as novels "about the inequality of capitalism and the need for socialism." Faced with such a hard line, Steinbeck and Albee reacted strongly. Said Luers: "I think that caused them to drink more and to get a little more irascible in certain things they did." At one midnight meeting, two Russian students attacked Steinbeck for betraying the working class because he had stopped writing books like *The Grapes of Wrath* and had "started lying."

Albee recalled that they had

> free-wheeling discussions with an entire spectrum of writers—from the brilliant, outspoken revisionist young to the stony-faced elders who had, with some honor or not, survived Stalin; we visited avant-garde painters in their studios; we had informal midnight sessions with university students; we placed a wreath on Pasternak's grave and nobody seemed to mind; and we had more than one night of vodka-drinking, table-thumping arguments with Stalinist holdovers in the bureaucratic apparatus of the Soviet Writers Union. It was an exciting time.

Elaine Steinbeck describes the nature of many of the meetings: "There would be a large crowd, and somebody would ask John a question, and John would answer, and Edward would say, 'I don't agree with you, John.' They talked about the war, politics, literature, all kinds of things." The Russians were surprised that the two American writers would disagree, especially in public. They were probably also surprised at their informality. Elaine Steinbeck recalled one dinner in Moscow. Her husband was being questioned so much that he scarcely had time to eat. "Suddenly he stood up to make a toast, and said, 'Natchez to Mobile.' I picked it up and said, 'Memphis to St. Joe,' and they all sat solemnly and drank, except for Edward who fell on the table laughing."

Early in the trip, Steinbeck wrote in a letter home, "The schedule is so heavy and every once in a while I begin to flag and fail. There is no time to write. I simply collapse into bed when I can." Albee was much better able to put up with the stress. Occasionally, they went to different cities, at one point, the Steinbecks going to Poland while Albee remained in Moscow. As Steinbeck wrote, "We left Edward behind in the big red city looking a little scairt. We will meet up with him in Prague."

According to Luers, Albee was always alert to the possibility that he was being misinterpreted or manipulated by the Soviet press for ideological reasons. At some point, Albee stopped being diplomatic. He was outraged at what was being done to writers in the Soviet Union, and he did not hesitate to express his opinion. "He didn't want to say what they wanted to hear," said Luers. "He wanted to say what he thought." He recalled one incident between Albee and an official Soviet guide. Albee pressed the guide for any points of disagreement he might have with his government. The guide refused to be specific and "Edward was drinking more vodka and getting angrier and angrier. Then he asked if he disagreed with the Stalin-Hitler pact prior to the invasion of Poland. The guide began to say it was done for the purpose of protecting Russia and to give the country breathing time. That so morally outraged Edward, that the man, particularly as a Jew, didn't see anything wrong with his country allying itself with Hitler—I remember Edward saying, 'I'm going to kill you.'" Luers said, "He meant it metaphorically."

Reflecting on the experience, Luers said,

> I hadn't been as close to anybody with his intellectual capacity as I was to Edward during the three weeks he was there. He had a tremendous impact on me personally. I grew to have a sense that he was one of the most meticulously honest people I had ever met. He clearly has two obsessions: one, he hates to repeat himself and he likes to be precisely responsive to specific questions asked; and he doesn't like to fall into patterns. He wouldn't design his answer to reflect a positive vision of America or a positive vision of himself. He just tried to get it right.

For Albee, the oddest experience that he and Luers had with Soviet writers was in Kiev: "We met several times with another one of the dissident writers. He stole wristwatches. He was a sleight of hand artist and he stole my wristwatch at one of our meetings. He stole everybody's wristwatch. He just liked to do it and he would keep them as memorabilia. He drank, as all Russian writers do. Bill said we would like to have another meeting with [this writer] to continue our conversation and 'Edward would like to have his wristwatch back.' [The writer] came to lunch with seven wristwatches, none of which, unfortunately, was mine."

The Steinbecks and Albee were in Leningrad when Steinbeck collapsed from exhaustion. While Steinbeck recovered, Albee and Elaine Steinbeck spent time together seeing the city. It was Albee's idea to black out everything that looked Soviet and to try and see the city as it was when it was St. Petersburg. They wandered through back streets and around canals. Steinbeck quickly recovered, and within the week, he and his wife left the Soviet Union for Poland. Albee and Luers went to Odessa at least partly because Albee wanted to see the setting of the famous scene in the movie *The Battleship Potemkin*, where the baby carriage rolls down the steps. In Odessa they went to the opera house and saw Rimsky-Korsakov's *The Czar's Bride*, which Albee described as "an obscure and foolishly lovely opera . . . shrieked by a bad, bad Russian soprano."

After the performance, they returned to their hotel and were brought joltingly back to the real world. Various members of the hotel management and staff were gathered around a radio, listening to a broadcast in English from the Voice of America. President Kennedy had been shot. A "semi-hysterical American eye doctor, who was visiting the famous eye clinic" in Odessa, was in his red underwear and he was crying. He led Albee and Luers to the radio, and they listened in horror.

In a letter to Flanagan, Albee wrote, "I'm sure it doesn't even make any *reality* sense in New York, but it's almost impossible to come to grips with it here. I miss everyone and everything so greatly, and have cried like a child (or maybe like a grownup)." In a subsequent letter to Barr, he said, "You cannot imagine what it is like to be so far and so frighteningly removed from home when such a thing hits . . . I suppose the whole experience has been—is being—what they call irreplaceable, or something, but it would be hard for you to imagine the depression and numb panic that sets in for a while each and every day." Luers later said, "It was so striking to see how frightened and concerned our Soviet hosts were, all of a sudden, over who might have killed him and what it meant. The concern that maybe their country had somebody involved—the death of the world's youngest, most appealing president. There was a great sense of solidarity which we had not felt fully during this trip." Albee and Luers stayed up late talking about Kennedy and about death, and, said Luers, that "became a theme that went through the next week or so." After the assassination, there were no more official functions.

Still not over their shock, Albee and Luers flew back to Moscow. Albee visited a few museums and then decided he wanted to go to Rostov-Veliki, a center of Russian culture outside of Moscow. Luers had never been there either, so he drove Albee (and Luers's wife) in his car. It was snowing when they left Moscow. Several miles from their destination, it began snowing heavily, and suddenly a bicyclist with no lights on his cycle was dimly seen ahead of them. Blinded by the storm, Luers accidentally struck the cyclist, knocking him to the side of the road. They took him to a hospital. Luers was questioned and the event was recorded in the files of the Central Intelligence Agency, which Albee later obtained through a Freedom of Information Act request ("Luers, while driving, struck a Soviet on a bicyclist [sic] and seriously injured him. This incident was fully reported to the Embassy and is a matter of record there").

Once again, Luers and Albee had a long night's vigil about death. Luers was afraid that he had killed the man, which he hadn't, and President Kennedy was still very much on their minds. From Luers's point of view, it was a moment of bonding with Albee, just as, he thought, Albee had previously bonded with Steinbeck. They had all lived through crises together. "I think the whole experience was troubling for Edward in many ways. He was alone; I think he called New York frequently. He was visiting this part of the world for the first time and experiencing a community of writers" that was in worse difficulty than he imagined. "Combine this with all the trauma of the Kennedy assassination and the automobile accident."

What Albee learned during the trip was to deepen his feelings about violations of human rights and encourage him to increase his activism in PEN, the international writers' association. As he was leaving Moscow in December, he held a press conference with American reporters and said that the Soviet writers he met were "not depressed and not optimistic, but ironic" about their situation, and they were living in "isolation from the mainstream of contemporary writing."

Back in New York, McNally had been working on his play *And Things That Go Bump in the Night*, which after several delays was scheduled to be done at the Guthrie Theater in Minneapolis. McNally had planned to meet Albee in Warsaw, or if he was delayed by the play, in Milan at the end of the month. He was filling in for Albee in the Playwrights Unit at the Actors Studio. In a letter dated December 1, McNally brought Albee up to date on the group's activities. As it turned out, Albee and McNally did not meet in Europe. Albee returned to America to confront two endings: *Ballad of the Sad Cafe* was in its final weeks and his relationship with McNally was over. McNally had taken up with the actor Robert Drivas, who was soon to star on Broadway in *And Things That Go Bump in the Night* and, after that, in other works by the playwright. Albee and McNally had a bruising argument at their last meeting. "We ended so badly," Albee said, tersely. It was to be seven years before they spoke again and many years before they were able to have any kind of friendship. In a final twist of irony, many years later, Drivas played the title role in Albee's *The Man Who Had Three Arms.*

After his Russian journey, Albee discussed his experiences with other writers and then raised the subject of the condition of Soviet writers with PEN, suggesting that the cultural exchange continue with a group of Soviet writers being invited to the U.S. In October 1964, he sent a formal invitation to Mykola Platonovich Bazhan of the Union of Writers of the Ukraine, forwarding a copy of his letter to Steinbeck. A Soviet delegation visited the U.S. in November of that year.

When *Ballad* closed after 123 performances, Albee was once again out of the country. This time he was in London for the opening there of *Virginia Woolf.* He wrote to Flanagan about *Ballad,* "It will be a great shame when the play goes away, for I am as fond of it as you are, as fond as anyone would be of a lovely child who has leukemia, or something. Silly audiences, they should want to go to it. Their loss." He added that he was "awful surprised by the thunderous British reception for Betty Woolf, was particularly gratified that they saw the writing in the play as better than average." At the end of the season, Dewhurst was nominated for a Tony as best actress in *Ballad of the Sad Cafe* but did not win. For the second year in a row, following *Virginia Woolf,* there was no Pulitzer Prize for drama.

Ballad was revived in 1977 at the WPA Theater, in a production starring Kaiulani Lee, and with one actor doubling in the roles of the Narrator and Marvin Macy's brother. The revival demonstrated that the play occupied a secure place in Albee's body of work as a haunting dramatic poem, a spoken ballad for actors. The production was harmonious in every detail and the fight scene was played with ferocious conviction and was a passionate, ritualistic battle for identity, control, and survival.

After seeing the revival, John Guare sent Albee a letter:

> Fourteen years ago I was going into the Air Force and the night after my last night in NY would be the first preview of *Ballad of the Sad Cafe.* I was ready to go AWOL to not miss this play. I didn't know what to do. I saw you in the street.

Ran up to you. Asked if there would be a dress rehearsal I could go to that night. You said Yes. I went. Then off to the Air Force. But the point is I saw the last performance at WPA yesterday and my god, it is such a play. I am still filled with the jolt *Ballad of the Sad Cafe* gave me yesterday and how good that I can write you as a friend and not run up, a stranger on the street. A beautiful experience. You transformed the Southern Gothic into a true Jacobean experience.

Many years later, Simon Callow made a film of the book, starring Vanessa Redgrave as Amelia. Although Albee was not involved in the production, he profited financially from it and played a role as defender of the property (his and McCullers's). Before shooting began, he advised the producer, Ismail Merchant:

> For the film to succeed to McCullers' intentions it must bring a mythic quality to the relationship. It is not the story of a shy, sexually repressed, mannish woman set on by a brutish punk. It is the story of two people who however unclearly to themselves they may comprehend it, are engaged in a bizarre "grand passion"—the one real chance in their lives for something very special—the one opportunity for them both to fully realize themselves. It is this quality, this awareness which reaches toward the mythic, and makes what happens when Marvin Macy comes back so poignant, so inevitable, and the stuff of true tragedy.
>
> It is this which is missing from the screenplay. As it is now, a punk gets rejected and comes back and does his dirty work. That is not what McCullers intended, is not what I intended, and is not what the screenplay should be offering us.

He concluded that McCullers was "not writing about small people."

10

The Play That Dare Not Speak Its Name

I say to myself, thank God, it's just dear old Irene.

A FTER the breakup with McNally, Albee became involved with William Pennington, an interior decorator. For several years, they lived together and took several trips together. In contrast to Albee, Pennington was very concerned with keeping up a high standard of living and he had a penchant for lavish spending. The two were never as close as Albee had been with Flanagan and McNally. Early in 1964, Albee and Pennington went to Europe. Relaxing, enjoying the countryside, and visiting friends, they spent most of their time in Italy. Albee bought a stylish Lancia convertible in Genoa, drove to Rome, stopping on the way in many Italian hill towns. Later he sent the car back to America. In Rome, he received a letter from McNally, responding to a letter Albee had sent to him from northern Italy. McNally, who was on Fire Island, had finished revisions on his play *And Things That Go Bump in the Night* (which would open and quickly close on Broadway in April 1965). McNally brought him up to date on shows and activities of friends. He had passed by Flanagan, who turned away the moment he saw him. Then at the end of the letter, he said that when he and Albee met again he hoped he would be spared an evening like their last one, which he still regretted.

On the ship returning home, Albee began to write *Tiny Alice*, a play that had been lurking in his mind for more than two years. He worked on it in August and finished it in September in his house at Montauk. Coming after the adaptation of *The Ballad of the Sad Cafe,* it was Albee's second full-length, original play and, as such, was the theatrical equivalent of a second novel by a writer whose first work has been a resounding success. As it turned out, it became Albee's problem play. Depending on one's point of view, it is either a tantalizing intellectual exercise, a deeply probing study of religious martyrdom, a work with a severely schizoid personality, or simply a flagrant act of hubris. Although these and other assessments all had their proponents, it was the charge of hubris that was most prevalent when the play was first produced on Broadway.

Before *Tiny Alice* opened December 29, 1964, Albee had consolidated his various successes and was in the enviable position of being able to write a play and have it presented as intended without undue concern about what the public and critical reception might be. *The Zoo Story* and *Virginia Woolf* were extraordinary accomplishments, and though *Ballad of the Sad Cafe* did not have a long run, it had its enthusiasts and did no damage to the playwright's reputation. Once again, there was great anticipation in the air as the world—or at least the theater world—awaited his next Broadway play. What would it be? After the play opened, the question changed to "What is it?" *Tiny Alice* remains his most discussed, dissected, and analyzed play, with no one, including the author, providing a totally satisfying explanation. One of the people who was most in the dark was the play's star, John Gielgud.

Before Steinbeck went to Ireland in late December with Elaine, he wanted very much to see a run-through or a preview of *Tiny Alice.* In a letter to Albee, he offered an observation about the play: "I happen to know who and what Tiny Alice is. Tiny Alice is Mary McCarthy, and Mary McCarthy is an anti-fertility symbol whose rites are celebrated on Walpurgis night, with the ritual sacrifice of a hecatomb of black cockroaches en gelees . . . So you see, I have found you out." When *Tiny Alice* opened, it was to be surrounded by mystery. There was great conjecture about its meaning and about the true identity of its title character. People called it many things, but never again was the name of Mary McCarthy invoked.

Several months after it opened on Broadway, and while a controversy was raging about the meaning and the author's intention, Albee held a press conference at the Billy Rose Theater, in order to "explain" his play. At the time, he carefully laid out the plot:

> A lay brother, a man who would have become a priest except that he could
> not reconcile his idea of God with the God which men create in their own im-

age, is sent by his superior to tie up loose ends of a business matter between the
church and a wealthy woman. The lay brother becomes enmeshed in an environment which . . . contains all the elements which have confused and bothered him throughout his life: the relationship between sexual hysteria and
religious ecstasy; the conflict between the selflessness of service and the con-
spicuous splendor of martyrdom . . . He is left with pure abstraction—whatever
it be called: God, or Alice—and in the end, according to your faith, one of two
things happen: either the abstraction . . . is proved real, or the dying man, in
the last necessary effort of self-delusion creates and believes in what he knows
does not exist.

Beneath this synopsis, there is an even more complex narrative. Julian, the
lay brother, is brought to the mansion of the rich woman, who is named Miss
Alice. There are three other characters in the play, all of them with generic
names: the Cardinal, the Lawyer, and Butler. In the library is an enormous
doll-house model of the house, a complete replica in every detail. Presumably inside that model is another model, and so on, like an infinite series of
Chinese boxes. Later that model itself becomes a part of the story, and eventually it is consumed by flames. Miss Alice is not the title character, but a sim-
ulacrum or substitute for her. When Julian first meets her, she is pretending
to be an old crone. Then she throws off her disguise and reveals herself as a
much younger and attractive woman.

At the end of the second act, in a scene of heightened passion, Julian suc-
cumbs to his seduction. In effect, Julian's body and soul are sold for 2 billion
dollars. He marries Miss Alice and is forsaken by her and everyone else. In the
climax of the play, after delivering an extremely long interior monologue,
with his arms wide as in a crucifixion, he dies. The play begins as a witty
philosophical dissertation between the Lawyer and the Cardinal, moves
through metaphor and religious symbolism, and ends in epiphany. It was that
epiphany that proved to be an obstacle for critics, theatergoers, and Gielgud.

The sources of the play go back deeply into Albee's childhood. Noel Farrand, to whom *Tiny Alice* is dedicated, always said that the house in *Tiny Alice*—and the model onstage—reminded him of the Albee family house on
Bay Avenue in Larchmont. In common, they were large and dark and mysterious, places to hide secrets. Imagine that inside the model are miniature versions of two small boys, Edward and Noel, moving from room to room to
basement to attic, sneaking through the house, burrowing into its crannies
and, in Noel's case, borrowing Frankie Albee's jewelry. The library itself ("pil-
lared walls, floor-to-ceiling leather-bound books") is a version of the Albee li-

brary in the Hommocks house, that room with untouchable books from which Edward extracted Turgenev, and was forced to pay the consequences.

Albee says that he once read a newspaper article about a family in Germany that kept a thirty-year-old son "in a terribly tiny room." It is curious that the son in the article was thirty, the same age when Albee emerged publicly, or in his words, was born as a playwright. Reading that story started him thinking about the idea of someone confined in a small space, a room within a room, or a box within a box, and that inspired *Tiny Alice*. But that, he said, "doesn't say anything" about the play itself.

Then there is the matter of the title "Tiny Alice" and the character of Miss Alice. It is impossible to think about them or the play without conjuring *Alice in Wonderland*, although here it is Julian the lay brother who is falling— through Alice's path (and kingdom). Combine all this with Albee's fascination with Jesus Christ and martyrdom, which began in his childhood when he was carried out of church crying, having heard for the first time the story of The Crucifixion. Albee has always insisted that it was Jesus the man, not Jesus the son of God who was his interest, but there is something about the self-willed martyrdom that has long fascinated if not obsessed him.

Albee's first choice (a reasonable one) for the role of Brother Julian was Albert Finney. Barr suggested Gielgud. After Albee finished writing the first two acts, Barr telephoned Gielgud in England and offered him the role. Albee never formally objected to the casting, but in retrospect he revealed his hesitation: "It wasn't my idea to have somebody whose sexual fires were dampened. I remember I wanted somebody younger and more sexual. But when John became available, I guess I was talked into it. What thirty-five-year-old playwright is going to turn down John Gielgud for a leading role?"

At the time that Gielgud was offered the role, only two of the play's three acts were written. He read the partial manuscript and was intrigued and also confused by the play. "I couldn't understand those two acts," he said, "but I thought it was a good part." He especially liked the first scene of the play between the Cardinal and Butler, in which his character did not appear. It was that scene that was later to capture the attention of critics. Soon after, Gielgud was having dinner in London with Irene Worth and told her that he had been sent a new Albee play. "What's it like?" she asked. "I don't know," he answered, candidly. "I don't understand it at all, but it's very interesting." He said he was thinking of doing it, adding, "It has a nice part for a woman." Her curiosity awakened, she asked if he thought that she would be suitable for the role. He said she was. When he called Barr back to say that he would do the play, the producer asked him if he had any suggestion as to who might play

Miss Alice. He proposed Irene Worth, and as he remembered, Barr "jumped at that."

One reason why Gielgud (as one of the three great knights of the English theater, along with Sir Laurence Olivier and Sir Ralph Richardson) was interested was that he felt out of touch with the contemporary theater and wanted to make the transition to the avant-garde. At that point, he had had no such offers, and he also had his blind spots. Neither then nor later had he liked Beckett ("I hated *Waiting for Godot* so much that I never bothered to see anything else he had written"). After Gielgud did *Tiny Alice*, he and Richardson were to do David Storey's *Home* and Harold Pinter's *No Man's Land*, but Albee was to provide his breakthrough.

At first, Gielgud had one question for Albee: What was Brother Julian's age? The playwright's tactful response: "I think all the men in the play should be around fifty." Gielgud was sixty, and although he felt he could disguise those ten years onstage, he thought it was "quite wrong and ridiculous my playing this chaste young man." Trepidations intact, he accepted the role.

In contrast to Gielgud, Worth loved the play. That is not to say that she understood it much more than he or anyone else did, but from the beginning she seemed to have a greater feeling for its mystery and an enthusiasm for the subject matter. She felt that it was "anti-clerical and anti-organized religion." In common with Gielgud, she was tantalized by the character she was to play. When Albee came to London to talk to her about it, he told her it was about "worlds within worlds," and she wondered if he had a kind of prescience about the expanding universe.

Later, she said, "The one thing I'm sure of is that the great theme of Edward's life is *pay attention*—and it is in every play." In *Tiny Alice*, she continued, "Edward writes about our fall from innocence, how we are destroyed by the camouflage, pretenses, and petty corruptions of life."

Alan Schneider agreed to direct the play although he, too, had serious reservations about it and felt that it became "murkier and murkier . . . ending in a scene I had difficulty believing on any level." He was also disturbed by the idea of Gielgud playing such a young innocent, a role that he thought was better suited to Marlon Brando or Montgomery Clift. William Hutt, Eric Berry, and John Heffernan were signed to play the Lawyer, the Cardinal, and Butler.

Gielgud did not get to read the third act until he arrived in America to begin rehearsals. "I was rather dismayed," he said, "because of this terrific monologue at the end that I thought was so difficult." "Dismayed" is putting it mildly. If he had read the third act in England and realized the demands that it would make on him, he might not have agreed to do the play. In fact, that monologue was one reason why Albee agreed to have him in the role, to give a Shakespearean eloquence to a long and complex confessional. At the time, Gielgud recognized that aspect of the play, saying that it had "a kind of grandeur and glamour which makes it exciting to me."

In his notes, Albee took a step toward an explanation of that final scene:

> Finally, Julian is left alone. I am not sure at this point whether or not he has been tied, arms spread, to the model. Julian begins a semi-hallucinated monologue, half to God, half to the true Alice . . . if she exists, if, in fact, there is a difference between her existence or nonexistence and between her identity and God's. It is a long monologue, ending in Julian's Christ-like statement of having been forsaken, having forfeited his life for a falsehood. In a semi-coma, he begins to call to Alice-God, as he is dying. He begins to hear a heavy breathing, sees one or two lights moving, going on and off in the model. The breathing is slow and enormous, filling the theatre. A great shadow begins to fall across the stage, the true Alice, enormous, transferable. Julian dies, accepting the existence, accepting his crucifixion.

Albee concluded, "Please don't ask me here to go into the psychological justifications or philosophical fine points. It will all be clear." Whenever Gielgud would ask him about the meaning of the play, he would respond, with variations, "You can't play the meaning of the play. You have to play the reality of the characters." The question remained: What was the reality of the characters?

In his autobiography, Schneider said that Gielgud "wanted to withdraw almost daily, and was sustained mainly by post-rehearsal brandy and Irene's good-natured joshing. Pleas to Edward to rewrite and clear up at least some of the confusion went unanswered. I don't think he knew what to do." Several years later, Gielgud looked back on the conflict and said, "We pleaded with Albee to consider rewriting parts of the second and third acts . . . It seemed to me that the elaborate sexual and religious melodrama which enveloped the play in the second act unbalanced its finer points."

As the production proceeded, Gielgud's nine-minute monologue became a primary stumbling block. Repeatedly the actor asked that it be reduced. Albee refused and Schneider ignored the request. Gielgud remembers saying at rehearsal that "nobody would ever sit through my death scene—they'll all be charging out getting their snow boots." Eventually, this stalemate led to a bruising encounter between the actor and the author. "It was a real fight," said Irene Worth, "but done in a gentlemanly way. The tension was dreadful. I kept trying to defuse it." Gielgud continued to ask questions, while she tended "to take everything on faith." Schneider did not offer satisfying explanations and Albee "was at his most teasing." It was her conjecture that Albee felt, "What kind of actor is this? He's driving me mad. Why don't you read what I've written." For Worth, there was right on both sides. "The accumulation of nervous energy within that speech was great, but it would be diffuse if spoken, and it would lose its power."

An irate Albee gave Gielgud three choices: "If you won't do the whole monologue we'll either do the first four and a half minutes, and put the curtain down, or you can start four and a half minutes in and we'll do the last half of the monologue, or I'll let you do 'hits from the monologue.' " Gielgud responded, "Very funny, Edward, very funny." Eventually the anger between Albee and Gielgud subsided. Gielgud said, "I think I persuaded Schneider to get rid of a bit of it." Some of the monologue was cut. As Albee says, "He eventually did 'hits from the monologue,' and did them very beautifully." The cuts were restored by Albee in the published version. From Gielgud's point of view: "I finally gave in and tried to play it as best as I could, but I was never happy with it."

As the play began giving previews, it quickly became the subject of cocktail party conversation throughout New York. Early in December, Albee offered an additional glimpse into the meaning of the play: "It's a mystery play, a double mystery, and also a morality play, about truth and illusion, the substitute images we create, that we substitute for the real thing . . . easy virtues, easy Gods, all the Gods that we create in our own image." He paused and retreated: "I've said too much." He said he was using the church because "I needed a power structure, and the church is one of the few absolute power structures available in the West. The play is not an attack on the church. It's like the corruption of wealth. There's nothing to attack in wealth, but there is in what people make of it." He added, in what turned out to be understatement, "It's a mighty peculiar play, instead of a sparkling new comedy."

On December 13, 1964, at Albee's request, Flanagan brought a copy of the play to Farrand and told him that it was dedicated to him. Farrand immediately wrote to Albee to say that he was "inexpressibly moved," proud, and grateful, and that this act of friendship came at a particularly dark time in his life. He had been "confronting specters" in his work and in his love life and was "virtually immobilized in consequence." He had been very close to despair. Evoking a shared memory, he said, "There is a line in Santayana about man's life being tragic in its essence and comic in its manifestation. Or something." Recalling a favorite line from their youth, he said, "Very 'Santayanayan'—'all the grace of a walking crow.' Which is all the grace I have these days." He read the play and the next day sent Albee a longer letter telling him that it was his best work. Farrand said that he and his brother Jack (Rev. Jack Farrand, a Jesuit priest) studied the play and found no possible conflict in the matter of Julian's vows, that lay brothers usually take "temporary" vows of poverty, chastity, and obedience, from which they can be released under diocesan authority, as in the play. Noel said that in spite of his health, he would like to go to the last preview and the opening and "to keep watch" in "the night vigil, or vesper mass," presumably waiting for the critical judgment. He apologized for his handwriting, "which surely has all the grace of a walking crow," and said "it was creepy coming across that old reference in *Alice*, after I had dredged it up, in my last letter to you. Creepy but nice." With the exception of Albee's old Choate teacher, Sandy Lehmann, who wrote the phrase in the school newspaper, probably no one else would have noticed.

One of the many scenes that bothered Gielgud before and after the opening was the seduction, what he refers to as "a kind of striptease melodrama," in which, with her back to the audience, Worth was to open her beautiful Mainbocher gown and, seemingly naked, embrace him with what Albee identifies as "her great wings." Gielgud later said, "We were embarrassed and the audience was embarrassed by the seduction scene. It was supposed to be sort of D. H. Lawrence. It was a very phony scene." He said that he and Worth never talked about it much, but "we soldiered on."

"It embarrassed him," Worth agreed, "I contrived to be fully dressed and yet give the impression of nakedness within the extravagant black lace dressing gown I threw back over my naked shoulders." In "a moment of panic," she said to Gielgud, "Oh, John, just imagine you and I suddenly got married." At that point everyone laughed. The night before the opening, Roddy McDowall went backstage after the performance to find Gielgud predicting, "We're going to be stoned, we'll be stoned tomorrow." Gielgud is as famous for his innocence as for his faux pas. McDowall asked him how he felt about that striptease. In characteristic fashion, Gielgud said, "I say to myself, thank God, it's just dear old Irene."

The scene and the act end with Miss Alice saying, "He will be yours! He will be yours!" and she cries out the name "Alice." Worth wondered what kind of sound she should make. "Once or twice just to be naughty I did a really sexy call-out. But I thought making an orgasmic cry was too obvious and rather cheap." She asked Albee what kind of sound she should make and he said the sound of relief. Subsequently she played her role in London, opposite David Warner, a much younger and seemingly far more appropriate actor for the role. "David, with the advantage of youth, was incredibly shy and reticent. Both men had superb tact and modesty. Both implied tremendous conflict between the spiritual and the physical."

For Gielgud, as for others, the Broadway opening night remains a bit of a fog. He managed to get through that final monologue, the curtain came down, and the well-wishers (who included Tennessee Williams) appeared, although when faced with congratulations, everyone must have felt some skepticism. Albee did not go to the opening night party, or as Gielgud recalls, "He ran away."

Because of Albee's previous accomplishments, the initial reviews were for the most part respectful and, to a certain degree, admiring—of the performances and William Ritman's monumental set as well as of the play. However, there was also an undertone of discomfort, a hedge perhaps against the possibility that the play would turn out to be specious. In the *Times*, Howard Taubman said, "Even if you find Mr. Albee's subject and treatment too enigmatic, *Tiny Alice* provides the kind of exhilarating evening that stretches the mind and sensibilities." Walter Kerr considered it to be "bloodless" and "uninteresting." In the *New York Review of Books*, Philip Roth wrote a scathing essay entitled "The Play That Dare Not Speak Its Name." The charge from Roth was that *Tiny Alice* was a homosexual daydream, in which "the celibate male is tempted and seduced by the overpowering female, only to be betrayed by the male lover and murdered by the cruel law." He ended with the question, clearly referring to Tennessee Williams and James Baldwin, among others: "How long before a play is produced on Broadway in which the homosexual hero is presented as a homosexual, and not disguised as an *angst*-ridden priest, or an angry Negro, or an aging actress; or worst of all, Everyman?"

After the Broadway opening, Albee, with the encouragement of Barr, churned the controversy (and presumably increased audience interest) through interviews and appearances on radio and television. In an interview in the *Times*, he confirmed that the champagne wedding supper between Julian and Miss Alice was intended as a Last Supper and that the six years that Julian spent in a mental institution was the same length of time it takes for a man to become a priest. "I don't like symbolism that hits you over the head," he said. "A symbol should not be a cymbal."

On January 21, 1965, the playwright appeared with his director onstage at the New School to talk about *Tiny Alice*. The moderator, Allan Lewis, said the play was "the inverse or reverse of a medieval mystery play," a reverse story of Christ. Schneider responded, "I don't think it has anything to do with the passion of Christ. I'm a Jewish boy from Baltimore and it has something to do with me in 1965." Albee admitted that "*Tiny Alice* examines the relationship or nonrelationship of man and God, which exists or which he created." And Schneider said, "I do not find that *Tiny Alice* is a play about the destruction of Julian's faith." After the long and finally aimless discussion, a woman in the audience said on the way out, "Just words, a lot of words."

The more Albee talked about the play, the cloudier it became. He said that, at first, he was reluctant to speak out, but then reread the reviews and the hundreds of letters he had received and decided there were things he could say about a play that "has been called everything from a hoax to a masterpiece." "It is the very simplicity of the play, I think, that has confused so many. It is, of course, neither a straight psychological study nor a philosophical tract, but something of a metaphysical dream play which must be entered into and experienced without preconception, without predetermination of how a play is supposed to go. One must let the play happen to one; one must let the mind loose to respond as it will." If, on the other hand, one tried to be too literal about the allegory, "the result is confusion, opacity, difficulty . . . all the things the play has been accused of." His final instruction to the audience: "Sit back, let it happen to you, and take it in rather as you would a piece of music or a dream."

Others contributed to the controversy. Elaine Dundy wrote a piece for the *Herald Tribune* in which she asked a number of people, many of them artists, who they thought Tiny Alice was. Tennessee Williams said that Tiny Alice was the Establishment, "the meaningless, monstrous, outrageously mysterious mysterious Mystery that defeats us all." Stella Adler said that in *Virginia Woolf*, Albee kept the betrayal downstairs: man betraying man. In *Tiny Alice*, it was upstairs: "It is not simply man's inhumanity to man anymore, but God's inhumanity as well." Calling it "middle-brow mysticism" and "a deplorable affair," Dwight MacDonald said that all of the characters except for Julian were "surrogates of the devil arranging for Christ's crucifixion." When the play was published, instead of writing a preface, Albee included a brief author's note, reaffirming the work's clarity while admitting that the play was "less opaque in reading than it would be in any single viewing." He acknowledged that he had restored the passages that were deleted for the Broadway production.

He sent a copy of the play to Noël Coward in Jamaica. Coward had seen *Tiny Alice* in New York and had told Albee that he was confused by it. In his letter, Coward struck some very responsive chords: "I have read *Tiny Alice* with the utmost concentration and considerable enjoyment. Your sense of theatre is superb and your writing brilliant. You were right, I did get more of it from the printed page but not enough to clear up my confusion. I know now, or I think I know, what happens but what I don't know is what *you* think is happening. Your basic premise still eludes me." He said he could think of several possibilities.

"Destruction of innocence," "Black over white," "The evil in good," "The good in evil," etc.: all facile and unsatisfactory. Your character drawing of Butler, the Lawyer and the Cardinal are clear and believable. Alice and Julian not only unbelievable but—to me—cracking bores. He seems to be a sex obsessed prig and she an over articulate shadow. Your other dimension is too vague for me to visualize. Perhaps my stubborn sanity clips my wings. Sex obsession and religious ecstasy I agree are on the same plane but it's not a plane on which I can move with much tolerance. I have enjoyed sex thoroughly . . . but it has never, except for brief wonderful moments, twisted my reason. Religious ecstasy I have never experienced. I suspect that my sense of humor is as stubborn as my sanity, perhaps they are the same thing. Your seduction scene neither moved, shocked nor appalled me. It made me want to laugh. You must forgive me for saying these things. I have a profound respect for your rich talent and a strong affection for you although I only know you a little. Expert use of language is to me a perpetual joy. You use it expertly all right but, I fear, too self-indulgently. Your duty to me as a playgoer and a reader is to explain whatever truths you are dealing with lucidly and accurately. I refuse to be fobbed off with a sort of metaphysical "what's my line."

Let me hear from you. Just an ordinary love letter will do.

At the time of *Tiny Alice*, some kind of apogee was reached with a cartoon by Whitney Darrow Jr. in *The New Yorker*, picturing a middle-class couple in bed, the husband sound asleep, the wife suddenly awake and nudging him to say, "Hayden, wake up! The meaning of *Tiny Alice* just came to me!"

Early in 1965, with the resignation of Elia Kazan and Robert Whitehead as the heads of the Repertory Theater of Lincoln Center, there was a search for a replacement. Among the candidates was the team of Albee, Barr, Wilder, and Alan Schneider, who had been working together for five years. In anticipation, Schneider wrote to Albee and Barr, saying that one reason to accept an offer if it came was to make Roger Stevens, David Merrick, "and all those other bastards sit up and take notice, even if they haven't yet." It would give the team "status, respect, respectability, a brand-new theater—several of them—the right time and place in history looming ahead of what's already been done." Schneider, however, was "reluctant, dubious, suspicious, and just plain scared" of being thrown into an area "where mistakes are not one's own to make and failure not one's own responsibility." In the past they had done well together "because you know exactly what you were doing, had goals and kept sights on them, functioned quietly and simply, in a small way but with very strong materials, and had Mr. Albee's plays in your clean-up position." He named all the other reasons why they should not make the move, but acknowledged that Barr and Albee were basically in favor of it and Wilder was opposed. Although he wanted to direct a play at the Vivian Beaumont Theater, he said, "I'd much rather do Edward's next five at the Billy Rose. Or the Cherry Lane. Or anywhere. Because I feel he—and we—have just begun. And, honest, I'm scared we might get off the tracks before we've gotten all the way home."

The post went to Herbert Blau and Jules Irving, who had headed the Actors Workshop in San Francisco. Their reign proved to be as fraught with problems as that of the previous management. All things considered, Schneider was prescient about the inadvisability of the group moving to Lincoln Center. Years later, Albee was to become one of a six-person artistic directorate at Lincoln Center. That did not last long either.

One day in May 1965, Albee suddenly received a call from a secretary in his father's office (the sister of Ted Lauder, the dentist and keeper of the family funds) telling him that his mother had had a heart attack and was lonely and unhappy. At that point, she was living alone in a house in White Plains. She and her son had not spoken or communicated in seventeen years. The secretary suggested that he might call her. He thought about it for several days, then telephoned her and asked her how she was. Taking the initiative, he suggested that he might come up and see her. He did and brought her a pin as a gift. The meeting was friendly but tentative. Albee had made the first effort and his mother immediately responded with a thank-you note: "Dearest Ed, I want to tell you again how happy I was to spend Sunday with you. My pin—what more can I say, your taste so fine and the thought of you—means so much." And with a sweep of her pen, she signed it, "Love. Mother." They resumed—or rather, began—a relationship. "I made the gesture," said Albee, "and it was very very slow and uncomfortable for both of us. Eventually we moved into civility but I wouldn't say it developed more than that. I was a very dutiful and good son, and took care of her to the extent that she needed taking care of. But she never quite approved of me, or forgave me for walking out."

As the character of A says in *Three Tall Women*:

We have a heart attack; they tell him; he comes back. Twenty plus years? That's a long enough sulk—on both sides. He didn't come back when his father died.

But he came to me. They call me up and they tell me he's coming to see me; they say he's going to call. He calls. I hear his voice and it all floods back, but I'm formal. Well, hello there, I say. Hello there to you, he says. Nothing about this shouldn't have happened. Nothing about I've missed you, not even that little lie. Sis is visiting; she's lying drunk and passed out upstairs and not even that little lie. I thought I'd come over. Yes, you do that. He comes; we look at each other and we both hold in whatever we've been holding in since that day he went away. You're looking well, he says; and, You, too, I say. And there are no apologies, no recriminations, no tears, no hugs; dry lips on my dry cheeks; yes that. And we never discuss it? Never go into why? Never go beyond where we are? We're strangers; we're curious about each other; we leave it at that.

Speaking about the resumption of the relationship, Albee paraphrases that line from *Three Tall Women*: "A 20 year sulk is long enough on both sides." Basking in her son's celebrity, she began going to his opening nights and visited him at his home in Montauk, and he visited her in Palm Beach, Florida. To a certain degree, he involved himself in details of her private life. For example, in October of that year, together with her chauffeur he took a close look at her newly purchased custom-ordered Chrysler Imperial and found it filled with flaws, including body parts that did not fit, paint that was chipping, and a window that squeaked loudly—and he sent a letter to that effect to an official at the Chrysler headquarters in Detroit. Although his mother always remained removed from his work and from his life, she took a pride in his accomplishments or, at least, in her position as the mother of Edward Albee the playwright.

In the play, A never forgives her son. As she says, "No; I never do. But we play the game. We dine; he takes me places—mother, son going to formal places. We never . . . reminisce. Eventually he lets me talk about when he was a little boy, but he never has an opinion on that; he doesn't seem to have an opinion on much of anything that has to do with us, with me."

It was, he said, "a semi-working relationship: the responsibility of the son and the woman who received the responsibility of the son. There was never great affection. She never opened up to me." But she told him things, in effect giving him an oral history of her marriage and the family, "facts, facts, but

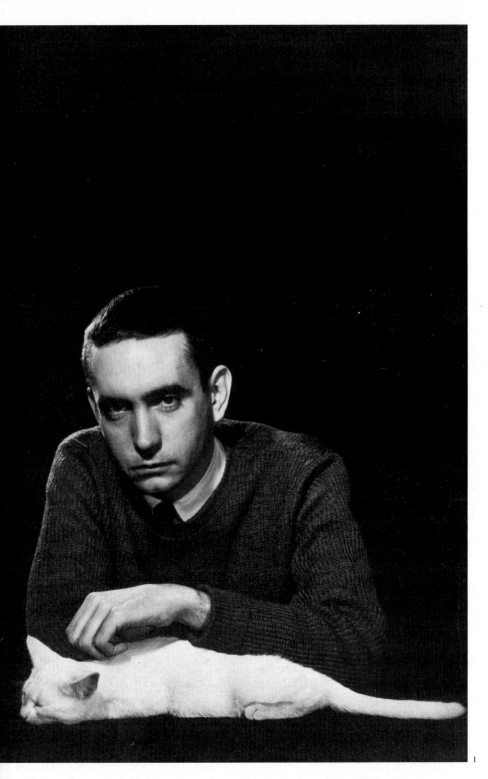

On the verge: Albee in 1961.

Dogs and horses: [TOP LEFT] *Edward (at about eighteen months) with his mother, Frances, the original "Tall Woman";* [TOP RIGHT] *with his mother (at right) and his nanny, Anita Church, in Palm Beach, where the Albees spent their winters, circa 1929;* [ABOVE] *with his mother, an accomplished horsewoman, and his cousins Barbara and Nancy, circa 1933.*

[RIGHT] *Reed and Frances Albee, 1939.* [BELOW LEFT] *Albee at Valley Forge Military Academy, where he spent an unhappy year in what he called "the Valley Forge Concentration Camp," 1944;* [BELOW RIGHT] *at Choate, 1945: "An ultra-poetical, super-aesthetical out-of-the-way young man";* [BOTTOM] *with Delphine Weissinger at her debutante party, 1949.*

5

6

7

8

*Albee at his typewriter,
which he "liberated"
from Western Union.*

9

*Albee with William Flanagan,
a composer and Albee's mentor.*

10

11

The look of YAM: a portrait of the Young American Man as playwright.

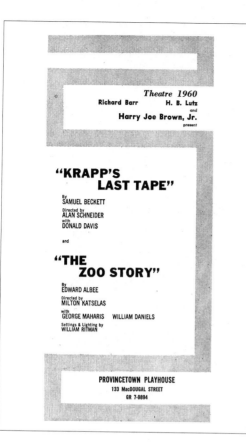

Theatre 1960
Richard Barr   H. B. Lutz
and
Harry Joe Brown, Jr.
present

"KRAPP'S LAST TAPE"

By
SAMUEL BECKETT
Directed by
ALAN SCHNEIDER
with
DONALD DAVIS

and

"THE ZOO STORY"

By
EDWARD ALBEE
Directed by
MILTON KATSELAS
with
GEORGE MAHARIS   WILLIAM DANIELS
Settings & Lighting by
WILLIAM RITMAN

PROVINCETOWN PLAYHOUSE
133 MacDOUGAL STREET
GR 7-8894

12

First edition: the program for the New York premiere of Samuel Beckett's Krapp's Last Tape *and Albee's* The Zoo Story, *January 14, 1960.*

"I've been to the zoo":
The original cast of The Zoo Story, *George Maharis as Jerry and William Daniels as Peter.*

13

"Well, now, aren't you a breath of fresh air!":
The American Dream, *1961, with Ben Piazza as the Young Man and Sudie Bond as Grandma.*

14

15

"You must be our little guests": Who's Afraid of Virginia Woolf?, 1962, *with Uta Hagen, Arthur Hill, George Grizzard, and Melinda Dillon.*

16

"I dance like the wind": *Melinda Dillon (far left) as Honey.*

After the success of Who's Afraid of Virginia Woolf?: *PLAYWRIGHT EDWARD ALBEE: ODD MAN IN*, Newsweek, *February 4, 1963.*

17

The author and Albee in Albee's apartment on West 10th Street, 1963.

18

19

Albee with his producers Clinton Wilder and Richard Barr, who went on to present more Albee plays.

20

21

Albee, with Colleen Dewhurst, working on The Ballad of the Sad Café, *his adaptation of the novel by Carson McCullers, 1963.*

Albee travelled to Russia with John and Elaine Steinbeck in 1963. Here he is pictured with Elaine in Leningrad (St. Petersburg).

22

"Pow! You're dead!": The film version of Who's Afraid of Virginia Woolf?, *(left to right) George Segal, Richard Burton, and Elizabeth Taylor. The movie won Taylor her second Academy Award as Best Actress.*

23

An Al Hirschfeld drawing of the film cast: Burton, Taylor, Segal, and Sandy Dennis.

24

Albee with his favorite director, Alan Schneider, working on Tiny Alice *in 1964.*

"Is the memory of something having happened the same as it having happened?": Irene Worth as Miss Alice in Tiny Alice.

25

26

A room within a room: John Gielgud, who played Julian in Tiny Alice.

At home in A Delicate Balance, *1966, with Jessica Tandy as Agnes, Rosemary Murphy as Claire, and Hume Cronyn as Tobias. The play won Albee his first Pulitzer Prize in 1967.*

Tony Richardson directed Kate Reid and Katharine Hepburn as Claire and Agnes in the film version of A Delicate Balance.

29

Amity: Albee and his mother backstage after the opening of Malcolm *in 1966, with Angela Lansbury and Ruth White (who starred in the play).*

30

[ABOVE] *Albee with Noël Coward,* [RIGHT] *with Harold Pinter,* [BELOW] *with Vaclav Havel.*

32

31

33

The New York cast of Three Tall Women: *Marian Seldes, Myra Carter, and Jordan Baker, 1994. The play won Albee his third Pulitzer.*

34

The London cast of Three Tall Women: *Samantha Bond, Sara Kestelman, and Maggie Smith.*

35

Albee in his Tribeca loft.

Jonathan Thomas, Albee's longtime partner, at the Montauk house.

The 1996 Lincoln Center production of A Delicate Balance, with George Grizzard as Tobias (Rosemary Harris as Agnes and Elaine Stritch as Claire are in the background). The production won a Tony Award for best revival of a play.

36

[LEFT] *Diana Rigg as Martha and*
[ABOVE] *David Suchet as George in* Who's Afraid
of Virginia Woolf?, *London, 1996.*

*Maggie Smith as Claire and Eileen Atkins as
Agnes in* A Delicate Balance, *London, 1997.*

41

At ease on the bed in Three Tall Women. *The happiest time? "Now. Always."*

very very very very very seldom did she let me in to her real feelings." During their meetings, they would have long conversations about his mother's earlier life and about her marriage. One subject they did not talk about was his homosexuality. "There was that barrier of things she could not discuss," he said, "and you cannot discuss anything unless you discuss my homosexuality. She could not talk about it, or I was not allowed to bring it up. At the very beginning of almost every meeting, she would say things about gay people—as to how much she despised them. 'I warn you not to talk about them.' So we shrugged and said, 'OK, you want to keep the relationship at arm's length, you want to keep it formal, you don't really want to become friends? OK, it's up to you now.' "

He says, assertively, "I never liked her," but he had a "grudging respect" for her. Asked if she was proud of his accomplishments, he said, "Yes, I guess so. Having bought me." He added, "I think she was too deeply ingrained with her prejudices and her decisions about everything. I don't think we could have ever broken through."

Especially at holidays, his mother would visit him at Montauk or at his New York apartment. Inviting a carefully selected group of friends, Albee would cook a lavish Christmas dinner. Irene Worth, who was a frequent guest, has vivid memories of Mrs. Albee:

> She had a kind of star radiance. She was irresistibly beautiful, with a tremendous magnetism, and she had the most marvelous white skin you have ever seen. She wore black dresses with low necklines, so the pearls were shown in their full beauty. I think they may be why Edward began to put pearls in his plays. In those days they had a polite and comfortable relationship. It wasn't until later that vituperation and anger began to overwhelm him. He went through some really bitter times. I remember he had a summer party at Montauk. We swam all day, but within the party and the glittering friends, his mother was irritating him, driving him mad.

Apparently he had asked her about his birth parents and she had refused to give him any information. "I don't know if she was taunting him, but she wouldn't tell him about his origins, and he was wild, absolutely obsessed." He said to Worth, "She won't tell me who I am." Despite the limits of their communication, he learned many things about her. Many years later, after her death, his memories of those conversations were to lead directly to *Three Tall Women*.

After Worth won a Tony award for her performance in *Tiny Alice* and by the time the play closed, Albee was in Montauk, diligently at work on another adaptation, his version of James Purdy's *Malcolm.* In June of 1965, he wrote to Flanagan:

"Life is placid on the surface, though I have four plays lined up to do, and such thoughts give me headaches." The plays were *Malcolm, A Delicate Balance,* his adaptation of Giles Cooper's *Everything in the Garden,* and *Box* and *Quotations from Chairman Mao Tse-Tung* (two interrelated plays). He continued,

> Also, I worry some about a growing tendency in Richard Barr to lean toward commercialism more and more. He's broke, of course, so that hurts the purity of aesthetic, but I sense the pressures beginning, and know I will have to battle on several sides the pressures to compromise toward the idea of theatre as a buyers market. I must talk to Richard, because I don't think he knows he's starting to resemble exactly what he left Broadway for years ago. There's too much talk, from Richard, from Alan, about "will the public take it?" and "We've got to think about what'll go."
>
> But, you know me as fairly stern when it comes to my own, and burned quite a bit from the pressures on poor *Tiny Alice.* Perhaps I will go overboard the other direction this year, be too unyielding. But, twixt the devil of compromising for public acceptance (V. Woolfs don't come along every day, with their acceptance coming from only partly the right reasons) and the deep blue sea of writing good plays as one wants to write them, having them done well, *be* good plays, and yet have them rejected, thereby becoming a "failure" because one does not have continuing public and critical "success." It is the double business that is so troubling . . . not troubling in the sense of what to write or how to write it, but of the two distinct criteria of success.

In his own life, he was sampling the profits of a successful career. A tennis court had been added to the Montauk house and he bought Maurice Evans's townhouse, a one-family brownstone, at 50 West 10th Street, a few doors away from the tenement-like building in which Albee had had his first New York apartment. In April, Evans, then a Broadway star, confirmed the sale (for $120,000) and ended a friendly letter with the suggestion that Albee might have a part for him in his next play. Otherwise, he said, he might have to haunt the house. It was Albee's most elegant residence, several steps up from the duplex apartment he had had on the other side of 10th Street and metaphorical miles away from his various walkups and cold-water flats. A former carriage house with a white brick facade, it had been redesigned and furnished by William Pennington. After Albee moved in June, there was a heavily atmospheric piece in the *Times* about the playwright and his new home: "The room looms back to tall draped windows at one end, its size exaggerated, elongated in lengthening shadows, in the beginnings of twilight, in orbs and cruces of light that pattern rather than illuminate." Albee was quoted as saying that the house had "a finality for him that no apartment could ever have." Actually, he sold it within a few years and, with Pennington, moved uptown to a Fifth Avenue apartment. One sign of the changing fortunes of people in the theater—and also of the changing taste of homeowners in New York—is that the carriage house went from Evans to Albee and then to Jerry Herman, the composer of *Hello, Dolly!*, who eventually sold it to a wealthy woman who owned a music company.

In his letter to Flanagan, Albee wrote, "I am growing old gracefully, drinking not much at all, and note only that the seasons, the years, swing by faster each time. One takes comfort, and dim at that, from the suspicion that one will outlast the planet, or, more accurately, terminate with it."

Flanagan freely interpreted earlier Albee remarks about failure and success:

It was good to get your letter—sad to find you so apprehensive about the future of your work. Yet it was difficult not to take a certain prideful pleasure in the very integrity of your apprehensions. In other words, that you'll do what you *must* as an artist in spite of the "rough years ahead," those "rough years" for you being those of a genuinely creative man who will be forced somehow to function in the philistine environment of the commercial jungle of the American theatre. And I sense as well that you realize that your downright bizarre fame will only enhance the conflict between what you *have* to write and what will be expected of you in the way of commercial success.

But keep one thing in your mind, if I may proffer the advice: As your greatest admirer and severest critic, *Tiny Alice*—that weirdly famous "failure"—convinced me for probably the *first* time that you just *might* have the finest natural gift for writing for the theatre of any American who has ever had a go at it. And that simple *fact* of what you've done to date has changed once, for all, and forever the standard by which we evaluate what is and is not serious in theatre in this country. It's the job of the rest of the people who are writing *for* the theatre and *about* it to cope with that problem; it isn't yours to worry about whether they can or will. And that bull shit of Kerr's and even Richard's about nothing in the theatre being of any value that isn't flocked to in its initial exposure is nothing more nor less than an inversion of the empirical fascism that the 12-

tone power group is wielding over the present creative musical scene. Much of what was done to *Tiny Alice* to make it more comprehensible to its preview audiences did, in my mind, lessen the play; but it didn't make it the hit that you very understandably wanted it to be.

I'm not suggesting unyielding Milton Babbitry and perhaps I even fear a reactive, perverse, masochistic high-browism from you. But I *am* suggesting that your responsibility is to the muse and not to Walter Kerr or even to Richard's paranoic fear of failure. You'll do what you'll do; and if you keep cool, retain your innate—if no longer always overt—humility that has always characterized your approach to your work, you'll go on growing in the almost incredible leaps and bounds that you've been developing in since the beginning of this decade.

Be thankful that you've made your pile on *Virginia Woolf,* that you can at least *afford* commercial failure, and fuck the rest of it. There just *isn't* any other way. In one way or another, in this solemn march to the grave, all of us have "rough years ahead." (And haven't I learned it!).

Then, more personally, Flanagan spoke about his own problems and the fact that he had "gone into another tailspin." He had been rescued by Ned Rorem and Muir Weissinger ("the only known beatnik with an English accent, a chauffeur driven Cadillac Fleetwood and a sense of the value or lack of it in other human beings" and an apartment "filled with visiting lady-firemen from, I *swear* it, Lebanon, and they speak only French and Arabic"). Weissinger had taken him uptown to his place where Flanagan "lay for a few days in deep depression." Then, deeply drunk, at the insistence of his psychiatrist, he made a "nightmarish midnight visit" to the psychiatric emergency room at Roosevelt Hospital and later returned to Weissinger's. Finally, he decided "that the cycle of psychiatrists, medication, crises and hospitals has been producing results that could scarcely be worse." Now holding himself together he was preparing to go to the MacDowell Colony with Howard Moss, to "take care of each other."

He said that Aaron Copland had called and was having a benefit and wondered if Flanagan and Albee could do excerpts from their opera *The Ice Age* as part of the musical program. Flanagan agreed but said that Albee was in Europe. Reading the first part of the first act of Albee's adaptation of *Malcolm,* he found it "very beautiful, funny and moving as theatre" and thought that music was really needed between the scenes. He had seen Purdy at a party given by Frank O'Hara and told him that Albee was working on the adaptation. "He seemed astonished. I hear he's awfully broke, and that may have explained the look of sudden cheer on his face." He also had seen William Inge at a party at Ned Rorem's. Mendy Wager, in explaining to Inge where he lived, said that he was on West 11th Street "in a house directly behind Edward's new one." Flanagan recounted: "Said Fam (laconically): 'Edward who?' Said Mendy (sardonically): 'You know, Bill, that *writer* fellow.' "

In March of 1966, the director William Ball saw *Tiny Alice*, and sent Albee a letter in which he called the play a classic. Several years later, as the founder and artistic director of American Conservatory Theater (ACT) in San Francisco, Ball apparently had second thoughts about the perfection of the play. He staged his own exceedingly eccentric version. It was hyperkinetic and freely interpretive, rewriting the text and stressing the ritualistic elements. In 1969 Ball brought the production to Broadway. Albee vigorously objected to the alterations and demanded that he return to the original as he wrote it. In 1975, Ball revived the play at ACT. Albee went to a preview and was horrified: This was a revival of Ball's original deconstructive version. At first the playwright demanded that the opening be canceled, then he decided to allow the production and to write a statement that would be inserted in the program. "William Ball, the director, has taken it upon himself to distort my play by cutting, juxtaposing and actually rewriting a good deal of the third act. Of course, this is inexcusable. And it is only out of concern for the actors who have put so much dedication and talent into the production that I am permitting the play to be performed tonight. I'm sorry that you the audience aren't seeing the play as I wrote it."

Another and far more rewarding revival occurred in 1972 at the Hartford Stage Company. It was the most faithful of the three versions, elevated by the odd fact that Jordan Christopher (previously a singer and not an actor) was more suited to the role of Brother Julian than Gielgud, who had seemed both too old and too worldly for the role of this innocent.

In my review in the *Times*, I said that director Paul Weidner "staged *Tiny Alice* simply, allowing the play to survive without directorial injections of adrenalin. As he rightly sees the play, it is a 'poetic metaphor,' sensory rather than intellectual . . . Clues are planted as in a mystery, and the resolution is, intentionally, an ambiguous one." The review went on to praise Christopher as "a little boy locked in a castle, lost and enchanted, yet longing to be sacrificed . . ."

Gielgud never saw the play again, never read it again, and, he said, never understood it. "I think I expunged it from my memory," he said in 1994 and marked it down as "one of those disasters," along with the *Medea* that he did with Judith Anderson. To Gielgud's surprise, some years later, Albee asked him to direct his play *All Over* on Broadway. On the other hand, Irene Worth remained unshakable in her belief in the brilliance of the play while affirming the fact that it is so difficult to act.

Albee eventually changed his mind or, rather, opened his mind about the play. By 1996, he was able to look back at it with a more objective eye. Speaking about his body of work, he said, "The only play I'm indifferent, really indifferent to is *Tiny Alice.*" He explained, "I don't relate to that play at all. I was going totally on instinct, as I remember, and I don't know whether it holds together intellectually or not. I'm not sure. There are a few misgivings about that play."

When he was reminded that that was what his critics had suggested, he responded, "Yes. Well. They may be right." About the characters, he said, "I'm still troubled as to who those three people in the house are: the Lawyer, Butler and Miss Alice? I knew at the time, or I knew enough about it that I thought it would work. But I can't defend that play intellectually at this point." Reminded that, in its time, he did defend the play intellectually, he said,

> I've developed elaborate theories about it, about molecular structure, and everything being part of something infinitely larger and infinitely smaller than itself. And the one thing that I do think is important, that I understand and am fascinated by, was the relationship between martyrdom and sexual hysteria. That's the most coherent part of the play, as far as I'm concerned. Fundamentally, Brother Julian's need for martyrdom is what *Tiny Alice* is all about. But the whole question, "Are these people the devil?" I don't know.

That part, he said, should remain "unresolved and free-floating." About the model of the house onstage: "That's the symbol for everything being part of something infinitely larger and smaller than itself. I've never accepted the Big Bang Theory. I'm sure that matter and anti-matter are mirror images of each other, of everything larger and everything smaller than itself."

Why did he write *Tiny Alice?* "I don't know. It was the next play to write. I don't remember what motivated it, unless it was that thing about religious ecstasy and martyrdom, the saints and sexual hysteria. Plus, creating God in one's own image. Things like that have bothered me for a long time. We create a God in our image, and the only thing that can be worshipped is that which cannot be comprehended. Faith does not permit intellectual investigation." Then he spoke about the question of martyrdom, and his fascination with Brother Julian's hallucination, that final, violent orgasmic scene. Asked if that scene came to him in a dream, he avoided the question and said, "Brother Julian thought of it."

Tiny Alice opened the door to self-indulgence, and the critical reception encouraged Albee to be stubbornly defensive. At various other points in his career, he succumbed to what might be called the *Tiny Alice* syndrome—he was so busy being metaphysical and reaching for profundity that he let the play get away from him. *Tiny Alice* was to remain a dream play, one that may never stand up under ratiocination, but one that does bear reassessment—from the author as well as his critics.

In 1997, Mark Lamos directed a revival of the play at Hartford Stage, in a production starring Richard Thomas as Julian. Seeing it at a preview, as a mature playwright looking back on an early work, Albee said to himself, "Come on, you childish, foolish young playwright fond of the sound of your own voice." He realized that Julian's final monologue was endless and cut it to about one-third of its length. Thirty-three years after *Tiny Alice* first opened on Broadway, he decided, "Of course, Gielgud was right."

Taylor! Burton! Lehman!

You know who I'd like to see as Martha and George:
  Bette Davis and James Mason.

T H E first formal announcement was in March 1964: The movie rights to *Who's Afraid of Virginia Woolf?* had been purchased by Warner Bros. Albee was paid $500,000, plus 10 percent of the gross after the film earned $6 million. Ernest Lehman was to be the producer and screenwriter. *Virginia Woolf* was a daring screen venture. At that early point, there was no director, and no actors were named to play the four roles. Those choices were left principally to Lehman, who, for all his success, was the invisible man of Hollywood screenwriting. Although he wrote original screenplays, beginning with *North by Northwest,* and adapted his own story into the film *Sweet Smell of Success,* he was best known (in Hollywood, if not to the general public) as the writer of the movie versions of the Broadway musicals *West Side Story, The King and I, The Sound of Music,* and, later, *Hello, Dolly!* In other words, his greatest skill was in transferring Broadway shows, in particular, musicals, to the screen, and in retaining whatever it was that made the shows theatrical successes. Mike Nichols, who was later signed to direct *Who's Afraid of Virginia Woolf?*, said, "The joke is that Ernie wrote one line in the movie of *West Side Story,* which is 'I and Graziella will take to the streets.'" Albee said that Lehman contributed two lines to the movie of *Virginia Woolf:* "Let's go to the roadhouse" and "Let's come back from the roadhouse." Both Albee and Nichols insist that all the other lines in the screenplay were Albee's. To give Lehman his credit, his fidelity to an original play or musical took a certain measure of courage, especially so in the case of *Who's Afraid of Virginia Woolf?*

Then and later, Lehman was to be defensive about his contribution as screenwriter. There was a shifting of scenes and some of the dialogue was cut in order to keep the movie at a reasonable length. Creative roles were played by the director, the actors, and the cinematographer—and by Lehman as producer, beginning with his surprising choice of Elizabeth Taylor to play Martha. Albee was a kind of absentee landlord. He had no say over the screenplay and his personal choices for Martha and George, Bette Davis and James Mason, were disregarded. Bette Davis was furious. It was a role "which I really want to kill somebody for. It was to be my part." She told Albee that if Uta Hagen had gotten the role, she would have been disappointed but not heartbroken. "But to cast Miss Taylor, this beautiful, gorgeous young woman, is sickening for your play." Albee's response to Davis: "What I hope they do is take the story up to the point where the play begins and leave us the play."

Albee had a few conversations with Nichols about specific lines in the play and met briefly with Lehman, but he was not involved in the production and did not visit the movie on location. He did not meet Taylor and her costar Richard Burton until the movie was completed. Considering the pitfalls of the movie, including the censorship and the self-censorship that might have taken place, Albee was immensely lucky in the results. Taylor seemed like a very doubtful choice. She was too young, too beautiful, and, it was thought, not serious enough as an actress to portray the savagely amusing, embittered faculty wife. Lehman thought otherwise. "Every actress wanted to play the role," he said at the time. "I was an open target for every agent. I had to barricade myself. Why do I think Elizabeth would be right? I sensed certain wavelengths in her personality akin to Martha. I don't mean she is a shrew or tears husbands to bits, but I think she has a deeply feminine vulnerability. Elizabeth said, 'All my friends say I'm a fool to play the role. The more they tell me that, the more excited I am to play it.' " He added, "People know how Uta Hagen played it. They certainly know how Bette Davis would do it, but they wonder how Elizabeth Taylor will do it." In an interview, Lehman elaborated on some of these thoughts: "I felt that of all the actresses I knew, no one in her public life and her public behavior was closer to Martha than Elizabeth Taylor, *the actress,* not the private woman . . . So I started getting very, very excited about the idea, which I kept a deep, dark secret, because everyone in town was playing the game of casting this picture."

When Lehman told Jack Warner his idea, Warner objected because of Taylor's youth. Still in her early thirties, she was almost twenty years younger than the character was supposed to be. Lehman insisted that through costume and makeup, the age differential could be overcome. Undoubtedly with an eye on the box office power of Taylor starring in the movie version of the prize-winning play, Warner agreed. Then it was up to Lehman to convince Taylor. At the time, Burton and Taylor were about to go to California to film *The Sandpiper*. Neither of them had seen the play on Broadway, and before they left New York on the Super Chief they were given a copy of Albee's manuscript. Taylor read it first and did not comment, then passed it on to Burton, who stayed up late that night reading it twice. He said in an interview with the writer Roy Newquist that he told his wife: "I think you're too young. I don't think you're enough of a harridan. Maybe you don't have the power. But you've got to play it to stop everybody else from playing it." Whatever small reluctance she had was quickly overcome by the challenge. As a reigning Hollywood star, she was paid $500,000 plus 10 percent of the gross over $6 million, which, not so coincidentally, was the same financial arrangement the studio had made with the playwright.

The next question was, who would play George? High on Lehman's list was Arthur Hill to repeat his Broadway performance. Though Taylor initially approved of Hill, her own first choice was her husband and frequent costar Burton, who had originally been one of the candidates for the role when the play first opened on Broadway. Although Lehman did not want the movie "to sound like another Dick and Elizabeth picture," he gradually came around to the idea of pairing them. As always, Warner's hesitation was largely financial. Having agreed to Taylor, he wondered if he could afford to have Burton. Two top, heavy star salaries scarcely left room for a name Hollywood director. The early choice, however, was Fred Zinnemann, who rejected the opportunity and went on to direct *A Man for All Seasons*, which turned out to be one of his greatest successes and the principal rival to *Virginia Woolf* for film awards in 1966.

Burton recalled the casting of the director: "Elizabeth and I both suggested we get a fresh, young director, because it's a young play, though it's about middle-aged people. Elizabeth suggested Mike and everybody was horrified. 'His first film,' they said. But we were in a pretty good position, because we had a veto on the director." Initially, Jack Warner was reluctant to hire Nichols, unwilling to trust a major property to an untried director. Lehman assured him that Taylor and Burton had great respect for Nichols and "we need that or else they'll eat our director alive." Until Nichols was signed, said Burton, "I was still convinced that I was too strong for the part and Elizabeth thought she was too young and not powerful enough for the searing dialogue."

Nichols had moved quickly from his career as an actor and stand-up satirist (with his partner Elaine May) to a new role as a Tony award–winning theater director. In the space of less than two years, he had directed three hit plays, *The Knack* Off-Broadway and *Barefoot in the Park* and *Luv* on Broadway, and was soon to follow that success with *The Odd Couple*. Although he had not yet made a film, he had been signed to direct *The Graduate*, a low-budget film starring an unknown Off-Broadway actor, Dustin Hoffman. *Virginia Woolf* was something else—a big-budget Hollywood movie with two titanic stars.

Nichols had first met Albee in 1960 when Nichols was appearing on Broadway in *An Evening with Mike Nichols and Elaine May*. One night Nichols and Albee had dinner before the Nichols and May show. Nichols recalled: "I remember two things that he said, that he loved what we did, and that the only thing he disagreed with were the blackouts. He thought they should be sort of gray-outs, that we should peter out rather than end with a punch, which was quite a brilliant point about us." Although Nichols thought Albee was correct in his assessment, he retained the blackouts. He said that he did not think either of them was influenced by the other, but that from the first he sensed a certain empathy with Albee, that both of them had "outsider feelings," which Nichols traced back to his childhood as a European immigrant in America and—something he shared with Albee—his unhappiness at boarding school. "Even though Edward was very austere and restrained socially, I felt a real connection to him and almost an affection, obviously because of his mind and his work, but also because of his wry cordiality."

When Nichols was offered the job, he said, "I couldn't turn my back on this piece of material. To turn it down out of fear would be cowardice." On the other hand, some of his friends, such as Lillian Hellman, thought that by making his first film with Burton and Taylor, Nichols was playing it safe.

Nichols had seen *Who's Afraid of Virginia Woolf?* soon after Elaine May's first play, *A Matter of Position* (starring Nichols), had closed in Philadelphia. "I thought it was the most exciting play and production that I'd seen with the exception of *A Streetcar Named Desire*. I always thought that it was Shakespearean in that the two main characters compete in recruiting the audience to their side, in a manner not dissimilar to *Taming of the Shrew*. Kate says, 'You see what he does to me? Watch this. He's out of the question,' and Petruchio says, 'Are you kidding? Look at her. She's a nightmare.' And the audience is shifted back and forth. That's what happens in *Virginia Woolf*." In that sense, Nichols related the play to the celebrated Pirandello sketch that he and Elaine May did, in which truth and theatrical illusion collide with one another. "To some extent it depends on who is playing the characters and how lovable each of the actors is, but to a large extent it depends on the power of the dialectic of the jokes, if they are—as they are by Edward—brilliantly balanced. The audience is bouncing back and forth between the characters. I'm on her side, I'm on his side, I'm on her side."

For the role of Nick, Nichols wanted Robert Redford, who had appeared for him in *Barefoot in the Park* on Broadway. Redford rejected the role because, said Nichols, "even then, he didn't want to play a schmuck"; it went to George Segal, who had worked for Nichols in *The Knack* Off-Broadway. Though some consideration was given to Melinda Dillon to repeat her Broadway role and to Barbara Harris, a favorite of Nichols from their days with the Compass improvisational theater in Chicago, the eventual choice was Sandy Dennis, who had recently scored a success in *Any Wednesday* on Broadway.

"I don't feel any enormous possessiveness," Albee said at the time, "no sense of loss, of desecration. I assume they will change the whole thing." Still, he was looking forward to seeing it when it was finished: "I wouldn't miss it for the world."

The first problem—and a continuing subject of contention—was Lehman's attempt to rewrite and explain Albee. Peremptorily, Lehman decided that George and Martha's son would no longer be imaginary. He would be real and would have committed suicide by hanging himself in a closet at the age of sixteen (his age would be lowered several years to make him a better match with Taylor as his mother). That closet would have been wallpapered over to hide the fact of the violent act. In defense of that change, Lehman said that when the play opened on Broadway the imaginary son had been the subject of criticism. But at the crux of Albee's play was an imaginary son; to change him into an actual person would be to undercut the entire work.

Lehman also wanted a scene over the opening credits in which George goes for a walk and sees two dogs fornicating. He lost both points. It was Nichols's feeling that to film it in color would give the work a certain literalization. He wanted something more stylized and abstract and also felt that Taylor's makeup would work better in black and white. As Lehman said, "We felt Elizabeth Taylor's makeup and aging wouldn't work in color. Somehow if you saw her wearing a red blouse and red patent leather shoes and lipstick, it wouldn't have been as harsh. And Jack Warner was equally harsh about having it done in color." A minor conflict between Nichols and Lehman was over Nichols's decision that, to emphasize the professorial aspect of the character, Burton should wear glasses in the picture.

"I had real fights on that movie," Nichols said, indicating that the battles were not with the actors but with Warner, Lehman, and the cinematographer Haskell Wexler. Wexler replaced Harry Stradling, who had been fired as cinematographer because it was believed that his work had been too flattering to Taylor. Nichols traced some of the problems to his own inexperience: "I was a New York theater director. I was cocky and I was afraid of Hollywood. I did really stupid things, like shooting the title sequence in Northampton. They tried to tell me I could have done it right on the back lot. But I didn't know anything about movies."

Despite the friendship between Taylor and Nichols, they were, said Burton, apprehensive of one other when the filming began: "She liked Nichols, but hadn't worked with him. She was afraid she was too young for the part, didn't have the big guns necessary for it. My wife is a fairly formidable woman. When those veils fall over her eyes strong men head for the hills. They were nervous with each other, so they took it out in all this kidding." With all the joking and the four-letter words flying, "it became almost liturgical."

Nichols decided that in the movie "the claustrophobia would take care of itself." He explained about George and Martha: "They've been married for a thousand years. They're together. These kids that are visiting them cannot leave, not because the doors are locked but because Martha has the power, and Nick needs the job. Claustrophobia did not seem to me to be so much an element. I also realized that the recruiting of the audience as a participant in the battle was no longer possible. Therefore the movie would be far more emotional than the play. In the play to a great extent emotion and tension are discharged in laughter, and although there are big laughs in the movie, it's not the same thing. It's frozen. That prize fight element of the play was gone, which left me with the emotional heart of it. I always thought it was like Erich Fromm's definition of love, that in a strong and productive love relationship, one partner wants the other partner to be his or her best self. Just as *Long Day's Journey* is, in my view, heartbreaking because the characters suffer only for one another, never for themselves. The boys are suffering for their mother. She's suffering for the boys. It's not what I think of as a Jewish family fight. It's never, 'Look what you've done to me.' It's 'Look what he's done to her.' In similar ways in *Virginia Woolf*, they are suffering for one another, and they love each other beyond measure, which is how and why we're able to stand the whole thing."

When he began working on the movie, he remembered a couple he knew in Chicago, a man who ran a book shop near the University of Chicago, and his wife. They had terrible fights, but, Nichols felt, at its base it was an honest relationship. "Their relationship is based on the truth." In contrast, with Nick and Honey "everything about them is based on lies. They got together over a lie. They continue to lie to each other and to themselves. George and Martha live with the truth. Even the imaginaryness of the child is perfectly clear to them. They just don't share it with anybody else." Nichols said that George and Martha's home in the movie was based on that of his friends in Chicago.

From the beginning, Nichols intended to emphasize the specificity of the dramatic situation and to avoid all thoughts about metaphor. At one point he asked Buck Henry, who wrote the screenplay for *The Graduate*, what he thought *Virginia Woolf* was about. Henry answered, "Well, it's about reality and illusion and the kind of games people play to fill in gaps of emptiness." Then Henry asked Nichols what he thought the play was about, and the director answered, "It's about a man and a woman named George and Martha who invite a young couple over for drinks after a faculty party. They drink and talk and argue for ten to twelve hours, until you get to know them." Henry's analysis of that summary: "He means that the immediate reality is all that counts. If you don't understand the first step, then the second and third steps will elude you completely."

By June of 1965, Nichols was deeply involved in preproduction of the film, studying the script and choosing locations and also studying movie technique. Privately he screened movies by Truffaut, George Stevens, Elia Kazan, and Fellini. He watched Fellini's $8^1/2$ four times, each time becoming so engrossed that he forgot to make notes about the director's technique. But he only got through the first twenty minutes of the film of *Long Day's Journey into Night*, Sidney Lumet's attempt to transfer a powerful stage experience to the screen. Nichols was dismayed by the fact that the director was not allowed to cut any of the dialogue and had chosen to substitute camera movement for action. This was to be an object lesson to him when he began filming his own movie on July 6.

Taylor said in her memoir, *Elizabeth Taylor* (ghost-written by Richard Meryman), that she had never seen *Virginia Woolf* onstage and had not even listened to the original cast recording. She wanted to create her own Martha, as distinct from that of anyone else, beginning with Uta Hagen. Then she—or Meryman—reached for a metaphor to describe the character: "I think she is a desperate woman who has the softness of the underbelly of a baby turtle. She covers it up with the toughness of the shell, which she paints red. Her veneer is bawdy; it's sloppy, it's slouchy, it's snarly." It's Elizabeth! "But there are moments when the facade cracks and you see the vulnerability, the infinite pain of this woman inside whom, years ago, life almost died but is still flickering."

Before shooting, the actors rehearsed for three weeks at the Warners studio in Burbank. At Taylor's request, filming did not begin until 10:30 A.M., which meant that because of the star's complicated makeup filming did not generally begin until after lunch. Sometimes there was an additional delay when Taylor and Burton would have a long lunch, one day a three-hour lunch with the Duke and Duchess of Windsor. Although the set was closed—no reporters or outside photographers were allowed to watch—occasionally a celebrity would visit. Nichols recalled the time that Marlene Dietrich showed up and, to Taylor's astonishment, inexplicably managed to avoid speaking to her.

Despite the fact that this was Nichols's first film, he already had vast experience directing actors onstage and apparently took an easy, confident approach even with his two stars. In her memoir, Taylor recalled one specific way in which he led her into an understanding of her character. In one scene as Martha, she had to open the door of the refrigerator. Inside she discovered "a complete portrait of the total disorder of Martha's mind and Martha's life," as personally designed by the director: "He had an ear of corn, all chewed and put away. There was a tangle of leftover spaghetti on a plate. A can of beans had been opened and left completely full, with the lid folded back." Nichols was, she said, an inventive director who soon had the actors participating in his inventions.

Burton credited Nichols with a certain ruthlessness: "His behavior, his manner, are silky soft. He appears to defer to you, then in the end he gets exactly what he wants. He conspires with you, rather than directs you, to get your best. He'd make me throw away a line where I'd have hit it hard . . . and he was right every time."

On August 21, the company came east to film exteriors in and around Smith College in Northampton, Massachusetts, having agreed that shooting would be completed before students returned for the fall semester. Because of bad weather, what seemed to be perpetual rain, the shooting was eventually extended from two to four weeks. A chartered plane flew from Los Angeles to Bradley Field, near Hartford, Connecticut, and from there the company was to be taken by car to Northampton. Nichols remembers: "There were sixty people aboard the plane. There was a first-class section for Elizabeth, Richard, Ernie, me and Sandy and George. And then a curtain. I said, 'Ernie, what have you done? You have kicked this production in the balls and we're not even off the ground. Now, open the fucking curtain and let's go in the back.' " Then and later, the Burtons were treated as royalty. As had happened when Burton did *Hamlet* on Broadway, they were surrounded—ambushed—by fans. "Everything was a circus because of Elizabeth," said Nichols. "She was so insanely famous that everything we did was on the cover of some magazine." He also said, in intentional understatement, "Publicity was not the main problem on this picture."

Landing at night, the Burtons (with Taylor's daughter, Liza Todd) were driven to a rented hideaway in Goshen, near Northampton. In the morning they discovered it was no hideaway. Walking out of their bedroom, Burton realized he was being ogled through a picture window by an army of neighbors. As Taylor said, "They applauded him." The couple immediately moved to a more secluded house, a fourteen-room estate on 112 wooded acres in South Ashfield, dispossessing Nichols, who moved to a different house in Goshen. So many people stopped at Edward Trevallion's general store in South Ashfield and asked directions to the stars' house that the owner nailed up a wooden sign, LIZ AND DICK, with an arrow pointing the way.

Filming took place at night, from 8:30 P.M. to 5 A.M., with the actors wearing thermal underwear to ward off the cold. Most of the scenes were shot at Tyler House, a faculty annex on the Smith campus, which had been altered somewhat (a front porch and bay windows were added) to simulate the home of George and Martha. An exact duplicate of that house was created for the studio interiors in Hollywood. The location shooting became a major Massachusetts event, bringing in tourists and also fascinating local residents and the local press. One reporter from Springfield, Massachusetts, got a job as a chauffeur and extra, then was fired after his identity was revealed. The movie company was surrounded by seventy guards recruited from five Massachusetts towns and the Deputy Sheriffs' Association. It was estimated that the studio was paying $150,000 for salaries to guards, chauffeurs, and extras, as well as for food, board, and drink.

Along with other journalists, I went to Northampton to write about the filming. Both the shooting itself and the stars were sheltered from visitors. It was clear that both actors had been deglamorized. Taylor's hair had been streaked with gray, her face lined to make her look older. Her clothes were intentionally unflattering. She had put on twenty pounds to play the role. "Martha walks stumpy," Taylor said and then demonstrated with a walk between a strut and a waddle. Wearing a baggy sweater, Burton was playing George as a seedy academic. Off camera, they took time to charm local residents. When Herbert Heston, the Smith College public relations man, was having difficulty keeping photographers at a distance, Taylor tried to soothe him by saying, "Mr. Heston—whenever I hear your name I think of Charlton. What is your first name? Herbert? May I call you Herbert? Call me Elizabeth."

In September, the company returned to California and continued shooting interiors through December. In February 1966, Albee flew to Los Angeles, and Nichols, without telling Lehman, showed him a rough cut. Watching his play unfold on screen, Albee said, "Part of my pleasure was relief." At least at that time, his doubts about the director vanished. "I found out that he had a pretty good idea of what the play was about. There was at least one considerable intelligence at work. I tend to suspect that Mike Nichols deserves a great deal of the credit."

On seeing the film, Geoffrey Shurlock, the head of Hollywood's Production Code Administration, refused to give it a seal of approval, but he was overruled by the Production Code Review Board, which said that the film "is not designed to be prurient" and was "largely a reproduction" of the play. In its statement, the board added that "this exemption does not mean that the floodgates are open for language or other material." In fact, the ruling proved to be a turning point in the fight against censorship.

The movie was released in June and received favorable reviews, better reviews, in fact, than the play. Stanley Kauffmann, who was briefly the drama critic of the *Times*, took a sidestep into his more customary role as a movie critic and reviewed the film for the *Times*. He began by saying that "the best American play of the last decade and a violently candid one, has been brought to the screen without pussyfooting." He concluded that this was "one of the most scathingly honest American films ever made." In an interview with Frances Herridge in the *New York Post*, Albee indicated that he was pleased with the movie: "I kept getting reports about terrible things happening to it—like their dropping the imaginary kid from the script or making him some kind of monster hidden away. And now it turns out nothing's been changed except for a couple of phrases that apparently were too strong for them." He said he had no desire to see his other plays filmed. "I'd rather stop while I'm ahead. I may not get Mike Nichols as director next time." The following April, Taylor won her second Academy Award as best actress and Sandy Dennis won as best supporting actress. The film also won Oscars for cinematography, costume design, and set decoration. There were those who felt that Burton should have been named best actor over Paul Scofield (for *A Man for All Seasons*).

When he finished the film, Nichols joked about having a nightmare: "After seeing *Virginia Woolf*, someone comes up to me and says, 'Do you want to do Albee's next play? I say yes, and then they send me . . . *Tiny Alice.*"

Although the movie was billed in advertisements as "Ernest Lehman's production of Edward Albee's *Who's Afraid of Virginia Woolf?*" rather than as a Mike Nichols film, Lehman was the forgotten man. For almost thirty years even as he went on to other projects, he apparently nursed a private grudge. Finally on June 19, 1994, after Albee won his third Pulitzer Prize (for *Three Tall Women*), Lehman sent a letter to the playwright unburdening himself of all his hard feelings, especially about Albee's lack of appreciation.

He listed some of the obstacles he faced in producing the film and in writing the screenplay, and he expressed his dismay about Albee's supposed suggestion to his agent that Lehman's name be removed from the screenplay. After summarizing his various resentments, he said that he hoped that Albee's return to being awarded Pulitzer Prizes was a sign that he would write more good plays in the future.

If Lehman had known Albee better, he might have realized that in his letter he was pushing all the wrong buttons, especially in his reference to the playwright's comeback. In his reply, Albee thanked Lehman for his congratulations, then said:

> I wrote 10 or so very good plays between my second and third Pulitzers, and you must know from your years in movies that the best work doesn't always win prizes, and that a prize is no absolute guarantee of excellence.
>
> I'm distressed by the body of your letter, because it suggests long-burning hurt on your part over things which are untrue, distorted, and/or exaggerated.
>
> I recall remarking when I saw the film that it was almost word for word my play, with a few excisions I felt unnecessary, and the addition of a couple of phrases about going to and coming from a roadhouse (a scene which I felt broke the claustrophobia of the play). I was delighted that what seemed to be no rewriting had been done. (It would be interesting to compare your script with the play some day.)

He added that he had

> no memory of ever suggesting to anyone at William Morris Agency that they investigate to see if your name could not be taken off the credits.
>
> I am grateful that your attentions to the project kept it faithful to my play. I'm grateful you fought the good fight against compromise and dilution. I'm not so certain I see the need for the film to have been in black and white, since I

wrote it in color, but perhaps back in those days black and white was "serious" and color was not.

Have we cleared the air? I hope so. Oh, by the way, where's the truth in what I remember Warner Bros. telling me that the film was all set for Bette Davis and James Mason? Between us, I think that would have been better casting.

I hope you're well and happy. I believe I am both. How right you are—"we are older, God knows."

Lehman replied with a letter of abject apology, bordering on self-mortification. He apologized for his rudeness and thanked Albee for the privilege of turning his play into a movie. He agreed that the roadhouse scene had a false ring to it, defended the choice of making the film in black and white, and said he was thankful that his variations had not been used in the film—that the result was more faithful to the play. Later he said that his behavior and the whole episode had been shameful. He blamed his letter on the fact that he was under medication.

Albee sent him a polite response and with that the case rested. Commenting on the correspondence, Albee said, "Lehman claims that he had to write so hard and do so much work to make the play work on film." Aside from two scenes, in the roadhouse and under the tree outside of George and Martha's house, "It's my play fucking word for word."

Despite Albee's initial relief about the fidelity of the movie to the play, over the years he was to change his mind about the film and about the actors. By 1996, he had seen the movie eight times, and he said, "In spite of everything, it's not bad. The only trouble with it is that it's completely humorless." Although he always thought that Taylor was far too young for the role, he thought it was "the best thing she's ever done." About the film, he said, "I still liked it best the first time I saw it, which was a rough cut before the movie music had been added and sentimentalized it."

Years later, after a long career as a film director, Nichols expressed his own reservations about the movie of *Virginia Woolf.* Asked if he would change anything in it, he said, "I would change everything. But it has a lot of life to it. It's a great script. It's a great play. It hasn't died in that way that some things from the stage died in being transferred. The strange thing about *Virginia Woolf* is that you think it's so much a play—and what kind of movie is it where people sit around a living room and talk? But it doesn't seem like a play, and I think that's more Edward's accomplishment than mine. I think that the things they're saying are forever shocking, not shocking because of the anger or the violence, but shocking because they're so alive. They're alive and recognizable and funny. The dialogue is so arresting. It was so outside and beyond all conventions."

Overcoming obstacles, the film is astonishingly successful at transferring the play into another medium. The dialogue was cut to bring the running time down to two hours and twenty minutes, and it was somewhat sanitized. The move away from George and Martha's home to the roadhouse is totally unnecessary and a few of the scenes would have benefited from being reshot. Burton's delivery of the "bergin" monologue, for one, is overly somber, missing the humor beneath the tragedy. On the other hand, when Burton walks into the room aiming the toy rifle, his intensity works to his comic advantage. In all important respects, the movie faithfully captures the brilliance of the play. Although Albee is, of course, correct, when he says Taylor is not a believable fifty-two-year-old, with the help of makeup and through her acting she is persuasively Martha: angry, embittered at her husband's failings, and thrashing through the remains of their life together. She is vulgar and savage—and brings a clear sense of comic proportion to her most devastating lines, from her opening declaration of "what a dump," and her saucy imitation of Bette Davis to her final expression of her fearful regard of a life without illusion.

Burton, the more natural actor, easily slips into his role, which is as comfortable as his professorial cardigan, and even his accent fits him well as an academic. He brings all his theatrical experience to bear on his scenes with George Segal, playfully prying into the younger man's private life and provoking him into his ruminations and revelations. More than in many other versions of the play, Taylor and Burton communicate the give and take and the connection in this partnership. They are battlers in close quarters, and beneath it all there seems to be a genuine admiration for each other's athletic verbal agility. They are in fact equal contestants.

In his first film, working with two titanic performers, Nichols wisely keeps his camera close, and at those rare moments when he pulls back for a long shot (to view the house through the trees), the film stops, as if in an intermission or a calm between storms. Then it is back to the bruising, continuing encounter.

Later, after their divorce, Burton and Taylor were to do *Private Lives* on Broadway, and their real relationship became the sole reason for that revival. They were unconvincing in character. The opposite is true about *Virginia Woolf*. Except for Taylor's youthfulness, they turned out to be excellent choices for these roles. Led by Nichols and drawn by Albee's dialogue, they underscore the credibility of the play, so that even the imaginary child seems to derive from the desperation of a childless couple in a real marriage. One of the additions is especially intriguing: The house becomes a part of the play, as the actors move from room to room. After the earlier party, Martha—still voracious—plunders the refrigerator for a chicken leg. She eats as she talks, while he quietly works on a crossword puzzle. She and George drink around the house, not limiting themselves to the living room, but revealing the house as a place of habitation: unmade bed, a sink with dishes, papers and books in disarray. Their life is in disarray and the camera is there as recorder and watchful observer.

The other two characters are their pawns, but both Segal and Dennis fill their roles substantially: They are catalysts and, to a certain degree, our surrogates, as they are drawn into this alien environment. *Virginia Woolf* avoids the pitfalls of so many filmed plays. It does not seem static. Nor has it been excessively opened up or expanded to bring in other characters, such as Martha's father. The movie of *Virginia Woolf* is a credit to all parties, beginning with Albee, Nichols, and the actors but also including Lehman and Warner for not interfering with the essence of the material.

Nichols continued to be fascinated by the play. In 1980, he and Elaine May played George and Martha in a production at the Long Wharf Theater in New Haven, directed by Arvin Brown. James Naughton and Swoosie Kurtz were Nick and Honey. Nichols said, "Arvin and I were both very constrained by the fact that I had done the movie and supposedly knew all about it. Out of conviviality, I made myself as blank and open as I could"—until several days into rehearsal when he began playing a more activist role in the staging. He suggested that Naughton dye his hair blond or wear a wig, so that Nick would be a Nazi. Naughton protested, saying that because of his coloring, he would look like a transvestite if he were blond. Nichols's primary problem was that he had "seen it played brilliantly twice"—on Broadway and in the film. "I'll never forget Uta and Arthur Hill. I remember every moment, every turn, every expression, every inflection. Uta was transcendant. And I always think, 'They did that in four weeks?'" In addition, it had been many years since Nichols had acted, and although May had appeared occasionally in movies, it was a long time since she had been onstage. Rehearsing the production, Elaine May would intentionally offer opposite line readings. She would whisper, "I don't bray." Nichols, in particular, worked very slowly and by the day of the first performance, the actors still had not rehearsed the end of the third act.

Naughton remembers: "In the top of the third act, Nick and Martha have this long scene. Since we hadn't rehearsed it, Elaine paraphrased the speech for the first two or three performances. But I've never felt so secure on the stage with anybody. Even though she didn't know the lines, she knew who Martha was. For the first couple of performances it was by the seat of your pants. By the time she had a chance to really work on it, she locked it in and it was fine." For Naughton, it remained a fascinating experience, and a lesson how to capture both the comic and tragic elements of the play.

Albee came to see it, went out to dinner with the actors and seemed respectful and polite, but asked Nichols and May if they could speak one at a time onstage. Because Nichols became sick, the run ended early, before the review was printed in the *Times*. The production became a footnote in the history of the play. As director or as actor, Nichols vowed never to do *Virginia Woolf* again: "I hear Uta and Arthur Hill and I hear Richard and Elizabeth and I hear Elaine and me. I can't get it all out of my head, and, of course, the joy of doing a play is to discover what it is."

12
Balancing Act

Where do I live?

The dark sadness

*I*n 1966, while Nichols was busy editing *Who's Afraid of Virginia Woolf?*, Albee had an extraordinarily active year with two plays on Broadway, *Malcolm*, adapted from the James Purdy novel, and *A Delicate Balance*; his adaptation of the musical version of Truman Capote's *Breakfast at Tiffany's*; and a screenplay about Nijinsky and Diaghilev for Rudolf Nureyev and Paul Scofield, to be directed by Tony Richardson. As it turned out, *Malcolm* was a disaster, closing after seven performances, *Breakfast at Tiffany's* closed during previews, and Richardson and Albee did not make the Nijinsky movie. But *A Delicate Balance* was one of his best plays and his first Pulitzer Prize winner.

As an admirer of Purdy, Albee wanted to give him a hearing on the stage and to expand his audience. In the *Candide*-like story, the title character is looking for his lost father. In a series of adventures, Malcolm loses his innocence and dies of acute alcoholism and sexual hyperesthesia. Albee had started writing his adaptation early in 1965 and by the summer was deep into it. He had sent the first two acts of the play to Flanagan, who was at the Mac-Dowell Colony in New Hampshire. Flanagan responded with enthusiasm: "I think Act II of *Malcolm* is funny, more *you* than Act I and quite without that sort of well-made neatness that worried me a little if it was to be continued throughout the play."

In a letter to Flanagan, Albee explained his approach:

I have tried to remove most of Purdy's extraneous camp, his moving away from the central figure, his shattering of concentration and direction. I'm trying to keep a kind of maelstrom descent for the poor boy . . . a Billy Buddish innocence-lost thing. Alan S. [Schneider] bothers me a little, because he keeps saying things like 'I wanna feel like hell for this kid all the time.' *I* don't think that should be it, really. I feel Malcolm as rather passive; I feel our reactions must be for *ourselves*, that we must have a kind of removal, a detachment in our involvement. But, I can iron all this out with him. It is one play I doubt he will be able to rationalize out of shape. I must keep telling him of the fine line dividing naturalism and too much stylization. I see the characters as vaguely distorted, but not out of shape. I have more or less, settled on a style for settings and lights. Projections of all backgrounds, some photographs (some in color, some not), some projected etchings, occasional projected drawings, with three treadmills in front of the full-stage scrim which will hold the projections, one for real furniture and stuff, the other two for the characters to more or less glide on and off stage.

Then he agreed that Flanagan might write a jazz score. He said he was working on the third act (the final version of the play was in two acts) and planned to finish it by August 1 and have the play in rehearsal in October. He did not finish it until the end of the year. He sent a copy to Purdy, who responded, "Thank you for your *Malcolm*, which I like *very much*. It's *very* strong, I think, and flows." Purdy had a few suggestions. He thought the death scene was somewhat long and could be more savage and he missed the character of Estel Blanc, who was cut from the final version. But his enthusiasm was clear: "You are the only person who could have adapted *Malcolm*—ever." In an article in *The New York Times*, Albee returned the compliment, praising the original novel as "deeply sad and terribly funny," and hoping that both aspects would be communicated to the audience.

Neither aspect was communicated, and the failure of the play could be shared by most of the participants, beginning with Albee. Clearly he was drawn to the novel because of its theme of the destruction of the innocent. His interest in that subject could be traced back to *The Zoo Story*, *The American Dream*, and *Tiny Alice*. But why tell it again, unless he had something to add to it, and why try to tell it in Purdy's voice? Of all Albee's plays, *Malcolm* is probably the one with the fewest admirers, the easiest to categorize as a mistake.

Alan Schneider, for one, was never enthusiastic about the project. In this case, Albee shifts a great deal of the blame to Schneider, or to himself for letting the director have his own way, for going along with his suggestions for changes. The fact is that he was not as involved in the production as he was in other projects. For Albee, it was "an experiment," in which "I sort of let Alan run the show. It wasn't quite what it should have been. I don't think it's a bad script, but maybe I'm blind to that whole issue." There were some problems on the casting. Michael Dunn had been the natural choice for the role of the midget but when he was unavailable, Albee altered the character to "the oldest man in the world," and it was played by John Heffernan. Without a midget (or a dwarf), said Purdy, the play simply "went off course." Also in the cast were such excellent actors as Estelle Parsons, Henderson Forsythe, and Ruth White. At that early stage of his career, Matthew Cowles had an air of innocence coupled with his inexperience. The actors tried their best to breathe life into the script. But the adaptation was artificial and undramatic and the production failed on basic levels. Even the treadmill that swept Malcolm through his adventures never worked properly. To compound the difficulty, the show was presented in the Shubert Theater, an enormous musical house and the wrong setting for a play that expected to get by on its charm.

"*Malcolm* was a mess," Barr wrote in his book. "Edward wrote the play with a sword instead of a pen and we overproduced it. Edward's adaptation was undramatic . . . the casting presented impossible problems; and we were a very unhappy team . . . Edward told me he cried at every performance; so did I when I saw the grosses!" Albee said, "The Christ-like innocence of the kid probably did affect me but I don't think I sat there in the third row blubbering every night. I don't cry in public very much. I remember being rather upset, annoyed and depressed that *Malcolm* was going away."

Stanley Kauffmann, who had just replaced Taubman as the *Times* drama critic, took a surprisingly generous view. Other critics were either greatly disappointed or dismissive. Brustein was angrily ad hominem, calling the play "Albee's most deeply homosexual work." Then in what sounded like a reprise of his attack on William Inge, he wrote, "As Albee gets closer and closer to his true subjects—the malevolence of women, the psychological impact of Mom, the evolution of the invert—he tends to get more abstract and incoherent until he is finally reduced, as here, to a nervous plucking at broken strings." The review was printed after the show had closed, coinciding with an infamous essay by Kauffmann in the Sunday *Times*. The headline on Kauffmann's piece was HOMOSEXUAL DRAMA AND ITS DISGUISES. In it, he said that "three of the most successful playwrights of the last 20 years are (reputed) homosexuals," and because of them "postwar American drama presents a badly distorted picture of American women, marriage and society." It was his charge that they invented "a two-sex version of the one-sex experience"; in other words, homosexuals were incapable of writing believable female characters. The playwrights he was referring to were clearly Williams, Inge, and Albee, who had created some of the most memorable women in dramatic history.

Twenty-five years later, Albee attacked the "disgusting article," saying in a *Times* interview, "It was absolutely preposterous to begin with—the notion that gays were writing about gays, but disguising them as straights and writing about men, but disguising them as women. Tennessee Williams knew the difference between men and women as well as I do."

Infuriated by the double critical assault, A. R. Gurney Jr. wrote to Albee in 1966. Speaking as a husband and the father of four children, he said,

> I think the homosexual has plenty to tell me about the world, and I think I've got a thing or two to tell him. There must be some sort of a life-line slung between the noisy family rooms of suburbia and the hushed bars of Greenwich Village. Every healthy society has had procedures for including and using the insights of its unmarried members. Plato's philosopher kings, Dickens's bachelor uncles, the preservation of marriages; somebody's got to air out the cave. Similarly, perhaps the family has given these single people some sense of continuity and extension in time. I hope that as our best playwright, you're not turning your back on just those who should listen to you most. *Virginia Woolf,* which I don't think could have been written by a married man, was so good, and such a success, precisely because it insisted that marriage means something. Hence it bridged both worlds. I hope you continue to let us have it.

When the closing notice for *Malcolm* was posted, Albee took out an ad in the *Times:* "To those who have come to see *Malcolm,* my thanks. To those who were pleased, my gratitude. To those who were disappointed, my apologies. See you next play."

The next play was *A Delicate Balance,* and it was the opposite of *Malcolm.* Albee had also begun that play in 1965 and had put it aside while he adapted the Purdy novel. After *Malcolm,* he retreated to Caneel Bay on St. John, where he tried to forget his "most recent theatrical triumph" by working hard on what he jokingly referred to as "a new frolic"—*A Delicate Balance.* "Greetings from Eden," he wrote Flanagan. "The sun purrs down, the water is smooth and blue, blue; there are no sharks to be seen. I sleep nine or ten hours a night, eat, lightly, of fish, three meals a day, swim, snorkle, talk to Anne Bancroft (who is here, so no fret) and *write!*" He turned again to A *Delicate Balance*, which "has been pressing at me for several months now, with almost an act done, and I am glad for the peace to be back at it. Funny play." He had some final thoughts about *Malcolm*, wondering why he had not been depressed:

> I began to feel guilty and uneasy about my well-being. Indeed, why was I *not* going into a decline? Why was I *not* sleepless, disoriented, and given to feelings of worthlessness and subject to writers-block? I have spent but one night when sleep would not come easily . . . and that was the night I lay awake and wondered why I was *not* sleepless, unhappy, blocked, etc.
>
> Maybe I shall have a collapse, months from now. Maybe I *will* fall apart and become a stone, or rage. Right now, though, I am of good mind, am working, resting, and—at most—mildly curious to know, when the time comes, whether or not the commercial failure of *Malcolm* was a true statement of its artistic value, as well. Otherwise, I couldn't care less about it. (Had it not been an adaptation!!!! Well now!!!).

In March, after seeing the rough cut of the movie of *Virginia Woolf,* Albee took an extended trip through Europe. Many years later, in the program for the 1997 revival of A *Delicate Balance* in London, he said that he was accompanied by Harry, his Irish "Woolfhound," as he called him. He was also accompanied by Pennington. On the *France* going over, he returned to A *Delicate Balance*, finishing the first act before landing at Le Havre. He wrote the second act while traveling through France, and he finished the play on the sea voyage home. In the Albee canon, A *Delicate Balance* is "the boat play." Later plays were to be written on planes, but this one was done the old-fashioned way, sitting in a deck chair on a luxury liner, which, of course, is how Noël Coward wrote *Private Lives.*

In Paris after visiting Italy, Switzerland, Germany, the south of France, and the Netherlands, he sent a letter to Flanagan:

> I have all but finished A *Delicate Balance*, for whatever that's worth. (More than the last three, I dearly hope.) I like it, but there might be some critical trouble. ("Nothing happens.") Quite true, because the dilemma faced by the characters is withdrawn just before they have to resolve it. The "action" of the play is therefore theoretical—how would they have behaved had the problem come to a head. They are altered by the whole thing, though, so perhaps it will pass as a play. I still like it.

He promised when he returned to give Flanagan "page after page of libretto" for *The Ice Age* and added that he was trying to buy "one of those lovely art-nouveau entrances to the Paris Metro" for his house in Montauk. Then, for fun, he enclosed a story as "an example of how I'm writing these days." It was entitled "My Weekend in Rome, a theme," and it was written in an intentionally childlike manner by "Eddie Albee. Age 3–8."

> My playmate [Pennington] and I went to Rome. We stayed a weekend. We lived with a nice Italian man. His name begins with Z [Zeffirelli]. He makes people move around in theatres. Now he is making them move in movies. He is nice. He has a house all full of people all the time. You never know who is going to be there . . . A nice dancing man [Nureyev] came to the house. The dancing man and the nice Italian man and I sat together and we talked. We are going to make people move around in a movie. The dancing man will move around in the movie . . .
>
> Then the nice Italian man took my playmate and me to dinner with two nice people. A man and a woman [Richard Burton and Elizabeth Taylor]. We sat in a little room so nobody could see us. Why? The man had a beard. The lady didn't. She had a white dress, and she had on lot of pearls and emeralds. She was very pretty. She came in with a big furry coat on. She took it off and said, I don't want to sit on my chinchill. What is a chinchill?
>
> We ate lots and drank a yellow wine, except the lady, who drank a yellow sparkling something. She had purple eyes. She was pretty . . .
>
> The nice lady and the man with the beard talked to me a lot. They asked me how I liked a movie they moved around in [*Who's Afraid of Virginia Woolf?*]. I said I liked it fine. They liked that. When we left the room, the nice pretty lady kissed me and asked me if she could move around in a play I made someday. I said that would be fun.
>
> There were other things, but that was most of the fun of the weekend. Oh, yes, the pretty lady smelled pretty, too. She said she liked to get presents.

This was Albee's first meeting with Taylor and Burton, and it was months before the movie of *Virginia Woolf* was released. All was friendliness and mutual admiration. "I liked it fine," Albee told them, and the hint was in the air that sometime Taylor might appear onstage in one of his plays. Years later, Albee said that during that meeting he had spent most of his time "watching the two of them being themselves." But why had he chosen to report on this event in such an intentionally childlike manner?

Without missing a beat, Flanagan responded to Albee's letter:

Of course, I *enjoyed* your latest, *My Weekend in Rome: A Theme,* as I enjoy all of your work, being such a fan of yours and everything. But, I must add that it is certainly the first blind item I've ever read in the style of Shirley Temple of the era of *The Good Ship Lollypop.* And I can't imagine even her, then, in the heyday of her steely innocence, inventing a new art form—like Truman Capote—called Non-Name Dropping. If anyone ever again accuses you of being a non-innovator, you just haul out the xerox I will have made of *My Weekend in Rome: A Theme*—which I suggest you retitle, *Aunt Bessie's Chinchilla,* by the way—and that will surely, surely silence them all.

Flanagan commented that from Albee's letter to him and from one he wrote to Howard Moss, the trip sounded "more frenzied than restful. Gambling, and buying the Metro and everything. But you always did have your flaming side and I suppose I shouldn't be surprised." Then he offered a brief description of the New York scene: "Degenerates and perverts, especially lovers of men, are being entrapped, beaten and shot down in the streets. (I'm almost not exaggerating)." On the cultural front, there was Julius Rudel's production of *The Dialogue of the Carmelites,* which struck him as "Rudel & Co." was "out to get the piece. . . . When I watch them do that it scares me— on the quaint assumption that it will one day be finished and that they will do something similar to *L'Age Glace* [*The Ice Age*]. As for the theatre, the disasters have been rolling in like the high tide."

He continued,

Richard [Barr] called me from Sardi's, stoned as usual, to tell me that you had "authorized" him and Clinton [Wilder] to read Acts I & II of your new play. He was very excited about it. I don't know what you mean by "nothing happens," but I would watch out for it—whatever it isn't—if I were you. I remember your saying to Howard and me, before you left, that you had written your characters into a situation that "you didn't know how to get them out of," and that you might have to start "all over again." Just make sure, in any case that you've written the play you want as opposed to a play you're settling on. If nothing else, it will save your having to think up a lot of explanations for yourself later.

That last reference, one assumes, was to *Tiny Alice.* Flanagan signed off by suggesting, "If you want to bring me something back from Paris, make it Jeanne Moreau's bank account."

To Moss, Albee jokingly referred to *A Delicate Balance* as his play about a "hack meeting Dvorak," said it was "getting longer, if no nearer completion," and went on to describe their gambling: "We run riot at the casinos, where Bill [Pennington] runs around acting The Last of the Big Spenders. I think he's twenty dollars ahead, and I'm forty behind, or is it that he's. . . . ?"

Howard Moss answered Albee's letter:

> The secret photo-copy of A Delicate Balance which was sent to me air-express from Lausanne has caused a great deal of amusement here. I can only say that I never read anything more unconsciously "funny," and the few hundred copies, mimeographed, that I have sent around more than confirm my opinion. I do think a second act which ends with its 2-foot high heroine strangling on a piece of spaghetti is cathartic. And the scene in the winter garden when Lorenzo throws the Dom Perignon at the Don has some very sharp writing. Sharp in distinction to the flatness that pervades so much of the rest of it. But I do think it will be an enormous success, standards being what they are, and I hope I'm invited to two or three undistinguished parties connected with its "launching."

He added, "I defended Tiny Alice at a dinner party and still limp noticeably. I lost the fight physically, as was to be expected, but I won it verbally, as was to be expected. What do those proletarian boobies know of emotion?"

From this and other letters between Moss and Albee, it is clear that they had a lively literary correspondence, filled with parodies and occasionally signed with false names. Sometimes, Albee would pretend to be William Shawn, threatening to replace Moss with Paul Goodman as poetry editor of The New Yorker. In that guise, he "rejected" Moss proposals for profiles of Luther Burbank and Stella Adler, saying they "just aren't quite 'up our street,' as the saying has it. Burbank is a little controversial, and the Adler girl is dead, is she not?"

A Delicate Balance was Albee's first family play since The American Dream, and it drew deeply from his memories of life in Larchmont, especially from his second childhood home, the Hommocks, the house that his parents moved to after the death of his paternal grandmother. The setting of the play is a representation of the Hommocks, and the three principal characters, Agnes, Tobias, and Agnes's sister Claire, were inspired by Frances and Reed Albee and by Frances's sister Jane. Although Agnes and Tobias eventually diverged widely from the Albees, Claire is closely based on Jane, who was an alcoholic and a frequent houseguest in the Albee home. The daughter Julia resembles Albee's cousin Barbara, one of his aunt Ethel's two adopted daughters. Barbara, he said, was "a spoiled brat" in contrast to her younger sister,

Nancy, who "was very slighted by my aunt in favor of Barbara." Edward and Nancy were friends in childhood.

Agnes and Tobias are an older married couple seemingly content with their life in suburbia, except for their problems with Claire and with their daughter, who keeps returning home after each of her broken marriages. Suddenly the couple's best friends, Harry and Edna, arrive uninvited, desperately frightened by an indefinable feeling of imminent disaster. As friends, they seek—and demand—shelter, and in so doing tilt the precariously balanced relationships within the family. Agnes and Tobias are forced to come to terms with this crisis, as Tobias asks himself what he owes his friends and what debt he has to their friendship.

As Albee wrote, one of the problems with A *Delicate Balance* was that Claire, the most colorful character, threatened to take over the play. "I seemed to be writing two plays at the same time," Albee said, "a play about Claire and about what the play was meant to be about. In act one, Claire went on endlessly. I cut a lot of stuff out and kept diminishing her role." Comparing the reality with the drama, he said, "There is a parallel to be drawn between the way my adoptive mother and father lived their lives and the way Agnes and Tobias lived theirs, and the kind of place they lived it in. My adoptive father tended to retreat and let other people run things for him. But here's an interesting delicate balance: Agnes says, 'I'll run it for you, but you ultimately make the final decisions.' In the end, Tobias says, 'You've never done that in your life. You've made all the decisions.' She says, 'No, ultimately I will do whatever you want.'"

In the transformation of autobiography into art, Tobias is also partly a representation of the author himself at a young age, as in the crucial third-act dialogue with Agnes:

TOBIAS

I remember when . . .

AGNES (PICKING IT RIGHT UP)

. . . you were young and lived at home, and the servants were awake whenever you were: six A.M. for your breakfast when you wanted it, or five in the morning when you came home drunk and seventeen, washing the vomit from the car, and you, telling no one; stealing just enough each month, by arrangement with the stores, to keep them in a decent wage; generations of them: the laundress, blind and always dying, and the cook, who did a better dinner drunk than sober. Those servants? Those days? When you were young, and lived at home?

TOBIAS (MEMORY)

Hmmm.

AGNES (SWEET; SAD)

Well, my darling, you are not young now, and you do not live at home.

TOBIAS (SAD QUESTION)

Where do I live?

AGNES (AN ANSWER OF SORTS)

The dark sadness. Yes?

Discussing that passage, Albee says, "The theory is that your only true home is your childhood home, and the rest is game playing. The homes that we make for ourselves are basically an imitation of the homes that we grew up in." They may be "different from or removed from them, but based on them in some way." Ultimately "your home has to be within your head; you accumulate an environment around you that makes you happy, secure, comfortable." For the author, the dark sadness is an "existential self-awareness." The play is not, as commonly accepted, just "about the requirements of friendship." For him, the crucial speech is delivered by Agnes in the third act:

Time happens, I suppose.
    To people. Everything becomes ... too late, finally. You know it's going on ... up on the hill; you can see the dust, and hear the cries, and the steel ... but you wait; and time happens. When you *do* go, sword, shield ... finally ... there's nothing there ... save rust; bones; and the wind.

He said, "The play is basically about these people who have accommodated to their own weaknesses and compromises, the adjustments they've made. When the time comes that there is a demand put on them, they have to figure out whether or not they are strong enough anymore to do what should normally be done: the Christian way, to take you in. That's why in Act Three, Agnes talks about the disease. 'A disease is sitting up there. Are we immune?' That terror. If we let them in, we let that disease, that terror in. Are we going to admit it to ourselves? Or do we throw them out?" Agnes asks which values are more important: "the value to others or self protection." The delicate balance is "between what we should be doing and what we ultimately decide we need to do to protect ourselves. . . . It's interesting to me that Tobias has finally decided to make a stand, to say, yes, you can stay. But upstairs they've already made the decision to leave. So he's talking into the wind. When he says, please stay, he's not begging people to stay so that he can be nice to them, he's saying, 'You've taken away my last opportunity to do something worthwhile in my life.' That's really what the play is about." In another conversation, he elaborated on the subject: "The play is concerned with the isolation of people who have turned their backs on participating fully in their own lives and therefore cannot participate fully in anyone else's life."

Explaining the title, he said, "These people are teetering between being able to survive and being thrown into chaos. The amount of self-deception they can maintain in their lives—that's why Agnes decides that the people have got to leave. Because the family can't survive. And so she says that they must go, and that is why Tobias is able to make his big speech asking them to stay after he knows that they can't. I very carefully placed it there. It's after Harry says, 'We're going.' Then he says, 'You may stay,' but only after he knows they're not going to. I assume that's why I called the play A *Delicate Balance*."

As before, Flanagan was one of the first to read the completed play and offer his comments, which turned out to be far more astute than those of the official critics after the play opened:

> In general: A *Delicate Balance* strikes me as the most controlled, mature and perhaps even the most artistically successful play you've done yet. If I mentioned V. *Woolf* on the phone the other night, it was only to point out that a vaguely similar human situation had been actually *written* in so totally different a way. In *Woolf* the speech rhythms are abrasive, corrosive, jarring; equally lethal verbal encounters—in terms of their substance—are, in the new one, curiously muted in tone, subtle of speech-rhythmic facture and, in spite of complexity of the literary style, clean and polished and paradoxically simple of "sound."
>
> I can't even compare it from these points of view with *Tiny Alice*—because I can't see that it even attempts the sort of outrageous theatricality and outsized gesture that makes me such a sucker for that play. But I sense, that preferences aside, biases aside, A *Delicate Balance* is probably the better—but not the "stronger" and more startling work of the two.
>
> The strongest impression the new play makes—in terms of what for a better word I call "growth"—is that it is less erratic, less given to virtuosic explosions of raw talent. I revert to the word "control." The clashes, the hatreds, the bitch-

ery—the Albee "trademarks"—are, in the characters themselves, muted and subtle. I guess that's what I must have meant when I said that it was V. Woolf written with a kind of Chekhovian, naturalistic, poetic restraint.

Then Flanagan named some problems. He said he had no objection to the move from "quasi-realism" to the second level and the arrival of Harry and Edna with their "Unknown Fear, the Angst, the Plague," but thought it was difficult to accept "their willing departure on the sweet-reason motivation you've given for their leaving." He wondered if the prior relationship between Tobias and Claire, "evidently terminated by Agnes," was clear enough. "It's important to know, for the play's sake, how Claire 'got that way.' And what the bone of contention between her and Agnes is." It is clear from this statement and from Flanagan's later comment that some of the play "is rather painful for me personally," that he identified with Claire, perhaps because of his problem with alcohol.

Striking upon one of the play's basic flaws, Flanagan questioned Julia's re-action to the fact that Harry and Edna have moved into her room: "She whines about it too much. Like Junior stole her Teddy Bear." Finally he said there was "a good deal of editorial nit-picking and stylistic cleansing that ought to be done" and volunteered to do it, if asked. "Syntax, my sweet, is not your strongest point."

Then he brought up the matter of their long delayed collaboration on *The Ice Age*. He was, he said, waiting for pages, and raised the possibility of an-other writer finishing the libretto. He added, with regret, "I probably never should have let you get mixed up with it to begin with."

Returning to *A Delicate Balance*, he reaffirmed his admiration and sug-gested that someone other than Schneider direct it and "careful, *choisi* cast-ing." "You yourself said that the prose is too convoluted. I disagree. But it needs careful pruning. And a production as stylish as *The Cocktail Party*, or something. Impeccable; subtle; muted; and actors with ears like musicians."

Four days later, Flanagan sent another letter, still worrying about *The Ice Age* and reminding Albee that the opera was commissioned by Julius Rudel in the spring of 1963. Except for a "Love Duet," the last work on it that he had received from Albee was during the summer of 1963.

In the meantime you've written four plays and produced three. Which is what you should, of course, be doing. But I think that until we're ready to get down to serious business on what is a major professional commitment for both of us that we had just better come clean with Rudel, tell him the exact truth, and do nothing more on it until we can go about it like artists. Otherwise . . . the opera is going to sound like it's been composed by four different composers at twelve different stages of his thinking and development. And it's going to turn out to be a big mess artistically. As I said before, I'm sorry I ever got you into this, but I honestly believed you when you said you *wanted* to do it . . . I don't mean any of this as either anger, vindictiveness or ultimatum setting. I could scarcely afford any of them. But I think it's time to be realistic about the situation . . .

The first choice to play Tobias and Agnes was America's first acting couple, Alfred Lunt and Lynn Fontanne, and Barr sent a script to them at their home in Genesee Depot, Wisconsin. They responded favorably but with qualifications: They wanted to open the play in England and to perform it for only six months. Schneider was willing to go along with these demands for the sake of having the Lunts in the play, but Albee did not want any strings attached to the production. Briefly there was talk about John Gielgud and Irene Worth. Later Emlyn Williams turned down the play. Jessica Tandy and Melvyn Douglas were proposed for the roles, and when Douglas dropped out, Tandy and her husband, Hume Cronyn, were signed. It turned out to be splendid casting. Cronyn had been an admirer of Albee since *The Zoo Story*. He had invested in *The Ballad of the Sad Cafe*, and letters had been exchanged between him and Albee about the possibility of Cronyn and Tandy appearing in *Virginia Woolf*. *A Delicate Balance* was to be the beginning of their working relationship. The Cronyns joined Albee in Montauk to read the play aloud.

In August the play went into rehearsal, with Rosemary Murphy playing Claire, Marian Seldes the daughter Julia, and Henderson Forsythe and Carmen Matthews as Harry and Edna, the couple seeking shelter. The scene was Albee's new home at 50 West 10th. All the principals were there, and the atmosphere was friendly and expectant. Albee made some quick conclusions and the next day he wrote a memo to Schneider. In it, he discussed some of the specific problems of the actors. Then he said:

Neither Harry nor Edna can be a figure of fun . . . If anyone in the audience ever laughs at Harry and Edna, we're sunk. There has to be a threat there—the Sword of Damocles, as you put it—and clowns ain't no threat.

As I said to you yesterday afternoon, I kept forgetting the threat during the reading. Also, the whole action seemed a little too . . . what . . . earthbound, too nitpicky, too . . . small.

But, hell, first day and all. I imagine the dimension, the underlying elements, the urgency . . . the whole thing! will have to come slowly, as you weave the actors into the complexity and the subtlety of their roles.

I'll get Agnes's new speech to you in a day or two. And do keep a look out for those areas that seem thin, that seem to be marking time.

In order to help Tandy and Cronyn understand the milieu and the role models for their characters, Albee took them to see his mother, who was then living in White Plains. As Cronyn recalled, "She lived in a very grand house, with acres of green lawn. You were ushered into the house and the madame was out on the verandah. The decor was very *House and Garden,* all green and white, white wicker furniture, settees, colorful cushions. Later I met Frankie numerous times, but this was the first introduction. The character that Jessie played was based on her." To Cronyn, Mrs. Albee seemed like "a grenadier guard. . . . She was six foot two and wore her hair in a very high pompadour, almost like a busby. We sat and chatted: Edward, Frankie, Jess, and me. I liked Frankie, but she was wrought of iron. Down at the end of the verandah, I saw a cushion with a legend on it. It seemed to be out of place. I was curious enough to get up when Frankie was talking to Jessie, probably lighting my pipe and wandered down until I could read it: It said 'Perhaps and that's final.' It was the most perfect summation of character." For Tandy, as well, that remark "always epitomized her for me."

Cronyn continues, "She must have been either utterly blind to her own characteristics or she had a sort of sense of humor about herself. In our presence and later on I thought I saw signs of real affection between Edward and Frankie. By this time he had had a degree of success and was recovering from whatever brutalities of rejection he had gone through, which must have been severe. I had heard just enough, some of it from Edward, about his adoptive father to get the feeling that Frankie really ruled the roost."

As rehearsals continued, Albee took an increasingly active part, often passing notes to Schneider, as in the following "Notes on the Nature of Tobias":

I find Hume's notes on Tobias to be fine. He catches the nature of the man . . . a man who is "retired" . . .

There are, of course, several things which Tobias is *not.* And we must not have him be any of them. Tobias is not smug, arrogant, cowardly, a figure of fun, ridiculous, shallow, asleep, stupid. We must always see in Tobias a reserve that is not used, may never be used (though it is), but potential, just the same. We must be aware of a good, intelligent man, a man whose passivity is choice,

not due to some lack in his nature. The tragedy of Tobias is that Time has happened to him. He is not a failure as a man, but when he takes the broadsword
and climbs the hill to do battle, there is only the wind left. (Shall I put that in
the play?).

   I find Tobias clear. The problem is to have him quiet, but visible, passive yet
capable of action. Never neurotic, never self-pityingly, a *man*. Never petty, a
large man, but a man never tried. Curiously an innocent.

   In these notes, Albee could have been describing his father, expressing his
feelings about him without a cover of cynicism and trying to look past his feelings of neglect, perhaps wondering and analyzing why his father stayed in the
background, did not interfere, but let his wife run the family and, in effect,
damage their relationship with their son. In the portrait in *A Delicate Balance*, Albee disregards the portrait of his father as a figure of fun—the one-
eyed penguin who liked to dance and was famously unfaithful to his
wife—and with compassion sees him as a variation of that favorite Albee character, Melville's Bartleby, who preferred not to. Reed Albee preferred not to
interfere, but in the guise—or the disguise—of Tobias in the play, he becomes a man of good though buried instincts.

   Some may question whether Tobias is in fact a portrait of Reed Albee. In
contrast to the husband in Albee's later play *Three Tall Women*, who is close
in detail to Albee's father, Tobias does not look or act like him, and he is faced
with a situation that Reed Albee never had to face in life. But almost as a re-
minder to himself about the origins of the characters, Albee imbues Tobias
with occasional Reed Albee mannerisms, beginning with his habit of jingling
coins in his pocket.

   Similarly, in his notes about Claire, Albee is also speaking covertly about
his Aunt Jane:

   The person who knows Claire best is Claire herself. She describes herself often and accurately throughout the play. She *is*, indeed, a hanger-on, a failed
person, someone who is fun part of the time but whom one cannot rely on. She
is aware of herself at all times. Also, she is aware of the needs and motivations of
other people. Tobias sees Claire as basically a hurt person who must be cared
for. He knows she's self-indulgent, but that is minor to him. Claire knows how
Tobias sees her. Claire does not dissuade Tobias from his opinion. Claire knows
that her relationship with Agnes is complicated, that Agnes needs her, especially her weakness, especially their corrosive moments. Claire clearly sees
Agnes' needs. Fortunately, or conveniently, Claire *is* all the things Tobias and

Agnes see her as. Claire *is* what she plays up. She emphasizes what she has become. Claire needs as much as she is needed, so there is a fine reciprocity there. Claire is passive, of course, in that she is where and what she will always be now. Claire doesn't really want a man of her own. She is content substituting liquor for sex (now) and being the defeated, failed relation. Also, she's set for life. The role is set, the patterns are arranged, and, given the possibility of a fresh start, I doubt she'd take it. Does she love Agnes? Yes. Is she envious of her? No longer. Does she care for Tobias? Yes; and she feels a sadness for him, a kind of comradeship. Does she like Julia? No, but she likes her more by the end of the play when she sees that Julia is home for good, is defeated. Is there viciousness in this? No, Claire sees the balance as clearly as Agnes. She was not named for nothing.

From her nephew's point of view, Jane—the real Claire—knew what was going on and had a greater self-knowledge than his parents, but could not be relied on to do anything or to say anything other than her occasional wry comments. Albee was amused by her, he liked her, but in the end she was less than an ally.

Albee had a more difficult time characterizing the daughter, Julia, the adult child who is unable to sustain a relationship outside of her family and incapable of taking a step to alter and improve her relationships within the family. She waits for others to take action. As he said:

> Julia is rather hard to describe, since she isn't "anybody" when the play begins, in the sense that her character hasn't formed. By the end of the play she has become somebody—an incipient Claire, a much older woman than when the play began. When she comes home, in act two, I doubt she knows she's home for good. It is only the events surrounding Harry and Edna's arrival—the threat to her "room" (her identity, whatever that may be), the threat to the family organization etc.—which brings her to the point of explosion and sudden fulfillment of her own nature. Julia has been an accumulator of attitudes, and if she has a personality, it is a "referred" one. Around her husbands, Julia takes on Agnes' attitudes and behavior—rather almost a parody of them. Julia is a child who, by the end of the play, becomes a middle-aged woman, another cripple in the house of life. She has had no children, probably a combination of the nature of the men who are attracted to her (and to whom she is attracted) and an unconscious resentment of Teddy [her dead brother], and fear of duplicating him. Julia loves and fears Agnes, fears her like an adolescent, and this is predominant, even though she strikes out—incipient hysteria, an important part of

her character, for the years of attrition have taken their toll on Julia, leaving her prime for the hysteria at home over the bar, the business of the gun, and the unrealized and unplanned coming home for good, Julia's feelings for Tobias are complicated, but I think she sees the true man through the "retired" person, and maybe, unconsciously, has incestuous feelings toward him. Julia's feelings toward Claire—resolved when she starts to become Claire—are mostly envy.

It would be unwise to equate Julia with Albee himself but there are points in common worth exploration. A loveless child, she left home but still feels curiously possessive about that home, about her room as a symbol of her childhood ownership. Perhaps in some transference, Albee is represented by Teddy, the dead son, the one who is never known and departs. The sibling relationship between Julia and Teddy, a kind of twindom, is one that conjures relationships in other Albee plays, especially the apprentice works but also *The American Dream*, in which, as mentioned, there are two characters who stand for the title, one who has died, and one who is returning home.

Julia was—and still is—the problem character in *A Delicate Balance*, a whiner without the saving grace of humor and, in contrast to her aunt Claire, a woman without self-knowledge, which, as Albee indicates, is one of Claire's outstanding traits. Is Julia really an incipient Claire? The important line in his analysis of Julia is the reference to her as "another cripple in the house of life." The "other" cripple is, of course, Claire, but by inference, all the characters in the play are, in various ways, crippled, unwilling, or incapable of altering their attitude and sentenced to a lifetime of solitude.

In these early notes to *A Delicate Balance*, Albee omits an analysis of Agnes, by all rights the central character in the play. That omission may be an accident, or more likely, it may have been a private admission of an inability to come to terms with his mother, then living and newly a part of his life again. It was only in *Three Tall Women*, years after her death, that he was able to understand—and to articulate that understanding—of her character and her behavior. In *A Delicate Balance*, Agnes is distinct from his mother in the way that she talks, as in her opening monologue, which has a Jamesian intricacy. Agnes is an imagined character, with hints of her real-life model. Speaking about Mrs. Albee and her relationship with her son, Jessica Tandy said, "Maybe she didn't like the way he turned out. Or maybe he was too smart for her." Both points are apt.

Richard Barr made a major contribution to *A Delicate Balance* when, a week into rehearsal, he suggested to Albee that Tobias could use another speech in the first act. Albee went home and that night wrote "the cat story," in which Tobias talks about his pet cat that suddenly stopped liking him. He resents that action as a kind of betrayal and has the animal put to sleep. That story became one of Albee's set pieces, along with the dog story from *The Zoo Story*. In both cases, characters are unable to relate to an animal and take drastic steps to remove it from their lives. The lesson: With regret one can do that to a dog or a cat, but a sane person cannot do it to another human. One has to learn to live with man's betrayal. "It needed something a little bit Chekhovian and metaphorical," said Albee. "I wrote it rather quickly, and after I had written it I became aware that it was sort of a metaphor for the whole play rather than simply a specific thing in Tobias's life."

During rehearsal, Cronyn was having difficulty with his long final speech in which Tobias pleads with Harry and Edna to stay with them, to bring their terror and their plague into his house. "I don't want you here!" Tobias shouts. "I don't love you! But by God . . . you stay!!" Then he tearfully adds, "Stay? Please? Stay?" Cronyn considered it a "kind of confessional" rather than an epiphany, and in the published text, Albee calls it an aria, which carries the character "to the edge of hysteria." Cronyn recalled, "Alan kept talking about it and I knew what he was saying, but I couldn't execute it. Edward and I met in the dressing room before rehearsal. He took a sheet of paper and he graphed an orgasm. He said, that's really what that speech is. That resolved my block. Immediately! I think it was one of the elements in the play I resolved more successfully. That speech and the cat speech."

As always, Schneider posed problems for the actors. Working with him, said Marian Seldes, was "extremely stressful, for me and for Rosemary Murphy, but I did not realize it was stressful for Jessica." Seldes remembered one day feeling that she simply could not please the director in any way. "His way of giving notes was to have his secretary write you." The notes were often "unintentionally cruel." One evening, she was in Tandy's dressing room when Tandy received one of the director's notes. "I just looked at her," recalled Seldes, "and I saw that her eyes were full of tears, and I knew mine were also. I remember saying to her, 'You too?' I thought it was something in the way those rehearsals were handled. It made the actors feel a kind of tension that had nothing to do with acting. There was some self-doubt. The interesting thing is, it never came from Edward. I never felt, wrongly or rightly, that I was not fulfilling what he wanted." One of Schneider's primary targets was Carmen Matthews. He had originally opposed her choice, saying that she was nothing more than a "stock" actress. Barr disagreed and she was hired. "He humiliated Carmen," said Seldes, "but she didn't bend. After the play was done, and when, in fact, I got the Tony [as best featured actress in a play],

Alan was so warm, reassuring, proud and kind. It was like one man had directed the play and one man afterward."

Apparently the actors were unaware of the extent of the humor in the play. Albee remembers the first preview, when Tandy "came offstage quivering because the audience was laughing, and she had forgotten that the play was funny." A *Delicate Balance* opened at the Martin Beck Theater on September 22, 1966, the first Broadway drama of the season. The opening was also to represent the first review by Walter Kerr in the *Times*. With Kauffmann having been relieved of his job, Kerr moved over from the *Herald Tribune*, which had merged into the *World Journal Tribune*. While the other daily critics wrote favorable reviews, Kerr continued in his role as dissenter. He thought the play was hollow, a "void in which the characters live and have their nonbeing." It is curious that, when reviewing Albee, Kerr seemed to use variations on the same imagery of emptiness. Schneider, for one, was furious. In his autobiography, he wrote that Kerr sounded "as though he was trying hard to rationalize a personal distaste," and added that he "did not like Ibsen or Chekhov, hated Samuel Beckett, and had strong reservations about Harold Pinter." Because he had no recourse to equal time in the *Times*, the director thought of this as "a most indelicate balance," which he had to face every day of his life.

Brustein said that the play "suffers from a borrowed style and a hollow center" and the result is "emptiness emptiness emptiness." He called it "a very bad play." A year after A *Delicate Balance* opened, he was still ridiculing it, accusing the author of "grinding out cocktail party chit-chat, in A *Delicate Balance*, with brandy being decanted over supernatural conversations in a 'House and Garden' setting." Arthur Miller has regretted the fact that he has "never had a critic in my corner," but he has never faced Albee's critical obstacles. For much of his career, Albee was confronted by the Janus-faced Kerr-Brustein, receiving negative notices from both ends of the theatrical spectrum, the most influential Broadway reviewer and the guardian of aesthetics.

In my review I wrote: "A *Delicate Balance* is Edward Albee in a reflective mood. It is full of Albee bite, bountiful bursts of colorful invective, repartee and shorthand character analyses, but the root of the play is something a lot more tender than anything he has ever attempted before . . . The actors, particularly Hume Cronyn, Jessica Tandy and Rosemary Murphy, are perfectly in key with their roles, and the play is marked growth for the author. For the audience, it is a strangely moving and disquieting experience."

As A *Delicate Balance* moved into a modest run, and before Albee could catch his breath, he received a call from David Merrick, with an unusual offer. Merrick, who was at the time the most dynamic and successful producer on Broadway, was in Boston with a Broadway musical version of Truman Capote's novella *Breakfast at Tiffany's*, which had been one of the most highly anticipated events of that theater season. Merrick had gathered such talents as Abe Burrows as book writer and director, Bob Merrill as composer, and Michael Kidd as choreographer, and as stars, two television luminaries, Mary Tyler Moore and Richard Chamberlain. The show hit the shoals during its out-of-town tryout. Burrows, who was known as a play doctor as well as director, was called off his own case and Joseph Anthony was brought in as the new director. Previously called *Holly Golightly*, the show regained its original title.

At Merrick's request, Albee flew up to look at the show and to rewrite the book. "I thought maybe it could be brought back to what Capote wrote. They gave me two weeks. I think if I had another two weeks, I could have done it, but it ended up as a terrible mishmash. I guess you don't have a lesbian policewoman slug Mary Tyler Moore in the belly in a Broadway musical, and get away with it." The new version of the musical moved to New York and began previews. At the first preview, said Albee, an "incredible wave of loathing came across the footlights." He explained, "They all bought tickets to see the Audrey Hepburn version, not this ugly Gogol-type nonmusical musical. It was nice of David Merrick to let me learn about the musical theater." What he learned was "to work alone—unless you're doing manufacturing like *Hello, Dolly!* or *Mame*."

In January, Albee received a letter from Harold Pinter, then on a visit to America. He had seen *A Delicate Balance* and "enjoyed it up to the hilt." He continued:

"For me, and I'm sure for you, this is as rare as rare. I mean in the theatre. I can't tell you how much I admired it. It possessed a quite unique distinction, authority and beauty. In fact I *basked*. But quite apart from basking, I was truly illuminated at certain points by some of the thoughts expressed by the characters. You hit quite a few nails on the head, for me. But I thought the work was unified, tough, caged in grace."

Pinter had also seen *Tiny Alice* in Boston and thought the conception was remarkable and wanted to talk about it and Albee's other plays with him. For what it's worth, he said, "I am so glad to know your voice." He added, "Kerr didn't like *The Homecoming* so the going is tough. We might survive for a while . . . I hope long enough for you to be able to see it."

By the end of 1966, there were discussions about a possible London production of *A Delicate Balance.* Through Toby Rowland, the play had made its way to Laurence Olivier, as director of England's National Theater. After reading it, Olivier passed it on to Kenneth Tynan, his literary manager. In his note to Olivier, Tynan said,

> This is beautifully written, an exquisite fandango of despair . . . Tobias's big speech (pp 159–162) sums up what the play is about—the fact that although we all hate each other, we are stuck with each other. Directed like the best productions of Pinter, it would certainly hold an audience—especially an intelligent and fairly jaded middle-class audience. *But:* Albee's people are so listless, so despondent, so cut off—not only from each other but from the outside world. You're not surprised that they drink, and tremble, and contemplate killing each other: the wonder is that they haven't committed suicide before the curtain rises. If we weren't doing *Rosencrantz* (another fatalistic play), I think the Albee would be a definite contender for this year. I'd recommend postponing it until 1968.

In his response to Rowland, Olivier agreed with Tynan about postponing a decision but hedged a bit in his enthusiasm. He added that he knew that Albee had been at the National the previous week to see *Othello,* "but didn't come round so it may well be that he hated the lot of us and wouldn't touch us with a barge pole anyway."

Rowland passed that comment along to Albee, who wrote to Olivier: "In point of fact, I would have come back to see you, would have loved to, but, since you were, at that time, considering whether or not to do *A Delicate Balance,* I thought my showing up, proper praise in hand, might have been seen as pressure or intimidation on you, so I did not come back." It was, he said, "an extraordinary performance . . . You must tell actors, some day, how you manage to change size, weight and age in the course of one short scene."

Olivier responded: "You must not be in the least disturbed. There was not a shred of bitterness in my remarking to Toby that you did not come round. I appreciate more than I can say your extreme delicacy in not doing so in the circumstances—talk about a delicate balance! I was only disappointed that I could not greet and embrace you as fellow artists should . . . I do so much hope that the next opportunity of our meeting will find nothing in its way, no matter how gossamer the delicate issues might be."

With three references to "delicate" in his brief note, it would seem that the play was very much on his mind. But Olivier decided not to do it, either as an actor (imagine Olivier as Tobias) or as a producer.

That season *The Homecoming* won the New York Critics Circle award and the Tony award for best play. On May 1, 1967, *A Delicate Balance* won the Pulitzer Prize for drama, the award that had been denied Albee for *Who's Afraid of Virginia Woolf?* in 1963. At that time, the Pulitzer judges John Gassner and John Mason Brown resigned in protest. This time the selection of the Pulitzer jury—Richard Watts, Elliot Norton, and Maurice Valency—was approved by the Pulitzer board. Albee thought about declining but then decided otherwise. At a press conference the day after the announcement, he offered his three reasons for accepting: "First, because if I were to refuse it out of hand I wouldn't feel as free to criticize it as I do accepting it. Second, because I don't wish to embarrass the other recipients this year by seeming to suggest that they follow my lead. And, finally, because while the Pulitzer Prize is an honor in decline, it is still an honor, a considerable one." He added that the prize "was in danger of losing its position of honor and could, foreseeably, cease to be an honor at all." He said he was planning to use his $500 award to start a memorial to Gassner, who had died the previous month.

We met that morning and I asked him how it felt to be a Pulitzer Prize–winning playwright. He qualified the title to "a complaining Pulitzer Prize–winning playwright." He said, "I couldn't very well reject the prize without being accused of revenge and petulance. In my quiet opinion it certainly was the best American play this past season," and he added that the only other good play that year was *The Homecoming*.

The playwright was flooded with congratulations. Mike Nichols wired, "Well you can't lose them all." Albee's aunt Jane offered her congratulations for his "brilliant play," adding that she was "very proud of you and your many accomplishments" and never underestimated his "sense of humor—it is great." His childhood friend Muir Weissinger wrote that the Nobel Prize was next and appended, "I sent the Pulitzer people my congratulations, but they were out dueling." Tongue in cheek (and ignoring the debacle of *Breakfast at Tiffany's*), David Merrick took credit for the prize: "Well, I set it right. The Pulitzer is better than the Tony anyway. Who are you writing all those new plays for? How about a drink soon. Congratulations."

Albee sent a telegram to the Cronyns thanking them for their contribution in "making the Pulitzer dishonor inevitable": "Now that you are playing in a national monument akin to Elvis Presley's first guitar, which is a prize exhibit in the U.S. Pavilion in Expo '67 by the way, don't forget the laughs and the slapstick so essential to the success of any of my plays."

It was left to John Simon to write a piece in the *Times* attacking Albee for accepting the award for what he called "one of Albee's weakest plays." He suggested that the playwright missed an opportunity to tell the Pulitzers "to go soak their heads." Irresistibly, Albee was drawn to making a response: "Mr. Simon's disapproval of my plays has been a source of comfort to me over the years, and his dislike of A Delicate Balance gives me the courage to go on, as they say." Then he defended his acceptance of the award he criticized as "both correct and salutary," adding that if he had refused the prize, the critic "would very probably have trotted out a piece quivering with the conviction that I should have accepted it." But having not won for Virginia Woolf, Albee retained a certain cynicism about the prize. Several years later when Richard Howard won a Pulitzer for his poetry, Albee said to him, "Congratulations on getting that award that nobody believes in."

In October, Jean-Louis Barrault staged A Delicate Balance in Paris, with Madeleine Renaud as Agnes, Edwige Feuillere as Claire, and Claude Dauphin as Tobias. Harold Hobson called it "the most brilliant opening of a Paris autumn season," characterizing the play as "an obsessional exploration of the abysses of the Albee mind."

Albee's next play was unplanned. Clinton Wilder had suggested that he, Barr, and Albee present Giles Cooper's Everything in the Garden on Broadway. The agreement was that the British play, first produced by the Royal Shakespeare Company in 1962, would be transplanted to an American setting. As Albee took over the project, he found himself revising and rewriting the play until, after Cooper was killed in an accident, it turned into an adaptation, or rather, in his words, an "intense collaboration." He said, "Perhaps his play is better than mine; perhaps it is not. I can only say that our work has become enmeshed to the point that I can no longer tell where his leaves off and mine begins . . . I would just as soon have a small credit in the back of the program under 'house physician.' " On the other hand, in a letter to Steinbeck, with a copy of the play to follow, he said, "Everything in the Garden is a complete re-casting, re-writing, re-thinking of an English play by Giles Cooper and, for better or worse, I think I've made it completely my own. I think you might find one or two chuckles in it."

Despite the fact that the story had been transposed to American suburbia, Albee and his partners decided to have an English director, Peter Glenville. Paralleling Jean Kerr's Mary, Mary, the stars were Barry Nelson and Barbara Bel Geddes, who had also appeared together in the early Broadway hit The Moon Is Blue. At the first rehearsal of Everything in the Garden (in Albee's 10th Street townhouse), the author urged silence about the subject: "We want everybody to think it's Mary, Mary." The central characters were a married couple with money problems. Enter Mephistopheles in the person of a Park

Avenue madame (Beatrice Straight) who offers the wife a job as a prostitute. It was soon clear that the play was not just a situation comedy about a respectful prostitute or a satire about the sour side of suburbia but a cautionary fable about money and the many guises of greed.

Also in the cast was Richard Thomas, then sixteen and later a major television star as John Boy on *The Waltons*, and much later a fine dramatic actor on stage (in 1998 he played Julian in *Tiny Alice* at the Hartford Stage Company). Thomas had lost out to Matthew Cowles for the title role in *Malcolm* and turned down a chance to be Cowles's understudy. He remembers Albee sitting in on rehearsals of *Everything in the Garden* and being "unfailingly polite and nice" to him, and also to Glenville, who would ask the playwright for new dialogue. In some cases, he would supply the lines on the spot: "Barry, you say this, Barbara, you say this." Looking back on the experience, Thomas said, "Albee was in that period of adaptation where his own unique voice was somehow missing. He was standing behind Carson McCullers or James Purdy or Giles Cooper. All of a sudden, where was he?"

As it turned out, it was Robert Moore, as a sardonic voyeur and commentator, who had the sharpest lines. Most of the reviews were dire. *Everything in the Garden* joined Albee's other adaptations as a failure, but because it was sold to the movies for $350,000 it also proved to be one of his better moneymakers. Anyone who doubted the work's veracity would have been startled a week after the opening to see a banner headline on the front page of the *Daily News*: SEXURBIA: NAB 4 HOUSEWIVES. L.I. SPLIT-LEVEL LOVE FOR SALE. Four housewives in Freeport, Long Island, were arrested in the neighboring town of Merrick for operating a prostitution ring, as life seemed to be imitating art.

In 1969, Albee had a major success in London. Peggy Ashcroft decided to play Agnes in *A Delicate Balance*. With Olivier passing on the play, Trevor Nunn agreed to direct it, but when Nunn proved to be unavailable, Peter Hall was brought in as director. Late in 1968, he sent Albee a progress report on the production, starring Ashcroft and Michael Hordern as Agnes and Tobias and Elizabeth Spriggs as Claire. Hordern was "calming down magnificently and is finding a great deal of power in the final monologue," Ashcroft was becoming "more formidable each day" and Spriggs was improving. At first, "she was enjoying playing the part from that seat on the sidelines in great comfort." Claire's "life and her anguish and the reasons why she drinks were being kept well away from her," but now she was recognizing the problem. Hall later said that there were early difficulties with Ashcroft: "She found Edward's language completely maddening and terribly difficult to learn. She of course got there and dominated the production. Peggy is one of the greatest actors that I've ever worked with, and I worked with her about twenty-six or twenty-seven times. She always went through some kind of trauma, almost a nervous breakdown in the creation of any part. It took different forms. With *Delicate Balance*, it was the language: 'Why can't he leave well enough alone, I know it's wonderful, but God . . .' "

Albee was present for the final rehearsals and the run-through. "I don't recall any friction," said Hall. "I just remember being highly diverted by the ironical teasing. He was not capable of saying, 'I don't like that.' He would say, 'Have you any views of that moment over there?' and I would say, 'Why?' There would be a long long dance and you'd finally get down to what was bothering him. It was always very clear, just tiny nuances of behavior: Would she go that far, or would she be that overt? He is an utterly practical man of the theater. He knows about actors, he knows about staging, so one was dealing with a professional, but to some degree a professional who wished to disguise that fact. He wishes to remain an enigma at all times. Edward is a very daunting personality. He makes a religion of putting people off. He loves destabilizing people." As for the play, Hall rates it higher than *Who's Afraid of Virginia Woolf?* "Clearly, *Virginia Woolf* is a more populist play, but I think of *Delicate Balance* as a classical work, using the word classical to mean well formed, completely defined, and centered. I very much admire the classical economy—and it's a wonderful yarn. I'd go for *Delicate Balance* any day." Comparing it to Henry James, he said, "It is so quintessentially American and yet so unAmerican. It's American of a certain past kind."

The play opened, said Albee, "to the confusion of the press: seven uncomprehending 'yeas,' two uncomprehending 'nos,' and two uncomprehending 'I don't knows.' " Later in the run, Hall wrote Albee: "The depth and flexibility of performance is increasing but now I am faced with something rather alarming. The public now enter the theatre in reverential awe and the critics have told them that it is 'an important American play.' If we're not all very careful the performance could become ponderous and the experience a companion piece to T. S. Eliot. I will watch and nag. The intellectual weeklies have been quite marvelous except for one which was quite terrible. But that's life."

13
Flanagan

We might all be dead or locked up when we turn the
next corner.

*I*N the spring of 1966, Flanagan was overcome by panic, partly because of
the glacial slowness of *The Ice Age,* but also because of his psychological and
financial problems. He felt that Albee was increasingly remote. During the
next two years, they seemed to communicate more by mail than in person.
On May 12, 1966, Flanagan wrote to Albee:

> Since I have known you for nearly twenty years now, the image of myself for-
> ever trying to penetrate your Iron Curtain is untenable. I am told you are plan-
> ning a trip to London next week. Since I have no way of knowing when we will
> confer again, I am submitting here a more or less formal brief of how I intend
> to handle the situation regarding Rudel.
>
> I plan to set the remainder of what you gave me in 1963 — composing, as I
> have from the beginning, sort of by the Braille system. I myself will try to make
> whatever cuts and slight alterations I feel to be necessary for clear projection of
> both text and plot, continuing to pretend as I compose that I have more than a
> foggy notion of what the rest of the libretto might be like.

When the partial score was finished, he planned to submit it to Rudel,
hoping that more money might be forthcoming from the Ford Foundation.
But without Albee's cooperation, he felt that all this would be a waste of time.
He had interviewed Albee for the *Paris Review* and was being pressed by the

magazine to turn over his tape recording of their talk so it could be included in an anthology of interviews.

The Ice Age never was finished, and eventually the commission was cancelled. Despite Flanagan's grave disappointment about that failure, his relationship with Albee continued, although at a greater distance. Albee still sent Flanagan his plays as he completed them. Next in line was the intricate double bill of *Box* and *Quotations from Chairman Mao Tse-Tung* (or *Box-Mao-Box*, as it was called). These two interrelated plays are among his most abstract works. Each play was inspired by a different author, *Box* by Beckett, *Mao*, which takes place on an ocean liner, by Paul Claudel and his play *Partage de midi*. In praise of *Box-Mao-Box*, Virgil Thomson found another legitimate comparison. He said that it made him think of the Gertrude Stein plays in which "everybody talks to himself." Albee started writing the plays in Montauk and finished them in Puerto Rico.

In his introduction to the published text, Albee said that they were "conceived at different though not distant moments" and can stand alone but are "more effectively performed enmeshed." *Box* is a play without actors and, ostensibly, without a narrative. An empty cube is onstage, the equivalent of a pictureless frame. In the background is heard the sound of a woman's voice. *Box* was written first and *Mao* was "an outgrowth and an extension" of it. In a letter to Steinbeck (in August 1967), he said about *Box:* "It is one of a series of shortish experimental plays I'm putting together. They will probably number eight or ten when I'm finished with the project, and they all have to do with the relationship of musical form and structure to the drama. The one I'm working on right now, for example, *Quotations from Chairman Mao Tse-Tung*, is an exercise in counterpoint." By September, *Mao* had grown. It was "longer and messier and threatens to ooze all over the evening, burying *Box* in its course." As a double bill, the show begins and ends with *Box*, which acts as "a parenthesis" around *Mao*. For the author, the work is technically complex, but "quite simple" in terms of content. He suggested that the audience "relax and let the plays happen."

In the case of *Mao*, he began with the monologue of the Long-Winded Lady, naming her after the character created by Maeve Brennan for her series of pieces in *The New Yorker*'s "Talk of the Town." Brennan was a friend of his and he dedicated the two plays to her and Howard Moss, thereby linking the works to *The New Yorker*. He describes his collage technique: "I put down the 'Over the Hill to the Poorhouse' poem in quatrains. Then I took the 'Quotations from Chairman Mao' in the order in which he wrote them. Then I took my scissors and I cut each quotation and kept them in exactly the same order.

I did the Long-Winded Lady monologue in paragraphs. I put all these things on walls all around me, and I constructed the psychologically proper order for them to go in. One from column A and one from column B, another from column A, then adding one from column C. I constructed the whole thing as if with paste and scissors. The order was governed by a sense of musical composition. Sometimes the quotations from Chairman Mao would relate to what the Long-Winded Lady was saying. Sometimes they wouldn't. I just kept inserting things between other things."

Several years later, trying to reconstruct the production for a possible British version, Albee wrote:

> My memory tells me the cube was 12 feet in each direction and was made of two inch square tubing. It was slightly distorted, in that each of its angles was not 90 degrees, but the distortion was not excessive—in other words, it wasn't expressionist as in Caligari.
>
> Everything began in darkness and a suffusing light, not harsh but not dim, and gradually enveloped the cube. The lighting gave the impression that its source was the tubular structure itself, though of course it was not. The fade at the end of the play was, as I recall, identical to the fade up at the beginning. I recall the sounds of bell buoys, waves and seagulls at the beginning and at the end.

In April 1967, as an experiment, using the pseudonym Rayne Enders, he submitted *Box*, the first and last third of the collage, to the Albee-Barr-Wilder Playwrights Unit. The first managing director of the Playwrights Unit was Edward Parone, the agent who had given Barr *The Zoo Story*. He was succeeded by Chuck Gnys. Albee had heard that Gnys had been erratic in his choices, turning down good plays and playing favorites. Unwisely, Gnys rejected Rayne Enders's *Box*. Checking the files of the Playwrights Unit, Albee discovered that Gnys had completely dismissed both the play and the playwright, describing it as "totally without point or interest; hopeless."

Flanagan, for one, was very amused by the Gnys episode and said so in a letter to Albee in July 1967. In the letter, he also offered expert criticism of the play. About Gnys and *Box*, he said:

> He's perfectly entitled to think it "hopelessly dull" (and, while if anything it has too much point, I can easily understand how Chuck might find it "pointless"). But how he could have concluded from it that you weren't "ready" for the playwrights unit, when the poise of the writing, the explicitly *experienced* hand behind the stage directions, etc., is a comment on something!—

something not so hot. Furthermore, once again the stage directions and even in the monologue itself, I can't imagine (personally) having been shown the piece (unidentified) without guessing to the point of certainty that *you* had written it. In Chuck's position, even with the *nom de malicieur*, I think I would have smelled a rat.

"Too *much* point": Well, I guess that assumes I know what the play is about. In part, it's a variation on the theme of *V. Woolf* in George's speech about how we'll "not have much music, much painting, etc."—humanism going to science; in *Box* art going to craft; both symbolic of our age. Order vitiates freedom of choice—this being an extension of *one* (I disagree with you that its the *principal* one) theme of *A Delicate Balance*. "Progress," then, isn't really progress at all. The *Box*, I presume, is a symbol of (the illusion) of order—"perfection," empty, flawlessly geometric, beautiful in its way, but dead. "Milk"—its senseless spillage with its inhumane implications—is a symbol of its opposite.

Flanagan observed that this was Albee's "first real anti-play" and that it needed great care in its visualization onstage. He admitted that Gnys's confusion might have derived from the fact that some of the references were "very special. . . . Who the hell is going to know what you mean by the whole musical analogy—its obvious symbolic reference to a world that produced the Box ('system as conclusion,' the New Music), and 'tension and the tonic' and its implications?"

In February 1968, *Box-Mao-Box* was announced for production under Albee's authorship and Barr's producing aegis. With the alias removed, Gnys sent Albee a sheepish letter: "Now I know why Rayne Enders was reluctant to send me *Box* again," adding, "Do you think you may have done it on purpose?" Albee answered, "Rayne Enders was reluctant to send you *Box* again but I persuaded him that it might go this time, especially in combination with *Mao*." In a subsequent letter he said that, of course, he had sent the play in under the pseudonym on purpose, explaining that he did it because he was "curious about a number of matters—primarily whether or not a system which allows only one of the several interested parties to make final judgement on a work is a good system." He said that he felt *Box* had "some merit" and that "it was rejected out of hand." In a letter to Albee, Gnys tried to rationalize his precipitous judgment:

I didn't like *Box* when Rayne Enders sent it in and it's painful to tell a friend that no matter what name it's submitted under I would reject it again for presentation at The Playwrights Unit. *Of course*, it has 'some merit'! Much of it is

brilliant, but I don't think it works as a visual or theatrical piece . . . I don't understand what you mean by 'it was rejected out of hand,' and I never said it was
'totally without point or interest; hopeless.' My opinion as written on the card
was that it was 'boring and pointless.' I don't have time to write exacting criti-
cisms of every play that comes in. I chose those words to record my general and
most predominant feeling about the play when I first read it. It was a brief and
cruel comment. I never imagined Rayne Enders would see my naked, unsoft-
ened critique.

Then he asked Albee's forgiveness and suggested, "Next time don't snoop.
Curiosity (or was it paranoia?) killed the cat." Or rather, it may have cost Gnys
his job. After a decent interval, he was fired, although supposedly not for his
rejection of Rayne Enders. Within several years, the Playwrights Unit was itself disbanded, but it left an indelible imprint on the American theater. It was
a primary training ground and launching pad for many writers who later had
significant careers.

Directed by Alan Schneider, and with a haunting minimalist set design by
William Ritman, *Box-Mao-Box* opened in March 1968 at the Studio Arena
Theater in Buffalo (with the voice of Ruth White speaking in *Box*). In Sep-
tember, with several cast changes (Albee favorites Wyman Pendleton as
Chairman Mao and Sudie Bond as Old Woman, and with Nancy Kelly as the
Long-Winded Lady), the play opened at the Billy Rose Theater on Broadway.

Both in Buffalo and at the Billy Rose Theater on Broadway, the reviews
ranged from confusion to boredom to, in several cases, outright insult. As was
often the case, Harold Clurman was the most thoughtful of the critics, calling
it "a polyphonic chamber work," in which "we are confronted with banality
on three levels: the despair of the middle class, the heartbreak of the dispossessed, the rote of the professionally insurgent." He concluded, "There is a
melancholy beauty in this play and genuine feeling without tears. The play
convinces me that we have in Albee a dramatist who is still growing. *Box-
Mao-Box* is like no other play he has written and like very few others written
by anyone else." With its recurrent waves of sound and light (and silence), it
is perhaps closest to Beckett's late, brief works like *Ghost Trio* and *Quad*. As
with those plays, it should be staged by a director knowledgeable about choreography.

In retrospect, it is amazing to think that such an experimental play could
be on Broadway, but it was there in repertory with other works during a Barr-
Albee season. Using a troupe of favorite actors, the team also presented revivals of *Krapp's Last Tape* and *The Zoo Story*, *The Death of Bessie Smith* and

The American Dream (with the latter directed by the author), and Beckett's *Happy Days.*

Flanagan had begun working on a book about Albee, which would discuss his work and also draw upon Flanagan's personal knowledge of the playwright. He had shown part of it to Howard Moss and Aaron Copland. Copland expressed his disappointment: "I imagined that it would draw upon to a greater extent the human side and your all-round view of Ed. Naturally I see the difficulties that result from your knowing perhaps 'too much.' "

Flanagan was hoping to enlist Albee in helping him with synopses of his plays. In a letter to Albee, he wrote, "The book, as you know, is being written in almost the style of a non-fiction novel. But after *The Ballad of the Sad Cafe,* beginning with *Tiny Alice,* my connection with you personally has grown increasingly remote; as a consequence, except for *Malcolm,* so has my fund of usable anecdote and detail." Working on the book, he had spoken at length to Barr and mistrusted some of what he said. He wanted to talk again to Clinton Wilder and, particularly, Alan Schneider, because in the book the director would be subjected to criticism: "He will get a pretty bad critical mauling" for his direction of *Tiny Alice, Malcolm,* and *The Ballad of the Sad Cafe.* Flanagan's theory was that "none of the plays he's messed up suit his temperament" and therefore he could not be blamed for being hired. He was thinking of ending the book with the Chuck Gnys story: "The book is full of ironies and, in a sense, after Pulitzer Prizes etc., this would be the crowning one."

"I'm 44-years-old today," Flanagan wrote, "and I haven't been so startled by any age since I turned thirty. In those days, one didn't start to 'think thirty' until the later twenties hit. Now, the middle-forties have me 'thinking fifty' already. It doesn't depress me so much as it sort of scares me. I've lost so much time in the last seven years—struggling to earn enough to eat with, spending two years in breakdown and a couple of more in recovery—that I just haven't finished what I want to do." He said that since April—it was now August—he had done more than in any comparable time span of his life: work on the Albee book, "a piano-sketch" of a musical piece, and freelance articles and reviews. "We might all be dead or locked up when we turn the next corner."

Flanagan seemed to be living on a runaway rollercoaster: He was up, he was down, he was spinning out of control. With Albee's financial help, he went into psychiatric therapy while still facing an economic crisis. He had applied for a grant to the Thorne Foundation but had been turned down because Copland, Thomson, and, he supposed, "everyone else in the music world" thought that, in the words of Francis Thorne, "Albee takes care of him." "Once the myth that I was literally being supported by you was squelched," he wrote Albee, "once it became clear to all what I had been trying to conceal—namely that *The Ice Age* was very definitely *not* in progress— things have been going noticeably better for me in terms of my career." Because of their financial needs, Flanagan's friend and lover Ruben had gone to work for Barr as a houseboy until Ruben himself suffered a breakdown.

"If, at 44," he wrote Albee, "I can't solve these problems myself, then I know I'll be half emotional cripple for the rest of my life." It was largely due to his therapist that "I can weather crises, that I can drink pretty much like anyone else, that I've learned something about my capacity for personal control—without which what would appear to be a fairly impressive talent would be useless to me or anyone else."

Still he wondered if they would ever do their opera and had decided after three years of stalemate to "proceed as if there weren't going to be one." He was also stalled on the book about Albee. He asked for Albee's continuing financial support of his therapy and added, "I sometimes think you've been shielded by your own affluence for long enough now that you view the problem of anxieties of this sort like a man from another planet; thus, what you begin with the most generous of intentions you create doubt and confusion less out of 'wicked' motivation than a kind of abstraction."

He also wrote to Albee about his meetings with Judy Garland: "Spent a bit of prime time with Frances Gumm lately . . . She's terrifyingly paranoid even at her best—charm, with sweetness one minute and absolutely inexplicably violent the next. And she demands such complete attention, even at her best, that the experience is ultimately exhausting. If anybody gave a damn about her, they'd get her into a hospital fast, reduced on seconal and amphetemine, while there's a chance. Let me tell you, it put the fear of God in me!" In a sense, this was another example of Flanagan's own cry for help. He ended the letter with an apology, "I know I've harrassed you terribly the last few months, but it won't go on any more."

Still the letters continued as Flanagan found himself under extreme emotional stress. He fell down at a party and injured his eye, requiring plastic surgery. Albee suggested that Flanagan had been drunk or drugged at the time. Flanagan responded, "I drink less than most of our friends and hold it far better than, for example, you . . . I do rather resent your suggestion that I'm a pill head." He said he took Valium and sleeping pills. If he has a few drinks, or even gets drunk, people think he is "on a bender." In contrast, "Richard Barr drinks all day and it's just fine, apparently."

He continued, "I know how you feel about tranquilizers and sleeping medicine and even, for yourself, about psychiatry. But for all of your control, and recognizing all possibilities of future personal decline in myself, I am at least two steps ahead of you at the moment: I don't like it, but I *can* live alone if I must and I've proven it; and although I have a healthy respect for its dangers, I've learned that *fear* of alcoholism only made me act the part out. I'm not afraid of it any more."

Flanagan and Albee spoke briefly at a party given by Morris Golde, and Flanagan followed up with a letter. He had hoped that he and Albee could write a song for Garland as Cocteau had done for Piaf. Referring to the party, he said, "I couldn't understand or make sense enough out of the rather sharp things you were saying to me to even get angry . . . I've been so determined to handle my own problems that, even though I was on the verge of starvation after *The Ice Age* fell through, I worked my way out of it alone." But again he found himself in debt. "Right now, I have no apartment, no money and owe a fortune because of this mess; but it was never my intention to ask you or anyone else for help." What he learned the last few years was that his work was all he had. With a new piece, *Another August,* he "seemed to have found the chords to set off a boom in my career that might very well be the last one if I fucked it up." Albee did not respond. In December, Flanagan sent him a new record of his songs, including one, "The Weeping Pleiades," that was dedicated to him. "I have the impression that I'm off your list, as it were," he said with regret. As it turned out, that was the last recorded message from Flanagan to Albee.

In May of 1969, David Diamond received his last letter from Flanagan. Diamond had visited New York, but Flanagan had been so busy he had missed him. Among other things, Flanagan had moved to a new apartment at One Sheridan Square and given himself a housewarming party, at which he gave a public performance of his songs, the first time in six years that he had done anything like that. Flanagan wrote, "Up 'til now at least, I've shown a resilience that, while it's unwise to count on it eternally, should be encouraging enough to spare my friends the anxiety of very probably unnecessary speculation if I don't answer the phone for the legitimate reason that I'm not at home. Some of my good friends—Ned, Edward, Howard, Morris—have come to the conclusion that if I'm in serious trouble they will hear from me; and that, unless they do, the assumption is that I'm in a strange way as tough as I am vulnerable."

In fact he was spiraling downhill fast, drinking far too much, and alternating between eating too much and going on starvation diets. "He sort of removed himself from civilization," said Albee. "We practically never saw each other except when he needed money, or needed to be gotten out of some problem. It kept getting more difficult, because he was being enormously self indulgent, and did not want to help himself. I thought he was trying to kill himself. I had moved away emotionally, as you have to in a situation like that. In a curious way, I felt, he was getting back at me: So I distanced myself." But Albee continued to give him money for his medical bills. A frantic call would come at two in the morning and Albee would arrange for Flanagan to be taken to the hospital. "He wasn't trying to help himself. It was almost as if he was saying, 'I deserve this. I deserve being helped.' "

On an evening at the end of August, Rorem was about to go to dinner with friends when the telephone rang. The caller asked, "Are you a friend of William Flanagan?" Rorem answered, "Who wants to know?" It was a policeman from the Charles Street police station. He said, in what Rorem remembers as a curious turn of phrase, "He's not living, you know." He told Rorem that Flanagan had been lying dead in his apartment for several days. During that time, no one—none of his friends—had found him. Rorem asked the police not to contact Flanagan's family. He tried to find Albee, and when he was unable to, he asked one of Flanagan's editors to go to Flanagan's apartment and identify the body. Eventually he called Terrence McNally and asked him to track down Albee. Later in the evening Rorem spoke to Albee in Montauk. After hearing about Flanagan, Albee walked outside to a terrace, sat down, and cried "for him, not for me, for him—and nothing more."

Although the obituary in *The New York Times* gave no cause of death, it was assumed among his friends that Flanagan died from a heart attack after consuming a combination of alcohol and drugs. Albee said, "He'd been out drinking, dancing and drugging, and he went home and had a heart attack and died." His death was "not unexpected." Albee came in from Long Island. Flanagan's parents had flown in from Michigan. Albee asked them to his apartment, where he met them for the first time. Inexplicably—considering his expulsion from the Eastman School of Music—Flanagan was buried in Rochester. Only a few people were at the funeral: David Diamond, Noel Farrand, and Flanagan's mother, who kept asking why her son was dead. Albee did not attend.

The following April, Albee and Rorem held a memorial for Flanagan at the Whitney Museum. Copland, Thomson, and Albee all spoke; Rorem played Flanagan songs on the piano; and there was a special performance of

The Sandbox (with Sudie Bond and Jane Hoffman), with Flanagan's score. At the time, Albee announced that he was planning to open a writers' colony in Montauk to be called the William Flanagan Memorial Creative Persons Center. In order to be in residence, he said, artists had to show "poverty and talent," both of which Flanagan had in abundance. He sent Flanagan's parents a copy of an article about the memorial that appeared in the *Times*. Mrs. Flanagan responded, thanking him for honoring her son's memory with a "school." She wrote, "The way he died still haunts us. We keep asking ourselves, could he have been saved if someone had been with him. We realize now he must of had some very serious problems. He did a great job in keeping everything from us. The fact he couldn't come to us for help, this is where we failed him. Those large Dr bills, what were they for, why did that Dr expect you to pay half of the account? Questions without answers."

Through all the years and all of Flanagan's problems—his drinking, his bouts of depression, the periods he spent in and out of various hospitals—and for all the complexity and contradictions of his relationship with Albee, he seemed to be devoted to the playwright and to his talent. In one of his last letters to Albee, he said, "The one thing I am certain we share in common is pride and respect in each other's talents and minds and work. Anything else about our relationship is past history." Flanagan's death not only shortchanged the world of his own promise as a composer, but it also robbed Albee of his most reliable and forthright critic. It was also a warning about what could happen to an artist without a core of resilience.

14
Death and Life

It is now scheduled to open in January under the title
Seascape. Stars will include Deborah Kerr, Barry
Nelson, and Frank Langella. The subject is about evo-
lution and will revolve around the character of Attila
the Nun, pictured as a "second-rate would-be dicta-
tor."

> −PALM BEACH [FLORIDA] DAILY NEWS

•

She sounds first-rate to us.

> −THE NEW YORKER

•

Your author wanted you all to have this in case the
press should pester you again about the "meaning of
the play."

> *love,*
> *your director*

> −ALBEE'S NOTE TO THE CAST OF SEASCAPE

*E*ARLY in 1967, Albee began writing two short plays, companion pieces entitled *Life* and *Death* to be presented as a double bill on one evening. Through an exceedingly circuitous route, each ended up as a full-length play, and *Death* was completed and produced before *Life*. *Death* became *All Over*, and *Life* turned into *Seascape*. In writing *All Over*, Albee might have been provoked by the death of Flanagan. Even more likely he was provoked by the death of Steinbeck (in December of 1968), perhaps also by the assassination of Robert F. Kennedy, who is mentioned in the play. *All Over* is Albee's meditation on death and dying, which The Nurse in the play regards as "the final test of fame." She poses the question, "Which is newsworthy, the act of dying itself, or merely the death?"

In June of 1970, he finished the first act in Montauk, then went to Caneel Bay in the Virgin Islands and worked on the second act. In the fall he returned to Manhattan, where he had been living for the past year in an apartment on upper Fifth Avenue, a baronial apartment that looked out on Central Park and the Metropolitan Museum of Art. The apartment had been Pennington's choice, and he had decorated it, but with characteristic Albee touches, including marble floors and cork-lined walls as Albee had had downtown.

By the first week of December Albee had completed *All Over* and it was immediately put into production. It was, he said, "a serious play about how people get through life. It takes place in a bedroom and living room of a rather important and famous man who happens to be dying. A whole bunch of people—his wife, mistress, best friend, son—are waiting for him to die. The action of the play is the last two hours of this man's life. He never appears and never speaks, but I hope that he's the most noticeable character in the play." The characters talk about their relationship with the dying man, a lawyer, and about their own lives, some with contempt, others with a mutual understanding. Albee later said, "The whole purpose of that play was to examine the power, both destructive and influential, of somebody such as the dying man, whose effect on everybody around him, whether intended or not, is so profound." Being the children of someone who is famous, the son and daughter suffer in a special way. "They feel they cannot possibly live up to the responsibility of their father, and therefore they revolt against it and become as unsuccessful as they possibly can."

Although there is no direct linkage between *All Over* and events in Albee's life, and his father was not famous in the sense of the dying man in the play, one can trace emotional roots. The expectations of his parents that he would succeed weighed heavily in his schoolboy failures.

The characters in the play were given generic names; the pivotal roles were The Wife and The Mistress. Comparing the characters in *All Over* with those in *A Delicate Balance*, he said that they were very different but that there was a closer kinship between The Wife and Agnes in *A Delicate Balance* than there was between The Mistress and Claire. The first choice for The Wife was Dame Peggy Ashcroft, who had had a great success as Agnes in the London production of A *Delicate Balance*. Albee telephoned her in England and then sent her a copy of the play suggesting that she might like to do it in New York for a limited run. Several days later he said she could choose either of the two leading female roles. Ashcroft reluctantly declined.

At the same time he had sent a copy of the play to John Gielgud, who agreed to direct it. Albee chose him despite the fact that the two of them had had their conflict with *Tiny Alice*. Gielgud was amazed and also flattered that Albee offered the play to him. "We fell out," said Albee, "and it got built up by others. We didn't talk for five years." Together, they gathered an all-star cast: Jessica Tandy as The Wife, Colleen Dewhurst as The Mistress, George Voskovec as The Best Friend, Madeleine Sherwood as The Daughter, James Ray as The Son, Peggy Wood as The Nurse, and Edgar Stehli as The Doctor.

As was now the custom, the first day of rehearsal was held at Albee's home. I was there, covering the event, and there were also several television reporters with cameras. Wearing a turtleneck sweater flecked with gray, Albee was in his hirsute phase, with his hair covering his ears. Before the rehearsal began, we sat in his study and talked as his dogs bounded around the room. He said that in contrast to his other plays, *All Over* did not have a long gestation period. I asked him if a growing sense of his own mortality had caused him, at the age of forty-two, to write a death-watch play. "A sense of mortality comes at thirteen," he said. "A sense of one's own mortality should come in the thirties."

Illustrating my piece in the *Times* was a photograph of Albee's women preparing for *All Over*, Wood, Dewhurst, Tandy, and Sherwood conversing in his living room, as Albee and Gielgud, smoking a pipe, looked on. At the far left was Stehli, cupping his hand over his ear, as if he was straining to hear what was being said. As was soon clear to everyone, Stehli was deaf. Two weeks later he blacked out during rehearsal and resigned from the cast. He was replaced by Neil Fitzgerald, and Peggy Wood, who, Albee said, could not remember her lines, was replaced by Betty Field.

Tandy felt some confusion about her role, especially when the character would seem to contradict herself. "Which is true?" she wondered and asked Albee. She recalled, "Edward said, 'I'm sure we all understand that. You understand that, don't you, John.' John the fink of course said, 'Well, not altogether, but . . .' I never got anything from either of them. I was lost in limbo." "I had a very good time in rehearsal," said Gielgud, "though Edward was not helpful. It was difficult because the Martin Beck Theater was so huge—a mausoleum when it's empty. The actors had to play it out front all the time. It needed a small theater really."

Frankie Albee flew up from Palm Beach to go to the opening night on

March 27. Afterward, she went to a benefit party at the Playwrights Unit on East 4th Street, and she was photographed there with Gielgud, two tall people beaming at each other. She told a reporter that during the summer when she returned to Westchester, she had lunch with her son twice a week. "I think it's a lovely thing that he takes the time," she said. "After all, when a fella is forty years old, your mother is just your mother."

Just before the opening, Gielgud sent Albee a note thanking him for asking him to direct *All Over*. He said that he found the play "so continually fascinating and stimulating to work on. I do so hope the critics will like it, and that the team spirit of the company will be recognized." They didn't and it wasn't. The second night, after the reviews were published, the theater was nearly empty. "It was absolutely a dead flop," said Gielgud. "Nobody would go near it. The public was so indifferent."

Several weeks later in *The Nation*, Harold Clurman, once again moving against the tide, proclaimed *All Over* as "the best American play of several seasons." After praising Gielgud's production as Albee's "most thoroughly realized interpretation," he said the play "conveys an existential shudder which has its origins in the soul's dark solitude." In a letter to Tandy, Tennessee Williams said that she gave "a brave and beautiful performance of a brave and beautiful play." To Albee, Williams said it was "my favorite of your plays . . . a marvel of controlled eloquence." The playwright Wallace Shawn said that *All Over* was "one of the great experiences I ever had in the theater."

Later, Albee tried to explain the critical reaction: "Maybe they became impatient with these wealthy, self-indulgent people who seem to be most interested in the precision of their language. Maybe the play seemed too distant, too elegant. Of course it does have the problem that so many of my plays have of being about an almost extinct society." He said that he thought Gielgud's staging was "a little cold, a little icy," but added quickly that he was moved by it. What the production missed was a sense of underlying irony. The play seemed sparse and sober and the few incidents of wry comedy were shortchanged, as in the Mistress's memories of the men in her life ("I have cared for only three men—my own two husbands . . . and yours").

All Over gathers its strength from the growing relationship between Wife and Mistress, each distinct, but together in mourning the man who is about to die and their life—or their lack of a life—with him. Awaiting the end, the Wife is becalmed, suppressing an anger: "Selfless love? *I* don't think so; we love to *be* loved, and when it's taken away . . . then why not rage." Finally, she does rage, in a moment, as Albee says in his stage direction, combining self-pity and self-loathing.

Before returning to England, Gielgud sent a follow-up letter, saying, "Let us hope that the public will confound those horrible critics." *All Over* closed after forty-two performances, and within a month opened in a new production at the Hartford Stage Company, directed by Paul Weidner and starring Myra Carter. That version was later taped for Public Television. That season the Pulitzer Prize and the New York Drama Critics Circle award for best play went to *The Effect of Gamma Rays on Man-in-the-Moon Marigolds* by Paul Zindel, who years before had stalked Albee as model and mentor.

Hearing about the Broadway reception of *All Over*, Peggy Ashcroft wrote to Albee: "I was stunned when I met Alan Schneider who told me of the hostile reception by those mongrels, the critics, of *All Over*. I can still hardly believe it, still less understand. I need hardly say it doesn't diminish my admiration and enthusiasm for it one jot—and I know Peter [Hall] is as obsessed by it as I am." She was about to open in Pinter's *Landscape*, on a double bill with *Silence*, and would follow that with another play. Then, she said, they could talk about doing *All Over* in London.

In 1972, Peter Hall directed the play at the Aldwych Theater with an all-star English cast, Ashcroft as The Wife, Angela Lansbury as The Mistress, Sheila Hancock as The Daughter, and Patience Collier as The Nurse. Albee was in London for rehearsals, and in a letter to Barr, he expressed his early dissatisfaction with Lansbury: "The production of *All Over* should be quite marvelous . . . *if!* . . . Angela comes up." On the other hand, he was already pleased with Ashcroft: "Peggy will be superb (it's so clear who I had in the back of my head while I was writing the part) and the rest of the cast goes from acceptable to wonderful." Within a week things had improved:

> The architecture and sense of the play are all there in Peter's simple and subtle direction and a few things on my part—putting the whole doctor thing back in, taking the wife's expositional stuff about being young and meeting the husband for the first time away from where it was (after the two "What will you do's") and putting it much earlier in act two—have helped as well, I think, and they are all acting with far more awareness of the dying man than we had in New York (and Peter has given up his desire to have the dying man visible, but in shadow—I've got my screen back).

But he felt it lacked "the necessary electricity and tension." "I wait, and look, and nudge Peter about it, and seek the proper moment to push hard."

As in New York, the London reviews were cool, or as the author summarized them: "*All Over* superbly done to bravoing audiences and generally mixed (up) critics." In his biography of Peggy Ashcroft, Michael Billington wrote that "once again Peggy gave a performance, like a shell slowly being cracked open, that revealed the soul-wrenching misery under the dignified facade." For Hall, in retrospect, "It was a continuation of the work we had done on A Delicate Balance. Although the experience of working with Peggy and Angela, two heavyweight actresses, was terrific, I remember less about the play emotionally than I do about A Delicate Balance. My memory of it is that the fact of death, the approach of death is almost leaned on too much for dramatic capital. It's a bit like Victorian melodrama relying on secret drinking. I felt the texture could have been a bit denser."

In 1973, Tony Richardson directed the film of A Delicate Balance for Ely Landau's American Film Theater. Four years earlier Schneider had tried, unsuccessfully, to put together a movie version with Anne Bancroft as Claire and the possibility of Katharine Hepburn and Henry Fonda as Agnes and Tobias. Albee and Richardson had worked together on the screenplay for a movie about Nijinsky and Diaghilev. In keeping with Landau's concept for his film series, Richardson thought of A Delicate Balance not so much as a film but as a recorded play. Once again, Henry Fonda's name was raised, then lowered. Paul Scofield, who had been set to play Diaghilev in their other project, was cast as Tobias, with Katharine Hepburn as Agnes. "I had seen the play several times and really didn't understand what it was about," Hepburn said. "When Ely Landau and Tony Richardson asked me to do it, I thought, yes, no, yes, no, yes, no—then yes, why not?" Kim Stanley, who in the 1950s had been the most acclaimed actress of her generation, was signed to play Claire. The cast was completed with Lee Remick as Julia and Joseph Cotten and Betsy Blair as Harry and Edna.

The first reading of Albee's screenplay took place at Richardson's house in London. In his autobiography, the director recalled Stanley's first scene, when she improvised, crawled on the floor, and sputtered. "Looked on one way it was a parody of the stereotypical view of Method acting. In a London first-floor drawing-room, expressing her emotions, her flesh, her bulk, it was almost obscene." Scofield was furious. Richardson felt that the performance "had the ugliness, the truth, the understanding of great art," but that truth "was at the expense of everything else—the other performers, the text of the play, and the exigencies of the production." Hepburn said she would not continue if Stanley stayed in the cast. Although Richardson felt guilty about the decision, Stanley was released from her contract and Kate Reid was hired to play the role. As he filmed, Richardson lost enthusiasm for the play, finding it "unsatisfying in its emotional underpinnings."

Albee concluded, "The movie's got faults but it's interesting. It's very fortunate that Agnes resembled Hepburn, since I don't think Hepburn would have
tried to become anybody other than herself." This was, in fact, a somber version of the play, missing most of the humor (especially in Kate Reid's performance). The house is dimly lit, as if this were a setting more for a mystery play
like *Tiny Alice* than for *A Delicate Balance*, except for scenes now set in the
dining room, and the ending, when Hepburn throws open the French doors
to greet—with unwarranted optimism—the beginning of a new day. Far more
than in other versions, there is physical contact between Agnes and Tobias, as
she unconvincingly tries to express her closeness to him. A great deal of acting
is afoot, except for Cotten, who is quietly persuasive as the uninvited guest,
and Remick, whose beauty and subtlety made this difficult role more believable. For once, it seemed that Julia really had options, which she has stubbornly undercut. As an adaptation of an Albee play, Richardson's *A Delicate
Balance* is far outclassed by Mike Nichols's *Virginia Woolf.*

Richardson and Albee's other collaboration, with Rudolf Nureyev playing
Nijinsky, was shelved when Harry Salzman decided he did not have the
money to produce it. Later Salzman filmed the Nijinsky story without
Richardson or Albee. Albee had two other unproduced screenplays, for *The
Death of Bessie Smith* and for a film about Stanford White and Harry K.
Thaw.

In April 1972, Peter Hall was in New York and ran into Albee, who told
him that he had nearly finished a new play, a comedy, "and that the only directors for it were either me or himself." The play was *Seascape*, and of all Albee's works it was the one to go through the most changes. In its original
conception, it was to be a one-act entitled *Life*, paired with *Death*, the play
that became *All Over*. By 1967, *Seascape* was a separate play and Albee hoped
that it would be on Broadway the following season. At the time, he said, "It's
about evolution—I think." In preparation for writing it he had been reading
books on anthropology and sociology by Robert Ardrey, Konrad Lorenz, and
others and was thinking about the "collective unconscious." "I'm doing a
study on the social structures of primate society and of fish society. I can't
make direct contact with gorillas, but I can dive under the water and look at
fish. I'm moving away from writing about people to writing about animals."
He said that most of his plays exist on a naturalistic level, and *Seascape* was to
be no exception: "Things occur which couldn't possibly occur, but I'm setting it completely naturalistically." Progress was very slow, and it was to be
eight years before the play appeared on Broadway (in January of 1975).

Seascape is Albee's exploration of anthropology, evolution, and life on sea and on land. Of the play's four characters, two are human (a married couple, Charlie and Nancy), and two are lizardlike creatures (Leslie and Sarah) in the process of evolution. The four meet on a beach, very much like the stretch of sand facing the playwright's home in Montauk. One can assume that looking out toward that beach Albee imagined two such creatures emerging from the sea. As he said, "My house is eighty feet above the beach. The windows of my study look out on nothing but the beach and the ocean, and I'm always aware of what's there. I suspect that had something to do with *Seascape*." Trying to explain the evolution of the play, he said, "There are still prehistoric fish at the bottom of the ocean. It's conceivable that they could evolve. In the course of the play, the evolutionary pattern is speeded up billions of revolutions." Paraphrasing a line of Charlie's in the play, he said that the shift from primordial soup "to string quartets and tangerines takes a very small amount of time—150 million years. Things evolve or devolve. Everything is always undergoing mutation in order to survive. It's the survival of the most adaptable. Whether or not it's for the better, I don't know, but it's certainly more interesting." On a thematic level, he said that the play addressed a number of matters that concerned him in all his plays: "People closing down, how people get along with one another, how they make a marriage." From *The Zoo Story* and *Who's Afraid of Virginia Woolf?* onward, "closing down" is in fact one of Albee's principal artistic concerns. Admitting that people had compared the relationship between Charlie and Nancy to George and Martha, he said that with George and Martha, "on the surface there are lots of fireworks and vituperation. With Charlie and Nancy, the feeling was one of regret: If I wanted to make them George and Martha, I might have called it 'Who's Afraid of Two Green Lizards?' "

He began the play in Montauk and completed it in London in 1974. Submitting it to Barr, he announced that he wanted to direct it, the first time he would stage the initial production of one of his plays. Charlie and Nancy were conceived as an elderly couple, and the first choices to play the roles were two stalwart mature actors, Henry Fonda and Helen Hayes. Both turned it down, although for a long time Fonda planned to do it. Having missed out on *Virginia Woolf*, Fonda felt obligated to explain to Albee the reason behind his reluctant decision not to go ahead with *Seascape*:

> For over a year I have confidently told myself, and even a few intimates, that I was going to do the "new Albee play."
>
> And when I finally read it last week it was everything I could have dreamed of. Brilliant, provocative, exciting, funny and a great part!

Would you believe, unannounced and unexpected, another script came in the mail the same day.

It's not a better play than *Seascape*—in fact, they can't be compared, but it's a challenge I can't resist, a one-man play on the order of Hal Holbrook's *Mark Twain*.

So—*Seascape*, like *Virginia Woolf* will be one of the plays I dream of doing for my own pleasure sometime in some regional theater.

Thank you for letting me read it. I can't believe I am really writing this letter.

With that, Fonda signed up to play Clarence Darrow in David Rintels's *Darrow*, which he single-handedly turned into a Broadway success. After several attempts at interesting other mature actors, Albee decided to make the characters younger—middle-aged. Though this would shift the tone of the play from a late-in-life rueful reflection to a midlife crisis, it opened up casting possibilities, and also making it possible for younger actors to play the sea creatures. In a startling switch, the choice for the role that had first been offered to Helen Hayes was someone from the opposite end of the acting spectrum: Maureen Stapleton. Putting the question of age aside, Hayes was known for her genteel, ladylike portrayals, Stapleton for the lusty vibrancy of her performances in plays like *The Rose Tattoo*.

In the summer of 1973, Albee and Barr gathered actors around Stapleton for a preliminary reading of the play: George Grizzard as Charlie and James Ray and Maureen Anderman as Leslie and Sarah. The reading was in Albee's apartment on Fifth Avenue. At this point, the play was in three acts, and in the second act the married couple accompanied the creatures in a journey beneath the sea. Fortified with a vase-size glass of white wine, Stapleton went through her role with an increasing sense of confusion. After the reading, the actors left together and Stapleton said, "What was that all about?"

When Anderman arrived home, her telephone was ringing: Barr said that Albee wanted her to play Sarah. During the next year, she participated in other readings. Augusta Dabney and William Prince, among others, read the older roles. Arthur Hill was considered for the male lead, but turned it down (he had also turned down a chance to be in *Everything in the Garden*; as with Uta Hagen, he ended up doing only one Albee play). In July 1974, the script went to Dorothy McGuire, who had expressed interest in doing it. Finally the play went full cycle, from Maureen Stapleton, the quintessential working-class actress known for her emotionalism onstage, to Deborah Kerr, who through her films (and her few Broadway performances) represented the most graceful and ladylike of women. In August, Albee was in Klosters,

Switzerland, giving a copy to Kerr, which, she said, "I fell in love with immediately." She accepted the role, and then Barry Nelson, who had previously
starred in *Everything in the Garden*, agreed to play her husband. Frank Langella was named to play the lizardlike Leslie.

Back in Montauk, Albee worked on two other short pieces while wondering about the future of *Seascape*. "I would seem to have Deborah Kerr to play
Nancy," he said to Howard Moss, "and I'm not entirely sure I know exactly
how I feel about that snippit of info." She had not appeared on Broadway in
twenty years (in 1953, she had scored a success in *Tea and Sympathy*), and
her enthusiasm was tempered by her questions about her character. Albee
sent her a letter with random thoughts about the play. In her response, she expressed her hope that she and the other actors could "keep the thread of wonder . . . the 'glimpse of the wonders' that both uplifts and deflates them, the
'sadness after intimate intercourse' . . . if we can keep all this going, and more
importantly make it *build*, then we shall bring it off . . ." She continued:

> I am floundering around with Nancy and will be for a while . . . although
> there is so much of me *in* her, that at times I worry that it is not more complex
> to me! No doubt you will rectify that! I want her to be gay and energetic and
> funny and sad, and, as you say, carrying enough life for both of them. So that
> 'I'm too old to have an affair' has much more depth than the apparent humour
> of it. She *could* take on Johnny Smythe or the Devlin boy quite passionately
> and successfully. The poignancy lies in that she never *would* . . . not that
> type . . . Sometimes I feel she should be more deeply funny, but you can help
> me with that. I don't want her to become *just* an interpreter in Acts II and III,
> that the Nancy we were getting to know, laugh with, be touched by, recognize,
> gets *lost*. And this tends to make things begin to go down-hill a bit, so that trying
> to jack it up again at the end seems a Herculean task. II and III are on the edge
> of being repetitive, i.e. Statement, Incomprehension, Explanation, Misunder-
> standing, Frustration. One *could* get impatient if one was watching and listen-
> ing . . . I arrive October 16th . . . shaking in my boots and exhilarated at the
> same time.

On the first day of rehearsal, the play, a long three acts, seemed inter-
minable to Albee. As he watched the actors go through it, he agonized over
what he might do in terms of cutting. At the end of the day, he told Barr that
he was about to make a drastic decision: He thought he would cut the scene
underwater. In a bold stroke, he excised the second act, in which Leslie and
Sarah take Charlie and Nancy back to their underwater home, and he put

some of the essential dialogue from that act into the scenes that took place on land. The next day, to the amazement of the actors, they discovered that the play had lost almost one-third of its dialogue and much of its action. In the underwater scene, the characters had been attacked by a killer octopus. Swimming around (a casting and design problem?) were also lobsters and moray eels. The new version kept the cast to four, two human, two creatures, all of them on dry land. Explaining the change, Albee said, "I was getting into intellectual depths I couldn't handle. The play was turning into a thesis." Too late to make the switch, and working from the original manuscript, a theater in the Netherlands staged the full version including the act that took place underwater. For all other future purposes, the play was now in two acts.

Whenever Anderman or Langella would ask Albee how their characters should behave, he would answer, "Like lizards" or "Like Sarah and Leslie." To help the actors, he would talk about marriage and love, but not about mortality or evolution. As always, he wanted the play to speak for itself. The following year, in a letter to a German director, he explained his approach. He said that he intended for Leslie and Sarah to be as real as Nancy and Charlie: "Just as civilized in their own way; just as middle class. I suppose I was most interested in equivalencies. Certainly Leslie and Sarah must be frightening and must very clearly be true lizards but, of course, we have to make an anthropomorphic adjustment in order to relate to them . . . Certainly Leslie and Sarah are a metaphor but they must be as real as possible."

For the first time, Albee took a play on an extended out-of-town tryout before coming to Broadway. *Seascape* opened at the Mechanic Theater in Baltimore, just before Thanksgiving. The theater was large and cold, and Kerr had difficulty being heard. The reviews were bad and the cast began joking that the show was a turkey special. Albee did more rewriting, and the show went back into rehearsal. Albee was merciless in his cutting, and the play got shorter and shorter. "He doesn't hold on to things," Anderman said. "That was my first lesson on that with him."

The production moved to the Kennedy Center in Washington, playing in the Eisenhower, another large theater. *Seascape* gradually began to improve. In Washington he finally found an ending, and the audience was more responsive, especially to Langella. It was soon clear that he had the choicest role, and he took full advantage of the histrionic possibilities. In the spotlight, the actor—in Anderman's words—started to misbehave. As Langella later demonstrated in Edward Gorey's *Dracula* on Broadway, he had a certain talent for playing grotesque characters. "Have you noticed?" said Albee. "He is most effective when he is not playing normal human beings." As Leslie, the amphibian, he began to upstage the other actors by striking lizardlike poses. On occasion, he bedeviled them during the performance, even to tickling Kerr and Nelson. One day Clinton Wilder, coproducer of the play, lost his temper and grabbed Langella—a much bigger man than himself—and shook him. Albee never forgave Langella for his actions, calling him "a selfish, cruel actor," explaining that "he had Deborah and Maureen in tears, stepping on lines—he was pushy and self serving."

By the time the play reached Philadelphia in December, it had begun to seem stronger and more cohesive. Opening at the Shubert Theater on Broadway on January 26, 1975, it received another set of mixed reviews, with most of the critics regarding it as one of Albee's slighter works. Clive Barnes in the *Times* was an exception. He began his review, "Hats off, and up in the air! A major dramatic event." Despite Barnes's doffed hat, the play struggled at the box office and closed after sixty-five performances. James Kirkwood's *P.S. Your Cat Is Dead!* lasted only two weeks in April, and Albee sent him a letter of commiseration: "As one presently involved with a near miss I can sympathize with you . . . I can tell you from my own experience that every author thinks that each one of his plays has been closed before its time, that a little more care and a lot more money would have made all the difference: (at the end of *Who's Afraid of Virginia Woolf*'s 800 performance run Uta Hagen was heard to complain that proper management would have given the play 'a good run')." He added, "The commercial theater is not a rational or even a decent place to work in; its disappointments are cruel and its rewards slippery at best."

As the other actors in *Seascape* expected, Langella won a Tony as best featured actor. The company took the play to Los Angeles and on the day that it closed there, it unexpectedly won the Pulitzer Prize for drama. Once again, there was a flare of admiration and invitations to Albee, including one to be a judge that summer at the Miss and Mr. Nude America Contests in Rose Lawn, Indiana. Politely, he declined, adding that Indiana in August was no place or time to be, even in the nude. That summer he also sent a letter to John Osborne praising his *Watch It Come Down*, a cantankerous play that had had a controversial run at the National Theater in London. Osborne thanked him for his "kindly, charitable act." "Life here is quite bloody—almost literally," said Osborne. "Hedged in by malice, vindictiveness and a passion to wound . . . There is so much giggling hatred in the air." Then he said about Peter Hall: "Captain Hall steering his Titanic straight for the ice." Inviting Albee to visit him in England, Osborne closed, "Onward, I suppose," words that could have been echoed by Albee.

In October, Albee went to Japan on a lecture tour. Before he left, he outlined a few special requests. He wanted more free time to visit museums and galleries and to see Bunraku and Noh performances. A little optimistically, he said, "I don't drink, and I hope this will not prove embarrassing to any of my hosts. Perhaps if they knew beforehand it would save my having to explain all the time . . . As to food: I do hope that I will be exposed to as much Japanese food as possible. I rarely eat beef in America, preferring fish, and I am found at Japanese restaurants all the time—usually eating sushi, oshinko, natto, miso soup and cold bean curd. I just don't want my kind hosts to mistakenly think they are honoring me by serving thick steaks and fried potatoes."

That December he had a poem "The Peaceable Kingdom, France" published in *The New Yorker*. It had been accepted by Howard Moss, and it was Albee's first publication in the magazine, a fulfillment of a youthful dream. The poem concerns a ruined village, "a vat of stillness," in which "The sunlight / Saturates the soil, the rock, the air, / Raising a perfume."

In April 1976, Albee directed a revival of *Who's Afraid of Virginia Woolf?* on Broadway. The production starred Colleen Dewhurst and Ben Gazzara as Martha and George, with Richard Kelton and Maureen Anderman as Nick and Honey. It was the third time that Dewhurst had done an Albee play and the first time she had worked with him as a director. She had recently scored a major success in *A Moon for the Misbegotten* with Jason Robards and was looking for another challenging role. She and her companion Ken Marsolais kept coming back to the idea of *Virginia Woolf*. Eventually she called Albee and suggested they do it on Broadway. Marsolais coproduced the revival with Barr. With some justification, Anderman felt she had been cast against type. Usually she played strong young women. She didn't look or feel like Honey. When the show was trying out (in New Haven and Boston), she colored her hair blond, then went back to her natural brunette. As director, Albee tried to emphasize more of the play's comic elements and to help Dewhurst locate a more human side of Martha.

The closest Albee has come to a unanimously favorable press was with this revival, when even several of his harsher critics joined the enthusiasts. Walter Kerr, writing in the Sunday *Times*, said that "the play stuns, and remains a stunning achievement, because its strength comes from actual pain, its demonic energy from real despair . . . It's reassuring to know that *Virginia Woolf* still has its wits about it, its wits and the fascination of a coiled cobra." No longer was it a play with a "hole in its head." Among the other favorable notices was one in the Columbia *Spectator*, the undergraduate newspaper of Columbia University, which called *Virginia Woolf* "certainly one of the wittiest and most gripping American plays," adding that the revival "does it full justice." The critic was a student named Tony Kushner, later a Pulitzer Prize–winning playwright himself. After seeing *Virginia Woolf* "in all its glory," he wondered why Albee "has chosen to waste his considerable talents on such hooey as *Seascape.*"

Despite the reviews, the revival had only a brief run. Perhaps not enough time had passed since the original production and the movie version. Albee spent June 8 on an uncharacteristic activity: He wrote personalized thank-you notes to the critics, including Walter Kerr. John Osborne would have groaned at the thought.

In January, Peter Hall had offered a much delayed response to *Listening,* a one-act that Albee had written the previous year, on commission for the *Earplay* series on National Public Radio. As the new head of the National Theater, replacing Laurence Olivier, Hall was about to move into the company's new building on the South Bank of the Thames in London. In his letter Hall suggested that Albee might direct *Seascape* at the new National, but expressed his reservations about *Listening:* "I must confess that I was a little disappointed in *Listening* in its present state of development. It seemed to me to extend itself—in length and in emotions—beyond its subject matter. But I'd be very happy to be proved wrong, by seeing you put it on in as ideal circumstances as we can give you." After taping *Listening* for radio, with Irene Worth, James Ray, and Maureen Anderman (codirected by Albee and John Tydeman), Albee answered Hall, "We all seem to feel that the play extends itself in its length and its emotions precisely to the extent of the subject matter." He said that *Listening* and its companion piece, *Counting the Ways,* which Hall had not yet read, would be his choice for the new intimate Cottesloe Theater, rather than *Seascape.*

Listening is a mysterious, abstract colloquy among a cook, a therapist, and a catatonic young woman, who encounter one another at a fountain in the garden of an insane asylum. *Counting the Ways,* which takes its title from Elizabeth Barrett Browning, is a series of twenty-one quick blackouts in which a husband and wife (He and She) quiz one another on love and death.

After reading *Counting the Ways,* Hall cabled his enthusiasm to the author and said he wanted to present it at the National with Michael Hordern and Beryl Reid, with Bill Bryden directing. Although he was not familiar with Bryden's work, Albee agreed in principle and suggested that *Counting the Ways* be paired with another short play, preferably *Listening.* Later he raised the possibility that it might be done with *Box* and sent Bryden a tape of Ruth

White's performance in New York. Eventually, Hall decided to do *Counting the Ways* by itself, with Michael Gough and Beryl Reid, and Bryden directing. In a letter to Albee, Michael Birkett, Hall's deputy, said that he thought the play could stand on its own, as the first time the National would do a world premiere of an American play. Then came another explanation. Beleaguered by delays on construction and by a strike of stage technicians, and greeted with poor reviews for their first productions in the new building, Hall and his team seemed to be acting at least partly out of desperation. The small Cottesloe Theater would not be ready for the Albee play and therefore they were putting it in the enormous Olivier Theater as a time filler. The National would have two epic productions in its repertory, each running more than four hours, Albert Finney in *Tamburlaine* at the Olivier and Peter O'Toole in *Hamlet* at the medium-size house, the Lyttelton. This meant that matinees of both did not end until 7 P.M. Birkett said that *Counting the Ways* would be presented at around 8:45 P.M. as a special solo production.

Did anybody stop to think that *Counting the Ways* was a brief one-act dialogue that would be lost in the vastness of the Olivier? The critics noticed: The reviews, in Hall's word, were "appalling." In his *Diaries*, he wondered if this were not "another nail in the coffin." In a letter to Hall after the opening in December, Albee acknowledged the National's problems, including its running battle with the press and the fact his play was caught in the middle:

> Most certainly I don't feel that the play was served well all by itself in the vast space. It *is*, after all, a curtain raiser, Peter, and while I understand your point in wanting to perform it by itself on the Tamburlaine and Hamlet matinee days, I fear I should have insisted that it be performed with its sister, *Listening*, or not at all . . . In essence it comes down to the fact that while I think both Beryl and Michael are intelligent and sensitive actors and could have performed my play as I wrote it, they were not asked to do so . . .
>
> The play I wrote was a forty minute, fast moving, light hearted existentialist comedy. What emerged on the stage of the Olivier was seventy minutes of slow moving, leaden sentimentality, punctuated occasionally by slow motion attempts at humor.
>
> Of course nobody told Bill that the play must last seventy minutes (I hope!) though I did suggest to him at one point in rehearsal that the play clearly created a new law: any play will expand to fill the time allotted to it. I told Bill over and over in rehearsal my feelings about briskness, about pace, about "attack." He just didn't seem to be able—or is it willing?—to transform his syrup into champagne . . .

He said to me one evening, "I'm not ready for Chekhov." And while I am certainly in no way comparing *Counting the Ways* to *Uncle Vanya*, or myself to Chekhov, there is a familyhood of subtlety, understatement and sophistication.

Perhaps to safeguard against possible future slow-motion productions, Albee decided to label the play "a vaudeville."

In January 1977, the two one-acts, *Listening* and *Counting the Ways*, were finally presented on a double bill, as intended. For a production at the Hartford Stage Company, Albee directed Angela Lansbury and William Prince in *Counting the Ways*, with Maureen Anderman joining them for *Listening*, recreating the role of the young catatonic she had played on radio. "It was a very strange play about the id, the ego and libido," said Anderman. She remembered that during rehearsal she had asked very few questions of Albee, but expressed her curiosity about the fact that her character "kept talking about blue, blue, blue." The author said she should be dressed in blue. She asked him, why blue, and he said that blue represented the sky and freedom.

At the end of the play, a woman remembers being in a park on a muggy spring day and seeing a girl in a "huge, oversize, ratty, matted fur coat, pulled tight around her, her hands jammed into deep pockets." The girl slowly took her hands out of her pockets, and they "were all blood, up through the wrists where she'd cut them, and she'd drawn her hands from the pockets, filled with her blood." That scene is directly from Albee's life. Once, at a dinner party at Albee's foundation in Montauk, a young playwright suddenly brought his hands up from under the table, showing that he had just slit his wrists. Albee said, "Oh, that's the wrong way to do it. Let's go upstairs and fix that." He led the playwright from the room, stanched the bleeding, and calmed him down. Then they returned to the table, one of several occasions when Albee responded quickly to an emergency.

15
Into the Woods

Somewhere in the middle, he got lost in a dark forest.

ALCOHOL always seemed to be a part of Albee's life. When he was a child, he was already tending his father's bar at home, mixing old-fashioneds for company (and, of course, for his Aunt Jane). As a young teenager, he would drink with Noel Farrand and Muir Weissinger. He drank at prep school, and during his brief excursion at Trinity College he spent more time at bars in Hartford than at his studies. At that point, drinking was a pastime. But real drinking, alcohol in earnest, began when he moved to New York in 1948. He and Flanagan and their friends drank prodigiously and indiscriminately—whatever they could afford, whatever was available: beer, boilermakers, whiskey, martinis. They drank for pleasure and, increasingly, they drank because they had to. Heavy drinking started in the 1950s and continued as Albee emerged as a playwright. For several years, he managed to compartmentalize the alcohol and the creativity. In the 1960s, there was a change: Occasionally Albee would drink so much that he would black out. Without knowing it, or at least without admitting it at the time, he became an alcoholic. It did not matter that almost from the beginning of his professional playwriting he was a success. Or perhaps it did matter. What provoked the drinking? Overconfidence from that success? A lack of confidence from that success? His failures? Was it, as he later thought, genetic? For a while, the drinking did not seem to affect his work, then it did. By his own estimation and certainly by the estimation of those who suffered from the effects of his alcoholism, Albee was a bad drunk who in the name of truth-telling and under the influence of alcohol would say the most savage things, even to friends. "When I was drinking, I would feel the need to set people straight," Albee said. "I knew what phonies they were, what duplicity and hypocrisy I saw. But I shouldn't have done that in public as much as I did." If you drink too much, "You're either going to be a nice Irish drunk or you're going to be a monster. I turned into a monster."

It did not help that others in his orbit, from Flanagan to Richard Barr, suffered from the same malady. While Barr was accusing Albee of drinking too much, he himself was drinking too much. Barr was, said Mark Wright, "a determined alcoholic. As the years wore on, we realized that any decision that was reached with Richard after twelve o'clock was questionable. But we all protected him. We didn't confront him with his drinking, and it's much to our sorrow that we didn't." On at least one occasion, Albee did confront Barr about his drinking. In an undated letter, he wrote, "Last night you were obviously drunk, and I don't think you should be back stage or around the cast— and their guests—when you're that drunk." Several times Albee was forced to have Barr removed from a theater. Barr seemed to become more blatant not only in terms of his drinking, but also sexually, inviting friends to orgiastic parties at his home. At least outwardly, and in his unpublished memoir, Barr maintained an air of discretion, but privately he was incautious.

In contrast, Albee's personal life and his drinking remained largely private, with the exception of the times he drank with Barr. With Albee as with Barr, the drinking simply was not spoken about within the circle, even though there were times when Albee was so drunk at parties that he passed out and had to be carried home. Glyn O'Malley, a playwright who was Albee's assistant and, later, his assistant director, remembers, "It was extremely difficult for anyone during this period to *tell* Edward anything." O'Malley himself had had a drinking problem and had gone through the program at Alcoholics Anonymous. Albee was not interested: "I didn't think it was the way to go." Or, as Bartleby would say, "I would prefer not to."

Trying to trace when the actual impairment began, Albee looked back to *Tiny Alice*. He remembered writing three or four sentences and not knowing what they meant. He cut them out during the production, but it was an early warning: It was as if someone else, another Edward, had sneaked in and put those lines into his play. The suddenly sober Edward removed them. The drinking continued over a long period: "Maybe it was beginning to be brain damage time." He said that after Flanagan and McNally, "I took a new lover—alcohol."

Especially in London in the early 1960s, Albee woke up in strange beds in strange places and wondered how he got there. One of his earliest blackouts was in 1962 when he was in London for *The Zoo Story*. In New York, one of his most frightening experiences occurred when he was drunk on the subway. Several thieves cornered him and threatened to cut his throat but ended up simply taking his wallet and running away. Years later he could look back on his alcoholism with some objectivity: "An inordinate amount of creative people don't take particularly good psychic or physical care of themselves. They become alcoholics, drug addicts, manic depressives, schizophrenics. I can't think of too many writers, with the possible exception of Arthur Miller, who haven't gone through some period of psychological or physical dependency. Some of us come through it and some don't. Tennessee and Bill Inge didn't pull through it. O'Neill pulled through it. I pulled through it." Trying to explain the causes, he ventured, "The creative act demands a kind of dislocation from the mainstream. One feels an outsider. I won't go so far and tie it into unhappy childhoods. The commercial and career pressures are heavy. I don't know whether the career pressures cause the drug addiction and the alcoholism. There may be a tie in between creativity and the cells in the brain that produce alcoholism and mental disarray."

As Claire does in A *Delicate Balance*, he makes a careful distinction between drunks and alcoholics: "A drunk does it merely for pleasure, and doesn't have to do it, but the alcoholic eventually can't control it. It's all chemistry," the moment after the third or fourth drink "where something clicks in the brain, and one becomes a different person." In his own case, there were those blackouts. "I couldn't remember what I had done. And I kept waking up in places and didn't know how I got there. Who are these people and what did I do?"

During his lowest point, he felt himself losing control of individual plays, of his career and of his life. By Albee's estimate, the period lasted for about five years and ended in 1972, followed by a series of lapses or "fallbacks." In fact, the heavy drinking lasted twenty years and the worst of the alcoholism spanned about ten years, from 1967 to 1977. There was an incident at Jacob and Marion Javits's house on Park Avenue, a party with many writers in attendance. Albee seemed to be playing a private game of "Get the Guests," beginning with the television newscaster Sandy van Ocher. Jerzy Kozinski became Albee's antagonist, advising the others at the party to ignore the playwright as a "poor, pathetic old drunk." Another night Joy Small, Alan Schneider's assistant, had a party in her apartment on 10th Street at Fifth Avenue. At the time, Albee was living nearby at 50 West 10th. Tallulah Bankhead was also at the party and both she and Albee were drunk. Two friends of his crossed their arms and carried Albee, as if he were sitting on a chair, down the street to his home.

The alcoholism and the recovery occurred during the time that Albee began his relationship with Jonathan Thomas, a Canadian painter and sculptor. Albee had broken up with Pennington, who in retrospect played a very small part in the playwright's life. "He was a mistake," Albee said. "I don't know how we met. I was drinking too much—and he was around for a while." Oddly, years later, when Pennington died in an automobile accident, he left Albee a small bequest. The relationship with Thomas turned out to be long-lasting. Albee says unequivocally that Thomas was responsible for the fact that he did not drink himself to death: "I'd be dead without him." The two met in 1971 when Albee went to Toronto to deliver a lecture at the University of Toronto, where Thomas was studying for his master's degree in art history. Then twenty-four, Thomas had previously studied mathematics. He remembers that at their first dinner, Albee's hand was shaking and stopped only after he had had two double scotches. Because of a snowstorm, Albee had to stay longer in Toronto. After several days together, Albee told Thomas that if Thomas were ever in New York he should look Albee up. Soon after, Thomas went to New York and then moved in with Albee in his Fifth Avenue apartment.

As their relationship grew so did Thomas's awareness of Albee's addiction to alcohol. As he said, "Edward could go in for the kill and be very cruel to someone, and say things he didn't believe in." When *All Over* was in previews (early in 1971), they followed a nightly ritual. They would meet Barr and others for drinks at Joe Allen's. Then they would go to the theater and the two of them would stand in back and watch the play. Afterward, they would go backstage. Occasionally the playwright would flagrantly disregard theatrical tradition and give notes on the performance directly to the actors. To Thomas's astonishment, he once badgered Jessica Tandy in her dressing room. Later, Thomas returned to Tandy's dressing room to apologize for his friend, saying that it was a terrible thing Edward had done and he did not mean it. Tandy replied, "Please, just leave," and Thomas realized that he himself had been unprofessional in intruding. But he remained on guard. When he was drinking, Albee could be overcome by paranoia and think that people were betraying him, that they were out to do him an injustice. Thomas and other friends had to be cautious about how far they were willing to go in restraining him.

Once Albee and Barr went to see a play on Broadway and were so drunk, said Albee, that "we shouldn't have been allowed in the theater." In the middle of an act, they decided to leave. As they walked out, they loudly insulted the actors, director, and playwright. Albee cannot remember exactly what he said or did—or even what the play was—but says, "I was quoted as saying something about the second-rate director and the third-rate actors and the fourth-rate play." Remembering that incident and others, he said, "I was a terrible drunk. I felt the need to expose people to the world for who they really were. I did not want to let them get away with anything anymore, even if that demanded embarrassing or humiliating them. I was a scourge." Years later, trying to explain his outrageous behavior, he said, "Something happens in the minds of certain people when they drink. That click, that twist, and you become the Evil Twin, and you can't stop. You can't do anything about it. I felt the need to injure. As the lady says in *Three Tall Women*, 'I can't remember what I can't remember.' "

As the drinking became worse, he began to resemble Claire in *A Delicate Balance*, who describes her symptoms: "Your eyes hurt and you're half deaf and your brain keeps turning off, and you've got peripheral neuritis and you can hardly walk and you hate . . . you hate, and you notice—with a sort of detachment that amuses you, you think—that you're more like an animal every day . . . you snarl, and *grab* for things, and hide things and forget where you hid them like not-very-bright dogs . . ." Claire visits Alcoholics Anonymous but refuses to believe she is an alcoholic. Albee refused even to go to AA, although he tried Antabuse.

It was clear to Thomas that Albee's drinking impaired his work. It is Thomas's theory that Albee's plays of the 1970s, *All Over, Seascape,* and *The Lady from Dubuque,* were largely written before 1971—and later revised. "Maybe he could still write based on material from his past and what he thought of in the past, but he was too isolated to be creative. No longer could he go into a bar and see 'Who's Afraid of Virginia Woolf?' written over the bar and think, 'I've got to remember that. That would be great for a play.' "

Sometimes as early as 10 A.M., Thomas would hear the sound of ice cubes clinking and know that Albee's drinking had begun. One day in his study in his Montauk house, Albee had a sudden start: He realized he was drinking in the morning and also that he had been hiding a glass of liquor behind the books in the bookcase. The other event that awakened him to his state happened in New York in 1976. "One day after a lot of drinking and a lot of smoking—I smoked three packs a day and I drank three packs a day—I went into fibrillation. My heartbeat went up three hundred beats a minute and I thought I was going to die." His doctor was called in and gave him chloral hydrate, "green footballs," and sedated him for four or five days. Around this time, his drinking was probably aggravated by his financial problems.

His accountant was Bernard Reis, who was a major figure in the scandal over the Mark Rothko estate. Because of Reis's mismanagement of his accounts, Albee suddenly found himself with an enormous debt ($600,000 to $700,000) to the Internal Revenue Service. By this time, he had amassed a large collection of modern art and was forced to sell some important work (by Rothko, Picasso, Kline, and Miró) at a substantial loss in order to pay his back taxes. Since he could not wait for an auction, he sold the paintings to Frank Lloyd at the Marlborough Gallery. According to Jonathan Thomas, what Albee sold for less than $1 million would have been worth $15 million in 1998. Albee was furious: "I had to get some money quickly. I was trapped. Those were the paintings that were most saleable. I was probably living too high on the hog, on the edge anyway. All of a sudden, the money stopped coming in and the bills were big." From then on, he began to take greater personal control of his finances.

In 1977, Albee paid $30,000 for a loft on Harrison Street in Tribeca and while the loft was being renovated, the two men lived temporarily in Thomas's studio on Lafayette Street. During this period Albee would stop drinking for a long stretch, then suddenly there would be another episode. "I think he used me as a bit of a crutch," said Thomas. "When I wasn't around he would drink. Somebody would offer him wine and he'd say, 'Oh, I don't drink anymore, but I'll have a taste.'" One of the danger spots was the Dramatists Guild, which had an open bar frequented by the Guild's members.

One of Albee's worst lapses occurred in January 1978. The occasion was a dinner party given by my wife and me at our apartment in Greenwich Village. It was intended as a festive evening to bring together friends who had the theater in common. The guests were Sybil Burton Christopher and Jordan Christopher (who had appeared in *Tiny Alice* at the Hartford Stage Company); Edith Oliver, the Off-Broadway critic of *The New Yorker*; Shirley Kaplan, a director and teacher; S. J. Perelman; Louise Kerz, a theater archivist; Al and Dolly Hirschfeld; John von Hartz, a playwright, and his wife, Kathy; Elizabeth Swados; Andre and Mercedes ("Chiquita") Gregory; Joe and Gail Papp; and Albee. Hume Cronyn and Jessica Tandy came late after their performance of *The Gin Game* on Broadway, as did Farley Granger after his performance in *The Torchbearers* at the McCarter Theater in Princeton. It was a snowy night, and some of the guests were late in arriving.

At first, the evening was friendly and sociable, although if one were closely observant, it should have been clear that there was immediate tension between Papp and Albee. (If only I had known beforehand how antagonistic each was to the other.) Papp left no doubt about his own position in the theater. He was at that point the most important producer in America and a man of great theatrical power. Encountering Albee, he casually called him "Ed" and then "Eddie." Piqued, Albee asked him if he preferred to be called "Joe" or "Joseph." "Joe," said Papp. "OK, Joseph," Albee said, adding, "I'm Edward." During dinner, everything suddenly went awry. As always, memories vary about what exactly took place, but within an instant there was a raging argument between Papp and Albee.

The conflict began with Albee raising his wine glass. He smiled as he toasted Papp, "Here's to megalomania." That remark seemed to open the floodgates to mutual criticism. Papp upbraided Edith Oliver for her negative review of David Mamet's The Water Engine at the Public Theater and Albee countered by agreeing with Oliver. Then he called A Chorus Line "a piece of shit." Papp had moved the Michael Bennett musical from the Public Theater to Broadway, where it was an enormous hit. "You have a middlebrow theater," Albee charged. "Too many of your plays lie." The talk turned briefly to the question of Pulitzer Prizes. In the past few years, the Pulitzer for drama had gone from Seascape to A Chorus Line to Michael Cristofer's The Shadow Box (the previous year) rather than to David Rabe's more deserving Streamers, which Papp produced at Lincoln Center. "Very few Pulitzers are deserved," said Oliver, politely, "except yours, Edward." Papp objected, suggesting that Albee was rewarded for his later plays because he did not receive a Pulitzer for Virginia Woolf. Albee then assailed Papp for second-guessing his writers and directors: "I've heard from writers that you meddle and interfere with artistic decisions." Papp, in character, responded in kind, and before anyone knew what was happening, the argument had turned bitterly ad hominem.

Suddenly, out of the blue, Albee began baiting Papp for his political past, asking him, "How long were you a member of the Party?" Without flinching, Papp counterattacked, "How long have you been doing what you do? You know what I mean," a reference, of course, to Albee's homosexuality. Albee continued to attack Papp's politics, suggesting that he had left the Communist Party too late to qualify himself as a liberal. Though both men had moved into forbidden territory, it was Albee's unrelenting assault that seemed more unconscionable, especially in the light of his own egalitarian beliefs.

Insults flew back and forth as all other conversation stopped, and no one else joined the fray. We all became onlookers. It was as if we were witnesses to a grudge fight or a head-on car collision. Those sharing the table with the two combatants watched in amazement as they went at each other. It seemed im-

possible to intercede. It was an even but not a fair fight, a real-life approxima-
tion of the war between George and Martha in *Virginia Woolf*, and there were
moments when it seemed as if it might end in violence. What had at first escaped my attention was that Albee had been drinking steadily—and heavily—
since Papp arrived. Though both remained articulate, Papp, drinking far less,
seemed to be more in command, and he was treating Albee with disdain and a
growing fury, as if Albee were Senator Joseph McCarthy returned to earth.

Each seemed to regard the other as a kind of symbolic nemesis. For Albee,
Papp represented all producers with private agendas, hypocrites who
stonewalled new and adventurous playwrights. For Papp, Albee represented
an intellectualism and an aesthetic arrogance that debilitated what he considered to be the societal demands of theater. The differences between the
two were deepened by the fact that at that moment Papp was at his height
while Albee was at a low point in his career. When Albee left the table for a
moment, Papp said, "It's a shame. A great playwright whose days are past.
There's nothing for him but to say all others are shit. It's sad."

Cronyn and Tandy arrived from their theater, followed soon by Farley
Granger. The Cronyns had been warmly praised by the critics, and *The Gin
Game*, as thin as it was, was a major success on Broadway. Later that year it
was to win the Pulitzer Prize for the playwright D. L. Coburn. Albee took
Cronyn aside and said, "Hume, why are you in that shit?" "I like the play,"
Cronyn said. "It's shit," repeated Albee. "That's your opinion," said Cronyn.
"It is, and you know it," he answered. "Actors must work," explained Cronyn,
trying to calm Albee down. "An Albee play is only written every five or ten
years. In between we must earn a living."

By dessert, tempers momentarily cooled, but sparks still flew. At one point,
Papp looked around and said, "You still here, Edward? I thought you left."
They began battling again. "You *want* to be attacked," said Papp. "You're a
masochist, but I won't be your sadist." The tension abated only after Papp's
departure. With the enemy gone, Albee kept drinking and finally fell asleep.
Sitting on a couch, he would occasionally stir himself to inject a few words
into a discussion, without knowing its nature. Granger, ever alert and telling
theatrical stories, said several times, "Oh, Edward, go back to sleep." Somehow, late in the evening, Albee awakened and was able to leave at the same
time as the Cronyns, who put him in a taxicab. He did not go home that night
and does not remember where he went. As Thomas remembers, Albee was
afraid to come home. Those who were there at the crash did not forget it. It
was a long time before my wife and I had another dinner party.

The next day a letter, hand-carried, arrived from Albee:

What a splendid party except for that Edward Albee person!

Sorry, Mel: Joe Papp brings out the worst in me—not an excuse; a reason.

I hope the enclosed (attached?) shows that while I can be hopeless socially, I still can write.

Attached was a copy of Albee's new play, *The Lady from Dubuque*.

But Albee felt something more was required. Five days later, a longer letter arrived, offering further comments on his behavior, a letter that is unmatched in terms of its regret and apology, not only to us and our other guests, but, I felt, to himself. Why had he acted that way? In the letter, he tried to come to terms with his demons:

> There is no veritas in vino for me. The reason I stopped drinking six years ago (with two or three awful slips, like the one at your party) is that I do not become merely an unpleasant drunk, or an ugly self-destructive drunk, but I become entirely another person.
>
> I have always held that the riveting objectivity (about oneself, for example, or oneself in a situation) that writers have is a kind of closely controlled schizophrenia.
>
> With some of us, though, doppelganger is an overpowering monster when uncontrolled.
>
> By nature, I am a gentle, responsible, useful person, with a few special insights and gifts.
>
> With liquor, I am insane.
>
> No degree of aggression etc—hidden or not—could provoke in *me* the following: attack on those one cares about; determination to humiliate the universe; self-destruction so sweeping, so uncanny in its aim.
>
> If some of us—all of us?—have, as Agnes speculates in A *Delicate Balance*, a "dark side to our reason," then I have it, in spades.
>
> It mortifies me—tears me apart—and more than ever because I know it is not . . . *me*.
>
> (I suspect the alcohol stimulates a chemical reaction in my brain related to, if not identical with the chemical found in the blood of general schizophrenics.)
>
> I know I must answer for my behavior at all times, drunk or sober—sane, or not. I ask you to understand, though, that the person I became at your house was not an extension of Edward Albee, but his demented other self.
>
> I am shamed that I behaved as badly as I suspect I must have. (I remember nothing after my attack on Joe Papp at dinner, or, rather I vaguely recall seeing Hume and Jessica through a fog. . . . then, nothing.)

I am appalled that I may have (must have!) attacked those whom I respect, admire, care about.

(Except Papp from that; doubtless I was excessive with him, and shouldn't have done it in public, but. . . .)

You know—I hope you know—that I like and respect you. I hope I haven't offended you—and your good wife—to the point of no return.

Can we lunch one day. . . . someday?

In terms of truth-telling that letter takes its place alongside the letter from the headmaster of Lawrenceville answering the inquiry from Choate about the advisability of accepting the young Edward Albee, despite his bad scholastic record. In this case, however, it was a heartfelt personal confession, not so much of guilt but of an inability to be in control from someone who prided himself on his self-control. Overcome by alcohol—and prodded by Papp (and that he realized was no excuse)—he had committed three terrible acts: attacking those he cared about, humiliating "the universe," and "self-destruction so sweeping, so uncanny in its aim." He was apologizing to us for the first transgression and to himself for the second and third. Writing the letter, delivering it, and realizing what he was doing to himself and his talent (and to his friends) must have been a step on his road to recovery.

After the party, there was no comment from Papp, who was accustomed to being attacked in print by critics and in public by disgruntled playwrights. He and I never talked about the incident, and neither did he and Albee, although several years later when Albee was asked by the American Academy and Institute of Arts and Letters to present a Distinguished Service award to Papp, he declined.

For others at that dinner the altercation was ingrained in their memories. Sixteen years later, I asked Hume Cronyn and Jessica Tandy if they remembered it. Cronyn said, "Of course I do. Edward really was loaded—crocked—and he was impossible. He took out after Joe." Tandy nodded in agreement and added, "Joe was no help either." Cronyn said, "I always liked Edward a lot. I'm sorry that he's dropped out of our lives, or that we've dropped out of his. The only thing I found very hard to take was his drinking. He became such a bloody bore. He became abusive and lost all sensibility. It got to be too much. I thought, oh God, I can't spend another evening with that."

Later that year, Albee had a brush with death that had nothing to do with his drinking, but that did reveal his vulnerability. He and Jonathan Thomas were in Los Angeles and a friend picked them up in his car. Thomas got in the front seat and Albee opened the rear door to get in the back seat. He was halfway inside when a car crashed into the back of their car, driving it against the curb. Albee's head struck the car door and he started to bleed profusely. His friends immediately took him to a hospital. Albee remembers the episode in slow motion, as a kind of near death experience. He almost lost an eye. "I was very lucky," he said. "I didn't die and I wasn't blinded either." But he has a scar over his eye. The accident was terrible, but the drinking was, he said, "far more insidious."

Describing Albee's life at this time, albeit from a distance, Mike Nichols said, "Somewhere in the middle he got lost in a dark forest." That "dark forest"—drinking, drugs, abusive behavior, suicide—is a hazard in many professions, perhaps most particularly in the arts. With Albee, there was clearly a determination, a willfulness that kept him working even when he was at his most self-destructive.

16
The Lady, Lolita, and The Man Who

Deeper and deeper into the quicksand.

A s far back as 1960, Albee began thinking about writing a play called *The Substitute Speaker*. Along with his play about Attila the Hun, it was often announced as a work in progress and then shelved. In 1967, he said, "I keep thinking it's almost ready. That may be the play I'm keeping myself from writing." Ten years later, in two months during the summer of 1977, after returning from a writers' conference in the Soviet Union, he completed the first draft. It was now entitled *The Lady from Dubuque*. That was the version he gave to several people in January of 1978. Eventually there were to be two more drafts—and there should have been more. With earlier plays, there had been problems in the writing and the production, but there had always been at least a serious attempt at clearcut resolution, as in the drastic surgery performed on *Seascape*. *The Lady from Dubuque*, however, was marked by irresolution and plagued with problems, financial as well as artistic. For the first time in their partnership, Barr found it difficult to raise the money to produce an Albee play on Broadway. *The Lady from Dubuque* was the first of three plays in which, in Albee's words, he "was not in control." The others were *Lolita* and *The Man Who Had Three Arms*.

Then in three acts, *The Lady from Dubuque*, was a menacing comedy-drama, with a jarring dramatic break as three young suburban couples are suddenly and inexplicably visited by an older woman, the mysterious Lady from Dubuque, and her urbane black male companion. The play dealt with such favorite Albee subjects as reality and illusion, surrogate parents and their relationship to children, and most of all, death and dying. Inspiration had been provided by Elisabeth Kübler-Ross's book *On Death and Dying*. It was perhaps no coincidence that the title character was named Elizabeth. Up to a point, the play was naturalistic, then it shifted into a kind of surrealism as one began to wonder about the identity of the Lady and her connection to the couples downstairs. One of the young women is dying and she is asked to accept the stranger as her real mother, which she finally does.

In March, the play was announced for fall production on Broadway, to be produced by Barr and to be directed by the author. Explaining the eighteen-year gestation period, Albee said, "I thought I would wait to write it until I ran out of other ideas," but now he thought he would "get it out of my system." He had changed the title "when the play was no longer about the substitute speaker." In the original conception, Jo, the wife who is sick, died in the first act, and her husband, Sam, dressed up in her clothes and assumed her identity: He became "the substitute speaker." In the revised version, the wife was dying (but not yet dead), the husband was disconsolate, and suddenly a strange older woman appears. She is ominous yet solicitous. Asked who she is, she answers cryptically, "The Lady from Dubuque."

The title, of course, derived from Harold Ross, the founding editor of *The New Yorker*. When he was asked to describe what the average reader of his magazine would be like, he said, "One thing I know, the magazine is not going to be written for the little old lady from Dubuque." Albee commented on his title, "Since nothing else the character says is true, she might as well say that she's the Lady from Dubuque." In common with the Long-Winded Lady in *Mao*, the character—and the title—was a whimsical tribute to Albee's favorite magazine, in this case a kind of reverse tribute since Elizabeth, the Lady in the play, is the very opposite of Ross's smalltown nonreader. "If *The New Yorker* is written for anyone," said Albee, "it's written for her."

Speaking about the changes in the play, he said, "Originally it was about how much anguish people will allow us to demonstrate before they stop us, before they cut us off. Now it says that our identity is created by other people's need for our identity to exist. Our existence depends on our usefulness. My assumption is that the play has evolved rather than devolved. It comes to a more complex conclusion." When we spoke, he had just turned fifty. At the time of his birthday, he had visited his mother in Palm Beach, "where the average age is seventy: That gave me a marvelous sense of being young." For him, he said, "Being fifty has no reality for me. I'm quite startled when anybody asks how old I am. I don't feel any different than I did when I was thirty, except I can't read the print in the telephone book anymore and I'm far more impatient than I was." He did, however, look very different. The handsome short-haired preppy look had disappeared long ago, replaced by a certain shagginess: He wore his hair long, almost to his shoulders, and had a drooping Fu Manchu mustache and a look of sad-eyed wonderment. He continued: "I don't think my values have become middle-aged values. I'm an aging child. I'll be very surprised when I'm seventy. I think we get through all birthdays. But I'm not amused by the idea that theoretically I have only twenty-five years left. I feel a terrible panic to write."

Then began the long process of putting together a production. The first step was to find an actress of stature to play the title role. In May, Albee sent the play to Ingrid Bergman, whom he had met years ago in Paris. Hoping that she would act in it in New York and London, he wrote to her: "This new play of mine is quite close to what I intend, though I still think I have a little work to do in making the audience willing to take the journey with me." Then he summarized the work and what he viewed as its problems: "Since the play is ultimately about the fact that our reality is determined by our usefulness—other people's view of us in a reality context (the final pragmatism)—and Jo's needs override Sam's, I must make the mystery less of a tease and more of a philosophical matter."

In her polite rejection, Bergman said she was tired of doing successful revivals and wanted to create a new play, but confessed her confusion about *The Lady from Dubuque*: "So I read your play and I can't understand it. Is it symbolism, is it fantasy, are they real people, what does it all mean? You must have something in mind. It can't be just words ending in a riddle. The only scene I can understand is between the husband and wife, after all the guests have left in the first act. I'm sorry to be so stupid." Then she changed the subject to an Albee play she would have liked to have done, *Seascape*, which she mistakenly referred to as "The Sea Shore." She had not wanted to play the Deborah Kerr role, but instead was drawn to the character played by Maureen Anderman: "I would have loved to have played the female Lizard (not the dull wife!) if she'd had some of the funny lines you gave to the male Lizard. I fell off my seat laughing when they said 'Whale shit' (I understand that was later cut). I played 'Lizard' for days at Choisel! Now you see I *understood* the Lizards. I mention this to encourage you to write more, write about simple people or animals I understand. I can't perform if I don't know what I am doing." She closed, "Maybe one day we'll play the same tune."

Peter Adam, a producer who was acting as intermediary, was still hopeful and felt strongly that the Lady had to be played by an imposing figure. He suggested that Bergman only needed a push, and she would do it. Albee was less sanguine and was ready to move on to someone else. Had she done the play, he said, he probably "would have had to spend eight weeks explaining it to her."

Early in December 1977, long before Bergman had read the play, a script had gone to Irene Worth, but it was not until the following September that she and Albee had lunch to talk about the possibility of her playing the title role. Having staged *Seascape*, Albee again wanted to direct the premiere of his play. Worth was enthusiastic about *The Lady from Dubuque*, but she was adamant about one point: If the author were also the director, she would not be in the play. This was an objection to Albee as director as well as, more generally, to authors as directors. Discussion discontinued. Evidently irritated, Albee sent her a letter:

> I was quite relieved when Richard told me that you had decided not to play *The Lady from Dubuque* for it saved me the embarrassment of having to tell you that I had decided, as a result of our meeting, that I was not going to ask you to play the role.
>
> As a friend and a co-toiler, I must tell you that I was quite disappointed by your attitudes. They struck me as being patronising, and suggested that you had not backed off from the positions that had made the original discussion so unprofitable.
>
> Perhaps I mis-read your attitudes at our lunch, but in any event, I came away with the conviction that we would be at each other's throat within two days of the beginning of rehearsal.
>
> I hope you will find a splendid play to do and an environment in which nobody's opinions supercede yours.

Worth responded politely, asking forgiveness for having offended him. Rewrites and the search for a star continued. Colleen Dewhurst didn't think she was right for the role. At one point, Alexis Smith, who liked the play, was under consideration. Leueen McGrath also read it and said she would dearly love to do it. Albee sent copies to several friends, including Noel Farrand, who was head of a music festival in Taos, New Mexico. After Flanagan's death, Farrand was, in a sense, standing in for him as house critic. Praising the play, he wrote, "It has some of the thematic burden of *Alice* freshly and arrestingly treated (you appear to quote yourself in one place). Tragic in its fate, comic in its manifestation, and, if less lyrical in its ideal essence here than formerly, there is even a telling touch of that, notably at the end in the exchange, between Elizabeth and Sam (I've indulged myself in a 'Santayanian' reference)."

In September, Albee received a surprising offer. For many months, Richmond Crinkley had actively pursued officials at Lincoln Center to name him as director of the theatrical constituency. Lincoln Center's theaters, the Vivian Beaumont and the Mitzi Newhouse, had been dark since Joseph Papp had resigned in 1977. Finally officials of the organization acceded and offered the post to Crinkley. Since he was a producer and not a stage director, Crinkley came up with the unusual idea of naming a small group of people as a directorate to share the artistic functions of the organization. Sarah Caldwell, Robin Phillips, and Ellis Rabb had accepted his invitation, as would Woody Allen and Liviu Ciulei at a later date. It was Crinkley's suggestion that Albee be the playwright member of the directorate, with the understanding that he would be an adviser about plays to be done, which might include productions of his own works. Albee accepted with alacrity. As it turned out, his contribution was minimal. He was in charge of a group of short plays done at the smaller Lincoln Center theater, the Mitzi Newhouse. None of his own plays were done (though, of course, *The Lady from Dubuque* would have been a distinct possibility). Before reopening the Vivian Beaumont, Crinkley made his reputation with his production of *The Elephant Man*, which moved from Off-Broadway to Broadway. But he presented only one season at Lincoln Center, then closed the two Lincoln Center theaters for alterations. The idea of a directorate proved to be a grave disappointment, and Lincoln Center's theaters were dormant for several seasons.

A year after Albee and Worth had curtly ended their discussions, Richard Barr telephoned the actress and asked her again if she would be in *The Lady from Dubuque* — and added that Albee was not going to be his own director. With that in mind, she immediately agreed, and Alan Schneider was signed as the director. From California, Schneider suggested to Albee that he and Barr audition Frances Conroy for the important role of Jo, the woman who is dying. With her in that role instead of Pamela Payton-Wright, who had been previously cast, the director said he would have a great sense of security. "You remember my fighting so hard for Melinda and George [in *Virginia Woolf*]," he said. "That's the way I feel about Frances." He added, "When you get back from all those lecture jaunts, take a look at that ending once more and think about how best to strengthen Elizabeth's and Oscar's exit. I do believe that's important, and has nothing to do with the star's exit; just the most interesting and powerful conclusion to those two characters."

When rehearsals began—with Conroy as Jo and Earle Hyman as Oscar—the primary object of Schneider's disaffection was the actor Kevin O'Connor. Close to the opening, O'Connor was fired and was replaced by Baxter Harris. Also in the cast were Maureen Anderman (in a role originally filled by Swoosie Kurtz), Celia Weston, and Tony Musante. During rehearsal, Albee wrote a new ending for the play, or rather, "extended the play beyond its existing ending," in which it was clear that nothing in the play had really happened. But the director and producer objected, and Albee acceded, returning to the original ending. In his eyes, the characters in the play, in common with those in *Tiny Alice*, are all real people, "but they don't exist, except by necessity. Some uncertainties you have to preserve, some balances you have to keep delicate."

In order to present the play on Broadway, Barr had to put together a consortium of producers, five others besides himself, plus one associate producer. In late December, he was still raising money. After several delays, *The Lady from Dubuque* finally opened at the Morosco Theater on January 31, 1980. Critics and theatergoers were mystified.

Reviewing in the *Times*, Walter Kerr cast a disparaging eye and found only unanswered questions. In my review on radio station WQXR, I called the play a dance of death on the grave of the American family and added, "Mr. Albee contemplates the appearance of truth, man's need for an identity even if assumed. In this game we can choose our own roles to play . . . For most of its duration, *The Lady from Dubuque* maintains a delicate balance between bitter comedy and mystery . . . The play winds down at its climax. Anxious for an apocalyptic vision, the author becomes manipulative and our interest slackens . . ."

Confronted with mixed reviews and an uninterested public, Barr and his six coproducers closed the show after twelve performances. Albee was furious and called the producing team "the seven dwarfs," despite the fact that the lead dwarf was a close friend and ally.

In May, a new production of *The Lady from Dubuque* opened at the Hartford Stage Company, the final production of Paul Weidner's tenure as artistic director of the company. Earle Hyman repeated his role. Playing the title character was Myra Carter, a Scottish-born actress who had previously played the mistress in the Hartford Stage production of *All Over*. Engraved in her memory was the fact that she had been rejected by Barr as Worth's understudy in *The Lady from Dubuque* on Broadway. "Oh, you never could do it," she remembers him saying. "We need somebody with some stage presence." In regional theater, Carter began to gather a reputation as an interpreter of Albee.

In different productions of *A Delicate Balance*, she played both Agnes and the neighbor Edna, the first at the Arena Stage in Washington early in 1982. It was not until 1991 in Vienna that she was to place her signature on one of his new plays, *Three Tall Women*. Looking back on the original production of *The Lady from Dubuque*, Albee said: "I realized that there were problems in the second act that I wasn't in control enough to solve. I was too rushed. We went into rehearsal too soon. There's more work to be done on that play. I know exactly what to do to fix it. It's all clear to me now, but I remember not being sober enough to do the work. That's an example of a play that suffered from my drinking."

The Lady from Dubuque was the beginning of Albee's down period, when nothing seemed to go right. Glyn O'Malley, who was an assistant to Albee on the productions of *The Lady from Dubuque*, *Lolita*, and *The Man Who Had Three Arms*, calls the period "the valley of the shadow." He continues: "Here I was relatively young, late twenties and early thirties, watching this hugely influential playwright get knocked around. It was extremely difficult for him and for everybody around him." He remembered an Albee poem from the sixties, in which the central image was of someone being carried aloft in a parade. In contrast, in this period, Albee "disappeared into the crowd—there was that sense that it was over."

He was already embarked on his next show, an adaptation of Vladimir Nabokov's *Lolita*. *Lolita* was to be Jerry Sherlock's first theatrical production. He had produced several movies and had just finished *Charlie Chan and the Curse of the Dragon Queen* (starring Peter Ustinov). As was also true of Albee's other adaptations, what seemed to be a relatively easy—or at least carefully prescribed—assignment turned into a time-consuming, demanding project. In the case of *Lolita*, it was more than two years before the play opened, and the work was to lead to a bitter battle with his producer and, tangentially, with the Nabokov estate. There was more acrimony than the playwright had experienced on any other project. After Albee agreed to write the adaptation, one of the first people he contacted was Peter Hall at the National Theater in London. Although Hall said he was interested in directing the play, he found himself trapped by the demands of his job at the National. Sometime later, another British director, John Dexter, signed on.

After Albee finished the adaptation, he sent it to Dexter, who was then head of productions at the Metropolitan Opera. As was his habit, Dexter read the play aloud to himself, clocking the reading at three hours and twenty minutes with no intermission. This was, he said in a letter, longer than he imagined. Commenting on the play he said that he thought that structurally it was "pretty near flawless." Then he arrived at his reservations, starting with the opening of the third act, where he felt the author seemed "to digress in the manner of a picaresque novel into another world and into a group of characters whose relationship in the main thrust of the narrative is minimum." He added that he had "an inkling of a way of staging it which is crisp, clean and, I hope, in the best sense of the word, classical." Two months later, he expressed his doubts about the casting of the show, admitting that he was aware of his lack of knowledge about American actors. Then, after the leading role of Humbert Humbert had been rejected by Alan Bates, Anthony Hopkins, and Dustin Hoffman, and Donald Sutherland had been suggested as a possibility, Dexter resigned. Albee sent him a letter, acknowledging his resignation and questioning his reasons. "In retrospect, it appears to me that you were probably bowing out once you found that Bates, Hopkins and/or Hoffman were not available, and that we all played a dying game for lack of a straight remark." Albee was irritated because he had heard through an intermediary that Dexter would not take the time to meet with Sutherland, because he was too busy "making history." He closed his letter, "Greetings and farewell from one branch of Olympus to another." Dexter answered with a correction. What he had said was that he was unable to meet with Sutherland not because he was making history but because his production of *Mahagonny* "was making me have an *ulcer.*"

In adapting *Lolita*, Albee used a similar approach to that of *The Ballad of the Sad Cafe*. A narrator was onstage commenting on the action. With *Ballad*, his first idea was to have Carson McCullers do her own narration. With *Lolita*, he wanted to have Nabokov onstage, or rather, an actor playing the role of Nabokov. Nabokov's widow, Vera, and their son, Dmitri, vigorously objected, partly because the character was there at all, largely because "the character that Edward Albee has created is basically the antithesis of the real man they knew and loved."

In July, Albee, his producer, and his agent, Howard Hausman, met to discuss the conflict. Albee explained that he had used the initials VN for the character in his original draft, but that the role was not intended to be specifically Nabokov. Rather, it was a "creature of his imagination." According to those representing the novelist's estate, the agreement was that the character would be called the "playwright," although Albee asserted that it "was no more a self-portrait than it was a portrait of Mr. Nabokov." In a subsequent letter from Albee's agent, there was a correction to the agreement: Albee had never definitively agreed that the character would be called "the playwright."

There continued to be trouble between Albee and the Nabokov heirs, which culminated with a cable from Dmitri Nabokov: "Shocked you have not kept word and taken no action re unacceptable use of my father in Lolita script. If no word by return cable Montreux shall initiate proceedings to prohibit production." Albee finally decided to call the narrator A Certain Gentleman, a character that was Nabokovian but not Nabokov.

With Dexter unavailable, Frank Dunlop was hired as director, Sutherland was named to play Humbert, and the search was on for the other actors, especially for someone to play the title role. Albee thought that Sue Lyon was too old in Stanley Kubrick's 1962 movie version of the book. Initially the idea was to find someone of Lolita's approximate age, eleven and a half at the beginning of the book. Open auditions were held for girls from eleven to thirteen. With Albee and Sherlock sitting at a table in a room at the Picadilly Hotel in Manhattan, seventy-five candidates appeared. Each was interviewed. No one was called upon to act, and similar open calls were scheduled for other cities. Most of the candidates were unfamiliar with the book. When asked what she knew about the character, one eleven-year-old said that Lolita was a little girl "who likes to act sexy to her father so she can get beautiful clothes." Albee said that in preparation he had been looking at girls in the subway and on the street through Humbert's eyes and had almost gone up to a few to ask if they were actresses. He said the book was not about sex but about "lost time." He added that "with any luck, people won't know which is Nabokov and which is Albee." When one child at the audition asked him who he was, Albee doubled the confusion by saying that he was Nabokov.

Eventually, it was decided to have a professional actress play Lolita. Blanche Baker, Amanda Plummer, and Trini Alvarado all read for the role, and Baker was chosen as someone who could convincingly pretend to be Lolita's age. In October, Albee drafted a list of actors for the other roles. Maximilian Schell and Ian Richardson (who was eventually hired) headed the list of those to play A Certain Gentleman, followed by Curt Jurgens, Hume Cronyn, Hal Holbrook, Barry Ingham, and Herbert Lom. For Quilty, there were John Heffernan, Clive Revill, Michael Lombard, Derek Jacobi, and others, including someone identified as Sereren Dartin, who must have been that genius of Second City, Severn Darden. He was available and would have been a brilliant stroke. The role went to Heffernan, who was later replaced by Revill.

As the play finally went into production, Albee put down some thoughts about pornography, the art of Nabokov, and the problems of adaptation:

A long time ago—back when I was an adolescent in both mind and body—
I was deeply interested in what, in those days, was referred to as "smut" . . . I was
fascinated, then, in the early fifties, when word reached the eager that there was
a book called *Lolita*—by "some Russian"—too hot to handle, certainly too sor-
did to publish in the land of the free, etcetera.

My curiosity was piqued—as whose might not be—by this "smut" about a
dirty old man (38) seducing and kidnapping (to what unspeakable ends one
could only hope) a mere infant (12). So I availed myself of a (French) copy of
the book and settled down for a bad read.

I was bitterly disappointed . . . for I found myself in the presence of a brilliantly written, violently funny, profoundly sad and highly moral novel whose
true subject was that which had concerned both Proust and Chekhov (to name
but two writers out of hundreds): the thrall of the past, pure first love and the
absurdity of that which we call adulthood, or maturity.

I suppose I should have been forearmed, for, much younger, I had taken
Joyce's *Ulysses* under the covers with me, so to speak, and had been shocked to
discover another masterpiece . . .

The play of *Lolita* is both Nabokov and Albee—some scenes, some characters are the playwright's invention, others (most, perhaps) the novelist's. But,
that being as it may—and it is a matter which will be apparent only to
supremely dedicated Nabokovians—the entire work is Nabokov; it is my valentine to the great man, he who suffered fools so badly and who, so clearly, loved
us all, even the Humbert Humberts and the Lolitas of this world.

Unfortunately, what followed was a series of arguments and battles, adding
up, finally, to a folly. Albee's "valentine" was, for Dmitri Nabokov "a horrendous grotesque of my father's work." Despite their disagreement about the
adaptation, Dmitri Nabokov and Albee felt similarly about Sherlock, whom
Nabokov later called "an utter vulgarian." The trouble started in New York
and, in Albee's words, it quickly became "a cesspool" of a production. One
day during rehearsal, Sutherland, angry at the adaptation, ripped pages out of
Albee's script and flung them into the orchestra. Then he cut out pages from
Nabokov's novel, deciding they were better, and tried to insert them into the
play. "Everyone was beside himself on that production," said Glyn O'Malley,
"and I had seen it go from Edward laughing his head off upstairs as he wrote
the scenes to the horror of the production." Every day was a fresh disaster.

In a letter to the other creative principals, including Albee, Sherlock, and
Dunlop, the set designer, William Ritman, forecast chaos. He said that the
lack of a support system made it inconceivable that the production would

ever resemble the original concept. The problems began with a lack of money. He said that instead of having an experienced professional handle the projections, there was a photographer in residence, someone who had no experience in slides. To save money, the lighting designer had been forced to reduce the wattage on light bulbs from 1000 to 750 watts. Ritman said he was appalled at the atmosphere, and he predicted disaster unless more money were made available. Albee said that to save money Sherlock had Ritman's sets redesigned without telling the designer.

By the time the play opened in Boston in January of 1981, the script had gone through several rewrites. It was almost as long as *Nicholas Nickleby*, and Albee wanted it to be presented in two evenings, as was the case with that Royal Shakespeare Company adaptation. Eventually *Lolita* was scaled back to a normal length, a fact that always displeased the playwright, who continued to regard the two-part *Lolita* as his authentic version. Every night there were rewrites, and by his own estimate, Albee was drinking too much. There was still rumbling backstage, among the actors as well as the designers. Sutherland sent Albee a note, suggesting the insertion of a new scene, which, in Albee's absence, he, Dunlop, and Sherlock had worked on. Panic was in the air. What finally ended onstage, said O'Malley, was "a hacked-up version" of Albee's original adaptation. Early audiences were offended, as much by Nabokov as by Albee, and the reviews were mixed.

Taste always seemed to be in question. For Boston radio, a commercial was prepared using Nabokov's famous line, "Lolita, my love, fire of my loins," but the station objected, and Nabokov was rewritten to "Lolita, my love, fire of my passion." In spite or because of the controversy, the show broke the box office record at the Wilbur Theater during the two weeks it was in Boston.

After the tryout, the play returned to New York and went back into rehearsal. By this time, Dunlop was in San Francisco touring with his revival of *Camelot* (starring Richard Burton) and Albee was leaving on a lecture tour. Who was in charge? Anticipating the worst, Sutherland hinted on television that the show might never open on Broadway. Suddenly the opening was postponed for two weeks, a red flag for gossips and naysayers in New York: The word was out, a disaster was on the horizon. With the *Times* eager to have its reviewer jump in before the opening, Albee decided to forestall such an event by sending a letter to the managing editor, insisting that the postponement was because of Dunlop's contractual complications and for the "professional requirement of playing a frozen show for a number of performances." He added, with barely suppressed outrage: "Our producer, Jerry Sherlock, is, indeed, a devious and arrogant amateur, but you must believe me, the decision to postpone is entirely an artistic one."

At this point, Albee and Sutherland were still communicating, or at least Albee was pretending to communicate. On March 7, Albee sent Sutherland a letter filled with false hope. He suggested some changes in the text, inserting two short speeches, cutting and simplifying one of Sutherland's long monologues, and having Quilty's death sentence poem read by Humbert (in the final version the poem was delivered by Quilty). "Dare, Donald," said Albee. "You are at your very best when you do; so is the play." From the playwright's perspective, the actor never took the dare, and in the end he shared the brunt of Albee's anger (along with Sherlock and Dunlop). Among other things, Albee accused Sutherland of trying to rewrite the play. Sutherland joined Frank Langella on a short list of actors whom Albee hated working with.

"My version," his two-evening version, "was vulgarized and cut to shreds by the actor [Sutherland] who just cut whatever he wanted to. I kept trying to stop it but I couldn't fight against all three of them. The three of them—the producer, the director and the actor—made up the cesspool. Any scene that Sutherland was not the star of, or that anybody else seemed to be doing terribly well, he would either try to get them fired or have the scene cut down. It was disgusting." Albee went to previews where he watched "people walking out at intervals, retching—it was awful."

When Lolita finally opened on March 19, it was picketed by fifty women representing Women Against Pornography. Shouting "Incest isn't sexy, rape isn't funny," they broke through a barricade and succeeded in delaying the curtain ten minutes. "We're not against the book," said one of the protesters. "The book is fine. Albee is exploiting sexual abuse, incest and rape." Sherlock said in response, "The protesters will have little effect on the success of the play."

The adaptation was neither faithful Nabokov nor imaginative Albee, but an amorphous amalgam, in which everything and almost everyone sank. At greatest risk, and in the end at greatest fault, was the concept of having a narrator walk on and off stage and lurk around the scenery.

In my review on WQXR, I said, "Vladimir Nabokov's Lolita is a grand comic novel about one man's obsession, a lepidopteran landscape of language by a master of English prose. Edward Albee's adaptation . . . is a serious but ultimately futile attempt to encapsulate the fair Lolita on stage . . . As a play, Lolita is literate, but in the end it is languorous and self-depleting."

Among the actors, Richardson survived best of all. As A Certain Gentleman, he kept his evident embarrassment covert and tried to give the lines a certain urbanity. Sutherland simply seemed ill at ease. The direction showed the slapdash quality of several hands, all of them at odds, and even the set was drab; instead of visuals, rooms and furniture creaked on and off stage. As should have been expected, the reviews were negative, with the curious exception of Robert Brustein. Having dismissed *The Zoo Story* as Beat Generation "claptrap," having called *Virginia Woolf* an "ersatz masterpiece," *Tiny Alice* a hoax, and *A Delicate Balance* "cocktail party chit-chat," he did an astonishing about-face. Describing himself as one of Albee's "most persistent critics," he said he had a new respect for him because everyone else was attacking him. Then he said, "with all its flaws, *Lolita* is engrossing, terse and above all, dangerous." He concluded that "unlike so much of Albee's recent work, it undeniably lives on the stage." Even Albee thought that it had died.

He steadfastly refused to accept blame for what happened on Broadway, declaring that it was not his adaptation, but some bastardized version put together by various other people. As he said in an interview with Terrence McNally in the *Dramatists Guild Quarterly*, "Something called *Lolita* with my name attached to it was produced on Broadway, but it was not my adaptation of Nabokov's *Lolita*. The only really truly ugly theater experience I have had in a long and reasonably happy career was the experience of losing control of the production of that play." He said he had thought about closing the play before it opened but instead sunk "deeper and deeper into the quicksand."

In an introduction to a collection of his plays, he said, "A combination of disrespect for Nabokov's and my text, directorial vulgarity, salacious short-changing of the production *by* the production, and a lax and insensitive turn by a leading performer whose aim, I could swear, was the undermining of the venture, resulted in a disgusting misrepresentation of a faithful adaptation of a book I cherish."

Confronted with devastating reviews and with no money to continue, Sherlock quickly closed *Lolita*—with a curious, beneficial result for Albee. Because the show had managed to give the requisite number of performances under the Dramatists Guild contract, Albee's rights to the play were merged with that of the Nabokov estate. This meant that Albee would receive half of any future dramatic or film version of the novel. When *Lolita* was sold years later to Adrian Lyne for his film version, Albee shared the million-dollar sale with Dmitri Nabokov. Albee's greatest failure, *Lolita*, was to become his second greatest moneymaker, next to *Virginia Woolf*—at least until *Three Tall Women*. Albee also sued Sherlock for back royalties and won $75,000.

Despite the profit, *Lolita* remained the "sore point" of his career. "It was a disaster," he said. "It shouldn't have happened. I'm the villain because I didn't close it down. I kept saying, 'We can save this. It will get better.' " Later, he received a consoling letter from James Mason, who had played Humbert in the Stanley Kubrick film. "I am writing to you because I am a great admirer of Nabokov's writings and I have a personal interest specifically in the adventures and misadventures of Lolita herself. And since I also have a great admiration for your work, I was puzzled by what in this case turned out to be a misadventure." Then, reading Albee's mind, he said, "I had a feeling that the producer was not the man to handle either Albee or Nakobov, nor perhaps was the actor, but I did not know where to pin the ultimate blame." He asked Albee for a copy of the play "so that I can have the pleasure of reading your findings." Finally, he commented on his fatal experience with Brian Friel's *The Faith Healer.* Mason and his wife "took on Broadway," and, he said, "we are still licking our wounds."

Looking back on the production of *Lolita,* Sherlock said, "It didn't work and everyone has to share the blame. Everyone was difficult. Edward was petulant with a capital P. Donald Sutherland was a very difficult individual. It was like a cabal. The director and Albee were buddy-buddy, then they became enemies. The star was Albee's enemy; the next week he's on his side." The experience, he said, "burned me for good." It was Sherlock's first and last theatrical venture.

In 1981, Albee wrote a new introduction to a collection of his early plays, saying he was nineteen plays into his career and hoped to double that number in the course of his life. Then he offered an astute analysis of where he was and what he thought about playwriting: "I have learned, for example, that experimental plays, dense, unfamiliar and lacking proper road signs meet with considerable critical and audience hostility," but when he felt like writing another one

> there was nothing to do but wince, write it, take the caning, and hope that the next one will be "easier" for everybody. I have learned that some of my subjects—how we lie to ourselves and to each other, how we try to live without the cleansing consciousness of death, for example—are not the stuff of box office smash, and sometimes, not very often, but sometimes I wish I could write about what Herbert Gold called "happy problems." I have learned that while I am especially fond of those plays of mine which have been misunderstood I must not misunderstand the feeling—that it is not necessarily a valid intellectual judgment and may, indeed, be nothing more than protective parenthood: touching but not always instructive. I have learned that being a playwright (like being a politician, or an ax murderer) is what one *is* more than merely what one does,

and that a playwright's perceptions are framed by the proscenium arch. The truth he tells is a playwright's truth but, with any luck "it transcends the personal and the private, and has something to do with the anguish of us all."

There is always the temptation for an artist to return to his greatest success, to wonder how he did it, and then to try to write a sequel. That temptation should be avoided. Invariably it is an attempt to turn back the clock and the impetus comes during a time of creative depletion. A bad case of writer's block may encourage a writer to reread and rethink an early work. Has there ever been a sequel that equalled the original? With plays and novels, in particular, disaster awaits the writer, unless the work was conceived as an interlocking series (as in Lanford Wilson's plays about the Talley family). The primary area of danger is for an author to try to imagine what happened to the characters in the future. Years after *Look Back in Anger*, John Osborne unwisely pondered the question of Jimmy Porter after anger and wrote a play aptly entitled *Deja Vu*. Neil Simon brought back Oscar and Felix in a needless movie sequel to *The Odd Couple*. Occasionally over the years, Albee would refer to the possibility (firmly rejected) of writing *Son of Virginia Woolf*. For him, as it should be, the play was the play: He would never revisit New Carthage and look into the later lives of George and Martha. Fortunately, he realized that such a return would only serve to demean the original. In 1981, however, he wrote a sequel to his first play, *The Zoo Story*, for a private benefit performance. Albee says it was never meant to be performed publicly. Glyn O'Malley referred to it as the gay version of *The Zoo Story*.

The play was called *Another Part of the Zoo*. In one act, thirty-three pages, it is a dialogue between characters initially identified as J. and P. At first, they seem like Jerry and Peter of *The Zoo Story*. The plays begin identically. P. is seated on a park bench absorbed in his reading. J. enters, looks at the other man, and then says:

I've been to the zoo. I said, I've been to the zoo. MISTER! I'VE BEEN TO THE ZOO!

With only minor alterations, the dialogue replays *The Zoo Story* until the line "It's northerly." Then P. asks J., "Why do you . . . just stand there?" A little later, J. says, "You look familiar," a line that he repeats. At first one notes the small differences: Peter is married and has two daughters, P. has two sons. After small talk about exercise and body building, J. asks him his name. After he says he is Peter, J. introduces himself as Jesus, not *the* Jesus but an Hispanic contemporary of that name. Suddenly Jesus plants a thought: "I think you and I have a mutual friend," someone named Nicky. Jesus persists in try-ing to make Peter remember him and finally takes out a knife and threatens him with it. As Jesus becomes more pointed in his narrative, Peter says, "What is this, a parable or something?" Nicky and the man who may be Peter had an affair that lasted 100 days and ended with Nicky being abandoned and trying to kill himself by slashing his wrists. Holding his knife close to Peter's face, Je-sus says, "How could you *do* that to him? To *any*one!?" Peter denies every-thing and begs for his life. As the play ends, he repeatedly denies that he is gay. Jesus leaves. Peter has the last line:

"I'm not; I am not gay; I am. . . . not. . . . gay!" The rhythm of the words sounds like the last line of *Virginia Woolf:* "I . . . am . . . George . . . I . . . am."

It is impossible to read the play without thinking of its predecessor, and, of course, Albee forces the comparison, even to calling the new version of Jerry, Jesus, underscoring the subtly symbolic elements of *The Zoo Story.* Artisti-cally, there is no comparison. *The Zoo Story* is a masterly play that builds su-perbly from a seemingly casual encounter to an explosive confrontation to a ritualistic act of violence. The sequel is simply an afterthought, a lesser ver-sion of what was an intuitive act of the imagination, and the references to the author's life (sons named Terry and Bill) are self-conscious. Albee denies the play is a sequel to *The Zoo Story.* Just as the beginning of *The American Dream* is a homage to Ionesco, *Another Part of the Zoo* is, he said, "a homage to me."

Early in 1982, Albee thought about doing the play on a double bill with a one-act by Terrence McNally, an early version of *The Lisbon Traviata,* and then decided not to. In a letter to McNally, he said,

> I am convinced that nothing is guaranteed to narrow the public and guaran-tee an unfair shake more than doing the play (either play) as a kind of homo-sexual evening—two gay playwrights, writing on gay themes. I have never made a secret of my sexual direction, as you and a couple of thousand others know, but I don't want to see either of our plays ghettoized. I am writing another one act play this summer—on a heterosexual theme—and I feel that and *Another Part of the Zoo* belong on a bill together, in the same way I feel *The Lisbon Traviata* will be best served on a bill with another play of yours, a play in nice contrast to it.

The Lisbon Traviata became a full-length play, although the first act, the original version, was always the stronger part of that bill. *Another Part of the Zoo* disappeared into Albee's files, but its existence says something about the playwright's state of mind at the time. Although outwardly he remained, as always, calm and rational, one could surmise that in terms of his creativity there was a kind of inner desperation, something that he probably had not felt since the days before he wrote the original *Zoo Story*.

The Man Who Had Three Arms was the play Albee had to write and probably should never have written, a long diatribe about the price of success and celebrity. Despite the author's protestations about the play not being autobiographical, it was inevitable that that would be the assumption. "Himself," the man who became famous because he had a third arm growing out of his back, an "accident of nature," a freak who lost his following when the extra appendage withered away, was generally accepted as a representation of a certain Famous American Playwright who, it was generally assumed, had lost his audience along with his talent. The fun and fervor of *Fam*, his lighthearted spoof of William Inge, had been replaced by the frenzy and the apparent self-pity of *The Man Who Had Three Arms*.

The play was commissioned for the New World Festival of the Arts in Miami (along with plays by Lanford Wilson and Tennessee Williams). It was written in Florida, away from all stabilizing influences. For one thing, Jonathan Thomas remained in New York, and while working on the play Albee had one of his periodic relapses into drinking. Trying to trace the roots of the play, Glyn O'Malley said he thought that it came from the shape of Albee's life at the time. "He had structured his life in New York and now he was spending 80 percent of his time on the road lecturing. The travel was, I think, a chance for Edward to break out" and, in a sense, to indulge himself. "As for the play, he was setting himself up. It was a challenge, calling everybody out, taking them all on: 'If you think you fucked me with Lolita, here I'll give you one.'" Although Albee has always denied ever writing a play with an actor in mind for a role, he came closest with *The Man Who Had Three Arms* and Robert Drivas, who played the title role and also found the financial backing to put the production together.

After a lengthy introduction and several halting delays, Himself begins a lecture by attacking the audience. Soon he is off on his talk about his own dismemberment. As he says, "I find it hard sometimes to distinguish between my *self*-disgust and my disgust with others." Gradually he tells his life story: his birth, his bisexual schoolboy crushes (on a "Nabokovian girl-child" and "the captain of the swimming team"), and on to his graduation. The play is strewn with cross-references from literature and life. Suddenly, while speaking about his parents, Himself quotes James Agee: "One was my Mother who was good to me; one was my Father who was good to me." After getting a job in advertising, the character marries and the couple has three children. Then, while taking a shower, he discovers a small bump between his shoulder blades, which a doctor identifies as the beginning of a third arm. When Himself is told that because of the appendage he can become world famous, he responds by describing the previous, limited reach of his ambition. He wanted to have an ordinary life, the fulfillment of the American Dream. All this is interrupted by the Third Arm, which launches him into a public career endorsing products, making public appearances, and writing his life story. "With great celebrity," he says, "the thighs of the world swing open," and he becomes sexually insatiable. Then, as suddenly as it appeared, the third arm begins to disappear; and with that act, all his fame is removed, and he finds himself over $2 million in debt. He declares bankruptcy, has a nervous breakdown, and drinks too much. Finally he cries to the audience, "You owe me something, you people! You loved me in the good times, and you're fucking well going to love me now!!"

In June 1982, the play opened at the Coconut Grove Playhouse in Florida, a theatrical setting with a lingering pall. In 1956 *Waiting for Godot* had its disastrous American premiere there. Albee rewrote some of his play and in October it reopened at the Goodman Theater in Chicago. The following April it was on Broadway, not under the auspices of Barr, but produced by Allen Klein, one of the Beatles' managers. There were three actors in the cast, Drivas, William Prince, and Patricia Kilgarriff playing a diversity of men and women (priest, doctor, parents). From Coconut Grove to the Goodman to Broadway, the reviews got worse and worse.

The play, Albee said later, was meant to be "a slashing act of aggression." It was slashing; it was also lacking in humor. Despite a few randomly amusing lines, it was, in Himself's words, an "oh-so-sad-sad story." The show was further undercut by the fact that it was on a Broadway stage instead of a small studio. Because it was a play by Albee, there were, as always, expectations. Before opening night, Jonathan Thomas told Albee that the word of mouth on the play was very bad and that the reviews were going to be awful. Albee remained, in O'Malley's words, "adamant, pigheaded." It was not so much that he was falsely confident but that he apparently did not care or did not care to think about what the reception would be. On opening night, he went to see a Monty Python movie.

In common with that third arm, *The Man Who Had Three Arms* might have quietly disappeared if critics had not taken it as a personal insult. Frank

Rich in the *Times* called it "a temper tantrum in two acts" and accused the author of "virulent and gratuitous misogyny" and "narcissistic arrogance," saying that the lost third arm represented the atrophied talent of a playwright "in mid-career crisis." Albee vigorously objected: the play was not about him, or about any artist. It dealt with an advertising man, "a talentless person raised to high levels because he grew a third arm. That's not me." And the third arm was literal not metaphorical. That may have been his intention but it was disingenuous not to anticipate the inevitability of the autobiographical interpretation. Adman or artist, the title character, in common with the author, had had great early success, followed by failure and public vilification.

Having received the most vicious reviews of his career, Albee did not get drunk and put his hand through a window. He bought a copy of the *Times* in Times Square, read the deadly notice, and said to Jonathan Thomas, "Oh well. That's that. Let's go home." His reaction, said Albee, was a case of self-protection. "If you realize the roof has fallen in, you don't just stand there. You walk away." For solace, he remembered a Peter Arno cartoon in *The New Yorker*: "An experimental plane has crashed in the distance. There are several large, large generals looking down with great anger and disdain at a little man with a moustache and a furled umbrella, who walks away, saying to himself, 'Well, back to the drawing board.'"

The Man Who Had Three Arms closed after sixteen performances, Albee's third quick Broadway closing in a row. During the whole process, Drivas was HIV positive and he soon died of AIDS. Against all criticism, Albee continued to like the play, although he eventually rewrote the ending. "I didn't soften it," he said. "It's still about false gods and the superstar mentality. There's a certain amount of revenge and self-justification during the course of that play. It's a very angry play." In the revised version, Himself still rips off his shirt and swears at the audience. Then the Woman consoles him and notices that something is growing out of his back again, not an arm but a foot. "It doesn't destroy anything about the play," said Albee, "but it makes it more ironic and funny." After this debacle, it was to be a decade before his plays were seen again in New York.

Somehow Albee survived the triple disaster, and eventually, with Jonathan Thomas's help, he completely stopped drinking. Searching for reasons for the cessation, Thomas says, "He just didn't want to present himself as a drunk. That's why he stopped—it was the ego. He didn't want people to see that." When Albee later learned that he had diabetes, he accepted the fact that alcohol was no longer even a possibility. Albee shifts the credit for his recovery to Thomas. "Jonathan has been a stabilizing force in my life," he said. "I don't think that I would have stopped drinking had I not been with him." Asked to be specific about that help, he laughed and said, "It's very hard when you're drunk all the time to know how somebody is helping you. If I was drinking at eleven in the morning, he would just be patient." And more than anything else, his patience paid off. "I don't think anyone else would have put up with it all." Asked to reflect on his partner, Albee said, "He's very complex. I don't mean this in any pejorative sense: He's a totally good person." By that, he meant that he was not a pollyanna, but completely trustful and giving. "I don't think he's capable of betraying anybody."

As Albee stopped drinking, the "demented other self" disappeared, and in its place, he resumed a mask of shyness—or was it withdrawal on several levels? When he and Thomas would go out to dinner, often Albee would not say a word, eating and not drinking and, said Thomas, "with nothing to contribute. I don't think he was taking anything in. He wasn't particularly interested in people. It was OK when we were at home. But whenever we went out in public, he would just clam right up. It took a long time for Edward to get used to the fact he wasn't drinking and for him to start interacting with people again. Then he started writing and I think that's when the writing became more vibrant."

For Albee, it was "back to the drawing board," and also a most serious attempt to find a life and a livelihood away from New York. While keeping Manhattan as his home base, he moved to regional and university theater and to other countries, beginning with Austria, as the English language theater in Vienna became a producer of his work. Countering the Broadway antagonism, he went on the road, giving lectures and accepting residencies and commissions from various colleges and universities. "His primary focus at that point was getting out of town," said Glyn O'Malley. He remained stubborn about New York. Were a play of his to be done there—and none were—it could only be done on Broadway. As O'Malley said, "He thought, fuck 'em all, I'll go where I'm wanted." It was O'Malley's observation that Albee "only knew who he was when he was in the presence of one of his plays. Otherwise he was grabbing at something that he seemed not to be anymore. I never had the impression that he had thrown in the towel or was resting on his laurels. He exhibited a kind of toughness and tenacity that amazed me."

Because of his early successes, he remained a highly regarded figure on campuses, gathering honorary degrees along with artistic honors. He was courted by academics who scrutinized his work, the good and the bad, finding good in the bad and subjecting the plays (even *The Man Who Had Three Arms*) to a continuing process of reevaluation. With a resilience and a sense of self-worth, he survived outside of the commercial theater and isolated from a critical contingent that followed its hostility with disinterest. His outside activities—teaching young playwrights, speaking out on political issues—all helped to sustain him. He did not stop writing. But after the missteps of *Lolita* and *The Man Who Had Three Arms*, the one imitative, the other self-indulgent, he had to find his own voice again.

The process was gradual and also experimental. Freed from the burdens of New York productions, he could take chances. He could fail and few would take notice. He returned to writing one-acts, and when they were presented even in an out-of-the-way environment, they took on a greater importance. In 1983 there was *Finding the Sun*, written on commission for the University of Northern Colorado. A roundelay about couples decoupling on a beach, it has a melancholic air. It is one of his few plays with overtly gay characters. Albee staged it in Colorado, then at the University of California in Irvine. At Irvine, it was on a double bill with another new Albee one-act, *Walking*, one of his most abstract efforts. In *Box*, there is a setting but no actors, simply the off-stage voice of a woman. *Walking* begins on a beach with no actors, with the offstage voice of a woman, saying "Walk with me!" Then inanimate objects speak. The voice of a rock and of a plant echo that of the Woman, who soon appears onstage as do characters identified as a White Boy and a Black Boy. In a long monologue, the Woman talks about riding horses in the morning and then having an affair with a stable boy, about posing for an artist and then having an affair with him. This is followed by the White Boy's story of incest. Albee saw one performance of *Walking*, decided he was dissatisfied with it, and closed the show. It is, he said, one of his abandoned works, along with *Another Part of the Zoo* and such juvenalia as *The Dispossessed*, the early version of *The American Dream*.

In 1986, he was looking into the possibility of doing *Finding the Sun* in New York when Tina Howe's *Coastal Disturbances* opened at the Second Stage. The two plays shared a beach setting and "some of the same general preoccupations." Albee decided to postpone a New York production of his play "for a while, at least until the sea air clears." *Finding the Sun* finally was done in New York in 1994 as part of the Signature Theater season of Albee plays.

While Albee was at the University of Northern Colorado, Sidney Berger, the head of the School of Theater at the University of Houston, invited him to do a play in Texas. After Albee directed three of his one-acts, he was asked to stay on and teach. Albee soon became a valued member of the Houston faculty (along with José Quintero), teaching playwriting and, eventually, dramatic literature. Houston became a second cultural home for him. He rented an apartment there, visited local galleries and museums, and occasionally worked at the Alley Theater. Every spring he was in residence at the university. Although he is reluctant to say that the teaching helped to compensate for the diminishment of his reputation in New York, it did provide him with a focus, and perhaps, more important, it gave him a substantial regular income.

For Albee, there were several disturbing events in 1984. Crossing a London street against the traffic, Alan Schneider was struck by a motorcycle and died—a grave loss to both Albee and Beckett, each of whom had come to trust the director as an interpreter, or rather, as a conduit for his work. At a memorial for Schneider, Albee named the things the director taught him: "Never direct a play you don't respect." "Get to know the play you are going to direct, thoroughly, long before rehearsals start." "Hire the right actor, one capable of vanishing into a role and filling it." "Listen to your author." About the last point, he explained, "He *did* write the play, and he may just possibly have some insights and good ideas; in other words, you are not there to correct Beckett or breathe death into Chekhov." Other friends died that year: William Ritman, who had been the set designer for many of his plays; two friends in the art world, the artist Lee Krasner and the gallery director Betty Parsons; and John Joseph, one of his favorite teachers at Choate and a regular correspondent through the years. In 1984, Albee found himself writing memorial tributes. About Ritman, he said that he was "calm, sensible, creative, a still, sure presence in the natural chaos."

Albee continued to be a protector of his early work. That summer, a young director, Dov Fahrer, announced plans to present an all-male version of *Virginia Woolf* at Theater Arlington, a small theater in Arlington, Texas. Over the years, there have been people who have suggested that Albee originally wrote the play about two homosexual couples. On several occasions the possibility of an all-male production had been raised, once with an all-star cast (Henry Fonda, Richard Burton, Warren Beatty, and Jon Voight). Albee has always been adamant that the play is about two heterosexual couples, and he has steadfastly blocked any attempt to betray that concept. Fahrer falsely declared that it had been Albee's idea to have the play performed by four men, and when that approach "wouldn't sell," he changed the characters to two men and two women.

When Albee learned about the production, he issued an unequivocal condemnation through the Dramatists Play Service, which informed the director of Theater Arlington that the approach "constitutes a gross distortion of the intentions and context of an established piece and reflects a kind of arrogance for which there can be no excuse." Albee later explained that several aspects of the play, such as Honey's hysterical pregnancy, would make a homosexual version seem ludicrous. His agent, Esther Sherman, demanded that the show be closed, and it was closed, with "sincere apologies" from the theater. Some years previously a director in France had wanted to do a production of *The Zoo Story* with two actresses as Peter and Jerry. Albee politely declined, saying that he could "see no virtue having the play performed in any other way than as originally written."

When he was the artistic director of the McCarter Theater at Princeton University, Nagle Jackson had the idea of freely mixing plays by Marlowe, Goethe, and Moliere into a compilation called *Faustus in Hell*, a circumnavigation of the world of John Faustus. He also commissioned seven writers (Christopher Durang, Amlin Gray, John Guare, Romulus Linney, Joyce Carol Oates, Jean-Claude van Itallie, and Albee) to write the Seven Deadly Sins, one sin, of course, for each writer. Jackson inserted the result as a play within the play.

Albee contributed "Envy," and it was the choicest of the seven small sketches, a light-hearted sendup of authorial aspirations, its tone a direct contrast to that of *The Man Who Had Three Arms*. In Albee's "Envy," a man is reading an unnamed popular book and covets the prose style ("safely decadent; seemingly profound; soft targets, blunted barbs"). He is so engrossed that he is slow to notice the presence of Faust (Harry Hamlin), who enters and watches. Still not noticing, the self-involved protagonist says, "Oh, God! How I aspire to the middlebrow! I don't want to be among the truly great—I couldn't bear the height, the cold, the expectation." His dream, he says, is "to envy no man," to tread a tightrope with a safety net below, to have the knowledge that "what is needed is what is wanted, that accommodation is its own reward." Then he says, in the play's pivotal line, "To know one's limits and aim a little lower." Finally he notices his mysterious visitor, recognizing him as "Goethe's boy." With that, he changes his tune and begins to wonder what it would be like to be famous—like Faust. He starts quizzing his guest, asking him to tell him about happiness and the condition of his soul. One hesitates to overread this vignette, except to suggest that for Albee accommodation has no reward, and there has always been the temptation to try harder even if it only means, in Beckett's words, to "fail better."

Coincidentally, in 1985 Albee succumbed to a small Faustian temptation. For a fee of £10,000 (about $16,000) he wrote a short story to be used in an

advertising campaign for Volvo cars. The piece was to be in the nature of a fable on the subject of long-term planning, and it was to be between five hundred and seven hundred words. Although Albee and the other writers Volvo
solicited were left free in terms of what they chose to write about and how
they chose to write it, the piece had to mention Volvo.

On commission, Albee wrote about a future Utopia. He began, "Once
upon a time, many many years from now, the world was a better place." There
were no more armies or nuclear weapons. People emerged from hiding and
created a universal language and an international government. Poets, sculptors, and composers were placed in positions of authority, which was a kind of
poetic justice. Politically and economically, true socialism prevailed. Workers
had a say in how businesses were run. The result was pride of accomplishment and dignity. Archaeologists digging in the frozen north, searching for
mistakes of the past, found a time capsule proving that—once upon a time—
"inequity was rife, selfishness abounded, duplicity festered," and all portents
were ignored. But in the time capsule there was information that one organization had run counter to the prevailing winds. "Their workers worked well,
were happy, had pride in their work." "Who were those people?" asked one of
the Elders. "What were they called?" "Volvo," said an archaeologist, "loud
and clear." Volvo rejected the piece, a final and untenable act of criticism. Albee protested and was paid his full fee.

Although the piece was written as a commercial assignment, the political
point of view expressed was deeply important to Albee. Increasingly, he had
become an activist for the rights of artists, joining Arthur Miller, Harold Pinter, and others in speaking out against censorship and in support of dissidents
around the world. With Miller and Pinter, there was underlying political content in their plays. Albee's concerns about repression and bigotry rarely appeared in his work (*The Death of Bessie Smith* was an exception), but as with
his fellow playwrights, those concerns were always embedded in his con-
science. Through his work in PEN, ITI (the International Theater Institute),
the Dramatists Guild, and on his various international trips, he was able to
become a spokesman for his ideas.

In 1985, William Luers, his guide during his first trip to the Soviet Union,
was the U.S. ambassador in Prague. Luers encouraged Albee to bring in a
production to the Czech Theater Institute. The choice was an adaptation of
Sam Shepard's *Hawk Moon*, which Albee had previously presented at the
English Theater in Vienna. Czechoslovakia was still under Communist rule.
The playwright Vaclav Havel was an outsider and his country's most famous
dissident. Because of local restrictions, the production was not advertised and

the audience was to be small and by invitation: about fifteen people from the U.S. Embassy plus a guest list prepared by the host country that was intended to be limited to the most conservative representatives of official state theaters. Trying to skirt the restrictions, Luers and his associates notified members of the dissident theater community about the performance. These artists gathered in the courtyard leading to the theater, hoping to elude the guards posted at the doors and sneak inside. Albee went out into the courtyard to talk to Havel, whom he had met secretly that afternoon.

Luers was supposed to introduce Albee, who would then introduce the play. With the performance about to begin, the institute chairman locked the gate to the theater, leaving Albee, Havel, and others outside. Albee shouted to the chairman: "You're going to have a hard time keeping your crowd happy if you don't let me in." His words were translated and the official reluctantly unlocked the gate. Albee entered, leading more than fifteen dissidents into the theater. Havel, though, waited outside and, according to Glyn O'Malley, finally slipped in at the end of the performance, shielded from view by his compatriots. "Everyone knew he was in the room," said O'Malley, "but no one could see him. The tension and energy were electric." After the performance, there was a dinner at the U.S. Embassy. At one end of the table Luers sat with the officials; at the other end were Albee, Havel, and his colleagues. It was, said Luers, the first time that the two opposing groups had had dinner together, although they conducted separate conversations.

For several years, Albee had been on the board of directors of ITI, and in the late 1980s he was elected president of the American branch, with Martha Coigney, who had been in that post, ascending to the presidency of the international body. Although the position was unpaid and the duties relatively limited, Albee immediately became an activist. He also made large financial contributions to the organization, in effect giving grants to ITI.

"As president," said Ms. Coigney, "he's very demanding and very critical about what we should be doing. I feel like a graduate student with John Houseman the professor. He's demanding the same way Harold Clurman was demanding. They have such regard for what they believe in that they want everything to be perfect. When Harold would talk, he would get angry because sometimes he thought people were belittling theater. He would support mistakes, he would support lunacy, but he would not support diminution of anything to do with theater. The same with Edward. The way he speaks is very dry and understated, but underneath there is a huge ongoing passion. If he yells at me, I can't imagine what he does to himself. I think Edward is a ferocious American. He is a curmudgeon. He's very impatient and furious at stupidities, but he's a real patriot. He wishes an enormous amount for theater in this country—and for this country. He wishes it could be the country that it has the potential to be." She said that one of the reasons he is so effective leading campaigns against censorship and repression is because of his name recognition and because his work was first done outside of America. He is "a tactical internationalist" and "a fanatic protector of playwrights." Speaking to representatives from Eastern Europe at one ITI Congress, he made a strong statement about the need to respect copyrights, declaring that he made a living as a playwright and all countries should pay for the rights to his plays and plays by other writers.

In one of his other roles, Albee was head of the Brandeis University Creative Arts program, inviting panels of experts to give annual awards to talented people in the arts. One of the prizes he had encouraged and took particular pride in was for Notable Achievement in the Creative Arts, presented in 1985 to William Shawn, the editor of *The New Yorker*. As a great admirer of Shawn and of *The New Yorker*, Albee himself wrote the citation for the award. Shawn did not attend the ceremony, asking Brendan Gill to accept for him, but he sent a note to Albee thanking him for "the perfection and beauty of your writing in the citation."

Albee's work for Brandeis was an indication of the broadness of his interest in the arts, which extended far beyond theater and deep into the visual arts. Beginning with works by Milton Avery, he had built up a substantial collection of art and, gradually, came to know many artists: Marisol, Jasper Johns, Lee Krasner, and Mark Rothko. Rothko would occasionally visit Albee at his home in Montauk. Asked how well he knew him, Albee said, "I don't know how well anybody knew Mark. He would sit there by the ocean at the house, with his bowler hat and tie and jacket and be very quiet. He didn't talk much. We had a perfectly pleasant relationship." When they talked, it was often about art, about, for example, Milton Avery, whom Rothko said had influenced him. In contrast, Albee said when playwrights get together they never talk about their art. They talk about "money, sex, and food."

Of all the celebrated artists in his life, Louise Nevelson was the closest friend, although he quickly adds, "She was always doing a performance. Nevelson in public was Nevelson in private, and even at home she never came downstairs without all the makeup." As an admirer of her work, he wrote the introduction to the catalogue for her 1980 retrospective at the Whitney Museum of American Art. One reason why Nevelson wanted him to write his essay was her feeling for *Tiny Alice*, which "with its specific construction of a miniature house onstage has been very important to the images in my work." Inspired by *Tiny Alice*, she created a series of small "dream houses," which led to the walk-in environment "Mrs. N's Palace." In the catalogue, Albee wrote, "Nevelson feels that she began making her 'worlds' as an alternative space, so to speak—to create for herself a fathomable reality in the midst of the outside chaos. What has happened, of course, is that the private has become public, the refuge accessible to all." Something similar could be said about Albee, himself.

17
Frankie

We let him come, but we never forgive him.

*H*E played his role: the dutiful son. She played her role: the proud
mother. They were together again. Every other week he visited her at her
home in White Plains and later at the Westchester Country Club, where she
had become a permanent resident. They met in New York for lunch or dinner at La Caravelle or "21" Club, restaurants that remained her favorites. Her
chauffeur would drive her to her son's house in Montauk or to his loft in
Tribeca. At holiday time and other special occasions—special was whenever
Frankie Albee was there—he invited friends over, mostly women, friends like
Elaine Steinbeck, Joanna Steichen, Lee Krasner, Irene Worth, and also
Richard Barr, and he cooked. He had become a masterly chef and went out of
his way to cater to his mother's tastes, preparing bacon and eggs for breakfast
and planning lavish luncheon and dinner parties. When they were in Montauk, sometimes they would go to Krasner's house or to other friends for dinner. Jonathan Thomas was often excluded. When Frankie visited Montauk
for a weekend, he would move out to avoid conflict, sometimes visiting his
family in Canada. Occasionally their paths crossed. Jonathan would join Edward for Thanksgiving dinner with her at the Westchester Country Club and
even for lunch at La Caravelle. She would be polite while never acknowledging him as her son's partner. When Frankie was present, homosexuality was
never discussed and the brief times that it was mentioned, she would say
something derogatory about "fairies," like her brother-in-law George
Vigouroux. (For his part Albee has never met Jonathan Thomas's family—he

has two sisters—but he has occasionally spoken to Jonathan's father on the telephone from Canada.)

When Frankie visited, she was at the head of the table and the center of the conversation. As always, opinions about her varied. "She was hideous," said Glyn O'Malley, "a big dragon. She would sit there in her Pauline Trigere outfit, the full makeup and the hair, the paste jewelry, drinking scotch. She was an extremely cold woman." "She was the grande dame," said Joanna Steichen. "Life circled around her. Her majesty came in and was seated and graciously greeted everyone and was catered to. She directed the conversation because we all knew there were areas of life one didn't discuss with Frankie present. She had all the prejudices of her time and from her youth. It's important to remember that she was certainly close to eighty by the time I met her. She was a very controlling woman who liked to be independent. She was vain—and she was marvelous looking, beautifully groomed, enormous diamonds, well dressed. She seemed to have a new fur coat every year. In her manner, she was a combination of aristocrat and showgirl, although she'd never actually been a showgirl. She was very dignified, but there was also a little racy humor—an earthiness."

On the relationship between mother and son, Steichen said, "It was a great charade—absolutely charming, mildly affectionate, pleasant reminiscences. None of the bad stuff, none of the scrapes or difficulties. This was for public consumption; other people were present. But I doubt if they spoke any differently when they were alone. I didn't know about Frankie, but Edward is a very affectionate, loyal person, and I think he wanted to have a caring relationship with his mother. He put tremendous effort into it."

Mother and son also spent time together in Palm Beach, which Edward still hated. Both of them would dress up for formal dinner parties. Outwardly, the two were friendly, but they were never close friends. They never revealed secrets or deep feelings. There was too much "blood under the bridge." She would tell him stories about her youth, her friendship and rivalry with her sister, and about her marriage. He would listen and was encouraging. He filed away the stories in his memory bank. Some of the stories were candid, some were bawdy. He learned intimate details about his parents' sex life.

She told him that once she was sitting at her dresser in her boudoir, naked except for her pearls and her diamond bracelets. Her husband walked into the room. He was naked, too, except for an expensive diamond bracelet encircling his penis. "Do you want it?" he said, offering the bracelet in return for a sexual favor. When she rejected his advance, his penis wilted and the bracelet fell off into her lap. "Keep it," he said and turned and walked out of the room. Is this the kind of story a mother tells her son? He remembered it.

Occasionally they had arguments, sometimes in public. Edward would try to keep the conversation away from controversy: if possible, no talk about race, sex, or politics, or even about art. From *Tiny Alice* onward, she went to opening nights of his plays, but offered no opinions about the plays or the reviews they received. She seemed pleased to be his mother and sometimes introduced herself formally as "the mother of Edward Albee, the playwright." She introduced him as "my son, the playwright." In conversation, she referred to him as "Albee," as in "Albee thinks this."

Frankie became a fixture in his life. By not making demands, by not asking for too much, Edward could even enjoy her presence. Others seemed to like her: She could be amusing; she could also be malicious. At times, her resentment flared. As his friends observed, something was missing in their relationship. They were not really like mother and son, but more like distant relatives reunited after a long separation. They shared few memories. It would be difficult to imagine one saying to the other, do you remember when? When I found out I was adopted. When I locked Noel in the guinea pig pen. When I broke down in tears in church the first time I heard about the Crucifixion. When I fell in love for the first time. When I was sad sad sad and lonely at Lawrenceville. When I left home. Why didn't you listen to me? Why didn't you try to know me? Why didn't you tell me? She kept talking, some of it gossip, some of it remembrance of her own past, and always her son wanted more. He wanted to hear it all. He wanted everything; he expected nothing.

On January 20, 1984, Frances C. Albee signed a new will, leaving the bulk of her estate to her only child, Edward. There were small bequests to her secretary Concetta O'Donnell Sieniewicz; her housekeeper Wilma Buseta; her friends Elyce Brennan (her pink rhodacrosite and pearl necklace and pin), Ruth Aken (her emerald bead set of two necklaces, bracelet, and earrings), and June Todd (her entire lapis lazuli set, except for her lapis lazuli ring, plus $25,000)—and the children of Robert F. Bryan ($50,000), one of her lawyers. At her death, her son would receive $100,000, "as much or all as he shall select" of her furniture, furnishings, works of art, jewelry (except for those pieces specifically designated for friends), and other personal effects—and the remainder of her estate in trust during his lifetime. After Edward's death, the trust would be terminated and the remainder of the estate would be given in equal shares to United Hospital in Port Chester and Christ's Church in Rye. Her son, her friend William H. Todd, and her attorney Richard B. Cooper were named as executors.

Two years later, Frances C. Albee suddenly changed her mind. She had a new will drawn up and on February 6, 1986, she met with Cooper and two of his assistants, Mary E. Nelson and John A. Maraia, who were there to act as witnesses to the will. They met at Mrs. Albee's home at the Westchester Country Club. As Mrs. Albee sat at her writing desk, Cooper gave her a copy of the new will and passed copies to the others in the room. Before the actual reading, he quizzed her on it to test her mental capacity and, because she was decreasing the bequest to her son, to forestall legal action. He asked her to identify each beneficiary and the specifics of each bequest. In his notes, Maraia commented that at all times Mrs. Albee was alert and attentive: "I remember that I was thinking that if I live to be older than eighty, that I would hope to be as strong and capable of carrying on an intelligent conversation as is Mrs. Albee." When Cooper came to the passage in the will referring to her son, he asked her who Edward Albee was. She joked that she wondered that herself because she had recently seen a newspaper headline, WHO'S AFRAID OF EDWARD ALBEE.

Then Cooper asked her to read the first line of the will. She put on her glasses and read: "I, FRANCES C. ALBEE, residing in Rye, County of Westchester, State of New York, do hereby make, publish and declare this to be my Last Will and Testament, hereby revoking all wills and codicils heretofore made by me."

Cooper continued reading the will, with Mrs. Albee and the others following along on their copies:

"To my son, EDWARD F. ALBEE, only if he survives me, $250,000."

That was the sole provision for her son. Mrs. Albee acknowledged the fact that under this will Edward was receiving less than in her previous will. What she did not say was that it was drastically less, a minimum bequest. In the original will, he was the primary beneficiary. In the new will, the cash bequest was about 10 percent of her entire estate, the bulk of which was now going, in three equal shares, to three institutions, United Hospital in Port Chester, Christ's Church in Rye, and the New York Chapter of the Arthritis Fund. The money to the hospital would go to the "Reed and Frances Albee Fund," and each of the others would be "in memory of my late husband, Reed A. Albee."

There were other changes, for the most part increasing bequests to the other beneficiaries. Edward was excluded as an executor. Cooper and William H. Todd were now the only executors. When Cooper reached the sixth and final paragraph about the powers of the executors, Mrs. Albee laughed and said she might live a long time and, if so, she might want to buy the Westchester Country Club.

Finishing the reading, Cooper brought the original to Mrs. Albee's desk and asked, "Frankie, is this your will?" She replied, "I certainly hope so." She laughed, as did the lawyer and the two witnesses. Cooper asked her to initial each page. She said, "How do you want me to do it?" He said, "The way you always do." She took out an envelope and, for practice, with a grand flourish of her pen, wrote her initials on it. Then she initialed the will page by page: FCA, for Frances Cotter Albee. FCA, she said, with a laugh, meant "Finally Caught Albee." The laugh was an echo of her young womanhood.

One month later, Mrs. Albee added a codicil, increasing the bequest to the children of Robert Bryan to $100,000 and changing the division of the residuary estate. Instead of going in three equal parts to the church, the hospital, and the Arthritis Fund, she decided to divide it into six parts, with half of it going to the hospital, one third to the Arthritis Fund, and one sixth to the church. In October, apparently at Mrs. Albee's request, Cooper sent her another copy of the will, with this pointed comment, "As you know, your previous Will left your entire residuary estate to Edward, in trust, with the principal to be given to the Hospital and the Church." She knew; the change was intentional. Until his mother died, Edward was unaware of the new will.

A friend later reported that Mrs. Albee had explained her action by saying that Edward had enough money, "he doesn't need any more." But in reality one conversation may have been crucial to the change in the will. Jane Volk, an old friend in Palm Beach and someone who also remained close to Edward, had taken Frankie aside for a serious talk. Volk told her that she would be able to see Edward more and have a better life if only she just accepted the fact that he was gay. Of course Frankie already knew this, but she did not want to hear it and she certainly did not want to confront it. She said she did not want Jane ever to mention it again. Her son surmises, "After that, she called the lawyer pretty quickly."

During the next two years, Edward, unaware of his mother's new will, remained solicitous. Frankie took friends to lunch at expensive restaurants and charged them to her son's account. Edward saw her and talked to her frequently. When he visited her, he brought her favorite things: orange dipped in chocolate, bouquets of freesia. She continued to make regular visits to Montauk. Then her memory began to fail. In 1988, she planned to come for a weekend in August. Ten days before the visit, he called her to remind her. She said, "No, I'm coming this weekend." He said, "You can't. I'm not going to be here. We're going to be away. It's next weekend." He heard her maid say, "No, Mrs. Albee, it's next weekend." She didn't come either weekend. She never came to Montauk again.

One morning soon after, at 4 A.M., she telephoned Edward in Montauk and said she had gone to the hospital. "Edward, you've got to come at once.

They're doing things to me." He drove from Montauk to Port Chester, arriving at 9:30 in the morning. The Todds were there. His mother was sitting up in bed, bright-eyed, cheerful. "Why, Edward, what a surprise." In March 1989, she took a turn for the worse; she was bedridden. Edward visited her. When he left, he kissed her, a peck on the cheek, no hug, no warmth, but a kiss nevertheless. He had the flu that day. "It is my ironic memory that I breathed on her and killed her. That was not necessarily my intention. After I left, it did occur to me that perhaps I shouldn't have gotten so close to her. She was so fragile. But I didn't go up there to kill the woman." She returned to the Westchester Country Club, then several weeks later moved back into the hospital and came down with pneumonia. Her son visited her there. She was "more or less comatose," but when he placed a bouquet of freesia under her nose, she seemed to sniff them. The doctor told Albee there was nothing more that could be done and perhaps it was time to let her go. Several days later Albee was called back to the hospital, but by the time he arrived she had died. "Nobody was in the room except the chauffeur and the maid," he recalled, paraphrasing a line from *Three Tall Women*. He concluded, "Final irony."

In 1963, the year after *Virginia Woolf* opened on Broadway, Albee began writing a novel, but only got as far as the first chapter (which was published in *Esquire*). In that chapter, the protagonist at fifty-seven faced the death of his mother in a strangely impersonal manner, "watching over" rather than "attending" the event. The room where she has died was empty except for "everything about her." The passage ended, "And is it possible to distinguish between the memory of a perfume, the things it accompanies, and the perfume itself?" He never finished the novel, but the writing of the chapter was prophetic. He watched himself watching his mother.

After his mother's death, Albee chose a casket and arranged for the funeral at Christ's Church. The funeral was attended by local friends. Edward was the only relative. "I remember I had to go up and touch the coffin. I was expected to stand there for a moment. I didn't feel any emotion whatever. I remember it as a theatrical performance. People were watching. I had to stay there with my hands on the coffin, and I had to sigh. I remember watching myself do it. But I'm not making the comment that it was phony and I was doing it for them." There were no eulogies. Then everyone drove up to the cemetery at Valhalla, where the Albees have a lavish mausoleum with a stained glass window by Stanford White, a window Albee coveted as a work of art. His mother was buried next to her husband, her husband's parents, and her mother. "There is one place left," said Edward. "I wonder who it's for." Then he answered his question: "I plan to be cremated and buried with the dogs and cats in Montauk. Totally illegal: You're not allowed to bury human beings on private property. I plan to be sprinkled there."

He tried to persuade the *Times* to print an obituary, but the decision was made: Frances Albee was of little importance outside of her son's life. Being the mother of a famous playwright was not enough to justify an obituary.

The lawyer called him in for a reading of the will. Fifteen different wills, dating back to the death of Reed Albee, were spread out on a long table. Every few years Frankie Albee had written a new one. In the early ones, Edward the prodigal was to receive nothing. After their reconciliation, he was to receive $250,000. Then her bequest to her son escalated to the will in 1986 when he became the primary beneficiary and was to receive almost everything for his lifetime. Finally there was the last will, the last message from his mother, a parting act of disloyalty.

Cooper sent Albee a copy of that will and the first and only codicil, reasserting the fact that he is "the principal legatee under Article SECOND of the Will." Edward realized that this was a total rewrite. He might be his mother's "principal legatee," but he was no longer her principal heir. He had been replaced by the hospital, the church, and the Arthritis Fund. While selling her jewelry, Frankie had also been drawing from her principal. Her estate had been depleted, but still was substantial. Edward did some quick addition. The three organizations would share more than $1.5 million, with $615,000 divided among him and the other minor legatees. On the letter from the lawyer, next to his figures, he wrote two words, "residual" and "aberration." The residual estate went to institutions at a distance from her life and, by his estimation, his mother's act was aberrant.

Although he later insisted that he did not remember having "any important emotional reaction," it was a devastating blow. He referred to it as a disinheritance—"again." It was not the money—he certainly had enough money and the $250,000 was a sizeable sum—it was the rejection, the final closing down of mother against son. Were their more than twenty years of reconciliation a lie? The cruelty was unimaginable. He was no longer to receive any of his mother's remaining possessions and personal effects, and he had been removed as an executor of her estate. This meant that in her eyes he was not as close to her as her lawyer or the church she rarely visited. "Obviously she was incapable of getting rid of her deeply held prejudices and still had never forgiven me for walking out." With her money, she could have established a foundation, perhaps one that would have encouraged artists and writers. Presented with that possibility, he responded with a catch-22. If she had started a foundation, "I would have been enormously startled. Then I would have realized that she had lost her mind. I would have contested the will: Obviously the woman is mad."

What had he done—or not done—to deserve this? It was another act of abandonment. Perhaps he remembered the words of James Agee: "One is my mother who is good to me." Who is his mother? Should he challenge the will? He was angry, but still dutiful. After the funeral, he sent a $500 contribution to Christ's Church and received a thank-you note from the Reverend Edward Johnston: "It was a pleasure to meet you even though the circumstances were difficult, and I want to say how much I admire the thoroughness with which you had thought out the kind of service you wanted for your mother."

A letter arrived from La Caravelle, billing him for $226.50, a charge dating back to 1987. As he had before, he asked for photocopies of the bills with his signature and suggested they may have been charges incurred by his mother. He paid the bill. Among her personal effects was a valuable crystal chandelier he had once loaned her. He claimed it and immediately sent it to Sotheby's for auction. Her pearls were gone; he thought she had sold them. The lapus lazuli ring mysteriously disappeared. William Todd gave Albee two boxes from Frankie's home. In them, Edward found photographs, clippings, trophies, and his mother's birth certificate (proving that she was born in 1897, had taken one year off her age, and was ninety-two not ninety-one when she died).

Deep inside one box were documents from the Alice Chapin Adoption Nursery and Surrogates Court, New York County. The documents indicated that he had been placed with his foster parents, Reed and Frances Albee, on March 30, 1928, eighteen days after his birth, and that he had been adopted by them on February 1, 1929. Reading the papers, he discovered that his natural father had abandoned his natural mother and that his birth name was Edward Harvey. It was at this point that, for the first time, he started thinking more seriously about trying to track down his real parents. "How did I get this way?" he wondered. "Where did I develop this peculiar mind?" What part did heredity play in his life?

Despite the years of bitter resentment, he still had to come to terms with a woman who shadowed him in life and now seemed to haunt him in death. Soon he would write a play about her, and it would not be a story of revenge. Instead it would be filled with understanding and compassion, along with dark humor. In a curious twist of fate, the play about his mother would revive and retrieve his career. It was a play he could write only after she had died. Her death gave him the freedom to write about her.

18

A Tall Woman

Sometimes I wonder why we all go through our lives
without touching one another very much.

I N 1989, the year that Albee's mother died, Richard Barr also died. Although they had had their differences, throughout their lives Albee and Barr remained loyal friends and Albee was always aware that he owed Barr a great debt, not just for producing so many of his plays on Broadway, but for being faithful to the spirit of the work. Howard Moss, another close friend, had died in 1987. These deaths, more than that of his mother, left him with a sense of personal bereavement. In his eulogy of Barr, he said, "Richard had two theories: 'excellence will win out' and 'the theatre belongs to the playwright,'" and not to the director, actor, theater owner, critic, dramaturg, or audience. "There is an historical continuum of pertinence and excellence in the theatre as an art form and it is the playwright who is the generator of it all. Brave theories; brave man."

Teaching at the University of Houston and encouraging hopeful playwrights soon became a major part of Albee's life. Every fall for more than ten years, he received—and read—approximately 150 plays. As he says, "That dreaded moment: A huge box of manuscripts arrives." He read them all and excised the hopeless, those who seemed to want to limit their work and be commercial, those who wanted to write screenplays, and those who thought "maybe I should take Albee's course." From the submissions, he chose a small class, usually about twelve. "If I'm going to work with a young playwright," he said, "it must be somebody who I think is a playwright—not someone pretending to be a playwright—and someone whose talent and mistakes are interesting. I'm interested in making the playwright understand exactly what he's doing and in having his work exposed exactly as he intended it. That's the only way the playwright can learn something. I don't know whether that's teaching. You can guide. You can shepherd. I suppose you can Mamet, for that matter. But I don't think you can teach anybody who is not a playwright how to be himself." He tells his students that if they want some teachers, they should look to Chekhov, Pirandello, Beckett, and Brecht. "Every time you go to see a famous play in Houston, read it and imagine a production that you see when you read it. Don't always assume that a production you see is an accurate representation of the play." In writing their own work, the students are urged to challenge themselves to the point at which they might fail. "As Dick Barr used to say, 'Move off into the unknown.' "

The plays were read in the class, followed by open discussion. Some of the students would later move into Albee's second class, a smaller group of about five who would have their plays staged. Kevin Cunningham, a playwright who studied with him and later went on to become an assistant at Albee's Montauk arts colony, the William Flanagan Memorial Creative Persons Center, says quite simply, "He's probably the best teacher I've had." He credits him with "a hands-on" approach to teaching: "He's very direct in his criticism. For a long time, he's pushed me to pare back to essentials." In his teaching as in his writing, Albee has "an unerring instinct for the inevitable." At one point, he also taught a course in the history of theater. In it, he showed videos of plays by Chekhov, Ibsen, Pirandello, and a particular favorite of the class, Wilder's Our Town. As a teacher, he continued his self-education. "I think I teach to learn," he said. In class, he could hear himself "articulating things that I didn't know I knew or hadn't thought about the need to articulate." Sidney Berger, the head of the university's theater program, often sits in on Albee's class. As he says, "I think he's got a stake in developing these young playwrights."

Earlier in his career, he had often directed secondary productions of his own plays, but beginning with Seascape, he had occasionally staged a premiere. Increasingly, during this period, he directed his own work and less frequently the work of others (including Beckett). Friends and associates are willing to express their criticism of Albee as a director, but prefer not to speak about the subject on the record. The criticism is that though Albee knows text, he is unable to approach a play from the perspective of the actor, in contrast, for example, to Harold Pinter, who was an actor before he was a playwright and understands the problems of the performer. Albee himself is clear that when he directs he is operating as an independent agent. As he said, "When I am directing a play of mine, I have frequent conversations with the playwright. Sometimes I have a few arguments with the playwright . . . I usually win them as director, because that is the job I have hired myself to do." Playwrights, he said, have a tendency to overwrite. "And I, as director, will say, 'Now Edward, you know you shouldn't have done that. Let me try it without it.' And I will say, 'Oh, all right, Edward, go ahead.' My basic instinct is that if anything in a play of mine bores me, it must go."

Teaching, lecturing, directing, accumulating honors (and honorary degrees), and having more than enough income from past successes and revivals, Albee was living well. After the disaster with Bernard Reis and the forced sale at a loss of treasured art objects to meet the demands of the I.R.S., he expanded his art collection. He had become a collector of some importance and frequented museums and galleries, buying art and also advising friends like William Lieberman, curator of twentieth-century art at the Metropolitan Museum. He was on Lieberman's Visiting Committee. "Edward probably sees more work of young artists around the country than anyone I know," said Lieberman. "He certainly knows the New York downtown scene very well. His eye for art is A-1. If he says I should see something, I see it. And I wouldn't do that for most people."

In art, as in everything else in life, Albee is self-taught. At various institutions, especially Choate, he found teachers who pointed him to areas of literature or painting or the arts in general. From his point of view, that was only the beginning of his education. "You have to learn how to make sense of what you receive and go on educating yourself. I like to think I'm always educating myself—every day."

Albee regards himself as less a collector than an "accumulator," gathering art objects that make him feel "comforted and stimulated," and defining his motivation in buying art as "informed joy." His loft in New York's Tribeca area is a spacious duplex apartment. The main floor looks like a gallery: an open room with a high ceiling filled with art and artifacts. Visitors have to be careful not to step on a work of art. African and pre-Columbian sculpture and abstract paintings share an environment with a Dogon granary door and an eighteenth-century French grain thresher. The paintings are by Kandinsky, Schwitters, Arp, Vuillard, Avery, and Chagall, among others. Regularly, packing crates with new purchases arrive on the hand-operated elevator. His life as an accumulator began after *The Zoo Story* and increased greatly after *Virginia Woolf*, when he was able to purchase Kandinsky and Avery. His interest in African art came later: "I began to realize how beautiful and energetic it was.

It might have had something to do with my feeling that the early part of most cultures is most interesting, before they become too sophisticated and decorative. All my intellectual decisions are, I suppose, highly intuitive." He said he likes "Tough art. I don't think anything that is merely decorative is worth the time." The test of toughness is one he applies to all art, including his plays. "I've said this to my students all the time. Art should expand the boundaries of the form and, simultaneously, it should change our perceptions. I despise restful art."

For more than a quarter of a century, Albee and Jonathan Thomas have been a couple. It is by far the longest of Albee's relationships. During this period, Thomas became a sculptor and painter and also took out his United States citizenship. As Thomas has gotten older, he has cultivated a "bandito" look, with a drooping moustache and often wearing a bandanna across his forehead. Because of Albee's teaching in Houston and other commitments, they are not always together. But when they are apart, they speak on the telephone two or three times a day. Asked how they have stayed together so long, Thomas answers, "I think we know each other. We can read each other's moods. We think alike now—ordering the same food at dinner and knowing each other so well. We're a family and we have this extended family of people. It's not as extended as he thinks it is. I think he tends to think he's a little bit closer to some people than they feel towards him."

About their differences, he said, "He's articulate. I'm inarticulate. I have a logical mind and his is illogical." Thomas is a whiz at the computer, but Albee refuses to learn how to use one and writes his plays in a barely legible longhand. On the other hand, Albee is very astute when it comes to contracts, and in his plays (such as *Three Tall Women*) he becomes, in Thomas's words, a logical thinker, following a clear line through an intricate plot. In common, they are "control freaks." When they have house guests, they plan the day for them. They want to know what's going to happen in advance, and when it's going to happen. Meals are not improvised.

In speaking about Albee, Thomas emphasizes several other traits: his extraordinary fondness for animals (habitually, he speaks to dogs he passes on the street) and his fierce sense of competition, at games and sports—backgammon, bridge (for many years he played bridge with Tallulah Bankhead and other friends), and tennis. He is always determined to win—and hates to lose. Albee is, Thomas said, a competitive driver, who cannot stand to follow other cars in traffic. He becomes irritated on the long drive from New York to Montauk and has been known to rush his car past the Hampton jitney. One time he was in such a hurry that he drove the jitney off the road.

Early in his life, Albee had a terrible fear of flying. Once during his drinking days, he fortified himself with five scotches at the airport before taking a plane to St. Martin. In order to conquer this fear, he went through a concerted course of challenging himself by going on every ride that frightened him at Coney Island, beginning with the rollercoaster. Since then, he has been much more relaxed about flying and is far more daring. Thomas said that Albee has been on all the major rollercoasters in amusement parks across the country. He has also gone hang gliding and has his eye on hot-air ballooning. Trying to explain Albee's later-in-life daredevilry, Thomas said, "He has this childlike sense of wonder that wasn't there when he was drinking." Some of it was there when he was a child: He would love to stand outdoors during a storm.

Since childhood, however, he has had a fear of being kidnapped. More than many other celebrities he has been pursued by stalkers, many of them women. One sent him a series of alarm clocks and, thinking they might be bombs, he was hesitant about opening the packages. Sometimes stalkers have appeared outside his home; on the opening night of *Lolita*, one stationed herself across the street from the theater. In the play *Fragments*, a man, speaking for the author, recalls his fearful childhood: "People tried to kidnap me, to steal me out of my carriage, come in windows in the dead of night, stand by my crib and breathe there in the dark, just staring at me." Every night before going to bed, Albee instinctively checks all doors and windows to make sure they are locked. He never says goodnight, but, as he did so many years ago with his nanny, he says, for luck, "See you in the morning."

Albee is frugal with his money, traveling business or first class and staying in deluxe hotels when producers and theaters are paying, but traveling economy and favoring small hotels when he is paying. In Paris, he and Thomas habitually stay at a Left Bank hotel that charges less than $100 a night. Once a friend was staying there on Albee's recommendation and saw Arthur Miller checking in. Are all playwrights cheap? Albee's two indulgences are art and landscaping his property in Montauk. Sometimes Thomas will suggest that they buy smaller trees. Albee responds: "I'm not going to be around to see them when they're ten feet tall. I want big now."

Beginning with his work in the late 1970s, Thomas has painted and sculpted in a totemic, abstract fashion. Although Albee can criticize his work just as Thomas criticizes his plays, Albee feels he is too close to offer an objective opinion to Thomas, except to say that he prefers his more nonrepresentational work. "If I thought he was a terrible artist," said Albee, "that would

be a hideous dilemma." That, however, is not the case. Thomas shows his art
work and sells reasonably well.

In an office at the rear of Albee's loft, David Briggs, the latest in a series of
young artists (in his case, a filmmaker) working as an assistant to the playwright, keeps track of his professional life, his engagements as well as the ap-
plications to his foundation in Montauk. The foundation has become a kind
of informal, cross-cultural version of the Albee-Barr-Wilder Playwrights Unit.
About two dozen poets, novelists, playwrights, painters, sculptors, and photographers are accepted every year and are given a month's residency in the
summer in a converted barn known appropriately as The Barn. Once a candidate is accepted, there are no requirements and few immediate services, not
even meals as at such colonies as MacDowell and Yaddo. The Barn is simply
a place to work. It is privately supported by Albee, who gave the foundation
stock and amateur rights to several of his early plays and has added other
money over the years. Albee chooses the painters and sculptors himself and
occasionally visits during the summer. He has left the operation of the foundation to Rex Lau and Diane Mayo, a married couple, both of whom are
artists. They met in 1979 when they came to look after Albee's dogs during his
absence—and stayed on as his loyal associates. Most of those in residence are
at the beginning of their careers.

Albee's house in Montauk has steadily expanded to include a tennis court
and pool and beautifully tended gardens with Japanese pines and hydrangeas.
He has two cars, a Mercedes, and a Jeep Cherokee. From the window of his
splendid study in which he does much of his writing, there is a vista of the
beach below, looking out toward the Atlantic Ocean. He also has a three-bed-
room house in Coconut Grove, Florida, near Miami (an hour and a half away
from Palm Beach, where he had spent so many unhappy months of his childhood), and he and Thomas visit it in the winter. In the spring of every year, he
is in residence in Houston, where he keeps an apartment.

Albee has always had dogs and cats in residence. Animals are very much a
part of his life: the cat that cries like a baby, the Irish wolfhounds that have accompanied him on his various trips, especially Harry, the wolfhound that
sighed. As he wrote in an essay about Harry, "Dogs bark; they whimper; they
groan; they growl—but Harry sighed." He said he asked Harry if he were
happy, and Harry responded with "a great rumbling sound"—but still a sigh.
Most of his dogs and cats have been cremated and then buried on his property in Montauk. When Harry died, he was at the vet, and Edward decided to
bury him whole. He and Jonathan dug a huge six-foot grave, but when they

picked up the body at the vet, the dog had been frozen and his tail stuck straight out. Rather than break off the tail, they dug another three feet to accommodate it. As always, Albee said a few words at the burial. In contrast to his feeling about his animals, he would never visit the cemetery where his parents are buried.

When Albee is in New York, he freely takes advantage of the city. As a theatergoer (and Tony voter), he sees most of the significant plays (and has very strong opinions about them), along with a fair selection of concerts, movies, and other cultural activities. Every Christmas he has a party in his loft, inviting several hundred of his friends and colleagues. At one party some years ago, Colleen Dewhurst and Elaine Stritch arrived early, as Stritch said, "so we could get in some serious drinking before the amateurs started." Dewhurst looked around the cool, art-filled expanse of the large room and said, "Makes you want to curl up with a good book, doesn't it?"

Handsome and well-groomed in his youth, Albee had become shaggy in his middle years, but in his sixties had seemed to take more care with his clothes and grooming and to find a new vitality. Because of his diabetes, he had to be careful about what he ate, but otherwise he was in good health. Working out, playing tennis, he kept himself in shape. Once when he and a neighbor who was a doctor were playing tennis, the doctor said he would play better if he stopped smoking. Taking the advice, Albee immediately stopped smoking. Though he has never been a figure of fashion, he began to look distinguished. By giving speeches, he had grown in confidence and now is able to speak without notes. He can hold—and amuse—an audience, and when he reads scenes from his plays at public events, it is with the panache of a trained actor.

Through his role as president of ITI, he continues to be a spokesman for the arts and against censorship and other forms of artistic repression. In all his public statements on artistic and political issues, he refuses to be pigeonholed. That also applies when he speaks about gay issues. He has never made a secret about his homosexuality, but neither has he made it an issue in his career. At Out Write, a 1991 conference of gay writers in San Francisco, he said that being homosexual was one factor in his identity and his personality. He was also white, male, a playwright, director, and teacher. Explaining his feelings on the subject, he made a distinction between a gay writer and a writer who is gay. "A gay writer is a writer who feels a responsibility because he is homosexual to write about gay themes. With some writers, there's a bit of opportunism involved there. Writing on gay themes has become big business, and some of the lesser ones are cashing in." At the conference, he warned against ghettoization. "I pointed out a whole bunch of writers in the twentieth century who happened to be gay: Henry James, Gertrude Stein, Thornton Wilder, Tennessee Williams. They didn't write about gay themes. It was just a small part of their identity. Why concentrate on it? This has nothing to do with trying to be popular or to avoid censure. But it could be a limitation. In my own writing, I have a couple of gay characters, but I never felt the need to write about a gay theme." Instead he wants "to write about our society in general—I don't think being gay is a subject, any more than being straight is a subject."

"Edward's configuration of qualities is individual," says Martha Coigney. "He is a person who leads a political life in order to write plays about what he chooses to write about. If that makes him a bete noir to the political gay activists, so be it."

It might be said that Albee had a rich, full life, except in one very important respect. As a playwright, he was known for his past successes, as the author of *The Zoo Story* and *Who's Afraid of Virginia Woolf?* Academics wrote treatises and scholarly studies of his work. But to the public at large in the 1980s, he was a voice from the past: a playwright of the 1960s, who long ago had written his best work. Of course, he had continued writing, but his plays had not been done in New York since 1983 and the debacle of *The Man Who Had Three Arms*, and with rare exception his plays were not regularly revived in major regional theaters.

In the mid 1980s, he wrote a new play, *Marriage Play*, a dialogue between a husband and wife, Jack and Gillian (as in Jack and Jill), a couple in their fifties who live in suburbia and have been married for thirty years. In the first scene, the husband says simply, "I'm leaving you," and he does, but not until after a duel by dialogue. At the time, Albee described it as "a two-character play about two people who are married, and who are trying not to be married, but find it very very difficult not to be married." Before he entitled it *Marriage Play*, he had thought about naming it "The Old One Two" or "News from the Front," titles he decided to reserve for future works. The play had been commissioned by the English Theater in Vienna. In 1984 that theater had done *The Zoo Story* and *Counting the Ways* (starring Tom Klunis), and the following year Albee had presented a quartet of four one-acts by Pulitzer Prize–winning playwrights David Mamet, Lanford Wilson, Sam Shepard, and himself (*The Sandbox*). Klunis and Kathleen Butler were signed for *Marriage Play*, and before going to Austria, Albee presented the opening scene for an invited audience at the Viennese consulate in New York. In abbreviated form, the play seemed sharp and funny. On May 17, 1987, directed by the author, it opened in Vienna, and then for five years it went nowhere.

As always, he sent the play to various producers and actors. At one point, there was a possibility that Colleen Dewhurst might do it, if a leading man of stature would play opposite her (her former husband George C. Scott declined). One surprising candidate was Julie Andrews, but she turned it down. The Manhattan Theater Club expressed interest; at that point Albee was holding out for a Broadway production. In 1989 the play was scheduled to go into production with Rosemary Harris, but Richard Barr died before it could be done. Revised, with Shirley Knight replacing Butler, playing opposite Klunis, it opened at the Alley Theater in Houston in January 1992 followed by another short run at the McCarter Theater in Princeton. The play was not a success. Considering the circumstances—a bickering, long-married couple—audiences expected another *Virginia Woolf*. Instead what greeted them was something like a rerun of *Counting the Ways*, more banter than bitterness and, in this case, a vignette in the guise of a full-length play.

Albee attributed the failure to Knight, while she blamed it on his direction. As she said, "I think Edward is a great writer and I don't think he should direct his own plays. He has in his mind a certain way his plays should be done. In a sense, the actor is not allowed to make a contribution to the depth of a character. It means you're more like a robot." In October 1993, with Butler returning to her role opposite Klunis, the play, now about ninety minutes long, finally opened in New York. What was most interesting was not the play but the auspices of the production. Two years before, James Houghton had formed the Signature Theater Company with the idea of doing a season of plays by a single playwright, new plays as well as revivals. Signature had opened with works by Romulus Linney, followed by Lee Blessing, and now in a third season had turned to Albee. It was to be the beginning of Albee's own return.

In March of 1990, about a year after his mother died, Albee started writing a play about her. "I wrote with considerable enthusiasm and intensity," he said later. "I got so involved in what I was doing that I didn't really think about why I was doing it. That always happens when I'm writing a play. I don't think about the metaphors and the messages. I just think about the reality of what's happened. I was not writing with one hand and thinking, I am ridding myself of this woman. I think I remember being quite amazed at my objectivity while I was writing. Remember that Frank O'Hara poem: You must write about the memory of your feeling. If you're deeply emotionally embroiled in what you're writing you can't control what you're doing artistically." About his motive, he said, "How childish it would have been to try to get back at her. It would have been a rant or a whimper. I didn't want that."

He began the play in Houston, where he was teaching. The first act flowed. He wrote it in "two very quick spurts," completing it in Florida in December. Glyn O'Malley, his assistant director, suggested that if he finished the play soon, the English Theater in Vienna might present the premiere (and pay him $14,000). In January, he sent over a copy of the first act to O'Malley who read it and was "flabbergasted." "I always felt he had ascended up to his cerebral cortex for protection after *Virginia Woolf* and had written interesting abstract structural exercises with cold aloof characters. This was the first play of his that I read that suddenly had a gut kind of resonance in it," and was deeply felt. His excitement was palpable, "not just because of the monster mother, but I thought it was some of the most tightly composed writing that he had done." He called Albee and said, "This is what I think everyone is waiting for." He asked him if he knew what would happen in the second act. Albee answered cryptically, "You might be surprised." O'Malley telephoned Franz Schafranek, the head of the English Theater in Vienna. Schafranek flew to New York, met with Albee, and on the basis of the one act agreed to produce the play in Vienna.

Asked if he could have written the play while his mother was alive, Albee said he thought that would have been foolish, adding with lingering cynicism, "I would have missed that wonderful death scene. I don't think it would have occurred to me to do it until 'the subject' was complete." Also, still dutiful, he would have wanted to avoid her adverse reaction: "I don't know if it had anything to do with my thinking but it probably would have hurt her feelings a lot."

In the introduction to the published version of *Three Tall Women*, Albee said that he began writing the play during his first "awareness of consciousness," as an infant held by his nanny, who was standing with his adoptive parents on a knoll overlooking the family's house. In other words, he had been living the play and thinking about it all his life. When he started the play, he said,

I was more aware of what I did *not* want to do than exactly what I did want to accomplish. I knew my subject—my adoptive mother, whom I knew from my infancy (that knoll!) until her death over sixty years later, and who, perhaps, knew me as well. Perhaps.

I knew I did not want to write a revenge piece—could not honestly do so, for I felt no need for revenge. We had managed to make each other very unhappy over the years, but I was past all that, though I think she was not. I harbor no ill will toward her; it is true I did not like her much, could not abide her prejudices, her loathings, her paranoias, but I did admire her pride, her sense of self. As she moved toward ninety, began rapidly failing both physically and mentally, I was touched by the survivor, the figure clinging to the wreckage only partly of her own making, refusing to go under . . .

I realized then that what I wanted to do was write as objective a play as I could about a fictional character who resembled in every way, in every event, someone I had known very, very well. And it was only when I invented, when I translated fact intact into fiction, that I was aware I would be able to be accurate without prejudice . . .

While insisting that he was not seeking to come to terms with her or to have a catharsis, he admitted that by writing the play he had gotten his mother out of his system, adding "I get *all* the characters in *all* of my plays out of my system by writing about them." Then he asked himself if the character in the play was "more human, more multifaceted than its source." He had no answer, except to say that very few people who met his adoptive mother in the last twenty years of her life "could abide her, while many people who have seen the play find her fascinating."

The character is fascinating, and in creating her, Albee brought to bear all his knowledge of his mother: the wildness of her adolescence, what she went through during the years of her marriage and her husband's infidelity, her fear of being rejected by the Albee family, her mixed emotions about her sister, and her strange unmotherly detachment from her son. He put into the play all that he felt about her and all that he imagined: the somewhat less-than-love and the something other-than-hate. Frankie is there onstage in the character identified as A, the oldest of the three tall women. In old age, losing her memory ("I can't remember what I can't remember"), facing death, and raging into the night, A is malicious in her feelings about her family but piercingly perceptive as she looks back on her wrong roads.

There are three principal characters in the play, identified only as A, an old woman; B, her secretary and caregiver; and C, a young lawyer, trying to straighten out her accounts. Each is separated from the other by more than twenty-five years. A, in the playwright's description, is "a very old woman; thin, autocratic, proud, as together as the ravages of time will allow." B "looks rather as A would have at 52," and C "looks rather as B would have at 26." The play begins with a fact from life. A announces that she is ninety-one. C corrects her: She is 92. "Be that as it *may*," says A. Soon she is laughing and then crying, self-pity turning into self-loathing.

Albee was not present when the lawyers witnessed his mother signing her last will, but in the play he had in effect been able to transport himself to that place, as the quibbles and quarrels start and as the characters sift through the artifacts of the woman's life. The stories repeat and parallel those from Frankie's life, and the almost forty years she was married to "the little one-eyed man" who "has the morals of a sewer rat." One character plays upon the other, revealing the embitterment behind the mask. Discontent is rampant; there is no end, and comedy underlies the most scathing observation. Soon we get a full picture of a woman devoted to herself and to her way of life, to her horses more than to her husband and son. She marries for money, security, and the fact that her husband makes her laugh—and she suffers for it. Around her are the indulgent and philandering husband, the alcoholic sister, the prodigal son—people who appear with variations in other Albee plays and who populated the author's own life. "Way back then," were things always the same? Which parent was "strict but fair?" Questions are raised; some of them are answered.

At the end of the first act, A has a stroke. The second act begins with A in bed, apparently in a coma. In a *coup de théâtre*, the figure in bed turns out to be a dummy. A herself enters and converses with B and C, who now become A at earlier stages of her life. These are three faces of the same woman, which is why the characters have no full names and are called A, B, and C. The characters in the first act have now merged. They play a game of ages: Who knew what when, and when will the youngest of the three find out about events that will shape her life? The son enters and stands silently by the bed. He is the prodigal, cast out but returning, still silent as the three aspects of a woman carry us through her life and the burden of her memories.

As always, Albee says he does not remember the exact moment he began the play, but in this case, he remembers "the happiness of writing it." He felt a special elation when A said, "I have a son." In an instant, he realized that the son, his surrogate, was going to be in the play, albeit without saying a word. "That surprised and delighted me." The boy enters, stands by the bed, and stares at A while B rages, "Get out of my house!" The character is close to the age that he was when he left home. The old woman suddenly sounds like a peacemaker. "He came back," she says. "He never loved me, he never loved us, but he came back." And then, "We have a heart attack; they tell him; he comes back. Twenty plus years? That's a long enough sulk—on both sides. He didn't come back when his father died." B, the mother in middle-age, is unrelenting: "He packed up his attitudes and left!" In contrast, A tries to be ameliorative. She does want to see him again. Speaking about herself, she says: "Be alone except for her upstairs passed out on the floor, and the piano top with the photos in the silver frames, and the butler, and . . . be all alone; you *do* want to see him again, but the terms are too hard. We never forgive him. We let him come, but we never forgive him." And then to the silent son, she says, "I bet you don't know *that . . . do* you!"

As the woman recalls her son's departure, Albee plumbs his own memories of his schoolboy crises, when he "gets himself thrown out of every school he can find, even one or two we haven't sent him to." Then, a line right from Frankie Albee: "I tell him, you just wait; I'll have you thrown out of this house so quick it'll make your head spin." Before that happens, he walks out of the house, "out of our lives," as Edward did. "He doesn't say good-bye to either of us. He says good-bye to Mother, upstairs; he says good-bye to the Pekingese, too, I imagine. He packs one bag, and he leaves." And she shouts, "Get out of my house!!"

Deep into the second act, there is a feeling of the woman's isolation: how she sold her jewelry, piece by piece, to support her way of life, how she lived by herself and thought about death. Then comes a scene in which she has a premonition of her death. For Albee, it was a scene directly from life, from his final visit to his mother, after she had died. "I may have made it a little more dramatic," he admitted. "Isn't that what a playwright does? I remember the visual image of going into the hospital room and finding her lying there dead in the bed, and the chauffeur and the maid sitting stage right of her. Isn't that interesting that I said my visual memories involve stage right and stage left? I suspect that when I wrote that part of that premonition scene I was commenting on the ritualistic things that I did." In that scene, he offers a portrait that is doubly harsh, of mother and son, of both his mother and himself, for her subconscious threat of disinheritance, for the coolness of his regard, for his inability to be moved. A is speaking to her son, who is by her bed:

> You brought me flowers, you brought freesia. You know I love freesia; that's why you bring them to me, because I *love* them! Why do you do that?! You hate me; why do you do that?! What do you want?! You *want* something. Well, you just wait. You'll get what's coming to you. In my premonition I knew I was dead, and it didn't seem to matter any, and I was all alone . . . No one! Just the chauffeur and the maid. I was there an hour, and I was *dead,* and then *you* came in, and you had your flowers, your freesia . . . you stopped at the door of the room, and you knew right away and you stopped and you . . . *thought!* I *watched* you *think!* And your face didn't change. Why didn't your face ever change? And there you were, and you thought, and you decided, and you walked over to the bed, and you touched my hand, and you bent down, and you kissed me on the

forehead . . . for them! They were there and they were watching and you kissed me for *them*! And then you stood up, still holding on to my hand, as if . . . what? You didn't know what to do with it? You held on to my hand, and my hand wasn't warm anymore, was it? My hand was cold, *wasn't* it?"

C denies that she will ever become the old woman. Then she wonders about the happy times in her life. "*I haven't* had them, yet, have I?" she asks. "All done at twenty-six?" B interrupts to say that the happiest time is now, "old enough to be a *little* wise, past being *really* dumb." With a quick look at her older self, she says, "No offense."

"You're both such children," says A. The happiest moment is "coming to the end of it" where you can think "about yourself in the third person without being crazy." In a clear, Beckettian moment, she concludes: "When it's all done. When we stop. When we can stop." The play is fearlessly personal and at that moment it is also prophetic — about the end in loneliness. Writing it, Albee said, was "a kind of exorcism." It was, for him, "a laying to rest."

Earlier in Albee's career, when he finished writing a play, he would show it to Bill Flanagan, who would criticize, analyze, and suggest improvements. Albee would pass the play on to Richard Barr, who would read it and then put it into production. With *Three Tall Women*, he gave copies to a few friends, as he had done with *Marriage Play* and his other recent short plays. "I was overwhelmed by it," said Joanna Steichen. "Reading it, I cried with delight. He had started out writing in anger, but what came out was like a psychoanalytic working-through. In a sense, it really is a work of love. In it, he says, 'I understand this woman, I understand what she went through.' It was a kind of forgiveness. And he made her story alive, compelling, complicated, beautiful."

People in New York were no longer eagerly waiting for the next Albee play. In fact, no one was interested. As he knew, he was still "persona non grata." In a sense, it was like a repeat of the start of his career with *The Zoo Story*, and in similar fashion, he found a stage away from America, in Vienna. Instead of waiting for stars to reject him, he gave the play to Myra Carter, an actress who was unknown in New York but whom he knew and liked from revivals of *All Over* and *The Lady from Dubuque* at the Hartford Stage Company and *A Delicate Balance* at the Arena Stage in Washington. She had a reputation, then and later, for being difficult. Albee felt that her temperament was more than offset by her talent. "How did I get the role?" Carter asks. "Are you kidding? It was easy to get it. I don't think anybody else would have done it. I was the best he could get." Reading the play, she knew it had problems and, of course, no second act, but, she said, "I thought it was major. I detected the rhythmic tension."

Before leaving for Vienna, he had a reading of the first act with the three actresses who were to play the roles, Carter, Kathleen Butler, and Cynthia Bassham. As he left New York the next day (with Jonathan Thomas), Albee had not written the second act, which meant he did not yet know that the young man, his surrogate, was going to appear in the play. He did not begin writing it until after he arrived in Austria. While the actresses were rehearsing the first act, he was still in his hotel room working on the conclusion. Carter was disturbed by that and by the fact that her character cried so much. "She must have been very depressed," she told the author. "Oh, well, she just cries," he said. "Just cry." "Do you think I have a bag of water in my head?" she asked. In the stage directions, she said, "it was weep, weep, big weep, despair, five minutes of weeping on page four."

Albee admits, "Within the first three minutes of the play the actress has to burst into genuine tears. To inhabit that role, right off the bat she has to get that almost schizophrenic thing. That's very difficult to do and Myra is an honest actress." There was also the problem of the quick change of moods, how the tears "suddenly turned into laughter, on a dime." She remembers Albee telling her, "Don't smile. Don't be liked." Under a deadline, with the opening approaching, he finished the second act and created his coup, having Carter walk onstage while the audience thought it was looking at her in bed. During rehearsal, Carter received constant coaching on her demanding role. Albee remembers hearing her coming down the aisle of the theater saying, "Fucking play, fucking lines, supposed to fucking cry." "It was the hardest work," said Carter. "It was murder to learn because there's no rational cueing. You're saying the same thing over and over and you don't know whether it's the sixteenth time or the fourth time. I went gray in Vienna." Asked how he could stand all her tantrums, Albee answered simply, "Because she's a great actress" and because "the abuse was never directed against me."

He recalled her offstage tirade: "How can I live in that fucking room they've given me, hearing that fucking traffic all night. They only speak fucking German. How am I supposed to do my laundry?" "Everything in life was unfair," said Albee. "Everyone was out to get her." She even complained about the life mask of her that was used in the second act of the play. She said, "It was made by the opera house in Vienna and they didn't have enough Vaseline and it stuck. They tore it off and I was bruised all down my chin." O'Malley says, "Myra is real heavy furniture. She's so contrary. There's so much drama about the drama—and then she's brilliant. I adore her when the lights go up."

For all of her anxieties, she had an intuitive grasp of the character and the play. As she said, "The music and the language are quite stunning at times—those arias! But you've got to watch out or you're singing. It's hard to make the character real and yet pull down the fourth wall." At one point, worn down by the work, with, she said, lesions on her windpipe, she told Albee to expand the role of the youngest woman and remove her role entirely from the second act. Naturally, he refused. Staying with it, slowly she captured the fullness of her character: "The play is an expose of a woman. By the end, she's seen from every point of view." Albee's conclusion: "Myra was dragged kicking and screaming into giving a great performance."

A week before *Three Tall Women* was scheduled to open in Vienna, Larry Hagman and Linda Gray, the stars of *Dallas*, flew in to do A. R. Gurney's *Love Letters* at the English Theater. With *Dallas* still popular in Europe, it was a major media event, "Hollywood on the Danube," said Glyn O'Malley, "with unbelievable paparazzi." Then after the opening night of *Love Letters*, the theater was struck by tragedy: Franz Schafranek, the head of the theater, suddenly died. Together, the two events, *Love Letters* and Schafranek's death, eclipsed *Three Tall Women*, which opened quietly, almost secretively.

Seeing the play at its first performance (on June 14), Thomas was excited by it. On the sidewalk outside the theater, he said to Albee, "Edward, you've got a great play here, but you've screwed up the ending"—by having three long monologues. The opening night audience was polite and reserved, as were the reviews. The next night, after the performance, O'Malley said to Thomas, "This is it. This is going to put Edward back on the map."

Jeane Luere, who taught English at the University of Northern Colorado and had often written enthusiastically about Albee, was at the opening of *Three Tall Women*. She wrote to me, enclosing her review and a note saying, "His play is a wonder. Even old men cried. Not just mothers like me who have failed their kids as the heroine in the play thinks she did (his mom). It's not like his earlier work. Better. The boy in the play (him) gets a second chance and reconciles with the mom . . . Mr. A has a cosmic theme?"

That month, David Richards wrote a long article about Albee in the *Times*, headlined EDWARD ALBEE AND THE ROAD NOT TAKEN, a wistful, whatever-happened-to profile of the man who was "once celebrated as the boy wonder of the American theater." Richards summarized *Three Tall Women* and suggested that perhaps Albee had begun to lay old demons to rest. In the piece, Albee commented, "All my plays are about people missing the boat, closing down too young, coming to the end of their lives with regret at things not done, as opposed to things done. I find that most people spend too much time living as if they're never going to die. They skid through their lives. Sleep through them sometimes. Anyway, there are only two things to write about—life and death."

In 1992, while he was in Houston, he wrote *The Lorca Play* on commission for the Alley Theater. It is a long rambling play about Federico García Lorca, one that barely skirts the surface of the playwright's life. Albee staged it that April at the University of Houston. "It's not the sort of play I should write," he admitted. "Other people are better at that kind of docu-drama." As was true of *Lolita*, where A Certain Gentleman became a combination of Nabokov and Albee, in *The Lorca Play*, there was a merging of Lorca and Albee. Speaking about the Young Lorca and by indirection about Albee, the Narrator says, "Doesn't our young self always stay with us—lurk around the edges of our consciousness? And do we ever *really* think we're grown up? Don't we always think we're . . . what? . . . 15, or something?"

Later in the play, Albee speaks through Lorca: "Do you know what it's like to fall in love with people who don't want you? Do you know what it's like to be completely misunderstood? . . . Do you know what it's like to know how special and dangerous your talent is? To live in a society . . . so rigid, so set in its ways you don't *dare* be yourself . . . except deep inside? Do you know what it's like to be filled with poetry, to be filled with music, to be filled with love, and pity, and fear, and anguish, and a deep, deep . . . terrible dread?"

Despite reports from Vienna, people in New York remained doubtful about *Three Tall Women*, and Albee's agent, Esther Sherman, found it difficult to interest anyone in producing it. A board member of the River Arts Repertory, a small regional theater in Woodstock, New York, happened to have seen the play in Vienna and told Lawrence Sacharow, the founder and artistic director of the company, that this was the sort of play he should do. Sacharow, the creator of *The Concept*, a communal play about a drug addiction center, which was a major Off-Broadway success in the 1960s, was a great admirer of Albee's work, beginning with *The Zoo Story*. He described seeing that play as a life-changing experience.

Both Sacharow and Albee had been vital forces in the theater of the 1960s, but they emerged from entirely different directions. As a highly individual playwright, Albee had never been particularly concerned with exploring the emotions of actors, or with the outer reaches of performance art. Sacharow was a stubbornly independent director, who believed that drama could emerge from an ensemble of actors under the guidance of a directorial vision. In the summer of 1991, Sacharow wrote to Albee expressing his interest in doing *Three Tall Women* in Woodstock. Albee responded with a postcard saying that "it's too early to discuss anything concrete about that now, but your enthusiasm will have me enthusiastic about discussing it further." Later Albee sent him a script. In contrast to many other directors and producers who either do not read plays or do not know how to read them, Sacharow prides himself on being able to see a play on the printed page. He loved *Three Tall Women* and decided he wanted to do it. They met and Albee agreed that Sacharow could direct the play at River Arts.

"I had heard all these stories about how impossible he is and how angry he gets," said Sacharow. "I thought maybe it comes with the turf, and maybe it doesn't. I wanted to do this play and I wanted to work with him, but I was prepared for a siege." At that first meeting, however, "I got a strong feeling from him that he wanted the same thing that I did—a good collaborative process. The more we worked together the more surprised I was at Edward's ability to negotiate artistically around logic. If you made sense to him, everything was clear. When it didn't make sense, he would be firm, argumentative, and combative—with a kind of seething sarcasm. We began to have this artistic dialogue around the clarity and the logic of the choices that were made on every single level, starting with casting, then with design, then with costume. I thought this was probably the highest dialogue I've ever had with a writer in my career." At one of their early meetings, Sacharow asked Albee what he thought the play was about. He replied, "I guess it's about a woman who you don't like in act one, and who you like a little better in act two."

Sacharow says that the first choice to play the role of A at Woodstock was Uta Hagen. Albee insists that he always wanted Myra Carter to continue in the role and to play it in America. In any case, the script was given to Hagen, and the director and playwright talked about the possibility of her doing it. Periodically over the years since *Virginia Woolf*, Hagen had spoken to Albee about appearing in another of his plays. Repeatedly, she had her doubts. "In each one of the plays," she said, "there was something fascinating, but I like to play real human beings with endless dimension. I don't like plays of ideas. I don't like intellectual parlor games onstage. I like human conflict," which, she said, is what drew her to *Virginia Woolf*. "I loved that," she said. She had put her signature on Martha in *Virginia Woolf*, and it remained the high point of her career and also that of the playwright. Were she to have done *Three Tall Women*, it would have been a major artistic reunion, as if Laurette Taylor had lived long enough to do another play of Tennessee Williams years after their success with *The Glass Menagerie*.

Hagen turned it down because she did not like the play. She told Albee and Sacharow that she preferred not to work under such a tight schedule, but they were aware of her negative reaction. After the play had become a great success, she was emphatic in her opinion: "I think that the old woman is re-lentlessly hateful-boring." About Albee, she has mixed feelings, remembered affection from their closeness in the 1960s, combined with resentment built up over the years: "I feel so disloyal, but I feel very strongly that this is a lost talent for the American theater. I think it could have been gigantic. Then again, I see him and he's like a little boy. I want to give him a hug." Looking back on the possibility of Hagen doing *Three Tall Women*, Albee says it would have been very difficult for him to find sympathy for her in the role: "I've seen Uta act a lot and I've never seen 'pathetic' in her quiver."

At one point, Albee and Sacharow talked about the possibility of Irene Worth, who had a long history of appearing in Albee plays. Mary Louise Wilson, Elizabeth Wilson, and others were considered. Very early, Marian Seldes, a favorite of the director, was signed to play the role of B; even then the feeling was she could also play the oldest woman. Myra Carter was always the ace in the hole. Sacharow had never seen her act. Hearing her read the role of A, he readily agreed with Albee that she was easily the strongest actress who had auditioned: "If we weren't going to get a name like Uta Hagen or Irene Worth, she was better than anyone else on that level." He knew nothing about her personally, only that she had done the play in Vienna and therefore would be an asset—and that Albee wanted her.

Jordan Baker (who was named after a character in *The Great Gatsby*), was signed to play the youngest woman, C., and Michael Rhodes was hired for the silent cameo role of the son. There were three weeks of rehearsal, followed by two weeks of performance. Albee came up to Woodstock for the first reading. The night before the reading, Sacharow had a dinner party for the author and the actors at his house in Woodstock, beginning the production on a note of harmony. The next day the actors read the play aloud for the author and the director.

Periodically during the next three weeks the author came back to Woodstock to look in on rehearsals. He made minor cuts, removing references to a character named Bob, who was one of his mother's financial advisers, someone he thought was robbing her. The most drastic cuts were at the end of the play in the sequence of monologues from the three women, in which each talks about what she thinks is the happiest time in life. For Albee, they were "musical cuts." "I evolved the theory that the last scene in the play was like *Don Giovanni*. Everybody comes out and sings and addresses the audience. It ends with a fugato. That's also what's happening at the end of *Three Tall Women*." He gave the director notes, many of them about the positions of the actors onstage: Why is B hovering over A when she is such a strong independent woman? He emphasized the point at which he wanted A's cruelty to be evident. One difference between the author and the director was that Albee wanted the second act to be staged as naturalistically as the first act whereas Sacharow wanted it done in a more stylized fashion. For Albee, the second act, like the first, was "absolutely real: It's happening." In order to create a more complete picture of their characters, Seldes and Baker, with the director's help, imagined biographical histories for B and C in the first act.

Carter, of course, drew on her earlier familiarity with the play. "I really really liked Myra in Woodstock," said Sacharow. "We had a wonderful time investigating the play. She was very helpful." Then, according to Sacharow, she became increasingly difficult. There were indications that offstage—at least unintentionally—she was playing the role of Albee's mother (life imitating art imitating life). Albee says he did not sense such an offstage kinship between Carter and his mother. "Myra was a compulsive complainer," he said, "but not secretive like my mother." Still, in a strange way, Carter's attitude seemed to bring her into a closer bond with Albee. "I think that's why Edward has a loyalty to her," said Sacharow. "He will not disown her. That's the exact dynamic of the relationship." He added firmly, "The role is Myra. You couldn't have gotten a better actress to play that character." Finding ways to look past the tears and the malice of her character to make her as human as she could, Carter held fast to what was the role of her career.

Offstage, she was often unsettled, for example, repeatedly changing the room in the house where she lived in Woodstock. Jordan Baker voluntarily became a kind of shepherd, driving the older actress to work and helping her with her shopping. "We became like a dysfunctional family," said Sacharow. "We learned how to accommodate Myra's idiosyncrasies—and it worked."

At Woodstock, Seldes associated her character with Albee, himself. As she said, "If I thought of Edward—the quiet way he watches everything, the glee with which he squelches a stupid or careless comment, the droll way he has of observing your face while he is thinking—if I thought of him, I knew how to play this woman." From *A Delicate Balance* through *Tiny Alice* (where she was a standby for Irene Worth) to *Three Tall Women*, Seldes had frequently appeared in his plays and had become a close student of his work. As she realized, the "silent or absent youth" haunts his plays: the imaginary son in *Virginia Woolf*; Teddy, the dead son in *A Delicate Balance*; and the son in *Three Tall Women*, who sits at his mother's bedside and never speaks.

Near the end of rehearsals, the actors did a run-through of the play, the first time the play was performed in America before an audience, albeit a very small one: several members of the River Arts staff, including the playwright

Michael Cristofer, who was Sacharow's artistic associate; the technical director and designer; and also Joyce Ketay, a theatrical agent who lived in Woodstock. Albee was not there. After the run-through, emotion filled the room.
Ketay was crying. "It really affected me very strongly," she said later. She was
moved by the thoughts the play raised "about one's life and where it was going," especially by the question, "What would your young self think of you?"
At dinner afterward, she, Cristofer, and others continued to talk about it.

Albee came up three days later for the dress rehearsal, and there was more
fine tuning. When the play opened July 30, the local reviews (in Albany, Troy,
and Poughkeepsie as well as Woodstock) were very favorable, and the play
sold out its run. Previously, said Sacharow, the theater had only sold out when
there was a star such as Paul Newman or Joanne Woodward onstage. This
time it was the play that drew audiences. The run was extended for a third
week. As word spread to New York, producers came up to see it, but there was
still a feeling of tentativeness, as if people were afraid to take a chance on Albee. Lynne Meadow, the artistic director of the Manhattan Theater Club,
which specializes in presenting new plays, saw it and did not like it—or at
least did not like it enough to want to produce it. Elizabeth McCann, an independent producer, was intrigued by it, but did not sign it up. According to
Sacharow, of all the producers who saw the play in Woodstock, only three expressed their enthusiasm and wanted to bring it to New York: Michael Harvey
(an old friend of Albee's), Albert Poland, and Lucille Lortel, who has a long
distinguished record for producing worthy new plays Off-Broadway. Harvey,
who had AIDS, tried hard to put together a production, but after six months
he still could not raise the money, and soon after, he died.

After the show closed in Woodstock, Sacharow and Esther Sherman sent
the script to many producers, not just commercial producers like the Shubert
organization, but people at institutional theaters, including Andre Bishop,
artistic director of Lincoln Center Theater, and JoAnne Akalaitis, then the
head of the New York Shakespeare Festival Public Theater. None of them
wanted to do the play. The few who were interested were unable to raise the
necessary financing. It was as if Albee were unknown and not a world famous
playwright, a two-time Pulitzer Prize winner who had helped to change the
face of the contemporary theater. The theater is fickle and Albee had not had
a success in many years.

"It was the most extraordinary saga of not knowing what you have," said
Sacharow. "Then you put it on in Woodstock and you know you've got a gem
and you have to fight for a year and a half to get it on in New York. It was no
easier to get a play done by one of the greatest dramatists of America of the

twentieth century than to get a play done by any first writer." Actually a play
by a new writer might have had a greater chance of being picked up: Theaters
pride themselves on discovering playwrights. Trying to explain the lack of interest, Sacharow blames it partly on the shortsightedness of producers: "How
many producers have a reference point of great writers like Beckett or Genet?
You have to make a leap into a highly imaginative realm."

Hoping to do the play in New York, the three actresses were on call, waiting for news of a production. During this entire period, Albee remained committed to the director and the cast, although as Sacharow says, "Loyalty in the
theater is almost a contradiction. You want to get a play, you get it on no matter who has done it before or not done it before and if the right actor that you
love won't work for the producer you change the actor or the director or whatever. Edward professed his desire to see this production get on, and he was
standing behind it as the production he wanted to see in New York. Loyalty to
the play was the issue." Finally, the script went to Douglas Aibel, the artistic
director of the Vineyard Theater, an adventurous small theater near Union
Square. He liked it and scheduled it for January 1994.

Meanwhile Signature's Albee season opened with *Marriage Play.* Though
slight, it was well staged and acted and was in its own way disarming. *Marriage Play* was followed by *Counting the Ways* and *Listening,* and then by a
trio of plays with a sandy setting, what Albee referred to as "sand plays," *Box,
The Sandbox,* and *Finding the Sun.* All three productions had merit and in
varying degrees, each received respectful reviews. People began talking about
the revival of Albee's reputation.

After *Marriage Play* completed its run and before the double bill of *Counting the Ways* and *Listening* opened, I visited Albee at his loft for a piece for
the *Times.* Our conversation ranged widely through his life and occasionally
returned to the subject of the changes in the theater since he began writing—
and his own survival technique: "I always get worse reviews in New York than
I do anywhere else. One tries not to be paranoid, but I get the impression
they're laying in wait for me. I seem to bring out an intensity of response in
critics. I don't get much indifference. If I'm going to be slammed, it's almost
with pathological hostility. Maybe I've offended too many people. They're
very very leery about trying a play of mine in a commercial arena, and maybe
the plays aren't that commercial." He said that except for several years after
The Man Who Had Three Arms, he had always continued to write and his
plays were done "wherever the environment is sympathetic," in Europe and
in regional theater, which, he said, aims "to educate and make the audience
intolerant of what passes for entertainment in commercial theater." The

piece in the *Times* emphasized the playwright's durability. Under the head-line EDWARD ALBEE, ELDER STATESMAN, IS IN A STATE OF PROFESSIONAL REPRISE, it began:

> Edward Albee is a thorn in the body theatric. Through all the critical buffet-ing he has endured, he has survived with his ego and his equilibrium intact. Unlike many of his talented contemporaries, he has never stopped writing, and a healthy sampling of his work, including a selection of premieres, is being pre-sented in New York this season . . .
>
> Unafraid to state an intemperate opinion and, at 65, still writing plays ex-actly as he wants to write them, he retains his ironic sense of detachment. At the same time, by lecturing, teaching playwriting and serving as head of the United States chapter of the International Theater Institute, he has become a theatrical elder statesman.

We barely touched upon *Three Tall Women*. It was, he said, "sort of" about his mother—"a kind of exorcism." Having written the play, he understood her a bit better and had a little more admiration for her "wrongheaded attitudes." Few people outside of the immediate family—the director, the actors, Jonathan Thomas, several friends—knew how good the play was. For all her problems in harnessing her character, and for all her criticism, Myra Carter said that she predicted—long before the play came to New York—that it would win the Pulitzer Prize.

Back in rehearsal for four weeks, the company began looking more deeply into the play. Sacharow said, "For me the play is almost like a Greek drama. It has a resonance that's classical. You really do feel a catharsis, and I never got tired of working on it: that cathartic build toward that premonition scene and then the release at the end with the three monologues. I've never had that kind of purging experience with a play I've directed." He said that Carter con-tinued to assert herself, making demands about the scenery and other matters, resisting the director's attempt to emphasize the harsh subtext, and criticizing the director and other members of the company. Despite their conflict, he said, "We knew the performance was stunning. We wanted that performance in New York."

In his conversations with his director, Albee never talked about his mother, but the linking of her to the character was undeniable. "This woman is a monster," he would tell Sacharow, and he would warn, "You can't like her." However, in performance, the character seemed to enlist compassion. Be-neath the animosity, there was always a kind of admiration, or at least respect.

As Sacharow said, "My opinion is that he created a character that by its very nature is so raw and unfettered by any restraints. As an audience you admire someone who is not bound by any conventional societal morality. The thought of living with her would be anathema and you wouldn't want her for your mother, but you would say, she's an interesting person because she has no boundaries. When the dark side gets loose, there is something incredibly cathartic about it. I think the sympathy is there simply because you understand the woman is old and she's a victim of old age and infirmity."

One of the great problems in rehearsal was the so-called premonition scene at the end of the second act, when A imagines her own death and how it was received by her son. The director had to help Carter move step by step, emotion by emotion, through the scene, underlining the subtext and encouraging her ferocity. With a natural understanding of the complexity of her character and her self-entrapment, she played her for her full determination, her desperate need to be in control or, at least, to seem to be in control. The play is filled with bitter, deprecating humor, enhanced by Carter's virtuosic performance. As the story of her childhood, adolescence, and marriage unfold, the character is seen in her old age, clinging to her memories and to the wreckage of her life.

In January 1994, *Three Tall Women* opened at the Vineyard—without fanfare. As Albee said, "I didn't expect it was going to explode in the way that it did. I've learned never to expect anything. I've always had a 'let's see what happens' attitude about things. I don't predict. If I said to myself, I sense this is a wonderful play and I'm going to be back in the spotlight again, and then it didn't happen—that would be foolish. Fantasizing about things like that is dangerous." The *Times* review by Ben Brantley was qualified in its assessment, for a moment preserving the fact that all Albee plays have received mixed reviews. But the other reviews warmly greeted Albee's return as a full comeback. For the first time since *The Zoo Story* he sneaked into New York, and the critics—caught by surprise—chorused their enthusiasm. Linda Winer in *Newsday* said it was time to stop measuring Albee against the man who wrote *Virginia Woolf*, calling the new play "a devastating look at a certain kind of woman's life to the end" and Carter's performance "a nonstop cadenza of mood swings, filled with the pride, cruelty, sorrow and playfulness of a difficult but worthy woman." Brustein shifted gears, saying, "I am happy to join his other former detractors in saluting Albee's accomplishment."

What Albee had done as a playwright was to wipe out—and also profit from—the intervening years. He obliterated the self-consciousness and artificiality that had damaged plays in his middle period, works that had more to do with the mind than the heart, plays like *The Lady from Dubuque* that had striking beginnings but seemed curiously unfinished. Of all his works, *Three Tall Women* was the nearest to autobiography. Aspects of his life and, in particular, of his mother, have appeared throughout his work, but not with this specificity. Frankie, undisguised, was the inspiration for the play, and even as events diverged from reality, as Albee carried facts onto a fictional plane, the heart of A (and B and C in the second act) was his mother. Those who knew her could see her onstage. Those who did not would be convinced that this is the way she was: formidable, fiercely defensive, and in Marian Seldes's word, invincible.

Thematically and stylistically, *Three Tall Women* was like Albee's version of *Krapp's Last Tape*, the play with which his first play, *The Zoo Story*, opened. In both *Three Tall Women* and *Krapp*, a character is projected back into the past to offer a prismatic view of a person at different crucial points in a life. What would your young self think of you? In Beckett's case, Krapp stood in for the author; with "A's Last Tape," it was Albee's mother, who through the playwright's eyes could reflect on the follies of her life. Speaking about the play's subject, Albee has said, "Throughout our lives, we make choices," and if one is lucky, at the end of life we will not be "filled with regret over what we have not done." Although the play is written very much in Albee's voice, it is also his most Beckettian work, down to the final words: "When we stop. When we can stop."

After the reviews, producers began circling the play. Elizabeth McCann saw it again, liked it even better than at Woodstock, and decided to move it. She visited Albee at his loft to talk about the transfer. The playwright had one stipulation: He did not want the play to close for any length of time, but to re-open within three weeks so as not to lose its momentum. As the producer was leaving, Albee looked out the window and said he had thought about buying the building across the street and started talking about real estate. McCann laughed and said, "It's really hard being a playwright, isn't it?" That comment broke the ice on what was to become a creative partnership. Almost immediately they began talking about reviving other Albee plays after *Three Tall Women*. When there was still no interest from Broadway managements like the Shuberts, McCann reopened the play Off-Broadway at the Promenade Theater, where it became Albee's longest running show in New York since *Who's Afraid of Virginia Woolf?* When it closed on August 26, 1995, *Three Tall Women* had given 582 performances.

Beginning with *Three Tall Women*, McCann became Albee's primary producer, with a relationship that approximated—but did not equal—the one he had had for so many years with Richard Barr. She attributed the playwright's survival during his long lean years to the fact that he continued to write and to teach: "He kept being involved in the theater as an educator, and I think that was probably his salvation. I don't know how completely his head was turned by being a celebrity. Being a celebrity destroyed Tennessee Williams: He became a caricature of himself, as Orson Welles did. Tallulah Bankhead is an obvious example. I don't think Edward was as badly destroyed by being a celebrity, and therefore wasn't as badly destroyed when he was no longer one. Maybe it's a certain kind of toughness, the tenacity of being an outsider as an adopted child." As Roddy McDowall said, "Edward is of tougher mental stock than Tennessee—and he wasn't numbed by chemicals." McDowall remembered that when Noël Coward received bad reviews, he simply said, "They're wronnng," and went on to the next play. Responding to Coward's statement, Albee said, "Noël was right. We all know we make mistakes. But if you don't take that attitude, whether you believe it or not, you're in serious trouble." Coward refused to be swayed by positive reviews, and he refused to be dismayed by negative ones. What he learned from his mistakes, he learned by himself.

In 1993, before *Three Tall Women* came to New York, Albee wrote a play called *Fragments* on commission for the Ensemble Theater of Cincinnati. He labeled it a "sit-around," to emphasize the informal improvisational air. In common with *Listening* and *Box-Mao-Box*, it was experimental and by "following its own logic," was intended to be experienced like music. In April it closed the Signature season. At the very end of the play, one man asks another how lonely he is, and the second man replies, "Very. Sometimes I wonder why we all go through our lives without touching one another very much. Everyone I know who's died I know I haven't touched enough, no matter how much I have—or been touched enough by them." In *Three Tall Women*, Albee finally touched his mother.

On April 12, *Three Tall Women* won the Pulitzer Prize for drama, eighteen years after Albee's last Pulitzer and eleven years after he had been assaulted for *The Man Who Had Three Arms*. As always with Albee (and often with Pulitzers) it was a split decision, with several of the five judges favoring *Keely and Du*, a play about abortion by the pseudonymous Louisville playwright Jane Martin, and one voting for Terrence McNally's *A Perfect Ganesh*. Albee accepted the award with calm rationality. The day he won it, he was in Houston, teaching his course in playwriting. When he received the call from the Pulitzer committee, he was working out in a gym. Later he said to *The New York Times*, "I suppose I will be very warm and cuddly and pleased with myself for a while," adding that he never counted on winning any prize. "You just have to make the assumption you're doing good work and go on doing it." Then in customary fashion, he needled his critics: "Of course, there are the little dolls you stick pins in privately." This was Albee's third Pulitzer, putting him one up on Tennessee Williams. Maybe, he said, "Tennessee didn't get as many Pulitzers as he deserved."

At the end of the season the New York Drama Critics Circle also gave its best play award to *Three Tall Women*. It narrowly edged out Tony Kushner's *Angels in America, Part II, Perestroika*, which won the Tony award as best play, an award that *Three Tall Women* was ineligible for because it played Off-Broadway. Albee also won an Obie award for Sustained Achievement. In his acceptance speech, he thanked all the people who had sustained him over the years and concluded, "I am sustained." For him, the play was not so much a turning point, as "a returning point."

While the play was still running in New York, Albee and McCann arranged for a London production. With its American success and its prizes, the play had become a valuable property. Maggie Smith, one of London's most popular and highly regarded stars, was signed to play the central role, with Frances de la Tour and Anastasia Hille as B and C. Karel Reisz was named as director (at Harold Pinter's suggestion; Reisz had directed Pinter's *Moonlight*), but was replaced by Anthony Page after two weeks of rehearsal. In contrast to New York, where it remained Off-Broadway, *Three Tall Women* was to be a major production on London's West End, the first Albee play on the West End in twenty years. Unlike Arthur Miller, who had found a home in the English theater, Albee had not achieved such favored playwright status. After the initial successes of the one-acts and *Virginia Woolf* and the productions of *Tiny Alice* and *All Over*, his work had not been readily seen in England. There had been occasional revivals of *Virginia Woolf*, and a few of his other plays had been done by regional companies, but he had become a forgotten man in London. Now, of course, there was anticipation, and led by Maggie Smith, the play was assured of a certain success.

On November 15, *Three Tall Women* (coproduced by McCann, Robert Fox, Jeffrey Ash, and Daryl Roth) opened at Wyndham's Theater. Ian McKellen, Richard Eyre, Peter Shaffer—and other members of the London theatrical community—were at the first night, along with the London critics. Dame Maggie, whose style of acting can be so idiosyncratic as to be imitable, immersed herself deeply within the role. Though not outdoing Myra Carter, she equaled her in portraying a character whose indomitability is matched by her unintentional humor, whose residual dignity is offset by her vulgarity. Artfully she caught the sarcasm as well as the pathos. With her mouth turned down even as she was laughing, she was properly imperious. She made the ribald bracelet story suddenly gather a poignance.

More than in New York, the actresses in the London cast were well matched physically, slender and of a similar height, de la Tour as the acerbic middle-aged character and Hille as the youngest, carefully shading the difference between her character in the first and second acts. Page's production was in all sense stylish—from the elegant set design to the performances. Comparing the London production to his, Sacharow said they were like "night and day, in terms of subtext and character." Few others seemed to notice, including the author. When Albee asked on opening night what he thought of the production, Sacharow said it was very different. Albee responded, "Really? I thought it was exactly the same."

Seeing the play in another production made it even clearer that it was not only about dying and death but also about the changes that cumulatively define a life. Why do we become what we are? In that second act, three ages of woman confront one another, asking what we know, when we know it, and whether one can ever learn from experience. The once hopeful young woman curdles into the sourly cynical wife and finally turns into the embittered old woman (a grande dame, in this case in two senses). The question is raised as to the place that love and self-loathing have in this triangle. This is a wise and prophetic play about the tragic mistakes of life. The woman is her own victim, but after her first step, perhaps she had no choice. The son, the author's silent surrogate, refuses to be her judge but remains her close, critical witness. A, as personified by Dame Maggie (and Myra Carter), dominates through force of will. The other two characters are catalytic. In the end, the play is cathartic, for the audience as it was for the author (even though he had said earlier that was not his intention in writing it).

Albee did not watch the opening night in London. He and Jonathan Thomas went to the movies. After the actresses took their final bow, he arrived at the theater. Standing by the entrance, self-possessed, he accepted congratulations. Afterward at Joe Allen's restaurant, there was a small opening night party, where Albee thanked all the participants. The reviews, naturally, were mixed, but many were filled with enthusiasm and a certain surprise. Benedict Nightingale in the *Times* of London said, "His play has the force of the deeply personal, yet somehow contrives to transcend it . . . It is also a living reproach to those of us who had written off the author of *Who's Afraid of Virginia Woolf?* and *A Delicate Balance* as a burnt-out volcano, or blown-out hurricane, a dramatist thirty years past his prime." Paul Taylor in the *Independent* zeroed in on Dame Maggie's performance and her character: "The brilliance of the performance lies in the way it hints at the younger selves who will only appear in person after the interval. Like layers in a shifting palimpsest, glimpses flash for the young, insecure, married-above-herself woman who, let down on all sides by adulterous husband, snobby in-laws, alcoholic sister and unfeeling son, was gradually compelled to metamorphose into a growling, radar-fitted guard-dog over her own life." One week later, *Three Tall Women* was named best play in the *Evening Standard* awards and Maggie Smith was named best actress. After a substantial run, the play closed and then reopened at the same theater with Dame Maggie heading a new cast (Sara Kestelman and Samantha Bond).

In a letter to Albee, Dame Maggie wrote, "Your play is a tough one to do at the best of times. . . . Every word is like an arrow with deadly accuracy in your piece. I am endlessly fascinated by the text and it is a joy as well as agony to do. So I have much to thank you for."

The play ran until December 1995. Albee was present for the closing night. If anything, that cast was even sharper than the one that originally opened in London, with Dame Maggie retaining her equipoise and the two new actresses an even more balanced pair.

Both times that the London production had closed, Albee had hoped that it would continue with a replacement for Dame Maggie. One possibility was Elaine Stritch. His suggestion was that she should be succeeded in the role by "the Great Scottish Actress: Myra Carter!"

After the play ran for a year in New York, Carter left the cast. "Towards the end of it, she couldn't take it anymore," said Sacharow. "There was no more distinction between the onstage and the offstage character. She would make it impossible for anybody to talk to her." During the run, she was given a week off to go to Hollywood to appear on *Frasier*. "She changed hotels six times on the first day," said Albee, "one of them because she didn't like the doorknobs in the room." The entire cast of the television show later went to New York to see her performance and sat in a front row at the Promenade. They filled her dressing room with flowers and came backstage to see her after the performance. Albee remembered that she berated them for sitting so close to the stage, and for giving her flowers when she had asthma.

One night Albee came to talk to her after a performance, and she threw him out of the dressing room. After an exchange of fuck yous, Albee left the theater. For Carter, the rehearsals—in Vienna, Woodstock, and New York—and the play itself was torturous. The play reestablished Albee's reputation, brought Sacharow to a new level as a director, and solidified the partnership of Albee and McCann. Carter had many offers, but despite the acclaim and the brilliance of her performance, she was not able to capitalize on her success. As Albee said, "Her reputation preceded her. I always thought she was a pill and a pain, but very funny at the same time, and also, very intelligent and right about a lot of things. She was no worse in her reaction to Larry Sacharow than Uta was to Alan Schneider." Underlying everything was Albee's admiration for her talent, and for all her criticism, she acknowledges her indebtedness, which began long before she did *Three Tall Women* when she was in revivals of his other plays. After a long conversation in which she unburdened herself of hostilities about the experience of doing *Three Tall Women*, she sent me a letter to retract what she had said and to explain her conflicting emotions. She wrote:

> I've always had such a personal and artistic affinity with Edward Albee and the plays of his that I've done, and have such appreciation, that his manner with actors sometimes rankles me probably more than it should. Perhaps it's shyness, but he can be very distanced, a little condescending, even pompous at times, as if he were dropping down from his higher place in the hierarchy of the theater. Actually I don't think he relates to actors, or truly believes we have to move his words into a completely different medium as equal artists and not just interpreters, and that this takes, and needs, a process of our own. After a performance, he'll come up many stairs to tell you you got a word wrong, but not anything you got right. Nothing about what he liked. Not much dressing-room encouragement, support.

Without Carter, the play toured the country for two years, with Marian Seldes ascending to A, and Michael Learned as B. Before going on tour, the company did a run-through of the play in New York for the author and director and McCann and Daryl Roth (as producers). That day, the actor playing the boy was absent and Sacharow asked Albee if he would fill in for him in the role. Following his text, Albee sat next to A's bed. In character, he shifted in his seat and fiddled with the sheet. "It was so extraordinary," said Sacharow. "With his little gestures, one got this whole sense of how you are when you're visiting someone who is dying—and you can't wait to get out of there. You're there, but you know you don't want to be there." In contrast to the actor, Albee was, he said, "totally aloof." "I missed a cue," said Albee, "because I was involved in being there, being the boy, acting—acting myself." He was in fact reenacting a scene from his own life when he sat by his mother's bed and, in effect, watched himself watching her.

When *Three Tall Women* was published, it was one of Albee's few plays without a dedication. The earlier plays had all been carefully dedicated—to Flanagan, Rorem, Albee's grandmother, David Diamond, Barr and Wilder, Noel Farrand, Steinbeck, Maeve Brennan and Howard Moss, Stefani Hunzinger. His adaptations had been dedicated to the original authors, McCullers, Purdy, Giles Cooper. "Who could I dedicate it to?" he asked about *Three Tall Women*. When the obvious choice was mentioned, he said, "I wouldn't do that. What could I say, 'To Frankie—Love and Kisses?' 'Mother Dear?' 'Mommie Dearest?' " Then he concluded, "It's not written *for* her. It's written *about* her. Possibly I should dedicate it to myself, as survivor." The play was also written for her, in absentia.

19
A New Balance

In your rebellion, the American theater was reborn.

W I T H the success of *Three Tall Women*, and Albee's reemergence as an acclaimed, prize-winning playwright, 1996 became a halcyon year. Honors descended on him, critics who had once carped now praised him, and as a natural next step, there was a wave of interest in his body of work. The year began with a Broadway revival of *A Delicate Balance*. Despite the fact that it won the Pulitzer Prize for drama in 1967, the play had never received its due. When it had opened in September 1966, critics were puzzled—and some were dismayed—especially by the presence of the uninvited guests arriving at the home of Agnes and Tobias. In the 1960s, it did not seem understandable that friends would suddenly demand lodging and protection from unnamed fears, and when the play won the Pulitzer there were those who regarded it as belated payment for *Virginia Woolf*, denied the award four years earlier. By the 1990s, however, the themes of the play—fearfulness, the test of friendship, the family as nuclear unit—were far more relevant.

In April, *A Delicate Balance* was revived on Broadway by Lincoln Center Theater, with Gerald Gutierrez directing a cast headed by Rosemary Harris and George Grizzard as Agnes and Tobias, and Elaine Stritch as Agnes's sister Claire.

For all three actors as for the play and the playwright, it was a case of a promise fulfilled. Grizzard, who had first emboldened Broadway as Nick in *Virginia Woolf*, and had then gone on to play Hamlet at the opening of the Tyrone Guthrie Theater in Minneapolis, had become a character actor with solid credentials (mostly on stage). He remained a friend of Albee's and had appeared in a revival of A *Delicate Balance* at the Berkshire Theater Festival in Stockbridge, Massachusetts. Although Harris, a distinguished actress who had specialized in classics, had never done a play by Albee, they had talked about working together as recently as *Marriage Play*. Stritch had replaced Kate Reid in the matinee company of the original Broadway production of *Virginia Woolf*, becoming one of the more notable actresses to tackle the role of Martha. After her performances as sharp-tongued characters in works by Stephen Sondheim and Noël Coward, the role of Claire, the sardonic, bibulous sister, seemed ideal casting. On a more personal level, she and Albee shared a background as recovering alcoholics—and both now had diabetes.

Looking at the play again, Albee changed only a few lines, such as an acknowledgment that Claire's shopping for a topless bathing suit was something from the past and that such a garment was not made anymore. He later wrote a piece he called "a non-reconsideration," declaring that the play did not seem to have dated and that seeing it again it was "exactly the same experience" as in 1966: "The play concerns—as it always has, in spite of early-on critical misunderstanding—the rigidity and ultimate paralysis which afflicts those who settle in too easily, waking up one day to discover that all the choices they have avoided no longer give them any freedom of choice, and that what choices they *do* have left are beside the point."

Gutierrez's approach to the play was to emphasize its timelessness and its reality. Whatever metaphorical emanations there were would come through indirection. The audience must believe in the presence of that family onstage and in the real possibility of an invasion by their neighbors. As Gutierrez said at the first rehearsal, he had an Aunt Kitty who lived in Brooklyn and would see A *Delicate Balance*. If she did not understand the play, there was no point in doing it. To erase the slate, he eliminated all the stage directions in the published script and gave the actors photocopies of the new version.

The first stage direction about Agnes, before she begins her opening monologue, was that she was "not sardonic, not sad . . . wistful, maybe." With Albee's assent, the revival eliminated wistfulness. As Harris said about her character, "She's much more aware of the irony of what she's saying. Edward and Gerry wanted the feeling that a row had just erupted at the dining room table. Claire had run upstairs and slammed her door. The tension is rather high. My astonishment at her behavior—that's the thing Agnes is boiling about, her bloody sister's ingratitude." In that monologue, Agnes also talks about the possibility of losing her mind. Harris related that fear to *Three Tall Women*, in which the character does begin to lose her mind. The actress wondered if Albee's mother had the same fear. From seeing both Myra Carter and Maggie Smith in *Three Tall Women*, she felt that she knew so much more about his mother and consciously or not she was drawing on that knowledge in playing Agnes. In other words, the performance of the revival of *A Delicate Balance* was partly influenced by *Three Tall Women*.

Albee was at the first reading, then only occasionally dropped in on rehearsals. "I would have loved to have talked to him about his mother," said Harris. When she first saw the play in 1966, she said, she was single and looked at the play from the daughter's point of view, of "someone coming home to her parents." Then when she read the play several years before she was asked to do it, "I saw it entirely from the other end of the telescope, from Agnes's point of view, and I found it heartbreaking." From her present perspective, the actress, twice married, with a daughter (herself an actress), understood the role viscerally. For most of her career, Harris had worn wigs onstage as a way of changing her personality. The fact that she played Agnes without a wig, in her own silvery hair, and wearing a dress that was a copy of one of her own that she had kept in her attic is an indication of how close she felt to the role.

At first she did not realize that the woman Tobias had the affair with in the play was actually his sister-in-law. That added another piece to the puzzle and to the delicate balance at the heart of the relationship: "The two sisters are in love with the same man, and the man is sort of rendered impotent by that fact. To me, Claire drinks because she's never been able to have the man she wants." One other question Harris pondered was about Teddy, the son of Agnes and Tobias. She believes he may have died in the swimming pool and that his sister Julia might have been told to watch him and let it happen, "or that we're all guilty in some way." Grizzard felt that Tobias's lack of interest in Julia as a child was because of Teddy's death, but that in the course of the play he discovers that his daughter needs him.

Stritch began the play with the conviction of her confidence. She knew this role as she had known Martha. "I knew about playing a woman who drank," she said. In both cases, she drew from her own experience as a drinker and a smoker. "Anything that's dysfunctional, dys-anything, has got to have some humor in it. It's got to." She could have been speaking about Albee as well as herself when she said, "I think humor is one of the most precious things you can have. I also think it's dangerous, because you can get away with so much through using it." At the same time the character should not know she is funny. The fear was that she would "overshoot the runway."

She had had two previous connections with Claire. In 1966, she played the role at the first reading of the play in Richard Barr's apartment in Greenwich Village before Rosemary Murphy got the part, and in the 1970s, she had played Claire on a BBC radio version (with Irene Worth as Agnes). "Claire has been part of my life for a long time," she said, "and of course I didn't understand what I was talking about then. Claire had a few drinks. So what? I didn't understand the terror, what it means to drink like that. She's a real drinker, a goner, and she doesn't give a shit." It is her underlying feeling that all the principals in the play are drunks, Tobias, Agnes ("who doesn't want to lose control"), and the daughter Julia who will become one.

"Claire breaks my heart. When I think about her, I think about myself. She's always in the back seat, the third party. She's never been with the man. She says, 'I have found several, and none my own.' I look right in my glass when I say that. She's got nobody, and living in that house, she can drink as much as she wants. I always felt she keeps herself looking good because she knows she's falling apart. Alcoholics do that."

Except for early disagreements between Gutierrez and Grizzard and the fact that John Cunningham was replaced by John Carter in the role of Harry (playing opposite Elizabeth Wilson as Edna), the production proceeded without major problems. "It's very interesting with Stritch," said Albee. "She was having great trouble during the rehearsals. She said she had been a lush for years and could play the character perfectly well but wanted to find the truth in it and build a character from there. It took her a long time to come up with the character, but I'm convinced that she's giving the same performance through exploration that she did the first day of rehearsal. It's a lovely, true performance. As the wisecracking, ironic, self-aware, ruined person. She's playing Elaine, who happens to resemble Claire, in the same way that Katharine Hepburn did in the film of A Delicate Balance. It was very fortunate that Agnes in certain aspects resembles Hepburn."

About the other stars, Albee said, "Rosemary is right on target: tough, steady, relentless, willing to be laughed at by the audience. I think George is a revelation." He added, "I find the ending beautifully bleak in this production. Agnes said, 'We can begin the day,' and nobody moves. Maybe eventually one of them will get up and move back into some semblance of familiar behavior, but nobody is going to jump to it at the end. It's so far from Tony Richardson's ending to the movie, where Hepburn thrusts open the window when she says, 'We can begin the day.' A terrible ending to a good film."

The play opened April 21 at the Plymouth Theater, Albee's return to Broadway after an absence of thirteen years. A Delicate Balance was a rediscovery, and for many who had not seen it before or had undervalued it in its

original production, it was a discovery. Gutierrez's production probed to the
heart of a drama about the "dispossessed and suddenly dispossessing," while
never overlooking the darkly comic undercurrents. In it, Albee looks behind a
suburban facade and exposes the nerve ends of a family in crisis: Tobias is settled and seemingly resilient but still vulnerable; Agnes is imperious but philosophical; and Claire, the always recovering drunk (but not an alcoholic).
What do they do when fear strikes and old friends show up on the doorstep
and claim shelter? The three leading actors were splendidly in touch with
their characters: Grizzard, jingling the coins in his pocket, mixing drinks, and
trying to provide an ameliorative sense of stability; Harris, a lovely presence
exuding well-being and vivifying her Jamesian dialogue; and Stritch captur-
ing the desperation beneath the self-deprecation. Only the daughter's role
(played by Mary Beth Hurt) remained problematic. But the play and the actors—despite their widely varied backgrounds—were in eloquent harmony.

After the opening, there was a party at Tavern on the Green. At their entrance, the actors were applauded and there was an ovation for the playwright. The next day the reviews were highly favorable, and they continued to
be so throughout the week, even from those critics who had had a negative or
reserved response to the play in 1966. Two months later, A Delicate Balance
won a Tony award as best revival of a play and Tony awards also went to
Gutierrez as best director and Grizzard as best actor. It had been expected
that Stritch, who had received adulatory personal notices, would also win, but
the best actress award went to Carol Burnett for Moon over Buffalo.

Although Albee and his childhood friend Noel Farrand had not seen each
other in several years, they had frequent telephone conversations and continued to exchange letters, and Albee sent him a regular supply of tapes of classical music. He remained one of Albee's most loyal friends. Farrand had
severe medical problems in recent years. Suffering from diabetes, he had had
one leg and the other foot amputated and was confined to a wheelchair. He
had been living in a nursing home in Freeport, Maine, but in February 1995
he had been able to move to a private apartment in Brunswick. He was always
faithful about sending Albee messages on his birthday and in March he sent
him his greetings addressing him as always as "Dearest Edward Reedivich," a
hangover from their days in the Rachmaninoff Society. "Escaped from Booby-
hatch," he announced and closed the letter, "Thinking of you with all love
(esp. Sunday) and walking Santayanayan and wagging my tale."

On August 21, 1996, Farrand died. In his last weeks he had apparently
been in one of his manic phases, drinking again and smoking heavily, and
had fallen into a diabetic coma. Albee was of course greatly saddened by his

death: Farrand was his last close link to his childhood, and when they talked they had an intuitive sense of what the other was thinking. For all his mania, Farrand had a sharp mind and memory. "I could drag up something from the past," said Albee, "and he would know it instantly. I don't think he forgot anything, and he could quote things at great length." Looking back, he said, "We grew up together. We were both outsiders. My oldest friend. No question."

A *Delicate Balance* had a healthy but not a long run, closing September 29 after 186 performances. Toward the end of the run, Rosemary Murphy, who portrayed Claire in the original production, replaced Elizabeth Wilson as Edna. The week before the closing, the production remained in superb condition and was still attracting large audiences. It could have been extended with additional replacements, except for the fact—as Albee said in the program for the play when it was revived the following year in London—that "some of the cast members had a bad falling out and refused to continue. Shame on them!"

He explained that the seeds of the dissension had been planted early, but the alliances kept shifting. When Stritch was onstage she was the center of attention. At one point, it was "everybody against Stritch." "I have the feeling," he said, "that the three principals did not like each other. I think there was some question of alignments and who liked whom, and if Gerry was being nicer to Stritch than he was to the others." Until the show closed, he was unconcerned about the private war: "As long as it doesn't get in the way of the performance, as long as they can use it in their interpretation. But it just makes it rather chilly backstage." When A *Delicate Balance* closed, Albee was in London for the opening of a revival of *Virginia Woolf* at the Almeida Theater. He sent the *Delicate Balance* cast a note saying he was sorry he couldn't be there "at our unnecessary closing."

Having established a working partnership with Robert Fox, Elizabeth Mc-Cann decided, with Albee's agreement, that the next play of his they would do in London would be *Virginia Woolf*, which had not had a major London revival since 1987 when Patrick Stewart and Billie Whitelaw did it. In 1981 Paul Eddington and Margaret Tyzack (replacing Joan Plowright) had played the roles at the National Theater. During the tryout of the National production, Albee took Plowright aside and encouraged her to express Martha's vulgarity, "to let out all the stops. . . . You can do it," he said. "Joan Plowright can do it," she replied, "but Lady Olivier cannot."

To ensure the success of the new production, the producers signed two important stars, Dame Diana Rigg and David Suchet, to play Martha and George. For Rigg, one of England's ranking actresses, Martha was to be her third queen-size "M" role in a row, coming after *Medea* and *Mother Courage*. Jonathan Kent had directed her in both those classics and it had been his idea that she should do Martha next. For Suchet, a valuable member of the Royal Shakespeare Company before he became a television star as Agatha Christie's Hercule Poirot, it was a fulfillment of a dream. (Coincidentally when Poirot was shown in the United States, it was on the *Mystery!* series on Public Television introduced by Rigg.) Suchet had first seen *Virginia Woolf* in the 1976 Broadway revival starring Colleen Dewhurst and Ben Gazzara. Ever since then, he had wanted to play George. In 1995, his agent happened to ask him if there was any role he coveted. He immediately said George in *Virginia Woolf*. The agent then asked if he had any suggestion as to who might be his Martha, and he said Diana Rigg. To his surprise, he was informed that she had recently been approached to play Martha in a London revival. "Fight for me," said Suchet. "I've got to do this." The fact that Suchet had recently starred in David Mamet's *Oleanna*, directed by Pinter, weighed in his favor.

Howard Davies, who has an affinity for American plays and had done works by O'Neill, Williams, and Miller, had been trying to put together a production of *Virginia Woolf* and was brought in as director. First he had to be interviewed by the playwright. The meeting took place at Albee's loft in New York. Davies remembers: "I was obviously meant to admire his art, so I said, 'That looks like a Chagall,' and he said, 'Yes, it's an early Chagall. Unsigned.' I got one passed mark on that. Then he said, 'So, *Three Tall Women*, which production did you like best, the one in New York or the one in London?' I said, 'The one in America because it didn't suffer from a star performance.' That seemed to go down quite well, except that I didn't tell him I hadn't seen the one in London."

Albee was at the Almeida Theater for the first days of rehearsal and then returned midway in the rehearsal period to give the director notes on the production. He also watched the final run-through before the first public performance, and it was a disaster. The lighting was still being adjusted, a photographer was taking pictures, and suddenly Rigg forgot her lines. "Everything went," she recalled, "and for the first time I wept hopelessly in my dressing room because they were going to bring in the audience on the following day. I was sobbing, 'I'm sorry I fucked everything up.' Edward said, 'It's a very difficult part in a very difficult play.' One felt that he understood."

George and Martha are written as equal competitors, bonded in love and engaged in battle. Their relative strength largely depends on the actors playing the roles. In the original production, Uta Hagen tended to dominate, but Arthur Hill eventually evened the balance. In the film, Taylor and Burton fought to a draw. As Suchet said, "History says that the play is a one-woman show. Richard Burton didn't think it was a one-woman show." However, in the Broadway revival, Dewhurst overpowered Gazzara. The opposite was true in a production at the Hartford Stage Company, matching Marlo Thomas's bland Martha with Robert Foxworth's forceful George. John Lithgow reportedly outshone Glenda Jackson in the Los Angeles revival. As with Kate and Petruchio, Beatrice and Benedick, so much relies on the pairing of the actors. As new actors come along, Albee considers their suitability. Meryl Streep and Kevin Kline—are they old enough? Kathy Bates, Susan Sarandon, Christine Lahti, Stockard Channing? Tommy Lee Jones, Alan Rickman? Albee once thought about Shirley MacLaine as Martha; occasionally he has wondered about Liza Minnelli and Bette Midler. Others have always had their ideas about casting. Easily the most eccentric production would have been the one discussed by Peter Sellars. He would have directed Ron Vawter and Karen Finley as George and Martha, and Wallace Shawn and Lola Pashalinski as Nick and Honey. When Vawter died, the idea was abandoned.

The opening of *Virginia Woolf* in London was glamorous, now the Albee standard on the West End. In the audience were Tom Stoppard, Peter Shaffer, Goldie Hawn, and a pair of Foxes (Robert the producer and Edward, one of his actor brothers). The set was semi-naturalistic, a living room with woods seen in the background. The opening line, "Jesus H. Christ," said offstage, was strangely muffled, and as Diana Rigg entered she seemed toned down and subdued. As the play continued, she smoothed out Martha's vulgarity. She captured the humanity but not the monstrous side of the woman. In performance, Suchet turned out to be the stronger (and also the more American, with a very convincing accent). As he took charge, the play shifted in George's direction. His scenes with Nick (Lloyd Owen) took center stage away from his arguments with Martha. The play remained tightly wound and tense, as it exposed the roots of marriage, betrayal, envy, cowardice, opportunism, and love bound together with hate.

Almost all the reviews were favorable. Albee summarized them: "Shattering dramatic experience, a masterpiece, blah, blah, blah, blah, blah." Rigg won the *Evening Standard* award as best actress.

This was one of four overlapping major revivals of the play. Within a two-week period in September, productions of *Virginia Woolf* had opened in Paris, London, and Stockholm (Albee had gone to all three), and there was also one at the Coconut Grove Playhouse in Florida, starring Elizabeth Ashley. The Stockholm revival had arbitrarily split the play in two. In the middle of Honey's dance ("I dance like the wind") in the second act, the curtain came down and there was an intermission. When the curtain went up, she was still dancing. Albee was horrified.

The morning after he saw the production, he held a press conference in which he said that splitting the play into two acts was intolerable. "No conductor would dare perform a three movement symphony and go through the first movement and into the second movement and then stop in the middle and have an intermission and then go on. No curator hanging a triptych at a museum would dare to cut the center panel in half and make it a diptych." He said that unless the original intermissions were restored, he would discontinue the production. The producer guaranteed that Albee's wishes would be respected, and the production continued. Some weeks later, Niels Astrup and Myriam Boyer, the actor and the actress playing George and Martha in Paris, gave too convincing a performance. A battle broke out onstage between them. He choked her so hard that she responded by slapping his face. Astrup, who was also the coproducer, fired the actress after the performance, and the show closed for a week. The actress later sued for wrongful dismissal.

Three Tall Women had also been done in Stockholm, and when the Swedish director Bjorn Melander was in New York, Martha Coigney invited him to dinner along with Albee and other guests. She showed Albee photographs of Melander's production at the Royal Dramatic Theater in Stockholm. In one picture there was a man standing in the background. Because the only male figure in the play is the young man sitting at his mother's bedside, Albee asked the director who that person was. Melander said that it was scenery. Albee said, "It looks to me like an extra human being, which means an extra character." "But he doesn't speak," said the director. "It's just an evocation." Evocation or not, the playwright was furious and demanded that the man be removed from the production or he would close the play. The man was removed. Coigney explains, "He is enormously protective of the truth in production of his plays in other parts of the world. He loses every bit of a sense of humor if he thinks anybody has done a piece of cosmetic surgery or addition to one of the plays."

For the production of *Virginia Woolf* in Florida, there was the question of who would play opposite Ashley. Michael Wilson, who was directing it, sent the author a list of possible candidates. Albee wrote in comments on some of them: Christopher Walken ("bad news"), John Malkovich ("if you want two headaches, ok"), Mandy Patinkin ("don't be silly"), William Hurt ("trouble"), David Morse, later to score a considerable success in *How I Learned to Drive* ("who he?"). Frank Converse was signed for the role. As the production began, the actress had apparently been demonstrating her temperament, reason enough for the author to refer to her as Dame Elizabeth. For the moment, he seemed caught between dames. Asked who was the best Martha and if there was a definitive Martha, he answered, unsurprisingly, "Not that I know of. I've seen a lot of good ones. Put them all together, they're fine." Then he said that he liked a lot of what Colleen Dewhurst did in his Broadway revival. His conclusion: "There is no definitive Martha, as there is a definitive A in *Three Tall Women*." Between Myra Carter and Maggie Smith, he said, "I would choose Myra, but only if I was pressed up against the wall and told to make a choice or they would shoot me. I thought Maggie was wonderful." He said that he loved the London production of *Virginia Woolf:* "It's very theatrical and detailed and well-acted."

Coincident with the London opening, he received a letter from the University of Central Florida. He had accepted an invitation to visit the university as part of a Distinguished Author series and was asked to choose a passage from one of his plays, perhaps *Virginia Woolf,* which could be printed in a limited edition as a broadside. Significantly, he chose a political passage in which George answers a challenge from Nick. In it, he says that a civilization is built of principle and order "to the point where there *is* something to lose . . . then all at once, through all the music, through all the sensible sounds of men building, attempting, comes the *Dies Irae*. And what is it? What does the trumpet sound? Up yours. I suppose there's justice to it, after all the years . . . Up yours."

A week after the opening in London, Albee sent Rigg a letter congratulating her on the *Evening Standard* award and pointing out "one danger area" in her performance, "a tendency—most probably when you're tired—to make Martha too pitiable in Act Three." He said it was important to remember that Martha said, "Some night I will go too far," not "I have gone too far." "What's so important is that George's revelation about the death of the son be a surprise to Martha (i.e., 'you can't do that'). I guess this is really a night like any other, except that Martha has broken the rules while not even realizing it." Another danger point came with the line "I don't like what's going to happen." That line, he said, should not be thrown away, it must be foreboding. "Now if George annoys and angers Martha sufficiently (the slaps, etc., leading up to the kids' reentrance), you will have the drive and energy to do the section beginning 'You want our son? All right, you'll have him not as a lament, but proudly, even joyously.' " Rigg answered, "Point taken about not becoming too pitiable, have generally toughened up in that area and become much more celebratory about the son."

With the help of its stars, the play had a long run on the West End. As Albee admitted on the day of the opening, "I've had a very good year."

For several years, Albee had been a member of the nominating committee for the Kennedy Center Honors in Washington, and in December of 1996 he was finally honored himself. He was the fourth playwright to be given that award after Tennessee Williams, Arthur Miller, and Neil Simon (one wonders why Simon got his first). In 1996, the other honorees were Johnny Cash, Benny Carter, Jack Lemmon, and Maria Tallchief. As his personal guests, Albee invited Jonathan Thomas, Elaine Steinbeck, Joanna Steichen, Maureen Anderman, and Mark Wright. The night before the award ceremony, there was a State Department dinner at which the honorees were given their medals. Each was individually toasted, Albee by Irene Worth, who delivered the toast from *Tiny Alice*.

On the afternoon of the presentation, a reception was held in the East Room of the White House. As a galaxy of politicians and artists watched, President Clinton spoke about each of the honorees. With Albee, he was specific, pointed, and accurate. He said:

> Edward Albee's life epitomizes the rebellious spirit of art. From childhood, he challenged convention. He left college for the streets of New York where he worked by day and wrote by night. For ten years he pursued his art with single-minded purpose, but without recognition.
>
> Then, in only three weeks in 1958, he wrote a play that took the American theater by storm and changed it forever: *Zoo Story*, a play about a young drifter and a well-to-do stranger who meet on a lonely park bench. It was the first of many plays by Edward Albee that dared us to look at ourselves in the same stark light he turned on our fears, our failings, and our dreams. For over forty years, his work has defied convention and set a standard of innovation that few can match. From *Who's Afraid of Virginia Woolf*, to *Tiny Alice* to *Three Tall Women*, his plays have invigorated the American theater and inspired a new generation of playwrights to do the same.
>
> Tonight our nation—born in rebellion—pays tribute to you, Edward Albee. In your rebellion, the American theater was reborn.

The fireplaces in the White House were blazing, the rooms were festooned with flowers, and a band played as guests celebrated and met the president. Seizing the opportunity to proselytize for the arts, Albee told Clinton that he should take a public stand in favor of the beleaguered National Endowment for the Arts. Clinton said that there was enough money in the budget to keep the NEA and National Public Radio going for another year. Albee said, "That's not enough." The next day he followed up that conversation with a letter urging the president to make a strong public statement in support of the NEA, reiterating that "people should pay attention to the forces of darkness that oppose the creative act," and "once you start censoring the arts in a country, democracy falls apart." At the reception on Sunday, surrounded by his friends, Albee was wearing his Kennedy Center medal around his neck and said he planned to keep it on when going to the gym or taking a shower. He seemed happy, or at least at ease.

I had a fantasy about the weekend. Because Albee had been born in Washington and had still not tried to trace his natural parents, I thought that at the ceremony that evening, a coat-check attendant or a new ambassador would reveal herself as Louise Harvey, Edward Albee's long-lost mother. "That would have been dramatic," Albee said later. "If they had wanted to do it right, they could have this old, old lady come onstage in a spotlight. And then, 'Son, Son'; 'Mother, Mother.' That would have been lovely. I would have burst into tears."

Albee and Thomas sat high up in a box watching the tribute unfold. After Johnny Cash, Maria Tallchief, and Benny Carter were honored, there was an intermission. Albee went to the presidential box and, among other things, he and Clinton talked about how women had risen in rank in the military. Albee said, "Women are still not allowed in combat roles, are they?" Clinton explained that they were not in combat but they did fly planes on and off aircraft carriers. As in their previous discussion about federal support of the arts, in a brief conversation there was healthy give and take.

When it was Albee's turn to be honored, Elaine Stritch came out on the stage and did the topless bathing suit speech from A Delicate Balance and then spoke for herself. She said she did not know anything about the playwright's personal life but she goes to his annual holiday party and in New York "that means a friendship." She then repeated one of Mark Wright's favorite stories about the original production of Virginia Woolf. An elderly couple was coming out of the show, and the wife was complaining that married people simply did not talk the way George and Martha did onstage. Her husband snapped, "For Christ's sake, shut up." Then, in a filmed collage of moments in Albee's life, there were glimpses of him as a child on horseback and at Choate, scenes from the early plays, my Newsweek cover about him as "Odd Man In" on Broadway, Richard Burton and Elizabeth Taylor in a visceral scene from the film of Virginia Woolf, and views of the changing face of Albee from youth to maturity. After the film, it was Grizzard's turn to speak. He said that on a previous occasion when he had been asked to say something about Albee, he had commented, "Edward is the smartest man I know and I've met four presidents." As laughter filled Grizzard's pause, he added, "Mr.

President, I had not met you at the time." Then the actor played Peter in a scene from *The Zoo Story*. Wearing her Mainbocher gown from *Tiny Alice*, Irene Worth talked about the reception of the original production: "They didn't understand the play, or the gown" and repeated the toast from the play. That was followed by Stritch as Martha and Rosemary Harris doing Agnes's closing speech in *A Delicate Balance*. After the segment honoring him, Albee stood up in the box and acknowledged the applause. He made a point of looking around the theater, downstairs in the orchestra and waving to the people in the balcony behind him.

Seeing the film, hearing the tributes, and then having to stand up and take a bow, Albee had a curious sensation. He later said, "I kept saying to myself, 'This is supposed to be a high point in my life, but here I am judging whether or not they did it well. It was interesting but I was feeling a little critical of the way it was done. I was so aware of the stage quality of the whole thing, that it was just another production I was looking at. I participated in it, but, as in everything else, I watched myself participating. And was this a high point? I wasn't feeling high-pointish. Some of my friends called it the High Time Award. High time, Edward. There it goes: I was observing again, observing what was happening to me and wondering why I wasn't in a flood of tears the way you're supposed to be at a time like that. Right afterward I turned to Johnny Cash and asked him if he was deeply moved, or was he sort of observing. He said, 'Yes, me too.' "

The next day Albee was knocked down from his pedestal and confronted with the absurd reality of life. *The Washington Post* ran photos of the Kennedy Center honorees, with one of Albee and Elaine Steinbeck, with Jonathan Thomas in the background. The picture was captioned, "Playwright Edward Albee and his wife, Percy, take center stage last night at the Kennedy Center." It was a howler of a mistake worthy of one of E. B. White's amusing newsbreaks in *The New Yorker*. Albee telephoned Elaine Steinbeck and asked her if she wanted a divorce. He immediately shot off a correction to *The Post*. His response appeared two days later under the headline DISTRESSING MISTAKE:

> While I was delighted that *The Post* photographed me at the Kennedy Center, I was shocked that the newspaper had given me a wife, and that her name is Percy. This kind of sloppy journalism is deeply distressing, for two people are with me in the photograph: Mrs. John Steinbeck—widow of the Nobel laureate, who is a dear friend, though to whom I am not married and whose name is not Percy—and Mr. Jonathan Thomas, with whom I have been living happily for 27 years.

20
A New Baby

Edward survives good news and success with fortitude.

*W*ITH his rediscovered success, Albee might have been expected to rest on his laurels, but he is enough of a realist to know that those laurels can be wrenched away from him in an instant. The fluctuating rhythm in his life of failure-success-failure-success made him constantly wary. Perhaps for that reason—in contrast to many other artists—he does not believe in surrounding himself with awards, photographs of himself with other famous people, posters of his shows, or other mementos. To him, to exhibit these things would be embarrassing, "showing off." None of his awards, including his Pulitzer Prize awards, are in evidence in his loft, except for a London *Evening Standard* award used as a stand to support a sculpture, an African animal mask. That award is useful.

As Jonathan Thomas says, "Edward survives good news and success with fortitude." He is also an indefatigable worker, and even as *Three Tall Women* continued exponentially, with productions at regional theaters and in other countries, and as his other plays were revived, and as he seemed to be continually feted and honored, he immersed himself in his writing. He had an idea for a new play called *The Play about the Baby*. In November 1995, he first mentioned that he was writing the play. He was pleased with the title. When people would ask him about his new play, he could say, "The Play about the Baby?" And they would answer, "But what's the title?" The dialogue could become an Abbott and Costello "Who's on First" routine. He said he had written about forty minutes of the first act and there were four characters, a

middle-aged couple, who is or is not related, and a young couple. The themes
were identity, people as possessions, and surrogate parents—themes that per-
sisted since *The Lady from Dubuque* and other plays where "reality is created
by our need for it." He had been working on the play on his various plane
trips, writing in longhand and carrying the manuscript in his soft black briefcase. On a plane, Albee with his neat briefcase might be mistaken for a diplo-
mat (or a spy). Going through security, the play set off no alarm.

   While writing *The Play about the Baby*, he was already thinking about another play, one that would deal with a doctor who injects himself with the
AIDS virus. In it, the author would examine society's reaction to that act. Coincidentally, a play by Austin Pendleton on the same subject opened Off-Off-
Broadway. "I searched around for an equivalent offense," Albee said. He had
three other ideas for plays: "They're like stacked airplanes above an airport
waiting to land." He added, "It's nice not to be in the position of waking up
one day without a play in your head."

   By June 1996, he had a clear conception where he was heading with *The
Play about the Baby*. Before going to Montauk to work on it, he said that it
was "finished in my head." He was thinking of it as a chamber play, not as a
large-scale piece. By November, he had finished the first act and was seventeen minutes into the second act. He knew the exact length because he had
read it aloud to himself and timed it. He was going to Florida in December
(after the Kennedy Center honors) and was determined to finish it by early
January, when he was due to return to Washington to receive a National
Medal of Arts from the president (along with Stephen Sondheim, Robert
Redford, and others). He said that he had a "wonderful visual idea for the end
of the play," which meant adding another character. Now there were five people in the play. The new character was, he said, "the baby," to be played, he
thought, "by a smallish female inside a large rubber baby," or perhaps the
puppetlike costume would be constructed out of some other material.

   On March 21, 1997, Albee gave me a copy of *The Play about the Baby*. It
was an absurdist comedy with farcical overtones about paternity, maternity,
and how the imagination can act to control reality. The four characters wear
generic names: Man, Woman, Boy, Girl. A young couple has a baby and an
older couple play games of possession and memory with them, trying to convince them that the baby, now inexplicably missing, never existed. In that
sense, there was an echo of *Virginia Woolf*, as the older pair outwit and "get
the guests." One suspected that the author had fun writing this play, but he
had to be careful not to evoke too many memories of earlier plays. In the play
there were visual surprises, including, as a trick ending, the appearance of the

title baby. Actors needed a light touch and a rhythmic sense: The dialogue seemed choreographed. Several lines lodged in one's memory: "The baby bundle." "We've come to take the baby." A week later I told Albee that I liked the play, but had some questions about it. He said he had favorable responses from Anthony Page, Howard Davies, and Jonathan Kent at the Almeida Theater. He had already begun casting it in his mind. He said he wished Fritz Weaver were younger and could play the older man. Because A *Delicate Balance* was being done in London in the fall, he said any production of *The Play about the Baby* would probably be postponed until the following year.

Where did the play come from? Then and later Albee would not—or could not—say, but it seemed apparent that it derived from his lifelong obsession with the meaning of parenting. Such questions had appeared in his apprentice plays and as early as *The American Dream* and had reappeared in *Who's Afraid of Virginia Woolf?* and subsequent works. One impetus for writing the play may have been his own curiosity about his birth and adoption.

In April 1997, he went to Wilmington, Delaware, for the presentation of the Common Wealth Award, a $25,000 prize given to people in a variety of arts and sciences. The playwrights who had previously won it were Harold Pinter, Tennessee Williams, Athol Fugard, Samuel Beckett, Arthur Miller, and August Wilson. That year, Albee was honored along with Seamus Heaney. In his acceptance speech, Albee took the opportunity to talk about censorship and self-censorship of artists, "the attempt of the forces of darkness in the Congress to destroy the National Endowment for the Arts."

In May he delivered a graduation speech at the University of Houston. In it, he referred to what he calls "the wounding of education," the fact that young people are wounded by being educated into awareness of racism and the intrusion of religion on government. He also said that within the next twenty or thirty years America was going to be a truly multiracial society, "and it is our responsibility to accept this with enthusiasm and love." He received a standing ovation (and an honorary degree). Several weeks later he got another honorary degree from the State University of New York at Purchase and would receive still another from Dartmouth College in June. Also in June there was a reading of *The Play about the Baby* at Albee's loft, with George Grizzard, Patricia Kilgarriff, an actor from Houston, and an understudy from *Three Tall Women.*

Recently he had been to a lunch that William Luers, the president of the Metropolitan Museum of Art, had given in honor of Vaclav Havel, the president of the Czech Republic. Havel had been invited to speak about Albee at the Kennedy Center honors, but because of illness was unable to attend. Albee said that at the lunch Havel (who was suffering from cancer) seemed healthy and in good spirits. He was there with his new wife. Albee said about Havel: "There's a curious thing he does. He speaks English perfectly well, but whenever he gets up to make public comments, he speaks Czech. It has to be translated. We all talk to him in English." Philip Roth was also a guest at that lunch. He and Albee had not talked since Roth's malicious essay about *Tiny Alice* in the *New York Review of Books* ("The Play That Dare Not Speak Its Name"), but that day they had a friendly conversation. He said Roth told him that now at sixty-five he had discovered that the only thing he cared about was writing. As always, Albee was the playwright who dares to speak his mind. He commented, "The main character in his new novel has prostate trouble and is impotent. Maybe Roth can't do much besides write."

After *Three Tall Women*, Maggie Smith was looking for another play to do on the West End. One evening she and Eileen Atkins shared a dressing room for a charity event. At the time Atkins was starring with Vanessa Redgrave and Paul Scofield in *John Gabriel Borkman* at the Royal National Theater. She and Redgrave, who had recently appeared together in *Vita and Virginia*, were playing sisters. In the dressing room, Atkins looked at Smith and realized for the first time that there was a resemblance between them. Both are very slender, have long faces and wide eyes. Atkins thought that every evening she had to go through the difficult process of trying to look more like Redgrave, "when I could easily look like Maggie" and wondered if there were some play that they could do together. She didn't say anything about that idea to Smith but, coincidentally, Smith had a similar thought.

The next morning Maggie Smith called Robert Fox and said that she had looked in the mirror and realized that she and Atkins resembled one another. Wasn't there a play in which they could play sisters? At that point, Fox was in negotiations to bring the Broadway company of the revival of *A Delicate Balance* to London. Instead he decided to do it with Smith and Atkins. Having her choice of roles, Smith decided not to play the leading role of Agnes, but Agnes's sister Claire, the smaller but showier part, the one that Elaine Stritch had turned into such a huge success in the New York revival. Atkins agreed to play Agnes.

When Atkins saw the play in its original Broadway production, she had had an adverse reaction to it, especially to the idea of the friends suddenly seeking shelter with Agnes and Tobias: "Two people turn up on your doorstep. Tell them to pull themselves together!" Subsequently she had turned down an offer to play the daughter in the first London production. But reading and working on the play she completely changed her mind about it and blamed her early opinion on the fact that she was being "terribly British" in her response.

Anthony Page, who had directed Smith in *Three Tall Women* and had followed with a Tony award-winning production of *A Doll's House*, was signed as director and John Standing was named to play Tobias. Rehearsals were, Atkins said, "agonizing and difficult, one of the worst rehearsal periods I've ever gone through." For her, the worst was at the very beginning. After the first day, Page told her that at Albee's request, her final speech at the end of act three was going to be given to Smith because Smith did not have enough to say in the last act. In that speech, Agnes muses on the passage of time. You hear the battle but when you finally ascend to the top of the hill, "there's nothing there . . . save rust; bones; and the wind." It is a lyrical statement and one that grows naturally out of Agnes's character. She is the philosopher, Claire the pragmatist. When Page told her of the switch, Atkins was enraged. The director explained that years earlier the original American producer of the play (Richard Barr) had felt that Claire did not have enough to do in the last act and suggested that Albee might give that speech to Claire. However, the speech stayed with Agnes in the original production. Atkins did not believe the story and felt that if it were true it undermined her position in the cast.

Although she went along with the change, she continued to feel it had been a mistake. As she said, "I still don't understand how such an absolutely marvelous writer could move that speech from one sister to the other. It's a wonderful introspective speech. For my money, Claire would never be that introspective. I was somewhat appalled that he did that, and it put me off on a very bad footing with him. It made me angry and mistrustful of both him and Anthony."

What followed sounds like backstage gossip but says something about an actress's feeling of possessiveness about the integrity of a character. To find out the truth about the speech in the New York production, Atkins called Zoë Caldwell, who asked Hume Cronyn (the original Tobias).

He said there was never any question: The speech always belonged to Agnes. Through the theatrical grapevine, Atkins's question to Caldwell eventually reached Elaine Stritch, who later said to Smith that she had heard she had stolen Eileen Atkins's speech. Atkins made it clear that her argument was not with Smith, who at one point offered to give the speech back to her. Atkins responded, "No, no. It was given to you, honey." "I don't resent Maggie," she said later. "I resent any writer with a play like that, which has been done for years, just casually giving a speech to another character."

Albee's version of the switch: "After listening to the first run-through, I remember sitting there thinking that speech belongs to Claire. It just seemed right for the character to have it—not Maggie Smith, but the character. It had nothing to do with Eileen Atkins versus Maggie Smith." In explanation of why he thought Claire would make that statement, he said, "She's been an outsider watching what happens in the family and commenting on it." But would he change it in future editions of the play? "I probably should," he said, tentatively. "It's much better that way. It balances better—more delicate." Claire, who dominates the early part of the play, then largely disappears. This also happened with Big Daddy in *Cat on a Hot Tin Roof*, and Tennessee Williams rewrote the play to bring the character back onstage. Perhaps Albee could have done something similar with Claire, writing a new scene for her in the third act. Page regards the question of the transferral of the dialogue as "a storm in a teacup."

As rehearsals proceeded there were other problems. Atkins did not like her character and felt that she was being pushed to make her more horrendous. Worrying about her accent, she telephoned Julie Harris to ask her to make a tape of what an upper-class woman living in a suburb of New York would sound like. Harris sent a message back, saying, "Think of Katharine Hepburn and cut it in half." Hepburn had, of course, played Agnes in the film version of *A Delicate Balance*.

Along the way, there were small changes. Early in the play, Claire, holding a brandy glass, lies down on the floor. Tobias lights a cigarette for her and Claire says, "That will give me everything I need. A smoke, a sip and a good hard surface." In New York, Stritch had played that moment with great panache and earned the audience's laughter. In rehearsal, Smith objected: "Why am I lying on the floor? Middle-aged people don't lie on the floor." When Smith refused to go on the floor and played the scene on a sofa, Albee rewrote the line to "A smoke, a sip and an attentive listener." On tour, Smith was still having problems with the scene and during a rehearsal asked Atkins what she thought she should do. She said, "I don't care whether you're on the floor or not, but 'a smoke, a sip and an attentive listener' is a lousy line compared with 'a smoke, a sip and a good hard surface,' because that line is about fucking and that's what this scene is about. You're inviting Tobias. If you say 'an attentive listener,' it means nothing." She added, "The sofa looks violently hard anyway, so say 'good hard surface.' " Smith returned to the original line.

Robert Fox wanted the play to be performed in two acts, putting a single intermission in the middle of the second act. The two-act version was tried one night and Albee was adamantly opposed: "The first act was fine. The second act was lugubrious and endless. It does not work dramatically."

In the end, little of this mattered. The two actresses looked and seemed like sisters and delivered a beautifully modulated double performance. Although, as Albee recognized, the setting seemed stolidly English and not like American suburbia, the production was assured and the accents (with uncredited thanks to Katharine Hepburn) were well measured. Before the play opened, Albee had said that he thought of himself as an international writer rather than as a regional one. With the exception of a few plays like *The Death of Bessie Smith* with a specific American background, his work could, he thought, be easily translated into another environment. This was not true, for example, with Tennessee Williams. "When I see my plays in England," Albee said, "they don't strike me as being terribly American."

As with the Broadway revival, the offstage conflicts seemed to have no ill effect on the performances. The play and the cast received generally favorable reviews, with the best notices going to Atkins. She, not Smith, received the *Evening Standard* as best actress, the third year in a row that an Albee actress had won that prestigious award. At Atkins's request, Smith presented the award. In her acceptance speech, Atkins said that acting was like tennis, and you only improve your game if you play with the best players: "I took this part for one reason only, to get up onstage and play with Maggie Smith." Then she worked her way around to the play: "I loathed Agnes at first. Having loathed and cursed Edward Albee for about six weeks, I suppose I am going to say thank you very nicely to him now, and admit that it was a good part." And she thanked the rest of the cast. The delicate balance of the production was preserved.

Albee continued to work on *The Play about the Baby*. In the revised version, he indicated that the baby's puppetlike appearance should be considered an alternate ending. Later he excised the scene entirely. While he was in London, there was a reading of the play at the Almeida with Jeremy Irons and Frances de la Tour, directed by Howard Davies. A production was scheduled for the next year, to try out in Malvern, England, and then to open in London in early September.

In New York on an evening in November 1997, Albee acted in one of his own plays. He and Irene Worth read *Counting the Ways* for charity. The reading had been won in a raffle and was presented in the home of Virginia Zabriskie, the art dealer, as an after dinner entertainment. Eighteen people were there, mostly well-dressed women. One man leaned back in his chair and snoozed through most of the twenty-five-minute reading. Undaunted, the two actors gave a stylish performance. The next day was Edward Albee day at the City University of New York. The theater critic Edwin Wilson led a panel discussion about the Albee-Barr-Wilder Playwrights Unit. John Guare, Lanford Wilson, and Paul Zindel spoke about their various debts to the Playwrights Unit and to Albee himself, who listened with obvious discomfort as, in effect, he was eulogized. Then he and I had a public dialogue. Later he said, "I've never heard myself referred to in the past tense so much. I wanted to crawl quietly out of the auditorium."

Although there were no Albee plays in New York that season, there were revivals of his work at various regional theaters. Sidney Berger directed *All Over* at Stages, an Off-Broadway–size theater in Houston, and Mark Lamos did *Tiny Alice* starring Richard Thomas at Hartford Stage. Glyn O'Malley had compiled a production of a one-man show called "Albee's Men" in California and then brought it to Robert Brustein's American Repertory Theater in Cambridge, Massachusetts. It was the first Albee play that Brustein had ever presented. Looking forward to the production, he wrote to the author, praising Stephen Rowe, who was to play all the men and pre-reviewing the play as "a beautiful collage of your writing, a broad canvas for an array of your male characters over the years." Then he said, "Personally, I look forward to renewing a friendship with you that has been suspended since the early sixties, when we used to share symposium tables and award meetings together. In the thirty-five year interim, it would seem that we have both grown somewhat greyer and more resigned." Albee had not grown more resigned and he was not about to forget Brustein's early attacks on his plays. Albee's response: "I have more of an elephant's memory than he does."

Generally Albee celebrates his birthday privately. For his seventieth on March 12, 1998, he flew back to New York from Houston for a small dinner party given in his honor by Elizabeth McCann. That afternoon he spoke about aging: "When the old man in *Finding the Sun* asks the boy how old he is, the boy says, 'I'm 16,' and the man says, 'Don't be silly. There is no such age.' Sometimes I feel sixteen, sometimes younger. Sometimes I feel a healthy forty. The only way I ever feel anything close to my age is the way people treat me: 'Tell us, sir, with great wisdom . . .' I read the actuaries and I don't enjoy the fact that I'm supposed to drop dead in six years. I have no intention of doing that. I really would like to go on until I become desperately, painfully ill, either mentally or physically. I would like to go on forever. What's the old phrase: dying on the upswing." At the dinner party, a message was read from Harold Pinter: "But you remain so young! And brilliant! Congratulations. Love, Harold P."

Then Albee described a climactic scene in Werner Herzog's film *Aguirre: or the Wrath of God.* The conquistadors are deep in the infested jungles of South America. Indians have been following them and killing them with their poisoned arrows. People are dying everywhere. "This young soldier, delirious with disease, stands up and looks at the blinding sun and says this is not the jungle and this is not the sun. An arrow hits him in the chest and he looks down and says, 'And this is not an arrow.' "

Albee added, "And this is not a birthday and I am not seventy."

After Albee turned seventy, Jonathan Thomas observed one curious change: He began jingling coins in his pocket just as Reed Albee did when he entered a room.

Because he liked Frances de la Tour's performance as B in the London production of *Three Tall Women,* Albee always had her in mind to play the leading female role in *The Play about the Baby,* as she had at the London reading of the play. There was difficulty finding a suitable actor available for the male lead. Several British stars had turned it down because of conflicts in their schedule and other reasons, and at one point he had thought about asking Pinter to play the part. Finally Alan Howard, who had been a stalwart member of the Royal Shakespeare Company, signed on and two promising newcomers, Rupert Penry-Jones and Zoe Waites, were named to play the younger couple. Albee was in London for the beginning and the end of rehearsals in July and then joined the company in Malvern, where the play was to open in August as part of a season presented by the Almeida Theater. During the tryout, he tightened the play and changed a few words from American to British to accommodate the actors and the environment.

The day before the opening in London, Albee said he was not nervous about *The Play about the Baby,* figuring he had written it as he wanted to and the cast had been well chosen and well directed by Howard Davies. He knew, of course, that the play's future life depended partly on the critics. "They're going to like it or not," he said, "and there is not necessarily a relationship between critical acceptance and the value of the work. What can be done about that? Should I send all the critics chocolates before tomorrow night? Why worry about that which can't be helped." Then he leaped into a figure of speech. "Theater," he said, "is very much like death," and he laughed. "I know I'm going to die. It will probably happen within the next twenty years, and there's absolutely nothing I can do about it. I take care of myself. I don't have any physical excesses. I don't drink. I don't smoke. I exercise. I eat well. I'm not encouraging rapidity of demise. I know it's going to happen. I don't think I'm going to be very amused by it. But why worry about things you can't do anything about? There is plenty to worry about that you can do something about." Then about the play, he admitted, "I could be living in a fool's paradise. But I've done everything I can with this play, brought it to a state that I think is fine—aside from the set." He did not like the set. "No one has contradicted me or stood in the way of my making a fool of myself on my own terms."

On September 1, *The Play about the Baby* had its world premiere at the Almeida, a London theater that had been having a streak of uncommon successes. As usual, Albee was not planning to stay for the performance. He and Jonathan Thomas were going off to dinner, but before the curtain, he was in the theater's bar greeting friends, including Mark Wright; Elizabeth McCann; and Stefani Hunzinger, his German agent, who had flown to London for the event. Harold Pinter and Antonia Fraser arrived, and Albee and Pinter were soon having a vigorous political discussion about the Kurds and the Turks.

The play began with the birth of a baby: an offstage cry at birth, and a couple welcoming a child into the world. Then Alan Howard entered, playing into the vaudeville aspect of the play, conversing with the audience and putting an informal imprint on the performance. Revealing an antic sense of comedy, Frances de la Tour added her own spontaneity. The dialogue was sharp, swift, and conversational as the older couple bedazzled the younger pair. In contrast, Penry-Jones and Waites were passionate, highly physical, and tactile. Clearly this was a couple in love. As Howard and de la Tour teased and mocked them, the tone gradually altered to one of fear and dread until at the end of the first act Howard announced "We've come to take the baby." While repeating the motifs of the first act, the second act accelerated the seriousness, as the Man and Woman tried to convince the younger couple that the baby never existed. Finally Howard lifted the blanketed "baby" over his head and became a kind of sideshow barker. "Ladies and Gentlemen!" he said. "See what we have here! The baby bundle!" He threw it up in the air and, of course, it came down empty. Although he said, "There's never been a baby," there had been a baby, and now it was gone. Missing? Kidnapped? Abandoned? Albee offered no answer, as the play arrived at its mysterious conclusion.

The reviews were mixed, with critics split between those who felt that Albee had cannibalized his earlier work and those who thought (as I did) that he had fascinatingly evoked favorite motifs in a different style. The actors and the production received high praise, but the reviews were not the kind to send producers hurrying to move the play to the West End or to Broadway. *The*

Play about the Baby would make its gradual way to New York. It was, as intended, a chamber play and had considerable value as a kind of poetic étude, variations on a provocative theme. In it, Albee once again demonstrated his agility with language. The direct confrontational style, in which the actors engaged the audience, was a novel step for him. As with Albee's own *Box-Mao-Box* (and with later plays by Beckett), it should earn its place in the body of work, and it would be performed in other productions.

The actors were not disturbed by the play's mysteries. Alan Howard was taken by the matter-of-fact quality of the events. When his character says, "We've come to take the baby," it was, he said, like "somebody saying I've come to take the sofa or I've come to clean your drains. Or it could be a brain surgeon, a schoolteacher, or a parental figure." Aware of all the metaphorical possibilities, he wanted "not to try and make some extraordinary construct of what it all means, but to play it on the line, to the point where the past and the future is contained in the present." He saw a connection between his Albee character and Vladimir, whom he had recently played in *Waiting for Godot*. Each is "a kind of stage manager or master of ceremonies." He was unapologetic about Albee echoing familiar themes. "Every worthwhile artist—every painter, sculptor, composer—has struggled with major themes and gone back to them again and again. They're trying to find another way of expressing it."

"The play is about life," said Frances de la Tour. "A baby's being born. It's the beginning of life and it's about what happens when fear comes into life, when you get older and when you're disappointed." Playing her character was "like walking a tightrope." In common with her costar, she moved artfully from moment to moment, each one of which made perfect sense to her. "It's hysterically funny, very painful, completely bemusing—it's all those things."

Two days after the opening, after all the daily reviews had been published, Albee said that he was disappointed in the critics' reception, but he remained confident in his work. "The play is where it should be," he said firmly. "If they don't like it, fuck 'em. You don't go and rewrite to make critics happy." He offered a few points of clarification. The baby is real even though we don't actually see it. "We see its blanket. She's not nursing a blanket. She's not crazy. And she has mother's milk, so obviously she's had a baby." What happens to the baby? He reiterated that "it's made evident that reality is determined by our need" and added that the younger characters in the play "realize they cannot take the pain and loss of having a baby, so it ceases to be real." This theme, self-determination of what is reality, has always been of primary concern to Albee.

In his first monologue in the play, the Man talks about that subject, the fact that "first we *invent*, and then we *reinvent*," and that "the greater need rules the game." The character recalls an embarrassing lapse of memory. As the host of a party, he was with two friends, when "this tall older woman" walked over to them. "I turned to introduce them to the older woman standing next to me, and I looked at her, and I knew she was familiar, but I couldn't, for the life of me, remember who she was." Then one of his friends laughed and said, "We *know* your *mother*, dear." The story is directly from Albee's life. It happened at one of his loft parties. With a laugh, he explained the oversight about his mother: "I had been trying for years not to recognize her, so I think it was probably a wish come true." If, as Albee says, reality is created by our need for it, then it might be said that he no longer had a need for his mother.

21
Lost and Found

I'm past yearning for my natural parents.

I N his book *American Dreams: Lost and Found,* Studs Terkel drew word portraits of some one hundred Americans who have triumphed over adversity—racial, economic, educational—and fulfilled their dreams. Typical of the people is a grandson of slaves speaking about the day he first registered to vote. In comparison, Albee has had an easy and comfortable life. Adopted into wealth, gifted with artistic talent, he had a relatively early success and, despite various roadblocks, some of them self-erected, has gone on to continuing accomplishment and reward. That, of course, is the cover story. Underneath he has faced great familial and psychological strain and, in common with other artists of his caliber, has had to search deeply within himself for his creativity. Like Terkel's one hundred, Albee has lost and found his American dream, and as he is well aware, there is always the danger of losing it again. He shares with Samuel Beckett an innate sense of realism. Life continues until it ends: We are "born astride the grave." But it is in man's nature to keep doing what he does until he can no longer do it. "I can't go on, I'll go on." Unlike Beckett, he has a great zest for living life to the absolute fullest degree, his life as he created it.

As he said, "The single journey through consciousness should be participated in as fully as possible by the individual, no matter how dangerous or cruel or terror-filled that experience may be." As an artist, he adds, "We must go on. We must not add to the chaos but deal honestly with the idea of order, whether it is arbitrary or not."

Several years ago, a teacher on Long Island sent Albee a questionnaire. These were among the questions, and Albee's pithy answers:

What do you believe was your greatest achievement? "I hope I haven't had it yet."

What has your career been like? "Lucky, precipitous (both up & down)."

What was your school life? "Chaotic."

When did you become interested in your field? "When I started reading & seeing plays."

Were you identified as "gifted" in school? "Yes."

Description of Family. "Adoptive—we never got along."

Description of Opportunities. "I don't know what this question means."

Aspirations Today. "To be a better writer."

Did you ever have a mentor? "Sure—Chekhov, Pirandello, Beckett, etc."

What was the role of your parents? "None."

Did any one else play a significant role in your life? "Too many to mention."

To what do you attribute your achieving prominence? "Talent & grit."

Do you have a passion for what you do? "Yes."

Were there times when you had to persevere even though you felt like giving up? "No."

Were there any obstacles you felt you had to overcome? "Of course."

What do you think the major factors were which contributed to your success? "See above: talent & grit."

Because each of the women in *Three Tall Women* speaks about the happiest time in her life, it seemed appropriate to add a question to the list: What has been the happiest time in his life? Without hesitation, he said, "Now. Always."

He explained, "That's the only way to avoid regret, isn't it? If one loses one's talent, if one's ill and poor and lonely, if something that hideous were to happen to me, I would hope that I would still find something interesting about the experience." He said he thought B, the middle-aged character in the play, was the wise one: "Standing in the middle of it, being able to see 360 degrees, to see the past and look to the future. Being right now: She's very sensible. She's given up illusions."

Albee is still shadowed by questions. What, if anything, does he owe his natural parents? Does creativity have genetic roots? What would he have been like if he had been brought up by his real parents, or if he had been adopted by someone other than Reed and Frances Albee? Would his real mother have been as harmful as his adoptive mother? What effect does environment have on creativity? It is certainly possible that he is a greater artist because of his circumstance, because of what he had to react against. His adopted world—the wealthy WASPs of Westchester—became the locus and the primary object of his art. Does this mean a debt is owed to the Albees for mistreating him? As he has often said, he suffered no physical abuse at their hands, no recovered memory haunts him, but the emotional neglect was tangible. In psychological terms, he was taken in by the wrong family. Despite Reed Albee's background in the business of the performing arts and Frances Albee's various social concerns and their supposed worldliness, they knew nothing about the needs of an artist and even less about the personal needs of their son. Almost from the moment of his arrival in Larchmont, on that hilltop in the arms of his nanny, he was deprived—pampered, but deprived—starved of affection and treated more as a possession than as a child who needed nurturing. It was a hostile environment. Very early, he understood intuitively that his life—and later his art—had to be found elsewhere.

Beneath his boyhood shyness, there must have been a confidence, a certainty that he would find his own way in life. Throughout his life, Albee has been a most independent spirit, self-reliant, self-motivated, and in the purest sense of the word, self-centered. He is centered and he has a sense of self, though he also has global interests, social and political awareness, and a genuine regard for the talents—and the travails—of others. But there are those who think of him as closed off, cool, unemotional. Although that charge has continually been contradicted, he retains, even for those who know him well, an edge of mystery. In certain ways, he withholds himself. Perhaps he is afraid of rejection. He has never been psychoanalyzed and though he can be introspective, he does not easily reveal thoughts and emotions.

Any attempt to link his art and his life causes Albee to wince. There you go again: looking for connective tissue. But connective tissue is the root of his art. His plays emerge directly from and converge with his life, but a life transformed so that, in the art, it would be unrecognizable to the outsider. Even in Albee's most personal play, *Three Tall Women*, the unnamed title character(s) is a fully imagined figure, drawn to the measure of Frankie Albee while transcending her and becoming a viscerally dramatic (and highly comic) woman. Her life and her feeling about her life certainly parallel those of the character but the character becomes truer than life. Had she lived to see her play, Frankie should have been proud of the transformation, although probably she would have held it at arm's length, as she apparently did everything in her son's life.

In varying degrees, Frankie Albee exists in many of the characters in her son's plays: Mommy in *The Sandbox* and *The American Dream*, Martha in *Who's Afraid of Virginia Woolf?*, Agnes in *A Delicate Balance*, the Wife in *All Over*. It could equally be said that she does not exist there: These are fictional characters, even A in *Three Tall Women*. As with any artist, Albee has been able to take the people of his life, including himself, and recreate them in different forms as the people of his imagination. A collage of "Albee's Women" would be a panoply of strong-willed, dominant females whose lives are inextricably linked with their mates. Wives and husbands take precedence over mothers and fathers. The family has come under the playwright's scrutiny and the prognosis for progeny is as dire as it is compelling. Parents maim their children in the world of Albee.

The novelist John Irving, who was adopted by his stepfather, has said that though he knew who his natural father was, he never felt a need to look for him, because of his love for his mother and stepfather. If he liked them less, he might have looked elsewhere for his parentage. Albee rejected his adopted parents. It was his decision to leave home, just as it was his decision almost twenty years later to renew relations with his mother, and it was his trauma when in her will she chose, in effect, to disinherit him, to disown him, as his natural parents had done at his birth.

As he said about this subject, "I used to care about it, but then I discovered that I was a writer. I started discovering *me*. I found out who I was through my plays. I'm past yearning for my natural parents. I don't need it. I'm sure that's the reason."

Along his path there have been surrogate parents: Nanny Church and his maternal grandmother; Florence Weissinger, the mother of one of his childhood friends; teachers at Choate. Older admiring friends and colleagues like Richard Barr and John Steinbeck, in some respect, played parental roles. Despite the closeness and even the mentoring of these people (and of William Flanagan, the most important early force in the nurturing of his talent), Albee remained apart. He has had lovers as well as friends, and he and Jonathan Thomas are as close as any long-married heterosexual couple. Their relationship endured Albee's alcoholism and his recovery, his years of public rejection as a playwright, and his subsequent reclamation. They seemed to share a permanent bond. "I know I love Jonathan," Albee said. "I suspect he loves me. I'm sure he does, and I'm grateful for all the bad times he stayed through, and I would never do anything to hurt him. He is my stability. He's a real centered person. Mind you, I think I'm sufficiently mature that I can survive, not terribly happily, if he were to die. I would feel the loss of his presence and his company. But I don't think I would collapse." Both agreed, however, that if either died, the other's world would collapse.

Albee found himself within his art. The closer he writes to his life, the more transforming the experience and the greater the art. Difficulties arise when he puts himself in a position of being a substitute speaker for someone else's ideas. He is, as Noel Farrand said, the outstanding imaginative dramatist of his generation. With every play, he tries to do and to say something different and exploratory, without worrying about expectations or perceived limitations of the form. It was once said about the artist Milton Avery (in a catalog for which Albee wrote the introduction) that each picture he painted "seems to have been created according to its own set of rules." Each Albee play is created according to its own set of rules.

Thinking about him, one remembers the lonely little boy at Lawrenceville "with a tiny scar over one eyebrow, looking like a mark of anxiety"; the swimmer intentionally sinking to the bottom of the pool and sitting underwater holding his breath; the teenager propped up on his dormitory bed and quietly and privately writing a novel well into the night; an underaged drinker listening and laughing in a New York bar as a classmate fumblingly orders a glass of "bergin"; the playwright who was "born at thirty" when he sat down at his kitchen table and wrote, for the first time, from his heart.

As Albee looks to his future, the new plays and continuing revivals, the reinterpretations and the reevaluations, the mystery of his birth and his sense of abandonment remain.

Late in September 1998, Albee and Jonathan Thomas were driving back to Manhattan from Montauk when Samuel Barber's *Knoxville: Summer 1915* came on the radio. To Thomas's astonishment, Albee began to cry.

> One is my mother who is good to me. One is my father who is good to me. By some chance, here they are, all on this earth; and who shall ever tell the sorrow of being on this earth, lying, on quilts, on the grass, in a summer evening, among the sounds of the night . . .
>
> After a little I am taken in and put to bed. Sleep, soft smiling, draws me unto her: and those receive me, who quietly treat me, as one familiar and well-beloved in that home: but will not, oh, will not, not now, not ever; but will not ever tell me who I am.

Acknowledgments

THIS biography began in 1994, but its origins go back to the early 1960s. The first play by Edward Albee that I saw was *The Zoo Story* in its original production Off-Broadway in 1960. I first met Albee in 1962, several days after the opening of *Who's Afraid of Virginia Woolf?* on Broadway. Our initial conversation was for an article in *Newsweek* magazine that followed my review of *Virginia Woolf*. Subsequently we had several long discussions for my cover story on the playwright that appeared in the February 4, 1963, issue of *Newsweek*. This book draws upon material from that story and also from the many interviews we have had during the intervening years. The principal source is an extensive series of conversations from 1994 to 1999 with Albee at his homes in Manhattan and Montauk, and in London when he was there for the opening of various productions. In these talks, he was candid and responsive to all questions. At the same time, he gave me access to files, papers, letters, manuscripts, and his voluminous scrapbooks of clippings. My thanks to him and to Jonathan Thomas, who has also been open in offering his thoughts and comments.

During the same period, I talked to many people who have been important in Albee's life and work. Some of them and others have also provided me with copies of letters to and from him. A number of people were especially helpful. Lin Emery has the clearest memories about their childhood in Larchmont and Palm Beach, as does Celeste Seymour about the time she and Albee spent together. Robert Heide was particularly informative about Albee's early years in New York. David Diamond, Ned Rorem, Richard Howard, Pinkas Braun, Stefani Hunzinger, Michael Wager, and Edward Parone offered their detailed knowledge about his apprenticeship and after. Mark Wright and Howard Atlee, surviving members of the Albee-Barr-Wilder producing team, were able to look back clearly on the days with Richard Barr and Clinton Wilder. Joanna Steichen and Elaine Steinbeck, who are among

Albee's closest friends, spoke frankly about him and, in the latter's case, supplied information about Albee's trip to Russia with John Steinbeck. William Daniels, Milton Katselas, Uta Hagen, Arthur Hill, George Grizzard, Roscoe Lee Browne, Lou Antonio, Irene Worth, John Gielgud, Mike Nichols, Hume Cronyn, Jessica Tandy, Maureen Anderman, Glyn O'Malley, Myra Carter, Marian Seldes, Lawrence Sacharow, Elaine Stritch, Rosemary Harris, Eileen Atkins, and Elizabeth McCann provided insights about the playwright and his various works.

Separate mention should be made of Albee's actresses, a gallery of great ladies of the theater, who include those named above and also Maggie Smith, Diana Rigg, Jane Hoffman, Angela Lansbury, Deborah Kerr, Colleen Dewhurst, Bibi Andersson, Haila Stoddard, Elizabeth Taylor, and Frances de la Tour. All of them made contributions to this book as well as to Albee's plays.

David Aldeborgh, who was Albee's roommate at Choate, provided a wealth of information, including copies of the school literary magazine, newspaper, and yearbook, all with work by and reference to Albee. Officials at Lawrenceville and Choate supplied additional material. David Briggs, Albee's assistant, was a helpful guide to the playwright's files and archives. Noel Farrand's contribution is inestimable. As Albee's oldest friend (and a friend of mine), with his sharp memory for details, he was able to shed particular light on their childhood and on various stops along the way. I regret that Noel did not live long enough to read this book. My thanks, in absentia, to William Flanagan, whom I met in 1962 and whose letters (supplied by Albee, Flanagan's mother Elma, David Diamond, and others) are a significant resource for this book.

In addition, the following people spoke about Albee and/or were instrumental in supplying letters and other information: Peter Alexander, Edward Ayres, Roger Baker, Sidney Berger, Elaine Boies, Andreas Brown, Francis James Brown, Frederick Buechner, Joseph Cali, Simon Callow, Martha Coigney, Betty Comden, David A. Crespy, Kevin Cunningham, Howard Davies, Donald Davis, Ben Edwards, Robert Farrand, Father Jack Farrand, Sanford Friedman, Athol Fugard, Jack Gelber, Morris Golde, Farley Granger, Jane Greenwood, Andre Gregory, John Guare, A. R. Gurney, Peter Hall, Shirley Herz, Alan Howard, Paul Jordan, Joyce Ketay, Mimi Kilgore, Shirley Knight, Perry Knowlton, Robert Lantz, Rex Lau, Ernest Lehman, Bethel Leslie, Lyle Leverich, William Lieberman, Romulus Linney, Jeane Luere, William Luers, Sara Lukinson, Roddy McDowall, Norman Mailer, Diane Mayo, Arthur Miller, Dmitri Nabokov, James Naughton, Anthony Page, Anne Paolucci, Arthur Penn, Harold Pinter, James Purdy, José Quintero, Mrs. Charles Rice, Sam Rudy, Jean Schneider, Wallace Shawn, Jerry Sherlock, Joy Small, Stephen Sondheim, Susan Specter, John Springer, Ernest Stiers, John Stix, Tom Stoppard, Barbara Strouse, Charles Strouse, David Suchet, Richard Thomas, Galina Volchek, John von Hartz, Delphine Weissinger, Muir Weissinger Jr., Edwin Wilson, Lanford Wilson, Robert A. Wilson, Ronald Winston, John Wulp, and Paul Zindel.

Farrand's unpublished memoir, *Footnotes*, which was made available to me by Richard Cameron Wolfe, was a help, as was Richard Barr's unpublished autobiography, *You Have to Hock Your House: The Story of a Producer,* a copy of which was given to me by Albee. Lou Antonio also supplied excerpts from his logbook kept during the production of *The Ballad of the Sad Cafe,* and Edward Parone offered an essay entitled *Six Degrees of Edward Albee.*

Barr is one of many people who, without knowing it, were helpful in the preparation of this book. Those include William Flanagan, Alan Schneider, Isabel Wilder, Thornton Wilder, Clinton Wilder, Carson McCullers, Henry Fonda, Bette Davis, Katharine Hepburn, Harold Clurman, Chuck Gnys, Michael Dunn, Tennessee Williams, Richard Burton, and Samuel Beckett, all of whom spoke to me over the years about Albee. Others, including Aaron Copland, Howard Moss, John Steinbeck, Noël Coward, William Inge, Burr Tillstrom, Billy Rose, Alan Heely, Ingrid Bergman, Louise Nevelson, John Osborne, John Dexter, Kenneth Tynan, Laurence Olivier, speak through their letters, as do Albee's relatives, George Vigouroux and Jane Cotter Bendilare. My thanks to Terrence McNally for allowing me to quote from several of his letters. Those who approved the use of letters include: Ellen Adler, Lisa Aronson, Edward Beckett, Robert Brustein, Arthur Cantor, JoAnn Kirchmaier, Floria Lasky, Myron Nevelson, Riggs O'Hara, Joan Plowright Olivier, Helen Osborne, Lars Schmidt, Anne Simmons, R. W. Tillstrom, William H. Wharfe, and A. Tappan Wilder. Previously unpublished letters by Tennessee Williams are printed by permission of The University of the South, Sewanee, Tennessee (Copyright © 1999 The University of the South). The inclusion of the letter from Leonard Woolf was approved by Leonard Woolf Papers, University of Sussex Library, and letters from Aaron Copland by the Aaron Copland Fund for Music, Inc. Lyrics from "Lush Life" by Billy Strayhorn, copyright © 1949 (renewed) by Music Sales Corporation (ASCAP) and Tempo Music, Inc. All rights administered by Music Sales Corporation. International copyright secured. All rights reserved. Reprinted by permission.

For the *Newsweek* cover story, I interviewed Albee and most of the other major figures in his life up to then. Additional reporting was provided by Richard Fithian and by the late John Speicher, and my thanks go to both of them. With his novelist's curiosity and eye, Speicher tracked down many of Albee's school friends and teachers, including Michael Campo, Ed Proctor, Porter Caesar, and John Joseph. Behind them was a team of *Newsweek* correspondents in the United States and in Europe. Dick Schaap edited that story and Gordon Manning was his editor (and has faithfully encouraged my work over the years). T. H. Wenning was the theater critic and a mentor.

I never met Frances Albee, but she, of course, plays a major role in this book, as she did in her son's life. She is seen through the eyes of others, beginning with her son.

A basic resource was, of course, Albee's plays. In addition to the published texts, Albee allowed me to read various drafts, and others were read at the New York Public Library for the Performing Arts at Lincoln Center (including Albee's apprentice work, poetry, and stories as well as plays, which the playwright gave to the library). Thanks are due to Robert Marx, Robert Taylor, and others for their cooperation in using the material in the library's archives. In addition, Maureen Anderman and Lawrence Sacharow both provided early manuscripts of plays they were involved with. I have seen all of Albee's plays and have reviewed most of them (for *The New York Times*, *Newsweek*, WQXR, or *Playboy*), and this book draws upon some of those reviews.

Nancy Boensch gave additional research assistance at the Harry Ransom Collection at the University of Texas in Austin, and Leslie Nipkow, a fine actress, took time away from her career to transcribe the taped interviews with her customary diligence and theatrical knowledge. At *The New York Times*, Carol Coburn has been constant in her help on theatrical and other matters. My thanks, too, to Pamela Kent at the *Times* London bureau. My son, Ethan, continues to be a faithful and adventurous theatrical voyager and, as always, was expert in solving computer problems. Special thanks go to my agent Owen Laster, who was a primary mover in bringing about this book, and to my editor, Bob Bender.

Two people were absolutely essential to this project. My wife, Ann, provided encouragement, advice, ideas, criticism, and research assistance, all of which were needed. She made suggestions all along the way and, as always, was the first and most perceptive reader and editor of the manuscript. The person to whom I am most indebted is, of course, Edward Albee, who offered me freedom of access and was generous with his time and interest. As he knows, his life is his work, and vice versa — and the singular journey continues.

Chronology of Plays

-> *The Zoo Story.* September 28, 1959, Schiller Theater, Berlin, Germany; January 14, 1960, Provincetown Playhouse, New York City.

The Sandbox. April 15, 1960, The Jazz Gallery, New York City.

The Death of Bessie Smith. April 21, 1960, Schlosspark Theater, Berlin, Germany; March 1, 1961, York Playhouse, New York City.

Fam and Yam. August 27, 1960, The White Barn, Westport, Connecticut; October 25, 1960, Theatre de Lys, New York City.

-> *The American Dream.* January 24, 1961, York Playhouse, New York City.

-> *Who's Afraid of Virginia Woolf?* October 13, 1962, Billy Rose Theater, New York City.

The Ballad of the Sad Cafe. October 30, 1963, Martin Beck Theater, New York City.

Tiny Alice. December 29, 1964, Billy Rose Theater, New York City.

Malcolm. January 11, 1966, Shubert Theater, New York City.

A Delicate Balance. September 12, 1966, Martin Beck Theater, New York City.

Everything in the Garden. November 16, 1967, Plymouth Theater, New York City.

Box and *Quotations from Chairman Mao Tse-Tung.* March 6, 1968, Studio Arena Theater, Buffalo, New York; September 30, 1968, Billy Rose Theater, New York City.

All Over. March 27, 1971, Martin Beck Theater, New York City.

Seascape. January 26, 1975, Shubert Theater, New York City.

Listening. March 28, 1976, BBC Radio Three, London; January 28, 1977, Hartford Stage Company, Hartford, Connecticut; November 5, 1993, Signature Theater Company, New York City.

Counting the Ways. December 6, 1976, National Theater, London; January 28, 1977, Hartford Stage Company, Hartford, Connecticut; November 5, 1993, Signature Theater Company, New York City.

The Lady from Dubuque. January 31, 1980, Morosco Theater, New York City.

Lolita. March 19, 1981, Brooks Atkinson Theater, New York City.

The Man Who Had Three Arms. October 4, 1982, Goodman Theater, Chicago; October 5, 1983, Lyceum Theater, New York City.

Finding the Sun. May 10, 1983, University of Northern Colorado, Greeley, Colorado; February 4, 1994, Signature Theater Company, New York City.

Marriage Play. May 17, 1987, Vienna's English Theater, Austria; January 8, 1992, Alley Theater, Houston, Texas; October 1, 1993, Signature Theater Company, New York City.

Three Tall Women. June 14, 1991, Vienna's English Theater, Austria; July 30, 1992, River Arts Repertory, Woodstock, New York; January 27, 1994, Vineyard Theater, New York City.

The Lorca Play. April 24, 1992, Houston, Texas.

Fragments. October 10, 1993, Ensemble Theater of Cincinnati, Ohio; April 8, 1994, Signature Theater Company, New York City.

The Play about the Baby. September 1, 1998, Almeida Theater, London.

200(1)? Who Is Sylvia or The Goat?

Notes on Sources

ABBREVIATIONS

EA: Edward Albee
FA: Frances Albee
RB: Richard Barr
DD: David Diamond
NF: Noel Farrand
WF: William Flanagan
MG: Mel Gussow
AS: Alan Schneider
JS: John Steinbeck
JT: Jonathan Thomas

Every chapter draws upon the author's interviews with Edward Albee and most of them draw upon Albee's plays, letters, papers, and other writings, as stated in the text. Unless otherwise noted, all Albee interviews were with Mel Gussow between September 29, 1994, and January 14, 1999. Quotations from these talks are not individually indicated. In addition, there were interviews in 1962, 1963, 1966, 1967, 1971, 1972, 1974, 1975, 1978, and 1993, and public conversations between EA and MG at the University of Houston (March 30, 1993), and in New York at the 92nd Street Y (December 12, 1994), City University of New York (November 21, 1997), and Cooper Union (December 9, 1998, sponsored by the Lincoln Center Library of the Performing Arts).

Lincoln Center refers to the Albee papers at the Lincoln Center Library of the Performing Arts. Albee's archives refers to his personal papers and manuscripts retained by the playwright.

PROLOGUE
13 "We are talking now." James Agee, *A Death in the Family*.
16 "He's a lone traveler." Martha Coigney interview with MG, June 12, 1998.
16 "I think he suffered." Irene Worth interview with MG, May 5, 1995.
17 "the last great playwright." José Quintero interview with MG, August 11, 1998.
18 "Nothing can alter." NF letter to EA and interviews with MG, September 1, 1994 and August 31, 1995.

20   "this vague, unreasonable kinship." Mike Nichols interview with MG, September 12, 1996.
20   "a kind of dark, strong personality." Stephen Sondheim interview with MG, May 5, 1998.
20   "a mysterious number." WF interview with MG, October 29, 1962.

1. EDDIE
21   "It's lucky." Muir Weissinger Jr. interview with MG, January 4, 1963.
21   EA, introduction to *Three Tall Women*. New York: Dutton, 1995.
22   Saul Bellow, *The Actual*. New York: Viking, 1997.
22   EA adoption papers: Chambers of the Surrogate Court, Borough of Manhattan, New York City, February 1, 1929; Alice Chapin Adoption Nursery, New York City, March 30, 1929.
23   FA, news release about Reed Albee sent to *The New York Times*, November 17, 1959.
23   Information about E. F. Albee and Groucho Marx's description of him. Robert W. Snyder, *The Voice of the City: Vaudeville and Popular Culture in New York*; *American Vaudeville As Seen by Its Contemporaries*, edited by Charles W. Stein; Abel Green and Joe Laurie Jr., *Show Biz from Vaude to Video*.
24   Larchmont Official Centennial Edition.
24   Headline in the *American*, March 1925.
26   "the right balance." Jane Cotter Bendilare letter to EA, undated.
26   EA, *The Merry Month of May*, in collection at Lincoln Center.
26   "billed as my favorite woman." Ronald Winston interview with MG, January 17, 1997.
28   "Tobias retired." EA notes for *A Delicate Balance*, Lincoln Center.
30   "almost from the cradle," etc. NF interviews with MG.
32   On Frances Albee, Peter Alexander interview with MG, September 11, 1994.
32   "Grenadier Guard." Hume Cronyn interview with MG, May 19, 1994.
32   "whole FAO Schwarz catalog." Robert Farrand interview with MG, January 14, 1963.
34   "Our governesses," etc. Lin Emery interview with MG, May 31, 1997.
35   "grave, handsome child." Mrs. Russell L. Law letter to EA, February 8, 1963.
35   "we stayed up as late as we could." Ethel Hofer letter to EA, December 16, 1962.
36   "There never was a kid." Ed Wynn interview with *Newsweek*, 1962.
39   "Let's press the button." Muir Weissinger Jr. interview with MG.
40   "He was particularly sensitive and observant." Joanna Steichen interview with MG, September 19, 1996.
41   "All the governesses." Emery interview with MG.
45   "Edward said." NF interviews with MG.

2. SANTAYANIAN FINESSE
46   "An ultra-poetical." *The Brief* of the Choate School, 1945.
46   "I'm not sure I am representative." EA speech to American Council for the Arts

at 1988 National Arts Convention, October 6, 1988, and with variations before other groups.
47 FA, application to Lawrenceville, June 24, 1940, signed by FA in name of Reed Albee.
48 "I began writing poetry." James Merrill, "A Different Person."
48 "Small for his age." Frederick Buechner interview with MG, May 1, 1995.
49 "I like Lawrenceville." EA letter to Alan Heely, undated.
49 Lawrenceville School Housemaster's report, December 1, 1942.
50 Lawrenceville School Subject Report, June 6, 1942.
50 "a Lawrenceville norm." John Joseph, interview with John Speicher, *Newsweek*, October 1962.
50 "lump in my throat." FA letter to Alan Heely, undated.
51 "Darkness stole." EA poem written at Lawrenceville, quoted by EA.
51 "my own fault." EA letter to Alan Heely, undated.
52 C. Wardell St. John letter to Heely, June 6, 1944.
53 "Young Edward Albee." Heely letter to C. Wardell St. John, June 7, 1944.
54 "I have a feeling." Frank C. Wheeler on accepting EA at Choate, 1944, discovered by Speicher in files at Choate.
54 Dedication, *The Brief*, 1946.
55 Edwin Proctor's report on EA.
55 "hour after hour." Charles Rice interview with *Newsweek*, 1962.
55 "nose out cliches." Rice letter to EA, November 2, 1962.
55 Porter Caesar's report on EA's first term.
56 "moody, eccentric." Caesar interview with Speicher, October 1962.
56 "never curled his lip." John Joseph interview with Speicher, October 1962.
56 Charles Rice's report, June 1946.
56 "When I was sixteen." George in *Who's Afraid of Virginia Woolf?*
58 The Choate literary magazine, February 1945: EA, poem, "To whom it may concern."
58 Kaleidograph: EA, poem, *Eighteen*.
58 "liked to dominate people," etc. David Aldeborgh interview with MG, November 15, 1995.
59 EA: *The Flesh of Unbelievers*, at Lincoln Center.
59 EA: *Schism*, first play. The Choate literary magazine, May 1946.
59 On *Schism*. NF interviews with MG.
59 "always in cahoots." Father Jack Farrand interview with MG, June 14, 1995.
60 EA: *Nihilist*. The Choate literary magazine, May 1946.
61 The *Choate News*, May 25, 1946, Alexander Lehmann: review of Albee's play and poem, and one of David Aldeborgh's paintings.
61 "a light deep in the water." Rice interview with *Newsweek*.
61 EA: *Each in His Own Way*, discovered by Rollin Mettler while going through papers preparing for the Choate class's 50th reunion, sent to EA and placed in his archives.
62 "My mother was crazy about him." Celeste Seymour interview with MG, April 14, 1995.

64   EA: *Sort of a Test*" The Choate literary magazine, November. 1945.
64   The *Choate News*, February 16, 1946.
65   "An ultra-poetical," etc. *The Brief*, 1945, 1946 yearbooks.
65   George St. John letter to Reed Albee, June 18, 1946.
66   Choate Alumni Bulletin. EA's speech, "Building Responsibility," 1972.
67   "the inscrutable person." Michael R. Campo interview with Speicher, October 1962.
67   EA: *Cocktail Party: The Women. Trinity Review*, December 1946.
68   EA: *The City of People*. Lincoln Center.
68   "Your irresponsible record." George St. John telegram to EA, February 25, 1947.
69   "blithe assurance." NF: unpublished memoir, *Footnotes*.
69   "I always knew." Delphine Weissinger letter to EA, February 7, 1963.
71   EA: *The Dispossessed*, at Lincoln Center.

3. ALBEE'S VILLAGE DECADE
72   "the most brilliant person." NF interviews with MG.
72   "When I told my family." WF, *Stereo Review*, November 1968, interview with Peter Reilly.
72   "totally disillusioned." Francis James Brown interview with MG, November 14, 1994.
73   "a mentor . . . a leader of the pack." Charles Strouse interview with MG, April 12, 1995.
73   "One of the most intellectually stimulating." John Gruen, *The Party's Over Now*.
73   "melodic curve." Marc Blitzstein, program for Carnegie Recital Hall, February 24, 1959.
73   "a contemporary Voltaire." Roger Baker interview with MG, November 21, 1995.
74   "Every homosexual." Brown interview with MG.
74   "He was kind of on the plump side." WF interview with MG, October 29, 1962.
74   "I can't recall a word." WF: "Albee in the Village," *New York* magazine, October 27, 1963.
75   On Rachmaninoff Society. NF: *Footnotes*.
75   On EA's meeting with W. H. Auden, etc. NF interviews with MG.
77   "nice, affable, slightly overweight." Ned Rorem interview with MG, October 5, 1995.
77   On paying back loans. EA letters to Richard Howard, undated.
78   On the gay world, etc. Robert Heide interviews with MG, September 23, October 4, 1996.
80   "Avoid martinis." EA: poem about drinking. Collection, Richard Howard.
81   "Whatever remarks." EA letter to DD, December 20, 1950.
81   "He went distinctly Bohemian." WF interview with MG.
82   On meeting EA. Thornton Wilder letter to Ruth Gordon and Garson Kanin, November 19, 1962.
83   "A reading of his poems." Thornton Wilder letter to MG, November 1962.
83   "whiskey and lake water." EA letter to Wilder, November 16, 1962.

83   EA: *The Making of a Saint*. Lincoln Center.
84   "Cultivate also a deeper concentration." Wilder letter to EA, November 22, 1954.
85   "He was vitiating his emotional resources." WF interview with MG.
85   EA: *The Recruit, In a Quiet Room, Ye Watchers and Ye Lonely Ones, The Invalid, End to Summer, The Merry Month of May, Black Is the Color of Mourning, The Dispossessed, Excelsior*. Lincoln Center.
86   WF: "Albee in the Village."
87   "He was dabbling in poetry." WF interview with MG.
87   "orphan of the storm." Richard Howard interview with MG, November 5, 1997.
87   "hoot himself out of the balcony." WF: "Albee in the Village."
88   EA's comments on plays, Howard interview with MG.
89   "Profound hypnotic effect." WF interview with MG.
89   "I did that." EA to WF, in *Paris Review* interview.

4. DIE ZOO-GESCHICHTE
93   "I am dislocated . . ." EA, *New York Journal American*, in a column filling in for Dorothy Kilgallen, May 11, 1960.
93   "There was no preparation." WF interview with MG.
94   "I live in a four-story brownstone." EA, *The Zoo Story*.
95   "The trouble is." Wilder letter to EA, August 17, 1958.
96   "I was very impressed." Aaron Copland letter to EA, undated. Reprinted by permission of the Aaron Copland Fund for Music, Inc., copyright owner.
97   "you might try writing a few more." William Inge letter to EA, August 13, 1958.
98   "The bulky object." EA letter to Richard Howard, September 24, 1958.
98   On changing the title of *The Zoo Story*. Howard interview with MG.
99   On doing Albee and O'Neill on same bill. Quintero interview with MG.
99   "a beautiful one-act play." WF letter to DD, October 1958.
100 "Attached is my play." EA letter to DD, October 2, 1958.
100 "I have finally come to a point." DD letter to EA, October 23, 1958. This letter, written from Florence, was to be a turning point in Albee's career.
101 "I don't mean thanks specifically." EA letter to DD, December 10, 1958.
102 "Well, I must be an exception." DD letter to EA, December 20, 1958.
102 EA letter to DD, January 23, 1959 about *The Death of Bessie Smith*.
102 "Mon cher, I knew B.S." DD letter to EA, February 10, 1959.
102 "I was convinced." Pinkas Braun letter to MG, October 27, 1995.
102 On blocking all calls. Stefani Hunzinger interview with MG, September 3, 1998.
103 "I have read it several times." Pinkas Braun letter to EA, January 21, 1959.
103 "Gian Carlo Menotti received me last week." EA letter to Richard Howard, January 31, 1959.
104 The poem "is a mess." WF letter to DD, March 19, 1959.
104 "dog-eared, high-middle Polish translation . . ." EA letter to Howard Moss, March 27, 1959.
104 "leaped off the page." Edward Parone, "Six Degrees of Edward Albee," an essay,

July 10, 1997.

105 "quadruple communion." EA letter to Richard Howard, May 16, 1959.

106 Howard: *Duet for Three Voices*, in *Quantities*, Wesleyan University Press, 1962.

106 Louis Calta, the *Times*, July 16, 1959; Harold Clurman, *The Nation*, August 15, 1959.

107 "thereby hangs a tale." Michael Wager interview with MG, September 15, 1995.

107 "He popped his head." Heide interviews with MG.

107 "I'm sorry—sorrier than you will ever know." WF letter to EA, undated.

108 "If one's life is the source of his art." Terrence McNally letter to EA, July 22, 1961.

109 "It has been a difficult." WF letter to DD, September 22, 1959.

109 EA letter to WF, in October 1959, undated from Berlin, describing his trip over ("The last few days on the boat . . .") and the opening night of *The Zoo Story*.

110 "The ship is full of priests." EA letter to Howard, October 1959.

114 Reviews: *Die Welt, Tagesspiegel, Telegraf, Berliner Morgenpost, Der Tag*.

114 EA letter to WF, October 13, 1959, about his last days in Berlin and his visit to the Berliner Ensemble.

115 "having asked none of the questions." WF letter to EA, October 4, 1959.

116 "Just as I was beginning." WF letter to EA, October 8, 1959.

117 "I don't know how I got roped into." EA letter to Richard Howard, October 13, 1959.

118 "It is nine-thirty at night." EA to Pinkas and Gisela Braun, October 18, 1959.

118 Samuel Beckett letters to EA, November 20, 1959, "Many thanks"; January 20, 1960, "It is good news."

118 "one of the most exciting." EA letter to Pinkas Braun, November 4, 1959.

118 "my own faintly idiotic." EA letter to Richard Howard, October 13, 1959.

5 . YAM

119 "That's the best." Norman Mailer at the Actors Studio.

119 David Merrick's reaction, etc. Parone essay on EA.

119 Submission to the Actors Studio. Michael Wager interview with MG, September 15, 1995.

120 "It was different from anything I had read." John Stix interview with MG, August 22, 1995.

120 "buttoned up young man." Lou Antonio interview with MG, August 2, 1997.

120 Norman Mailer interview with MG, April 14, 1997, about his reaction to reading of *The Zoo Story* at the Actors Studio.

121 "the play worked like a pistol." Romulus Linney interview with MG, August 4, 1997.

121 "I distinctly remember," etc. RB, unpublished memoirs.

123 "everybody's outsider." Donald Davis interview with MG, April 14, 1996.

123 "I was very torn about it," etc. William Daniels interview with MG, August 23, 1997.

124 "I said I've been to the zoo," etc. Milton Katselas interview with MG, October

15, 1997.

124 Conflict on *The Zoo Story*. Mark Wright interview with MG, October 8, 1995.

125 Reviews, Brooks Atkinson, *The New York Times*; Walter Kerr, the *New York Herald Tribune*; Richard Watts Jr., the *New York Post*; Harold Clurman, *The Nation*; Robert Brustein, *The New Republic*.

126 Brustein letter to EA, February 26, 1960, letter to MG, December 2, 1998.

127 Mention of a new play called *Exorcism*. EA interview with Frances Herridge in the *New York Post*, February 5, 1960.

127 "As you know." RB letter to Katselas, January 28, 1960.

127 "hottest young playwright." WF letter to DD, January 18, 1960.

128 "All eyes turned." Robert Heide interviews with MG.

128 "disaster device." EA letter to RB, March 28, 1960.

128 Clurman in *The Nation*.

129 "You can't imagine the debt." John Guare, October 1994, in program for London production of *Three Tall Women*.

129 "where one wanted to be." Tom Stoppard interview with MG, December 3, 1994.

130 "These little bumbles." EA letter to Daniels.

130 EA letter to Ned Rorem, June 28, 1960, about directing for first time.

131 Milton Shulman in the *Evening Standard*.

131 "a torrential suicide note." Robert Stephens in *Knight Errant*.

131 "the audience identifies completely with Peter." EA letter to Joseph J. Mandata, March 19, 1968.

131 "All you need to know." EA in public readings of *The Zoo Story*.

132 "no abortive scripts." Geri Trotta, *Horizon* magazine, September 1961.

132 "Outrage over the racial prejudice." EA letter to Pinkas Braun, January 24, 1959.

133 "If the characters." Braun letter to EA, April 27, 1959.

133 "Your comments on my Bessie Smith play." EA letter to Braun, May 2, 1959.

134 "dazzles with terror." Ned Rorem letter to EA, July 3, 1959.

134 Braun letter to EA, June 22, 1960, opening of *Bessie Smith*.

135 "Muscle-brained actor." EA letter to DD, April 8, 1961.

136 "The Kuklapolitans held forth in the driver's seat." Burr Tillstrom letter to Terrence O'Flaherty, January 26, 1971.

137 EA, "My Favorite Grandmother," the *Theatre* magazine, March 1961.

138 William Inge letter to Rorem, September 15, 1960, about *Fam and Yam*.

6. MOMMY AND DADDY

139 "Is the play offensive?" EA in Preface to *The American Dream*, New York: Coward-McCann, 1961.

141 Martin Esslin, *The Theatre of the Absurd*.

142 EA letter to DD, January 14, 1961, about *The American Dream* and success.

142 AS letter to EA, December 25, 1960, about *The American Dream*.

143 Jane Hoffman interview with MG, April 3, 1998, about acting in *The American Dream*.

143 Reviews: Kerr in *Herald Tribune,* Watts in *Post.*

144 "Damn those drama men." EA letter to DD, January 30, 1961.

144 WF letter to DD, March 20, 1961, "the straw" that broke his back.

144 DD letter to EA, February 17, 1961, on Flanagan and *Bartleby.*

144 Reviews: Judith Crist in *Herald Tribune,* Clurman in *The Nation.*

145 "hell on the ears and a boot in the ass." George Vigouroux letter to EA, May 1961.

146 John M. Lupton letter to *Westport Town Crier,* July 20, 1961.

146 EA letter to Ned Rorem, July 18, 1961, about protests to *The Zoo Story.*

147 EA letter to WF, July 29, 1961, about Argentine tour of *The Zoo Story.*

147 EA letter to WF, September 22, 1961, from London.

148 "Dearest of the New Exquisites." WF letter to EA, September 27, 1961.

148 "the same dirt-cheap." EA letter to WF, October 5, 1961.

148 "Brunhilde, dear." WF letter to EA, October 10, 1961.

149 EA letter to WF, October 1961, about *The American Dream.*

149 Reviews: Robert Muller in *Daily Mail,* Bernard Levin in *Daily Express.*

149 Kenneth Tynan "writes about you as if you were dead." McNally letter to EA, October 30, 1961.

150 Tynan in *The Observer.*

150 EA, Preface to *The American Dream.*

150 Stefani Hunzinger interview with MG, on mention of *Virginia Woolf.*

7. BLOOD UNDER THE BRIDGE

151 "unlikely to appear." *Time* magazine, February 2, 1961.

152 *Exorcism* as title. EA interview with Frances Herridge in *New York Post,* February 5, 1960.

153 "half-way through" *Virginia Woolf.* EA letter to DD, November 18, 1960.

154 EA letters to Ned Rorem, June 3, 1961, "die trying"; June 22, 1961, "right on schedule."

154 "The play—I think—is going to be three acts." EA interview with Paul Zindel and Loree Yerby in Wagner literary magazine, 1962.

154 "He is chastened" (about WF). EA letter to Rorem, July 18, 1961.

154 "I'm bored when people read aloud." Rorem interview with MG, October 5, 1995.

155 "razor-blades . . . clean slices." McNally letter to EA, December 4, 1961.

155 EA letter to DD, January 26, 1962, about WF's collapse.

158 On the dialogue in *Virginia Woolf.* Richard Howard interview with MG, November 5, 1997.

158 "like hearing Bill talking." Charles Strouse interview with MG, April 12, 1995.

159 "It is mind-boggling." Elaine Stritch interview with MG, August 10, 1996.

159 "Mommy and Daddy." EA letter to DD, April 8, 1961.

162 Influence of James Thurber, *Vintage Thurber.*

163 "The dialogue crackled." AS in *Entrances.*

164 "I felt like I was riding some wave." Roger Baker interview with MG, November 21, 1995.

164 On *The Male Animal*. Mark Wright interview with MG, October 9, 1995.

165 "The reactions were not mixed." RB in his memoir.

165 "free-swinging, bold." EA, *The New York Times Magazine*, February 25, 1962.

166 "best American play." Michael Wager interview with MG, September 15, 1995.

166 "I was scared." Cheryl Crawford, *One Naked Individual*.

167 On potential tax problems. Roger Stevens letter to EA, February 18, 1966.

167 "Lee didn't want to." Arthur Penn interview with MG, March 18, 1997.

168 Henry Fonda on not seeing the script of *Virginia Woolf*, interview with MG, March 1974; *My Life*.

168 "There was no question about it." Uta Hagen interview with MG, April 19, 1995.

168 "Alan had a sadistic streak." Wright interview with MG.

168 "I was floored." Hagen in her diary, and in note to EA, 1962.

169 On casting. AS in *Entrances*.

170 "a surprising range." Penn interview with MG.

170 "I was absolutely knocked out." Arthur Hill interview with MG, July 17, 1997.

170 "brilliant script . . . rotten part." George Grizzard interview with MG, April 27, 1995.

171 "thickest looking play." Lou Antonio interview with MG, August 2, 1997.

171 On reading *Virginia Woolf*. Harold Clurman letter to EA, August 31, 1962.

172 Hagen in her diary and in interview with MG.

173 "exploded like a sudden storm." AS in *Entrances*.

173 On his connection with George. Hill interview with MG.

173 On Schneider. Hagen interview with MG.

173 On Melinda Dillon. Grizzard interview with MG.

175 "astonished, excited." Barr in memoirs.

175 "I think you're a nickel phone call away." Billy Rose letter to EA, October 4, 1962; ad in *The New York Times*, October 1, 1962.

176 "running on all eight cylinders." Hill interview with MG.

176 "excessive importance." EA in *The New York Times*, October 7, 1962.

8. FAM

178 Headline in *New York Daily News*, October 21, 1962; MG in *Newsweek*, October 29, 1962.

179 Reviews: Robert Coleman in the *Mirror*; John Chapman in the *Daily News*; Kerr in *Herald Tribune*; Howard Taubman in the *Times*; Watts in the *Post*; MG in *Newsweek*; Clurman in *The Nation*; Brustein in *The New Republic*. EA interview with Paul Gardner in the *Times*, October 15, 1962.

181 On matinee company. Hagen interview with MG, April 19, 1995.

181 After the opening. EA interview with MG, October 18, 1962.

182 EA letter to WF, December 1963, about throwing bottles.

182 EA letter to Charles Rice, December 10, 1962, about *Newsweek*.

182 Tennessee Williams telegram to *Newsweek*, January 31, 1963, disowning quotation about EA.

183 "a dog's last dinner." Williams interview with *Newsweek*, 1962.

183 "a gimlet eye." Harold Pinter interview with *Newsweek,* 1963.

183 WF letter to MG, January 23, 1963, about his knowledge of Albee.

183 EA letter to MG, March 1, 1963, about the cover story.

183 EA, "How *Who's Afraid of Virginia Woolf?* Has Changed My Life."

185 Elaine Boies interview with MG, January 9, 1997, about rumor that she and her husband were the models for Martha and George.

185 Dominic Lagotta letter to EA, June 10, 1983, on same rumors.

185 *Staten Island Advance,* May 8, 1994, ibid.

185 Paul Zindel interview with MG, July 31, 1997, on Boieses and Willard Maas, and letter to EA, October 9, 1962, enclosing his two reviews of *Virginia Woolf.*

186 "I am in the middle of severe facial neuralgia." EA letter to Zindel, October 1962.

187 About adoption. Letter from woman to EA, January 11, 1963.

188 "how moved I was." Peggy Wood letter to EA, October 16, 1962.

188 "Never was terror more delightful." Boris Aronson letter to EA, October 1962.

188 "same dreamy searching eyes." Clara Wortman letter to EA, April 30, 1963.

189 Pulitzer Prize rejection in May 1962: articles in *Post, Times, Herald Tribune, Variety, Time*; Turner Catledge's *My Life and the Times.*

190 Reception of *Virginia Woolf* in South Africa: articles and reviews in the *Cape Argus,* Port Elizabeth; Sunday *Tribune,* Durban; Sunday *Times* and Sunday *Express,* Johannesburg; *Variety.*

190 "Eduardo mio." Uta Hagen letter to EA, September 1963.

191 Franco Zeffirelli letter to EA, October 3, 1963, about his production of *Virginia Woolf.*

191 About European productions of *Virginia Woolf.* Mark Wright interview with MG.

191 "very Strindberg." Bibi Andersson interview with MG, June 5, 1995.

192 Clinton Wilder letter to EA, May 24, 1963, about Lord Chamberlain and *Virginia Woolf.*

192 On London production of *Virginia Woolf.* Arthur Hill interview with MG, July 17, 1997, and Hagen interview with MG.

193 Leonard Woolf letter to EA, January 28, 1965.

193 Virginia Woolf, *Lappin & Lapinova* in *A Haunted House and Other Stories.*

9. "Our" ballad—and Travels with Steinbeck

194 About *Bessie Smith* and *The Ballad of the Sad Cafe.* Carson McCullers letter to EA, August 5, 1960.

195 "I have stayed out of contact." EA letter to DD, January 30, 1961.

195 "the sun, the hay." McCullers letter to EA, August 4, 1962.

195 Dr. Mary E. Mercer letter to EA, August 6, 1962.

195 McCullers on EA, EA on McCullers in *Harper's Bazaar,* January 1963.

196 On "the McCullers part" in *Ballad.* McCullers letter to EA, May 28, 1963.

196 EA conflict with Joseph Hayes and Evan Hunter: articles and letters in *Times,* August 11 and 18, September 1, 1963.

198 RB letter to EA, signed Joseph Hayes, undated.

199 EA in *Transatlantic Review*.

199 On EA and Carson McCullers. AS in *Entrances*.

199 "a midget mentality." Michael Dunn interview with MG, November 1963.

199 Lou Antonio interview with MG, August 2, 1997, and his logbook of *Ballad of the Sad Cafe*.

199 "signs of cowardice." Colleen Dewhurst in *Her Autobiography*.

200 On AS, Michael Dunn, Colleen Dewhurst, and George C. Scott's participation in *Ballad*. Roscoe Lee Browne interview with MG, July 26, 1997.

203 Reviews: Chapman in *Daily News*, Kerr in *Herald Tribune*, Brustein in *The New Republic*.

203 "He could insult anybody." WF letter to DD, December 1, 1963.

204 "It clicked." Antonio interview with MG.

204 "the flash of the moment of truth." JS letter to EA, October 1962.

205 "a kind of grey weariness." JS letter to Leslie Brady, May 13, 1963, in *Steinbeck: A Life in Letters*.

206 On EA's trip to Russia. William Luers interview with MG, May 4, 1995.

206 "There would be a large crowd." Elaine Steinbeck interview with MG, April 12, 1995.

207 "We left Edward." JS letter to Elizabeth Otis, November 8, 1963, in *Steinbeck: A Life in Letters*.

208 On the Kennedy assassination. EA letter to WF, November 1963.

208 "You cannot imagine." EA letter to RB, November 1963.

209 "Luers, while driving." Central Intelligence Agency, file obtained by EA through the Freedom of Information Act.

209 EA at Moscow press conference, reported in *Times*.

210 "It will be a great shame." EA letter to WF, February 12, 1964.

210 On seeing *Ballad*. John Guare letter to EA, November 7, 1977.

211 On McCullers's intent. EA letter to Ismail Merchant, November 3, 1989.

10. THE PLAY THAT DARE NOT SPEAK ITS NAME

212 "I say to myself . . ." Roddy McDowall quoting John Gielgud during interview with MG, October 10, 1997.

213 "I happen to know who and what Tiny Alice is." JS letter to EA, November 19, 1964.

213 Transcript of EA's statement at press conference on *Tiny Alice*, March 22, 1965.

215 "I couldn't understand." Gielgud interview with MG, November 12, 1994.

216 "anti-clerical." Irene Worth interviews with MG, May 5, 1995 and January 8, 1999.

216 "murkier and murkier." AS in *Entrances*.

217 "Finally, Julian is left alone." EA's notes on *Tiny Alice*, at Lincoln Center.

217 On Gielgud. AS in *Entrances*.

217 On *Tiny Alice*. Gielgud interview with MG.

217 "It was a real fight." Worth interviews with MG.

218 "It's a mystery play." EA interview with MG, December 8, 1964.

218 "inexpressively moved." NF letter to EA, December 14, 1964.

219 On seduction scene. Gielgud, Worth, and McDowall interviews with MG.

220 Reviews: Taubman in the *Times*, Kerr in the *Herald Tribune*.

220 Philip Roth in the *New York Review of Books*, February 25, 1965.

220 On symbolism. EA interview with Paul Gardner in the *Times*, January 21, 1965.

221 EA on New School panel, January 21, 1965. MG notes.

221 Elaine Dundy in *Herald Tribune*, January 31, 1965.

221 "less opaque." EA, Author's Note, *Tiny Alice*, New York: Atheneum, 1965.

221 "I have read *Tiny Alice*." Noël Coward letter to EA, February 18, 1965.

222 Whitney Darrow Jr. cartoon in *The New Yorker*, 1965.

222 About Lincoln Center. AS letter to EA and RB, January 20, 1965.

223 "Dearest Ed." FA letter to EA, May 10, 1965.

224 "We have a heart attack." EA, *Three Tall Women*.

225 FA's "star radiance." Irene Worth interviews with MG.

226 "Life is placid on the surface." EA letter to WF, June 1965.

227 "The room looms." Article about EA in the *Times*, June 1965.

227 "I am growing old gracefully." EA letter to WF, July 1965.

227 On "rough years." WF letter to EA, June 20, 1965.

229 EA, program insert for Ball's production of *Tiny Alice*, Stanley Eichelbaum, *San Francisco Examiner*, October 5, 1975.

229 Review of Hartford revival of *Tiny Alice*. MG in the *Times*, April 17, 1972.

229 "I think I expunged it from my memory." Gielgud interview with MG.

11. TAYLOR! BURTON! LEHMAN!

232 "The joke is." Mike Nichols interview with MG, September 12, 1996.

233 On the film of *Virginia Woolf*. Bette Davis, in a dialogue with EA, January 28, 1965, for *Redbook*, unpublished; interview with MG, January 5, 1977.

233 On Elizabeth Taylor. Ernest Lehman interviews with MG, August 29 and 30, 1965; and with John Brady in *The Craft of the Screenwriter*.

234 "I think you're too young." Richard Burton interview with Roy Newquist, *McCall's*, June 1966, and with *Newsweek*, October 10, 1966, for cover story by MG on Nichols, November 14, 1966.

235 On meeting Albee. Nichols interview with MG.

236 On Taylor's makeup. Lehman in *The Craft of the Screenwriter*.

238 Reality and illusion. Buck Henry, *Newsweek* interview, 1966.

238 On Martha. Elizabeth Taylor in her memoir *Elizabeth Taylor*.

239 About Nichols's direction. Burton interview with *Newsweek*.

240 "Everything was a circus." Nichols interview with MG.

240 On location with *Virginia Woolf*, as seen by MG, for article in *Newsweek*, September 13, 1965.

241 "part of my pleasure." EA interview with MG, October 14, 1966.

241 Production Code Review Board's ruling on *Virginia Woolf*, Vincent Canby in the *Times*, June 1966.

241 "best American play." Stanley Kauffmann in the *Times*, June 24, 1966.

241 "reports about terrible things." EA interview with Frances Herridge in *Post*, July 1, 1966.

242 Having a nightmare. Nichols interview with MG, March 15, 1965.

242 "I worry, of course." EA letter to Lehman, July 12, 1994.

245 "as blank and as open." Nichols interview with MG.

246 On Elaine May. James Naughton interview with MG, June 17, 1998.

246 "I hear Uta." Nichols interview with MG.

12. BALANCING ACT

247 On *Malcolm*. WF letter to EA, July 17, 1965.

248 "I have tried to remove." EA letter to WF, July 1965.

248 On *Malcolm*. James Purdy letter to EA, August 31, 1965.

249 Without a midget, the play went "off course." Purdy interview with MG, December 5, 1998.

249 "with a sword instead of a pen." RB in his memoirs.

249 "Albee's most deeply homosexual work." Brustein in *The New Republic*.

249 "Three of the most successful playwrights . . . are (reputed) homosexuals." Stanley Kauffmann in the *Times*, January 23, 1966.

250 "disgusting article." EA interview with David Richards in *Times*, June 16, 1991.

250 "plenty to tell me." A. R. Gurney Jr. letter to EA, January 23, 1966.

250 "See you next play." EA in ad in *Times*, January 1966.

250 "Greetings from Eden." EA letter to WF, January 20, 1966.

251 EA letter to WF, including "My Weekend in Rome, a theme," March 1966.

253 Response to "My Weekend in Rome." WF letter to EA, April 2, 1966.

254 A play about a "hack meeting Dvorak." EA letter to Howard Moss, March 26, 1966.

254 "The secret photo-copy." Moss letter to EA, March 28, 1966.

255 EA, notes on *A Delicate Balance*, August 16, 1966, at Lincoln Center.

255 "I remember when." EA, *A Delicate Balance*.

257 "the most mature." WF letter to EA, April 22, 1966.

258 On *The Ice Age*. WF letter to EA, April 26, 1966.

259 On the characters in *A Delicate Balance*. EA, notes to AS, at Lincoln Center.

260 On meeting Frances Albee. Hume Cronyn and Jessica Tandy interview with MG, May 19, 1994.

260 "I find Hume's notes on Tobias." EA, notes to AS, at Lincoln Center.

264 On working with Schneider. Marian Seldes interview with MG, January 29, 1998.

265 Review by Kerr in *Times*, September 23, 1966.

265 Response to Kerr's review. AS in *Entrances*.

265 Brustein in *The New Republic*, October 1966.

265 "never had a critic in my corner." Arthur Miller interview with MG, October 11, 1996.

265 MG in *Playboy*, on *A Delicate Balance*.

266 "enjoyed it up to the hilt." Harold Pinter letter to EA, January 11, 1966.

267 "an exquisite fandango of despair." Kenneth Tynan letter to Laurence Olivier, January 12, 1967, quoted in Olivier letter to Toby Rowland, January 13, 1967, and in *Kenneth Tynan: Letters*.

267 "but he didn't come round." Olivier letter to Toby Rowland, January 13, 1967.

267 "I would have come back to see you." EA letter to Olivier, March 30, 1967.

267 "talk about a delicate balance." Olivier letter to EA, April 6, 1967.

268 "still an honor." EA at press conference, May 2, 1967, on receiving the Pulitzer Prize for *A Delicate Balance*, as reported in *Times*; "a complaining Pulitzer Prize–winning playwright." EA interview with MG, May 2, 1967.

268 Nichols telegram to EA, May 2, 1967; Jane Cotter Bendilare's letter to EA, May 1967; Muir Weissinger's letter to EA, May 13, 1967; David Merrick's letter to EA, May 2, 1967.

268 "Now that you are playing in a national monument." EA telegram to the Cronyns, undated.

268 John Simon in the *Times*, on EA's acceptance of the Pulitzer; EA's response in the *Times*.

269 Harold Hobson in the Sunday *Times* of London.

269 An "intense collaboration." EA writing in the *Times*, November 26, 1967.

269 "a complete recasting." EA letter to JS, August 29, 1967.

270 On rehearsals of *Everything in the Garden*. Richard Thomas interview with MG, August 24, 1994.

270 On London production of *A Delicate Balance*. Peter Hall letter to EA, December 16, 1968.

271 "I don't recall any friction." Hall interview with MG, July 4, 1996.

271 "The depth and flexibility of performance." Hall letter to EA, January 26, 1969.

13. FLANAGAN

272 On trying to penetrate EA's "Iron Curtain." WF letter to EA, May 12, 1966.

273 Reminded of Gertrude Stein plays. Virgil Thomson letter to EA, October 28, 1968.

273 "at different though not distant moments." EA, Introduction to *Box-Mao-Box*, New York: Atheneum, 1969.

273 "It is one of a series of shortish experimental plays." EA letter to JS, August 29, 1967.

274 "My memory tells me." EA letter to Bill Bryden, July 12, 1976.

274 On Chuck Gnys's rejection of *Box*. WF letter to EA, July 8, 1967.

275 "Now I know why Rayne Enders was reluctant." Gnys letter to EA, February 9, 1968.

275 Explanation of Rayne Enders episode. EA letters to Gnys, February 1968.

275 "I didn't like *Box*." Gnys letter to EA, February 1968.

276 "A polyphonic chamber work." Clurman in *The Nation*.

277 On WF's book about EA. Aaron Copland letter to WF, July 26, 1968. Reprinted by permission of the Aaron Copland Fund for Music, Inc., copyright owner.

277 WF's book as "a nonfiction novel" and on turning forty-four. WF letter to EA, August 14, 1967.

278 "Albee takes care of him." WF letter to EA, February 16, 1968.

278 "prime time with Frances Gumm." WF letter to EA, April 7, 1968.

278 "I drink less than most of our friends." WF letter to EA, April 29, 1968.

279 About the Garland lyric and *The Ice Age*. WF letters to EA, September 9, 1968, and undated 1968.

279 "I have the impression that I'm off your list." WF letter to EA, December 18, 1968.

279 "I've shown a resilience." WF letter to DD, May 29, 1969.

280 On WF's death. Ned Rorem interview with MG, October 5, 1995.

281 "The way he died still haunts us." Elma Flanagan letter to EA.

281 Sharing of "pride and respect." WF letter to EA, undated 1968.

14. DEATH AND LIFE

282 *The New Yorker*, "News Break," commenting on item in Palm Beach (Florida) *Daily News*, October 1974.

283 On EA's Fifth Avenue apartment. Glyn O'Malley interviews with MG, May 17 and 25, 1998.

283 "a serious play about how people get through life." EA interview with MG, February 8, 1971.

284 "I was lost in limbo." Jessica Tandy interview with MG, May 19, 1994.

284 The Martin Beck as "a mausoleum." John Gielgud interview with MG.

285 "when a fella is forty years old, your mother is just your mother." FA interview with Enid Nemy in the *Times*, March 29, 1971.

285 "so continually fascinating." Gielgud letter to EA, March 27, 1971.

285 "a dead flop." Gielgud interview with MG.

285 "an existential shudder." Clurman in *The Nation*, April 12, 1971.

285 "a brave and beautiful performance." Tennessee Williams's letters to Jessica Tandy and EA, April 29, 1976.

285 "One of the great experiences." Wallace Shawn interview with MG, November 11, 1998.

286 "confound those horrible critics." Gielgud letter to EA, April 2, 1971.

286 "I was stunned." Peggy Ashcroft letter to EA, undated, 1971.

286 On London production of *All Over*. EA letter to RB, undated.

287 "like a shell slowly being cracked open." Michael Billington, *Peggy Ashcroft*.

287 "a continuation." Peter Hall interview with MG, July 4, 1996.

287 "I had seen the play several times and really didn't understand what it was about." Katharine Hepburn interview with MG, November 1975.

287 On Kim Stanley at first reading for film of *A Delicate Balance*. Tony Richardson, *The Long-Distance Runner*.

288 On *Seascape*. EA interviews with MG, May 3, 1967; October 22, 1974; December 17, 1975.

289 Rejecting *Seascape*, Henry Fonda letter to EA, September 10, 1974.

290 On reading of *Seascape* with Maureen Stapleton. Maureen Anderman interview with MG, January 6, 1998.

291 "I fell in love with immediately." Deborah Kerr letter to MG, November 20, 1997.

291 "I would seem to have Deborah Kerr to play Nancy." EA letter to Howard Moss, August 7, 1974.

291 "Keep the thread of wonder." Deborah Kerr letter to EA, October 2, 1974.

291 On rehearsal of *Seascape*. Anderman interview with MG.

292 "Just as civilized in their own way." EA letter to Peter Lackner, October 26, 1976.

292 "He doesn't hold on to things." Anderman interview with MG.

293 "Hats off." Clive Barnes in the *Times*, January 27, 1975.

293 "As one presently involved with a near miss." EA letter to James Kirkwood, April 21, 1975.

293 "Life here is quite bloody." John Osborne letter to EA, August 22, 1976.

294 EA letter to William D. Miller, September 15, 1975, about trip to Japan.

294 "a vat of stillness." EA, "The Peaceable Kingdom, France," *The New Yorker*.

294 Kerr in *Times*; Tony Kushner in *Columbia Spectator*.

295 "I was a little disappointed." Peter Hall letter to EA, January 19, 1976.

295 "We all seem to feel." EA letter to Hall, February 1, 1976.

296 "another nail in the coffin." Hall, *Peter Hall's Diaries*.

296 "I don't feel that the play was served well." EA letter to Hall, December 13, 1976.

297 "It was a very strange play." Anderman interview with MG.

15. INTO THE WOODS

298 "Somewhere in the middle." Mike Nichols interview with MG, September 12, 1996.

299 RB as "a determined alcoholic." Mark Wright interview with MG, October 9, 1995.

299 "Last night you were obviously drunk." EA letter to RB, undated.

299 "It was extremely difficult." Glyn O'Malley interviews with MG, May 17, 25, 1998.

301 On his relationship with EA and on EA's behavior. JT interviews with MG, December 6, 1995; February 3, 1996; October 5, 1998.

303 The dinner party, January 22, 1978: recollections from MG, Ann Gussow, John von Hartz, Hume Cronyn, Jessica Tandy, Farley Granger.

306 "What a splendid party except for that Edward Albee person!" EA letter to MG, January 23, 1978.

306 "There is no veritas in vino for me." EA letter to MG, January 28, 1978.

308 Mike Nichols's interview with MG.

16. THE LADY, LOLITA, AND THE MAN WHO

309 "Deeper and deeper." EA interview with Terrence McNally in *Dramatists Guild Quarterly*, reprinted in *Broadway Song & Story*.

309 "I keep thinking it's almost ready." EA interview with MG, May 3, 1967.

310 "I thought I would wait to write it until I ran out of other ideas." EA interview with MG, March 23, 1978.

311 "This new play of mine." EA letter to Ingrid Bergman, May 25, 1978.

311 "So I read your play and I can't understand it." Bergman letter to EA, June 4, 1978.

312 Bergman needed a push. Peter Adam letter to EA, June 9, 1978.

312 "I was quite relieved." EA letter to Irene Worth, September 26, 1978.

312 "It has some of the thematic burden." NF letter to EA, February 21, 1979.

313 On Frances Conroy. AS letter to EA, September 14, 1979.

314 Reviews: Kerr in *Times*, MG on WQXR.

314 On her rejection as understudy for *The Lady from Dubuque*. Myra Carter interview with MG, March 16, 1998.

315 "the valley of the shadow." O'Malley interviews with MG.

315 On *Lolita*. John Dexter letters to EA, August 8, October 30, 1979.

316 "Greetings and farewell." EA letter to Dexter, November 13, 1979.

316 On his production of *Mahagonny*. Dexter letter to EA, November 19, 1979.

316 Objection by Vera and Dmitri Nabokov to "the character that Edward Albee has created." Joan C. Daly letter to Howard Hausman at the William Morris Agency, June 27, 1979.

317 "Shocked you have not kept word." Dmitri Nabokov telegram to Jerry Sherlock, undated.

317 On preparation for *Lolita*. EA interview with Eleanor Blau, *Times*, September 17, 1980.

318 "A long time ago—back when I was an adolescent." EA, "A Note on *Lolita*," written in 1981.

318 "horrendous grotesque." Dmitri Nabokov interview with MG, September 10, 1998.

318 On Sutherland ripping out pages. O'Malley interviews with MG.

319 On production problems. William Ritman letter to Albee, Jerry Sherlock, Frank Dunlop, undated.

319 "a hacked up version." O'Malley interviews with MG.

319 Change in *Lolita* radio commercial, reported by John Corry in the *Times*, February 6, 1981.

319 "Our producer . . . a devious and arrogant amateur." EA letter to Arthur Gelb at the *Times*, February 27, 1981.

320 "Dare, Donald." EA letter to Sutherland, March 7, 1981.

320 On picketing of *Lolita* and Sherlock's statement about protesters having no effect on the success of the play. *New York Post*, March 20, 1981.

320 Reviews: MG on WQXR, Brustein in *The New Republic*.

321 "Something called *Lolita*." EA interview with McNally.

321 "A combination of disrespect for Nabokov's and my text." EA, Introduction to Fireside Theater collection of eight plays, August 1987.

322 "I have a personal interest . . . in the adventures and misadventures of Lolita herself." James Mason letter to EA, November 18, 1981.

322 "Everyone has to share the blame." Jerry Sherlock interview with MG, January 8, 1998.

322 "experimental plays, dense, unfamiliar and lacking proper road signs." EA, Introduction to collection of early plays, 1981.

323 EA, *Another Part of the Zoo*, EA archives.

324 "nothing is guaranteed to narrow the public." EA letter to McNally, May 15,

1982.

325 "He had structured his life." O'Malley interviews with MG.

326 "Adamant, pigheaded." JT interviews with MG.

327 "a temper tantrum." Frank Rich in the *Times,* April 6, 1983.

327 "He just didn't want to present himself as a drunk." JT interviews with MG.

328 "His primary focus." O'Malley interviews with MG.

329 EA, *Walking,* EA archives.

330 EA at memorials for AS and Ritman.

332 EA on future utopia for Volvo ad.

332 On performance of *Hawk Moon* in Prague. William Luers interview with MG, May 4, 1995.

333 "Everyone knew he was in the room." O'Malley interviews with MG.

333 On EA's role at ITI. Martha Coigney interview with MG, June 12, 1998.

334 "the perfection and beauty of your writing." William Shawn letter to EA, May 29, 1985.

335 On importance of *Tiny Alice* to her work. Louise Nevelson letter to Thomas Armstrong, August 9, 1979.

335 "a fathomable reality in the midst of the outside chaos." EA, Introduction, *Louise Nevelson: Atmospheres and Environments.*

17. FRANKIE

337 "She was hideous." O'Malley interviews with MG.

337 "She was the grande dame." Joanna Steichen interview with MG, September 19, 1996.

338 FA, Last Will and Testament, January 20, 1984; New Last Will and Testament, February 6, 1986; First Codicil, February 6, 1986; Memorandum from Mary E. Nelson re: Execution of Will of Frances C. Albee. All were prepared by Austrian, Lance & Stewart, 30 Rockefeller Plaza, New York City.

341 "the memory of a perfume." EA, "A Novel Beginning," *Esquire,* July 1963.

342 "principal legatee." New Last Will, February 6, 1986.

343 "It was a pleasure to meet you." Reverend Edward Johnston (Christ's Church, Rye, New York) letter to EA, May 10, 1989.

343 EA's adoption papers, February 1, 1929.

18. A TALL WOMAN

344 "Richard had two theories." EA's eulogy of RB, 1989.

345 "He's probably the best teacher." Kevin Cunningham interview with MG, July 20, 1997.

345 "I think he's got a stake." Sidney Berger interview with MG, November 22, 1997.

346 "Edward probably sees more work of young artists." William Lieberman interview with MG.

347 "We're a family" and EA's traits and fears. JT interviews with MG.

349 "Dogs bark; they whimper." EA, "Harry Sighing," EA archives.

351 "Edward's configuration of qualities." Martha Coigney interview with MG.

352 "I don't think he should direct his own plays." Shirley Knight interview with MG, April 3, 1997.

353 On the writing of *Three Tall Women*. O'Malley interviews with MG.

353 First "awareness of consciousness." EA, Introduction to *Three Tall Women*, New York: Dutton, 1995.

357 "I was overwhelmed by it." Joanna Steichen interview with MG, September 19, 1996.

357 "How did I get the role?" Myra Carter interview with MG, March 16, 1998.

358 On Myra Carter and the opening in Vienna. O'Malley interviews with MG.

359 The opening. JT interviews with MG.

359 "His play is a wonder." Jeane Luere letter to MG, July 6, 1991.

359 "the Road Not Taken." EA interview with David Richards in *Times*, June 16, 1991.

360 "it's too early." EA postcard to Lawrence Sacharow, August 27, 1991.

361 "I had heard all these stories." Lawrence Sacharow interview with MG, May 13, 1998.

361 "I like to play real human beings with endless dimension." Uta Hagen interview with MG, April 19, 1995.

362 On casting. Sacharow interview with MG.

363 "If I thought of Edward." Marian Seldes interview with MG, January 29, 1998.

364 "It really affected me." Joyce Ketay interview with MG, June 29, 1998.

364 "The most extraordinary saga." Sacharow interview with MG.

365 "I always get worse reviews." EA interview with MG, November 5, 1993.

367 Reviews: Linda Winer in *Newsday*, Brustein in *The New Republic*.

368 "a great liberation." Irene Worth interview with MG, January 8, 1998.

368 "It's really hard being a playwright, isn't it?" Elizabeth McCann interview with MG, November 26, 1996.

369 "Edward is of tougher mental stock than Tennessee." Roddy McDowall interview with MG, October 10, 1997.

369 On winning the Pulitzer Prize. EA interview with David Richards in the *Times*, April 13, 1994.

371 Reviews: Benedict Nightingale in the *Times* of London, Paul Taylor in the *Independent*.

372 "a joy as well as agony." Maggie Smith letter to EA, November 25, 1995.

373 "I've always had such a personal and artistic affinity." Myra Carter letter to MG, March 17, 1998.

373 On Myra Carter and on EA acting. Sacharow interview with MG.

19. A NEW BALANCE

375 "In your rebellion." President Clinton, December 8, 1996.

376 EA. A "non-reconsideration" of *A Delicate Balance*, August 1996.

376 On playing Agnes. Rosemary Harris interview with MG, April 25, 1996.

377 On playing Claire. Elaine Stritch interview with MG, August 10, 1996.

379 "Escaped from Booby-hatch." NF letter to EA, March 9, 1995.

380 "a bad falling-out." EA, in program for *A Delicate Balance* in London, August

1997.

381 On playing George. David Suchet interview with MG, November 5, 1996.

381 On playing Martha. Diana Rigg interview with MG, November 5, 1996.

382 Comparing the characters. Howard Davies interview with MG, November 4, 1996.

383 On fight between actors in Paris production of *Virginia Woolf, Evening Standard*, London, November 1996.

383 "He is enormously protective of the truth in production." Coigney interview with MG.

384 "one danger area." EA letter to Diana Rigg, November 13, 1996.

384 "Point taken." Diana Rigg letter to EA, November 1996.

385 "Edward Albee's life epitomizes." President Clinton speaking at ceremony awarding EA Kennedy Center Honors, December 8, 1996.

386 "the forces of darkness that oppose the creative act." EA letter to President Clinton, December 9, 1996.

387 *The Washington Post*, caption on photograph of EA and Elaine Steinbeck, December 9, 1996, and EA's letter of correction, December 11, 1996.

20. A NEW BABY

388 "Edward survives good news." JT interviews with MG.

390 On censorship and the "wounding of education." EA speeches at Common Wealth Award and at University of Houston.

391 On playing Maggie Smith's sister and rehearsals of *A Delicate Balance*. Eileen Atkins interview with MG, December 5, 1997.

395 On *Albee's Men*. Brustein letter to EA, December 4, 1997.

398 On performing *The Play about the Baby*. Alan Howard interview with MG, September 4, 1998.

398 "The play is about life." Frances de la Tour interview with MG, September 3, 1998.

21. LOST AND FOUND

400 Studs Terkel, *American Dreams: Lost and Found*.

400 "The single journey through consciousness." EA in program for *Tiny Alice* at Hartford Stage Company, May 1998.

401 EA's answers to questionnaire from Starr Cline, June 20, 1995.

403 On adoption. John Irving interview with MG, April 7, 1998.

404 Each picture "seems to have been created according to its own set of rules." John Canaday on Milton Avery in *Milton Avery: American/1885–1965*.

404 "One is my mother." James Agee, *A Death in the Family*.

Selected Bibliography

WORKS OF CRITICISM

Amacher, Richard E. *Edward Albee*. New York: Twayne Publishers, 1969.

Bloom, Harold, ed. *Edward Albee*. New York: Chelsea House Publishers, 1987.

Clurman, Harold. *The Collected Works of Harold Clurman*. New York: Applause Books, 1994.

Esslin, Martin. *The Theatre of the Absurd*. Garden City, N.Y.: Doubleday, 1961.

Kerjan, Liliane. *Albee*. Paris: Editions Seghers, 1971.

Kerr, Walter. *The Theater in Spite of Itself*. New York: Simon & Schuster, 1963.

Kolin, Philip C., ed. *American Playwrights Since 1945*. New York: Greenwood Press, 1989.

McCarthy, Gerry. *Edward Albee*. London: Macmillan, 1987.

Paolucci, Anne. *From Tension to Tonic: The Plays of Edward Albee*. Carbondale and Edwardsville, Ill.: Southern Illinois University Press, 1972.

Roudane, Matthew C. *Who's Afraid of Virginia Woolf?: Necessary Fictions, Terrifying Realities*. Boston: Twayne Publishers, 1990.

Rutenberg, Michael E. *Edward Albee: Playwright in Protest*. New York: Avon Books, 1970.

OTHER WORKS

Agee, James. *A Death in the Family*. New York: McDowell, Obolensky, 1957.

Albee, Edward. *Plays, individual and collected*. New York: Coward-McCann, Atheneum, Dutton.

Billington, Michael. *Peggy Ashcroft*. London: John Murray, 1988.

Brady, John. *The Craft of the Screenwriter*. New York: Simon & Schuster, 1981.

Bryer, Jackson R., ed. *The Playwright's Art: Conversations with Contemporary American Playwrights*. New Brunswick, N.J.: Rutgers University Press. 1995.

Carr, Virginia Spencer. *The Lonely Hunter: A Biography of Carson McCullers*. New York: Doubleday, 1975.

Catledge, Turner. *My Life and the Times*. New York: Harper & Row, 1971.

Coward, Noël. *Three Plays by Noël Coward*. Introduction by EA. New York: Dell, 1965.

Crawford, Cheryl. *One Naked Individual.* Indianapolis; New York: Bobbs-Merrill, 1977.

Dewhurst, Colleen. *Colleen Dewhurst: Her Autobiography.* Written with and completed by Tom Viola. New York: A Lisa Drew Book/Scribner, 1997.

Fonda, Henry. *Fonda: My Life.* As told to Howard Teichmann. New York: New American Library, 1981.

Garfield, David. *A Player's Place.* New York: Macmillan, 1980.

Guernsey, Otis L., Jr. *Broadway Song & Story.* New York: Dodd, Mead, 1985.

Green, Abel and Joe Laurie Jr. *Show Biz from Vaude to Video.* New York: Henry Holt, 1951.

Gruen, John. *The Party's Over Now.* Wainscott, N.Y.: Pushcart Press, 1989.

Hagen, Uta. *A Challenge for the Actor.* New York: Charles Scribner's Sons, 1991.

Hall, Peter. *Peter Hall's Diaries.* Edited by John Goodwin. London: Hamish Hamilton, 1983.

Hall, Peter. *The Autobiography of Peter Hall: Making an Exhibition of Myself.* London: Sinclair-Stevenson, 1993.

Harmon, Maurice, ed. *No Author Better Served: The Correspondence of Samuel Beckett and Alan Schneider.* Cambridge, Mass.: Harvard University Press, 1998.

Heide, Robert and John Gilman. *Greenwich Village.* New York: St. Martin's Griffin Edition, 1995.

Ionesco, Eugène. *Four Plays.* New York: Grove Press, 1958.

Kolin, Philip C., ed. *Conversations with Edward Albee.* University Press of Mississippi, 1988.

Larchmont: Official Centennial Edition. Village of Larchmont, N.Y., 1991.

McCullers, Carson. *The Ballad of the Sad Cafe and Other Stories.* New York: Houghton Mifflin, 1951.

Merrill, James. *A Different Person.* New York: Alfred A. Knopf, 1993.

Nevelson, Louise. *Atmospheres and Environments.* Introduction by EA. New York: Clarkson N. Potter, 1980.

Parini, Jay. *John Steinbeck: A Biography.* New York: Henry Holt, 1995.

Paris Review Interviews. Writers at Work: Third Series. WF's interview with EA. New York: Viking, 1967.

Parone, Edward, ed. *New Theatre in America.* New York: Dell, 1965.

Purdy, James. *Malcolm.* New York: Farrar, Straus & Cudahy, 1959.

Richardson, Tony. *The Long-Distance Runner: A Memoir.* New York: William Morrow, 1993.

Rorem, Ned. *The New York Diary.* New York: George Braziller, 1967.

Rorem, Ned. *Knowing When to Stop.* New York: Simon & Schuster, 1994.

Schneider, Alan. *Entrances.* New York: Viking, 1986.

Seldes, Marian. *The Bright Lights: A Theatre Life.* Boston: Houghton Mifflin, 1978.

Sheppard, Dick. *Elizabeth: The Life and Career of Elizabeth Taylor.* Garden City, N.Y.: Doubleday, 1974.

Snyder, Robert W. *The Voice of the City: Vaudeville and Popular Culture in New York.* New York: Oxford University Press, 1989.

Stein, Charles W. *American Vaudeville As Seen by Its Contemporaries.* New York: Alfred A. Knopf, 1984.

Steinbeck, Elaine and Robert Wallston. *Steinbeck: A Life in Letters.* New York: Viking, 1975.

Stephens, Robert (with Michael Coveney). *Knight Errant.* London: Hodder & Stoughton, 1995.

Taylor, Elizabeth. *Elizabeth Taylor: An Informal Memoir.* New York: Harper and Row, 1965.

Thurber, James. *Vintage Thurber,* vols. 1 and 2. London: Hamish Hamilton, 1963.

Tynan, Kenneth. *Kenneth Tynan: Letters.* Edited by Kathleen Tynan. New York: Random House, 1994.

Wasserman, Julian N., ed. *Edward Albee: An Interview and Essays.* Houston: University of St. Thomas, 1983.

Woolf, Virginia. *A Haunted House and Other Short Stories.* New York: Harcourt Brace & Company, 1972.

UNPUBLISHED

Albee, Edward. Unpublished plays, novels, stories, poems, essays, and early versions of plays in Albee archives and at Lincoln Center.

Barr, Richard. *You Have to Hock Your House: The Story of a Producer.*

Farrand, Noel. *Footnotes.*

Index

Billy Rose Theater, 165, 166, 174–75, 177, 213, 223, 276
Bingham, Barry, 189
Birkett, Michael, 296
Bishop, Andre, 364
Black Is the Color of Mourning (Albee), 26, 85–86
Blacks, The (Genet), 118, 130
Blau, Herbert, 223
Blessing, Lee, 352
Boies, Jack and Elaine, 185
Bond, Samantha, 372
Bond, Sudie, 137, 142, 168, 276, 281
Boulanger, Nadia, 73
Bowden, Charles, 121
Box and *Quotations from Chairman Mao Tse–Tung* (Albee),17, 226, 273–76, 295–96, 310, 329, 365, 369, 398
Boyer, Myriam, 383
Boyle, Kay, 185
Bradbury, Lane, 166, 171, 173, 204
Brady, Leslie, 205
Brady, Scott, 90
Brandeis University, 334
Brantley, Ben, 367
Braun, Gisela, 113, 117
Braun, Pinkas, 100–103, 110–11, 113, 117, 133
Breakfast at Tiffany's (Capote), 247, 266, 268
Breaking Up of the Winships, The (Thurber), 162
Brecht, Bertolt, 115, 132, 188, 345, 381
Brecht on Brecht, 166
Brennan, Elyce, 338
Brennan, Maeve, 273, 374
Brief, 54, 55
Briggs, David, 349
Brown, Arvin, 245
Brown, Francis James "Jim," 72, 73–74, 75
Brown, Harry Joe, Jr., 123, 127
Brown, John Mason, 188–89, 268
Browne, Roscoe Lee, 199, 200, 201–2, 203
Browning, Elizabeth Barrett, 295
Brustein, Robert, 126, 180, 203, 249, 265, 321, 367, 395
Bryan, Robert F., 338, 340
Bryden, Bill, 295–97
Budge, Don, 37
Buecheler, Kurt, 111
Buechner, Frederick, 47–48, 50, 55
"Building Responsibility" (Albee), 65–66
Burbank, Luther, 254
Burnett, Carol, 379
Burrows, Abe, 178, 266
Burton, Richard, 168, 170, 233, 234, 235, 237, 239–40, 241, 244, 246, 252–53, 319, 330, 381–82, 386

Buseta, Wilma, 338
Bush, Prescott, 146
Butler, Kathleen, 351, 358

Caesar, Porter Dean, 55–56, 57
Caffe Cino, 88, 187
Caldwell, Zoë, 392
Callas, Maria, 116
Callow, Simon, 211
Cameron, Kenneth, 67–68
Campbell, Frank, 30
Campo, Michael R., 67
Capote, Truman, 247, 253, 266, 268
Caretaker, The (Pinter), 149
Carr, Virginia Spencer, 203
Carroll, Lewis, 215
Carter, Benny, 385–86
Carter, John, 378
Carter, Myra, 13, 286, 314–15, 357, 358–59, 361, 362, 363, 366, 367, 370, 371, 372–73, 377, 384
Cash, Johnny, 385, 386, 387
Catcher in the Rye, The (Salinger), 50
Catledge, Turner, 189
Cat on a Hot Tin Roof (Williams), 196, 393
Chamberlain, Richard, 266
Chapman, John, 179, 188, 203
Chekhov, Anton, 17, 88, 136, 265, 297, 330, 345
Choate Alumni Bulletin, 66
Choate News, 57, 60–61, 62
Choate School, 18, 44, 46, 47, 52–66, 156, 158, 307, 330, 346, 386, 403
Chopin, Frédéric, 61–62
Chorus Line, A, 304
Christopher, Jordan, 229, 303
Christ's Church, 338, 339, 340, 341, 343
Church, Anita (Nanny Church), 21, 33, 34, 35–36, 37, 38, 42, 188, 403
Circle in the Square, 88, 129, 130
Citizen Kane, 121
City of People, The (Albee), 68, 141
Clark, Bobby, 37–38
Claudel, Paul, 273
Clinton, Bill, 385–86, 387
Clock Without Hands (McCullers), 194
Clurman, Harold, 96, 100, 101, 106, 126, 128, 144–45, 171, 180, 276, 285, 333
Coastal Disturbances (Howe), 329
Coburn, D. L., 305
Cocktail Party, The (Eliot), 88
"Cocktail Party—The Women" (Albee), 67
Coconut Grove Playhouse, 326, 382
Cocteau, Jean, 88, 103, 279
Coigney, Martha, 16, 333–34, 351, 383
Coleman, Robert, 179, 188
Columbia *Spectator*, 294–95
Columbia University, 69